HOUSE DIVIDED

LIONEL LOKOS

HOUSE DIVIDED

THE LIFE AND LEGACY OF MARTIN LUTHER KING

ARLINGTON HOUSE

New Rochelle, New York

For My Mother and Father

Contents

HOUSE DIVIDED

Introduction

I will not insult the intelligence of the reader with that old cliché, "Some of my best friends are Negroes." The truth is that Negroes are not, and never have been, among my circle of friends, although I was acquainted with a few colored classmates at college. They and I exchanged only the smallest of small talk, and even those bare civilities were considered something of a breakthrough in my college days—in those days of racial innocence, before America was divided into those who would overcome and those who would watch the walls of their society come tumbling down.

All the impassioned rhetoric of the civil rights movement has not made me "pro-Negro." Conversely, all the excesses of the blood-soaked Long Hot Summer of 1967 have not made me "anti-Negro." As carefully as I can, I haltingly walk a racial tightrope that seems to get thinner and more fragile every year. Like Blondin walking the high-wire over Niagara Falls, I strive to maintain a sense of intellectual balance, and refrain from leaning too far in either direction —rejecting the Negrophiles *and* the Negrophobes, because I consider the obsequious condescension of the former every bit as degrading as the blatant bigotry of the latter.

My primary concern in this book is to present the documented facts about Martin Luther King—to discuss what Dr. King did for, and to, his people and his country, from the time he first groped his way through the Montgomery bus boycott, right up to his political love affair with Ho Chi Minh.

Admittedly, I am writing from my own total frame of reference, a reference which defies rigid classification. I am writing this book not as a liberal, but as a conservative; not as a WASP, but as a Jew, and something of a rugged individualist; not as a champion of an American apartheid, but as one who now lives in a heavily integrated neighborhood; not as a long-distance onlooker, but as one who has been in Harlem, and, more than that, part of whose family once lived and worked in Harlem.

The Harlem experience always reminds me of that sardonic French saying, "The more things change, the more they are the same." It is now generally forgotten that Harlem was not always all-Negro, but was once an integrated community. Before Martin Luther King was born—before Trinidad was graced with the presence of Stokely Carmichael—whites and Negroes were living in Harlem, albeit on different blocks. For a time, 125th Street was the racial dividing line between the two neighborhoods. Then, as Negroes moved below 125th Street, whites moved to other blocks, and eventually moved out of Harlem altogether. Then, as now, white tenants voted with their feet, and elected to forego racial togetherness on the same block.

It has similarly been forgotten that some of the white merchants, still grimly hanging on in Harlem, opened their stores during this integrated period. They and their families represent the last vestiges of a once-integrated community, and a few of them were in the neighborhood long before the great influx of Negroes from the South. (For example, Blumstein's Department Store in Harlem first opened its doors around 1886.)

My grandfather opened a men's clothing store in Harlem in 1910. In the half-century of its existence, the Lokos Clothing Store apparently achieved a certain renown; a Negro co-worker told me it was considered the "Brooks Brothers" of Harlem. After my grandfather died, the store was run by my uncle and his family until 1962, at which time they were "persuaded" to get out of Harlem. Lest anyone, at this point, accuse me of being an embittered member of some fallen white power structure, I hasten to add that neither I nor my parents have ever had any financial interest in that store.

My father moved from Harlem in 1922, but our visits to that neighborhood continued, on and off, for many years thereafter. In 1938, my mother and I stopped in at my uncle's store, and on our way back to the subway we had our first brush with reverse discrimination. It was a warm day, and we went to a hot-dog stand around 125th Street to get something to drink. The colored counter girl ignored us. We were there for about fifteen minutes, but she pointedly refused to acknowledge our existence, much less wait on us. Whereupon, as I recall, we did not stage a sit-in, call in the American Civil Liberties Union, or launch an impromptu demonstration. We just left quietly, thinking some rather uncomplimentary thoughts about the Brotherhood of Man, Harlem Style.

Dr. King's social scientist allies would, of course, offer the usual prefabricated textbook explanations for the incident—but no explanation I have ever heard could excuse this act of utter stupidity against a woman and her ten-year-old son. It need only be stressed that neither then, nor later, did it occur to either of us that the counter girl should be *compelled* to serve us against her will.

Curiously enough, this experience did not evoke a backlash reaction in me. On the contrary, I became very much interested in Negro problems, and, while still in my early teens, came to the conclusion that the black man had been subjected to gross discrimination at almost every turn. One of the first books I read on the subject dispelled any notion I may have had that Negroes were oblivious to their lot in our society. The book was called *The Negro Caravan*, and was a compilation of some of the best Negro prose and verse, from Phyllis Wheatley to a short-story writer named George Schuyler. The one work which I remember to this day is Paul Lawrence Dunbar's "We Wear The Mask."

In all the long history of racial protest, it would be difficult
to find anything more haunting and compelling than this:

> We wear the mask that grins and lies,
> It hides our cheeks and shades our eyes,—
> This debt we pay to human guile;
> With torn and bleeding hearts we smile,
> and mouth with myriad subtleties.
> Why should the world be over-wise,
> In counting all our tears and sighs?
> Nay, let them only see us, while
> We wear the mask.
> We smile, but O Great Christ, our cries
> To thee from tortured souls arise.
> We sing, but oh the clay is vile
> beneath our feet, and long the mile;
> But let the world dream otherwise,
> We wear the mask.

Without violence, or the implicit threat of violence—without substituting one form of discrimination for another—
Paul Lawrence Dunbar touched a chord of conscience in
me that Martin Luther King could never have reached, with
all his oratory.

When I enlisted in the Navy, I found that it was becoming less and less necessary for Negro servicemen to "wear
the mask." President Truman had ordered the desegregation of the armed forces—an act which, mild enough in
today's civil rights context, was considered practically revolutionary at the time. The Navy's integration efforts would
probably be dismissed as mere "tokenism" by today's rights
militants, but even a token is a beginning, and even that
beginning infuriated many white Southern sailors. Their
reaction often summed itself up into some of the more vivid
four-letter words, and yet—having expressed themselves at
some length—they obeyed. Whether they liked it or not
(and they obviously didn't) they complied. I have often
wished that Negro militants showed the same willingness
to obey laws with which they disagree.

After I was discharged, I found myself gravitating towards conservatism (I was one of the few Brooklynites who supported the late Senator Taft for the Presidency in 1952). When the time came to write a college paper, I selected a topic that seemed to combine my concern for civil rights and conservatism—"Racial Discrimination by Labor Unions." I went back to Harlem to the offices of the Brotherhood of Sleeping Car Porters, and secured information about alleged discriminatory practices by the other Railroad Brotherhoods. The entire subject was one on which the liberal press had maintained an embarrassed silence for all too obvious reasons, for all too many years. The silence has since been broken, but the rate of overall progress has been glacial (and, in some unions, even that might be an overstatement).

That was fifteen years ago—my last visit—shortly before "Whitey" became persona non grata in Harlem.

The memory of the public being what it is, it needs to be repeated at regular intervals that Negroes are not the only minority group in this country, and that they have never had a monopoly on hardship. White America has not been an earthly paradise of affluence and plenty, no matter what "Afro-Americans" or "Soul Brothers" or "Black Nationalists" may think. The tapestry of our nation's history is interwoven with remembrances of poverty-stricken immigrants who *lived* the words from Emma Lazarus' "The New Colossus." They were the struggling, breathing embodiment of her words:

> Give me your tired, your poor,
> Your huddled masses yearning to breathe free,
> The wretched refuse of your teeming shore,
> Send these, the homeless, tempest-tossed to me:
> I lift my lamp beside the Golden Door.

These immigrants did not ask for special treatment or special legislation. They asked only to be let alone—to make their own way, to work out their own destiny. They were discriminated against, they knew unimaginable want and deprivation. But they never lost faith with the future. They never lost faith that tomorrow would be better—*that through their own efforts, they would make it better.*

I belong to one of these groups. I belong to a religious minority which knew backlash, frontlash, and whiplash long before the first slaver set out for the Congo.

If Dr. King could look back on almost two and a half centuries of Negro bondage, Jews can trace their bondage back thousands of years, from the days of Pharaoh to the lash of the Cossacks and the pogroms of Europe.

If Dr. King mourned the "spiritual death" of Negroes, Jews mourn the physical death of millions of their co-religionists in the human slaughterhouses of Nazi Germany a generation ago. The descendants of slaves have shown a fantastic increase in population; the survivors of a madman's "final solution" of "the Jewish problem" are an all too pitiful few.

If Dr. King could talk of poverty in the Negro ghettos, Jews can recall their fathers and grandfathers coming over in steerage with very little more than the clothes on their backs, then lifting themselves up by their own bootstraps. Dr. King said that it is a cruel jest to tell a man to raise himself by his own bootstraps when he has no boots; in reply, I would say that it is possible to save a little at a time until you have the price of a pair of boots, then buy them, and then begin the lifting process. It can be done—and has been done—over and over again, without waiting for a Federal anti-poverty program.

If Dr. King could talk of job discrimination because of color, Jews can recall many years of job discrimination because of religion. Such incidents are legion, and certainly do not require repeating here. My own experience is probably as typical as any. Some years ago I sent my resumé to one of New York's largest advertising agencies. I was called in for an interview, and told that I had all the necessary qualifications. Then I was asked about my religion.

When I replied that I was Jewish, the interviewer, somewhat sheepishly, confessed that the job was with an out-of-town client who would not "approve" of my religious affiliation. I icily commented that I would not want to work for someone like that, and left the office.

If Dr. King could recount cases of Negroes "passing" for white to circumvent job discrimination, Jews can recall instances where a few co-religionists "passed" for gentile. A distant cousin of mine worked for a company for thirty years, concealing his religion all that time. He lived in fear of the company ever discovering that he was Jewish. I think he was one of the kindest, gentlest persons I ever met; I know he was one of the unhappiest. It was not until he died that his employers finally learned that he was Jewish —and only then after attending the funeral chapel.

In greater or lesser degree, Jews and Negroes have had similar encounters with the various forms of overt or covert, open or masked, discrimination. This is probably the reason why, of all white groups, it is the Jewish groups that have traditionally been most sympathetic to Negro aspirations.

For myself, I still subscribe to the broad principles of Negro equality. But I will never sign a blank check to the new Machiavellism that sanctions the use of any and all means—however deplorable—to achieve this end.

If I had to summarize, in a single sentence, the major difference between Dr. King's civil rights position and my own, I would say that it is the difference between "ought" and "must." I think "men of good will" (to employ one of Dr. King's cherished euphemisms) can generally agree that a restaurant owner *ought* to serve anyone who comes into the store, that an employer *ought* to do all his hiring without regard to race, color, or creed, that a landlord *ought* to rent his apartments on a basis of color-blind equality, etc. . . . But Dr. King went much further than that. He believed that hostile, reluctant or unwilling restaurateurs, landlords and employers should be *forced* to do these things, and it is at this crucial juncture—where the element of coercion is brought into play—that Martin Luther King and I parted company.*

I was opposed to the same two provisions of the Civil Rights Act of 1964 that Barry Goldwater found repugnant, and for basically the same reasons. I opposed the Public Accommodations section of the Civil Rights Act, because it seemed a perfectly obvious infringement of the "involuntary servitude" clause of the 13th Amendment to the Constitution.

In Establishment circles, it may no longer be fashionable to quote this clause—but not even the zealots of the Left can ignore out of existence the plain and simple meaning of its provisions:

Neither slavery nor involuntary servitude, except as a punishment for crime whereof the party shall have been duly convicted, shall exist within the United States, or any place subject to their jurisdiction.

Certainly there was not a particle of doubt in the mind of Dr. Alfred Avins, formerly a Professor of Jurisprudence at Cambridge, and of Constitutional Law at Chicago-Kent College. In an article which met with massive silence from what were usually the most vocal civil rights adherents, Dr. Avins wrote:

The fact that Negroes, or those who sympathize with their aspirations, may believe that white persons who refuse to serve them are being arbitrary or capricious, does not alter in any way the legal effect of the Thirteenth Amendment. This provision bans absolutely and in the most express terms, the claim of any person to force any other person to serve him for any reason whatsoever. Correspondingly, it confers on every per-

---

* Hoping to discuss these differences—and ask various questions, as well—I wrote to Dr. King in February, 1968, requesting an interview. I received a reply from his secretary, Miss D. McDonald, stating that because of his almost constant traveling during this period, King would be unable to see me.

son the absolute and unfettered right to refuse, for any reason
or none at all, to serve any other person.

In this article, published in the 1964 Winter issue of the
Cornell Law Quarterly, Dr. Avins concluded that the ban
of the 13th Amendment against involuntary servitude guar-
antees to "every person the right to refrain from working
for any other person" and that this guarantee covers "bar-
bers, hotel clerks, shoe-shine men, sales clerks, waitresses,
just as much as . . . field hands, cotton pickers and farm
laborers."

I objected to the Fair Employment clause because I
believed that, in actual operation, it would be anything but
fair. Where employers may previously have discriminated
against Negroes, I felt companies might now feel compelled to discriminate in *favor* of Negroes—adding some
Negroes to their staff, for display purposes, if nothing else
—and that to this extent, there would be discrimination in
reverse. For example, I couldn't help wondering how the
Equal Employment Opportunity Commission would rule in
a case where a Negro, a Puerto Rican, and a White Anglo-
Saxon Protestant all applied for the same unskilled job. If
the Anglo-Saxon got the job, would the employer be accused of anti-Negro and anti-Puerto-Rican bias? If the
Negro got the job, what objective proof could the company
offer that it had not discriminated against the Puerto Rican?
And if the Puerto Rican got the job—and the Negro filed
a complaint—how could the employer come up with convincing evidence that he was not motivated by prejudice
against one minority group in favor of another? It seemed
that only the Anglo-Saxon would not have the proverbial
leg to stand on—unless he could accomplish the unlikely
feat of proving discrimination because he was *not* a member of a minority group!

It will hardly surprise the reader that my views did not
exactly endear me to my liberal acquaintances. Nor did I
recoup my loss in popularity by stating that, unlike Dr.

King, I felt a landlord has a right to pick his tenants and rent his apartments as he sees fit. But, I was told, it was wrong to discriminate against colored applicants. I agreed with the opinion, but maintained that in this country a man has a right to be wrong—to do something which others may consider wrong—provided only that he does not infringe upon any of the enumerated constitutional freedoms of others.

It is one of liberalism's favorite homilies that nothing is ever all black or white—well, hardly ever—nothing except the Civil Rights Act of 1964. One either swallowed whole all eleven sections of the Act, in toto (trying not to gag over the "involuntary servitude" implicit in the Public Accommodations clause), or be denounced as a backlasher, crypto-racist, or mindless minion of segregationists. All of which simply reaffirmed what I had long known to be a melancholy truism—that liberals disdain all conformity except their own.

In my experience, the most fervent endorsements of the Civil Rights Act of 1964 came from "long-distance liberals" who lived in rural or suburban areas far removed from the scene of urban disturbances. Apparently, absence made the liberal's heart grow fonder—and the more absent they were from Negro neighborhoods, the fonder they were of this most sweeping civil rights law since the days of Reconstruction. On the other hand, I—a villainous conservative—lived then, as now, on an integrated block in a heavily integrated neighborhood.

Having lived on this block, off and on, over a period of twenty-five years, I can attest to the "before" and "after" of integration in this particular area. "Before," the neighborhood was predominantly Jewish, with a random scattering of Catholics and Protestants. Then about ten years ago Negro families started moving in, block by block. The reader can more or less fill in the rest of the paragraph. As Negro families moved in, some white families moved out. At the present time, my neighborhood is about equally divided between whites and Negroes. But I seriously doubt that it will remain that way. As Negroes advance from house to house, a number of whites—with the inevitability of Greek tragedy—fall back and retreat to suburbia. Other white families, with growing children, stay out their lease and then move (moving vans have been doing a very brisk business here for quite some time). Only the elderly poor remain; they have nowhere else to go.

The smallest white and Negro children play well together (possibly because children can see a human being, where their elders can only see A Cause). Teen-agers on both sides of the color line seem more reserved about social integration, away from the school. As for Negro and white adults, communication between the two is virtually nil, a fact which appears to occasion little or no regret by either group.

The main business street of the neighborhood used to draw shoppers from all over Brooklyn. Now there are stores for rent and other stores conducting "going out of business" sales. A drugstore that has been on this street as long as I can remember was gutted by fire and never reopened. Five blocks away is one of the largest high schools in Brooklyn. As far as a passer-by can ascertain from the composition of the lunch-hour crowds, Negro students are in the overwhelming majority.

All of this leads me to believe that in time my neighborhood will become nearly all-Negro, and if that happens I will feel obliged to move. The reason is as inescapable as the headlines that tell of growing anti-white hostility among young Negroes. In all fairness, I must admit that I have not yet had any personal difficulty with Negroes in the neighborhood. Perhaps it would be safe enough; perhaps the Black Muslims and SNCC have not yet won any converts in this area. But the problem is, I could never really be sure. And were the neighborhood to become nearly all-Negro, I could never really be comfortable, feeling I risked a game of Racial Roulette every time the mercury soared.

At this writing, however, the neighborhood is still integrated. How long? Only as long as whites can feel it is reasonably safe to leave their homes at night, and re-enter in the early hours of the morning, without fear of robbery or assault. We have learned to avoid walking down certain streets at night. But that isn't always enough; sometimes, the trouble comes very close to home.

Half a block away is a large playground with basketball courts, handball courts, and swings and seesaws for the youngsters. Two and a half years ago, this was the scene of a racial murder. Some Negroes and whites were hotly disputing who could occupy one of the basketball courts. The argument was temporarily settled with fists, and then finally resolved with more lethal weapons. A white boy was killed, and a young Negro sent to prison. If there have been any other major assaults at the playground, I have not heard of them, so you could take the broad view and call it "an isolated incident." There is always something rather comforting about that phrase—whether or not it has the ring of credibility.

Another "isolated incident" took place almost at my doorstep, during the Long Hot Summer of 1967. Some friends had just left my apartment and had taken the elevator down to the lobby. I was catching up on my reading when I heard loud and angry voices coming from the street. I looked out of my window and saw a group of Negro teen-agers milling around the sidewalk. Three policemen were watching them. Each was virtually stalking the other, and each seemed equally the hunter and hunted. I had the feeling that just one wrong word, one wrong move, anything or nothing, would have turned the whole block into a battlefield faster than a Blood Brother could scream "Police Brutality!" It was not some ex-post-facto news summary on television that I could turn off at will. It was happening right outside my apartment house, and I felt besieged. At this point my friends returned and told me the police had ordered them back into the house, for their own safety. On the elevator they had met one of my neighbors, who was so badly frightened that she had asked for and received a police escort into the house. She has made up her mind to move out as quickly as possible, and I fully expect others to follow suit. As usual, Dr. King would probably have placed the onus on "society" (that battered whipping boy for all group and individual problems since time began), but by now that long-playing record is wearing a bit thin.

I will cite just one more "isolated incident," and be done with it. While writing this introduction, I decided to "take a breather" and walk around the neighborhood. I walked along a nearly all-Negro block and noticed three cars on a side street, waiting for the light to change. Without any warning, two of the cars—with Negro occupants—swerved around the third car, and crossed against a red light. Luckily, there were no oncoming cars, so an accident was avoided. And luckily—just a minute later—they jammed on the brakes in time to avoid running over some children. And then a chilling thought occurred to me: if police had seen what these Negro drivers did and attempted to arrest them on this Negro block, it could have provided all the ingredients for a full-fledged race riot. After all, just two weeks before, the Newark riots had followed close on the heels of a routine arrest for a traffic violation. A trifling incident had turned a city to flames.

The contemporary group of Negro writers takes great pride in "telling it like it is." I propose to do no less in this book.

In the wake of the Newark, Plainfield, and Detroit riots, I think it is more than coincidental that the criminal disobedience of today came after prolonged periods of civil disobedience under Dr. King's tutelage. Nor is it mere chance that today's violent defiance of governmental authority in the North came after prolonged periods of nonviolent defiance of governmental authority in the South. When Dr. King knowingly and repeatedly breached the forces of law and order, he created an atmosphere in which *all* forms of racial disobedience—and *all* forms of racial defiance—could flourish, with or without the limitations he imposed upon himself and his followers.

Recently, on a television program, Dr. King confessed that some of his dreams had turned into nightmares. It was a rare burst of candor, and on that much, at least, he and I agreed. This is the story of Martin Luther King's willful destruction of his dreams. This is the story of "an American nightmare."

LIONEL LOKOS
Brooklyn, N.Y.

CHAPTER 1

A Bullet in Memphis

卐 卐 卐 卐 卐 卐 卐 卐 卐 卐 卐 卐 卐 卐 卐 卐 卐 卐

He had gone three years without a major congressional victory—nothing since the Voting Rights Act of 1965. 1966 had been a series of humiliating frustrations and failures. 1967 had seen his role shifting to a largely ceremonial one as the prematurely elder statesman of the civil rights movement, along with a growing estrangement from many of his "natural allies" over Vietnam. And now it was 1968, and Martin Luther King's last stand. It was 1968, and everyone—friend and foe—knew that if King didn't achieve something big, something bold, something epic-making this year, he was probably finished as a civil rights leader. Because now the new name of the game was Relevance, and such were its stony ground rules that Martin Luther King, like any fledgling aspirant, had to prove himself still relevant to the civil rights movement, or take his awards, his honorary degrees, and his Nobel Prize and retire from the fray with as much grace as he could muster.

Whatever else might happen, Martin Luther King had not the slightest intention of fading away. But what to do? And where and when to do it? No one knew better that the time was past to march against some obscure Southern official. It had been a useful ploy, and gained King the instant headlines which had become the breath of life to the movement. But the South had learned its lesson well, and the supply of fire-eating segregationist officeholders was beginning to run out. Like an impresario searching for a new star, King desperately sought *the* issue which would hurtle him out of journalistic limbo and back on page one —*the* issue which would bring together the New Left, the Old Left, radicals of all shadings and assorted liberals, all arrayed in one mighty assault against society. But what kind of assault? And to what end?

America was given the answers on December 4, 1967. On that date, Martin Luther King announced plans to lead an extended campaign of massive civil disobedience in Washington to force Congress and the Administration to provide "jobs or income for all." King saw the confrontation in Washington as a "last desperate demand" by Negroes, an attempt to avoid "the worst chaos, hatred and violence any nation has ever encountered." King's strange idea of avoiding chaos was to threaten that his followers might tie up transportation in Washington, jam the hospitals, boycott schools and sit-in at government offices as part of the demonstration.[1]

How much would King's program cost? He tossed off a figure in the billions, as airily as a housewife adding something to her charge account. For a time he spoke of a minimum amount of 10 to 12 billion dollars to finance his program.[2] Then he eyed the $70 billion the federal government had earmarked for defense, and decided that if this country did away with defense it could take "the $70 billion it spends annually for war" and use it instead to provide "jobs or income" and wipe out the ghettos.[3] Which figure came closest to financing King's program (the details of which were left vaguely suspended in air) depended upon which newspaper or magazine you read in a given week. All that was certain was that the poor were to be made financial wards of the paternalistic state, even if this country had to dismantle the Pentagon to do it. Those who worked for a living would be obliged to support those who did not (regardless of whether they could not or would not work) quite conceivably for the rest of their lives.

The marchers in Washington would not be presenting detailed legislative proposals to Congress, so one could not turn to them for any hard and fast definition of the word "poverty." On previous occasions, where a definition of "poverty" had been attempted, it was sometimes met with angry cries of protests by Negroes themselves. Thus, in early January, 1968, the Negro newspaper *The Amsterdam News* acknowledged that its editorial desk had been "virtually swamped" by furious critiques of a column by H. Carl McCall, city commissioner in New York's Human Resources Administration and former head of the Council Against Poverty. A letter by Mrs. Myrtle G. Whitmore, vice president of the Crown Heights Taxpayers and Civic Association in Brooklyn, charged that an attempt was being made "to turn Crown Heights into a 'Poverty Pork Barrel . . .' " Mrs. Whitmore stated that Crown Heights organizations had tried many times to meet with McCall when their area was being incorporated into poverty areas bordering it, but McCall was never available. Mrs. Whitmore pointed out that McCall wrote that a certain percentage of "families" have incomes below $4,000, but he didn't say "families of four," which was the federal government's definition of poverty levels. She noted that the "families" to whom McCall referred could be elderly couples on Social Security or private pensions (many with savings accumulated during their productive years), mother and child, daughter and elderly parent.

Mrs. Whitmore wrote, "This may come as a shock to Mr. McCall, but many persons earning $75–$80 per week do not consider themselves poverty stricken. They are hardworking individuals who are proud they are paying their own way." As for a comment by McCall that over "half" of the population over 25 had not completed high school, Mrs. Whitmore said, "This has no significance because over 25 could include persons over 65 or many of the European immigrants who migrated here in the 1900's, when the lack of a diploma did not prevent one from succeeding. Many persons without diplomas are well-off manufacturers, property owners, and businessmen, not in the least poverty stricken. If he had said 18 and 35, that would have meant something: but of course the figures Mr. McCall used appear to be purposely distorted in order to help a weak case."[4]

Possibly it was to avoid being confronted by the Mrs. Whitmores of the Negro neighborhoods that Martin Luther King avoided details and definitions and largely confined himself to generalities about "an Economic Bill of Rights for the Disadvantaged." In about the broadest possible terms, King's Economic Bill of Rights "would guarantee a job to all who want to work and are able to work. It would also guarantee an income for all who are not able to work. Some people are too young, some are too old, some are physically disabled, and yet in order to live, they need income. It would mean creating certain public-service jobs, but that could be done in a few weeks."[5] How old was "too old," how young was "too young," what was the minimum physical disability that would preclude self-support (especially in view of the "Hire the Handicapped" campaign), King declined to say. He even declined to predict that his Economic Bill of Rights would stave off riots in the ghettos. The most he would say was, "A program that would really deal with jobs could minimize—I don't say stop—the number of riots that could take place this summer."[6] What he seemed to be advocating was the old social planner's millennium of full employment for those who worked, and full welfare for those who did not. "I hope," he said, "that a specific number of jobs is set forth, that a program will emerge to abolish unemployment, and that there will be another program to supplement the income of those whose earnings are below the poverty level."[7] Did the world owe the poor and the unemployed a living? Martin Luther King would have replied "Yes" without a moment's hesitation—

along with a stern admonition to Congress to stop holding up the paychecks.

King pointed to a poll by Louis Harris which had revealed that 56 per cent of the people felt that some kind of program should come into being to provide jobs to all who want to work.[8] But the support of "some kind of program" did not, in itself, provide carte blanche for a tax program running into many billions of dollars.

In an earlier work, the author quoted an article in which Seymour Martin Lipset wrote: "Knowing the electorate's *general* position on the principles involved may result in serious errors concerning how they will vote on a *specific real* measure." As an example, Lipset cited heavy support in polls for the general principle of civil rights legislation; but when specific civil rights measures were subjected to referendum in various Northern cities, a large majority of the whites voted against them. Lipset concluded: "So, the pollsters may make considerable public errors, and for all anyone knows, they have made similar mistakes in many of their private surveys."[9] Quite possibly, the same statement could be made about the results of this poll by Louis Harris.

King had selected fifteen areas—ten cities and five rural districts—from which to recruit his initial cadre. The plan was to have 200 poor people from each area, for a total of 3,000, to get the protests going.[10] These 3,000 were to act as marshals for the thousands King expected to come to Washington for weeks of demonstrations.[11] And in a touch that seemed more attuned to a drama critic than a news reporter, King planned to have a shanty town built in Washington, symbolizing the lot of the poor and recalling the bonus marchers of the thirties. The shanty town would be built on public property, in the expectation—more likely, the fervent hope—that, with photographers looking on, they would be run off from a succession of sites until they ended up on private property belonging to a sympathizer.[12]

Sometimes on and sometimes off the record, moderates

expressed misgivings about the march on Washington. A top ranking leader of the NAACP, Dr. John A. Morsell, feared that King's proposed civil disobedience campaign in Washington might lead to violence and repressive measures. Morsell felt the demonstration would be met as insurrection and put down as such, and that would lead to violence. As Morsell summarized it, "I don't think you can pressure Congress by sitting down in Congressional offices. I think the results are more likely to be the opposite."[13]

King himself acknowledged that the ugly mood of many Negroes in the nation's slums made the campaign "risky," but he asserted that "not to act represents moral irresponsibility."[14] But it may well have been the penultimate in moral irresponsibility and naiveté to state, as King did, that Negro militants, including SNCC, would be asked to participate in the Washington march but must pledge nonviolence for the duration.[15] King hardly reassured moderates by scheduling a meeting with Stokely Carmichael to see if they could work together in the Washington campaign.[16] Since Carmichael's return from North Vietnam and Communist Cuba, he had been spending most of his time in Washington.[17] Early in January, 1968, Carmichael had called more than 100 local civil rights leaders to a secret two-hour "Black Power" meeting at the New School for Afro-American Thought in Washington. Out of this meeting emerged a new loose coalition called the "Black United Front,"[18] and it was this front for Stokely Carmichael that decided not only to endorse King's march on Washington, but to support it with food and housing for delegates as well.[19]

There was ample reason to believe that King was encountering difficulty in his quest for 3,000 marchers. A month before the Washington campaign was to commence, King found it necessary to undertake a three-week recruiting drive in a number of cities.[20] He toured Mississippi counties that were among the poorest in the nation, and exhorted "whole families" of poor Delta Negroes to come to Washington during the week of April 22 and "plague Congress and the President until they do something."[21] He went to New York City, where the New York *Times* described his audiences as "small but enthusiastic crowds."[22] The following day, he made a whirlwind eleven-hour tour of Newark, Paterson, Jersey City and Orange, where he was "literally mobbed by hundreds of spectators wherever he went."[23] But there was nothing in the news stories to indicate that he was mobbed by hundreds of volunteers.

Most of the news about the march on Washington came in bits and pieces—a paragraph reference in a larger news story, accounts of King's frenetic dashes from one city to another. Undoubtedly, one of the most cogent accounts of the march appeared less than a month after the initial announcement, in a January issue of *Christianity and Crisis*. This issue was devoted to an interview with the Rev. Andrew J. Young, executive vice president of the Southern Christian Leadership Conference. The subject was the projected march on Washington by poor Negroes, and the picture Young drew was one of the Nation's Capitol brought abjectly to its knees in a near-paralysis of governmental functions. Young said of this projected march on the Capitol by poor Negroes, "We have been reluctant to tie up a big city like we did [sic] in Birmingham. But we decided that we had better go ahead and dramatize these problems, *and if it means tying up the country, then we just have to do it*" (emphasis added).

King's long-time aide told *Christianity and Crisis:* "No laws say a man has a right to a job. And yet we know that our society will be destroyed unless people have jobs and an income. So it may be necessary for us to create such disruption and disturbance in the system that it will either have to reform itself or destroy us." Rev. Young declared, "to dramatize the 'gold drain' out of the city into the suburbs, we may decide not to let people get back out to the suburbs or into the city. The way Washington is, a few hundred people on each of those bridges would make it impossible to get in or out—or at least *extremely* difficult. It would mean that every day, going back and forth, you are thinking about three or four hours each way. That's another kind of civil disobedience." Rev. Young blandly labeled these proposals "a last resort"; he considered it much more to the point "to have a thousand people in need of health and medical care sitting in around the Bethesda Naval Hospital so that nobody could get in or out until they get treated."

The SCLC's executive vice president declared, "We're prepared to go for broke. But we're not going to destroy any people and we're not going to destroy any property." And yet it's not at all clear just how inclusive is that word "we." Rev. Young stated that a group of 3,000 would be trained for the demonstrations, but conceded that "succeeding waves of people coming in could be less disciplined." Just how undisciplined will they be? And what will they be capable of doing to society?

Rev. Andrew Young said of the coming confrontation in Washington, D.C., "The choice now is between either massive changes through nonviolent demonstrations or destruction through riots." In effect, this becomes a kind of reverse Machiavellism—enunciating the spurious doctrine that nonviolent means justify virtually any conceivable end.

Christianity and Crisis asked King's assistant if the planned civil disobedience campaign would enlist the support of violence-oriented groups in the ghettos. He replied, "Even the black nationalists and people who are proclaiming violence, other than those who are just sick, are interested enough in the progress and well-being of black people to agree to stand aside and let us have our way for a season." He went on: "We intend to have the kind of relationship with the violent groups that would say if you can't adopt nonviolence and join us, let us try our way until the first of August *then you can take over with another approach*, but let's not try to mix the two."[24] This spectre of "the other approach" was envisioned some years ago by Dr.

Jerome D. Frank, a professor of psychiatry at Johns Hopkins University. Dr. Frank stated, "leaders of nonviolent movements constantly remind their opponents that if their demands are not met, they may not be able to keep their followers in check. Is the threat of violence an integral part of the success of nonviolence? Can nonviolent campaigns succeed in the complete absence of this threat? If not, are they truly nonviolent?"[25]

From the very moment this campaign was announced, there was fear that the massive demonstrations in Washington, D.C., might prove uncontrollable. Among those expressing deep apprehension was Richard H. Sanger, recognized as one of this country's foremost authorities on causes and patterns of political violence. Sanger felt that King's demonstration in Washington "could be potential dynamite." He expected that most of the demonstrators would be conscientious and law-abiding, but feared that "a small percentage of extremists might try to cut off Washington's lights and water, cripple movement by turning over big trailer trucks on the main arteries, occupy key buildings, and temporarily take over parts of the city. Things like these have been done in parts of Detroit, in parts of Watts, in parts of Newark, and elsewhere. It might be tried in Washington." He stressed that while King envisaged nuisance demonstrations, "I'm sure there are people in the wings who will take advantage of the opportunity to provoke greater violence."[26]

It was hardly conducive to law and order to find the Rev. James Bevel cast in one of the leadership roles in the march on Washington. One of King's long-time aides in the Southern Christian Leadership Conference, Bevel had been one of the prime organizers in the anti-Vietnam assault on the Pentagon[27]—an assault which had been pockmarked with violence and conspicuously infiltrated by Communists and brandishers of the Viet Cong flag. Bevel was in charge of nonviolent workshops to train the Washington demonstrators,[28] but in view of his background (which will be considered in greater detail in the chapter on the Vietnam protests) one was entitled to shudder at the thought of the training and the trainees.

The federal government was becoming more and more uneasy about the prospects of the Long Simmering Spring that lay ahead, right at its doorstep. And undoubtedly this was why the New York *Times* reported, "When the Rev. Dr. Martin Luther King, Jr. leads the vanguard of his 'poor people's campaign' toward the Capitol next month, the federal and city authorities will be better and more massively prepared to police and protect the demonstrators than at any such protest in history . . ."[29] It seemed highly likely that for a time at least, the forces of law and order would clearly outnumber the marchers. More than 10,000 policemen and federal troops were estimated to be available in the Washington area.[30] A stand-by Army communications and command post had been set up at police headquarters, and the Washington police had received special riot-control training and equipment, including chemical mace.[31]

King pledged that during the Washington march "we will never destroy life or property and if the demonstrations become violent, if the people who come to Washington do not abide by nonviolence, we shall call them off. We may be greeted by violence—I cannot guarantee you that we won't—but we will never respond with violence."[32] A writer repeated King's words to a young man whom he had seen at the Atlanta headquarters of the Southern Christian Leadership Conference. The man exclaimed, "Man, *he* can't call it off! You can't call off things like that no more!"[33]

Much has been said of King's doctrine of nonviolence, but as we will see, in his hands it was a two-edged sword— sweetly perfumed on one edge, and machete-sharp on the other. And this was bluntly evident once again, in the article he wrote for *Look* in April, 1968. One finds at least three references to the threat of violence, riots, and even guerrilla warfare by the disenchanted if King did not achieve his aims nonviolently. The reader is invited to judge for himself. Here are three blatant appeals to fear and terror:

"As committed as I am to non-violence, I have to face this fact: if we do not get a positive response in Washington, many more Negroes will begin to think and act in violent terms."

"I think we have come to the point where there is no longer a choice now between non-violence and riots. It must be militant, massive non-violence, or riots."

"I'm convinced that if something isn't done to deal with the very harsh and real economic problems of the ghetto, the talk of guerrilla warfare is going to become much more real."[34]

To be sure, King opposed rioting for various reasons, one of which should be of immense interest to anyone who considers himself a conservative. King wrote, "I am convinced that if rioting continues, it will strengthen the right wing of the country, and we'll end up with a kind of right-wing take-over in the cities, and a Fascist development, which will be terribly injurious to the whole nation."[35] This was not the first time Martin Luther King had depicted American conservatism as a kind of Frankenstein monster, thirsting to erect a Fourth Reich in the nation's cities. As we will see, King's Beloved Community was open to all—all on the Left, including the most anarchic and demagogic elements of our society. Only those to the right of Nelson Rockefeller (at least 26.5 million of them, according to the 1964 election returns) were personae non gratae in King's hymn to brotherhood.

King wrote, "We welcome help from all civil-rights organizations . . . I think both the NAACP and the Urban League play a significant role. I also feel that CORE and SNCC have played *very* significant roles"[36] (emphasis added). In a strangely opaque choice of adverbs, King wrote that "Some of the Black Power groups have *temporarily* given up on integration. We have not. So maybe we are the bridge, in the middle, reaching across and connecting both sides."[37] And maybe Stokely Carmichael, Rap Brown, and Floyd McKissick would like nothing better than to cross over that bridge and take over the NAACP and the Urban League.

Martin Luther King liked to depict himself at the middle of that bridge, but with him directing the traffic, it was all too evident that all roads led in just one direction—Left and Far Left. In an interview with a writer for the New York *Times*, King conceded, "In a sense, you could say we are engaged in the class struggle, yes." He quickly added, "this isn't a *purely* materialistic or class concern," but at the same time he frankly admitted "our program calls for a redistribution of economic power."[38] This same writer went to the headquarters of King's Southern Christian Leadership Conference and found posters of Che Guevara in one of its offices.[39]

In view of King's verbal brilliance, and his ceaseless and meticulous search for the mot juste, men of reason must conclude that he meant exactly what he said. One must also conclude that he meant exactly what he said and did, by his words and presence, on the evening of February 23, 1968, in Carnegie Hall.

On that evening the author saw a spadeful of earth being dug for the grave of American democracy. He saw the ground being broken, sometimes quietly, sometimes raucously, sometimes by well-manicured gentlemen of great renown, sometimes by street thugs turned "liberators." He saw Black Nationalists, Communists, genteel members of the peace movement, and the usual motley gullibles uniting as the fingers of one well-integrated fist, hoping to bring down our society in a kind of racial Armageddon. And they have every confidence of eventual victory.

On the surface, it could have been a lodge meeting, flanked by the ladies' auxiliary and the young people's group —until you noticed that one of the sweet, motherly-looking white ladies was passing out a letter from H. Rap Brown. And there was an apple-cheeked teen-ager who looked like the kid down the block—until you noticed that he was hawking the *Worker*. A few others, who could have blended right into Rotary Club meetings, were passing out leaflets advertising a benefit for Max Stanford of the Revolutionary Action Movement (one of those arrested in the plot to assassinate Roy Wilkins and Whitney Young), a demonstration in Madison Square Garden to restore the title of Muhammad Ali, and copies of the *Vietnam Courier*, direct from Hanoi.

Why this gathering of the ultra-radical Left? The official poster outside Carnegie Hall told it all: "An international cultural evening sponsored by *Freedomways* magazine, observing the 100th Anniversary of the birth of Dr. W. E. B. DuBois . . . Special Keynote address by Dr. Martin Luther King, Jr."

In testimony before the House Subcommittee on Appropriations on January 29, 1964, J. Edgar Hoover stated that *Freedomways* was one of the publications which "The Communist Party, USA continues to use as media of propaganda . . ."

In the lobby, the author bought a most impressive looking brochure, titled "The DuBois Centennial—An 'International Year' 1968." It offered DuBois' lofty pronouncements about the Afro-American freedom movement, the world and Africa, colonialism, peace; and towards the end of the brochure, as conspicuous as "a word from the sponsor" was this:

I have studied socialism and communism long and carefully in lands where they are practiced and in conversation with their adherents, and with wide reading. I now state my conclusion frankly and clearly: I believe in communism. I mean by communism, a planned way of life in the production of wealth and work designed for building a state whose object is the highest welfare of its people and not merely the profit of a part. I believe that all men should be employed according to their ability and that wealth and services should be distributed according to need.

Quotation from Autobiography
by W. E. B. DuBois

On the preceding page was a list of honors accorded Dr. DuBois, among them the Lenin International Peace Prize in 1959.

The author turned to the page listing United States sponsors of the DuBois Centennial Year. Two members of the old Highlander Folk School were listed—Jim Dombrowski and Mrs. Septima Clark. Long-time officials of the Southern Christian Leadership Conference were listed—Rev. C. T. Vivian and the Rev. Wyatt Tee Walker (who has been working for Governor Nelson Rockefeller for quite some time now). Marlon Brando and Harry Belafonte were on the list, as was the new mayor of Cleveland, Carl Stokes, and Roy Wilkins of the NAACP. Altogether there were almost 200 U.S. sponsors of the DuBois Centennial Year, among them ministers and rabbis, professors, and even a congressman (Charles C. Diggs, Jr., D-Mich.). Two long-time SNCC officials were included in the list of U.S. sponsors of the DuBois Centennial Year—James Foreman and Elizabeth Sutherland.

The program was late getting started. The author took advantage of the lull to glance through the leaflets and other literature he had picked up at the door. The letter from H. Rap Brown was written from Parish Prison in New Orleans, dated just two days before the meeting. It is an extraordinary document—extraordinary in the depths of its hatred for this country. The last sick paragraph reads:

America: if it takes my death to organize my people to revolt against you, and to organize your jails to revolt against you, and to organize your troops to revolt against you, and to organize your children, your God, your poor, your country, and to organize Mankind to rejoice in your destruction and ruin, then here is my life! But my soul belongs to MY PEOPLE. Lasime Tushinde Mbilashaka. (We shall conquer without a doubt.)

H. Rap Brown

At this point, a few in the audience began clapping insistently for the program to begin. The author looked around, and as far as he could see, it was a sell-out. The audience was about 60 per cent New Left, 40 per cent Old Left, including a large number of young Negroes.

The program got under way about 25 minutes late, and the first speaker was J. H. O'Dell, contributing editor of *Freedomways* magazine. These days, he calls himself J. H. O'Dell; in the past he has also been known as Jack O'Dell and Hunter Pitts O'Dell. Under one or another of these names, O'Dell once worked for the Southern Christian Leadership Conference. O'Dell had the rare privilege of being hired, fired, hired again, and fired again by Martin Luther King's organization. The story broke in 1963. Joseph Alsop wrote that King finally dropped O'Dell "when he was warned by U.S. government officials that O'Dell was the genuine Communist article." King himself acknowledged that O'Dell "may have had some connections in the past" with communism. He said that O'Dell left the Southern Christian Leadership Conference on June 26, 1963, by "mutual agreement" because of concern that his affiliation with the integration movement would be used by "segregationists and race-baiters." And now in 1968 King and O'Dell were appearing on the same platform and the same program, at the same meeting.

In his speech, O'Dell declared, "For 60 years, DuBois worked to develop the spirit of Afro-American internationalism," a phrase he defined as "a socialist transformation of society the world over." He introduced the gentleman who was to be master of ceremonies for the evening—Ossie Davis.

Ossie Davis reeled off a list of his heroes—Paul Robeson (much applause); Robert Williams, chairman of the Revolutionary Action Movement, who was "driven from us" (more applause); and Malcolm X (still more applause). With great fanfare Davis introduced the next speaker, who had come from Hollywood, where he was working on a script about Malcolm X. The applause intensified as James Baldwin came out on the stage.

Baldwin told the audience, "I've never known a Negro

who was not obsessed with Black Power." He said that he
might not always agree with Stokely Carmichael, "but I
get his message." To Baldwin, this was the message:
"Stokely Carmichael is saying: 'if I can't live here, well,
neither will you. This land is mine as well as yours. We'll
share it, or we'll perish. I don't care.' " Carmichael was saying, "The U.S. will fall. I hope I live to see the day," and
"every black man is saying this in many ways, over and
over again."

Baldwin concluded, "If this country cannot change, remember, we come of a long line of runaway slaves who
managed to survive without passports."

The meeting would hardly have been complete without at
least one song by the New and Old Left's Musical Laureate,
Pete Seeger. Seeger and Len Chandler did a song that had
been written for William Epton (who was convicted of
conspiring to commit criminal anarchy and riot). Epton
undoubtedly would have approved of the song; certainly
the audience expressed its delight by singing and clapping
along, and chanting with the singers, "We will not bow
down to genocide." The phrase was used to describe the
war in Vietnam—or as Seeger and Chandler called it, "the
war against the poor." No pacifist he, Seeger told the audience, "People who know how to fight will inherit a world
we can all love."

Now came the moment everyone had been waiting for.
The applause was long and loud and some stood up as the
featured speaker of the evening, Dr. Martin Luther King,
Jr., strode out on the stage.

King expressed his delight at being "a part of this important meeting." He gave a resumé of DuBois' life and
works, summarizing, "He died at home in Africa, among
his cherished ancestors. History cannot ignore Dr. W. E. B.
DuBois." All through King's dissertation, one could almost
feel the audience waiting, listening for THE WORD. And
then it came, after King had eulogized DuBois as a "restless
militant black genius . . . a model of militant manhood and
integrity . . . . a radical all his life." It came when Martin

Luther King almost smugly observed, "So many would like to ignore the fact that DuBois was a Communist in his last years." A great wave of applause greeted his remark. King denounced "our irrational obsessive anti-communism [that] has led us into too many quagmires—" here the rest of his sentence was drowned out by a thunderous ovation. "All over the world," King declared, "we must live together as brothers, or we will all perish as fools."

And now King was ready to discuss his own strange concept of brotherhood—his march on Washington in April. He stated, "We have to go to Washington because they declared an armistice in the war against poverty," because so much was being spent on the "senseless, cruel, unjust war in Vietnam." He had to wait for the applause to subside before he could continue: "We will stay in Washington until the government responds. If it means forcible suppression, we will accept it. If it means jail, we will accept that." He concluded, "DuBois will be with us when we go to Washington in April, to demand our right of life, liberty, and the pursuit of happiness."

The invitation was all but engraved. Given King's now open contempt for moderates and the anti-Communist movement, his obeisance to the most famous Negro convert to communism, and his very presence at the DuBois Centennial, there could be no doubt that the Communists felt not only invited, but *expected* to be present at the march on Washington in April, 1968. There could no longer be any doubt that King intended to be the Trojan Horse of the civil rights movement—either not knowing or not caring that he would bring Communists with him—and depend more and more upon their support as his future campaigns escalated in radicalism and desperation.

COMMUNITY OR CHAOS?

Martin Luther King had made his choice—and it seemed obvious even to his staunchest apologists that the darkest days of An American Nightmare were still ahead.

In and out of government—in white and Negro neighborhoods—the talk, the exhilaration, the fears revolved around and around the march on Washington—Part 2—with Martin Luther King in one corner, and the Congress of the United States in the other. And given King's awesome string of victories in the years gone by, no one pretended for a moment that the contenders were not evenly matched.

Newspaper article after article fed the public's voracious appetite for any and all details about the forthcoming march. Anything else seemed superfluous. A garbage strike? Well yes, there had been a sanitationmen's strike in New York City—and now there was one in Memphis. And King was going to Memphis. But then, King was always going somewhere. And almost that perfunctorily, the public shifted its attention from garbage collections in a Tennessee city to the massive civil rights confrontation that would soon blitz Washington, D.C.

Under normal circumstances, there would have been nothing in the strike of the Memphis sanitationmen to absorb the public interest very long. The basic details could hardly have been more prosaic. It all started a week and a half before King's speech in Carnegie Hall—on February 12— when 1,300 garbage collectors and sanitation workers went out on strike. Their demands were: 1) recognition of Local 1733 as bargaining representative of the sanitation men; 2) establishment of grievance procedures; 3) payroll deduction of union dues; 4) "fair" provisions for promotions; 5) health, hospital and life insurance; 6) a uniform pension program; 7) sick leave, vacation, and overtime pay; 8) a wage increase.[40]

Mayor Henry Loeb had said flatly that he would not recognize the union (which had been chartered two-and-a-half years before) and would not permit a union dues checkoff.[41] And this apparently was the crux of the controversy. The city garbagemen were making $1.70 an hour,[42] but wages were almost incidental to the question of union recognition. The city had offered, and the workers were ready to accept, a 10-cent raise immediately, and five cents more an hour in July.[43]

So far, this could have sounded like a perfectly straight-forward union dispute, interlaced with serious policy problems about the right of civil service workers to strike against a city and withhold essential services necessary for the health and well-being of its citizens. But soon these valid and legitimate issues were shunted aside and the racial issue became paramount. Most of the strikers were Negroes, the Mayor would not recognize their union, and the entire matter escalated into a full-blown civil rights issue. It was no longer labor versus management, but black versus white.

The Memphis chapter of the NAACP estimated that 98 per cent of the Negro vote went against Mayor Loeb in the 1967 election in which he won a second term.[44] Inevitably the sanitationmen's strike evolved into a polarization of support for and against the mayor along substantially rigid racial lines.

This same polarization was the reflex reaction to Tennessee Governor Buford Ellington's preparations for the Long Hot Summer. In early March, the Governor announced his determination to allow a National Guard riot training exercise in which troops would be concentrated in the state's four metropolitan areas.[45] He stood his ground in the face of furious charges by Negro leaders that it would heighten racial tensions and might even lead to civil disturbances. They indignantly cited the report that the Guardsmen would go through anti-riot drills in the North Nashville Negro section, including the campuses of the predominantly Negro Fisk University and the state-operated Agricultural and Industrial University.[46] A year before, this had been the scene of three nights of rioting in which policemen and students were injured and a number of buildings were destroyed by fire.[47] The Governor replied that there was "nothing to be excited about," and denounced critics for spreading false rumors about the operation. He said there had never been any intention to assemble troops in the Negro section, but acknowledged that the exercise was aimed at preparing the Guard to combat civil disorder that might occur in the summer.[48] Perhaps he had the ghastly Newark and Detroit riots in mind when he emphatically declared, "We are going to take advantage of all the training we can get in this area."[49] As for his critics, he grimly noted, "There are people who would like to see riots, and they are not all in the North Nashville area. Martin Luther King is training 3,000 people to start riots, and when we say we are going to train the Guard to protect the lives of people and their property, there is a big hullabaloo about it." Governor Ellington said he had planned to invite newsmen to travel with the troops and witness the exercises.[50]

Three weeks later, 4,000 of these troops were called up by Governor Ellington at the request of Mayor Loeb. A total of 8,000 more troops were placed on alert.[51] What had begun as a massive protest march in support of the sanitationmen, led through downtown Memphis by Martin Luther King, had been accompanied by violence in which a group of Negro youths smashed windows and looted stores.[52] Negro students, prevented by the police from leaving high school to join the march, hurled missiles at the officers. The youths dashed along, shattering store windows with sticks.[53] In all, 155 stores had their windows smashed, with about 35 per cent of their window displays rifled.[54] Forty-one persons were arrested on looting charges. A number were beaten and gassed, a 16-year-old boy was killed, and 60 were injured.[55] Mayor Loeb said he called for the National Guard "two minutes" after the first window was broken on Beale Street. President Johnson offered federal assistance if Memphis needed it, and said, "We will not let violence and lawlessness take over the country."[56]

Charges were made that the police had lost their heads, launching a full-scale offensive instead of moving in and arresting the 30 to 70 teen-agers actually involved.[57] But Mayor Loeb was convinced that firmness was the deciding factor in containing the disorders.[58] The mayor's convictions

seemed borne out by the tragedy that was only a week
away. Certainly in the frightening days that lay ahead,
riots swept many of its sister cities, but Memphis remained
relatively quiet by comparison.

At the first sign of trouble, King was whisked away from
the march.[59] The front-page photo of him in the Memphis
march shows him stunned—dazed—by the violence.[60] That
the rioting was a tremendous embarrassment to King was
all too evident, in view of the many doubts and misgivings
that had been raised about the potential for violence in the
forthcoming march on Washington.[61] To reassure the
doubters, King was practically compelled to promise to
return to Memphis "as quickly as possible" to stage a "massive" march without disorder.[62] This is a fact that has already been lost sight of by far too many Americans—that
Martin Luther King was back in Memphis that fateful day
preparing for a second march, because of the Negro violence
which had marred the first procession.

At first, King had scheduled this second march for Friday, April 5, but he put it off until Monday, April 8, in
order to give union men from across the country time to
come to Memphis and join in the protest. He expected about
5,000 marchers to come in from other cities.[63] Tensions
were running high in the city, and Mayor Loeb instructed
City Attorney Frank Gianotti to seek an injunction in United
States District Court forbidding the march. After hearing
the arguments on April 3, United States District Court
Judge Bailey Brown issued a temporary restraining order
forbidding King to hold that march on Monday. The order
was not only against King but also on all persons under his
authority and those acting in concert with him.[64] King
angrily called the order "illegal and unconstitutional" and
said that there was a "real possibility" that he would not
obey it. King said he would first attempt to have the restraining order set aside in the courts. He said his lawyers
would go into Federal Court the following day in an effort
to have the order dissolved. "Beyond that," King declared,

"it is a matter of conscience. It will be on the basis of my
conscience saying that we have a moral right and responsibility to march." He recalled that he had been "forced" to
defy court orders in the past, and cited as a case in point
his week in jail in Alabama the preceding year for having
defied a court injunction in Birmingham back in 1963.[65]
This is a second fact which must be remembered—that
Martin Luther King was in the middle of planning a demonstration which would flout a court injunction, issued to
avoid precisely the kind of violence that ended his life.

On the evening of April 3, King addressed a cheering
crowd of 2,000 supporters. He had flown in from Atlanta
to Memphis, and told them that his flight had been delayed
because of a baggage search that airlines officials said resulted from threats to him. In King's words:

And then I got into Memphis. And some began to say the
threats—or talk about the threats that were out. Or what would
happen to me from some of our sick white brothers. Well, I
don't know what will happen now. We've got some difficult
days ahead. But it really doesn't matter with me now. Because
I've been to the mountain top. I won't mind. Like anybody, I
would like to live a long life. Longevity has its place. But I'm
not concerned about that now. I just want to do God's will. And
He's allowed me to go up to the mountain. And I've looked
over, and I've seen the promised land. I may not get there
with you, but I want you to know tonight that we as a people
will get to the promised land. So I'm happy tonight. I'm not
worried about anything. I'm not fearing any man. Mine eyes
have seen the glory of the coming of the Lord.[66]

Many have interpreted this statement by Martin Luther
King as a premonition of a sudden and violent and imminent
death, and this may well be. But the thought of death was
never very far from King's mind. He referred to it in many
of his books, and directly or indirectly in his major campaigns. And after he won the Nobel Peace Prize in 1964,
his wife said, "I have lived with the threat of death always

present."[67] Ten years ago, he had been excruciatingly close to death from a stab wound at the hands of a Negro woman in a Harlem department store. He was stabbed in the upper left side of his chest with a steel letter opener.[68] A photo in the *Amsterdam News*—captioned "A Sneeze Away from Death"—shows him sitting, with the letter opener protruding from his chest, calmly waiting for an ambulance.[69] At the hospital, the doctor said that the blade of the letter opener, seven inches long, impinged on the aorta, a blood vessel near the heart. He said a puncture of the aorta would have caused "instant death."[70] King's Negro assailant, Mrs. Izola Ware Curry, told a police inspector she stabbed King because then "he would listen to my problems because I've been followed in buses and people have been making me lose my job." A month later, at Bellevue, Mrs. Curry was adjudged insane.[71] In 1958, it occurred to no one to condemn the Negroes of Harlem because of the act of one Negro woman. It now seems equally absurd to condemn the entire white community because of the act of one white man in Memphis (or a few cohorts, if such should prove to be the case) in 1968.

On the morning of April 4, Memphis Police Director Frank Holloman was in Federal Court, in support of the temporary restraining order against the march granted by Judge Brown the day before. Holloman said that the Negro community was so worked up that another mass demonstration in Memphis could "be worse than Watts or worse than Detroit." The Police Director stated he had received reports that "Negroes are buying guns from wholesale houses in our neighboring state of Arkansas." He also said that Negro youths "have been supplied for several weeks with specific instructions on how to make Molotov cocktails and firebombs."[72]

That evening, Martin Luther King was in his room on the second floor of the Lorraine Motel. He went outside, and leaned over the railing to chat with an associate, Rev. Jesse Jackson, standing just below him in a courtyard parking lot. Jackson introduced him to Ben Branch of Chicago, a musician who was to play that night at a rally in support of the striking sanitationmen. King asked Branch to play a Negro spiritual, "Precious Lord, Take My Hand," at the rally. Suddenly a shot burst out. King toppled to the concrete second-floor walkway. Blood gushed from the right jaw and neck area. His necktie had been ripped off by the blast. Later, Jackson recalled that King "had just bent over. If he had been standing up, he wouldn't have been hit in the face."[73]

King was apparently still alive when he reached the St. Joseph's Hospital operating room. He was carried in on a stretcher, a bloody towel over his head. King received emergency surgery, but it was too late. He was pronounced dead at 7:05 p.m. Central Standard Time by staff doctors.[74]

That night, Mayor Loeb reinstated a curfew which had been in effect, and declared: "After the tragedy which has happened in Memphis tonight, for the protection of all our citizens, we are putting the curfew back in effect. All movement is restricted except for health or emergency reasons."[75] Governor Ellington called out the National Guard and pledged all necessary action by the state to prevent disorder. He stated, "I can fully appreciate the feelings and emotions which this crime has aroused, but for the benefit of everyone, all of our citizens must exercise restraint, caution and good judgment."[76] Police said the murder of Martin Luther King had been followed by sporadic shooting, fires, bricks and bottles thrown at policemen, and looting that started in Negro districts and spread all over the city.[77]

At this time, details about King's assassin were sketchy at best. Memphis Chief of Detectives W. P. Huston said a late model white Mustang was believed to have been the killer's get-away car.[78] Police Director Holloman said the assassin had fired the fatal shot "50 to 100 yards away in a flophouse."[79] A high-powered 30.06 caliber rifle was found about a block from the scene of the shooting. "We think it's the gun," Chief Huston said.[80] All that was certain was that with the Memphis police patrolling the area, the killer made an incredibly perfect escape.

The days following the assassination were a grotesque nightmare, with eulogies approaching deification competing for newspaper coverage with reports of rioters running amok in over 100 cities. Sometimes in the same city, an integrated procession or service was being held while only blocks away store windows were being broken and stores looted. The mood of the ghetto would fluctuate from hour to hour, from day to day, from grief to fury to a bellicose cry for vengeance. A city might be tormented by rioters one day, quiet the next, then confronted by rioters the day after. Another city might be quiet in the first 24 hours after the assassination, then suddenly erupt into violence and looting. It was a frenzied grief coexisting precariously with a frenzied madness, with madness carrying the day. It was a funeral procession marching through a still smoking battlefield, a wake lit by the flames of a Molotov cocktail.

One of the worst riots in the country ravaged a city where "it couldn't happen"—in Washington, D.C. Washington, D.C. is the only city in the United States with a Negro majority. It has a Negro mayor and is watched over by a benevolent federal government. Unfortunately, it also has Stokely Carmichael, and this racist demagogue was given totally free rein by a supine Attorney General of the United States to say and do as he wished in the feverish days that followed.

U. S. News & World Report called it "The Second Sacking of Washington,"[81] and it had not even slightly overstated the case. The trouble began about an hour after the announcement of the murder of Martin Luther King. The night of April 4, at around 9 p.m., mobs began forming in Washington's Negro business center. They forced shops and theaters to close, smashed windows and looted.[82] The looting followed a protest march led by Stokely Carmichael down 14th Street, N.W., the center of a principal Negro commercial and shopping area. Carmichael exhorted Ne-

groes to "go home and get your guns."[83] By midnight, rioting had spread over many blocks. Police tried only to break
up crowds, and made only felony arrests. Police Chief John
Layton said, "We just didn't have enough men to disperse
them in the beginning."[84] And yet as head of the police
department, he hardly gave a better account of himself the
following day. At 9 a.m. on April 5, arson and looting began
again after a lull. No police were in sight in some riot areas.
Only about 500 of the 2,800-man force was on duty.[85]

At 10 a.m., Stokely Carmichael called a news conference
at the 14th Street headquarters of the New School for Afro-
American Thought. Before television cameras, he asserted
that "white America has declared war on black America"
with the murder of King. "Black people have to survive,
and the only way they will survive is by getting guns," he
said.[86] Asked what he would tell Negroes who would have
to die to do as he said, Carmichael answered, "That they
take as many white people with them as they can." The last
question asked Carmichael was, "Do you fear for your life?"
Carmichael snapped back, "The hell with my life! You
should fear for yours. I know I'm going to die. I know I'm
leaving!"[87]

Less than an hour after the 30-minute news conference
ended, Carmichael was in the street with a following of
50 Negroes.[88]

By noon, police in many areas began to radio for tear
gas and help. Where Negro mobs threatened their lives,
they fell back under orders to avoid shooting. By 1 p.m.,
fires and looting spread to new areas. By 2:30 p.m., bands
of looters began to prowl through the downtown shopping
area, wrecking stores and carrying off merchandise. Several
sections of the city were in flames. By 3 p.m., police set up
blockades, then retreated as mobs became overwhelming.
Marauding bands wrecked stores within two blocks of the
White House. Finally, at 4 p.m.—nineteen hours after the
first window-smashing and looting had begun—Mayor Walter E. Washington telephoned President Johnson for federal

troops. The President authorized mobilization of Army and Air National Guard units.[89]

By now, black smoke was rising above the Negro slum area. As night fell, swiftly moving looters—many of them arriving and leaving in automobiles—hit almost every store in the central downtown block bounded by 13th, 14th, F and G Streets. Pedestrians, in a frantic exodus from the city, were seen streaming across the Memorial Bridge over the Potomac.[90]

Army troops from Fort Myer reached the White House and Capitol. Soldiers deployed around the Executive Mansion and machine guns were set up around the Capitol.[91] The President ordered 4,000 regular Army and National Guard troops into Washington, D.C., after determining that "a condition of domestic violence and disorder" existed in the Nation's capital.[92] The army troops were ordered to protect firemen and ignore looters at the outset.[93] At 11 p.m., that first day after the assassination, the police in Washington reported six dead. A total of 353 persons were treated at hospitals, including seven policemen and six firemen. There were 639 arrests of adults and 109 arrests of juveniles.[94] Tom Wicker of the New York *Times* wrote, "It was hard to view what happened here as a direct and bitter reaction to Dr. King's murder. . . . Most of the looters, far from appearing angry or mournful at the news from Memphis, appeared to be having a good time."[95]

Three blocks from the White House, cars loaded with Negroes pulled up at a shoe store. Looters piled into the street, broke the windows, and cleaned the place out. Police, looking on, did nothing to stop them.[96] A regular Washington policeman said, "I think we could have stopped this thing if they hadn't put us under wraps so. Looters would break a window, then stand aside to watch our reaction. When we did nothing, the mob would move in and ransack the place. We just had to stand there."[97]

Intelligence sources in Washington said that Carmichael was unsure about what to do after the assassination of King until he got a call from the Cuban press agency, Prensa Latina, in New York. After the call, Carmichael appeared in the streets of Washington demanding that Negroes "get guns."[98]

King's successor, Ralph Abernathy, said, "You and I know that just folk, poor people that had a hard time" were rioting over the nation.[99] And yet the Washington *Post* did not find the rioters in the Nation's capital quite that downtrodden. The *Post* reported that "The first riot suspects in court here yield a portrait of a typical suspect about 29, who has attended 11 grades of school, has a job paying $85 to $95 a week, and has not been in trouble with the law before." Of the first 119 riot suspects, only 13 were unemployed, 27 were high-school graduates, nine had attended college, and two were college graduates. An interviewer for the D. C. Bail Agency called them "an amazingly respectable crowd, compared with the people we usually get here. They have firm home addresses, families, and few criminal records."[100] The usual descriptive verbiage—"deprivation," "want," "neglect," "the disinherited"—was virtually impossible to apply to the overall Negro population of Washington, D.C. The Nation's capital is now almost two-thirds Negro in population. It has a Negro mayor. Negroes have majorities on the city council and the school board. The police force is nearly one-fourth Negro, and has tried to establish friendly relations with Negroes. Washington's biggest employer is the federal government, which counts Negroes as more than 30 per cent of its local employes. Schools and public accommodations long have been integrated. Racial discrimination in housing is forbidden.[101] And this was the city that writhed in agony and jumped when Stokely Carmichael cracked the whip.

The more moderate Negro leaders maintained that King would have been outraged by the riots that swept America's cities after his death. But as we will see, Martin Luther King had a unique facility for opposing riots in the aggregate, and yet somehow, in some way, for some reason, excusing the individual rioters. He would not even attempt to assume moral responsibility for riot prevention, but simply washed his hands of the matter, as witness this statement:

Riots are here. Riots are part of the ugly atmosphere of our society. I cannot guarantee that riots will not take place this summer. I can only guarantee that our demonstrations will not be violent . . . if riots take place, it will not be the responsibility of Martin Luther King or the Southern Christian Leadership Conference . . . There's no point in turning to us.[102]

Within hours after the assassination, tributes and condolences (and some shabbily camouflaged anti-American tirades) began pouring in from all over the world, with many of the eulogists comparing the death of King with the death of John F. Kennedy. The influential French newspaper, *Le Monde*, wrote of the murder of King: "Hatred and passion disfigure the visage of a white America that wants to be respectable and cannot help being racist."[103] In Britain, members of all parties in the House of Commons introduced a motion expressing "horror at the brutal and senseless murder" and pledged to eliminate racial discrimination in their country.[104] In Geneva, Secretary General U Thant sent Mrs. King a cablegram praising her husband for having "worked so unceasingly and by nonviolent methods for the cause of peace, international understanding and human rights."[105] In West Germany, both houses of Parliament stood in silence to pay tribute.[106] The Soviet newspaper *Izvestia* headlined "United States Is a Nation of Violence and Racism."[107] And quite probably with an eye and ear on Stokely Carmichael's press conferences, North Vietnam's premier Pham Van Dong sent this message to the Southern Christian Leadership Conference: "The murder of Martin Luther King has deepened the Afro-Americans' hatred and sharpened their will to fight for their sacred rights. . . . Once again, I share with our Afro-American brothers this deep grief and voice the strong sympathy and support of the Vietnamese people for the just struggle of the Afro-American."[108] In India, after a speech of tribute by Prime Minister Indira Gandhi, the members of Parliament stood for a minute of silence.[109] In South Africa, Dr. W. F. Nkomo, a Negro leader of Pretoria, believed that "The assassins have now strengthened the hands of the likes of Stokely Carmichael and black-power advocates. They will now have all the evidence in their possession for propagating race hatred." An Afrikaans-language paper, *Die Vaderland*, expressed shock at the killing and said that King was a "victim of evil racial passions he helped to stir up and eventually could not control, so that he had to compete with the Rap Browns and Stokely Carmichaels to retain his position as Negro leader."[110]

In America, President Johnson proclaimed the following Sunday, April 7, a national day of mourning for Martin Luther King. The President ordered that until King's interment, the American flag was to be flown at half-staff on all buildings, grounds, and naval vessels of the federal government, as well as all U.S. embassies abroad.[111]

"Together," Johnson stated, "a nation united and a nation caring and a nation concerned and a nation that thinks more of the nation's interests than we do of any individual self-interest or political interest—that nation can and shall and will overcome."[112]

Former Vice President Nixon described King as "a great leader—a man determined that the American Negro should win his rightful place alongside all others in our nation."[113] One of the few who dared strike a discordant note was Texas Governor John B. Connally, Jr., who was wounded by a sniper when President Kennedy was assassinated. The Governor said that King had "contributed much to the chaos and turbulence in this country, but he did not deserve this fate." He called the murder of King an act "which tends to crumble away our society."[114] And former Governor George Wallace termed the assassination "a senseless, regrettable act."[115]

In a Palm Sunday sermon at St. Peter's Basilica, Pope Paul VI associated the memory of King's murder "with that of the tragic story of the Passion of Christ which we have just heard."[116] In Switzerland, the Rev. Dr. Eugene Carson Blake, General Secretary of the World Council of Churches, concurred with a statement that "By international consensus, Dr. King was a first citizen of the world. In the United States, he was a main hope for a tortured nation."[117]

In the emotional proliferation of those soul-searching days, few, if any, would call into question some eulogies that bordered on sacrilege. There was Bishop James A. Pike, who told an audience at the Central Presbyterian Church in New York City that Jesus was a revolutionary like the Viet Cong and a freedom fighter like Martin Luther King.[118] There was the Rev. George Clements, pastor of St. Dorothy's Church, largest Negro Roman Catholic parish in Chicago, who said that Martin Luther King "is a saint" and should be canonized. Rev. Clement said, "I am hoping that people will let me know of any miracles that have occurred because they prayed to Saint Martin Luther King."[119]

Among the more thoughtful and temperate eulogies was that of Dr. Norman Vincent Peale at Marble Collegiate Church. Dr. Peale declared, "Let us take over Dr. King's ministry for him and carry it on by preaching understanding, love and peace as he did in applying Christianity to social conditions. Let us set a wave of love rolling across the country that will sweep aside the wasteful hate and destruction that now threatens us all. At tragic as Dr. King's end was, we must not allow it to be the source of hatred, waste and more misery for more people."[120]

Reactions to King's death varied widely but with fair predictability among Negro leaders and would-be leaders. Floyd McKissick of CORE stated, "Nonviolence is a dead philosophy and it was not the black people that killed it. It was the white people that killed nonviolence and white racists at that. It's a horror for us, for all Americans, that the apostle of nonviolence should be gunned down on an American street."[121] A few days later, at a memorial meeting in New York's garment center, McKissick wondered aloud how many of the white mourners "are here because it's a fad."[122] Roy Wilkins of the NAACP felt that "Dr. King was a symbol of the nonviolent civil rights protest movement. He was a man of peace, of dedication, of great courage. His senseless assassination solves nothing. It will not stay the civil rights movement; it will instead spur it to greater activity."[123] Whitney Young of the National Urban League called it "a bitter reflection on America. We fear for our country. The only possible answer now is for the nation to act immediately on what Dr. King has been fighting for—passage of the civil rights and anti-poverty bills and a true and just equality for all men."[124]

Washington, scene of some of the worst rioting, was also the scene of some of the most violent diatribes by Negro leaders. Julius Hobson, head of Associated Community Teams (ACT), said, "The next black man who comes into the black community preaching nonviolence should be violently dealt with by the black people who hear him. The Martin Luther King concept of nonviolence died with him. It was a foreign ideology anyway—as foreign to this violent country as speaking Russian."[125] And Lincoln Lynch, chairman of Stokely Carmichael's Black United Front (which had already endorsed the March on Washington), hoped that black people would "adopt a position that for every Martin Luther King who falls, 10 white racists will go down with him. There is no other way. White America understands no other language."[126]

In Atlanta, the Rev. A. D. King, brother of Martin Luther King, delivered an angry sermon titled, "Why America May Go to Hell." King's brother preached, "America has come to the hour now. You are a dying nation. But America has a chance; you don't have to go to hell."[127] Hell, the minister made clear, was Vietnam, and Heaven on earth was located equidistant between the subtreasury and the

Economic Bill of Rights. A much more worthy and poignant note was struck by the Rev. Martin Luther King, Sr., at this same service. He said, "You and I know these are serious, bewildering times in which we live. But don't you lose your way and don't you ever let it get so dark that you can't see a star."[128]

In city after city, marches, processions, parades were held in King's memory. On a march from the Ebenezer Baptist Church to Morehouse College in Atlanta, the participants included Harry Belafonte, Godfrey Cambridge, Hazel Scott, Aretha Franklin, Clara Ward, Diahann Carol, Leslie Uggams, Diane Ross, Lena Horne, and Leontyne Price of the Metropolitan Opera. The march stopped directly in front of the office of Governor Lester Maddox in the state capitol. The group began singing the civil rights anthem "We Shall Overcome." As Gertrude Wilson, a white writer for the *Amsterdam News*, recalled it:

[Leontyne Price] climaxed the message to Maddox with a ringing note somewhere in the stratosphere above high 'C' which virtually pierced the highest windows of the state capitol. As all eyes focused on Leontyne, comedian Godfrey Cambridge looked at her and said, "Take it easy, soul sister, we want to shake up the Governor but we don't want to wake up Dr. King."[129]

In Memphis, Mrs. Martin Luther King, Jr. led a silent march through the streets of the city—the march her husband had planned to lead in support of the demands of the striking sanitationmen. Bayard Rustin, one of the march organizers, told the rally that his assistants had counted 42,000 marchers. The police estimate was slightly more than 19,000.[130] In any case this parade was silent and orderly, in marked contrast to the first parade led by King, which had been accompanied by Negro violence and looting. The new head of the Southern Christian Leadership Conference, Rev. Ralph D. Abernathy, strode beside Mrs. King and held her hand tightly clasped in his.[131]

At the three-hour City Hall rally, Abernathy pounded the wooden lectern repeatedly with his clenched fists. It could have been a prayer meeting—a prayer to the sanctity of civil disobedience. Abernathy cried out, in impassioned tones, "We are bound for the promised land and we aren't going to let nobody, whether it be Mayor Loeb, whether it be the governor of the state of Tennessee, whether it be the National Guard or the police force, whether it be Lyndon Baines Johnson or the Congress of the United States, we aren't going to let nobody turn us around."

The crowd responded fervently with "Amen, amen," and "Tell it like it is."

The way it was, Abernathy had discussed it all with God, and this was the reverend's transcript of the conversation. In Abernathy's words:

I have been on top of the mountain. I have talked to God about it and God told me that Martin did not get there but you have been so close to Martin I am going to help you get there. If God will lead me I am going to lead my people into the promised land.[132]

In New York City at the Central Park bandshell, more than 10,000 people stood shoulder to shoulder to sing two verses of "We Shall Overcome." Mayor Lindsay said of Martin Luther King, "Not even death itself can defeat him. He was a man with a dream and that dream lives on."[133] In the line of march to the park was a man carrying a large photograph of Malcolm X. Fixed to a corner of this photograph was a smaller picture of King.[134] In the march, Governor Rockefeller strode arm in arm with the leader of the Harlem Mau Maus.[135] At the bandshell, James Foreman, director of SNCC, mounted a bench in front of the platform and demanded help for H. Rap Brown. "Free Rap Brown," he shouted, and others in the audience echoed his demand.[136]

Some motorists in New York City were signifying their

respect for King by driving with their headlights on.[137] (But the author's own observation in Brooklyn was that no more than a fourth of the cars along the main thoroughfare of Flatbush Avenue had done this.) Among those with lights on were drivers of police radio cars in parts of all five boroughs. A police department spokesman said no general directive for this action had been issued, but noted that commanders in many precincts had ordered their men to join the tribute.[138]

In Chicago, Mayor Richard Daley called a special memorial meeting of the City Council, the first he had called since the assassination of President Kennedy in 1963.[139] And also in Chicago, fires blazed on the West Side after a day of uncontrollable looting, fires, and deaths.[140] Three thousand National Guardsmen were ordered into the city's streets.[141] Scores of persons were injured, struck by rocks as they drove in their cars or attacked by gangs on the street.[142] Half the Chicago fire department was fighting the fires and what was obvious arson. While firemen were struggling to subdue one blaze, two more buildings would go up in flames. A fireman said, "There is no way in the world the fires could have spread by themselves like this."[143] While the firemen worked, looters carried off appliances, television sets and liquor. Some Negro youths hurled bricks at firemen.[144] Other youths roamed through downtown Chicago streets and the slum areas breaking store windows, looting, stoning buses and automobiles.[145] Circuit Judge Richard J. Fitzgerald was bombarded with rocks and bricks while driving to the Criminal Courts Building.[146] In some blocks along Madison Street, more than half the stores had been smashed, looted or burned. One store that had not been touched was a small grocery owned by a Negro, Hooker Brown. Heavy metal gates had protected his store, and even though he was open, he insisted on keeping the gates in place. Said Brown, "Without the bars, these people in here, they'd take all they could steal. You've got to look out for yourself."[147]

On April 6, at Mayor Daley's request, President Johnson ordered about 5,000 troops to Chicago to help put down what Lt. Gov. Samuel Shapiro called an insurrection. Also on duty were 6,700 Illinois National Guardsmen and 10,500 Chicago policemen, with half of the police force on the streets at a time.[148]

The police listed eleven Negroes dead, seven in the rioting and four others indirectly related to it. About 1,800 persons had been arrested, about 1,450 of them adults.[149] About 500 Negro families were burned out of their homes.[150]

In Chicago, damage to 210 buildings burned down in the rioting was put at $10 million by insurance adjusters. But the figure was subject to revision—upwards. Looting, loss of business, and a great deal of other damage was expected to increase the total by many millions.[151]

Five Negro militants were arrested in Chicago on charges of arson and conspiracy to commit arson. Among them were Doug Andrews, described by the Police Superintendent as a known advocate of "violence and the overthrow of lawful authority," and Edward Crawford, president of the National Negro Rifle Association.[152]

Among those attempting to "cool it" were leaders of the two major South Side Negro gangs, who decided that they did not want their neighborhood pulverized by the rioting that had destroyed much of Madison Street on the West Side. Nearly 4,000 of the gang youths faced off in a dramatic confrontation as their lieutenants talked peace and order "out of respect for Martin Luther King."[153]

In Baltimore, violence did not begin until the second day after the assassination of Martin Luther King, but when it did begin, it grimly made up for lost time. The violence began about 5 p.m. on April 6, subsided during the early morning hours, and then broke out again like a racist epidemic about 8 a.m. on April 7.[154] In a ten-and-a-half hour period, the Baltimore police recorded 137 cases of looting. About 350 fires were reported in a single evening. Forty-one more fires occurred the following day.[155]

To help the city and state police cope with the crisis, 6,000 National Guardsmen were ordered into the city by Maryland's Governor Spiro Agnew,[156] a liberal-to-moderate Republican who had won the election with overwhelming Negro support. The looting, burning, and violence flared again and became worse as evening came on. Now Governor Agnew asked for federal troops. In all, nearly 5,000 federal troops were sent into Baltimore, at the Governor's request, serving along with nearly 6,000 Maryland National Guard troops and about 1,500 local and state police.[157] The police confirmed four separate incidents of sniping around the city. At one time a fire in a delicatessen threatened to consume an entire block of Lombard Street in East Baltimore, after firemen were driven away by snipers firing from a nearby public housing project. Finally the firemen managed to return and pour water on the blaze.[158] The Fire Department said it had been called to about 500 fires since the riots began. Police and firemen were being pelted with stones and bottles more frequently, and soldiers had to start using tear gas several times to disperse crowds in Negro slum areas.[159] Mounted policemen patrolled downtown streets. Policemen with dogs on leashes were seen in Negro areas. At first much of the looting was done by children and teen-agers. Then adults began joining in.[160]

On April 11, Governor Agnew called 100 Negro leaders to his office for a meeting,[161] including many who had walked the streets of Baltimore under special curfew passes, trying to persuade Negroes to stay indoors.[162] Outside the meeting and barred from entry were the militants—in Agnew's words, the "ready-mix, instantaneous, circuit-riding, Hanoi-visiting, caterwauling, riot-inciting, burn-America-down type" Negroes. Governor Agnew explained that his exclusion of these ultra-militants was "no accident, ladies and gentlemen, it is just good planning. I do not communicate with lawbreakers."[163] Governor Agnew charged that the young militants had inflamed the Negro community, thereby inciting the riots. He told the Negro leaders that "the looting and rioting . . . did not occur by chance," and stated, "It is no mere coincidence that a national disciple of violence, Mr. Stokely Carmichael, was observed meeting with local black power advocates and known criminals in Baltimore April 3, 1968—three days before the Baltimore riots began." Then Agnew accused those at the meeting of "breaking and running" when criticized by the black militants for disunity.[164] He charged that they were afraid to repudiate militant Negroes because of "a perverted concept of race loyalty" and because they didn't like being called "Mr. Charlie's boy" and "Uncle Tom."[165] Eighty of the 100 Negro leaders present walked out.[166] Later the Governor's press aide said, "It was nothing done lightly. The Governor personally drafted this speech. It was all done with very sober thought. With the riot he felt very strongly that the time had come to speak out. He feels it very important and vital that the responsible voice of the black community be heard. He feels it is being subdued, either voluntarily or otherwise." Governor Agnew commented that the walkout was not a surprise, although the number involved was. A reporter asked him, "What if everyone had walked out?" The Governor replied, "I would simply be faced with a situation where I would have to find other Negro leaders."[167] Governor Agnew had won election with the help of a Negro electorate that voted for him by margins as large as 50 to 1 in some precincts.[168] He assured the Negro leaders that he remembered this and asked, "Don't you think I know I'm committing political suicide when I sit here and do this?"[169]

Washington, Chicago, Baltimore—on and on went the grisly dishonor roll of 110 towns and cities plagued by disruption, disorder, and worse, far worse. To those in other countries, it must have appeared for a few eerie days as if America trembled on the edge of revolt. And then suddenly, on April 9, 1968, all eyes turned to one city—

one event—one procession—almost to the exclusion of everything and everyone else in the world.

On April 9, the body of Martin Luther King was borne to its final resting place. His African mahogany coffin was carted through the streets of Atlanta on a crude farm wagon pulled by two Georgia mules. Behind the wagon marched some of the most famous personages in this country.[170] Governor Rockefeller and Senator Robert Kennedy made the trek.[171] At the funeral service were Vice President Humphrey, Richard Nixon, Attorney General Ramsey Clark, The Most Rev. Terence J. Cooke, newly appointed Archbishop of New York, Archbishop Iakovos, Primate of the Greek Orthodox Church in the Americas, Rabbi Henry Siegman, executive vice president of the Synagogue Council of America, Harry Belafonte, Marlon Brando, Eartha Kitt, 50 members of the House of Representatives and 30 Senators.[172] In general, the visiting politicians got a courteous reception, although the temperature was lowered by several degrees when Nixon arrived at the church. Cries of "politicking" greeted the former Vice President as he entered the church, and some of the younger militants murmured audibly about "crocodile tears" and vote-seeking.[173]

Stokely Carmichael appeared at the church, accompanied by six bodyguards. The church was already jammed. Carmichael had been invited—there was a seat for him—but the doormen were dubious about admitting the bodyguards. Some of Carmichael's followers, thinking their chieftain was being kept out, shouted, "You'd better let him in," and "He's a black man." Finally the whole group was allowed to enter.[174]

The live television coverage of the funeral service ran seven and a half hours. It was estimated that about 120 million people in the United States watched some part of the funeral services. The services were beamed by the Early Bird communications satellite to Europe, where they were transmitted by Eurovision, the European broadcasting union. Later, some reporters said that they had instinctively joined in the singing of "We Shall Overcome."[175]

At the services, a prayer was given by the Rev. Ronald English, assistant pastor of the Ebenezer Baptist Church[176] (where King had served as co-pastor with his father). Rev. English all but depicted King's career as the Second Coming of Christ. He told the congregation of dignitaries, "We have witnessed the life of the crucified Christ and we have seen the slaying of Martin Luther King . . . like Jesus, not only did Martin Luther King challenge the status quo, but he challenged our mode of existence. Therefore, like Jesus, he had to die as a martyr for a cause that challenged the world's assumed posture of security."[177]

At times, it was difficult to determine where Rev. English's prayer ended, and his political lobbying began, as when he beseeched the Almighty:

Grant that the Congress and President of this nation who have been so generous and gracious in their memorial tributes will be guided by the memory of this suffering servant and return to the legislative halls determined to pass without compromise or reservations legislation so vitally needed to preserve domestic tranquility and prevent social disruption.[178]

And again, where he uttered this plea, which could have been penned by Dr. Benjamin Spock:

Grant, oh lover of peace, that we will effectively negotiate for a peaceful settlement in Vietnam to end the brutal slayings and communal atrocities committed in the name of democracy.[179]

Martin Luther King was buried beside his grandparents. An epitaph on the tombstone, derived from a Negro spiritual, read: "Free at last; free at last; thank God Almighty I'm free at last."[180]

In New York City, on the day of the funeral, public and parochial schools were closed, most department stores and retail businesses were closed until 1 p.m., and the New

York Stock Exchange closed for the first time in honor of a private citizen (the American Stock Exchange also closed).[181] A memo from A. O. Sulzberger, publisher of the New York *Times*, went to all employees, offering to grant a day off with pay to all those wishing to attend the funeral in Atlanta. The *Times* was even prepared to advance its employees the economy round trip air fare to Atlanta, with the sum being recovered through payroll deductions.[182] In the heavily Negro Bedford-Stuyvesant area of Brooklyn, stores and other commercial and industrial places were shuttered and signs read: "Closed all day in memory of Dr. Martin Luther King."[183] But there was good reason to believe that not all of these closings were voluntary. While an employee of a restaurant pulled the iron gate into place outside, the owner said, "The mob just came in and ordered us to close." Asked "What mob?" he replied, "Some youths from CORE."[184] Other such incidents were cited. In Greenwich Village, the police had received anonymous reports from merchants in the area near New York University of threats by Negro youths to the effect that "if you don't close, your store will be burned."[185] And the pressure applied against some workers was almost as unsavory; in many areas, labor union members had been *directed* by their national leaders to stop work at least part of the day.[186]

In the predominantly Negro New Cassel area of Nassau County, N.Y., the police said that about 75 Negroes, divided into three or four groups, stopped motorists and ordered them to turn on their automobile lights in honor of King. Persons who refused to do so had their cars stoned. After several cars were stoned, the Police Commissioner closed 20 blocks to traffic. Bus service was suspended after the evening rush hour because of the disturbances.[187]

In Washington, D.C., the word "closed" was repeated thousands of times on the doors of restaurants, banks, office buildings, and stores, big and small.[188] Again, while a great number may have closed voluntarily in honor of a fallen civil rights leader, others had apparently been intimidated by threats of violence. A typical phone call went "Are you going to be open Tuesday [the day of the funeral]?" If the merchant replied "yes," the caller would warn, "Okay. We'll get you tonight." One of the largest automobile dealers in a predominantly white suburb was notified that on the day of the funeral he would have the choice of being "closed down or burned down." Not too surprisingly, he decided to close.

Two beauty operators received a telephone call from the shop's owner. He had just been threatened and he told them to lock up right away. They did. A law firm in one community was threatened with being fire-bombed if it opened its offices on the day of the funeral. It did not open. One businessman said, "I think it must have been planned, with callers going by listings in the yellow pages of the phone book. There were just too many calls for it not to have been."[189]

In the midst of the five days that shook the nation, the House of Representatives was debating the passage of the Civil Rights Act of 1968, with its controversial provisions for "open housing." The Civil Rights Acts of 1964 and 1965 had been passed in times of crisis, violence, and threats of violence. The Civil Rights Act of 1968 was to be no exception. Even as the House debated the measure in the besieged capital, tourists seeking to watch had to show passes issued by their Congressmen. Several hundred Marines and soldiers stood guard in battle dress.[190]

The day after the assassination, the New York *Times* wrote: "The slaying of the Rev. Dr. Martin Luther King, Jr. could assure passage of a landmark civil rights bill next week, Congressional leaders said today."[191] And one of the civil rights bill's chief opponents, Rep. William Colmer of Mississippi, chairman of the House Rules Committee, agreed that this would probably be the result. Colmer termed the shooting "a dastardly act." He continued: "These dumb, would-be or self-styled patriots who commit this type of act are doing the cause they believe in a grave injustice and hastening the enactment of ill-advised legislation in a period of anger and emotion."[192]

On April 10, the House passed the Civil Rights Act of 1968 and sent it to the President. The vote was 250 to 171.[193] In the House, as in the Senate, Republicans provided the margin needed for the passage of the rights bill.[194] The Act immediately bars discrimination in federally-owned housing and in multi-unit dwellings insured with federal funds. On December 31, 1968, it covers all multi-unit dwellings and homes in real estate developments except those occupied by the owners with up to four units (such as boarding houses). Effective January 1, 1970, it will extend to all single-family homes that are sold or rented through brokers. Those who consider themselves discriminated against can complain to the Secretary of Housing and Urban Development within 180 days. HUD will try to settle the matter informally. If the case does go to federal court, and if the complaint is upheld, the complainant can be awarded his court costs, actual damages, and up to $1,000 in punitive damages.[195]

In death, as in life, Martin Luther King forced passage of a civil rights act—an irony he probably would have relished.

Since the evening of April 4, the country had been asking the questions: Who killed Martin Luther King? What was his name? What did he look like? How did he manage to escape? Where did he go? When would he be caught? The answers were tangled in a massive labyrinth of false names, false trails, and uncertain identities. The news stories served only to headline the confusion:

FALSE POLICE REPORTS OF CHASE AFTER DR. KING'S DEATH GIVE IMPETUS TO CONSPIR-ACY THEORIES

ALABAMIAN NAMED IN DR. KING INQUIRY

MYSTERY DEEPENS IN DR. KING INQUIRY
(Data on Man FBI Seeks to Question Are Few)

NEW THEORY TOLD IN DR. KING INQUIRY
(Man Sought by the FBI May Have False Identity)

FBI ACCUSES GALT OF A CONSPIRACY IN DR.
KING SLAYING; GALT ELUDES FBI AGENTS
IN CALIFORNIA; THOUSANDS OF WANTED
POSTERS DISTRIBUTED IN NATION

FBI SAYS 'GALT' IS AN ESCAPED CONVICT

HOW MANY 'GALTS'? WITNESSES DIFFER
(Three Earlier Descriptions of Suspect Vary Widely)

FBI HUNT FOR RAY IN DR. KING'S KILLING
STUNS PRISON OFFICIALS AND OTHERS
WHO KNEW HIM

A CONVICT SAYS RAY SOUGHT KING BOUNTY

GALT TRIP FROM COAST TO NEW ORLEANS
RECALLED BY COMPANION

On the night Martin Luther King was shot, Memphis
policemen were drawn to the north side of the city 34 minutes after the shooting by a false report from "police car
160" that a white Mustang automobile, believed to be the
getaway car, was speeding along city streets. Detectives
later investigated the possibility that the report was relayed
by an accomplice of the killer to the central police radio
in an effort to draw pursuers to north Memphis while the
killer escaped across the Mississippi River into Arkansas
or down U.S. Highway 55 into the state of Mississippi.
That night, at 6:36 p.m., the police radio reported that a
blue hardtop 1966 Pontiac had joined the chase for the
white Mustang. In the next ten minutes, several progress
reports on the "chase" were relayed through the headquarters radio to other police cars headed to the area. The
police dispatcher making the broadcast said that the descriptions of a chase were being fed to him by "police car
160." At 6:47 p.m., the police radio broadcast a report
that someone in the white Mustang was shooting at the

blue Pontiac. That ended the broadcasts about the chase.[196]
The Commercial Appeal, a Memphis paper, quoted Lieut.
R. W. Bradshaw, who was assigned to police car 160 that
night, as having said that he saw no white Mustang and
did not chase one that night.[197]

A week later, the FBI issued a fugitive warrant charging Eric Starvo Galt with conspiracy in the slaying of
Martin Luther King. The FBI said Galt conspired beginning about March 29 with a man "whom he alleged to be
his brother," to "injure, oppress, threaten or intimidate"
King. The conspiracy was said to have continued until
about April 5.[198] In Memphis, Galt was charged with first-
degree murder on a state warrant.[199] The FBI released two
photographs of Galt.[200] In Birmingham, Alabama, Galt's
former landlord was asked if the photos were of his former
tenant, and replied, "I don't think so." In Memphis, a witness said an FBI photo of Galt did not resemble the man
seen leaving the scene soon after the slaying. In Atlanta
a taxi driver could not identify the picture.[201]

Two days later, the FBI announced that an escaped
convict named James Earl Ray was the man being sought
under the alias of Eric Starvo Galt for the murder of Martin Luther King. Galt's true identity was discovered after
latent fingerprints uncovered in the King investigation were
compared with the prints of more than 53,000 persons
listed as wanted by the Bureau. Ray had escaped from the
Missouri State Penitentiary on April 23, 1967.[202] A 40-
year-old native of Illinois, Ray had served seven years of
a 20-year sentence for armed robbery and car theft in St.
Louis.[203]

This was by no means the last piece in the puzzle. Descriptions given the police and the FBI of the assassin had
varied so widely that it appeared as if as many as four
men may have been under suspicion. A source in the Justice
Department said that credible witnesses in Memphis and
in Birmingham who saw Ray (or Galt) seemed to be describing different men. Before the bulletin on Ray there

were at least three separate descriptions from witnesses who had known a Galt in the last six months:

A long-nosed man in his late 20's who was seen in the Memphis rooming house from which the shot was fired.

A 30-year-old quiet-spoken man who talked about the weather at a Birmingham rooming house last fall.

A 36-year-old "avid dancer" who bought a rifle in Birmingham and who took dancing lessons in New Orleans.[204]

On the basis that the suspect could not have been in two places at the same time, it was now believed that more than one man had used the name Eric Starvo Galt.[205] This was offered in evidence: On March 1, 1968, an Eric Galt telephoned the Alabama Highway Patrol to ask for a duplicate copy of the driver's license he got in September of 1967. The copy was mailed to a Birmingham address and a bill of 25 cents that was enclosed with the duplicate was returned to Montgomery on March 6 with the 25 cents. *But the FBI had said that Galt had been in California during this time.*

In its bulletin describing Galt as an avid dancer, the FBI said that he had taken dancing lessons in New Orleans in 1964 and 1965. *But the FBI said that Galt, under the name James Earl Ray, had been in prison in Missouri from 1960 until he escaped in April, 1967.*[206]

Prison officials and inmates at the Missouri State Penitentiary were described as "stunned" that James Earl Ray had been accused of conspiring in the slaying of King. Warden Harold R. Swenson said, "I was floored. This guy's penny ante. It doesn't shape up, does it?" One of the warden's aides stated, "We've got 2,000 prisoners in here, and none of them recognized him [from the FBI photos]."[207]

In Whitfield County Jail in Dalton, Georgia, Raymond Curtis, a convicted murderer who had been in prison with James Earl Ray, said he had once heard Ray say he would be willing to try to collect $1 million for killing Martin Luther King. Curtis said that he and Ray had been inmates at the Missouri State Penitentiary when they heard the news that President Kennedy had been assassinated. Curtis added that a third prisoner had told them a "K-K businessman's association" was offering "a million dollar bounty to get King." Curtis went on, "King was running his mouth pretty good, then, and Ray said, 'If there is a million dollar bounty on King, I believe I can collect it.'" Curtis said he had heard Ray mention "a King bounty" several times. At one point he said Ray referred to the Kennedy assassination by saying: "Boy, probably somebody made a nice little penny off of that. I sure wish it was me."[208]

In Los Angeles, James Earl Ray was reported to have driven to New Orleans in December, 1967, to talk business with "a man with an Italian name." The statement was made by Charles Stein, a bearded song writer who said that he had made the trip with Ray (who was traveling as Eric Starvo Galt), and that he had been told the "Italian" name "but I don't remember right now what it was. But it was a man with an Italian name and he either lived on the industrial canal in New Orleans or he had a business there."[209]

Questioned about a possible conspiracy, Attorney General Ramsey Clark answered, "There's no significant evidence that it goes beyond the single actor."[210]* And there the matter stands, as of this writing (April 28, 1968) — the statements, the revisions, the re-revisions, the names and the aliases, the photos and more photos. Where it will all end, no one can say. Whether or not an arrest is made,† whether or not James Earl Ray is tried and convicted of the slaying of Martin Luther King, it seems safe to predict that the rumors will never really die—that the theorists will offer bits and pieces of evidence or simply conjecture that some other person or persons, in concert or conspiracy,

---

* Later, Clark sounded far less certain. If others were involved, he said, the F.B.I. would find them.

† On June 8, 1968, James Earl Ray was arrested in London as he was preparing to board a plane for Brussels. Ray had a loaded gun, and was carrying two fraudulent Canadian passports.

really committed the murder. After all, not even a panel headed by the Chief Justice of the United States Supreme Court was able to squelch dissenting views about the assassination of John F. Kennedy—and it may well be that academic and political figures for years to come will be working feverishly to uncover new evidence that some far-out group paid or instigated or committed the murder of Martin Luther King. The charges and countercharges will probably go on and on, and may never be fully resolved in our lifetime.

The assassin killed his body, but did not and could not kill his thoughts. In death, Martin Luther King is very nearly as powerful as he was in life. When Ralph Abernathy took over as new president of the Southern Christian Leadership Conference, one of his first announcements was to pledge that the group would be "more militant than ever" but would continue to pursue its goals through "nonviolent" protest.[211] Two weeks after her husband's death, the newspapers reported Mrs. Coretta King had agreed to speak in her husband's place at the anti-Vietnam War rally to be held in Central Park on April 27. David Dellinger, coordinator of the parade committee, told the press: "Coretta King is coming to speak because she is concerned that since his death her husband is being remembered by many people only for his civil rights activities. She is anxious to re-establish his role in people's minds as an anti-war leader."[212] And in an article written by him for *Look*, King had said of the march on Washington, "This will be an attempt to bring a kind of Selma-like movement, Birmingham-like movement, into being, substantially around the economic issues."[213] So the doctrines of Martin Luther King did not die with him in Memphis; his ideas and beliefs quite obviously survive him, and will continue to permeate our society, in and out of government. And now more than ever it becomes necessary to know who he was—what he was—what he really said and did and wanted, and why, as he himself ruefully admitted, his dream had become a nightmare. We must look beyond the legend, beyond the applause and eulogies, beyond the degrees and Nobel Prize, and find a man named Martin Luther King and know him well. We must know—by studying his campaigns in Birmingham and Selma—just what a "Selma-like movement, Birmingham-like movement" was, and the potentialities for chaos such a campaign can bring to the nation's capital and elsewhere in our beleaguered country. We must study King's role in the anti-Vietnam movement and the company he quite willingly kept during those marches. We must study his many associations with the Far Left. Above all, we must ask ourselves if the doctrine and dogma of Martin Luther King's campaigns unwittingly created a fertile breeding ground in which the urban riots could flourish. But first we must begin as King did, with a knowledge and understanding of the three most potent words in America—the words that have transformed our lives and our country: "nonviolent civil disobedience."

CHAPTER 2

To Prison with Love

✿✿✿✿✿✿✿✿✿✿✿✿✿✿✿✿✿✿✿✿

Civil disobedience, in fact and theory, casts a long if erratic shadow over the pages of American history. It starts with the Boston Tea Party, when about 60 colonists protested an "unjust" import duty on tea by tossing 342 chests of it into Boston Bay. It turns up again in the Whiskey Rebellion, when President Washington was forced to call out the militia to cope with rebellious mountaineers refusing to pay an "unjust" tax on distilled liquors. It shimmers in the waters of Walden Pond, when Henry David Thoreau decided that "the only obligation which I have the right to assume is to do at any time what I think right." It stages a 20th-century sneak preview in the frenetic forties, when A. Philip Randolph threatened to lead a civil disobedience movement to protest segregation in the Army[1] (an earlier attempt at civil disobedience had been postponed because of the riots of 1943).[2] But it remained for Martin Luther King to elevate civil disobedience to virtually the level of a constitutional right; to carry civil disobedience to the verge of martial law in one of the largest cities in the South; and to do all this with the indulgence of the President, much of the Congress, and very nearly all the members of the Supreme Court.

In the entire English language, one can hardly find a

more appealing word than "nonviolence," implying, as it does, the presence of peace. It was Dr. King who welded nonviolence to resistance, and then emphasized that non-violent resistance "does resist."[3] It was Dr. King who needed, and even welcomed, a violent reaction to his non-violent civil disobedience. It was Dr. King who, in Birmingham and Selma, drew up "battle plans," deployed hundreds and even thousands of nonviolent "troops," and generally out-maneuvered, out-fought and out-thought his foes in one engagement after another. And after Birmingham, it was Dr. King who now labeled it "the nonviolent revolution" and stressed that it was "just coming of age."[4]

Dr. King outlined his basic strategy as follows, in the pages of the *Saturday Review:*

1) Nonviolent demonstrators go into the streets to exercise their constitutional rights.
2) Racists resist by unleashing violence against them.
3) Americans of conscience in the name of decency demand Federal intervention and legislation.
4) The Administration, under mass pressure, initiates measures of immediate intervention and remedial legislation.[5]

Obviously, if a hundred demonstrators could not provoke violent Southern resistance, more hundreds would be thrown into the breach—and more after that, if necessary —until the desired goal of violence was unleashed against them. Only then could the stage of crisis be reached where "Americans of conscience in the name of decency demand Federal intervention and legislation," and only at that point would "the Administration, under mass pressure, [initiate] measures of immediate intervention and remedial legislation."

As we will see, this is precisely what took place in Birmingham.

King always considered his doctrine a combination of Christianity and Gandhism. He once wrote: "I had come to see early that the Christian doctrine of love operating through the Gandhian method of nonviolence was one of the most potent weapons available to the Negro in his struggle for freedom. . . . In other words, Christ furnished the spirit and motivation, while Gandhi furnished the method."[6]

In an incisive article, a young Indian author, Ved Mehta, disclosed substantial differences between the Gandhian doctrine and its American transplant. For one thing, wrote Mehta, "Dr. King, unlike Gandhi, is fighting for minority rights. The struggling people in British India constituted the entire labor force, and the realization of this fact placed a powerful economic lever in their hands." At the same time Mehta pointed out the ambivalence of King's position, vis-à-vis the law, in that "Dr. King must uphold favorable legislation for Negroes, and at the same time harness disobedience to unjust laws."[7]

In a television debate with James J. Kilpatrick, editor of the Richmond *News-Leader*, King flatly declared, "an unjust law is no law . . . the individual who discovers on the basis of conscience that a law is unjust, and is willing in a peaceful sense to disobey that unjust law and willingly and voluntarily suffers the consequences, is expressing the highest respect for law."[8] King was still equating disobedience with respect when he told the New York *Times:* "I say obey the law when the law is right, when the law is just and when the law is in line with the moral law of the universe. When conscience tells someone that a law is unjust, then I think a righteous man has no alternative but to conscientiously disobey that law."[9]

Could segregationists practice civil disobedience if *their* consciences led them to a contrary view of "the moral law of the universe"? At one time, King conceded the right of "sincere whites" to oppose desegregation, as long as that opposition took a nonviolent form.[10] Then New York *Times* correspondent Claude Sitton observed that the prime argument for Southern white compliance with the Supreme

Court school desegregation ruling was that it was now the law of the land. "This argument," Sitton emphasized, "would get short shrift by King's standards."[11] Possibly this was the reason why less than a year later King revealed some dour second thoughts, and railed against the "uncivil disobedience" of the segregationist.[12] In what may have set a new international track record for infinite gall, King complained that "in the face of laws they consider unjust, the racists seek to defy, evade and circumvent the law, and they are unwilling to accept the penalty. The end result of their defiance is anarchy and disrespect for the law."[13]

No estimate has ever been made of the total number of dollars spent to finance Dr. King's doctrine of civil disobedience. But the cost may well have been staggering. At the height of the Birmingham crisis, the NAACP Legal Defense Fund was compelled to take out full-page ads and practically plead for funds.[14] Their desperation was readily apparent when they revealed that they were "defending every one of 2,497 Negro citizens jailed in Birmingham for peaceful protest against segregation," and "appealing the convictions of Rev. Martin Luther King, Jr., and ten Negro ministers sentenced to jail for criminal contempt." Frankly admitting "our resources are inadequate for this gigantic task," the NAACP estimated that "legal costs for the defense of nearly 2,500 individuals may come to $500,000."[15] It was, and is, difficult to reconcile these mammoth legal defense efforts with Dr. King's professed willingness "to pay the penalty" for his resistance to the law.

More than anyone else, Martin Luther King must have known what even a fraction of that $500,000 could have done for the Negro poor, in terms of vocational guidance and training classes and any number of self-help projects to elevate their economic status. But instead, these hundreds of thousands of dollars were expended on litigation involving almost 2,500 practitioners of civil disobedience.

Ironically, Dr. King—the high priest of selective lawlessness—had developed a considerable following in the legal profession. When he addressed the Association of the Bar of the City of New York, Judge Rosenman told him that out of six thousand people who had wanted to hear him, only fifteen hundred could be admitted to the building. Since the meeting hall seated only 650 people, 850 others were sitting in five anterooms to listen to his speech over loudspeakers.[16] In a remark that must be considered the ultimate in tastelessness on the part of a jurist, Judge Rosenman facetiously thanked Dr. King for finding time between jail sentences to address the Association of the Bar of the City of New York.[17] In his remarks—delivered at the height of the crisis in Selma, Alabama—Dr. King told his audience of lawyers that even though devotees of nonviolent action practiced civil disobedience, they also respected the law and felt a moral responsibility to obey just laws. Predictably, he added that advocates of nonviolence were justified in disobeying unjust laws because they did so peacefully and openly, and willingly accepted the penalty for their disobedience. He concluded his prepared text with the prediction that "one day all of America will be proud of the glorious achievement of the nonviolent heroes during this historic decade."[18]

But some renowned lawyers could scarcely be considered proud of the means King utilized to reach his achievements. Among these distinguished dissenters were Morris I. Leibman, Chairman of the American Bar Association Standing Committee on Education Against Communism. In an address before the criminal law section of the American Bar Association, Leibman expressed his conviction that "we have an affirmative and daily duty to eliminate discrimination and provide opportunity—full opportunity and meaningful equal justice for all our people." But he was equally convinced that civil disobedience represented a threat to our law-oriented society.[19] He recalled to mind these words spoken by Abraham Lincoln more than one hundred years ago:

Let every American, every lover of liberty, every well-wisher to his prosperity, swear by the blood of the revolution never to violate in the least particular the laws of the country. . . . Let every man remember that to violate the law is to trample on the blood of his father and to tear the character of his own and his children's liberty. Let reverence for the laws . . . be taught in schools, in seminaries, and in colleges; let it be written in primers, spelling books and in almanacs; let it be preached from the pulpit, proclaimed in legislative halls, and enforced in courts of justice, and in short, let it become the *political religion* of the nation; and let the old and young, rich and poor, the grave and gay of all sexes, tongues and colors and conditions, sacrifice unceasingly upon its altar.[20]

Leibman believed that the very phrase "civil disobedience" was basically a misnomer. Specifically, he asked his audience of experts in criminal law to consider "whether there can be 'civil' disobedience when there is a specific intent to disobey the law." He reminded the attorneys that "such a specific state of mind is ordinarily treated as the essence of criminality, hence not civil." Leibman summarized, "it seems to me that there is an inherent contradiction in the concept of premeditated 'righteous' civil disobedience."[21]

Leibman stressed, "let there be no question of where we stand on human rights and our rejection of discrimination. Surely, the continuing social task for the morally sensitive citizen is to impart reality to the yet unachieved ideal of full and equal participation by any and all in our values and opportunities."[22] Having made his position perfectly clear, the lawyer turned the other side of the civil rights coin, and saw a corresponding need for full participation in civil *obedience*—the need for all members of society to obey all law, while reserving the right to seek its change or amendment through the ballot and the legislature. He reminded his listeners that "no society, whether free or tyrannical, can give its citizens the 'right' to break the law. There can be no law to which obedience is optional, no command to which the states attach an 'if you please.' "[23]

It is a somber reflection upon the temper of our times that in 1964—175 years after the ratification of the Constitution—a distinguished member of the bar found it necessary to prepare cogently worded arguments in behalf of compliance with the law. It is no less depressing to reflect that in this adversary proceeding in the court of public opinion, Leibman was acting as attorney for the *defense*.

If, on occasions such as this, the story of the civil rights movement seems to assume a bizarre, almost surrealistic air, the dubious credit must be laid at the door of Dr. King. After all, it was he who, on gilded wings of rhetoric, succeeded in convincing much of the American public that massive resistance was massive good will, and that one served the law best who reserved the right to disobey it.

It bears repeating that Leibman deferred to no one in his personal sympathy for equal opportunity. But he refused to be mesmerized into rubber-stamping anything and everything done in the name of civil rights. Regardless of the intensity and even fervor of one's own personal beliefs, he was convinced that "lawyers must insist on the integrity of the means."[24]

Leibman cut straight through to the heart of the issue, in these few words:

While the idea of civil disobedience may evoke sympathy where the claim is made that the cause is just, once we accept such a doubtful doctrine, we legitimatize it for other causes which we might reject. We must be even more careful in the sympathetic case because, in effect, that sets the standard of conduct which then becomes acceptable for cases not as appealing or for groups not as responsible. Thus, we substitute pressure for persuasion, and squander the carefully nurtured value of self-restraint and jeopardize the system of law.[25]

At no point in his speech did Leibman so much as mention the name of Martin Luther King. But no shoe yet fashioned has ever provided a more perfect fit.

Leibman's speech was delivered at the height of the blistering Presidential campaign of 1964. It had threatened to be a Long Hot Summer; already, there had been rioting and looting by Negroes in several urban areas. Fearful of a white backlash that could lead to disaster at the polls, the major civil rights leaders urged their members to observe a "broad curtailment, if not total moratorium" on all mass demonstrations until after the Presidential election.[26] The announcement of the moratorium was made on July 29, 1964—less than two weeks before Leibman's address to the Criminal Law Section of the American Bar Association.

Perhaps it was with this expedient moratorium in mind—and the patently obvious political motivation for it—that Leibman warned his audience to harbor no illusions about the perilous potential of mass demonstrations. As he expressed it:

The plain fact of human nature is that the organized disobedience of masses stirs up the primitive. This has been true of a soccer crowd, and a lynch mob. Psychologically and psychiatrically, it is very clear that no man—no matter how well intentioned—can keep group passions in control.[27]

Martin Luther King had had this truth forcibly brought home to him a year before, in Birmingham, Alabama. During his nonviolent campaign a riot broke out, as at least 2,500 Negroes rampaged through the business district—and the New York *Times* noted that, at that point, Dr. King was apparently no longer in control of this violent demonstration.[28]

The young Indian author, Ved Mehta, related an incident in which Gandhi had called off a "startlingly successful" mass civil disobedience campaign because of one act of violence in a remote village. "According to Gandhi,"

Mehta wrote, "a whole campaign of nonviolence was negated by one incident of violence, however small."[29] As we will see, Dr. King took a much more cavalier view.

King conceived of nonviolent resistance as embodying the best—and, equally important, avoiding the worst—of two worlds. He placed it at a point equidistant between what he considered the two extreme reactions to racial oppression. At one extreme, he saw those who resigned themselves to oppression. "There is such a thing," he maintained, "as the freedom of exhaustion," in which one simply gave up, accepted injustice, and acquiesced in his own degradation. Those who followed this course, were, in effect, cooperating with their oppressor, and incurring not his friendship, but his contempt.[30] King was withering in his indictment of this passive submission. In his words, "to accept passively an unjust system is to cooperate with that system; thereby the oppressed become as evil as the oppressor. Noncooperation with evil is as much a moral obligation as is cooperation with good."[31]

At the other extreme, King saw those who dealt with their oppression by resorting to "physical violence and corroding hatred."[32] King objected to violence and hatred on moral grounds:

It thrives on hatred rather than love . . . destroys community and makes brotherhood impossible.

and on coolly pragmatic grounds:

It solves no social problem; it merely creates new and more complicated ones.[33]

As the ultimate solution, King proposed "nonviolent resistance." His movement was to be nonviolent, in the sense that there would be no physical aggression against the oppressors; there would be a willingness "to accept blows from the opponent, without striking back." And yet he and his followers would resist, in every other conceivable way,[34] just short of violence.

Over and over, one encounters the word "suffering" in King's civil rights vocabulary. He cited as one of the characteristics of nonviolent resistance, "a willingness to accept suffering without retaliation."[35] But since we are dealing with human beings, and not gods, the insistent question arises: how much suffering will an ordinary person endure, before he turns to retaliation, with or without Martin Luther King's benediction?

King himself had written that "realism impels me to admit that many Negroes will find it difficult to follow the path of nonviolence."[36] What of those who leave this path? What turn in the road do they take? Do they turn to acquiescence or violence? And what of those who are violence-oriented, and barely set foot on King's path at all? Dr. King's own *personal* commitment to nonviolence is readily conceded—but can the same be said of all those in, and on the fringes of, his movement? Specifically, just how nonviolent is nonviolence?

The doctrine of nonviolence had always been the fixed star in Martin Luther King's civil rights firmament. And yet he had often muddied the ideological waters with a none too subtle threat of violence if his methods should fail. He had often implied that if Negroes do not achieve their objectives through nonviolence, they will then feel justified in resorting to force and violence.

In the 1964 campaign, it was made abundantly clear that one of the overriding objectives of the civil rights forces was the defeat of Barry Goldwater in his race for the Presidency. Goldwater had voted for the Civil Rights Acts of 1957 and 1960, and supported nine of the eleven provisions of the Civil Rights Act of 1964. However, because he considered two provisions of the 1964 bill unconstitutional he felt compelled to vote against it, and this act of conscience made him an anathema to Dr. King and his entourage.

King was tireless in his savage denunciations of Gold-water, and his predictions of racial violence if the Arizona Senator were elected. Thus, on September 13, 1964, the New York *Times* reported:

The Rev. Dr. Martin Luther King, Jr., forecast today a "dark night of social disruption" in the United States, if Senator Barry Goldwater is elected President. The American Negro leader said he was convinced that the discontent, frustration and despair of disinherited, poverty-stricken groups would then erupt into "violence and riots the like of which we have never seen before . . ."[37]

This raw forecast of violence becomes all the more meaningful when read against the background of King's own book, *Stride Toward Freedom*. In this work, King wrote that "the [white] reactionaries were not in retreat. *Many of them had predicted violence, and such predictions are always a conscious or unconscious invitation to action.*"[38] The parallel could hardly be more obvious—even to Dr. King.

In demonstration after demonstration, in city after city, King's predictions of violence were sometimes obliquely worded, sometimes bluntly phrased, but almost invariably present in one form or another. In the November 7, 1964, edition of the *Saturday Evening Post*, a few days after Lyndon Johnson's landslide victory, King wrote:

Nonviolence can exist only in a context of justice. When the white power structure calls upon the Negro to reject violence but does not impose upon itself the task of creating necessary social change, it is in fact asking for submission to injustice. Nothing in the theory of nonviolence counsels this suicidal course. The simple fact is that there cannot be nonviolence and tranquility without significant reforms of the evils that endangered the peace in the first place.[39]

As Lerone Bennett, Jr., senior editor of *Ebony*, noted in his biography of Martin Luther King:

Time and time again, King had warned that "nonviolence could not exist in a vacuum." As early as 1961, he had said, "If something isn't done in a hurry and in a vigorous way, explosive situations will develop, particularly in the large industrial areas of the North, where you have great numbers of Negroes with these frustrations emerging."[40]

How nonviolent is nonviolence? At a Conference on Nonviolence and Social Change, which was held at Howard University in November, 1963, a few troubled experts seemed to doubt that the doctrine of nonviolence was quite as beatific as its name implied. Foremost among them was Dr. Jerome D. Frank, a professor of psychiatry at Johns Hopkins University. So far, he said, "Only groups that believe that they cannot hope to win by violence have adhered to nonviolent tactics." "Furthermore, these nonviolent movements could potentially mobilize superior violence on their side. The British knew that too harsh suppression of Gandhi and his followers would stimulate violent revolutionary movements, and they were fighting for their existence at the time. . . . In our country, the federal courts can mobilize overwhelming power in defense of Negro rights as Mississippi has learned." Dr. Frank continued, "Leaders of nonviolent movements constantly remind their opponents that if their demands are not met, they may not be able to keep their followers in check. *Is the threat of violence an integral part of the success of nonviolence?* Can nonviolent campaigns succeed in the complete absence of this threat? If not, are they truly nonviolent?"[41]

Given this viewpoint, it is of more than passing interest to read King's statement that "in the long run, destructive means cannot bring about constructive ends because the ends are pre-existent in the means."[42] By raising the threat of violence as a means of bringing about social and legal change, it may well be that King himself began the slow, steady obliteration of the constructive end he sought, of a "beloved community" at peace with itself.

On at least one point in his philosophy, King could not be more clear—the glorification of going to jail. To Martin Luther King, imprisonment was practically a form of purification, an act of heroism very nearly comparable to that of the early Christian martyrs. In King's strange scale of values, no stigma attached to the prisoner, only to the jailer. And certainly no one—in or out of the clergy—had ever more consistently practiced what he preached.

In his book, *Ebony* editor Lerone Bennett. Jr. compiled a record of King's arrests from January 26, 1956, through June 13, 1964. There were 29 entries on King's personal police record, among them:

Being indicted with other leading figures of the Montgomery boycott on the charge of being a party to a conspiracy, to hinder and prevent operation of a business without "just or legal cause."

Being arrested in an Atlanta sit-in, and jailed on the charge of violating the state's anti-trespass law.

Being arrested in a "prayer vigil" in Albany, Georgia, city hall, and jailed on charges of failure to obey a police officer, obstructing the sidewalk, and disorderly conduct.[43]

Other entries included minor traffic infractions, and release on bail; in one case, a fourteen-dollar fine was paid almost immediately—over King's objections—by Montgomery Police Commissioner Sellers. In Albany, Georgia, he was released against his will, after a $178 fine was paid by a "mystery man."[44]

Notwithstanding the nationwide publicity given his many arrests, through a maximum number of suspended sentences King had actually served very little time in jail. During the eight-and-a-half-year period noted above, King's total time in prison amounted to approximately one month.[45] But this had not prevented him from extolling the virtues of imprisonment to a whole generation of college students.

King stated that the way of nonviolence might mean

"going to jail," and felt, "if such is the case, the resister must be willing to fill the jail houses of the South."[46] He reiterated that the nonviolent resister "does not seek to dodge jail. If going to jail is necessary, he enters it as a bridegroom enters the bride's chamber."[47]

King had called for an elite corps of student volunteers who would go to jail, rather than pay fines imposed for their protest activities.[48] Small wonder that this famous commentary was made by Adlai Stevenson in an address to the graduating class of Colby College, in Maine: "I think especially of the participation of American students in the great struggle to advance civil and human rights in America. Indeed even a jail sentence is no longer a dishonor, but a proud achievement. Perhaps we are destined to see in this law-loving land, people running for office not on their stainless record, but on their prison records."[49]

To King, it was far more than "a proud achievement." Writing in the *Nation*, he rhapsodized, "Words cannot express the exultation felt by the individual as he finds himself, with hundreds of his followers, behind prison bars for a cause he knows is just."[50]

In pursuit of this "just cause," King obviously was prepared to escalate nonviolent resistance to the brink of nonviolent revolution. He had declared that the young Negro "is carrying forward a revolutionary destiny of a whole people consciously and deliberately. Hence the extraordinary willingness to fill the jails as if they were honor classes, and the boldness to absorb brutality, even to the point of death, and remain nonviolent."[51]

The response from students sometimes approached the fanatical. In this same article, King disclosed, "I am no longer surprised to meet stylishly dressed young girls whose charm and personality would grace a Junior Prom, and to hear them declare in unmistakably sincere terms, 'Dr. King, I am ready to die if I must.'"[52]

J. Edgar Hoover once remarked, "those who seek equal rights under the law should be taught to assume equal responsibility before the law."[53] By this criterion, King's hosannas to imprisonment, and selective anarchy, reached the nadir of irresponsibility. Besides defeating the process of law and order, it ultimately defeated the cause of civil rights itself. In the carefully considered opinion of Charles E. Whittaker, a former Justice of the Supreme Court:

Minority groups, in preaching and practicing defiance of the law, are in fact, advocating erosion and destruction of the only structure that can assure to them, or permanently maintain for them, due process of law, and the equal protection of the laws, and that can thus protect them from discriminations and abuses by majorities.[54]

No matter how many times King drew the fine line between just and unjust laws—no matter how many times he consulted the universe to decide which laws he would obey or disobey—the fact remained that he could not uphold integration laws on odd days, flout segregation laws on even days, and simultaneously proclaim his "highest respect for the law."

Just what did he hope to find at the end of the nonviolent road? What was his ultimate goal? Paradoxically enough, it was not desegregation per se. King considered desegregation "only a partial, though necessary step toward the ultimate goal which we seek. . . . Something must happen so to touch the hearts and souls of men that they will come together, not because the law says it, but because it is natural and right." King stressed that "the aftermath of nonviolence is reconciliation and the creation of the beloved community."[55]

In terms of this ultimate goal, it can hardly be doubted that nonviolence has failed, and failed dismally. The community is less beloved—and more bristling with interracial hostility—than ever before. Even King seemed grimly to admit this, as witness the title of his recent book: *Where Do We Go From Here: Chaos or Community?*

Where do we go from here? Dr. King had posed a most interesting question. But before there can be any definitive answer, we must first see where we have been. We must first retrace our steps along the King itinerary, from Montgomery to Albany, Georgia, to Birmingham and to Selma. We must relive the pitched battles in which civil disobedience "lovingly" emerged victorious over law and order. We must see how he brought civic authority to its knees as the Federal government applauded.

Chaos or community? Perhaps both. Perhaps a chaotic community that bows and scrapes to the will of the mob, while an impotent government stands helplessly by. And if that should be the unhappy result, history—in searching for first causes—may well inscribe this epitaph for The Beloved Community:

IMPALED UPON THE LOVING SWORD OF CIVIL
DISOBEDIENCE.

CHAPTER 3

The Montgomery Bus Boycott

✼✼✼✼✼✼✼✼✼✼✼✼✼✼✼✼✼✼✼✼

In all the frenetic history of the civil rights movement, there has never been anything quite like the Montgomery bus boycott. Beyond question, it stands triumphantly alone among all the campaigns in which Martin Luther King participated.

In other campaigns, King was, quite frankly, an outsider—and not always a welcome one—in the target city that was to come under nonviolent siege; in Montgomery, he was one of the local Negro leaders heading up a campaign composed entirely of local residents. In other campaigns, civil disobedience was encouraged and practiced; in Montgomery, there was no civil disobedience as such (even though King seemed to regard the campaign as an act of massive noncooperation). In other campaigns, there was a working alliance of religious and secular groupings, moderate and radical elements, with militant student representation; in Montgomery, almost the entire movement was under the guidance and control of the clergy (this was four years before the formation of the Student Nonviolent Coordinating Committee). In other campaigns, King invariably issued an urgent call for Federal intervention and remedial legislation; in Montgomery, the primary objective was to bring about a local solution to a local problem.

Ebony's Lerone Bennett, Jr., wrote: "It is a point of

immense interest that the Montgomery movement began in irony and ended in irony."[1] Possibly the crowning irony was that Martin Luther King did not initiate this campaign. If anything, he was more or less pulled into it, and apparently "played it by ear" at the outset of the campaign.

The immediate cause of the Montgomery bus boycott was not an impassioned sermon by the Rev. King—or even one of his Gandhian films—but a colored seamstress with aching feet.

On December 1, 1955, Mrs. Rosa Parks boarded the Cleveland Avenue bus in downtown Montgomery. Mrs. Parks had been on her feet for many long hours, and she was very tired. Wearily, she sat down in the first seat behind the section reserved for whites. Soon the bus driver ordered her and three other Negro passengers to move back in order to accommodate boarding white passengers. By this time, every seat in the bus had been taken, and Mrs. Parks saw no reason to stand in order that a white male passenger could take her seat. While the other three Negro passengers immediately complied with the driver's request, Mrs. Parks alone refused, and was subsequently arrested.[2] Out of this most unlikely raw material was molded the eleven-month-long bus boycott heard around the United States, and probably the world as well.

The city fathers could hardly have made a more controversial arrest. Mrs. Parks was active in her church, and equally active in the local chapter of the NAACP (of which Dr. King had been vice-president for a few months).[3] The arrest of Mrs. Parks came as the proverbial last straw in a long-simmering resentment against an antiquated system of bus segregation. Under this system, if white passengers were already occupying all of their reserved seats and more white people got on the bus, Negroes sitting in the unreserved section immediately behind the whites had to get up, so that white passengers could take their seats. If the Negroes refused to stand and move back, they were arrested.[4]

Negroes were just as incensed by the rudeness and

abusiveness of some bus drivers. Some of the white men who drove the buses referred to Negro passengers as "niggers," "black cows," and "black apes."[5] King wrote that frequently Negroes paid their fares at the front door, and then were forced to get off and reboard the bus at the rear. Often the bus left "with the Negro's dime in the box before he had had time to reach the rear door."[6]

Mrs. Sadie Brooks testified under oath, in court, that she heard a Negro passenger threatened because he did not have the correct change. "The driver whipped out a pistol, and drove the man off the bus."[7] Mrs. Martha Walker also gave sworn testimony about the day she was leading her blind husband from the bus. She had stepped down, and as her husband was following, the driver slammed the door and began to drive off. Walker's leg was caught. Although Mrs. Walker called out, the driver failed to stop, and her husband was dragged some distance before he could free himself. She reported the incident, but the bus company did nothing about it.[8]

The arrest of Mrs. Parks galvanized the Negro community into mass, unified action. And yet no civil rights campaign in any city ever had a more uncertain beginning.

Mrs. Parks appeared in court on December 5. In protest, a committee of Negro leaders called for a *one-day* boycott of buses on that date.[9] They arranged for the distribution of an unsigned leaflet which read: |

Don't ride the bus to work, to town, to school, or any place Monday, December 5.

Another Negro woman has been arrested and put in jail because she refused to give up her bus seat.

Don't ride the buses to work, to town, to school or anywhere on Monday. If you work, take a cab, or share a ride, or walk.

Come to a mass meeting, Monday at 7:00 p.m. at the Holt Street Baptist Church for further instruction.[10]

By the morning of December 3, 7,000 leaflets had been

mimeographed, and by 11 a.m. the job of distributing them had begun. One of the great imponderables will always be whether or not that first day of the boycott would have succeeded, had it not been for the unwitting assistance of the Montgomery news media. A Negro maid, who could not read very well, gave one of the leaflets to her employer. The white employer read it and gave it to the local newspaper, the Montgomery *Advertiser*.[12] On Saturday morning, the newspaper made the contents of the leaflet a front-page story.[13] In Dr. King's words, that newspaper story "turned out to the Negroes' advantage, since it served to bring the information to hundreds who had not previously heard of the plan. By Sunday afternoon, word had spread to practically every Negro citizen of Montgomery. Only a few people who lived in remote areas had not heard of it."[14]

The New York *Times* reported that "the full text of these appeals appeared in the Montgomery newspapers, and their substance was broadcast over the Montgomery radio stations. As a result, the one-day protest was almost 90 per cent effective."[15]

To virtually everyone in Montgomery, this was a boycott, pure and simple—to almost everyone except Martin Luther King. He related the action taken in Montgomery to Thoreau's *Essay on Civil Disobedience*. "From that moment on," he wrote, "I conceived of our movement as an act of massive noncooperation. From then on, I rarely used the word boycott."[16] That may be. But a boycott it was understood to be, by Negro and white alike, above and below the Mason-Dixon line. Dr. King to the contrary, civil disobedience was not even slightly at issue. The Negroes of Montgomery were *not* disobeying the law; they were physically removing themselves from the jurisdiction of the segregation laws by refusing to ride buses.

At the meeting in the church, there certainly was no hint of civil disobedience in the resolution read to the assembled Negroes by Ralph Abernathy, himself a minister, who would remain one of Martin Luther King's closest

associates. The resolution called upon the Negroes not to
resume riding the buses until:

1) courteous treatment by the bus operators was guaranteed.
2) passengers were treated on a first-come, first-served basis
   —Negroes sitting from the back of the bus toward the
   front, while whites sat from the front toward the back.
3) Negro bus operators were employed on predominantly
   Negro routes.[17]

The motion was carried unanimously.[18] There was clearly
nothing overly startling about the demand for courteous
treatment by bus drivers. The second demand was not
really aimed at obliterating segregation; it was more in
the nature of a modification of the prevailing segregation laws in Montgomery. The third demand for Negro
bus operators—because they were Negroes—to be employed on predominantly Negro routes—because they were
Negro routes—was nothing less than reverse discrimination. We will encounter more of these demands by
King for preferential hiring, in other target cities North
and South, in the course of this book. And no matter how
perfumed the phrases used to sweeten the concept, simple
frankness compels one to call it by its right name: *racial
bigotry in hiring*.

The Montgomery bus boycott was not the first of its
kind in America. At an earlier date, the Rev. Theodore
Jemison (a friend of Dr. King) had led a bus boycott in
Baton Rouge, Louisiana.[19] Rev. Jemison had set up an
effective private car pool during the boycott in Baton
Rouge, and King suggested that the Negroes of Montgomery do the same.[20]

For the Negroes of the South, there was a special symbolic significance not only in what was happening, but
where. It was all taking place in Montgomery, Alabama—
"The Cradle of the Confederacy"—where Jefferson Davis
took command of the secessionist cause for the entire South.

It should be stated at this point that present-day Montgomery is by no means a museum-piece of the Confederacy. A native of the city commented, "It's the stock images—what we call the mildew-and-magnolia approach—that depress us."[21] And in all fairness, the New York *Times* stressed, "The reality is that outside of a few trees with hanging moss, the 'Heart of Dixie' tourist slogans on the license plates and the brass star imbedded on the front portico of the capitol to mark the spot where Mr. Davis became the first Confederate President, Montgomery, Ala., could just as easily be Hartford, Conn., or Des Moines, Iowa."[22]

Indeed, Montgomery had made the transition from a rural economy to a combination of cotton, cattle and manufacturing. It was also home for the Maxwell Air Base, Gunter Air Base and the Air University.[23]

But segregationist sentiment in Montgomery had become a cherished tradition in the eyes of many whites, and discrimination would die hard, if at all. Ten thousand persons jammed the City Coliseum to hear Senator James O. Eastland of Mississippi deliver a fiery defense of segregation.[24] The next day, the Alabama Council on Human Relations held its statewide conference at the Negro Alabama State College in Montgomery. Two hundred persons were present.[25]

Probably to the initial astonishment of segregationist and integrationist alike, the Montgomery bus boycott was adjudged from 95 per cent to nearly 100 per cent effective.[26] Many Negroes got up at three in the morning and walked to work, some of them six miles each way.[27] Others utilized the car pool, which turned out to be a resounding success.[28]

In his book about the Montgomery campaign—*Stride Toward Freedom*—King wrote that the private car pool was so efficient that "they had to admit in a White Citizens Council meeting that the pool moved with military precision!"[29] And a Northern reporter marveled, "For most of this past year, Montgomery Negroes operated their own transit service with 'pool' cars and station wagons, maintaining better schedules than the city system had established."[30]

It was the Montgomery bus boycott that first made King a national figure. After the first few uncertain months, his ascent as High Priest of the Church Militant was rapid, if not meteoric. On March 4, 1956—three months after the boycott began—the New York *Times* was referring to him as "Martin King, Jr., a 27 year old Baptist minister."[31] A month later, that newspaper was writing about "the Rev. M. L. King, Jr."[32] But shortly after, the practice began of reporting his name in full—Dr. Martin Luther King, Jr.—and so it has remained. His burgeoning renown was pretty well established by December 22, 1956, when the *Times* enthused about "the Rev. Martin Luther King, Jr., whose name should be remembered."[33] For those few malcontents who might wish to forget, Dr. King was to inaugurate annual memory courses in the target cities of the North and South.

King was president of the MIA—the Montgomery Improvement Association,[34] the forerunner of his own Southern Christian Leadership Conference. It was the Montgomery Improvement Association that was running the car pool and had to shoulder the growing expenses of the campaign. The price tag on success was getting higher and higher; the cost of running the MIA had increased to $5,000 a month.[35] Yet King never made a public appeal for funds.[36] As it developed, such an appeal might well have been superfluous. By this time the nation's press was giving extended coverage to the boycott, and unsolicited donations started pouring in from as far away as Tokyo.[37] MIA leaders were invited to other cities to appear at fund-raising meetings.[38] When everything was added up, from all sources, the total came to nearly $250,000.[39] The largest response came from church groups.[40]

The sum total of vehicles in the car pool was equally impressive. By the time the boycott had ended, the "fleet" totaled 300 private cars and twenty station wagons, many of them lent to the MIA by churches and other groups from all over the country.[41]

It is curious how certain acts of Martin Luther King, over the years, recall the policies of some of the most rabid Negro sects in America today. In a move that had distinct separatist overtones—and probably would have been heartily applauded by the Black Muslims—King requested permission to establish an all-Negro bus company "owned and operated by Montgomery Negroes." He asked that it be licensed to "provide adequate transportation for our people." His request was denied by the city authorities.[42]

Meanwhile, the city bus company was skidding toward a financial disaster area. Before the protest began, some 70 per cent of their passengers were Negroes. Eleven months after the boycott began, the bus company was estimated to have lost more than $750,000.[43] In addition, downtown white merchants reported substantial losses.[44]

And yet, with all this, the city authorities wanted no part of violence. One Saturday, photographers were busy snapping photos of hooded members of the Ku Klux Klan; while the negatives were still being developed, Montgomery was, in fact, giving the KKK the bum's rush. The Klan was told it could not hold a rally in town and could not parade within city limits.[45] One of the grinning white spectators said, "Looks like they been lost outa one of them old movies." Two Negro teen-agers looked at the Klansmen, smiled, and then burst into laughter.[46]

As the New York *Times* expressed it: "There is a tacit agreement by the bulk of both the Negro and white communities that violence must not erupt, that at all costs the campaign for and against Jim Crow must be confined to the propaganda forums, to the courts, to any peaceful channels."[47]

Unfortunately, a few trigger-happy simpletons shattered

the uneasy racial peace of Montgomery, during and then after the boycott. While Dr. King was attending a mass meeting at the First Baptist Church, an explosion rocked his house. A bomb had gone off on his porch.[48] Two nights later a stick of dynamite was thrown on the lawn of E. D. Nixon, a member of the Negotiating Committee of the MIA.[49] Luckily, in both instances no one was hurt.[50] Large crowds of Negroes assembled but they did not lose control, thus averting what one policeman felt could have developed into a race riot.[51]

Notwithstanding these unsavory incidents, there was a surprising degree of *local* white assistance for the Negroes' campaign that has never been equaled in any other civil rights protest. The Mayor appealed to white employers not to serve as chauffeurs to the boycotters, but a great many whites ignored him, and not only picked up and delivered their own Negro employees but carried other Negroes to and from jobs.[52] And one day a white Southerner who lived in Montgomery drove up to a group of Negroes waiting for an MIA station wagon. "You people waiting for your pick-up?" he asked. The Negroes hesitated, then one replied: yes, they were. "You people stay off the city buses, mind!" the white man said. "You'll never win, once you get back on those buses." Then he drove off.[53]

The city administration made a few abortive efforts at negotiation, but no real agreement was reached.[54] When further talks proved fruitless, all three city commissioners let it be known that they had joined the White Citizens Council.[55] Whatever kid gloves the commissioners had claimed to be wearing were now taken off, and the city started a "get tough" policy to break the boycott. They started giving out traffic tickets in practically wholesale lots to Negroes involved in the car pool. Many of them were booked at the police station and others were taken to jail.[56] It was in Montgomery that Martin Luther King was first arrested. The charge against him can only be described as ludicrous: he was arrested on the charge of traveling thirty miles an hour in a twenty-five mile zone. At the time of the arrest, he had stopped to let off three passengers that he had picked up from the downtown district.[57]

For the first time in his life, King was put behind bars, in a jail that presumably featured separate but equal enclosures. King languished in the prison only long enough to go through the finger-printing process. By now, a large group had gathered outside the jail. The jailer became a little panicky, and his panic increased along with the size of the crowd. Evidently, he feared that the situation would soon get out of hand. As King recalled, with obvious relish, "Rushing into the fingerprinting room, he [the jailer] said: 'King, you can go now,' and before I could get half my coat on, he was ushering me out, released on my own bond."[58] This was the first time—but hardly the last—that the threat of violence would come to the rescue of nonviolence.

In his encounters with the city authorities in Montgomery, King could always rely upon the expert legal services of Fred Gray, one of the two Negro lawyers in that city. King was effusive in his praise of Gray in *Stride Toward Freedom*,[59] but at no point in his book did he so much as acknowledge how a kindly Federal providence intervened to keep Gray out of the Army. Chronologically, it is undeniable that Gray's draft status was changed *after* he became active in the Montgomery bus boycott.[60] But then, his occupational status had apparently changed as well.[61] Gray had held a deferment as a minister until he was reclassified by his local board. The chairman of the local draft board explained that Gray, although a lawyer, had received the deferment as acting pastor of a Negro church. That church had since acquired a pastor, and the board therefore felt free to reclassify him.[62]

The local board ordered Gray to report for induction on August 16, 1956[63] (by then, the bus boycott was in its eighth month). The NAACP took Gray's case to the Presidential Appeals Board in Washington, but the appeal was

turned down.[64] That should have ended the matter but it
didn't. On the day Gray was scheduled to go into military
service, an order from Selective Service Director Lewis B.
Hershey stayed his induction "indefinitely."[65] Thereupon,
three local draft board officials resigned, protesting Hershey's "continued" intervention in Gray's case.[66] Gray contended that he spent at least half his time in ministerial
duties.[67] Certainly Martin Luther King, if anyone, would
have known if Fred Gray was a minister, whether part-
time or full-time. But he nowhere referred to a "Rev. Fred
Gray" in his *Stride Toward Freedom*. In this book, he
listed "Mr. Fred D. Gray, Att'y" as a member of the MIA
Negotiating Committee and the Executive Board.[68] And in
the body of the text of his book, he referred to Fred Gray
on five occasions, but always as an attorney and never as a
minister.

While some members of the local draft board resigned,
other Alabama draft boards engaged in their own brand
of civil disobedience. Members of the Bullock County draft
board said they were setting up a new "F-G" [Fred Gray]
classification for the duration of the dispute. A member of
that board said the group would not "send anybody from
Bullock County until Fred Gray goes."[69] Two other county
boards followed suit.[70] After nine months of refusing to
call up any more inductees, the National Director of Selective Service ousted the entire draft board in Bullock
County.[71] The controversy eventually died down when Gray
passed the draft age.[72]

In 1956, there could scarcely have been a busier lawyer
in Montgomery, black or white, than Fred Gray. Far-reach-
ing legal action was taking place on two fronts. The MIA
was no longer satisfied merely to revise the segregated
seating policies on the buses. Accordingly a suit was filed in
the United States Federal District Court, asking for an end
of bus segregation on the grounds that it violated the Four-
teenth Amendment.[73] In a two-to-one decision, the judges
of the District Court declared that the city bus segregation

laws were unconstitutional.[74] The attorneys for the city of Montgomery promptly filed an appeal with the U.S. Supreme Court.[75]

Meanwhile, the city officials, in their search for more legal artillery, fired a new broadside against the MIA—a rarely used and almost forgotten 35-year-old state law against boycotts. Specifically, they invoked Title 14, Section 54, which provides that when two or more persons enter into a conspiracy to prevent the operation of a lawful business, without just cause or legal excuse, they shall be guilty of a misdemeanor.[76] The Montgomery County Grand Jury was called to determine whether Negroes who were boycotting the buses were violating this law. After about a week, the jury found the boycott illegal and indicted more than one hundred persons, including King.[77]

King noted that "at the jail, an almost holiday atmosphere prevailed. . . . Many Negroes had gone voluntarily to the sheriff's office to see if their names were on the list, and were even disappointed when they were not."[78] In a sentence that could almost have been a harbinger of the civil disobedience to come in Birmingham and Selma, King wrote: "Those who had previously trembled before the law were now proud to be arrested for the cause of freedom."[79] But it must be reiterated that the campaign in Montgomery was in no way an exercise in civil disobedience.

Far from admitting that the Negroes had disobeyed the law, their defense attorneys presented arguments to show that the prosecution's evidence was insufficient to prove violation of Alabama's anti-boycott statute.[80] In addition, the defense attorneys declared that no evidence was produced to show that the Negroes did not have "just cause or legal excuse"[81] (as required by the anti-boycott law).

The defense attorneys called 28 witnesses to the stand, who told their stories of crude, and sometimes cruel, treatment at the hands of various bus drivers.[82] After four days of arguments—in a trial attended by scores of reporters from all over the United States, as well as India, France, and England—Judge Carter found King guilty of violating the anti-boycott law. The penalty was a fine of $500 and court costs, or 386 days at hard labor in the county of Montgomery.[83] The trials of the other defendants were continued at the request of the prosecutor, pending an appeal.[84]

In *Stride Toward Freedom*, King exulted: "I knew that I was a convicted criminal, but I was proud of my crime. It was the crime of joining my people in a nonviolent protest against injustice. . . ."[85] This sounded as if King had been sent to prison. But as the New York *Times* noted, nearly seven months after the trial: "Dr. King has been free on bond since [the trial] serving actively as the boycott leader."[86]

The guilty verdict against King in the anti-boycott trial was to be the city authorities' sole touché in the entire eleven-month duel. The final thrust was dealt by the Supreme Court, and it did not disappoint Dr. King in the slightest. It affirmed the decision of the District Court in declaring Alabama's state and local laws requiring segregation on buses unconstitutional.[87]

If the city commissioners were disconsolate, some of the bus drivers were all but inconsolable. Montgomery's bus drivers had been among the bitterest opponents of desegregation, and now they had an even more bitter pill to swallow. After the Supreme Court decision had been announced, the bus company assembled its one hundred drivers—all white— and made it clear that it was not going to defy the court. Those who were opposed to non-segregated buses were told to step forward and quit. Six bus drivers resigned on the spot.[88]

The first day of bus integration was deceptively calm— perhaps, at least in part, because much of the world was looking on. That first day, for the first time, all the Negro passengers entered buses through the front door. They sat in the first empty seats they saw, in the front of the buses and in the rear. They did not get up to give a white passenger a seat. And whites sat with Negroes. Dr. King rode one of the buses accompanied by a white minister, the Rev. Glenn Smiley of New York.[89]

Two days later, a shotgun blast ripped into King's home. Panes of glass were shattered, but no one was hurt.[90] And soon it became clear that if you rode an integrated bus in Montgomery, you just might be taking your life in your hands.

Bitter-end segregationists, unable to enforce bus segregation by any other means, turned to terror and violence. Three days after King's house was attacked, two Montgomery buses were struck by gunfire.[91] Two days later, a Negro woman riding a bus was wounded by a sniper's bullet.[92] The Police Commissioner ordered all buses halted for the rest of the night.[93] With New Year's Eve approaching, the city canceled night bus runs for the holiday weekend.[94] In a ten-day period, between the first day of bus integration and New Year's Day, there were four shooting incidents on the Montgomery City Lines buses.[95] The city ordered an eleven-day curfew on night bus runs, extending into January.[96] The day after the curfew was lifted, a city bus was struck by a shotgun blast from a passing car, and the Mayor immediately reinstated the ban on night bus operations.[97]

But all this was a mere curtain-raiser for the senseless havoc of the night of January 9. That night there were bombing attacks on four Negro churches and the homes of two integrationist ministers.[98] City authorities halted bus service "indefinitely."[99] James E. Folsom, then Governor of Alabama, inspected the damage and offered a $2,000 reward for the arrest and conviction of the bomb throwers. Governor Folsom declared: "Any person who would bomb the House of the Lord endangers the life of every man, woman and child in Montgomery. I call on all people of Alabama to help stamp out such lawlessness, wherever it may occur."[100] (Later, the city of Montgomery offered a similar reward.)[101]

The Montgomery *Advertiser* carried an editorial calling

for the resumption of bus travel even "if they run empty." It urged that special police details be assigned to the buses. As the editorial bluntly expressed it: "The issue now is no longer segregation. The issue now is whether it is safe to live in Montgomery, Alabama."[102] That same paper carried an ad signed by business and professional leaders in Montgomery, deploring the outbursts of violence.[103]

After a six-day stoppage, the city and buses tried once more, on a limited daylight schedule. Police guards were assigned to buses, finishing their last runs after nightfall. Some buses carried Negro passengers only. Others carried a few whites, and no Negroes. In buses that were integrated that day—whether from force of habit, or habit born of fear of force—Negroes took seats from the middle of the bus back, while the whites stayed in the front.[104]

Now a group of segregationists took a page from King's book, colored it white, and asked the city commission for permission to operate a "private" bus line, for members only, as a means of combatting the bus integration order. In turn, the city commission petitioned a three-judge Federal Court panel for instructions. While the judges refused to hand down an advisory ruling, two of them made it clear that in their "personal" opinion, the new bus line would in effect be a public transportation system and thus subject to the court restrictions against segregation.[105]

A year later, in February, 1958, the New York *Times* still found Negroes riding the buses "in amiable, voluntary segregation."[106] But at the end of that year, it was assuring its readers that "today, Negro bus riders sit where they please."[107]

That the Negroes of Montgomery won an impressive victory is incontrovertible. But to whom—or what—should the victory be attributed? As Lerone Bennett, Jr., pointed out in his biography of King, the Montgomery movement "ended not as a triumph of passive resistance, but as a confirmation of the NAACP theory that lawyers are the Negro's best friend." (He quickly added that "Montgomery transcended lawyers.")[108] King himself had wondered in print whether the Montgomery bus strike could have succeeded if the Supreme Court decision had not come through in the nick of time.[109]

But all this was now behind him. The Montgomery bus boycott was history, and now King had his eyes fixed firmly on the future. He told a cheering crowd that he would never again pay a fine in court for any charge stemming "from our fight for freedom." And he emphasized that "we no longer have to fear going to jail."[110]

Many regarded King as a moderate. And yet even at this early date, his philosophy left scarcely any room for a middle ground. He himself acknowledged this polarization of views in Montgomery, in which nearly everyone was forced to choose one side or the other, with precious little room for compromise. Without a trace of regret, King noted that "the moderate finds himself now in a position where he can hardly function."[111]

For the most part—as we will soon see—moderates were hardly allowed to function any more effectively in Birmingham and Selma, Alabama.

CHAPTER 4

1962: Checkmate in Albany, Georgia

❧❧❧❧❧❧❧❧❧❧❧❧❧❧❧❧❧❧❧❧❧❧

If there is a skeleton in the civil rights closet of Martin Luther King, it is Albany, Georgia. The folklore of the civil rights movement is filled with tales of Birmingham and Selma, Alabama—but strangely silent about this little southwest Georgia community. Dr. King's followers were ready, at the drop of a metaphor, to relate his extraordinary successes in "loving" combat with Bull Connor and Jim Clark, in 1963 and 1965—but simply wouldn't discuss King's experiences with Police Chief Laurie Pritchett in Albany, Georgia, in 1962.

Whoever originated the civil rights anthem, *We Shall Overcome*, had to be thinking about some other town. King never did overcome in Albany, Georgia. It would be much more accurate to say that Albany, Georgia, very nearly overcame him.

On the surface, there is nothing of the giant-killer about Albany, Georgia, and little, if anything to suggest its "crinoline and magnolia" past. Its population in 1961–'62 was then around 56,000, with whites outnumbering Negroes by something more than a 3-to-2 margin.[1] Albany had almost doubled in population between 1950 and 1962, and was fast diversifying its industrial base.[2] It had rug and mattress factories, thread and cotton mills, a golf-club factory, and other industrial plants. It was the economic beneficiary of two big Federal payrolls, courtesy of nearby Turner Air Force Base and a big Marine Corps supply center. The principal crops were peanuts, pecans, and some cotton. Considerable livestock was raised near there.[3]

This was the site of Martin Luther King's next campaign. All civil rights systems were "go," and it was confidently expected that a successful nonviolent launching was just a matter of routine. But a few insuperable technical difficulties presented themselves, and Project Albany never did quite get off the ground. By August, 1962, the Rev. Wyatt Tee Walker, executive director of King's Southern Christian Leadership Conference, stated, "nowhere in the South have we ever had such a concentration of personnel and resources."[4] Yet Mrs. Ruby Hurley, southeastern regional director of the NAACP commented, "Albany was successful only if the goal was to go to jail."[5] And Reese Cleghorn of the Atlanta *Journal* (once a classmate of King's) flatly declared, "Almost everybody outside King's immediate camp thinks the Albany protest was a failure."[6] Why? Perhaps because for the first and only time in King's career, his own "weapons" were turned against him. *U.S. News & World Report* capsuled the town's winning strategy in the headline: "Now It's Passive Resistance by Whites—The Albany, Ga., Plan."[7] The plan was devised by the city's police chief, Laurie Pritchett, a man who, as a sheer tactician, won the grudging respect of his most adamant rights opponents.

When Chief Pritchett saw trouble developing, he began rebuilding and retraining his force. He held daily classes in how to handle demonstrators without force or violence. He hammered home the idea that physical contact should be avoided, that no police dogs were to be used, no tear gas fired or night sticks swung—except in extreme cases.[8] Years before Daniel Moynihan had made the phrase famous, Chief

Pritchett had come to the conclusion that in civil rights campaigns, the first side to resort to violence lost—and he was determined that it would not be the police department of Albany, Georgia.

It must have been one of the most frustrating civil rights campaigns of King's career. He was practically moving heaven and earth to force Pritchett to come out swinging—the better to raise the cry of "Police Brutality!" Instead, Chief Pritchett responded with a mildness that virtually approached Alphonse and Gaston. In an action, and reaction, that seemed as carefully staged as a Wednesday matinee, the Negroes demonstrated, and the police arrested them, pleasantly, courteously, and with what rights militants must surely have regarded as the most maddening good nature—arrested them for illegal assembly, unlawful parades, and disturbing the peace. In Albany, Georgia, at least, martyr status was impudently denied Dr. King and his allies, and for this, we may assume, he never quite forgave Chief Pritchett.

In Birmingham and Selma, Alabama, the police officials made one tactical blunder after another, and the Federal government was to intervene massively and decisively on the side of the Negroes in these civil rights campaigns. But in Albany, Georgia, the Federal government could only look on helplessly, its hands effectively tied by Pritchett's refusal to give it any pretext for intervention.

A dozen cities in six states had observers in Albany, Georgia, to see how it was done—how Negroes threw stones and spit at white policemen without encountering even a billy club drawn in response; how a group of white police turned back a mass of marching Negroes without a riot developing; how white residents stood aside from the street demonstrations, avoiding racial conflict.[9]

In his account of the Montgomery bus boycott, King said of the city fathers that they "were not aware that they were dealing with Negroes who had been freed from fear. And so every move they made proved to be a mistake . . .

Their methods were geared to the 'old Negro,' and they were dealing with a 'new Negro.' "[10] Similarly, King's methods were geared to the "old Southern white" and he was dealing with the "new Southern white" in Albany, Georgia. And he really didn't understand the "new Southern white" at all. Nor did the Student Nonviolent Coordinating Committee, which had arrived in Albany, a month or more before King.

The Student Nonviolent Coordinating Committee charged —privately, at first, then publicly, as its annoyance increased—that in effect it planted the seed, while King reaped the harvest, in one Southern community after another.[11] And this was especially true in Albany, Georgia.[12] That the "harvest" in Albany became, upon closer inspection, a famine, in no way lessens the accuracy of the SNCC statement.

Members of SNCC arrived in Albany in the fall of 1961. They were all primed and ready for nonviolent action on November 1—the date the ruling of the Interstate Commerce Commission barring segregation in terminals was to go into effect.[13] For the next few weeks, the SNCC workers were talking to students in Albany about testing the ICC ruling.[14] SNCC joined forces with the Youth Council of the NAACP, the Baptist Ministers Alliance, and other groups, and on November 22 they formed a coalition group called the Albany Movement, with local osteopath Dr. William G. Anderson as president and real estate man Slater King (no relation to Martin Luther King) as vice president.[15] That Thanksgiving weekend—three weeks after the ICC ruling—three members of the local NAACP Youth Council entered the Trailways bus terminal, went into the restaurant there, and were met by Police Chief Pritchett. He called them outside, and told them that if they re-entered the lunch room he would arrest them. They went back into the restaurant, and were thereupon arrested. A half hour later, they were released on bond.[16]

This was little more than a skirmish. The real confrontation came in mid-December. On December 10, 1961, four

SNCC members rode a train from Atlanta to Albany, accompanied by members of King's Southern Christian Leadership Conference, a writer from Denmark, a white girl from Georgia, and Tom Hayden of Students for a Democratic Society (one of Hayden's most recent claims to fame was his trip to Hanoi, in the company of an admitted Communist, Dr. Herbert Aptheker). The group was integrated, and ignored a conductor's request that they move. They got off the train at Albany, Georgia. There, they went into the white waiting room briefly, came out again, began to get into cars to take them downtown, and at that point were placed under arrest by Pritchett.[17]

The Albany Movement now swung into action. On the day that the Freedom Riders were to be tried in city court, over four hundred high school and college students marched downtown to protest. The police ordered them to disperse but they refused. Police then herded hundreds of them into an alley alongside City Hall, where they stood for two hours in the rain before being booked.[18] Slater King was arrested as he and seventy others knelt in prayer in front of City Hall.[19] That same night, three hundred people marching to City Hall were arrested for parading without a permit.[20] This was one of the rare occasions when Pritchett enunciated his own personal segregationist sentiments loud and clear, as he told reporters: "We can't tolerate the NAACP or the SNCC or any other nigger organization to take over this town with mass demonstrations."[21]

At this point, Martin Luther King was invited to Albany by the executive committee of the Albany Movement.[22] King arrived from Atlanta with the Rev. Ralph Abernathy, and called for a continuation of the "nonviolent protest." Addressing 1,000 people packed into the Shiloh Baptist Church, he told his audience, "Don't stop now. Keep moving. Don't get weary. We will wear them down with our capacity to suffer."[23]

The following day, King was arrested, along with 264 other Negroes and one white youth, as they marched on City

Hall for a prayer demonstration; they were protesting the city's refusal to release Negroes held in earlier arrests. King and the other demonstrators were charged with parading without a permit, congregating on a sidewalk, and obstructing traffic.[24] That day's arrests brought to 749 the number of Negroes seized in five demonstrations and related incidents.[25]

What followed has been genteelly described as a "leadership conflict" by some, and more bluntly labeled a "power struggle" by others. Whatever the *mots justes*, it was quite apparent that a battle for top position in the Albany campaign was taking place between King's Southern Christian Leadership Conference and SNCC.

In an amazingly short time, SNCC had succeeded in arousing considerable antagonism in civil rights ranks. Slater King conceded that a purpose of the Albany Movement was to eliminate friction between local members of the NAACP and SNCC.[26] But the major—and not overly loving—tug o' war took place while Dr. King was in jail. Claude Sitton of the New York *Times* reported that "an open break occurred between the Southern Christian Leadership Conference and the Student Nonviolent Coordinating Committee."[27] Much of the story seemed to emanate from one of King's closest advisers, Rev. Ralph Abernathy,[28] who had been jailed with King, then posted bond and was released. He was quoted as having said that he, King, and Dr. Anderson, the leader of the Albany Movement, had conferred while in prison and agreed that the Southern Christian Leadership Conference should take over.[29]

"However," the reporter added, "it was apparent at the Albany Movement's news conference, and in private remarks by members of the student group, that the latter was in command."[30] With SNCC representatives sitting at his elbow, the acting chairman of the Albany Movement read a statement to newsmen, rejecting, in effect, the leadership bid of King's group.[31]

The controversy didn't last very long. Their differences

were papered over, with Dr. King's release from jail. He left his cell after a $400 security bond had been posted for him, after an agreement was reached in the city's racial dispute.[32] The Negroes agreed to wait at least a month before initiating new negotiations on their demands for lowering racial barriers, and also obtaining better job opportunities.[33]

In return for the cooling-off period, Albany Mayor Asa D. Kelley, Jr., and other city officials agreed to take the following steps:

Assure police compliance with an Interstate Commerce Commission ruling against segregation in bus and rail terminals.

Release all prisoners who were property owners, or could show evidence of employment, on signature bonds.

Reduce bonds for two local Freedom Riders, facing a state charge of unlawful assembly, from $750 to $200, and for eight other riders from outside the community, from $1,000 to $400.

Give the Albany Movement an opportunity to present its demands for other changes in racial customs to the new City Commission on January 11.[34]

Charges filed against the demonstrators for parading without a permit, congregating on a sidewalk, and obstructing traffic were to be held in abeyance, at the discretion of Chief Pritchett. It was indicated that they would not be revived except on renewal of the demonstrations.[35]

Along with King, 300 other Negroes were released from prison, but there was little enthusiasm for the agreement. One Negro leader commented, "It's nothing to shout to the rafters about." And King himself was less than satisfied with the plan, but stated, "I would not want to stand in the way of meaningful negotiations."[36]

The Southern Christian Leadership Conference had not been included among those who negotiated the agreement. The Negro representatives in these meetings with city officials were Marion S. Page, secretary of the Albany Movement, and Donald L. Holowell, an Atlanta lawyer retained by SNCC.[37] This seemed to indicate that smoldering rivalry between the two civil rights groups was not very far below the surface. But the leaders of the groups met in a show of unity and apparently patched up their differences, temporarily at least. At this meeting were officers of the NAACP, the Southern Christian Leadership Conference, and SNCC. "If there was an indication of division, it grew out of a breakdown of communications," King declared. "The unity is far greater than our inevitable points of disagreement."[38]

The Albany Movement did have one spectacular success during its campaign; not surprisingly, it was the weapon of the boycott—the weapon of "green power" turned against businessmen who were most vulnerable to a heavy loss of Negro patronage. As in Montgomery, the obvious target was the city bus company, which faced the wrath of City Hall if it desegregated its buses, and almost certain financial ruin if it did not. The bus boycott heated up after the arrest of Ola Mae Quarterman, an 18-year-old student and one of thirty-seven suspended by Albany State College, a state Negro institution, for having taken part in protest demonstrations.[39] Miss Quarterman was seized by police on the complaint of a bus driver. He had ordered her to move from the front of the bus and stated that she had answered, "I paid my damned 20 cents, and I'll sit where I please." The bus driver, a sensitive soul, was distressed at her profanity, and the court evidently shared his dismay. Miss Quarterman was fined $100 and sentenced to thirty days in jail, twenty-five of which were suspended.[40] After this, Negroes were urged to step up their boycott of the buses. This order proved to be the handwriting on the wall for the bus company, 80 per cent of whose passengers were Negro.[41] Four days later, Negro leaders called the bus boycott in Albany 90 per cent effective.[42] The buses ran for two more days and then the service was shut down.[43] The effectiveness of the Negro boycott can be gauged by the fact that receipts from bus fares had dwindled from approximately $400 a day to $110 a day.[44]

The bus company had agreed to the Albany Movement's demands for desegregation.[45] However, the City Commission had refused to give a written pledge not to interfere with the step.[46] Mayor Asa D. Kelley, Jr., had split with the commission on this issue. "I'm very hopeful that action by private citizens will bring a reinstatement of bus service with or without commission action, because the commission is not going to change its attitude," the Mayor said.[47] A few weeks later, the bus company hired its first Negro driver, in the hope that this would bring about a cessation of the boycott.[48] Then the company tried operating limited bus runs for white patrons, but had to shut down again because of heavy financial losses in the continuing boycott.[49] During this time, a committee of white merchants had sought to negotiate desegregation of bus seating, in an effort to prevent the bus company from going out of business.[50] Hedrick Smith of the New York *Times* wrote:

Negro negotiators rejected the offer and the bus company closed. The Negroes had demanded a firm commitment from the City Commission itself and had asked for concessions on other racial issues. Their demands cost the Negro movement sympathy among white business men.[51]

It took three years until bus service was reinstated.[52] Once again, King had demonstrated the same disdain for compromise recalled by his statement in Montgomery that "the moderate finds himself now in a position where he can hardly function."

The position of white moderates was made even less tenable by the threat of the Albany Movement to organize a full-scale boycott against white merchants downtown.[53] R. E. McTigue, president of the Albany Chamber of Commerce and executive of a local candy company, had planned to meet with other business and civic leaders in an attempt to find a solution to the city's racial problems. His reaction to the impending Negro boycott of the stores was, "It makes it more tense. That's the one thing that we had hoped wouldn't enter into it."[54] This new boycott was not quite as devastating as the bus boycott, but the loss of Negro customers unquestionably made itself felt in the downtown area. The boycott had started in early February, 1962. By September, a store owner downtown was commenting, "A year ago on Saturday afternoons, this street was so full of people you could hardly get through the crowd. Today, I could fire a cannon down the street and not hit anyone."[55]

The slump in downtown retail sales was also having a heavy impact on Albany real estate and rental prices. The president of a chain of stores said, "Because of our Albany losses, we're trying to sublease our store there for as little as half of the rent we're paying." After a month of advertising the location "we still haven't had the first inquiry," he added.[56]

Mrs. Ruby Hurley, the NAACP's southeastern regional director, maintained that "the cash register has a way of talking to the Southern businessman that beats anything I know of."[57] But Mrs. Hurley failed to realize that economic reprisals could be a two-edged sword. Slater King estimated that 20 per cent of the Albany work force of Negro maids and cooks lost jobs because of white hostility aroused by the Albany protest movement.[58] And while the cash register may have spoken with unsurpassed eloquence to the downtown merchants, its message was presumably lost on the city officials. If anything, the City Commission was now more intransigent than ever.

Eight months after his arrival in Albany, the New York *Times* noted that "Dr. King's group has spent roughly $10,000 *in the last month alone*, and has forfeited another $20,000 because its leaders were unable to appear at fundraising rallies in other cities."[59] But in terms of hard gains, King emerged from the Albany campaign virtually empty-handed.

The Negro tactics may have changed, but their basic goals in Albany were still the same. The objectives were:

Establishment of a bi-racial committee to work out a time-table for desegregation of schools, parks, libraries, lunch counters, and other places of public accommodation.

Recognition by the city that Negroes have the right to protest segregation peacefully under the Constitution.

A declaration from the city that it would abide by the Inter-state Commerce Commission's decision desegregating travel terminals.

Desegregated operation of city buses if they resumed service.

Fair and just disposition of nearly 1,200 cases of arrested demonstrators, and the exchange of surety bonds for $8,000 in cash bonds.[60]

The city's reply was to dispose of Dr. King's case by arresting him. On July 11, 1962, King and Rev. Abernathy were convicted of having violated a street and sidewalk assembly ordinance, by leading a street demonstration without a permit the preceding December. The sentence was $178 in fines, or forty-five days in jail.[61] They both refused to pay the fines or post bond through appeals, and went to jail to await assignment to prison street gangs.[62] Since, of the three alternatives, King and Abernathy had chosen prison, there was little, if anything, that the Federal government could do, and so a concerned President Kennedy was informed by Assistant Attorney General Burke Marshall.[63] With King in jail, the long-simmering resentment among Negroes quickly changed to open hostility, seeking only a target to strike out at. The confrontation came a day after King began serving his sentence, when Chief Pritchett narrowly averted a clash between his police force and 200 or more Negroes outside the Shiloh Church. Bricks and bottles were lobbed at the police who were stationed across the street. Accompanied only by two officers, Chief Pritchett walked through the menacing crowd into the church.

He conferred briefly with Negro leaders, and then spoke to the audience, telling them his men were there to protect them. "This business of throwing rocks and bottles is not good," he said. "We're here to plead with you and to solicit your cooperation, knowing that we will get it."[64]

Once again, as in Montgomery, the threat of violence released the nonviolent Dr. King from jail, although this time in spite of his vehement opposition. Dr. King was released from prison against his will, after "an unidentified well-dressed Negro man" had paid his fine. Chief Pritchett said that he did not know who Mr. X was,[65] and in a touch of high farce, King stoutly denounced the "subtle and conniving" tactics that had led to his release.[66] Less than a week later, in an address to the National Press Club in Washington, King remarked:

As the Atlanta *Constitution* suggested the other day, we have now reached a new landmark in race relations. We have witnessed persons being ejected from lunch counters during the sit-ins, and thrown into jails during the freedom rides. But for the first time, we witnessed persons being kicked *out* of jail.[67]

More than 1,000 Negroes packed the Mount Zion Church and the Shiloh Baptist Church to hear King urge a "nonviolent protest which will turn Albany upside down."[68] The city officials promptly applied for an injunction to prevent King's participation in these demonstrations.[69] The ban was handed down by Federal District Judge J. Robert Elliott, and King promised to abide by it. "Out of respect for the leadership the Federal judiciary has given, the enjoined parties and organizations have agreed to obey the order . . . and to work vigorously in higher courts, to have said order dissolved."[70] The ban on demonstrations was lifted by Chief Judge Elbert P. Tuttle of the U.S. Court of Appeals, and the police then had to disperse a crowd of 2,000 Negroes after bricks, bottles, and rocks had been thrown.[71] "Did you see them nonviolent rocks?" Chief Pritchett asked newsmen.[72] In the best Gandhian tradition, King canceled plans to lead a mass demonstration, and declared a day of penance for the outbreak of violence.[73]

S. Ernest Vandiver, then Governor of Georgia, had offered to dispatch the state's 12,000 National Guardsmen to Albany to maintain the peace, but Mayor Kelley said the city had no intention of accepting the offer unless the situation deteriorated.[74] Neither state nor Federal troops were ever used in Albany.

On July 27, King was arrested for a third time.[75] By now, the Negroes were beginning to show signs of battle fatigue. No more than 500 turned out for a mass meeting, and of these only fifteen expressed a willingness to take part in a third demonstration. As one reporter expressed it, "It appeared that the long struggle, which has brought few tangible rewards, had taken its toll."[76]

Of the city commissioners, Mayor Kelley appeared to be a minority of one. He was in favor of some "lines of communication" with responsible, law-abiding Negro leaders, and revealed that he was in daily, unofficial communication with Dr. W. G. Anderson, president of the Albany Movement. However, he believed that the city had reached an impasse on racial issues. "I just wish there was something I could do about it," he said.[77]

The New York *Times* noted that "Albany is governed by a group of urbane segregationists who have left the city's white racial moderates no middle ground. This has given Dr. King only a limited opening in the white community."[78] In a rare if grudging tribute, King called city officials "subtle, sharp, and tough" opponents.[79] Contributing to this impasse was James Gray, editor of the Albany *Herald*, and a transplanted Northerner who managed to be more Southern than some of Albany's native sons. Gray was a native of Massachusetts, a graduate of Dartmouth College who still wore white bucks, and an articulate and outspoken segregationist. His support for Chief Pritchett and the city commissioners undoubtedly helped tip the racial scales against the Albany Movement.

During a court proceeding, City Attorney H. G. Rawls and Recorder's Court Judge A. N. Durden, Sr., had asserted that local segregation ordinances in Albany were unconstitutional and would not be enforced.[80] Mayor Kelley's reaction was that the court statements represented no change in the city's position. He said that Negro demonstrators had been arrested for creating disturbances and not for violating segregation laws.[81] King quickly arranged for small groups of Negroes to "test various facilities to see if that [desegregation] policy holds true."[82]

The following day, the city of Albany shut down its three public parks and two public libraries after small groups of Negroes and whites sought to desegregate them.[83] Police Chief Pritchett said that he was ordering the parks and libraries "closed indefinitely in the interest of public safety."[84] Later, eight integrationists were arrested in a test of segregation at a bowling alley. They were arrested for refusing to obey the management's request to leave the bowling alley. They were charged with loitering.[85]

Mayor Kelley said the city would close its recreational facilities rather than place whites in "bodily contact" with Negroes.[86] He made the statement in August of 1962, and proved to be as good as his word. The city of Albany closed its tennis courts, swimming pools, park, recreation and teen center, as well as its library, to avoid having to integrate these public facilities.[87] In March, 1963, they were still closed except for the library, which was being reopened for a 30-day trial period, on a stand-up basis, to both whites and Negroes.[88] The trial reopening barely squeaked through the City Commission by a four-to-three vote,[89] the majority apparently finding stand-up integration less sinister than the sitting variety. At the same time, the City Commission voted six to one to repeal all segregation ordinances, to strengthen its hand in fighting the Albany Movement's omnibus desegregation suit before the Federal courts.[90]

Eighteen months after the formation of the Albany Movement, Claude Sitton of the New York *Times* reported: "Despite wave after wave of demonstrations led by the Rev. Martin Luther King, Jr., and his Southern Christian Leadership Conference, Albany is as segregated today as ever."[91]

Albany, Georgia, stands as King's sole defeat in the nonviolent campaigns. Why did he fail? Many reasons have been suggested; the author believes that King basically was unable to out-general a law enforcement officer who met nonviolence with nonviolence. Lerone Bennett, Jr. saw the problem as an organizational one, in that "King allowed himself to be pushed into action, without adequate preparation, on a battlefield he did not choose, with a faction-ridden army he never completely commanded."[92] Reese Cleghorn quoted an executive of another rights group who had commented, "As a professional, I was appalled by the lack of planning in the Albany campaign. They just charged off."[93]

But some of King's supporters told a different story; in their version of the Albany fiasco, the villain of the piece was the late President John F. Kennedy. In a special "JFK Memorial Issue," T. George Harris, senior editor of *Look*, wrote that "in the desperate drive to integrate Albany, Georgia, Negroes charged that Kennedy men kept King on the telephone for two solid days, when their leader could have turned failure into victory."[94] The operative word in that last sentence is "could"—and there seems little, if any, basis for even that cautious optimism.

The Albany story begins with an arrest, and ends with an arrest. But in this ending, Chief Pritchett was not lurking in the background. This time, the indictments were returned by a Federal grand jury at Macon, Georgia. In August, 1963, nine leaders and members of the Albany

Movement were indicted on Federal charges of obstructing justice; six were charged with perjury before the grand jury.[95] Attorney General Robert F. Kennedy personally made the announcement, and stated that the action grew out of an alleged conspiracy to boycott and picket the grocery store of a juror who had voted against a Negro plaintiff in a Federal civil suit.[96] (The store closed as a result of the boycott.)[97] The indictment also charged that six of the defendants committed perjury in denying before the grand jury that they had either participated in the conspiracy or taken part in the actual picketing of the juror's store.[98] Prison sentences were imposed on two of the persons convicted of perjury, two others were put on probation, and one was treated as a young offender.[99] The case was appealed to the U.S. Court of Appeals *by the Department of Justice*, under the command of a new Attorney General.[100] The Justice Department sought a reversal of the convictions on the ground that in four years "only four new Negro names" had been added to the jury list of the district court in Macon.[101] However, the Justice Department opposed dismissal of the indictments, arguing for new trials instead.[102] On July 21, 1966, the appeals court was unanimous in reversing the convictions, and then by a five-to-four vote dismissed the indictments as well.[103] The court's sole basis for reversal was its finding that "the methods of selecting prospective jurors have, over a large period of time—list after list—resulted in Negroes' being substantially underrepresented."[104] The court majestically ignored the fact that there were five Negroes on the 23-man grand jury that had issued these particular indictments.[105]

Probably to the great relief of its white citizens, Albany, Georgia, faded out of the headlines, and today has been largely forgotten by militants and moderates alike. The community re-emerged briefly in the news following the passage of the 1964 Civil Rights Act. In January, 1965, those testing public accommodations in Albany, Georgia, found that the owners had stuck to their decision to comply. The press noted that in virtually every restaurant, motel and drive-in, Negroes received courteous service. As one businessman commented, "We in Albany have always said we would obey the law, even if we don't like it. And we are doing that."[106]

It is possible to deplore the segregationist sentiments of the city commissioners and still conclude that, in many respects, Albany, Georgia, was a rather remarkable community.

CHAPTER 5

1963: War in Birmingham, and the Civil Rights Act

❀❀❀❀❀❀❀❀❀❀❀❀❀❀❀❀❀❀❀❀

Like a gambler plunging his last stack of chips on a final spin of the wheel, Martin Luther King staked his career and his future on Birmingham. After the humiliating defeat in Albany, he needed a sweeping victory, whatever the cost. A King biographer, Lerone Bennett, Jr., expressed it in these words: knowing that "a defeat in Birmingham would probably wreck his career and the nonviolent crusade, King sent Walker and other SCLC [Southern Christian Leadership Conference] aides to Birmingham to secretly recruit workers *and to lay the groundwork for a crisis.*"[1]

King knew that the crisis he envisioned for Birmingham would almost certainly provoke a violent and bloody reaction—especially since a die-hard segregationist like "Bull" Connor headed the city's police force. He knew that Birmingham had one of the most terror-ridden histories of any city of the South. In its early days as a railroad terminus, mining camp and mill town, disputes in Birmingham were frequently settled by the knife, the club or the gun—and the combatants had been known to use dynamite, as well.[2] Since World War II, there had been 50 bombings of Negro buildings, and not one of these bombings had been solved.[3] One law enforcement official noted that "kids in the back country around Birmingham grow up knowing how to handle dynamite. And dynamite is readily available. So they know how to get it and what to do with it. As a result, they're expert in hit-and-run dynamite raids."[4]

The other side of the racial coin was nearly as ominous. At the height of the Birmingham struggle, Roy Wilkins of the NAACP warned that Negroes in Birmingham, Alabama, were "some of the roughest in the United States." Wilkins stated, "If there is an incident there, I shudder to think what will happen, because they will not—the great rank and file of the 140,000 Negroes will not—accede to the fine discipline of Dr. King."[5]

In the midst of these inflammable social ingredients, King brought the kerosene-soaked cloth of "confrontation," lit it, and then delivered an impassioned polemic against the inevitable fire that seared the streets of Birmingham and the hearts of its citizens, black and white. A few years before, in an editorial about the Freedom Riders, the New York *Times* had expressed its belief that "non-violence that deliberately provokes violence is a logical contradiction."[6] Of Birmingham, it might well be said that never had so much violence followed so close on the heels of so many protestations of nonviolence.

In his search for recruits in the Birmingham war, King stopped just short of robbing the cradle; he had some demonstrators younger than ten years of age, and told an anecdote involving a child of "no more than eight" walking with her mother in a Birmingham demonstration.[7] Most of his youthful demonstrators were teen-agers who were encouraged to stay out of school in order to demonstrate.[8] In *Why We Can't Wait*, King related with great relish how, at one school, the principal gave orders to lock the gates to keep the students from joining the demonstrations.

The youngsters climbed over the gates "and ran toward freedom."[9] King wrote: "Looking back, it is clear that the introduction of Birmingham's children into the campaign was one of the wisest moves we made."[10] The New York *Times* disagreed, editorializing that "the presence of hundreds of children among the marchers made all these marches especially perilous adventures in brinkmanship."[11] The clear and present danger lay in the city's violent past and the terrifying possibility that Birmingham's bloody racial history might well repeat itself during these demonstrations, and that the children might be among its victims. There is no polite way to say it: King was knowingly, willingly, callously risking the lives of hundreds of children to achieve his objectives in Birmingham.

Again it must be emphasized that whatever the saccharine-sweet qualifying adjectives—call it "loving" or "nonviolent"—it was still war in Birmingham, and still clearly understood as such by the participants and the more astute observers. One of the most moderate of all civil rights leaders, Roy Wilkins, said, "The Negro in this country is engaged in a war for his rights, and for his status as a citizen. *It's literally a war.*"[12] *Ebony* editor Lerone Bennett, Jr. wrote that in Birmingham, "James Bevel and other SCLC aides had recruited an enthusiastic cadre of students who were demanding assignment to the front lines."[13] Rev. Bevel declared, "We need an army of captains and sergeants and privates to fight the white man this summer. I want captains to march whole schools to jail after graduation."[14] The New York *Times* noted that "the desegregation effort here is organized like a military campaign."[15] And King himself left no doubt that it was war. Writing in *The Nation* in 1964, he declared that:

The keys to victory in Birmingham were the refusal to be intimidated; the indomitable spirit of Negroes to endure; their willingness to fill the jails; their ability to love their children—

and take them by the hand into battle; to leave on that battlefield
six murdered Negro children, to suffer the grief, and resist
demoralization and provocation to violence.[16]

The reader may find it incredible—as did the author—that
Dr. King, the apostle of nonviolence, could regard "six
murdered Negro children" as one of "the keys to victory
in Birmingham."

Today, most Americans think of the Birmingham war
as wending its tortuous way through history with all the
inexorability of a Passion Play. And yet there is reason
to believe that much of the suffering might have been
avoided if only Martin Luther King had been willing to
wait just seven weeks.

James E. Mills, president and editor of the Birmingham *Post Herald*, and C. B. Hanson, Jr., president and
publisher of the Birmingham *News*, maintained that very
few of the reporters sent to Birmingham knew or tried to
find out the background of the struggle.[17] Certainly the
Birmingham story they told *Editor and Publisher* was substantially different from the version given to millions of
readers by the mass circulation magazines, and it ought
to be recorded in these pages.

Publisher Hanson emphasized that the first step needed
to correct the segregation problem was a change in the
city's government. Up until early April, 1963, there had
been a three-man commission form of government. Leading citizens of Birmingham agreed that with this form of
government, it would be impossible to reach accord between the Negro and white populations. Both Birmingham
papers endorsed a change to a city government consisting
of a Mayor and nine councilmen; the voters supported this
change in a referendum.[18] Next, there was a mayoralty
campaign between T. Eugene "Bull" Connor, an adamant
segregationist and a power on the city commission for
twenty-five years, and Albert Boutwell, author of the Alabama Pupil Placement Laws, but nevertheless regarded

as more moderate in race relations than Connor. Both newspapers supported Boutwell, who won the mayoral election by more than 8,000 votes out of 50,000 cast.[19]

The New York *Times* considered the Negro vote "decisive not only in the referendum . . . but also in the election of Mr. Boutwell."[20] But King never gave Boutwell a chance to cope with the city's racial problems. In the words of the Birmingham *News* publisher: "Virtually the day after the election, when at last the road was open for a solution of the segregation problem, the Rev. Martin Luther King and other outsiders—some of them frankly publicity seekers—came to Birmingham and started raising Hell."[21]

On April 15, 1963, Boutwell was sworn into office, but for the time being, at least, he was Mayor in name only. His right to take office was challenged by "Bull" Connor and the other city commissioners who contended that theirs was still the legitimate city government.[22] In effect, Birmingham had two city administrations in April and early May, 1963. The new city government was headed by Mayor Boutwell, who was not yet permitted to assume power; the old city government was headed by the three city commissioners, who were still in physical control of the reins of government and still insisting they could not be replaced until the expiration of their terms in 1965.[23] It was a question of law that could be decided only by a court, and the State Supreme Court set a hearing for May 16.[24] And until that date, any actions of Mayor Boutwell—in spite of the recent election—would have raised the knottiest questions of legality. Until that date, it was highly dubious whether or not Boutwell could have taken actions that were legally binding and had the sanction of high office.

All this, of course, was known to King and his followers, and everyone else in Birmingham. And although King had scant regard for Boutwell, he most emphatically regarded him as a moderate, compared with Connor.[25] King stressed, "we were hopeful that Connor would be so thoroughly defeated that at least we would not have to deal with him."[26] He went even further than this passive hope; he purposely postponed Negro demonstrations until the day after the run-off election, to keep Connor from capitalizing "on our presence by using it as an emotion-charged issue for his own political advantage." He held off the demonstrations because "we might actually have had the effect of helping Connor win."[27]

King wrote a book largely about the Birmingham campaign, entitled *Why We Can't Wait*. As we have seen, he did wait for "Bull" Connor to be defeated at the polls. It had been agreed that no member of the staff of the Southern Christian Leadership Conference would return to Birmingham until after the run-off election.[28] Having waited this long, he could then have waited until Boutwell was confirmed in his position by the state's highest court.

It has been largely forgotten today that King's entry into the Birmingham racial conflict was greeted with mixed emotions on the part of its Negro community. King went into Birmingham not only against the advice of some of its Negro leaders but without even informing them.[29] As early as April 6, 1963, a New York *Times* reporter noted that "many prominent members of the Birmingham Negro community are known to have opposed a direct-action campaign at this time. They believe that the new administration should be given an opportunity to disclose its intentions."[30]

One of the few Negro leaders who was willing to make his opposition public was C. Herbert Oliver, secretary of the Inter-Citizens Committee of Birmingham. This committee, composed of eight Negro and two white clergymen, had been formed two years before and had been a strong spokesman for removal of racial barriers in Birmingham. Oliver issued a statement that the direct-action movement was "operating in a vacuum." He explained that "there is no one to go to, to negotiate grievances. The old commission has been repudiated by the voters, the new one has not taken office."[31] The New York *Times* noted that the opposition in the Negro community took two forms—opposition to "pressing the campaign just as a new and moderate city administration is taking office and to the participation of Dr. King, even though he has said he was asked to come."[32]

The invitation to Dr. King came from the Rev. Fred Shuttlesworth, head of the Alabama Christian Movement for Human Rights—an affiliate of King's Southern Christian Leadership Conference. King's group had decided to hold its annual convention in Birmingham, and had decided to give "serious consideration" to joining Shuttlesworth and the ACHR in a massive direct-action campaign.[33] The ACHR met with the white Senior Citizens Committee (a group of prominent Birmingham business and community leaders) and had presumably come to some basic agreements. Some of the merchants removed Jim Crow signs from their stores; others agreed to join in a suit with the ACHR to seek nullification of city ordinances forbidding integration at Birmingham lunch counters.[34]

After the Southern Christian Leadership Conference held its convention, the Jim Crow signs reappeared in the stores.[35] King cited a rumor that "Bull" Connor had threatened some of the merchants with loss of their licenses if they did not restore the signs. King summarized, "we reached the conclusion that we had no alternative but to go through with our proposed combined-action campaign."[36]

Keeping in mind the results of the mayoral election, King's statement was arrant nonsense. Obviously there was a very clear-cut alternative, and that was to bring about Connor's defeat at the polls, which is exactly what happened. It was "Bull" Connor who was the most implacable opponent of integration in Birmingham, and it was Connor who had been handed his walking papers by the voters. King had decided to hold massive demonstrations, however, no matter who won the election. To that end, before the campaign began he sent confidential letters to the NAACP, CORE, SNCC and the Southern Regional Council, telling them of his plans and advising them that they might be called on for aid.[37] He corresponded with the seventy-five religious leaders who had joined him in the Albany Movement.[38] He discussed his campaign plans with some seventy-five New Yorkers, including unofficial representatives from the offices of Mayor Wagner and Governor Rockefeller.[39] In short, King notified nearly everyone of the start of the Birmingham campaign—except the Negro leadership of Birmingham.

Not before, but *after* the Birmingham campaign began, it was necessary for King to spend the better part of eight days racing from meeting to meeting, soothing ruffled feelings, and trying to drum up support from cool, if not hostile, Birmingham Negro leaders.[40]

The Rev. Albert S. Foley, chairman of the Alabama Advisory Committee to the Federal Civil Rights Commission, charged that King had agreed to secret negotiations with Birmingham business and professional leaders and then reneged. Rev. Foley, a sociology professor, pleaded with King, who "at first agreed" and then changed his mind without notice.[41]

King's commitment of thousands of "troops" into battle with the outgoing rabidly segregationist city commission; his initial refusal to meet with Birmingham's community leaders; his unwillingness to wait until the new and concededly more moderate mayor was confirmed in office—all are explicable only in terms of some larger goal, of which the Birmingham battle was merely an appendage. Quite obviously, that goal was a massive civil rights act of a sweep and intensity unprecedented in this country's history. King himself admitted that in January, 1963, "high government officials here in Washington were telling me that we did not need civil rights legislation. Even President Kennedy was saying that."[42]

Before Birmingham, President Kennedy had asked Congress to enact three pieces of civil rights legislation relating to voting rights, the Civil Rights Commission, and school desegregation.[43]

A month after the war in Birmingham began, President Kennedy sent a special message to the Congress on civil rights and job opportunities, in which he proposed "that the Congress stay in session this year until it has enacted —preferably as a single omnibus bill—the most responsible, reasonable and urgently needed solutions to this problem, solutions which should be acceptable to all fair-minded men. This bill would be known as the Civil Rights Act of 1963 and would include—in addition to the aforementioned provisions on voting rights and the Civil Rights Commission—additional titles on public accommodations, employment, federally assisted programs, a Community Relations Service, and education."[44]

Martin Luther King's feet may have been in Birmingham, but his eyes were on the White House—and his gaze never wavered for a moment. He needed a crisis and he knew "Bull" Connor would play right into his hands. He knew Connor would react with maximum violence and take the most repressive measures to put down the demonstration. The martyrdom which had been denied King in Albany, Georgia, was handed to him on a silver platter in Birmingham, and King played the role to the hilt as the nation cheered the hero and hissed the villain. Beyond any question, the Civil Rights Act was born in Birmingham, and the bumbling "Bull" Connor was its unwitting father. John F. Kennedy said later—with an equal mixture of truth and irony—that "the civil rights movement owes Bull Connor as much as it owes Abraham Lincoln."[45]

King publicly opened the Birmingham campaign on April 3, 1963, with a declaration that he would lead demonstrations there until "Pharaoh lets God's people go," i.e., until the city established fair hiring practices, formed a biracial committee, and desegregated facilities in downtown stores.[46]

King himself did not participate in a demonstration for

a week; he had his hands full trying to mobilize support in the Negro community.[47] The campaign started very slowly, gradually increasing in tempo. In the first few days, 35 demonstrators were arrested.[48] After that the probing operation abruptly ended and the foot-soldiers were moved into the streets. On April 6, 1963, a protest march on City Hall was stopped three blocks from its goal. Forty-two participants were arrested on charges of parading without a permit.[49] This first street demonstration in Birmingham was led by Rev. Shuttlesworth,[50] and it was on that day that the Battle of Birmingham began.

King had begun his campaign not only in defiance of the expressed wishes of various Negro community leaders, but the Justice Department as well. No less an official than Burke Marshall, chief of the Civil Rights Division of the Justice Department, had asked King for a delay in direct action until the new and more moderate administration of Mayor Boutwell could take office. King declined.[51] By now the Negro community was apparently closing ranks behind Dr. King. There was still some resentment against King's intrusion into the local situation, but it was no longer very vocal. As the New York *Times* saw it, "some Negro leaders were said to feel that the city's entire Negro population of 150,000 had now been committed, whether they liked it or not."[52]

King now added a new weapon of outright defiance to his civil disobedience arsenal. Besides endowing himself with a supposed right to disobey "unjust" laws, he now asserted the lordly prerogative of flouting "unjust" judicial decisions. And to King, there was nothing more unjust than a County Court injunction against continued demonstrations. King and some local leaders announced their intention of defying the injunction at noon.[53] Three hours later, seven pickets appeared before a local department store.[54] The following day, King was arrested when he openly violated the court injunction and led a march of Negroes toward the downtown section. The marchers were halted after four and a half blocks; by then, they had been joined by more than a thousand other Negroes.[55]

It was the first Birmingham march in which King had participated—perhaps partly in answer to some reported grumbling that he was letting local people get arrested, and staying safely behind the lines himself.[56] King did get his wish; he was arrested, his thirteenth arrest in the South.[57] And to those irate citizens who expected the Federal government to wave a magic wand and release him from jail, Assistant Attorney General Burke Marshall had somber news. As he apparently had told the President, Marshall told newsmen: "The Federal government has no authority to take legal action to intervene in Birmingham as the situation now stands." King's refusal to abide by the injunction, although he regarded it as unconstitutional, had tied the hands of the Justice Department.[58] Federal officials pointed out that the constitutional right of free assembly was not absolute, but subject to certain recognized limitations. They pointed out that in many cities there are police regulations against the number who may demonstrate and the locations and kind of demonstrations that are permitted without specific authorization. Even Washington, D.C. had similar regulations. For example, while pickets were permitted in front of the White House, their numbers were regulated by the local police and no demonstrations were permitted before the Capitol.[59]

Some Negro community leaders had tried to stop the demonstrations, and failed. The Federal government had tried, and failed. Now members of the clergy in Birmingham made one last attempt. Eight leading white churchmen of that city issued a statement calling the street demonstrations "unwise and untimely."[60] The signers included the Rev. C. C. J. Carpenter, Protestant Episcopal bishop of Alabama; the Rev. Joseph A. Durick, auxiliary bishop of the Roman Catholic Diocese of Mobile-Birmingham; and Rabbi Milton L. Grafman of Temple Emanu-el. The clergymen urged "our own Negro community to withdraw support from these demonstrations and to unite locally in working peacefully for a better Birmingham. . . . When rights are consistently denied, a cause should be pressed in the courts and in negotiations among local leaders, not in the streets. We appeal to both our white and Negro citizens to observe the principles of law and order and common sense."[61]

From his prison cell, King penned a reply to these churchmen. His answer—*Letter From a Birmingham Jail* —is one of the most famous of all civil rights documents, and was excerpted and reprinted almost ad infinitum by secular and religious journals (which seldom, if ever, quoted as much as a paragraph from the statement of the Birmingham clergymen).

In *Letter From a Birmingham Jail*, King stated that "Birmingham is probably the most thoroughly segregated city in the United States." He recalled the number of unsolved bombings of Negro homes and churches, and reiterated that "the purpose of our direct-action program is to create a situation so crisis-packed that it will inevitably open the door to negotiations."[62] He acknowledged that some had asked, "Why didn't you give the new city administration time to act?" His reply was, "I have hope that Mr. Boutwell will be reasonable enough to see the futility of massive resistance to desegregation. But he will not see this without pressure from devotees of civil rights."[63] That last sentence was a rather arrogant assumption, considering that Mr. Boutwell had not yet taken office.

King wrote, "I have almost reached the regrettable conclusion that the Negro's great stumbling block in his stride toward freedom is not the White Citizen's Counciler or the Ku Klux Klanner, but the white moderate who is more devoted to 'order' than justice; who prefers a negative peace which is the absence of tension to a positive peace, which is the presence of justice; who constantly says: 'I agree with you in the goal you seek, but I cannot agree with your methods of direct action'; who paternalistically believes he can set the timetable for another man's freedom. . . ."[64]

As always, King was unable to defend the nonviolent philosophy without raising the fearful specter of violence as the sole alternative; in his words, if his nonviolent philosophy "had not emerged, by now many streets of the South would, I am convinced, be flowing with blood."[65] King acknowledged that each of the white clergymen signing this statement had taken "some significant stands on this issue."[66] Specifically, he conceded that Reverend Stallings had welcomed Negroes to his worship service on a nonsegregated basis, while Catholic leaders had integrated Spring Hill College several years before.[67]

But in almost the same breath, he stated that "few members of the oppressor race can understand the deep groans and passionate yearnings of the oppressed race."[68] Reese Cleghorn had this telling comment about his old college classmate's *Letter From a Birmingham Jail:* "More than a 'treatise,' it sounded like a declaration of black independence in the civil rights crises of the future."[69]

Meanwhile, violence was being unleashed outside the Birmingham jail. Negroes, protesting the arrest of leaders of an attempted march, hurled rocks at policemen. Several Negroes were clubbed as the police tried to hold in check a crowd of about 2,000.[70] This was not the last occasion on which Negro violence would coexist with one of Dr. King's nonviolent protests.

King could have been free on bond at the very outset of his imprisonment, but he refused to do so. Finally, after being in jail about a week, he posted a $300 bond and was released.[71] King said he had been "persuaded" to post bond so he could consult with members of his strategy committee.[72] On April 26, 1963, he was found guilty of contempt of the Circuit Court injunction forbidding demonstrations. The penalty was a surprisingly mild five days in jail and $50 fine.[73] In addition, he was allowed to remain at liberty, pending an appeal to the State Supreme Court.[74]

The two competing city governments of Birmingham were agreed on one action, at least; on April 30, they both denied requests by Negroes for permits to stage peaceful protest marches.[75] Mayor Boutwell said the permit had been denied by his group because its approval might invite public disorder.[76]

In retrospect it is surprising that the Negroes even condescended to seek a permit, since they were going to march in any case, regardless of any decisions made by Connor and Boutwell. Two days later, on May 2, hundreds of young Negroes—many of them in their teens, or even younger—demonstrated through the streets of Birmingham. About 500 of them were arrested.[77]

And then in a sudden and terrible sweep of vicious fury, May became mayhem, as the worst fears of Negro and white moderates were realized. Suddenly all the hate, all the violence, all the rage flooded the streets of Birmingham. Few can forget May 3, 1963, the date "Bull" Connor singlehandedly guaranteed passage of the Civil Rights Act when he used fire hoses and police dogs to disperse Negro students protesting racial segregation. The demonstrations followed less than three hours after King had declared that the protests would continue in increasing intensity until there were both "promise and action" from the city authorities and white merchants to start to end segregation.[78]

Boutwell had still not yet been confirmed in office; his hearing before the State Supreme Court was almost two weeks away. All he could do was ask for an end to the demonstrations until his group assumed office.[79] All he could do was promise that "immediate and determined attention" would be given to the city's racial problems as soon as the new administration was confirmed.[80]

Harry Ashmore, Pulitzer Prize-winning editor for the *Arkansas Gazette* and now executive vice president of the Center for the Study of Democratic Institutions, thought that "one of the great still photographs of our time" may have done as much to arouse the nation as "Bull" Connor's police dogs. This was the famous photo of a scene in a Birmingham park where Negro children held hands under the pelting spray of riot squad fire hoses. It was not until

later, Ashmore recalled, that "I learned that we had all
been put on."[81] One of Dr. King's field marshals, the Rev.
Wyatt Tee Walker, provided this inside view:

. . . they'd been saying, "turn the water hose on, turn the water
hose on." Then somebody threw a brick and they started turning them on. So they just danced and played in the spray. This
famous picture of them holding hands, *it was just a frolic*,
they'd get up and run back and it would slide them along the
pavement. This went on for a couple of hours. All in good
humor. Not any vitriolic response.[82]

This is certainly not to minimize the gravity of the racial
crisis in Birmingham. It is simply to suggest that while a
news picture is worth a thousand words, the effect can
be mischievous in the extreme if the *fons et origo* is an
optical illusion.

In Washington, Attorney General Kennedy warned that
"increasing turmoil" would be made inevitable by a refusal
to grant equal rights to Negroes. Nevertheless, he questioned the timing of the demonstrations.[83] He pointed out
that Boutwell had made clear his intention to "resolve the
difficulties facing the community." Kennedy called on King
and other Negro leaders in Birmingham to use their influence to end the conflict. He said he hoped "for the sake
of everyone" that a solution could be worked out in meetings between both sides, and "not in the streets."[84]

King's answer was less than 24 hours in coming. The
following day the demonstrations continued with fierce intensity. Again firemen turned water hoses on groups of
Negro spectators who disregarded police orders to disperse.
Tough Negro steelworkers stormed out of the bars and
joined the Negro crowds, to very nearly breach the police
lines guarding the downtown section of Birmingham. At
the height of the disturbances, King's lieutenant called
off further demonstrations for the day because he had seen
several pistols and knives being carried by spectators.[85]

The children were sent home.[86] By now, more than 1,100
arrests of both adults and juveniles had been made within
the last three days.[87] One reporter noted that on that day
"again the demonstrators were all young people. Some were
no older than 10 or 12 years."[88] And still King would not
tolerate any let-up. He told a mass meeting, "Today was
D-day. Tomorrow will be Double D-day."[89] If by "D" he
meant "disaster," he could hardly have been more accurate.

Double D-day came, not precisely "tomorrow" but the
day after, when about 1,000 more Negroes were arrested,
of whom about 40 per cent were juveniles. At one Negro
school, 87 students were present and 1,339 absent. A flyer
distributed by King's supporters urged students to "fight
for freedom first, then go to school."[90] Birmingham Negroes who couldn't have cared less about Thoreau and
Gandhi understood perfectly the commonly accepted meaning of the word "fight." Or perhaps it was just the over-
long arm of coincidence that Double D-Day was immediately followed by R-R-Day—the day of the Race Riot. On
May 7, a riot broke out after 2,500 to 3,000 Negroes had
rampaged through the business district in two demonstrations and were driven back. The police and firemen drove
hundreds of rioting Negroes off the streets with high-
pressure hoses and an armored car. The Negroes hurled
rocks, bottles and brickbats at the law-enforcement officials
as they were slowly forced backward by the streams of
water.[91] The New York *Times* noted that "Dr. King and
his lieutenants appeared to have little control of the demonstrations, which were joined by hundreds of bystanders."[92]
An official of King's Southern Christian Leadership Conference accused leaders of SNCC of "whipping up" the
emotions of the many teen-age participants,[93] but King
could not evade a heavy share of the responsibility for the
riot. For more than a month he had escalated the battle
in Birmingham until Negroes and whites alike had reached
the breaking point. For more than a month he had locked
the city in a vise of unendurable tension, until the nerves

of thousands had finally snapped.

The New York *Herald Tribune* editorialized, "what was billed as a non-violent protest went beyond the bounds of peaceful assembly. There was a real danger of serious injuries and even death—a threat made especially ominous by the Negroes' use of school children as front-line troops." The *Herald Tribune* wrote of a "majestic inevitability to the Negro's progress in America," but added, "ironically, Birmingham seemed on the verge of a new era when Dr. King moved in on it as his target . . . there was an air of optimism that harmonious racial progress was about to be made."[94]

Two days later, with the President, the Attorney General, and the Congress virtually looking over their shoulders, an agreement was reached that ended the five weeks of racial crisis—but not before King had sharply reduced his demands. The agreement provided for:

Desegregation of lunch counters, rest rooms, fitting rooms and drinking fountains in large downtown department and variety stores within the next 90 days.

Promotion and hiring of Negroes on a nondiscriminatory basis in stores and industries, hiring of Negro clerks and salesmen within 60 days by the stores, and appointment of a private fair employment committee.

Release of jailed Negro demonstrators on bond or on their personal recognizance.

Establishment of a biracial committee within two weeks.[95]

The settlement terms fell far short of those sought originally by King. He had demanded *immediate* steps toward desegregation; now he was settling for promises of future action. The most serious shortcoming (from the Negro viewpoint) was the fact that the agreement in no way obligated any government official to do anything; the accord was an entirely private one, reached between King and white business and civic leaders. Thus, it had no official standing with the city, and neither the Mayor nor the old City Commission was bound by its terms. In addition, it took almost a week to induce the white business leaders to have their names made public.[96]

These negotiations marked the fourth major effort in the preceding five weeks to solve the racial dispute.[97] There was no longer any choice in the matter. Sheriff Bailey reported that the local law-enforcement agencies had been "strained to the utmost of their capacity." The sheriff was convinced that unless the demonstrations were stopped, and order restored, the next step would be the declaration of martial law.[98] With Dr. King's nonviolent gun pointed at their heads, the white business and community leaders hammered out the settlement with the Negro leaders.

A key provision of this agreement between the white and Negro negotiators was that hundreds of demonstrators still in jail would be released on nominal bail.[99] King's Southern Christian Leadership Conference was hardly destitute. Tidal waves of money flowed into Conference headquarters during the Birmingham battle. In a single rally, the Western Christian Leadership Conference in Los Angeles raised some $75,000 for King's group;[100] the National Maritime Union sent King a check for $32,000.[101] But immediate sources of funds for collateral to back bail bonds had been dried up by the drain of five weeks of demonstrations. About 3,200 demonstrators had already been arrested, and their bonds had been paid by sources all over the country.[102] Now it was necessary to raise $160,000 in bail money, and raise it quickly if the agreement were to stay intact, because King had promised the Negroes of Birmingham that the demonstrators would be released from jail.[103] Some years later, a former Justice Department lawyer revealed that Attorney General Robert Kennedy persuaded the labor movement to put up the $160,000. Kennedy called Walter Reuther of the United Auto Workers, who in turn consulted with Joseph Rauh of Americans for Democratic Action. A plan was worked out whereby the AFL-CIO, the United Steelworkers of

America, the United Automobile Workers and the Industrial Union Department of the AFL-CIO would raise $40,000 each. The following morning the $160,000 was sent to Birmingham.[104] The Negro bondsman there used the money to provide the security he needed to write the rest of the bonds. Within that same day, the bondsman wrote bail bonds totaling over a quarter of a million dollars.[105]

And then Birmingham's most vicious bigots spoke in the only language of which they were capable. Just a day after the public announcement of the agreement, a Negro motel and the home of an integration leader were bombed.[106] Widespread rioting by Negroes went on at the edge of the city's business district. Angered by the attacks, thousands of Negroes poured into the streets and fought with the police, firemen, state highway patrolmen and Jefferson County deputy sheriffs in a running battle that raged through four or five blocks. About 50 persons were injured, including a policeman and a taxicab driver who were stabbed. The mobs attacked the police and firemen, wrecked scores of police and private automobiles, and burned six small stores and a two-story apartment house. Firemen who attempted to fight the blaze withdrew under a hail of rocks from the rioters.[107] On another day in May, a crowd of more than 1,000 Negroes tried to block fire engines responding to a fire alarm. Three Negro children burned to death.[108]

Mayor Boutwell, who was still awaiting the State Supreme Court confirmation of his right to take office, condemned the bombings and riotings. "I want to make it plain to the hoodlums," he said, "that this city will not tolerate violence, especially the dastardly hit-and-run bombers who wreak vengeance without regard for life and property."[109] Bombers attacked the home of King's own brother;[110] nevertheless, he conducted a "pool-hall pilgrimage" to calm down the Negro population. "We must not beat up any policemen, as brutal as they may be," Dr. King said. "We must not stab anybody, we must not burn down any stores."[111]

Meanwhile, there appeared to be substantial differences of opinion over the terms of the biracial pact. The first white businessman to admit his participation in the agreement was Sidney M. Smyer, Sr. Smyer told newsmen that at least one store would have one Negro salesman within 60 days. However, he said, this employee's position would be discontinued "if there is violence on either side."[112] King contended the pact called for hiring or promotion of at least one Negro in seven stores.[113]

But perhaps the most serious obstacle was that, as one young businessman commented, "we're operating in a political vacuum. The white people don't know whom to follow."[114] Another businessman warned that the agreement was predicated on the court confirmation of Boutwell as Mayor. "If the court rules in favor of the Commissioners," he commented, "this agreement isn't worth a tinker's damn."[115]

The day before the State Supreme Court was scheduled to hear the competing claims to office of Mayor Boutwell and "Bull" Connor, some sixty business and industrial leaders—most of them Boutwell backers—gave implied support to the token desegregation plan. The list of leaders included no merchants at all, and since the pact provided for desegregation of lunch counters, they were the only businessmen involved directly in the agreement. Furthermore, a mild statement accompanying the names expressed no endorsement of the desegregation plan.[116]

Anthony Lewis wrote that "Any fair reading of the Birmingham experience and other recent events in the South would have to show the moderate forces gaining." Lewis noted the days it took to divulge the names of those who supported the racial agreement, but concluded that in light of Birmingham's turbulent racial history "it was progress to go that far."[117]

During the last days in office of the City Commission,

the Board of Education ordered the expulsion or suspension of some 1,100 Negro students who had been arrested in the anti-segregation demonstrations. The Board voted to expel all arrested students 16 years old or older, for the remainder of the term, and to suspend all those under 16.[118] It was probably the shortest expulsion in the annals of education. That same day, the Supreme Court ruled that a city that made segregation a policy by ordinance or official statement could not prosecute Negroes for seeking service in privately owned stores. In such a setting, the Court reasoned, a refusal to serve Negroes could not be attributed to the store owner alone; he was so influenced by public policy, the judicial argument went, that the discrimination could be laid to the state and was therefore unconstitutional.[119] Two days later, a Federal judge ordered the education officials in Birmingham to reinstate the 1,100 Negro students who had been suspended. The judge based his decision on the Supreme Court ruling, in that the Negro students were illegally arrested for engaging in legally permissible activities.[120]

While "Bull" Connor was still reeling from this blow, the Alabama Supreme Court dealt his administration the final *coup de grâce*. In a unanimous decision, the state court upheld Mayor Boutwell's claim to office, and he and nine councilmen immediately took over from Connor and the other Commissioners.[121] One of Boutwell's first acts was to declare his support for the racial peace pact.[122]

While Boutwell was still settling down at City Hall, Attorney General Robert Kennedy asked James Baldwin to arrange a secret meeting between himself and several prominent Negroes. The meeting was held in the Kennedy family apartment at 24 Central Park South, in New York City. With the exception of Baldwin, all the other participants (only one of whom was an official of a civil rights organization) seemed to regard the meeting as an abysmal failure. Baldwin said that the Negro group repeatedly sought to impress on the Attorney General that race relations in the North had reached a crisis, and that the masses of whites and Negroes were moving toward a serious and perhaps violent collision. Among the participants were folk singer Harry Belafonte, one of King's earliest supporters and fund-raisers, and Clarence Jones, attorney for both Baldwin and King. James Reston wrote that Assistant Attorney General Burke Marshall opened the meeting by explaining what the Justice Department had done to arrange a settlement in Birmingham. When he finished 40 minutes later, some of the Negroes laughed at him. Reston stated that "an attorney for the Negro leader Dr. Martin Luther King came up and thanked Attorney General Kennedy for his efforts to settle the Birmingham case, but he did not speak up for the Justice Department in the meeting itself." Kennedy was said to have asked the attorney why he had remained silent while militant Negroes in the meeting condemned the Administration. In Reston's words:

The reply given to these questions was that militants in the movement for Negro leadership were now in the ascendancy, that "moderation" or "gradualism" or "token integration" were now offensive words to the Negro and that sympathy by a Negro leader for the Administration's moderate approach was regarded as the work of "collaborationists."[123]

In short order, a letter from the attorney—the aforementioned Mr. Jones—was published in the New York Times. Jones wrote: "The reply ascribed to me, partially by paraphrase and partially by quote, in Mr. Reston's column is factually inaccurate. No such statement or reply was made by me or anyone authorized to speak for me to the Attorney General during or after the meeting on Central Park South." Jones expressed concern that "because of my association with Dr. King, actions or inactions which have been ascribed to me are a reflection of the 'moderate' movement being 'intimidated' by the 'militants.'"[124]

Jones coyly failed to note whether he considered himself in the moderate or militant camp. Certainly in 1964 he defended such clients as Jesse Gray, the rent-strike leader, who called for "100 men ready to die for freedom,"[125] and three Mobilization for Youth workers who went to court to prevent New York City from subpoenaing them in an investigation of Communist infiltration of that agency.[126]

Regardless of Jones' protestations to the contrary, it was becoming more and more apparent that "moderation" was now an offensive word to Martin Luther King. Some 10,000 civil rights marchers in Kentucky heard King say that Negroes must continue to press for equal rights at the risk of being called immoderate. Bluntly, he proclaimed that "if moderation means slowing up in our fight, then moderation is a tragic vice which members of our race must condemn."[127] Little wonder that *Ebony* editor Lerone Bennett, Jr. wrote of "King contributing to the radicalization of the Negro people, and the growing radicalization of the Negro people pushing King to new postures."[128] And nowhere was this radicalization more evident than in Birmingham.

In 1963, it sometimes seemed as if nothing was happening in the country except in Birmingham, and that nearly all of the country's civil rights activity was taking place in that beleaguered city. Actually, during 1963 there were 930 protest demonstrations in the South alone, and a total of 20,000 demonstrators were arrested.[129] It was just that Birmingham had become the demonstration showcase, the city that sometimes seemed to have at least as many reporters and TV cameramen as policemen. It was the tormented city of Birmingham about which television viewers knew more intimate details than they knew about their next-door neighbors. The entire city was being continuously X-rayed; the Battle of Birmingham was being fought and refought in almost every conceivable medium of communication.

Attorney General Robert Kennedy had met with the Negroes on May 24, 1963. During this meeting, they had urged that the President make an address or a series of addresses to the nation on the issue of Negro rights as one means of stating his "moral commitment" to equal rights.[130] Less than three weeks later, President John F. Kennedy delivered an address to the people on a nationwide radio and TV hook-up. In it, he stressed that:

. . . the events in Birmingham and elsewhere have so increased the cries for equality that no city or state or legislative body can prudently choose to ignore them. The fires of frustration and discord are burning in every city, North and South. Where legal remedies are not at hand, redress is sought in the streets in demonstrations, parades and protests, which create tensions and threaten violence—and threaten lives. We face, therefore, a moral crisis as a country and a people. It cannot be met by repressive police action. It cannot be left to increased demonstrations in the streets. It cannot be quieted by token moves or talk. It is time to act in the Congress, in your state and local legislative body, and above all, in all of our daily lives.[131]

A week later, JFK acted. He sent to the Congress a special message in which he urged passage of a "Civil Rights Act of 1963."[132] One section—which could almost have been written by King, in Birmingham—provided for "Equal Accommodations in Public Facilities." Reasons of commerce, convenience, and human rights were given for its passage—but literally the most forceful reasoning was given in this paragraph:

There have been increasing public demonstrations of resentment directed against this kind of discrimination—demonstrations which too often breed tension and violence. Only the Federal government, it is clear, can make these demonstrations unnecessary by providing peaceful remedies for the grievances which set them off.[133]

Arthur Krock wrote: "The fact is that the Administration is highly apprehensive of racial violence throughout the nation." Attorney General Robert Kennedy was quoted by one Senator as painting "a terrible picture of a situation which could become uncontrollable" in an attempt to secure Southern support for the civil rights bill.[134]

In Birmingham, Mayor Boutwell was moving slowly and carefully to restore order and control to his city. Given the history of Birmingham—given the knowledge that segregationist feelings were still intense, that Governor Wallace and the Kennedys were all watching in the wings—the Mayor did as well as he could, considering the bitterly conflicting elements he had to work with.

The peace pact had provided for the establishment of a biracial committee "within two weeks." The two weeks stretched into two months, but the committee was formed in the middle of July.[135] More than 200 leaders of Birmingham's churches, professions, business and industry formed a biracial committee on community affairs. Mayor Boutwell, who had appointed the committee on authorization of the City Council, called the gathering "an historic occasion" and expressed the belief that "this can well be the beginning of our finest hours."[136] At the same time, Negro moderates in Birmingham moved to regain control in their community. Some of them formed a "self-enforcement committee" to restrain any attempts by individuals to speed up integration by unauthorized sit-ins.[137] Little by little, quiet but substantial progress was being made. A group of Negroes, protesting the shooting of a Negro youth by a policeman, were able to go straight to City Hall and receive an explanation by the chief inspector of the Police Department.[138] And a few days later, the City Council unanimously repealed all racial segregation ordinances on the pragmatic grounds that they were unenforceable in court.[139] In August, Claude Sitton was able to report that "lunch counters and other facilities in many downtown department and variety stores have been desegregated. Negroes have been promoted to other than menial positions, and still others have been hired. City officials have reopened public parks on a desegregated basis."[140] To those who grumbled that the pace of desegregation was not fast enough, political supporters of the mayor had this comment: "Many white people are willing to act with the mayor and council as long as they feel they're not being pushed."[141]

It would be pleasant if the Birmingham story could be ended here. But the racial agony of that city had not yet run its course. In September, 1963—in compliance with Federal court order—school boards in various Alabama communities made plans for desegregation of classes.[142] A score of Negro children were admitted to formerly all-white grade schools in Birmingham, Mobile, and Tuskegee.[143] Then Governor George Wallace, self-proclaimed champion of states' rights, stepped in, and proceeded to crush the rights of the communities to educate their children. With helmeted and armed state troopers at the ready, Wallace had little difficulty getting the Birmingham Board of Education to accede to his "request" to close temporarily three schools scheduled to integrate.[144] A furious Birmingham *News* commented:

Wallace now not only defies Federal courts, he defies wishes of legally constituted local authorities. Immediate disruption of careful local planning in four Alabama cities is the first result. Turmoil and confusion follow closely. What Federal court orders make inescapable still will come. But in the interval, a Governor so enthralled with his own sense of power will have created near-havoc. . . . George Wallace is not "saving Alabama." He is in process of destroying self-government and the educational system of this state.[145]

Under Federal pressure, the Alabama schools were reopened and integrated, but not before counter-demonstrations were held by white Birmingham students.[146] And then came the bomb blast that shook the racial peace pact to its very foundations, and reverberated in the halls of the Capitol.

Five days later, in Birmingham, a bomb severely damaged a Negro church during Sunday School services, killing four Negro girls.[147] (Ironically, the morning lesson was "The Love that Forgives," from the fifth chapter of Matthew.)[148] This wanton savagery touched off racial rioting and other violence in which two Negro boys were shot to death. At one point, three fires burned simultaneously in Negro sections. Mayor Boutwell and other city officials and civic leaders appeared on the local television station and urged an end to "this senseless reign of terror."[149] President Kennedy, in an unmistakable allusion to Governor Wallace, stated: "It is regrettable that public disparagement of law and order has encouraged violence which has fallen on the innocent."[150] And Birmingham realtor Sidney Smyer, who had been one of the prime movers in the racial peace pact, said, "There wouldn't have been any trouble if Wallace had stayed out. Why did he do it? Why didn't he let us alone?"[151]

The Birmingham *News* condemned violence on both sides. The newspaper criticized Negroes for "open law-violating street demonstrations," then added:

But Negroes of Birmingham have a hard right to ask why the bombings of the past have not been solved, for it is their flesh and blood, their property, which has been the target of dynamite planters. Every white man certainly should be asking himself how he would feel if for years the unidentified had made his wife, his children, his home, his church, the object of such hatred.[152]

This same Birmingham newspaper rejected the thesis that the bombing may have been the work of a Communist "agent provocateur." The Birmingham *News* wrote that "it would be a gross misconception to accept the 'Communist' theory as being behind Negro efforts to win new privileges. . . . The Negro leadership on local level is not Communist-inspired, and it will have to be dealt with, if it is to be dealt with satisfactorily, as a citizens' movement, not any Red conspiracy."[153]

In New York, a group of Negro writers and artists called for a nationwide campaign against Christmas shopping to protest the killing of the Negro children. James Baldwin said that Americans "have no right to celebrate Christmas this year." The group said it had written to the major Negro civil rights organizations asking support of the boycott.[154]

King's Southern Christian Leadership Conference gave serious consideration to a national civil disobedience campaign drafted by Mrs. Diane Nash Bevel, field secretary of SNCC and wife of Rev. James Bevel.[155] The plan was given to Rev. Shuttlesworth but he refused to endorse it.[156] The Rev. Wyatt Tee Walker, one of King's top aides, seemed to be highly receptive to the entire concept, however. Walker asked the meeting of King supporters:

Is the day far off that major transportation centers would be deluged with mass acts of civil disobedience; airports, train stations, bus terminals, the traffic of large cities, interstate commerce would be halted by the bodies of witnesses non-violently insisting on freedom now?
I submit a nationwide work stoppage might attract enough attention to persuade someone to get this monkey of segregation off our backs, once, now, and forever.[157]

The Southern Christian Leadership Conference endorsed the call for a nationwide boycott, but a week later was forced to reverse itself when virtually every other civil rights group rejected the idea.[158] At that point, Martin Luther King had second thoughts, and decided to go along with the thinking of the other civil rights leaders.[159] And so the giving and receiving went on, as always. And the children of the country were spared the ordeal of seeing a picket line around Santa Claus.

With the Christmas boycott put to rest, national attention again focused on Birmingham, where there was little optimism about the chances of apprehending the church bombers, even though 25 FBI bomb experts were working on the case.[160] Such bombings were considered particularly difficult to solve because the explosion usually destroyed the physical evidence, and law officers had to rely on eyewitnesses, if any, and on informers.[161]

Martin Luther King demanded that President Kennedy have Birmingham occupied with Federal troops who would "take over this city, and run it. . . ."[162] Instead, the President named a two-man committee to try to bridge the ever-widening gap between the races in Birmingham.[163] In addition, Assistant Attorney General Burke Marshall urged white leaders to appoint Negroes to the police force as soon as possible. He made this recommendation after noting that Birmingham Negroes were now patrolling their own areas, carrying arms, because they felt they could not trust the regular law enforcement processes to protect them. Marshall felt that no new Federal statute could cure the crisis in Birmingham, where the two racial communities were torn apart. "There isn't any magic piece of legislation," he said. "The city of Birmingham must continue to be run by the people of Birmingham. The cure will have to come from here."[164]

Martin Luther King warned of more mass demonstrations unless city authorities acceded to four demands, including the recruiting of Negro policemen.[165] By indirection, two leaders in the Birmingham Negro community (one of whom had been a defense lawyer for King in Birmingham) rejected this threat.[166] They opposed "additional outside interference," an action which the New York *Times* considered "a sharp reply to a four-point ultimatum given city leaders by the Rev. Dr. Martin Luther King, Jr. . . ."[167]

By now, as the Birmingham *News* pointed out, "other voices" were beginning to be raised in the white community. Fifty-three Birmingham lawyers issued a public statement calling for obedience to decisions of the U.S. Supreme Court and an end to racial violence.[168] A week later a group of 90 prominent white citizens in Birmingham petitioned the Mayor and City Council, asking that "immediate consideration" be given to the hiring of Negro policemen.[169] The first Negro policeman was put on the force in Birmingham, but not that year, or the year after, or even the year after that. The first Negro policeman was not placed on the force until the end of March, 1966.[170] In the intervening two and a half years, some Negroes had turned down jobs on the force, prompting Mayor Boutwell's assistant to comment, "We have concluded that they prefer the issue to the job."[171]

What progress was made in Birmingham took not just weeks or months but years—and nothing at all was accomplished until the State Supreme Court of Alabama told Albert Boutwell he could take office as Mayor. There is not a particle of evidence that all of King's demonstrations and foot-soldiers—all of King's crisis-ridden confrontation —accomplished anything in Birmingham that could not have been accomplished if he had never set foot in the city at all.

Birmingham had served its purpose for Martin Luther King. It had wiped out the humiliating defeat in Albany, Georgia. It had made him a revered, if not adored, national hero, a sepia David smiting Whitey Goliath with the loving slingshot of nonviolence. Most of all, the Birmingham war had fashioned for him a long red carpet extending right into the White House, and with it the key to the Congressional committees that produced the Civil Rights Act.

The monumental measure of the emotional impact of Birmingham upon the country took place on August 28, 1963, when more than 200,000 Americans, black and white, joined in the March on Washington. Their objective was passage of the public accommodations measure proposed by President Kennedy and a Federal Fair Employment Practices Act barring discrimination in all employment.[172] During the March, the ultra-militancy of the Student Nonviolent Coordinating Committee almost caused a Catholic prelate to withdraw. Archbishop O'Boyle refused to deliver the invocation unless SNCC's John Lewis agreed to delete the following paragraph from the text of his speech to the marchers:

We will not wait for the President, the Justice Department, nor the Congress, but we will take matters into our own hands and create a source of power, outside of any national structure, that could and would assure us a victory. . . . We will march through the South, through the heart of Dixie, the way Sherman did."[173]

King's dream of a Civil Rights Act of 1963 died in Dallas the day a demented assassin snuffed out the life of John F. Kennedy. But the same pressure that had been applied to JFK was simply transferred to his successor in 1964. There was no longer a "Bull" Connor in office, obligingly providing martyrs for Dr. King. Instead the racial arena widened from coast to coast, with upheavals from Brooklyn to Seattle, from Chicago to Atlanta and Nashville. Two weeks before the passage of Lyndon Johnson's Civil Rights Act, the press noted the President's concern about the possibility of violence and a "Long Hot Summer" in 1964.[174] The Administration's fear was not that the bill went too far, but that it did not go far enough![175]

The Civil Rights Act of 1964 gave Martin Luther King the public accommodations clause he demanded—prohibiting discrimination or refusal of service on account of race in hotels, motels, restaurants, gasoline stations and places of amusement if their operations affect interstate commerce[176] (and there is hardly any business enterprise in the 50 states that the Justice Department cannot link to interstate commerce, if it is so inclined). Also included was a Fair Employment Practices Act, with an escalator clause increasing the amount of employer coverage over a four-year period. Alone of all eleven provisions of the Civil Rights Act, the fair employment provisions became effective *after* the 1964 Presidential election had come and gone[177]—after Lyndon Johnson had renewed his lease on the White House and Barry Goldwater had been defeated.

In the words of the civil rights anthem, Martin Luther King had overcome. In Birmingham, King had overcome law and order; he had overcome Negro and white moderates alike; he had overcome parents who wanted their children in school instead of in jail; he had overcome the Justice Department, which wanted a solution at the conference table and not in the streets.

King had left behind him a fear-ridden city that had come to the outermost edge of civil collapse.

And now he proposed to do the same in Selma, Alabama.

CHAPTER 6

1965: War in Selma, and the Voting Rights Act

If, in 1964, you had walked along Times Square and asked the first ten New Yorkers you saw where the city of Selma was located, it is doubtful that even one of them could have given you the correct answer. Had you asked that same question in March, 1965, you would have been deluged with an avalanche of data about the black-heartedness of the community, its officials, and just about every (white) man, woman, and child who lived there. The difference was that in 1965, Selma, Alabama, had become the staging ground for Martin Luther King's next "loving" war, and the publicity wheels started turning with an almost computer-like speed.

The man in the street may have been under the impression that, alone among the civil rights leaders, it was King who "discovered" Selma, planted the flag of nonviolence on its soil, and then initiated the fight heard almost literally around the world. And King would probably have been the very last person to issue a correcting statement. But the fact of the matter was that King arrived in Selma about a year and a half *after* the Student Nonviolent Coordinating Committee had sent field secretaries into the town and became solidly entrenched in the Negro community. Again, as in Albany, Georgia, their leaders could only comment in helpless rage that it was SNCC that planted the seed in Selma, while it was King who reaped the harvest. Nor was it any ordinary harvest, but a bumper crop of sweeping Federal laws, brought about through the careful cultivation of Uncle Cornpone in the White House.

To be sure, King's interest in Negro voting strength dated back almost to the days of the Montgomery boycott. During the Prayer Pilgrimage of May 17, 1957, in Washington, D.C., King shouted: "Give us the ballot and we will no longer plead—we will write the proper laws on the books. Give us the ballot and we will fill the legislature with men of good will. Give us the ballot and we will get the people judges who love mercy. . . . Give us the ballot and we will transform the salient misdeeds of the bloodthirsty mobs into the calculated good deeds of orderly citizens."[1]

And yet even in those areas where Negroes had the ballot, the results were hardly anything to sing hosannas about. One had to agree with Bruce M. Galphin, race-relations reporter for the Atlanta *Constitution*, that in 1960 "without the Negro vote in key states . . . John Kennedy would not now be wearing his paper-thin mantle of victory." But as Galphin also noted, outside the "black-belt" counties "the plain truth is that Negroes themselves are in no small part to blame for their failure to realize their voting potential. . . . The net increase [between 1952 and 1961] is little more than 200,000. This is true even though more and more of the South's Negroes live in cities, where they encounter little or no official opposition to registering." Galphin told of a pre-mayoralty primary registration drive in Atlanta, sponsored jointly by long-standing Negro organizations and King's Southern Christian Leadership Conference. Despite an enormous pool of qualified Negroes and the "complete cooperation" of the County Registrar, the voting drive fell far short of its goal.[2]

In 1961, civil rights experts in the Kennedy Administration were convinced that Negroes were on the verge of a political breakthrough in the South. They predicted that Negro registration and voting would increase sufficiently by 1964, so that many Southern politicians would have to ease their stand for white supremacy. Attorney General Robert Kennedy believed the ballot would be the key to Negro progress in the South.[3] But the New York *Times* noted, as did Galphin, that "many students of the problem, including the Civil Rights Commission, have said that Negro apathy has accounted in good part for the low registration figures."[4]

This same article would have been just as timely in 1965. At the height of the demonstrations in Selma, Alabama, King led a mass march in Montgomery to encourage Negroes to register to vote in that city. In the reminiscent phraseology of a twice-told tale, the New York *Times* wrote that "the greatest obstacle to Negro voting here, as in many places in the South, is apathy." The article noted that Montgomery Negroes had been registering freely for over two years, but that only 40 per cent of the city's eligible Negroes were registered to vote, compared with 75 per cent of the whites.[5] At any rate, King did have his Montgomery demonstration, and the result was neatly summarized by one reporter in this single delicious sentence:

The Rev. Dr. Martin Luther King, Jr., led a march against Negro voter apathy here today, and apathy won.[6]

That day, only 195 Montgomery Negroes showed up to register to vote, and it developed that many of them were registered already.[7]

The percentage of registered Negro voters was low, but obviously it would have been ludicrous for King to use Montgomery as his showcase to point up the need for Federal voting rights legislation; it was a little difficult to castigate that city's officials, considering that they had actually *helped* Negroes attempting to register.[8] What was needed was a community where overt intimidation or coercion was used to prevent Negroes from voting—a community where Negro voter rolls were almost nil. In this respect, the answer to a civil rights militant's dream was Selma, the governmental seat of Dallas County, in Alabama. King knew exactly what to expect in Selma and picked it for exactly that reason. He knew that after the Supreme Court ruled against desegregation in 1954, Dallas County was the first to organize a Citizens Council.[9] He knew what had happened when SNCC had tried to organize a voting campaign in Selma. The SNCC voter campaign had started there in February, 1963, with the arrival of Rev. Bernard Lafayette and his wife.[10] Thirty-two schoolteachers who tried to register to vote were fired.[11] John Lewis, then leader of SNCC, was arrested for leading a picket line at the courthouse.[12] Between September 15 and October 2, 1963, over three hundred people were arrested in Selma in connection with voter registration activities.[13] In October of that year, SNCC decided on a large-scale offensive. They set October 7 as the day to bring hundreds to the Dallas County courthouse to register, and on that day assembled some 350 Negroes on the registration line. Howard Zinn, a white teacher at a Negro college in Atlanta, averred that he had made notes that day, almost minute by minute. His records made extensive references to Sheriff Jim Clark's special posse, with their "green helmets or white helmets, guns at their hips, long clubs"; Clark himself, with "the confederate flag stamped on his helmet, an open collar, epaulets on his shoulders, gun at his hip." Clark refused to let SNCC workers bring food to those who had been waiting in line for hours. Finally, two SNCC field secretaries, with arms full of food, approached the line, ignored white commands to move on, and then, as Zinn told it:

The next thing I saw was Chico Neblett [one of the SNCC

workers] on the ground, troopers all around him. They poked
at him with clubs and sticks. I heard him cry out and saw his
body jump convulsively again and again; they were jabbing at
him with the cattle prods. Photographers were taking pictures,
and the Major yelled, "Get in front of those cameramen!"[14]

The New York *Times* gave a considerably different version of the events. *Times* reporter John Herbers wrote
that several officers tried to push the two SNCC workers
away. But the two Negroes lay down on the sidewalk,
whereupon twelve troopers then surrounded the Negroes,
picked them up, and prodded them with nightsticks.[15]

In either case, the SNCC campaign faltered, then petered
out. A few last attempts at demonstrations were made the
following year, just a few weeks before the civil rights
moratorium of 1964.[16]

Interestingly enough, Martin Luther King and Sheriff
James Clark had clashed in 1963, not in Selma, but in
Birmingham. During the Birmingham race riot in May,
1963, Colonel Al Lingo, State Director of Public Safety,
moved his troopers into the riot scene, armed with carbines
and shotguns—all despite the objection of that city's chief
of police. Assisting Lingo was Selma Sheriff Clark and a
deputized group of irregulars from Dallas County, who
sealed off a 28-block area and refused to allow anyone but
residents and officials in or out of the section.[17] (Selma was
the home town of "Bull" Connor.)[18]

The repression of Negro voting rights in Selma was no
longer typical of the South, much less the entire country.
On the contrary, Martin Luther King himself admitted
that Negro voting registration in the South in 1964 had
nearly doubled since the Presidential election of 1960. He
conceded that about two million Negroes were registered
in the South, compared to 1.1 million in 1960.[19] About 90
per cent of the Negro voters cast their ballots for Lyndon
Johnson[20] and it was freely admitted on all sides that their
votes helped swing into the Johnson column several South-

ern states that otherwise would have gone to Goldwater. Mr. Johnson was reminded of this fact—sometimes privately, sometimes publicly, sometimes delicately, sometimes bluntly—by various civil rights spokesmen, North and South.

In addition, the Civil Rights Act of 1964 prohibited registrars from applying different standards to white and Negro voting applicants, and from disqualifying applicants because of inconsequential errors on their forms. The Act also made a sixth-grade education an unrebuttable presumption of literacy.

But as far as King was concerned, this legislation might just as well never have been written. He never gave the voting section of the 1964 Civil Rights Law a chance to work. The day after the election, King was telling reporters that he planned to engage in civil rights demonstrations in Alabama and Mississippi "based around the right to vote."[21] Furthermore, he declared, the landslide vote given LBJ should convince the President that he had "a definite mandate from the American public" to support such demonstrations.[22] One could see King drawing the blueprint for 1965 as he continued, "We hope that through this process, we can bring the necessary moral pressure to bear on the Federal government to get Federal registrars appointed in those areas, as well as to get Federal marshals in those places to escort Negroes to the registration places, if necessary."[23]

Sheriff Jim Clark could hardly have received a more clearly enunciated storm warning. If this were not enough, he had only to read the Sunday New York *Times* early the following year to find the statement of the Rev. Andrew Young, program chairman of the Southern Christian Leadership Conference, that "just as the 1964 Civil Rights Bill was written in Birmingham, we hope that new Federal voting legislation will be written here [in Selma]."[24]

Anyone who had followed the battle of Birmingham in even the most casual manner could hardly have failed to grasp that King was about to zero in on Selma with yet another loving blitzkrieg. It bears repeating that King saw the necessity for four events to take place before he could achieve his goals:

1) Nonviolent demonstrators go into the streets to exercise their constitutional rights.
2) Racists resist by unleashing violence against them.
3) Americans of conscience in the name of decency demand Federal intervention and legislation.
4) The Administration, under mass pressure, initiates measures of immediate intervention and remedial legislation.[25]

Obviously, segregationist violence was the *sine qua non* of the success of King's nonviolence. King *needed* Clark— *needed* a brutal response by the Sheriff of Dallas County— to secure Federal legislation. It was a bizarre war in which the violent became the vanquished, but war nonetheless. And if Sheriff Jim Clark blustered and blundered his way to defeat, it was because he obligingly fell into every baited trap King set for him.

Perhaps at this point it should be made clear that the phrase "the Selma campaign" is something of a misnomer. Jim Clark was Sheriff of Dallas County, of which Selma was the government seat. The chief law enforcement officer of the town of Selma was Wilson Baker, a moderate, and—had he been left alone by County Sheriff Clark—a match for Dr. King.

At times, the conflict between Baker and Clark was almost as intense as that between Clark and King. Wilson Baker, as Public Safety Director of Selma, sought a more moderate course in race relations. In early January, before a Negro rally began, he said that whites who might cause trouble would be kept out of the area.[26] He arrested two white youths who allegedly set off a tear-gas bomb in the Negro section of town.[27] During King's first month in Selma, he registered as the first Negro guest of a hotel built more than a century before by slave labor. A member of the segregationist National States Rights Party punched and kicked King and was thenceforth collared by Baker and dragged to a patrol car. The segregationist assailant was charged with assault and disturbing the peace.[28] He was fined $100, and sentenced to 60 days at hard labor.[29]

This was more or less typical of the judicious way in which Baker conducted himself in disturbances taking place within his jurisdiction. Unfortunately, the bulk of the civil rights incidents took place in and around the Dallas County Courthouse, and this was under the direct supervision of the unyielding segregationist Jim Clark. On these occasions, Baker could only stand helplessly by and watch Clark playing right into King's hands.

Wilson Baker was a new face in Selma, a native of North Carolina who had recently been appointed by a new city administration. His differences with Clark were so fundamental that, at one point, they stood ten feet apart in front of the Dallas County Courthouse and glared at each other. They did not speak to each other directly, communicating through representatives.[30] Baker belonged to the Laurie Pritchett school of law enforcement; Clark subscribed to the blunderbuss tactics of "Bull" Connor, and was similarly doomed to failure.

The battle lines between white officials and Negro rights leaders were clearly drawn on January 3, 1965, when Martin Luther King told an audience of 700 cheering Negroes he would assist in "a march on the ballot boxes" throughout Alabama. In King's words:

If they refuse to register us, we will appeal to Governor Wallace. If he doesn't listen, we will appeal to the Legislature. If the Legislature doesn't listen, we will dramatize the situation and seek to arouse the Federal government by marching by the thousands by the places of registration. We must be willing to go to jail by the thousands.[31]

But by now it was getting more and more difficult for civil rights demonstrators to be arrested. Southern sheriffs were becoming much more sophisticated about civil rights campaigns—much more aware of the television cameras waiting in the wings—and, realizing that abstention was the better part of valor, refraining, as far as possible, from making any more arrests than absolutely necessary. And the new city government of Selma was no more interested in filling its jails than its sister Southern communities. The New York *Times* noted that "Dr. King found in Selma not the monolithic community that it had been in 1963. A new leadership had emerged, committed to a reluctant compliance with the Civil Rights Law of 1964 and a policy of making the minimum change necessary to preserve the peace and reputation of the community."[32] This leadership exerted pressure on Sheriff Clark to avoid making mass arrests—and especially to avoid arresting King. For a time this policy prevailed—so much so that King's arrest was at least two weeks behind schedule, according to a blueprint his group drew up before the first of the year.[33]

As in Birmingham, the Selma campaign started slowly, with the usual limited forays. In the middle of January, 62 Negroes trying to register were arrested for refusing to return to a courthouse alley that had been assigned to them.[34] A few days later, 105 Negro teachers lined the steps of the Dallas County Courthouse in a voter registration drive (less than half of them were registered). Mr. Frederick D. Reese, King's chief aide in Selma, asked that the registration board set aside a Friday for registration of teachers. The chairman of the Selma School Board told the group, "Any of you will be permitted at any time to leave any school and register. But you cannot come in here and register now. The board is not open." Reese replied, "We want to see for ourselves if the board is open." At that point, Clark ordered the teachers to clear the steps. When they refused, he took his club and began punching the teachers, who began retreating down the stairs.[35]

The NAACP's Legal Defense and Educational Fund filed suit in the U.S. District Court, asking that Clark be enjoined from arresting applicants for registration at the courthouse.[36] Federal Judge Daniel Thomas issued an order to Clark to stop interfering with Negro voter applicants. He served notice that "violence on either side will not be tolerated." In effect, the judge blamed both sides for recent events; he said that "unnecessary arrests have been made, provoked by unnecessary assemblage by people at improper places." He directed the sheriff's office to issue applicants consecutive numbers, 1 through 100, on a first-come-first-served basis. Registrants were to line up at the street entrance, instead of in the alley as Clark had insisted.

Judge Thomas noted that since the voting rights drive had started, only 36 Negro applicants had been processed, but he felt both sides were at fault. He observed that "no sufficient reason has come to this court why some of them [Negroes who appeared Monday through Wednesday] could not have appeared on registration days in which the registrars had practically no applicants to process."[37] The next few days saw a continuing dispute over how many Negroes should be permitted in a voter registration line at one time. Officials interpreted Judge Thomas' order to mean that only 100 applicants should be permitted in line at one time. Negroes contended that this was merely a suggested figure.[38] In three days of registration, the board processed about 70 applications, most of them from Negroes. The applicants were told they would be notified in about three weeks whether they had passed the registration test,[39] which included questions on government and the Constitution such as:

If no national candidate for Vice President receives a majority of the electoral vote, how is a Vice President chosen? In such cases how many votes must a person receive to become Vice President?[40]

The answers (the second of which the author ruefully admits he would not have known, himself) are, respectively, the Senate, and 51 votes. It was with excellent reason that the Justice Department charged that the test was more stringent than standards applied to persons registered in the past, that it violated the 1964 Civil Rights Act because it required higher than a sixth-grade education, and that it was intended to freeze the present racial imbalance of the Alabama electorate.[41]

Meanwhile, Judge Thomas clarified his ruling in an order that civil rights workers could not be arrested for standing around voter registration lines and encouraging Negroes to vote, as long as they remained "peaceful and orderly."[42]

On February 1, Wilson Baker delighted Martin Luther King by arresting him and more than 770 other Negroes in the town of Selma for parading without a permit. About 500 of those arrested were students who stayed out of school and picketed the Dallas County Courthouse. It was the mass arrest King had been seeking, but Baker, having made his point, released the adults who were residents of Selma after they had spent six hours in jail (pending arraignment later in the month). A $200 bond was required of non-resident defendants; King refused to post the bond, and remained in jail.[43] He had to stay. It would almost have been the height of police brutality to force King to leave his cell. How else could that dramatic ad have appeared in the New York *Times*, datelined February 1, 1965, and headlined:

A LETTER FROM MARTIN LUTHER KING FROM A SELMA, ALABAMA JAIL.

King wrote about the jailing of hundreds of Negroes in Selma, the enormously difficult registration test, the small number of applicants taking the qualifying test at all, and concluded with a throbbing appeal for contributions.[44] Throughout his lengthy letter, he never so much as hinted that the entire question was undergoing the most thorough scrutiny in the Federal courts—courts which had proved exceptionally friendly to civil rights causes in the past. King stayed in jail just long enough to dramatize the voter drive. Five days later bond was posted. As one reporter expressed it, King now found it "more dramatic to come out than to stay in."[45]

There were still more mass arrests. This time it was Jim Clark who arrested about 520 Negroes, most of them high school students. A number of them were kept overnight in penal camps.[46]

Now Judge Thomas ordered the board of registrars to relax its literacy test and to speed the registration of Negroes.[47] The New York *Times* found that "the initial reaction of civil rights leaders was not one of jubilation but of disappointment." The Negroes felt the judge's decision was taking the steam out of their campaign, coming at the time it did.[48] They needn't have worried. With Jim Clark's near-genius for doing the wrong thing in the wrong place at the wrong time, it was predictable that the campaign would heat up again in short order. With his glandular reactions to civil rights demonstrations, Clark was practically Martin Luther King's secret weapon in Selma, and almost everyone realized this except Clark. By now, almost everyone was coming to understand that every time Clark used excessive force against the Negroes, he was aiding the passage of the Voting Rights Act of 1965.

In this context, the forced march became the last nail in the coffin of segregation in Selma. Admittedly, there was no gainsaying the fact that the student demonstrators had taken a special delight in taunting Clark. On one of those days of mass arrests, a high school student leader told his fellow marchers, "They don't want to arrest us. We want to make them arrest us. We'll lock arms in front of the courthouse."[49] Admittedly, Clark was on the verge of being hospitalized for exhaustion.[50] But nothing that had happened in that whole turbulent month could have condoned the action Clark saw fit to take on February 10,

1965. On that date, he and a group of deputies used night-sticks and electric cattle prods to lead 165 Negro demonstrators, all children and teen-agers, on a forced march into the Dallas County countryside. While Clark and his posse rode, the youngsters were compelled to march over two miles, until the exhausted children fled into a private yard. The sheriff then gave up the march, and returned to Selma.[51] Not surprisingly, this brutal stupidity infuriated the Negro parents and instilled new drive into the civil rights campaign.

By this time, almost 3,400 persons had been arrested, and Clark began yielding to growing pressure to stop making mass arrests.[52] For his part, King, with laudable magnanimity, decided to let the students go back to their studies; they had been out of school campaigning for two weeks, and most of them had been in jail at least once.[53]

Such as it was, this thaw didn't last very long. Less than a week later Clark struck one of King's assistants on the mouth, after he had goaded him with a string of invectives that included "brute" and "Hitler." The assistant, the Rev. C. T. Vivian, was arrested and subsequently charged with criminal provocation and contempt of court. Another staff member of the Southern Christian Leadership Conference sardonically commented, "Every time it appears that the movement is dying out, Sheriff Clark comes to our rescue."[54]

By the end of February, about 2,400 Negroes had signed the registrar's appearance book, which assigned priorities for voting registration in the coming weeks.[55] Around this time, there were persistent reports that a group of influential white community leaders were looking seriously for a solution to Selma's racial difficulties.[56]

In Montgomery, Governor Wallace ordered troopers to stop night marches by Negroes in Selma.[57] King responded by calling for a march on Montgomery to protest barriers to Negro voting.[58] At first he said that Negroes had no intention of abiding by the ban,[59] but he subsequently backtracked and decided that night marches might be suspended until a Federal District Court could be petitioned to overturn Wallace's order.[60] Roy Reed, of the New York *Times*, wrote:

The Negroes' rationale in holding night marches is to provoke the racist element in white communities to show its worst. As a result, Negroes have often been attacked. Both whites and Negroes acknowledge that the risk of violence is heightened considerably after nightfall.[61]

In this same article, it was reported that Wilson Baker persuaded 100 Negro youngsters marching on the courthouse to turn back just before nightfall, thus avoiding a clash with Clark and his posse (Baker had persuaded Clark to move in only if necessary).[62]

The month of March began with King receiving strong intimations from important business leaders of a desire to see an early end of racial violence and discrimination in Alabama.[63] And Judge Thomas issued two more orders to the Dallas County Board of Registrars. The board was directed to produce virtually all voter records and documents since the preceding September, and machinery was set up for appeals to a Federal Voter Referee.[64]

All this was forgotten in the march to Montgomery. Actually, it almost becomes necessary to number them since three different marches were scheduled between Selma and Montgomery. The 3,400 arrests were a Bobbsey Twins frolic compared with what was about to come. In March, 1965, it was nothing less than war in Selma—war on both sides, with precious little quarter given or asked —culminating in a Federal troop operation that resembled an anti-guerrilla campaign in Vietnam.

March No. 1 took place on March 7, 1965. Perhaps "march" is not quite the right word; it was more like a battlefield. It was the most militant demonstrators, determined to be an irresistible force, cheek by jowl against the immovable opposition of Jim Clark and Governor Wallace's man in Selma, Al Lingo. That day, Wallace and Clark won the battle, and Alabama lost the war.

On that day, Alabama state troopers and volunteer officers under Jim Clark's command ripped through a column of Negro demonstrators starting the first lap of a protest march from Selma to Montgomery. The troopers used tear gas, nightsticks, and whips to enforce Wallace's order against the march. At least 17 Negroes were hospitalized with injuries, and about 40 more were given emergency treatment for minor injuries and tear gas effects.

Mounted possemen spurred their horses and rode at a run into the retreating mass. Ron Gibson, a reporter for the Birmingham *News*, said that he had seen Sheriff Clark lead a charge with about half a dozen possemen to try to force the Negroes back into their church. Wilson Baker intervened and persuaded the Negroes to go inside. Baker held back Clark and his men, who were regrouping for another assault.[65]

This may well have been Baker's sole appearance on the scene; that bloody day, it was noted that Lingo and Clark's troopers had "all but replaced Selma's moderate Public Safety Director, Wilson Baker, and his city police, in dealing with Negroes protesting barriers to voter registration."[66]

The Selma *Times-Journal* reported that Mayor Joseph T. Smitherman had ordered Baker to have the city police join the state and county troopers in using force to break up the scheduled march. Baker said he would resign rather than carry out the mayor's orders. Some members of the City Council supported Baker's position, and worked out an agreement whereby the city police would not participate in the violence, but Baker would not stop the Negroes from marching into the force of troopers and possemen.[67]

The repression of this first march was the subject of scathing editorial comment all over the country. *Newsweek* called it "An American Tragedy."[68] Herblock of the Washington *Post* depicted a moronic "Special Storm Trooper" chuckling with satisfaction as he washed a Negro woman's blood from his club. The caption: "I got one of 'em as she almost made it back to the church."[69] Sanders of the Kansas City *Star* portrayed the troopers as ape-like dimwits, held on a leash by Governor Wallace.[70] And the criticism was by no means limited to the North. Montgomery's *Alabama Journal* editorialized: "By dumb, cruel and vastly excessive force, we have made new civil rights legislation almost a dead certainty: we have stained the state and put the lie to its claims of peace and harmony: given enough rope, as if they haven't already been supplied it, our strategists will hang the state in vainglorious self-immolation."[71]

Wallace's reply was that the state troopers had probably saved Negro lives by forcing them to turn back from a highway where they might have been attacked by angry whites.[72] But at best it was a distinction without a difference—being clubbed by state troopers, instead of being clubbed by white hooligans on the highway.

Beyond any question, when the troopers galloped after the retreating Negroes they trampled over the legitimate exercise of law enforcement as well. They openly engaged in a brutal racial vendetta, armed with the awesome police powers of the state. They showed scant interest in making arrests; they apparently were much more interested in breaking heads.

But it would be less than fair to saddle the troopers with all of the responsibility for the grisly events of that day. Herblock to the contrary, the marchers were not quite ready to qualify for sainthood. They marched in violation of the Governor's ban, before it had been reversed by a court of competent jurisdiction. In fact, they marched without Martin Luther King, who was in Atlanta. He had agreed *not* to lead the march after he learned the troopers would block it.[73]

As the television viewers saw the battle, it looked as if

the troopers had moved right in, without giving the marchers a chance to withdraw. But it was not quite that simple.
About 525 Negroes left Browns Chapel and walked six
blocks to Broad Street, then across Pettus Bridge. More
than 50 troopers, and a few dozen possemen, were waiting
300 yards beyond the end of the bridge. The confrontation did not come until the Negroes had left the town of
Selma, walked over the bridge, and then approached the
troopers. When the Negroes were 50 feet away, they were
ordered to stop, and did so. Then Major Cloud, the leader
of the troopers, told the marchers, "This is an unlawful
assembly. Your march is not conducive to the public safety.
You are ordered to disperse and go back to your church
or to your homes." After a further exchange of words
between the Major and Hosea Williams, leader of the
marchers, Cloud told the Negroes, "You have two minutes
to turn around and go back to your church." When the
Negroes refused to move, the Major ordered the troopers
to advance.[74]

One of England's best-known political commentators,
Henry Fairlie, wrote, "Every reliable reporter I know who
was present points out that there was first a period during
which police and demonstrators faced each other without
violence, in an atmosphere of unbearable tension." Fairlie
stressed that "Television news broadcasts did not and could
not show this preliminary encounter."[75]

One could vigorously condemn the bloody brawl that
took place that day in Selma and still be compelled to
emphasize that the troopers, in upholding the Governor's
ban, were clearly acting under cover of law, while the
marchers were engaging in civil disobedience. It was
equally necessary to emphasize that these disciples of nonviolence knew perfectly well that they were marching directly into a maelstrom of violence, and couldn't have cared
less. They were so certain that violence would result that
they had their own doctors and ambulances on the scene,
before the march began. The Medical Committee for Hu-

man Rights had three white doctors, some Negro and white nurses, and four ambulances moving right along with the marchers until they reached the bridge.

Three hours before the march, one of these doctors learned that state troopers were going to meet the marchers with tear gas. Addressing the Negroes gathered into the Methodist Church that was their meeting place for the march, the doctor told them, "There'll be tear gas, but don't panic. Don't rub your eyes. Wash them with water, if you can. And we'll be on hand to help."[76]

In view of this admonition to the marchers—and the conspicuous medical presence at the site of the march—it is difficult to see how Martin Luther King could have said, with any degree of seriousness, "When I made a last-minute agreement not to lead the march, and appointed my able and courageous associate, Hosea Williams, for this responsibility, I must confess that I had no idea that the kind of brutality and tragic expression of man's inhumanity to man as existed today would take place."[77] King announced plans to begin a second march from Selma to Montgomery two days later, and stressed his determination to seek a court order barring Alabama authorities from interfering.[78] At the same time he said he was "calling on religious leaders from all over the nation to join us on Tuesday in our peaceful, nonviolent march for freedom."[79]

Under Dr. King's leadership, that Tuesday march—in the eyes of the ultra-militant—became nothing less than a pious fraud. The march was undertaken in the face of a Federal District Court temporary restraining order against it.[80] Attorney General Katzenbach was on the phone at 5:00 a.m., urging King to call off the march.[81] But John Lewis, then chairman of the Student Nonviolent Coordinating Committee, was deaf to all entreaties to postpone the march. Invoking the I-Am-The-Law civil disobedience doctrine so beloved by Martin Luther King, the SNCC leader declared, "I understand there's an order from Judge Johnson. I believe we have a constitutional right to march whenever we get ready, *injunction or no injunction.*"[82]

During his campaigns, King had violated local court injunctions with gleeful abandon. But he had never before knowingly violated a *Federal* court injunction.[83] He wanted to abide by the injunction; he wanted to retain the allegiance of hundreds of ministers and civil rights advocates and workers who had come to Selma, specifically, to use their marching shoes; he wanted to keep the SNCC leaders from carrying out their ultimatum to lead the march themselves, if he would not.[84] Columnists Rowland Evans and Robert Novak wrote: "The sad truth is that Dr. King at times abdicated command of the Selma, Ala., demonstration to John Lewis and James Foreman, the two hothead extremists who lead the Student Nonviolent Coordinating Committee (usually called SNCC). And there is no doubt whatever that SNCC is substantially infiltrated by beatnik left-wing revolutionaries, and—worst of all—by Communists."[85]

On the morning of March 10, 1965, Americans picked up their newspapers and learned that the day before Martin Luther King had led 1,500 Negroes and whites on a second attempted protest march from Selma to Montgomery. State troopers turned them back on the outskirts of Selma, after they had gone one mile—but this time there was no violence. The marchers approached the Pettus Bridge, across the Alabama River. They stopped 50 feet from the trooper ranks. Four of the march leaders began praying. When the last prayer had ended, the marchers turned and went back to town.[86]

If all this sounds like bad melodrama, it is because this peaceful confrontation had been worked out in advance, with the Federal government as mediator. Both sides knew that the marchers would turn back after a prayer session, and that there likely would be no use of nightsticks and tear gas.[87] In a news conference held after the march,

Martin Luther King said: "We agreed that we would not break through the lines." He admitted that, "In all frankness, we knew we would not get to Montgomery. We knew we would not get past the troopers."[88]

Governor Wallace wanted to avoid another bloody confrontation, and had ordered Sheriff Clark's possemen kept off the streets.[89] By now, law enforcement in Selma was back in the more moderate hands of Wilson Baker.[90]

What had happened at the Edmund Pettus Bridge was now a matter of public record. As to what had happened behind the scenes, the reader can take his choice of these two differing versions.

According to a spokesman for Martin Luther King, "Governor Collins, head of the Federal Community Relations Service, asked him to call off the march in compliance with the Federal court injunction and President Johnson's wishes. They found there was no ground for compromise."[91] But according to a Federal government source, Collins had received a pledge from King that no attempt would be made to march against orders of the authorities.[92]

What happened next is clear enough. Collins then conferred with Col. Al Lingo, Alabama Public Safety Director, and Jim Clark. A plan had already been worked out whereby the marchers would not be stopped until they had gone some distance down U.S. 80 toward Montgomery.[93] Collins commented: "I think good people on both sides were anxious to avoid violence."[94]

Testifying in Federal Court, King confirmed that he had had no intention of leading a march of Negroes and civil rights partisans that day from Selma to Montgomery, in violation of the temporary injunction.[95] Judge Johnson asked, "Is it correct to say that when you started across the bridge, you knew at that time that you did not intend to march to Montgomery?" King replied, "Yes it is. There was a tacit agreement at the bridge that we would go no further."[96] King's testimony saved him from a contempt citation but, as the New York *Times* noted, it "had done little to heal the open contempt for his leadership expressed by some more militant Negro and white civil rights spokesmen. Many of these spokesmen privately charged that King had betrayed them by his behind-the-scenes bargaining."[97]

The SNCC leaders were among those most contemptuous of anything resembling a moderate racial settlement. Nowhere was this more definitively expressed than in a speech by SNCC's chairman to a staff meeting just a few weeks before this abortive march. Read the lines, and you see the oratory of then SNCC chairman John Lewis, in 1965. Read between the lines, and you can perceive some of the first faint outlines of Stokely Carmichael and Black Power, in 1966.

Lewis told the SNCC workers:

I think past history will testify to the fact that white liberals and the so-called affluent Negro leader will not support all of our demands . . . They will be forced to support some of them in order to maintain an image of themselves as liberal. But we must also recognize that their material comforts and congenial relations with the establishment is of much more importance to them than their concern for an oppressed people. And they will sell us down the river for the hundredth time in order to protect themselves.[98]

In this speech—delivered in 1965 to a still-integrated Student Nonviolent Coordinating Committee, in the midst of the Selma campaign—chairman Lewis declared: "If the movement and SNCC are going to be effective in attempting to liberate the black masses, *the civil rights movement must be black controlled, dominated, and led.*"[99]

At the same time, Lewis reiterated his conviction that "this country is a racist country. The majority of the population is white and most whites still hold to a master-slave mentality."[100] Had this been true, of course, the Civil Rights Acts of 1957, 1960, and 1964 would never have been reported out of committee, much less made the law of the land by Congress. Lewis would have been the first to object to any stereotyped views about "most Negroes," but had not the slightest hesitancy about stereotyping "most whites."

Within a few weeks, Lewis—who had been a Baptist minister—was among those playing host to hundreds of white clergymen who had come to Alabama for the express purpose of joining the second march from Selma to Montgomery. Among these ministers was James J. Reeb, a 38-year-old Unitarian clergyman from Boston. Reeb came to Alabama to march—his first time in the South—and died there.

Rev. Reeb had participated in the march led by Martin Luther King,[101] the march that turned back at the Pettus Bridge after observing the ritualistic niceties of a carefully-devised script. Four hours later, he and two other white ministers had dinner in a Negro restaurant. After the ministers left the restaurant, they were beaten by five white men. Reeb was knocked unconscious with a club and taken to University Hospital in Birmingham. There he underwent emergency surgery. He had suffered multiple skull fractures, resulting in a large blood clot over the left side of his brain. The following day, Wilson Baker announced the arrests of three white men on charges of assaulting Rev. Reeb, and added that a fourth man was being sought.[102]

Demonstrators kept a 24-hour prayer vigil for Reeb. As 200 of them were praying in the rain, Baker stepped out of his car and told them, "Reverend Reeb has died in the hospital in Birmingham."[103]

President Johnson telephoned the widow of Rev. Reeb to offer his condolences.[104] And Martin Luther King said, "Had policemen not brutally beaten unarmed, nonviolent persons desiring the right to vote, on Sunday, it is doubtful whether this act of murder by other Alabamians would have taken place on Tuesday."[105] This was a highly questionable statement, given the history of Birmingham a few short years before. In Birmingham, *after* a more moderate mayor was installed—*after* a biracial committee was formed —the church bombing took place that snuffed out the lives of the Negro children. And in the hours before the savage attack on Rev. Reeb took place, Governor Wallace had shown a desire to avoid further violence by acquiescing in the formula that kept Jim Clark and his possemen off the streets, and kept the state troopers from using any force at all during the second march. Perhaps one would just have to say that Rev. Reeb, in dining at a Negro restaurant in one of the most fervently segregationist communities in the South, was walking into a seething lion's den of hatred and hostility. Even with a police escort, the action would have been a dangerous one. Without such protection in the Selma, Alabama of 1965, Reeb's action was almost suicidal. That Rev. James J. Reeb was a victim of man's inhumanity to man is indisputable—but it would be fallacious to say that this particular act of inhumanity could not reasonably have been foreseen.*

* There was one other death during this civil rights campaign. A 26-year-old Negro wood cutter, Jimmie Lee Jackson, was shot by a state trooper in nearby Marion, Alabama. Jackson had gone to a mass meeting the night of February 18, 1965. The meeting turned into a protest march and state troopers broke it up with nightsticks. Jackson and a number of other Negroes fled into Mack's Cafe. That day, three generations of his family were in the hospital as a result of assaults by state troopers. Jackson's 82-year-old grandfather had a knot on the back of his head. Jackson's mother had five stitches in her scalp. Three Negro youths—Jeremiah Dobyne, Charles Pryor and Willie Smith—said Jimmie Lee Jackson attacked a state trooper when he saw the officer beating his mother. They said one of the troopers took out his pistol and shot him. Shot in the stomach, Jackson was taken to the Good Samaritan Hospital in Selma, where his condition was described as poor. At first, King's interest in Jackson seemed somewhat perfunctory. On February 23, 1965, the New York *Times* reported that King went to the hospital for a five-minute visit with the wounded Negro. Although Jackson still was in critical condition, King found him "in good spirits." King added: "I told him we were very concerned about him and he was very much in our prayers. I prayed with him"—rather a great deal to squeeze into a five-minute visit. Three days later, Jimmie Lee Jackson was dead; the immediate cause of death was listed as infection and respiratory difficulty. About 4,000 Negroes attended two funeral services

The day after the death of Rev. Reeb, 70 priests, nuns and laymen from the Catholic Interracial Council of Chicago flew into Selma to participate in civil rights activities.[106] They lost very little time getting started. As it was reported the following morning: "Civil rights demonstrators, *including ministers and nuns*, tried to break through police blockades today, setting off a riotous disturbance that lasted more than an hour." There was a confrontation in which "The demonstrators lined up facing the officers. Nuns stood face to face with state troopers."[107] Archbishop Thomas J. Toolen of the Mobile-Birmingham Diocese strongly disapproved of the Northern clergy's demonstrating in Selma.[108] He told a St. Patrick's Day audience that Martin Luther King was "dividing the people." Archbishop Toolen stated, "I do not believe that priests are equipped to lead groups in disobedience to the laws of this state." He felt that priests and nuns "are out of place in these demonstrations—their place is at home doing God's work."[109]

The 79-year-old Archbishop was no segregationist. In April, 1964, he ordered that all the Catholic schools in Alabama be integrated by September, 1965.[110]

Small groups of nuns from the Midwest made the trip to Selma to join or relieve those already there. A spokes-

---

for him, one at Selma and one at Marion. More than 1,000 walked three miles to bury him on a pine hill.

Later, King was to protest—with some justice—that President Johnson mentioned Reeb in his speech to Congress and sent flowers to Reeb's widow, but somehow "forgot to mention Jimmie, who died first." He felt this only reinforced the belief of SNCC militants, Stokely Carmichael among them, "that to white America, the life of a Negro is insignificant and meaningless."

In the author's opinion, King's basic point was a valid one. Certainly it was the death of Reeb, and not Jackson, that provided the almost irresistible emotional motivation for the passage of the Voting Rights Act. But the reasons for the heavy emphasis upon Reeb's death, and deemphasis of Jackson's death, were not necessarily sinister or racial. At the time, nine out of ten press stories concerned with the entire campaign centered on Selma, and it was in Selma that Reeb died. There was also a substantial difference in the manner in which the two met their deaths. Reeb was bludgeoned by a civilian bully boy without provocation. Jackson was shot after he had attacked a state trooper.

man for the Detroit Diocese said, "They have done it and they will continue to do it with our blessing."[111] In all, hundreds of priests and nuns from about 50 dioceses went to Selma—from Washington, Baltimore, Chicago, St. Louis, Oklahoma City, Tulsa, Wilmington, San Antonio, Boston, Pittsburgh, Brooklyn and New York.[112] John Cogley, former editor of *Commonweal*, observed a "crisis of obedience" among the young priests and nuns. He noted that "it is customary for visiting priests and religious to defer to the local bishop," and that Archbishop Toolen had disapproved of their activities. He disclosed that "on the technical grounds that the case was not covered by specific canon legislation, clearances from the local chancery office were not sought."[113]

To the non-Catholic, it looked like out-and-out clerical disobedience. On one occasion, more than 300 Roman Catholic clergy—who had arrived in Selma for the civil rights march to Montgomery—publicly rejected the Archbishop's efforts to curb participation by Catholic priests and nuns in the demonstration.[114] He had forbidden those who lived in Selma to take part and said those from other areas should be home "doing God's work."[115] The visiting Catholic clergy flatly stated their disagreement with the Archbishop; they pledged not only to march on Montgomery, but also to return to Alabama any time Martin Luther King asked them to.[116]

By now, Selma and voting rights had crowded almost everything else in the world off the front pages. There would be an article about something—anything—that was happening in Selma—while a press vigil was maintained at 1600 Pennsylvania Avenue and the Capitol. And few seemed concerned at the incongruity of Congress considering legislation that would affect over 195 million Americans, on the strength of events taking place in an Alabama community of 30,000.

At the same time that Johnson's emissaries prevailed upon King to turn back at the Pettus Bridge, the President served notice that the Federal government's best legal talent was preparing voting rights legislation "which will secure that right for every American."[117]

Eight days after the bloody confrontation of March 1, President Johnson was speaking before a Joint Session of Congress. He was interrupted 36 times by applause, twice by standing ovations, as he demanded immediate action on legislation "designed to eliminate illegal barriers to the right to vote."

Johnson told the Congress, and the American people:

What happened in Selma is part of a far larger movement which reaches into every section and state of America. It is the effort of American Negroes to secure for themselves the full blessings of American life. Their cause must be our cause, too. Because it's not just Negroes, but really it's all of us, who must overcome the crippling legacy of bigotry and injustice. *And we shall overcome.*[118]

The New York *Times* wrote that Johnson had made "what was probably the deepest commitment to the Negro cause of any American President."[119] King praised the President and his voting rights legislation, but he called for continued demonstrations until the Administration's bill became law. He told a news conference, "we must keep the issue alive, and the urgency of it before the nation."[120]

In Montgomery, Alabama, the Justice Department asked for a sweeping Federal court order to prevent Alabama officials from interfering with peaceful demonstrations in behalf of Negro rights. Specifically the Justice Department asked for an order preventing state and Dallas County officials from "summarily punishing, by striking, beating, tear-gassing or other means" any person for his participation in a civil rights demonstration.[121]

At the same time it was protecting civil rights demonstrators in Alabama, the Justice Department was ejecting demonstrators from its own building in Washington, D.C. Justice Department building guards had to eject forcibly demonstrators staging sit-ins in front of Attorney General Katzenbach's office on the fifth floor.[122]

Governor Wallace said that he would allow a peaceful march from Selma to Montgomery only if the Federal Court directed him to do so, and the court order was subsequently upheld on appeal.[123] In an appearance on CBS-TV's "Face The Nation," Wallace stated:

The reason we issued that order was not to not allow them to demonstrate but because on a 50-mile stretch of road with embankments, having to walk on the highway part of the way, with curiosity traffic by the hundreds of automobiles . . . we have an element of people in our state the same as in New York that are sometimes uncontrollable . . . We didn't want any of the demonstrators to get hurt. We were afraid if they got on the highway, that it would be impossible to defend them, it would be impossible to protect them, and at night, sleeping along wooded areas, no telling what could have happened, because we have had people to come in our state, black and white, who were intent on seeing that trouble does develop.[124]

Under oath, in Federal District Court, Alabama state troopers testified that the planned protest march would present hazards. They believed that the presence of a large number of pedestrians on U.S. Route 80, between Selma and Montgomery, would "pose a traffic hazard." The speed limit on Route 80 was 60 miles an hour, and one of the troopers testified that it had "very heavy traffic" and "many wooded areas."[125]

Five attorneys for the Selma Negro voter-registration movement submitted a "Proposed Plan for March From Selma, Ala., to Montgomery, Ala." Under the plan, the march was to take five days, with stopovers at designated private fields where the permission of the owner had already been granted. A street-by-street route of the march in Selma and Montgomery was included. The attorneys assured the judge that the following supporting services would be provided:

A. Food.
B. Truck-borne washing and toilet facilities.
C. Litter and garbage pickup by truck along route and at campsites.
D. Ambulance and first-aid service.
E. Transportation for return to Selma of those marchers in excess of the 300 (or fewer) persons who will continue on the march after the first day.
F. Lines of communication among the marchers and leaders and certain supporting services, to be established by walkie-talkie radios and other means.[126]

Finally, the attorneys concluded with an assertion that "the march will be orderly and peaceful and otherwise observe the highest standards of dignity and decorum."[127]

The following day, Federal District Judge Frank M. Johnson, Jr. authorized the mass march from Selma to Montgomery. At the same time, he ordered Governor Wallace and other Alabama officials to refrain from "harassing or threatening" the protest marchers on the 50-mile trip, and to extend them full police protection from hostile whites. This court order gave the President legal grounds for the use of Federal troops to protect the marchers, if necessary.[128]

Judge Johnson declared that "It is recognized that the plan as proposed . . . reaches under the particular circumstances of this case to the outer limits of what is constitutionally allowed. However the wrongs and injustices inflicted upon these plaintiffs [the civil rights demonstrators] have clearly exceeded—and continued to exceed—the outer limits of what is constitutionally permissible."[129]

The judge said that the proclamation by Governor Wallace forbidding the first march, and the enforcement of this order by state troopers and Jim Clark's possemen, had "stepped across the 'constitutional boundary line' that lies between the interests of the public to use the highway . . . and the right of American citizens to use it for the purpose . . . of protesting their grievances."[130]

"In this case," Judge Johnson stated, "the wrongs are enormous. The extent of the right to demonstrate against these wrongs should be determined accordingly."[131]

Governor Wallace asked President Johnson to send U.S. marshals to Alabama "to provide for the safety and welfare" of Negro and white members of the march to Montgomery. Wallace told a joint session of the Alabama Legislature that the number of Alabama highway patrolmen and other state and local lawmen was not sufficient to protect the "colossal demonstration" imposed on the state by a "mock court." He said that "maximum security" for the five-day 50-mile march would require the assignment of 6,171 law officers on eight-hour shifts;[132] it was estimated that the costs would run to $360,000.[133]

In short order, Lyndon Johnson signed two legal documents federalizing the Alabama National Guard and directing the Secretary of Defense to use whatever Federal troops "he may deem necessary" because of the danger of "domestic violence" during the march.[134]

Wallace blasted the marchers and their leaders as "Communist-trained anarchists trained in street warfare."[135] But at the same time, he urged Alabamians to exercise "restraint" and "superior discipline" by staying away "from points of tension" during the march. "I do not ask you for cowardice," he said. "I ask you not to play into the hands of the enemies of our nation and our freedom" by interfering with the marchers in any way.[136]

The New York *Times* wrote that "Violence is not expected. Almost 4,000 troops stand ready to provide security."[137] In that same edition, another article noted that the day before the march began, a 22-year-old Boston college student was slashed on the face by two white assailants.[138] He escaped with his life. As we will see, another was not quite so fortunate.

The march was the culmination of the uneasy partnership between SNCC and King's Southern Christian Leadership Conference in Selma. The radicalization of the civil rights movement was now all too evident even to the New York *Times*, which wrote that "the spirit of the Selma movement has been to bypass the moderates and bring about a change by increasing the tensions and appealing to outside forces. In the process, the movement has taken on a new militancy that was not apparent in previous campaigns led by Dr. King."[139]

In the few days preceding the march, hundreds of sympathizers poured into Selma. Two years later a shrewd analysis of the Who, What, and Why of the Selma marchers was provided by Dr. Price M. Cobbs, a practicing psychiatrist in San Francisco, who held an academic appointment at the University of California Medical Center. Writing in *Negro Digest*, Dr. Cobbs identified the basic participants in the march as "Negroes, diverse clergy, the young, and a recognizable group of older, liberal-intellectual establishmentarians, who could be called the Old Left." The psychiatrist believed that "The old rebels had to find a new cause to redefine themselves. To some, Selma became the most important focus since unionization in the Thirties. Many of the songs and slogans were similar, and struck the same responsive chord." Dr. Cobbs was convinced that "Martin Luther King, Jr. was the idea symbol to coalesce all these elements. He was black enough, young enough, radical enough, and religious enough to appeal in some measure to all groups. His forays into mysticism and vagueness . . . only served to enhance his appeal to all groups." Dr. Cobbs saw King functioning "as Bishop and Pope to religious leaders and as the idealized adult to the young. To the Negro he gave hope for black assertion. For the liberals he could speak the phrases and deliver the rhetoric which transported them to a past era."[140] All of these elements gathered in Selma, along with some 40 to 50 historians[141] (one wonders how many of them will claim to be objective about the Selma march in their books and lectures).

On March 22, 1965, Americans read in their newspapers

what sounded like an Army communiqué, direct from the front: "Backed by the armed might of the United States, 3,200 persons marched out of Selma today on the first leg of a historic venture in nonviolent protest . . . Hundreds of Army and federalized National Guard troops stood guard in Selma and lined the highway out of town to protect the marchers." Two Army helicopters hovered overhead.[142]

This was the first dispatch from the battlefield. The second war communiqué told the nation that "The Federal presence was everywhere, even in the air. About a dozen planes and helicopters, many of them manned by military personnel, flew over the procession constantly." Federal agents gave minute-by-minute radio reports to the Justice Department and the Pentagon. MP's guarded every cross-road.[143] The third dispatch from deep inside enemy territory stated: "The possibility that snipers were hiding in the trees worried the Army troops, who were responsible for security at the perimeter of the camp." Sentries were posted, and MP's checked cars coming down the road. When the marchers resumed their march—going another 16 miles—they were ringed by Army and National Guard troops. Soldiers walked four feet apart across the field chosen as the next night's campsite; they were searching for explosives.[144]

At times, it seemed as if still another war was being fought between the Southern Christian Leadership Conference and the Student Nonviolent Coordinating Committee. The New York *Times* found some of the SNCC leaders complaining "that their organization had done the groundwork in Selma and Dr. King and his organization were now getting the credit."[145] This had been a long-standing grievance against King and his group, but the SNCC leaders were now becoming much more vocal about it, and venting their fury for more, and still more, public consumption. The *Times* commented that for a time the two groups had managed to submerge their differences and work together, but that their "antagonisms came to the surface after the march on Highway 80, in which a large number of whites participated."[146] That newspaper noted the SNCC criticism that King came into the community for a short time, dominated the publicity, and then left without achieving lasting results.[147] One of the bitterest of all SNCC militants, James Foreman, said, "Remember one thing. They [the state troopers] aren't about to beat up white people. What do you think will happen to the Negroes when the white folks leave?"[148]

By now, do-gooders in the civil rights movement were fast losing favor even with some members of King's own entourage. Martin Luther King let it be known that he welcomed outside support from Negroes and whites.[149] But one of his assistants, with obvious disdain, told a group of Negroes, "As much as I dislike middle-class whites, we need their help."[150]

At this time, one of the more moderate members of the Southern Christian Leadership Conference (there were still a few left) vigorously criticized SNCC, but his incisive comments were lost sight of while the War in Selma was occupying and preoccupying the public's attention. In an eloquent and forceful sermon, the Rev. Jefferson P. Rogers told a congregation of Washington Negroes that there were "deep strands of the irresponsible" in the movement, manifested by a "foolish kind of radicalism"—a radicalism that does not have any capacity for reconciliation. Rogers, president of the local affiliates of the Southern Christian Leadership Conference, acknowledged that SNCC was his principal target. Rev. Rogers said that SNCC often seemed "more interested in protest than achievement." He objected to its demands that all other rights workers pay "obeisance" to it. He also said he deeply resented being "badgered" because he had shown the temerity to "call irresponsibility by its name," and declared that "I had one of the roughest weeks I ever had last week." He said that he and another minister had angrily demanded

Federal help, but that now that such help had been provided, "we should display neither anger nor cynicism but at least some sense of gratitude." Finally, this moderate Daniel in a lion's den of militants told his congregation that a man "cannot stand on the periphery and say to the man in the center, 'Bring me a millennium which will do away with caprices of human nature.' It can't be done."[151]

What a pity that Martin Luther King was not sitting in the audience. Few needed that sermon more.

But this courageous voice of moderation was drowned out by the tramp of marching feet on U.S. 80. King was still seeking the millennium on the road to Montgomery. The press reports poured in like war dispatches from the front. And then "De Lawd" (as the SNCC workers sometimes mockingly referred to him) led 25,000 Negroes and whites to the State Capitol in Montgomery.[152] A delegation was sent to see Governor Wallace, but was told that the Governor had closed his office for the day.[153] Federal troops were out in force at the Capitol. Eight hundred troops lined the street, one soldier about every 25 feet behind wooden barricades set between the street and the sidewalks. Troops stood on the roofs of buildings along the march route through downtown Montgomery, and on various office buildings overlooking the rally.[154]

To urban dwellers accustomed to thinking of population in terms of millions, 25,000 marchers may not seem like a very large turnout. But it is quickly placed in its proper perspective when one considers that there were almost as many marchers to Montgomery as there were citizens of Selma. Considering the handful who demonstrated at the very outset, it was as if one of Gulliver's Lilliputians had shot up to Brobdingnagian proportions overnight. James Reston found little difficulty in tracing the cause:

It is the almost instantaneous television reporting of the struggle in the streets of Selma, Ala., that has transformed what would have been mainly a local event a generation ago into a national issue overnight. Even the segregationists who have been attacking the photographers and spraying black paint on their TV lenses understand the point.[155]

In all, thousands of troops had been assigned to patrol the march,[156] to make very sure that Martin Luther King would overcome anything and everything that stood in his way.

One report noted that "the military operation accompanying the Alabama Freedom March shared the time and attention of the Pentagon with the war in Vietnam."[157] There was actually a "hot line" telephone to the War Room available to field commanders in Montgomery and at the National Guard Armory in Selma. Army spokesmen said both hot lines were used "fairly frequently."[158]

Army command and communications officers spread out on the fourth floor of the Post Office Building, filling a ten-room suite of connecting offices. The Army Chief of Staff had a personal representative on the scene. John M. Doar, the Assistant Attorney General in charge of the Civil Rights Division, was assigned as the principal Federal liaison man with Martin Luther King. The Chief United States Marshal accompanied then Assistant Attorney General Ramsey Clark in a separate border patrol radio car along the line of marchers.[159]

The Pentagon disclosed that it cost the Defense Department $510,000 to protect the marchers. This raised to nearly $13 million the cost of using Federal troops and federalized National Guardsmen in five major civil rights crises dating back to Little Rock in 1957.[160]

And yet all this mountain of dollars and overpowering military strength did not prevent the murder of Mrs. Viola Gregg Liuzzo.

Mrs. Liuzzo, a Detroit mother of five, was a member of the transportation committee of the civil rights march. A white worker for the Southern Christian Leadership Conference, she was shot to death while returning to Montgomery from Selma, where she had delivered a carload of civil rights workers who had participated in the march.[161] At the time of her death, there was only one other passenger in the car—a teen-age Negro named Leroy Moton. When he heard the shots, he ducked to the floorboards immediately. He said he kept his head down and could not identify the killers or their vehicle.[162]

It looked like another unsolvable racial killing without witnesses or clues. But less than 24 hours later, in a television appearance, President Johnson personally announced the arrest of four Klansmen in connection with the slaying. The President identified the four as Eugene Thomas, William Eaton, Gary Rowe, Jr., and Collie Leroy Wilkins, Jr. Mr. Johnson said all four arrested men were members of the United Klan of America, Knights of the Ku Klux Klan, Inc., the largest of a number of Ku Klux Klan organizations. During this announcement he declared war on the Klan, and urged its members to get out of the KKK while there was yet time.[163]

Wilkins' mother protested that President Johnson's TV address had made it impossible for her son to have a fair trial,[164] and some civil libertarians apparently agreed.[165] Paradoxically, less than a month later, Attorney General Nicholas Katzenbach announced a new set of rules substantially restricting the flow of pre-trial publicity in Federal criminal cases. The Attorney General's order stated that "at no time shall personnel . . . furnish any statement or information for the purpose of influencing the outcome of a defendant's trial." The New York *Times* found it interesting to speculate "on the effects this order might have had on President Johnson's television address in March announcing the arrest" of the four Klansmen. In any event, that newspaper was convinced that this new rule by the Attorney General "would surely forbid his office to make the kind of announcement the President made in the Selma case."[166]

Mrs. Liuzzo's sole passenger at the time of her murder, Leroy Moton, told investigators that they had been harassed a number of times by passing cars. He said that he and Mrs. Liuzzo had spent much of that day driving partici- pants in the rally back to Selma. One car drove up behind them and almost forced them off the road. Two or three cars trailed them. Then, in that last grisly encounter, a car pulled alongside. Moton heard the breaking of glass, then saw Mrs. Liuzzo slump against the door. She had been shot in the head. Moton remained in protective cus- tody in Selma. "How long do you think he'd live if we turned him loose?" a Selma policeman asked.[167]

At the time President Johnson made his television ad- dress he disclosed that he had been in frequent contact during the night with J. Edgar Hoover. The President said, "I cannot express myself too strongly in praising Mr. Hoover and the men of the FBI for their prompt and expeditious handling of this investigation. It is in keeping with the dedicated approach that this organization has shown throughout the turbulent era of civil rights contro- versies."[168]

Governor Wallace denounced the murder of Mrs. Liuzzo as an "outrageous" and "cowardly" act.[169] Both Wallace and Alabama Attorney General Richmond Flowers went on record as pushing for state murder indictments.[170]

Three of the four Klansmen were indicted in Federal Court on charges of conspiring to injure persons in the exercise of their constitutional rights. Charges against one of the men, Gary Rowe, were dismissed at the request of the Federal government. The Federal grand jury indicted Thomas, Eaton, and Wilkins, but returned no indictment against Rowe.[171]

The reason was revealed less than a week later, when Gary Rowe emerged as a paid informant for the FBI.[172]

Those who have long memories may recall liberals rant- ing against the use of paid informants in the days of Joe McCarthy's investigations of loyalty and security risks.

Since the Klansmen, however, were charged with nothing as trivial as subversion and infiltration, scarcely a liberal voice was raised in protest against the use of Rowe's services for the government. For himself, the author defended the use of paid informants when it was most unfashionable to do so, and unhesitatingly defends their use in the case against the Klansmen.

A state grand jury lost little time returning three murder indictments against the Klansmen, and, as expected, Rowe's testimony was crucial. Rowe testified that he and the three Klansmen followed Mrs. Liuzzo's car out of Selma and tried unsuccessfully three times to overtake it. The fourth time, Rowe testified, Wilkins thrust a .38 caliber pistol out the right rear window of the Klan car as it pulled even with Mrs. Liuzzo's car on U.S. Highway 80. He recalled: "The lady looked around and looked directly at us. Just as she looked at us, Wilkins fired two shots through the window of her automobile. Then Gene [Thomas] said, 'All right, men, shoot the hell out of them.' Then everybody started shooting."[173] Rowe testified that as the Klan car sped away, he told Wilkins, "I don't think you hit them." He gave Wilkins' reply as: "Baby brother, don't worry about it. That bitch and that bastard are dead and in hell. I don't miss."[174] Ballistic corroboration was quickly forthcoming. At the state trial, FBI agents traced the bullet found in Mrs. Liuzzo's head to the same pistol which Rowe testified had been fired at her car by Wilkins.[175]

Of all the observers at the trial, only one person—a Justice Department lawyer—was heard to predict that the jury would convict Wilkins. Most expected either outright acquittal or a hung jury, with one or two members holding out for conviction.[176] But to the surprise of just about everyone in the courtroom and the rest of the country, the all-white Lowndes County jury deadlocked ten-to-two *in favor of conviction*. It is probable that the verdict was caused, at least in part, by resentment at the verbal viciousness of the defense lawyer, Imperial Klonsel Matt H. Murphy, Jr. Murphy suggested that Mrs. Liuzzo may have had sexual relations with the 19-year-old Negro passenger, Leroy Moton. He told the jury: "The nigger is an African, and everybody knows that the Africans lived by the tooth and claw for 3,000 years and never built anything on earth more advanced than a hut with a thatched roof." The Negro, he said, "hasn't got any sense . . . morals . . . courtesy . . . decency." The New York *Times* reported that "Some of the jurors appeared to be embarrassed and stunned by Mr. Murphy's final speech . . . A few shook their heads as he spoke."

Edmund Sallee, a farmer on the jury, told reporters after the trial, "I think a great many of us were insulted to a great extent and he [Murphy] must have thought we were very, very ignorant to be taken in by that act." Sallee acknowledged that he was a segregationist, but added, "We can't allow murder on the highway here."[177]

Since a unanimous verdict was necessary for either acquittal or conviction, the judge had to declare a mistrial.[178] A second state trial was held five months later. At this second trial, the jury included six self-described white supremacists and present or former members of the Citizens Council. Not too surprisingly, this time Wilkins was found not guilty. Upon pronouncement of the verdict several spectators burst into applause,[179] but it developed that the applause was a trifle premature. There was still a Federal trial ahead.

The Federal trial was held in the court of Judge Frank M. Johnson, Jr., who was known as one of the strictest judges on the southern bench. The three Klansmen were tried under a civil rights law passed during Reconstruction. This 95-year-old law made it a crime for two or more persons to "conspire to injure, oppress, threaten or intimidate any citizen in the free exercise or enjoyment of any right or privilege secured to him by the Constitution or laws of the United States or because of his having so exercised the same."[180] The Justice Department's attorneys did not build their case upon whether or not murder and assault were covered under this law. Instead, they argued that the law had been violated because a Federal judge had specifically enjoined anyone in Alabama from intimidating participants in the march. The Justice Department contention was that the three Klansmen had violated the judge's ruling, and thus the law, by conspiring to kill Mrs. Liuzzo.[181] During the second full day of deliberations, the jurors told Judge Johnson that they were "hopelessly deadlocked." He sent them back to the jury room with the stern order to "try again." He told them, "it is very desirable that you should agree on a verdict," although no one should surrender his conscientious convictions. But he urged the minority (whatever its view) to consider how it had arrived at a decision contrary to the majority.[182]

That same day, this all-white Federal jury found the defendants guilty of conspiracy charges. Judge Johnson thereupon sentenced the Klansmen to ten years in prison, the maximum confinement permitted under that law.[183] Slightly more than three months later, one of the Klansmen—William Eaton—died of an apparent heart attack.[184] The other two—Wilkins and Thomas—were free on bond, while the case was taken to the U.S. Court of Appeals. Wilkins re-emerged in the news briefly in October, 1966, when he was sentenced to 30 days in jail at hard labor on charges of resisting arrest, public intoxication, and assault and battery.[185] He surfaced again in April, 1967, when the U.S. Court of Appeals upheld the civil rights conspiracy conviction of himself and Eugene Thomas.[186]

Leroy Moton, the teen-age Negro who was with Mrs. Liuzzo when she met her death, left Alabama and went to live in Connecticut. When last heard from—in August, 1967—Moton and three other men were being held on $20,000 bail each, in Hartford, on charges of two counts of arson in the fire bombing of a restaurant and food market in a predominantly Negro section.[187]

Perhaps most bizarre of all was the disposition of the Liuzzo car. Mr. Liuzzo had been financing the car through the General Motors Acceptance Corporation; after his wife's death, he arranged for the company to dispose of the car. The car passed into other hands and became the subject of this ghoulish advertisement in the Birmingham *News:*

Notice—Do you need a crowd-getter? I have a 1963 Oldsmobile two-door in which Mrs. Viola Liuzzo was killed. Bullet holes and everything intact. Ideal to bring in crowds. $3,500.[188]

One of the author's most vivid recollections of the Liuzzo case was the pillorying of William F. Buckley, Jr. Buckley's popularity with many liberal commentators has invariably been something less than sub-zero, but after making a speech mentioning Selma and Mrs. Liuzzo he was practically depicted as embodying the less admirable qualities of Simon Legree, Nero, and Torquemada all rolled into one "right-wing extremist." The Buckley speech was delivered before the New York Police Department Holy Name Society on April 4, 1965. In this speech he stated:

It was generally conceded—most specifically conceded by the Governor of Alabama—that everyone arriving in Alabama to protest the existing order under the glare of national klieglights, precisely needed protection against the almost certain recourse to violence of the unrestrained members of almost every society who are disposed to go to criminal lengths to express their resentment. That, after all, is why the President mobilized the National Guard of Alabama—at the Governor's urging. So the lady drove down a stretch of lonely road in the dead of night, ignoring the protection that had been given her, sharing the front seat with a young Negro identified with the protesting movement; and got killed. Why, one wonders, was this a story that occupied the front pages from one end to another, if newspapers are concerned with the unusual, the unexpected? Didn't the killing merely confirm precisely what everyone has been saying about certain elements of the South?[189]

Buckley compared the tremendous newspaper coverage given the Liuzzo story with the New York *Times*' two-inch story on page 58 about the unprovoked killing of a policeman in Hattiesburg, Mississippi, by a 20-year-old whose car he had stopped.[190] Buckley's point was that "here was an act surprising enough, outrageous enough, to occupy greater space in the daily newspapers,"[191] yet it was barely mentioned; on the other hand, the Liuzzo death, occurring in a context where death had been feared from the very beginning, was front-page news all over the country.

As Buckley saw it, the famous old yardstick of newsworthiness had been inverted; "dog bites man" was now considered news, while "man bites dog" was not. His point was appreciated, and applauded, by his audience of some 5,600 policemen.[192] But various liberal commentators saw it as a dark plot to glorify the segregationists of Alabama. The New York *Post* railed at Buckley's "spirited white-wash of Southern police terrorism" and his supposed "attack on Martin Luther King." Roy Wilkins asked then Mayor Wagner to rebuke—presumably en masse—the almost 6,000 policemen who had cheered the speech.[193] And in a most injudicious statement, New York State Supreme Court Justice Samuel H. Hofstadter charged that the policemen "cheered an attack on civil rights leaders that would have done credit to the most rabid race baiters."[194] Actually, the one civil rights leader mentioned in the Buckley speech was Martin Luther King, but he was in no wise attacked. If Buckley attacked anyone, it was the American Nazi Party—which he referred to as "George Lincoln Rockwell and his Nazi maniacs"[195]—and the KKK, or as he expressed it, "the grand wizard of the Ku Klux Klan . . . and a band of his fellow cretins."[196]

Much of the press criticism centered around Buckley's statement about the fearful risk that was taken when Mrs. Liuzzo drove down a stretch of lonely road in the dead of night, without protection, and with a young Negro demonstrator sharing the front seat. And yet, exactly a month after Buckley's speech, FBI informant Gary Rowe said that it was the sight of a white woman riding with a Negro man that caused the Klansmen to follow the Liuzzo car.[197]

Two of those who took part in the protest march were personal representatives of Governor Rockefeller. They were Alexander Aldrich, the Governor's cousin, and George Fowler, chairman of the New York State Commission for Human Rights. Both men agreed that the marchers would not have been able to go five miles without Federal protection.[198] And Mrs. Liuzzo was working without any protection at all. At the very least, she must have known that she was taking a considerable risk, and might have asked herself whether, as a mother of five, she had the right to assume this risk. *Time* called the wanton murder of Mrs. Liuzzo "moronic savagery,"[199] and the author fully agrees —but it is still necessary to state that in going to Alabama, Mrs. Liuzzo put her work in the civil rights movement above her duty to her children.

The Selma campaign did not end with the march to Montgomery. King had pledged to keep up the pressure until the civil rights bill became law, and he was more than ready to redeem that pledge. He first unleashed his loving bombshell on NBC's "Meet The Press." It was to be the ultimate economic weapon against George Wallace—no less than a national boycott of Alabama, including a refusal to buy its products and a withdrawal of Federal support for activities in the state.[200] This national boycott was to have two aims. One objective would be to commit Alabama to register at least 50 per cent of its Negroes of voting age; the other would be to get a vigorous stand against police brutality.[201] King must surely have been becoming intoxicated, if not delirious, with a sense of his own power, to tell the country: "I'm in a few days planning to call on the trade unions to refuse to transport or use Alabama products. I hope to call on all Americans to refuse to buy Alabama products. I hope to call on the

Secretary of the Treasury of the United States to withdraw all Federal funds that it has on deposit in Alabama banks. And finally I think it is necessary to call on all Federal agencies in line with the 1964 civil rights bill to withdraw support from a society that has refused to protect life and the right to vote."[202]

With these words, "De Lawd" revealed his clay feet to many of his staunchest admirers. The New York *Times* editorialized that "The Rev. Dr. Martin Luther King's proposal for a boycott of Alabama is wrong in principle and would be unworkable in practice." It stressed that this boycott would hurt the innocent and guilty alike, and probably do more harm to the powerless than the powerful. Specifically, the editorial underscored the very real possibility that Alabama Negroes might "suffer as much or more from such a boycott as the members of the so-called white power structure."[203] Administration sources responded coolly to the idea; they feared such a boycott might obliterate growing white moderate sentiment in Alabama, and saw no guarantee that the boycott would affect those most responsible for discrimination against Negroes.[204]

Whitney Young, Jr., executive director of the National Urban League, stated, "I have some reservations about a total boycott that makes no distinction between the good guys and the bad guys." He felt that a distinction must be drawn between "those industries that are arrogant and are rigidly exclusive in their policies," and those that "have made some progress in not only the employment of Negroes but also in providing some leadership in the community."[205] And even one of the charter members of King's senatorial fan club, Jacob Javits, felt that "an economic boycott which will hit the good as well as the bad would probably be ineffective."[206] Faced with mounting opposition to his proposal, King promptly took one step forward and two backward, and then quietly eased out of the entire affair. First he reiterated his determination to press his plans for the boycott, to "arouse the conscience of the good people of the state, so they can rise up against the irresponsibility of Gov. George C. Wallace." Then he complained that criticism of the boycott proposal was premature since its details had not yet been worked out; at that point, he indicated that the boycott might merely be selective and symbolic rather than a total refusal to purchase goods made in the state.[207]

When the oratory had ended, and the newsmen had departed, what had the march from Selma to Montgomery actually accomplished? Nothing, really, that had not already been accomplished before the marchers set foot on U.S. 80. The week before, President Johnson had already sent proposed voting rights legislation to the Capitol, and pledged to Martin Luther King, the Congress, and the country that "we shall overcome." The aforementioned Dr. Cobbs told the readers of *Negro Digest:* "While the purpose of the march was ostensibly to dramatize the plight of the Negro, there have been few benefits in terms of lasting gains." The psychiatrist wrote that the Negro's "confrontation with the Alabama storm troopers and rednecks was daring and courageous, but when all the visitors were gone the Negro was about where he started."[208] Harry Truman—who by now was getting a little too old to be impressed by King's theatrics—described the march as "silly." "They can't accomplish a darned thing," he said. "All they want is to attract attention."[209]

The march did score one substantial gain for Martin Luther King: a torrent of cash, checks, and money orders poured into his headquarters. The New York *Times* reported that "The emotional climate produced by the Selma, Ala., march two months ago was a financial lifesaver for the Southern Christian Leadership Conference."[210] A month before the march, the SCLC owed $95,845 to Negro-controlled financial institutions. It had completed 18 months of steady deficits. But a few months after the march, the conference's chief fiscal officer, the Rev. Ralph D.

Abernathy, exulted that "We're not in debt now." He said that the emotions and feelings aroused by the Selma event had produced a flow of contributions that would give King's Southern Christian Leadership Conference the biggest year it had ever had. Abernathy predicted, "We're going to have our first million dollar year," but was still far from satisfied. He believed that churches and unions could contribute much more than they had, and maintained that the churches should include the SCLC as a budget item.[211] And in the enlightened year of 1965 A.D., God help the churchmen who did not consider the Southern Christian Leadership Conference a worthy cause.

Of all the civil rights organizations, it was the Student Nonviolent Coordinating Committee that apparently was having the greatest financial difficulties. The Committee members, then numbering about 225, seemed to vie with each other to see who could be the most militant, the most aggressive, the most politically obnoxious. In 1966, Stokely Carmichael would hold the title against all comers, but in 1965, the Demagogue of the Year was undoubtedly James Foreman, one of SNCC's two top officials. At a rally in Montgomery, Foreman told his audience:

They have a voting bill up in Congress. But I want to know, is the President lying, or is he going to tell the truth? If those crooks in the White House, those crooks in the Senate, and those crooks in the House don't do something, we're going up there to Washington and we're going to stop traffic; we're going to stop every car, every cab, every truck; we're going to show them the biggest piece of civil disobedience the world has ever seen.[212]

But at this stage of the political proceeding, the question was no longer whether the voting rights bill would be passed, but when; the question was no longer whether the bill would infringe upon the states' constitutional right to fix voting qualifications, but whether they would be shorn of virtually all their powers in this field.

Southern Senators went through their ritualistic shadow-boxing and went down to their wholly predictable defeat, by a four-to-one margin. The New York *Herald Tribune* applauded the Senate vote, but there was a discernible note of hesitancy intertwined with its hosannas. "The time is long past," the *Herald Tribune* editorialized, "to put a decisive end to racial discrimination in the voting booth." And yet, that newspaper continued, "it's too bad this bill was made necessary; for there's more than a little merit to Southern complaints that it does violence to legislative, judicial, and even constitutional principles . . . so successful have been the states righters in thwarting the writ of the Fifteenth Amendment that *genuine rights have now to be swept away with the accumulated wrongs*"[213] (italics added).

The Senate balked on enacting a flat ban on poll taxes in state elections. By a hair's-breadth margin of 49 to 45, the Senate defeated such a ban. However, it did agree to insert a provision directing the Attorney General to test the constitutionality of poll taxes.[214]

Near the end of July, 1965, the Senate and House conferences convened to hammer out a final draft of the voting rights bill. What happened at that conference might have faded into the limbo of conveniently forgotten Washington in-fighting but for Rep. William Cramer of Florida (R). In a speech on the floor of the House, Rep. Cramer insisted that "a letter addressed to the conference by the Attorney General which influenced the conference's decision at the eleventh hour on the question of poll taxes should be made public."[215]

Cramer had the following letter by the Attorney General entered in the *Congressional Record*. The letter was addressed to another representative, whom Cramer declined to identify.

July 29, 1965

Late last night I discussed with Dr. Martin Luther King the proposed voting rights bill as it now stands in conference, and particularly the new poll tax provision. Dr. King strongly expressed to me his desire that the bill promptly be enacted into law and said that he felt this was an overriding consideration. He expressed his understanding and appreciation of the difficulties in achieving a satisfactory compromise in conference.

With respect to the poll tax provision, he expressed his view to me thusly:

"While I would have preferred that the bill eliminate the poll tax at this time—once and for all—it does contain an express declaration by Congress that the poll tax abridges and denies the right to vote. In addition, Congress directs the Attorney General to 'institute forthwith' suits which will eliminate and prevent the use of the poll tax in the four states where it is still employed. I am confident that the poll tax provision of the bill—with vigorous action by the Attorney General—will operate finally to bury this iniquitous device."

Dr. King further assured me that he would make this statement publicly at an appropriate time.

While you are free to show this letter privately to whomsoever you wish, I would appreciate it if you did not use it publicly without informing me so that I, in turn, may discuss it with Dr. King.[216]

This letter bore Attorney General Katzenbach's initials. Rep. Cramer was convinced that "this letter, after having been read in conference, unquestionably influenced a number of the conferees in that on Tuesday they took the position they should stand by the House version of the poll tax ban, and on Thursday, after this letter was read . . . changed that position."[217]

Rep. Cramer asked, "Why should a conference be influenced by opinions of one individual expressed at a time after both the House and Senate had worked their will? Why would the Attorney General want it kept secret for an indefinite period of time after he discussed the poll tax question with Dr. King, as he says in his letter? Why should the release of the letter be subject to Dr. King's approval?"[218] The Florida representative asked those questions on August 4, 1965; he may still be waiting for satisfactory answers. But beyond any question, Rep. William Cramer bluntly refused "to be muzzled at the direction of the Attorney General on any letter or any other matter which I believe to be properly within the public domain."[219]

Two days after Cramer bared the contents of this letter, the Voting Rights Act of 1965 was signed into law by President Johnson. The law provided for the automatic suspension of literacy tests and other "devices" in any state or county where less than 50 per cent of the voting age population was registered on November 1, 1964, or voted in the 1964 Presidential election.

Professor Andrew Hacker of Cornell University pointed out that "areas of low voting in the South are not always those with high Negro populations."[220] Professor Hacker noted that in Chattahoochee County in Georgia, a grand total of 439 citizens turned out to vote in 1964—less than one in twenty of legal age. Yet that county was more than 80 per cent white. He was hardly more impressed by the voting turnouts in Onslow County in North Carolina, and in Hardin County, Kentucky, where fewer than 25 per cent voted and the Negro portion of their population was less than 10 per cent.[221] And since almost 40 per cent of adult Americans failed to vote in the 1964 Johnson-Goldwater imbroglio, and more than half stayed at home during the 1962 Congressional elections,[222] the "less than 50 per cent" figure cited in the voting rights bill was hardly relevant to the single hard question: "Did this particular county, through these particular actions, violate the 15th Amendment to the Constitution?" This was the crux of the matter, since the voting rights bill had been drafted "to enforce the Fifteenth Amendment to the Constitution of the United States."

If the only criterion of voting discrimination had been "less than 50 per cent voting," there would have been Standing Room Only in the Federal courts, led by the President's own home state of Texas, where less than 45 per cent of its adult population went to the polls in 1964.[223]

And the most liberal city in the nation—New York City— would barely have escaped the Act's enforcement provisions, since only 51.3 per cent of its voting-age population voted in the 1964 election.[224] And the Voting Rights Act surely would have been applied to Washington, D.C., despite its exceptionally large Negro population. The 1964 voter turnout in the nation's capital was a wan 38.4 per cent of the voting age population—a lower proportion than in four of the states where Federal registrars were subsequently sent.[225]

What saved Texas, Washington, D.C., and others from running afoul of the registrars was as sly a bit of legal gerrymandering as this country has ever seen. It was the two-pronged test of "less than 50 per cent voting" *and* the use of a literacy test or "device" which automatically dropped the Damoclean sword of Federal registrars on the necks of offending states and counties. Even the New York *Times*, which was devout in its support of the Voting Rights Act, conceded that "passage of such a bill, which now seems assured, would have been inconceivable only a year or two ago."[226]

These two tests, taken together, comprised what James Jackson Kilpatrick called "a carefully rigged trap"[227]—a trap that caught the states of Louisiana, Mississippi, Alabama, Georgia, South Carolina, Virginia, and Alaska, 34 counties in North Carolina, one county in Arizona, and one in Maine.[228] It has perhaps occurred to the reader— as it did the author—that most of these states were in the Goldwater column in the 1964 Presidential election. Other states like Texas and Arkansas that were in the "less than 50 per cent" category—but went "all the way with LBJ"— were spared the ordeal of Federal registrars.

In effect, the offending state or subdivision thereof which had a literacy test, and had not dragged 50 per cent of its eligible voters to the polls in 1964 (never mind whether they *wanted* to vote, or not), was presumed guilty until proven innocent. The burden of proof was not on the

Justice Department to show that racial discrimination existed, but on the state or county to show it did not. It bears repeating that the Voting Rights Act was an act "to enforce the Fifteenth Amendment to the Constitution of the United States." The Fifteenth Amendment forbids the denial of the right to vote on account of color.

Had anyone seriously contended that Alaskans, citizens of one county in Arizona and another in Maine were victims of racial discrimination on the part of local voting registrars? If they were not, where was the constitutional justification for Federal registrars, as provided by the Voting Rights Act? Certainly not in Article I, Section 2, which provides that it is the *states* which fix the qualifications of electors who may vote in state elections. And certainly not in the Seventeenth Amendment, providing for the popular election of Senators. And least of all in the constitutional provision which provides that Presidential electors in each state shall be chosen "in such manner as the legislature thereof may direct."

As for the Southern states involved, Georgia Congressman Bo Calloway pointed out that at least some of the low voting figures were directly traceable to the ennui of the one-party tradition. Rep. Calloway disclosed that in November, 1964, on the same ballot with the Presidential electors, four of Georgia's ten congressional seats were uncontested, 191 of 205 House seats were uncontested, and 34 of 35 candidates for Solicitor General were uncontested.[229] Where Mayors and local commissioners also were being elected, it was estimated that there were probably no more than 25 contests in 1,000 separate elections.[230] Having no choice to make, it was not too surprising that many of these voters chose to stay home on Election Day.

President Johnson had barely finished handing out the pens with which he signed the Voting Rights Act, before Attorney General Katzenbach was designating counties in Alabama and Mississippi and parishes in Louisiana for Federal registrars.[231] "Let me again emphasize, as President Johnson has," said the Attorney General, "that these examiners will serve only so long as necessary. When local officials demonstrate their willingness to deal fairly with Negro as well as white applicants, the examiners will be withdrawn promptly."[232] The voting examiners sped through the offending counties like whirling dervishes; in a two-day period, they registered 2,877 Negroes in nine counties.[233] Seven months later, Attorney General Katzenbach stated that Federal examiners had registered more than 100,000 Negroes in 36 counties, bringing the total five-state Negro registration to about 950,000.[234] This represented less than 40 per cent of those eligible.[235] King made no secret of his disappointment, and characteristically blamed everything and everyone except Negro apathy and inertia. The villain now was no longer Jim Clark but the Attorney General—the same Mr. Katzenbach who now told civil rights leaders that private organizations, rather than the Federal government, had chief responsibility for getting eligible Negroes registered.[236] Considering the ultra-paternalism of the Johnson Administration, the Attorney General's views must have stunned the civil rights movement.

Certainly his views were considered the rankest heresy by Martin Luther King, who had been beating the drums for more registrars on the ground that "we will not be able to go into all the counties where there is a need with voter education projects."[237] In a quote that must have evoked hearty guffaws in Selma, King warned, "It looks like we will have to have more demonstrations to get examiners."[238] He noted that examiners had been appointed in Birmingham after his Southern Christian Leadership Conference had conducted street demonstrations there.[239]

Martin Luther King's nonviolent war was beginning to come full circle; he now seemed to be chanting "We shall overcome" the Administration which, a year before, had been chanting "We shall overcome."

The great furor over Selma obscured the fact that for years Negro voter registration in the South had been quietly but steadily rising—and this even before the advent of the Voting Rights Act. Pat Watters, Information Director for the Southern Regional Council, supplied these statistics: In 1940, Negro registration in the eleven states of the South was perhaps a little over 100,000. By 1947, it was a little over a half a million. From 1954 to 1960, it grew hardly at all. Between 1960 and 1964, the Negro vote increased another half a million—more in four years than it had in a decade previously. Since the Voting Rights Act, the Negro vote had increased about a million. As of the Spring of 1966, Watters concluded that the total Negro vote in the South stood at approximately 2,406,000, or 46 per cent of its potential.[240] (Since Watters' remarks came a month and a half after Katzenbach's vote estimate, this may account for the variance between the two figures.)

Watters believed that "at its full strength, the Negro vote could perhaps elect one-third of the Mississippi Legislature; 13 per cent of South Carolina's; 12 per cent of Alabama's. There are, I think, two congressional districts which the full strength of Negro votes could control—one in Mississippi, one in Southwest Georgia."[241]

Negro voting strength in Alabama had climbed to 228,000, representing about one-fourth of total registration, in 1966.[242] Alabama's 11 gubernatorial candidates took one look at the statistics and did drastic rewrites of their campaign speeches. "The word 'segregation' has virtually disappeared from the political vocabulary," said an editor of the Birmingham Post-Herald.[243] A similar reaction was voiced by an Alabama political reporter, who said that he had been covering political rallies almost daily for the last month and had yet to hear the word "nigger."[244] Four of the five major candidates promised to alter state resistance to civil rights.[245] Lurleen Wallace made few speeches; she preferred to let George do it. And even in his speeches Wallace omitted the word "segregation," while promising no change of policy.[246] The handwriting on the wall was read and duly noted by one of Wallace's hitherto staunchest supporters, Al Lingo, of both Birmingham and Selma fame. Lingo was running for sheriff of Jefferson County (which included Birmingham). He appeared before leaders of the Southern Christian Leadership Conference, dropped a contribution into a collection plate, and promised to appoint Negro deputies and clerks if elected.[247]

The election results were not unexpected. Lurleen Wallace won a sweeping victory in the Democratic primary; she got more votes than all her opponents combined.[248] Al Lingo was resoundingly defeated.[249] And Jim Clark learned the hard way that taking Negro youngsters on a forced march was no way to win friends and influence voters.

When the Voting Rights Act became law, Clark's first reaction was pure vitriol. "The whole thing's so ridiculous I haven't gotten over laughing at it yet," he said. "In fact I'm nauseated." He said he would not worry about Negro voters in 1966 when he ran for re-election. "My political future is not of importance," he stated. "It's the people of Alabama and my children that I'm worried about."[250] But then 1966 came around and Clark took a long, hard look at those voting rolls in Dallas County. By that time, out of some 23,000 registered voters, almost half—nearly 11,000—were Negroes.[251] To add to Clark's woes, an old political foe, Wilson Baker, had resigned as Public Safety Director of Selma to run against Clark in the Democratic primary.[252]

It was not overly difficult to determine which side the sheriff's political bread was buttered on. In his campaign for re-election, Clark took off his "Never" button and invited all the Negroes of Dallas County to eat barbecue and drink beer with him at a picnic. Only twenty-eight Negroes showed up, and they were photographed by Negro spectators who stood in the brush nearby.[253]

In Dallas County civil rights forces rallied around Wilson Baker, the man who, the New York *Times* noted, "kept the Negroes' constant, if grudging, respect all through the civil rights turbulence last year."[254] With Negroes now accounting for nearly half the Dallas County electorate, the outcome of the Democratic primary was never really in doubt—assuming all the votes, Negro and white, were counted. But after the Primary Day of reckoning, Clark challenged the validity of the ballots in six of the county's 80 voting precincts. He contended that the six boxes, in predominantly Negro neighborhoods and supervised by Negroes working in an election for the first time, had been improperly handled.[255] The Dallas County Democratic Executive Committee agreed with him and disqualified these votes.[256] The Justice Department had been watching the Democratic primary closely, and now asked the Federal court to overturn the Democratic executive committee's action and enjoin the alteration or destruction of the disputed ballots.[257] In its suit, the Justice Department said that Baker had won the election with 8,994 votes to 7,537 for Clark, and slightly over 1,000 for minor candidates.[258] It said that the six boxes challenged by Clark contained 1,672 Negro votes and 162 white votes, of which 1,412 had been cast for Baker. Baker needed these votes to win a clear majority and avoid a runoff.[259] The Dallas County Democratic Executive Committee contended that the Voting Rights Act gave the Federal government the right to register Negroes but not to "interfere" in local elections.[260] But Federal Judge Thomas ruled that the act gave the Federal government the right to intervene in local elections to insure that Negro votes were counted fairly.[261] Within a week, Dallas County Democratic officials bowed to a Federal court order and agreed to count the disputed ballots.[262] This done, Wilson Baker became the new sheriff of Dallas County, and Jim Clark suddenly joined the ranks of the unemployed.

One more barrelhouse right was aimed at Clark on February 27, 1967, when the same judge held him in civil contempt of a Federal court. Judge Thomas ruled that Clark had violated a decree by forcing the march of 200

Negroes in 1965. The former sheriff was ordered to pay $1,505 to a civil rights attorney, plus court costs.[263]

Like the soap that is 99 44/100 per cent pure, the Negro vote was nearly that monolithic in the 1966 elections, with only a few scattered exceptions. Martin Luther King was all over Alabama urging a "unified Negro vote"—in effect, a reporter noted, "a plea for support of Negro candidates, and for Attorney General Richmond Flowers in his race for Governor against Mrs. George C. Wallace . . ."[264] King said he expected criticism for advocating a bloc vote. "But for all of these years, whites have bloc-voted to keep us down," he added, "and now we got to bloc-vote to get ourselves out of this dilemma."[265]

It was a shabby denial of his dream—the recurring dream in which, as a kind of modern Moses, King saw himself leading America into the promised land of integration. Some disenchanted Negro leaders—notably in Macon County—saw bloc-voting as a mindless steam-roller, flattening everything in its path, including the first tentative steps toward political integration in Alabama. In 1964, the Macon County Democratic Club, the county's dominant Negro political organization, had supported an integrated slate of candidates for City Council. All won.[266] In 1966, one of these Negro councilmen, the Rev. K. L. Buford, supported the incumbent white sheriff, Harvey Sadler.[267] But King's Southern Christian Leadership Conference supported a Negro candidate for sheriff, Lucius Amerson.[268] Leadership Conference officials piously proclaimed support of Amerson because he was "the best qualified candidate" and not because he was a Negro.[269] The Negro candidate's "qualifications," in his race against an incumbent sheriff, consisted of his enrollment in investigative courses while in the Army. (He left his job as a postal clerk to run for sheriff.)[270] Rev. Buford openly accused the Leadership Conference of "preaching racism." Buford said he considered Sheriff Sadler a moderate on racial issues, and declared, "I don't see how we can build confidence between the races if we kick white moderates in the teeth."[271]

With a top-heavy Negro registration—and the Southern Christian Leadership Conference backing them—the result was a foregone conclusion. Naturally Lucius Amerson won,[272] and just as naturally, integration lost.

The Student Nonviolent Coordinating Committee urged Negroes to boycott the Democratic primary and wait until the November general elections, at which time they were to support candidates of SNCC-organized political parties.[273] The Student Committee was strongest in Lowndes County, where it organized the Black Panther Party.[274] SNCC's senior field secretary in Alabama declared, "To ask Negroes to get in the Democratic Party is like asking Jews to join the Nazi Party."[275] Martin Luther King avoided Lowndes County like the proverbial plague[276] and avoided even the mildest criticism of the Student Committee. The Black Panther Party was soundly beaten at the polls,[277] but that senior field secretary went on to become the head of the Student Nonviolent Coordinating Committee. Soon, very soon, the country was to hear more from Stokely Carmichael, and to wonder if he had overcome Martin Luther King.

CHAPTER 7

1966: Chicago and "Open Housing"

✿✿ ✿✿ ✿✿ ✿✿ ✿✿ ✿✿ ✿✿ ✿✿ ✿✿ ✿✿ ✿✿ ✿✿ ✿✿ ✿✿ ✿✿ ✿✿ ✿✿ ✿✿

Throughout Martin Luther King's campaigns in Montgomery, Albany, Birmingham and Selma, Northerners waxed long and loud over the satanic rascality of the South —orating, at a moment's notice, about the Calvinistic predestination that doomed white Southerners in this shiny new era of the Civil Rights Revolution. Northern mayors, governors, and civil leaders interspersed stern diatribes over the shortcomings of the South with glowing self-praise for their own reputed accomplishments in race relations. Reams and reams of self-serving statistics were paraded to show how infinitely better life was for the Northern Negro. Martin Luther King studied the statistics—listened to the speeches—visited the Northern Negro ghettos—and decided to make Chicago his next target.

By now, perhaps only Chicago was large enough to contain King's ego. Winner of a Nobel Peace Prize; holder of an almost interminable number of honorary degrees and awards; the master strategist who had maneuvered the President and the Congress into passage of two sweeping Civil Rights Acts—he had acquired an aura of near-invincibility. Perhaps King Canute could roll back the waves, but nothing could roll back King Martin Luther's relentless advances on the civil rights front.

There was something disquietingly different the following year, though. Something wasn't quite right. King's entry—or, more accurately, his re-entry—into Chicago was analogous to that hoary old chestnut about the vaudevillian playing the two-a-day in tank towns year after year, who finally gets to play the Palace. The only trouble was that at this point, King was beginning to lose his audience. There was life in the old act yet, but some of his lines were getting a little stale. The plot seemed more contrived and more predictable than ever before. Possibly that was why the cheers now seemed more mechanical, more perfunctory than ever—because in the droning sameness of all he said and did and wrote, King was starting to bore his public. And America was finding it increasingly difficult to applaud, and stifle a yawn, at the same time.

Martin Luther King was assuredly no stranger to the North. He had traveled all over the country and had visited many Northern cities on many occasions. But his base of operations had always been South; he had stoutly resisted attempts to form a Northern counterpart of the Southern Christian Leadership Conference. His own home was in Atlanta, and he had never evinced any desire to move himself, his family, or his organizational operations above the Mason-Dixon line. He therefore came to Chicago not precisely as a stranger, but certainly not with the deft, sure-handed expertise that had marked his confrontations in Alabama.

The differences between all his past campaigns and Chicago were more than merely geographical. For the first time, King was in a city that had not a single segregation law on its books. He would be conferring with a Mayor who, for years, had been garnering the lion's share of Negro votes. Far from being cowed by any supposed white power structure, Negro civil rights leadership in Chicago was highly articulate, and capable of highly militant action.

This was no Selma. Chicago had Negro congressmen and aldermen. And the Mayor was not exactly swathed in obscurity; he was Richard J. Daley, one of the most powerful officeholders in the country, with access to the White House under both Presidents Kennedy and Johnson.

In every campaign, Martin Luther King had invariably encountered some local Negro opposition, which he had managed to cajole, spellbind, or brush aside. But it was not that simple in Chicago. There he met an old adversary whose prestige and power, well-known among Negroes, was only rarely reported in the white press. In an article called "Quest and Conflict," Charles H. King, formerly president of the Evansville (Indiana) NAACP, pinpointed this confrontation-within-a-confrontation. In his words: "Chicago was to become the battleground between two men whose individual philosophies and activities had already split the Negro masses in general and the National Baptist Convention, U.S.A., Inc., in particular . . ."[1] The two men were Martin Luther King and Dr. J. H. Jackson, president of that aforementioned Baptist organization—the largest Negro religious body in the world. Chicago was Dr. Jackson's home; there he was pastor of that city's Olivet Baptist Church.

It is remarkable that the head of SNCC, with his few hundred motley activists, could command nationwide attention and press coverage while Dr. Joseph Harrison Jackson, president of the five-million member National Baptist Convention,[2] was virtually unknown to white America. Dr. Jackson was a vice president of the World Baptist Alliance and a member of the Central Committee of the World Council of Churches.[3] Often called a "citizen diplomat," he had traveled throughout Africa, Asia, Europe and the Middle East.[4] He had helped to write campaign literature for John F. Kennedy during the 1960 Presidential race, and had attended the 1962 Second Vatican Council in Rome at the invitation of Pope John XXIII.[5] *Ebony* wrote of Dr. J. H. Jackson: "One of the most effective preachers

214

in Protestantism, he began moving the Convention beyond its traditional 'once-a-year-get-together' attitude about its role to one of church-national-world involvement in which Negro Baptist power began to be more institutional and more influential."[6] Throughout the years, Dr. Jackson remained one of Martin Luther King's most steadfast opponents, and, for his pains, received ever shorter and shorter shrift from militants, black and white.

Dr. Jackson's opposition to King can be traced back at least as far as the March on Washington in 1963. He felt that "We must not fight the United States. We must not intimidate him [the President] or Congress . . . We cannot afford to demonstrate against Congress."[7] His convictions made him persona non grata at a civil rights rally in Chicago that same year. The New York *Times* reported that "A great cry went up from the 10,000 at the open-air meeting when Dr. Jackson was announced as the next speaker. The audience rose to its feet, booed and yelled when he moved forward to the podium." The outcry was so great that it became necessary to withdraw Dr. Jackson as a speaker. As he started to leave, a group of about 50 pursued him, shouting, "Kill him! Kill him!" They pinned him against the wall before ushers were able to extricate him and escort him to a car.[8]

Civil rights pickets periodically marched outside Dr. Jackson's church and denounced him as an Uncle Tom.[9] Asked by a Southern reporter how he would answer this charge, Dr. Jackson replied, "the age of the nonviolent doctrine has witnessed more violence on the part of the Negro than any other time in history. I believe the Negro has been used by persons with interests contrary to the best interests of the United States."[10] As for "this Uncle Tom business," Dr. Jackson said, "let me ask you what you think the term means." The reporter defined it as "a Negro who curries the favor of white men for his own gain." Dr. Jackson agreed this was the commonly accepted definition, "and I think it is the meaning attached to it by those who indict me. Yet I don't work for white people, so I have nothing to gain from them by my views on the racial problem." He pointed out that "My church in Chicago has called me for life, so I have no problem of finding a job. I have no political ambitions, so I don't need the favors of the white man in this area." On the other hand, he wryly noted, "The men who call me Uncle Tom, these men *do* receive money from white people. About 80 per cent of CORE's income comes from white people, for example."[11] At the height of King's demonstrations in Chicago, Dr. Jackson reiterated his long-held belief that civil disobedience and nonviolence would not carry the civil rights movement any higher and might lead to disrespect for law and order and to possible violence.[12] He urged his fellow Baptists to concentrate their efforts on voter registration campaigns and Congressional lobbying.[13] But perhaps his entire philosophy was best summarized in this one challenging paragraph.

I do not believe there is any other system in the world whereby a man can use his powers to become as strong and great as under the Stars and Stripes. It is my responsibility as an American to uphold this system and to oppose those, white or Negro, who attempt to destroy it.[14]

Between Dr. J. H. Jackson and Martin Luther King there existed a gap of Grand Canyon proportions—almost as wide as the gap between Chicago officials who insisted Negroes never had it so good, and civil rights leaders who, with equal insistence, felt that they had never had it so bad.

One of the few dispassionate dissections of Chicago's Negro ghetto was made by Horace R. Cayton and St. Clair Drake, authors of the famed study of Negro urban life, *Black Metropolis*. Almost 17 years later, Cayton and Drake revisited the Black Metropolis in Chicago, and drew a picture that was neither as ecstatic as the pronouncements

of Mayor Daley, nor as doom-laden as that of the rights
leaders.

In Chicago, the authors found that "by 1961, money had
been circulating freely and rapidly for over a decade. Credit
had been made easy through budget plans and wage assignments." In Chicago, Cayton and Drake wrote, "Thousands
of Negroes are now living in fine apartment buildings and
in relatively new, attractive homes vacated during the last
ten years by white people who were 'getting ahead.'" But
they emphasized that most Negroes were still living in
badly overcrowded quarters. Compounding the social con-
gestion was the fact that *the Negro population of Chicago
had doubled between 1950 and 1960.* At the same time,
slum clearance was tending to reduce the total housing
available, since, as the authors noted, "public 'relocation
housing' has never kept pace with demolition."[15]

Virtually all of Martin Luther King's campaign in Chicago was to revolve around the issue of "open housing."
Yet, surprisingly, Cayton and Drake found that not all
Chicago Negroes were exactly pining away for integration. Certainly the Black Muslims, with their passion for
a Negro apartheid, were championing a separatist movement that practically outsegregated the segregationists. The
Muslims wanted nothing less than a Black nation, and
white "devils" need not trouble to apply.

The authors of *Black Metropolis* felt that the era of
integration posed some rather discomfiting dilemmas for
the Negro community. They realized that "Bronzeville's
political power is based upon the existence of a segregated
community," and then wondered "what kind of political
influence and rewards could Negroes hope to expect if
the Black Belt were to disappear?" They asked if middle-
class Negroes should cooperate with whites to maintain a
"realistic racial balance" in integrated neighborhoods (to
prevent the overcrowded Black Belt transforming such
communities into sections of the Black Ghetto). Equally
important, they asked "are there values and cultural prod-

ucts which have developed among Negroes that will be lost if full integration ever becomes a reality?"[16]

Cayton and Drake were convinced that "the prosperity of Negro business and professional men rests upon the existence of a Black Belt." The authors had observed that Black Chicago's doctors, dentists, lawyers and businessmen "captured a sizable share of the dollars circulating in the expanded, and to some extent, 'captive' Black Belt market," and asked, "Could they survive under conditions of general competition?" In 1961—even before Martin Luther King had crossed nonviolent swords with Laurie Pritchett, in Albany, Georgia—the Chicago Negro Chamber of Commerce met to discuss "How Does Integration Affect Negro Business?" A Negro publication reported expressions of grave concern.[17]

But in general, the portrait Drake and Cayton drew of Black Metropolis in 1962 was one of buoyancy. As they put it, Negroes stopped moaning "I've Been Down So Long, Down Don't Bother Me," and started singing "Happy Days Are Here Again."[18]

The authors did send up one storm warning. They cautioned, "If the masses are driven too far, they are likely to fight back, despite their sometimes seemingly indifferent reactions to discrimination and segregation. *A potential for future violence within Black Metropolis exists that should not and cannot be ignored.*"[19]

Perhaps most significant was that "sleeper" statistic about the Chicago Negro population doubling between 1950 and 1960. Block by block, the Negro ghetto expanded, adding one notch after another to the Black Belt. As a 1965 survey by the Urban League reported: "Much like a monstrous giant, this expansion continually reaches out for the blocks that are located on the periphery of the already existing Negro ghettos."[20] As Negroes moved into areas along the "ghetto" fringes, whites moved out. Result? A block that was once all-white rapidly became all-Negro. The schools in these areas almost invariably mirrored these changes, turning from racially mixed to almost solidly Negro.[21] In 1965, there were more nonwhites than whites in Chicago's public schools.[22] The Chicago *Daily News* wrote: "The population trend will, if nothing is done to change it, turn Chicago into a Negro city while the white population flees to a ring of suburbs."[23] The same grim prediction was sounded by an official panel headed by Philip M. Hauser, University of Chicago sociologist and population expert. This panel warned: "Unless the exodus of white population from the public schools and from the city is brought to a halt or reversed, the question of school integration may become simply a theoretical matter, as it is already in the nation's capital. For integration, in fact, cannot be achieved without white students."[24] Civil rights leaders charged that the school board had gerrymandered school district boundaries in a way that aggravated school segregation to appease white neighborhoods.[25] They asserted that 90 per cent of all Negro children attended de facto segregated schools,[26] and Dr. Hauser considered these schools "unequal and inferior." Hauser reserved his most stinging barbs for Dr. Benjamin Willis, Chicago's Superintendent of Education. Willis, he said, had become "the symbol of segregation" and "a representative of the status quo" in Chicago. Hauser declared that "Willis is performing the same thing for the civil rights movement in Chicago as Governor Wallace has in the South. Some day they may erect a monument to him."[27]

By the wildest stretch of the imagination, Superintendent of Schools Willis could scarcely be held responsible for the influx of nearly half a million Negroes and the exit from the city of about half a million whites.[28] And the burgeoning expansion of the Negro ghetto and shrinkage of previously white neighborhoods hardly fell within the scope of a school official's duties. Where Dr. Willis ran afoul of the civil rights leaders was in his support for the neighborhood school. Negroes indignantly pointed to a survey showing that 84 per cent of Chicago's Negro youngsters attended schools that had 90 per cent or more Negro enrollment, while 86 per cent of Chicago's white youngsters attended schools that were 90 per cent or more white in enrollment.[29] Eliminate the concept of the neighborhood school, rights leaders contended, and you would eliminate de facto segregation in Chicago's school system.

The logic of their argument was, and is, a little difficult to follow. The term "de facto segregation"—or "segregation in fact"—was clearly a misnomer, because, in fact, there were some Negro students in predominantly white schools, and some white students in predominantly Negro schools. It was much more accurate to refer to it as "minimal integration"; it was much more pertinent to note the statistical studies showing that, limited as this integration was, year after year, the percentage of white students in Chicago schools had decreased, while the percentage of Negro enrollment had increased. What would be the effect of massive integration in the city schools? One can only conjecture—but it seemed reasonable to conclude that such a course would only accelerate the white flight to suburbia, still further decrease the percentage of white students in the school system, and accomplish the direct opposite of all that civil rights leaders hoped to achieve.

Compounding the problem was the fact that Chicago had absorbed a number of illiterate Negroes from Mississippi and surrounding states.[30] Obviously these pupils could not cope with their studies on the same achievement level as white students who had had a better education. Put them in the same class, in the same school, and you had a two-pronged dilemma; either you ignored the Negroes and taught the more educationally advanced white students—an obviously unacceptable proposal to civil rights leaders—or you ignored the whites and had them, in effect, sitting on the sidelines while you helped the Negroes catch up. This latter solution may have been desirable to Negroes but was unthinkable to white parents wanting the most comprehensive education for their children.

It was this damned-if-you-do and damned-if-you-don't dilemma that faced School Superintendent Willis, and the neighborhood school seemed the only feasible way to educate both groups satisfactorily, without goading still more indignant white parents into leaving Chicago. And it was all but inevitable that Willis would become the special target of civil rights groups casting about for an educational scapegoat.

There has probably never been such a sustained, vehement, implacable campaign to remove an educational official from office. Almost as institutionalized as the annual school threats were the anti-Willis boycotts. The success of these Willis-Must-Go boycotts reached astounding proportions. On October 22, 1963, more than 224,000 pupils stayed out of school in a one-day protest.[31] On February 25, 1964, 172,350 pupils did a repeat performance.[32]

The school board remained unmoved. In 1965, it made known its decision to grant a new contract to Dr. Willis; the decision carried a provision that he retire on his 65th birthday, some 19 months from the date his contract was renewed.[33] By way of outraged protest at the decision, civil rights groups called for a five-day city-wide boycott of Chicago's public schools.[34] The day after this announcement was made, rights leaders halved the projected protest to a two-day boycott.[35] A few days before the boycott was to take place, a Circuit Court judge granted the Chicago school board an injunction restraining the boycott[36] and a federal district judge refused to dissolve the injunction.[37] Despite the court order, civil rights leaders estimated that on one of the days originally selected for the boycott, 110,000 of the approximately 500,000 Chicago public school pupils were absent from class. The school board refused to give any estimate.[38]

As in Selma, members of the Catholic clergy were actively involved in demonstrations. On one occasion, civil rights demonstrators—protesting the retention of Dr. Willis—staged a sitdown at State and Madison, in the heart of the Loop (Chicago's downtown area). Traffic was tied up over a large area before 150 persons were arrested, among them Catholic priests and nuns.[39] A week later, the Catholic Interracial Council urged its members to avoid breaking the law in school demonstrations. At a news conference, John A. McDermott, the Council's executive director, stated, "The Catholic Interracial Council believes that civil disobedience—the conscious violation of law and acceptance of the consequences—is a valid form of protest against injustice only under certain extraordinary conditions." He said such conditions existed when clearly unjust laws were enforced or when valid laws were enforced in an unjust manner.[40] By implication, at least, McDermott did not consider this to be the situation in Chicago.

A similar disenchantment with clerical demonstrations against Willis was expressed by Msgr. Daniel M. Cantwell, Associate Editor of the *New City* magazine (published by the Catholic Council on Working Life). Monsignor Cantwell asked: "Is the trend among clergy to envision themselves as ward committeemen any healthier for religion or politics than the distant unhappy situations in which we recall knight-bishops, cardinal-chancellors, pope-kings, or the voice of Royal Oak, Mich.?" The Monsignor's reply was that "What Chicago needs is not only a new superintendent of public education, but men of God who know the difference between religion and politics and are willing to live with the difference."[41]

Verbal sparks flew all over Chicago when Mayor Daley said police files showed that many rights marchers in Chicago were Communists, and that Communist funds were helping to finance the demonstrations.[42] Joseph Morris, deputy police superintendent, said the names of more than 50 demonstrators had been checked, and of these 11 were found to be Communists or members of Communist-front organizations.[43] The NAACP asked Daley for evidence to substantiate these charges.[44] Daley replied that he had not said the civil rights movement was Communist-inspired or Communist-dominated. However, he still insisted that the Chicago police and the Federal government had evidence of Communist infiltration of civil rights demonstrations in the city.[45]

A group of Catholic priests issued a statement condemning Daley's charges as "a harmful action that may bring about anarchy by destroying the character of responsible leaders."[46] But Bishop Cletus F. O'Donnell, administrator of the Roman Catholic Archdiocese of Chicago, swiftly disavowed their views. "I was not informed of the matter nor did I consent to the statement," Bishop O'Donnell said. "Again I call upon all Catholics, especially clergy, to give all officials of the government, particularly law enforcement officials, the respect and cooperation necessary to preserve law and order in our city."[47]

The three weeks of demonstrations had a certain nuisance value, but little else. Then the Coordinating Council of Community Organizations (CCCO)—the prime civil rights organization in Chicago—decided the only effective way to help Chicago school children was to deprive them of Federal school funds. It fell to Albert Raby, head of the CCCO, to put this bizarre scheme into effect. He asked Francis Keppel, U.S. Commissioner of Education, to withhold some $32 million in Federal funds from the Chicago public school system on the grounds that it was racially segregated and discriminatory.[48] Members of the Chicago Board of Education angrily charged that children were being used to apply pressure, and that cutting off these funds would hurt most the children who most needed the special help provided by Federal aid.[49] Keppel had previously used the threat of withholding Federal money, under Title VI of the Civil Rights Act of 1964, to speed integration in Southern schools.[50] A preliminary investigation of the Chicago School Board was said to have uncovered at least an indication of deliberate discrimination against predominantly Negro schools.[51] Keppel issued a "hold order" and said that the complaints "must be satisfactorily resolved before any new commitments are made."[52] Martin Luther King hailed the freeze as "creative pressure."[53]

Almost every elected official in Washington from Illinois put pressure on Education Commissioner Keppel's office.[54] Albert Raby recalled that the Illinois congressional delegation backed the 1964 Civil Rights Act, and then caustically commented, "Yet they are the first to squeal like stuck pigs when the bill is enforced in the North, while they applaud enforcement in the South."[55]

Vehement protests from practically everyone who was anyone in Illinois—from Mayor Daley to Senator Dirksen[56] —so irritated President Johnson that the press quoted him as saying, in effect, "negotiate a settlement and do it fast."[57] The "freeze" on Federal funds was quickly removed.[58] The Federal investigation was called off, but an agreement was reached to discontinue any training at a supposedly segregated trade school and to appoint a special School Board committee to review the school boundary problem with at least 60 days to report.[59]

It was a laborious face-saving device for the U.S. Office of Education, and everyone knew it. Rep. Roman Pucinski, a Chicago Democrat who championed Dr. Willis, called it "an abject surrender by Keppel—a great victory for local government, a great victory for Chicago."[60] The Negro magazine, *Jet*, called it "a serious civil rights defeat."[61]

Less than a month after the "freeze" had been rescinded, Illinois released to the Chicago public schools $6 million of the Federal aid funds that had been withheld.[62] Ray Page, State Superintendent of Public Instruction, said the money would be used to implement Willis's proposals for after-school classes and improved education of children from low-income families.[63] A delegation of civil rights leaders went to the state capitol for an explosive meeting with Page. During this brief and bitter encounter, Meyer Weinberg, the civil rights group's research director, accused Page of having violated the Federal act by releasing funds without knowing what specific schools would be involved, or getting a breakdown of costs. Page said, "Let's be honest about this." Weinberg asked if that implied he was not being honest; he and Raby said none of the delegation would speak until the "accusation" was withdrawn. Page said, "That's up to you," whereupon the delegation walked out of his office.[64] Later, Raby charged that Page had been "hostile and insulting" to the delegation. Page fired back that the group had been "grandstanding" in its walkout, and that since the CCCO had never seen Chicago's full application for the Federal funds, its charges of illegality were meaningless. He added that his department would not be "part of an attempt to hold children as hostages with the neck of the superintendent [Willis] as ransom."[65]

The Chicago school board did make one concession to the CCCO. It voted for "immediate" appointment of an assistant superintendent in charge of integration.[66] Upon Willis's recommendation, the school board appointed to the position Dr. Virginia F. Lewis, a top Negro in the Chicago school system. Assistant superintendent for education extension at the time of her appointment, she had been with the school system for 39 years.[67] Nevertheless, Raby opposed her appointment, chiefly because Willis had recommended her. He commented that "Mrs. Lewis, like all of Willis's immediate staff, Negro and white, has not shown the requisite understanding of the scope of the problem, the specific training to deal with it or the capacity to do anything other than act in subservience to the superintendent and whitewash the superintendent's failure."[68]

The graphic revelation of Mayor Daley's "clout" (Chicagoese for "political influence") was not lost on Martin Luther King. A few weeks before the Federal "freeze" on school funds for Chicago, King had announced his intention to make Chicago a major target of a "nonviolent" school integration campaign.[69] After the "freeze" was rescinded, King's plans became considerably more vague. He said that after November 1, 1965, he would spend "a good deal of time" in that city to "grapple with problems of education, housing and employment that plague the Negro in Chicago."[70] Absent were ringing pronouncements about de facto school segregation.

With his showmanlike flair for timing, King first announced his selection of Chicago for the SCLC's first major Northern campaign a few days after the Raby group had asked for the "freeze" on Federal school funds.[71] Raby joined King in announcing a new alliance of the CCCO with King's Southern Christian Leadership Conference.[72] Near the end of July, King opened his Northern campaign with a whirlwind three-day tour to build support for a march he planned to lead on City Hall. He described Chicago as a "very critical" target in the civil rights struggle.[73] He told his audiences that Chicago housing patterns were as segregated as any in the country.[74]

Then came his much-touted march on City Hall to challenge "those who now wallow in the mire of petty politics."[75] King warned his followers that "there is no city of Jerusalem on Lake Michigan," and shouted, "I have found the North to be no better than the South."[76] King's long-time associate, Ralph Abernathy, seconded these sentiments. He maintained, "We came to Chicago with the civil rights movement because we have discovered that we live down South, and you are living up South."[77] During his tours at 18 rallies, King had appealed for a turnout of 10,000 persons for the march.[78] When that day came, he counted the marchers at 20,000 to 30,000. An early police estimate set it at 8,000. To many observers, it looked like 15,000.[79] Among those not observing the march was Mayor Daley, who just happened to be in Detroit.[80] In any case, whichever of the crowd estimates was correct, it was undeniably the biggest civil rights demonstration in Chicago's history.[81]

It has often been remarked that while Martin Luther King himself was, virtually, Nonviolence on a Pedestal, violence somehow never seemed far behind him. King left Chicago after his triumphant civil rights march; less than a month later, Chicago had a riot on its hands.

A fire alarm was sounded in the predominantly Negro

district on Chicago's West Side. A hook and ladder truck went to answer the alarm without the tillerman aboard to control the rear portion. A Negro woman was killed in an accident caused by the wildly swinging rear section of the long ladder truck; the rear section knocked over a traffic light standard which fell on her and caused her death.[82]

The tillerman was in the shower when the fire alarm sounded. He jumped into his clothes, but did not slide down the brass pole because his body was wet and his clothing damp.[83] This fire company had answered 3,200 alarms the previous year without a single accident,[84] but this one freak accident was enough to set a Negro mob hurling bottles and Molotov cocktails at the fire station.[85] The following day, 150 policemen battled rioters after a street-corner civil rights rally (called by a group not belonging to the CCCO) degenerated into a looting, bottle-tossing mob melee.[86] Looters smashed nearly every window of stores in a business district.[87] Sixty persons were injured.[88] A white policeman in civilian clothes was slashed when a crowd of Negroes attacked him.[89] Firemen had to call for police escorts to answer alarms, after rioters pelted engines with bottles and bricks as they drove from the station.[90]

Integration leaders had previously noted the absence of Negroes in this fire company, and demanded immediate integration of the company's crew.[91] In reply, the Fire Commissioner stated that the 4,400-member fire department had 208 Negro members and an open civil service employment policy. He said 23 fire companies were racially mixed, and that no Negro firemen had applied for transfers to this company. "I see no reason for transferring men around the city against their will just because some group wants it," he said.[92] However, he did shift an all-Negro company to the fire company in question, to replace those who had been suspended, while the accident was under investigation.[93]

The riot flared up suddenly and ended suddenly. Its quick ending was attributed to intensive pacification efforts, the psychological effect of calling up the National Guard, and calling attention to the death and devastation wrought by the Los Angeles riots.[94]

A month later, a coroner's jury declared that the death of the Negro woman that touched off the rioting was an accident.[95] And the fire alarm that sent the truck speeding out of the fire house that tragic day without the tillerman? It was a false alarm![96]

Residents felt that "police brutality" was one of the primary factors responsible for the violence.[97] It has, of course, become mandatory under the New Enlightenment that the lawless are to be deified and the lawmen are to be censured. But at the risk of engaging in perilous flights of reason, let us examine the official records. In Chicago, from January to August, 1965, 289 complaints against Chicago police had been filed. Of these, after investigation, 274 were judged "unfounded" or "not sustained," eight resulted in "exoneration" of the policemen involved, and *only seven complaints were sustained.*[98] If anything, some Chicago policemen would have had reason to complain of "civilian brutality" and judicial indifference. The preceding year, two off-duty Chicago policemen were told of two men, both Puerto Rican migrants, who were threatening people with a broken beer bottle. The officers identified themselves, drew pistols and ordered one of the men to drop the bottle. Instead the two men attacked the officers, severely slashing one. But a criminal-court judge, a Negro, dismissed battery charges against the two men. The judge said that the policemen had used "excessive force."[99]

This was not the only occasion on which lachrymose officials had bent over backwards to give most favored treatment to minority groups. Almost as incongruous was the proposal that would have made a farce of nursing education. Seymour Simon, the president of the Cook County Board of Education, quite seriously proposed that Negro girls be admitted to the County School of Nursing even if they failed to pass the entrance test. He said Negro girls should be tutored before the examination, and then if they

failed "there should be some adjustment in entrance qualifications." Simon denied that this was "discrimination in
reverse." He called it "an effort to bring equal opportunity
for employment to those who haven't had it."[100] The president of the Cook County Board of Education had a rather
curious concept of "equal opportunity." For opportunity
really to be equal, Negro nursing applicants, like their
white counterparts, would have to stand or fall on the
grades they received in the entrance exam. What was really
sought for them was not equal opportunity but preferential treatment, because of, and only because of, the color
of their skin. And pity the patients who would be so many
sacrificial offerings on the altar of civil rights.

Incidents such as this were hardly reassuring to white
parents who wanted educational excellence for their children, and were hardly designed to stem the flow of white
students out of Chicago and into the suburbs.

It was scarcely more encouraging for white parents to
read about an upsurge of violence in public schools in a
heavily Negro district on Chicago's South Side. In a four-
and-a-half week period, at least 14 incidents had been reported in the area's schools. The violence included three
stabbings, one shooting, the trampling on a lunchroom at-
tendant and an attack on a teacher, who was knocked
down a flight of stairs. One knife-wielding assailant was
only ten years old. Most of the violence occurred in integrated schools where Negroes outnumbered whites more
than three to one. The president of the Chicago Teachers
Union called for searches of students "in the presence of
police." He recommended that these be made several times
a month.[101]

Nineteen sixty-five came to an end, and at that time a
racial weather forecast for the Windy City might have
read: *cloudy, with gusts of hostility and suspicion. Frozen
lines of communication, with little relief in sight.*

And then in January, 1966, Martin Luther King began

his Chicago campaign, and proceeded to make the climate for race relations infinitely worse.

Why, of all Northern cities, did King choose Chicago for his first Northern campaign? Because, in his words, "it epitomizes all the problems found in urban centers of the North."[102] King told a strategy conference: "If we can break the backbone of discrimination in Chicago, we can do it in all of the cities of this country."[103] He believed that slum conditions in Chicago were typical of those creating urban race problems throughout the North, and knew he could count on the eager support of active local civil rights groups.[104] Accordingly, he announced "a full-scale assault" against the slums of Chicago.[105]

Before the campaign had even formally begun, the executive director of the Southern Christian Leadership Conference disclosed that the groundwork had cost $10,000 a month. Now he expected the field staff to be doubled and costs to rise sharply.[106]

With the usual high drama and fanfare, Martin Luther King took occupancy of a four-room flat in a West Side slum apartment house in Chicago. He planned to live in the third-floor walk-up while conducting the campaign.[107] In this way, he fully expected to experience first-hand the slum conditions of the Negro ghetto;[108] much to his chagrin, however, his landlord—with insufferable insolence—insisted upon having King's apartment freshly painted and well heated.[109] Nevertheless, 200 persons were on hand to cheer his symbolic entrance into the Chicago ghetto.[110]

Forty-one per cent of the Negro ghetto dwellings were rated as dilapidated, deteriorating and lacking in adequate plumbing, compared with 18 per cent for whites.[111] King's solution was to run the taxpayers through a fiscal wringer. He told his supporters that President Johnson's $2.3 billion city rebuilding proposal was "encouraging, *but we will need billions and billions*."[112]

For the first time, Martin Luther King was *welcomed*

into a target city by the Mayor. Daley was not precisely
effusive in his greeting to King, but he did say that all
city departments were anxious to be of help to King, and
noted that the Negro leader had already met with Police
Superintendent O. W. Wilson and top department personnel. "I believe this is the first police department in the
country that he has met with," Mayor Daley added.[113]
King had already announced his willingness to "break any
law" for the cause of civil rights.[114] Daley's cautious reaction was "I am hopeful and confident there will not be any
reason for breaking the law."[115]

An event which elicited little or no comment from other
civil rights leaders was King's 45-minute meeting with
the Black Muslim leader, Elijah Muhammed, in his 19-
room Tudor-style brick mansion near the University of
Chicago.[116] Curiously, the same stigma did not attach to
meeting a Negro racist as meeting a white one. King announced that the two had agreed to form a "common front"
to campaign against slums. King commented, "The time
has come when we, the Negroes, must see our mutual
problems. It is not the time for us to be fighting each
other."[117] Since the Muslims wanted a segregated society
and King an integrated community, one can only wonder
what their "*mutual* problems" could have been, and how
they could possibly arrive at a *mutual* solution.

In his orations on civil disobedience, King acknowledged
an obligation to comply with "the moral law of the universe." Among the most solemn of these are the Ten
Commandments, but this in no way deterred King from
elbowing the Decalogue aside to suit his convenience in
Chicago. Certainly, when Martin Luther King baldly
walked right in and commandeered a slum dwelling, he
was bending, if not breaking, the commandment: "Thou
Shalt Not Steal."

Acting in the name of three civil rights organizations,
King took over a West Side slum building without the
owner's permission.[118] King blandly commented, "I won't

say that this is illegal, but I would call it supralegal (above the law). The moral question is far more important than the legal one."[119] King said the civil rights organizations would collect $400 a month rent from four tenants in the six-flat building and use the money to clean and renovate the structure. King delicately referred to it as a "trusteeship until we can get the job done." He said lawyers were studying whether they should make mortgage payments of $150 a month on the building, but conceded that "we do not know whether we will be able to take care of it."[120]

In his takeover of the slum dwelling, King was not fighting a burly Jim Clark, but an 81-year-old invalid who was confined to his home. The octogenarian landlord, John Bender, said that the building had not been profitable, and told the press that he would be willing to *give* the building to King if he would take over the mortgage.[121] King did not accept the offer.

The civil rights groups contracted verbally for $600 worth of electric wiring for the slum dwelling.[122] Meanwhile, the Cook County Welfare Department announced it would withhold rent money provided to two welfare recipient families in the building if it was not paid to the owner of the building.[123] This sum totaled $155 a month, and would have reduced to $245 a month the rental payments that King said he would spend on the building.[124]

A spokesman for the First Mutual Savings Association, which held a mortgage on the building, said legal action would be instituted if the mortgage payments were not kept up.[125] At the same time, the city was filing suit in Municipal Court, charging that 23 violations of the city building code existed in the slum structure.[126] While King asserted the right to receive the rent moneys, the landlord was still being charged with all the legal and financial responsibilities for the dwelling.

The elderly landlord, in his lawsuit, again made obvious his desire to be rid of the property. Besides asking the court to prohibit King from collecting rents, he requested that a receiver be appointed for the building.[127] Almost without exception, when such requests were made they were made by the city. But city spokesmen noticeably shied away from the receivership bid on the grounds that the building—which contained 23 violations—did not include any major structural deficiency.[128]

King's "trusteeship" brought nothing but misery to all concerned, even those supposed to benefit from his "loving" usurpation. The landlord's attorney said eviction notices had been served on occupants of five of the apartments because no rental payments had been received for at least three months.[129] The Cook County Welfare Department was as good as its word, and began withholding rental allowances for three families in the building who were on public aid.[130] And if there were ever any doubts that the slum dwelling was a realtor's white elephant, they were dispelled by the Rev. Owen McAteer of St. Agatha's Roman Catholic Church, a civil rights leader. Rev. McAteer said rents had been collected, and the proceeds (presumably the full $400) applied to expenses of $889 for repairs to the building's electrical system and $150 for coal. To avoid financial disaster, King's Southern Christian Leadership Conference had advanced $2,000 to help pay for repairs and improvement of the property.[131]

King's takeover of the building was condemned by Chicago's Committee of 100, a moderate interracial civic organization. The group stated that "Dr. King has advocated that bad laws should be disobeyed. Perhaps in those parts of the South where the law has two faces, one black and one white, this may be appropriate. But in the North, particularly in Chicago, the law has just one face applicable to all. No one is above the law here."[132] And Chicago's Judge James B. Parsons, the first Negro ever appointed to a Federal district bench in the continental United States, bluntly described King's "trusteeship" as "theft."[133]

Eventually, Martin Luther King was enjoined from interfering with the operation of the slum building. The court ordered him not to enter the structure, not to collect any rents; in addition, he was told to submit an accounting in 20 days of any rents collected. The court also appointed a receiver for the property.[134] A very final ending to the controversy came three weeks after the court decision. The 81-year-old landlord was found dead, apparently from natural causes.[135] Martin Luther King had, after all, overcome the octogenarian—permanently!

King's seizure of a slum dwelling brought him copious publicity but little in the way of concrete accomplishment. He had no lack of money or volunteers or slogans, but he was sadly lacking in a living, breathing hate-object—the role that Jim Clark had so obligingly played in Selma. For the first time, a King campaign was aimed against a condition not directly traceable to malevolent law or segregationist officialdom. On the contrary, Mayor Daley greeted his arrival in Chicago by asserting that the city's slum eradication program was well under way and that the city was pleased to have King join in.[136] How much simpler life in Chicago would have been for him if the Mayor had proved intransigent. But under the circumstances, about all King could do was shout "Faster! Faster!" and call for twice as much money as Daley was spending, or, for that matter, more money than Chicago had in the city till.

King's supporters had rallied round him with dizzying speed. During a two-week period alone, some 12,000 persons paid prices ranging from $2.50 to $100 each to attend a fund-raising Freedom Festival.[137] The United Automobile Workers dispatched 125 paid organizers into the slums for four days as the first step in organizing tenants into "slum unions" to bargain with landlords for repairs and improvements.[138] But nothing in King's experience had prepared him for Mayor Richard J. Daley—one of the last of the old-time political bosses, who had an unbroken string of political knockouts to his credit in this citadel of infighting. While King was groping for a program, Daley was bombarding ministers with "fact sheets" showing what had been achieved before King had arrived on the scene. Among Daley's accomplishments:

29,000 apartments sealed and sprayed for rats and insects within the last year.

6,000 suits filed and $194,000 in fines levied in 1965 alone against owners of substandard houses.

31,000 public housing units constructed over the last 20 years, and 3,000 more to be made available over the next four years.[139]

One observer was quoted by the New York *Times* as saying, "If Daley makes a mistake, it will not be for a lack of interest in slums. He has always beaten his enemies by taking their programs and running with them. Before he's through, his crusade will make King's look minor league."[140] The newspaper noted that "while Dr. King's staff is searching for solutions, a growing number of Chicagoans are becoming skeptical of his [King's] chances of succeeding in unfamiliar Northern terrain and against problems that have baffled a small army of social workers."[141]

Mayor Daley challenged critics of the Chicago slums to form nonprofit construction and rehabilitation corporations for new housing. He said the Federal government would make 100 per cent mortgages on such projects, and revealed that he had suggested this program during a three-and-a-half hour meeting with King in his office.[142] Dr. King went right on "searching for solutions." But the Rev. Wilbur N. Daniel, pastor of the 5,000-member Antioch Missionary Baptist Church, announced plans to raise funds for a $6 million integrated housing project for moderate income families. Most of the money was expected to come in the form of an FHA loan. The church had already purchased a 21-acre site for the project.[143]

Rev. James Bevel, who directed the voter registration drive in Selma for the Southern Christian Leadership Conference, had come to Chicago as program director for the

West Side Christian Parish.[144] He subsequently became King's Chicago project director once the campaign got under way.[145] Elsewhere in this book, reference is made to Bevel's staunch affinity for the Far Left. But even he may have outdone himself when he participated in a meeting of the Committee for Independent Political Action (CIPA) in Chicago.[146] Represented at this meeting were the ultra-leftist Students for a Democratic Society and SNCC, as well as such gullible respectables as Prof. Robert J. Havighurst of the University of Chicago.[147] Among others, Bevel shared the speaker's platform with Lawrence Landry, organizer of a super-militant civil rights group called ACT.[148] In 1965, Landry made an inflammatory speech to a Negro crowd which, the Chicago *Tribune* charged, incited the riot in which 62 persons were injured.[149] The Committee for Independent Political Action elected an executive committee of 45 members, three of whom had been identified as Communists by the House Committee on Un-American Activities.[150]

Considering the company he kept, it should have occasioned no great astonishment that Bevel viewed the Chicago slums as "internal colonialism."[151] In an interview, Bevel stated, "The Northern slum is no different from the African colonies. Both are exploited—that is, outsiders take things out and don't put anything in." As an example, Bevel cited a druggist who "may make $20,000 profit from a drugstore in the slums but he doesn't use even as much as a dollar to paint a house there because he doesn't live there."[152] Bevel did not explain why a druggist—who gave value for value received—should feel *obligated* to go beyond the quid pro quo and spend extra money of his own in the ghetto.

Bevel went on, "The landlord collects rents, but won't make repairs. When there's a bank, it takes deposits [Author's Note: *and gives interest*] and maybe finances a car, but it won't make loans for a new slum business or for repairing a house. Even the schoolteachers, and most of the ministers and political precinct captains, don't live here."[153] Bevel wanted to reverse the process "so you have money coming in as well as going out. When this happens, people won't have to leave the slums to find a better life. They can stay right here and the slums will disappear."[154]

Bevel refused to commit himself to the 18-month deadline Martin Luther King had set for Operation Chicago.[155] Bevel had plans for a union of slum dwellers embracing virtually all the 300,000 Negroes estimated to live on Chicago's West Side. Ultimately he expected this to be expanded into the South Side, where even more Negroes lived.[156] Bevel said such a "slum union" could wage rent strikes and hold street demonstrations, boycotts and "cold cut weekends" during which Negroes would refuse to use gas and electricity for cooking.[157]

With King in Chicago—and Bevel out-Kinging King— the city of Chicago announced a massive crackdown on building violations.[158] The Building Department spread its dragnet for slumlords and, wonder of wonders, Illinois' top Communist leader fell right into it!

It was a kind of political slapstick worthy of Mack Sennett. On February 14, 1966, a Building Department inspection of a three-story six-flat stone building at 3443 West 12th Place turned up 11 building code violations, plus charges that three of the six flats were overcrowded. The violations included "evidence of rats and roaches," and toilets, windows, back porches and back stairs were in disrepair. The back stair conditions "were hazardous to life."[159]

Investigation revealed that this slum dwelling was owned by Claude M. Lightfoot, the top Communist Party leader in Illinois.[160] The proletarian slumlord sputtered, "I made no profit on the building and my income taxes will show it this year."[161] This was the first—and last—time the Communist Party was to consider profitability even vaguely relevant in landlord-and-tenant cases. Months later, Lightfoot was summoned to answer charges of building code violations, but by then the Communist chieftain had taken care to liquidate his profitless capitalist holdings.[162]

While the Building Department was lowering the boom on slumlords, Mayor Daley was presenting to the City Council a record $195 million bond issue for sweeping civic improvements, to be voted upon in the primary.[163] Daley pushed for its passage with the plea that it was needed to remove slums and blight by December, 1967.[164] But the outlook was far from promising. Four years before the voters had rejected a $66 million bond issue with heavy opposition from white property owners.[165]

Not even this record bond issue appeared to placate King. He wanted to weld the people together into the nucleus of a protest movement, a coalition of Negroes and other minority groups, unions, churchmen and liberals to make *"demands greater than Chicago is willing to give . . . so that direct action will become necessary."*[166] His ultimate objective was to create a situation where "the Federal government will be forced to act."[167]

King made public a list of these demands in June, 1966. Among them:

A minimum wage of $2 an hour.

Total school integration by September, 1967.

The dispersing of Negroes from concentrated areas throughout the city, through enforcement of open-occupancy measures and through the erection of low-income, low-density public housing units in each of the city's 50 wards.

The creation of ten "new towns," each with 100,000 population, 30 per cent Negro.[168]

A month later, King would make still more demands, and he knew full well what the answer would be. He was already preparing Chicago Negroes for the invariable next step. "A riot can always be stopped by superior force," he told a rally, "but they can't stop thousands of feet marching nonviolently."[169]

What King had in mind was about 200,000 feet. He hoped to draw as many as 100,000 people to a rally in Soldier Field.[170] A rally that huge would provide him with a powerful bargaining lever in his negotiations with Mayor

Daley—and by now it was dawning on him that he was going to need all the levers he could get. King railed against what he considered the failure of public officials to respond to conventional methods of nonviolent protest. "When they drain the steam out of the nonviolent movement and give no concessions," he said, "they are planting the seeds for a Watts-like situation."[171] He complained that in the North, officials would "let you march all summer and not give you one thing."[172] It was not necessary to read between the lines; King went on to spell it out: "In Chicago, for example, Mayor Daley's response was to play tricks with us—to say he's going to end slums but not doing any concrete things."[173]

It is difficult to see what could have been more concrete than the $195 million bond issue for capital improvements proposed by Mayor Daley. The bond issue had sailed past the City Council, and the Mayor had put his political neck on the line—staking the prestige of his Democratic organization on its passage. On June 15—three weeks before Martin Luther King bemoaned Daley's supposed failure to do "any concrete things"—the Mayor's record-breaking bond issue won voter approval by a margin of more than two to one.[174]

As always, King reverted to form when he said, "if gains are not made and made in a hurry through responsible civil rights organizations, it will open the door to militant groups to gain a foothold—and those that have tried to be responsible will be driven to more irresponsible deeds and words."[175]

In a call for "immediate action," King demanded:

That real estate agents handle only property available to all races and that banks and lending institutions give a pledge of nondiscrimination.

That public housing be built outside the black ghetto.

That the city purchase only from concerns with "full-scale fair employment" policies.

That business and local government publish racial employment statistics and that labor take on at least 400 Negro and Latin-American apprentices.

That the county public aid department recognize unions of welfare recipients that the civil rights movement was promoting.

That a citizen review board be set up for the police department.

That an immediate desegregation plan be adopted for schools.

That businesses be boycotted to force the hiring of Negroes.[176]

The purpose of his rally in Soldier Field was to dramatize these demands and to make Chicago "a just and open city."[177] A few days before, Dr. J. H. Jackson announced that he would not support the rally. In reply, King snapped, "I don't think Dr. Jackson speaks for one per cent of the Negroes in this country."[178]

Whether it was the opposition of Dr. Jackson, the 98-degree temperature, a monumental apathy or all combined, attendance figures at the rally in Soldier Field were far below King's expectations. A public relations aide for the Southern Christian Leadership Conference estimated the crowd at 45,000. Police estimated the crowd at 30,000.[179] Either figure fell far short of the projected 100,000 attendance figure sought by the civil rights leader.

King asked his followers "to decide to fill up the jails of Chicago, if necessary, in order to end slums."[180] He led the three-mile march to City Hall; more precisely, he rode in an air-conditioned car at the head of the sweltering column.[181] With his usual flair for drama—in the manner of Martin Luther posting 95 theses on the door of the castle church—he affixed a list of demands on the LaSalle Street door of the City Hall as the marchers cheered.[182]

Roman Catholic Archbishop John P. Cody sent a message to the rally endorsing many of King's demands. Pledging the Archdiocese of Chicago to the elimination of the last "vestiges of discrimination," Archbishop Cody made the strongest Chicago Archdiocesan statement yet on civil rights.[183] In addition, the Archbishop declared "Your struggles and sufferings will be mine."[184]

At Soldier Field, King made one of his characteristic pleas for nonviolence. He told the audience, "Our power does not reside in Molotov cocktails, knives and bricks. Our movement's adherence to nonviolence has been a major factor in the creation of a moral climate that has made progress possible."[185]

As always, his speech was warmly applauded. And less than 48 hours later a riot erupted in Chicago's Negro ghetto, featuring Molotov cocktails, knives, and bricks.

The immediate cause of the Negro riot was that policemen had turned off two fire hydrants being used by children on a hot afternoon.[186] After the police turned off the hydrants, a group of Negro youths stepped forward and opened the hydrants again. A fight then broke out between a Negro policeman and one of the youths.[187] Several gangs of up to about 250 youths each formed and began rampaging throughout the neighborhood, tossing Molotov cocktails at police cars and looting scores of stores.[188] The windows of every store in one large shopping plaza were shattered and the shelves of a supermarket emptied before the police arrived.[189] At a church meeting, Martin Luther King encouraged members of the audience to speak from the floor "to relieve the tension." Whereupon a number of Negro youths scoffed at him and walked out.[190] Gangs continued to roam the streets and break windows.[191]

The next night still more violence erupted, still more rocks were thrown, still more windows were broken, and still more Molotov cocktails were hurled.[192] Martin Luther King reeled off any number of reasons for the rioting; indeed the only ones he excluded from culpability were the rioters themselves. He blamed the disturbances on Mayor Daley's refusals to make concessions on King's civil rights program. King raised the venerable specter of "police brutality" and demanded a civilian review board.

He scored the lack of swimming pools and parks in the area, and said that Daley "can do much more to stop riots than I can."[193]

Then came the third successive night of violence. Now roving gangs and snipers in the predominantly Negro West Side exchanged gunfire with heavily reinforced police patrols. More than 1,000 policemen were unable to contain 5,000 Negroes in the streets, despite King's efforts to help. The police called for tear gas to repel armed Negroes at one point. Elsewhere, gangs of Negroes moved from street to street smashing windows in stores, looting, tossing fire bombs and retreating when the police rushed in.[194] At Chicago Police Superintendent Wilson's request, Governor Kerner called out 4,000 guardsmen. That night, 1,500 guardsmen cruised the troubled area, armed with carbines and fixed bayonets.[195] King sped from the scene of one battle to another trying to calm the crowds and preach nonviolence, but he remained in his car most of the time.[196] The largest fire in the riot zone consumed a bottling plant and adjacent packing company filled with cardboard boxes. Three hundred firemen and 60 pieces of equipment were used to fight the fire, which caused $100,000 damage. The owner of the packing company reported that he had been told by an employee that his Negro employees had been warned to get out of the building because "it will be burned to the ground this afternoon."[197] During the riots, Chicago police arrested several members of the virulently pro-Communist Revolutionary Action Movement in a tenement building; there they found marijuana and loaded weapons, with instruction sheets on their use.[198]

Mayor Daley angrily said of the riots that strife had been "planned." He said King's aides were "in here for no other purpose than to bring disorder to the streets of Chicago."[199] Daley said that King's aides "showed pictures" of techniques in violence. King acknowledged that Rev. Bevel had been showing motion pictures of the Los Angeles riots to Negroes in Chicago. The movies were used, he said, "to show the negative results of rioting."[200] But to those viewers who were so inclined, the movies could have served as an audio-visual seminar in violence. The New York *Times* reported that King arranged to have teen-age gang leaders shown the movie on the Los Angeles riot "to demonstrate how the rioters destroyed their own neighborhood and accomplished nothing." But this was not at all the way the gang leaders reacted. When police officers appeared on the screen they were hissed. When Negroes were shown attacking policemen they were cheered.[201] Possibly Dr. J. H. Jackson had in mind incidents such as this when he commented, "There is danger of using nonviolence in such a way that it will create violence."[202]

The guardsmen patrolled under publicly announced orders to shoot to kill if fired upon.[203] Their presence quickly "cooled" the ghetto. Relative peace and calm returned, and Martin Luther King was able to walk out of City Hall with agreements to four requests. The city agreed to install sprinklers on fire hydrants, so children in the ghetto could cool off on hot summer days; to request Federal funds to construct swimming pools; to appoint a citizens committee to determine how the police department could improve its relations with minority groups; and to assign two workers to each precinct in the riot zone to work for an end to the rioting.[204]

A spokesman for the city's Water Department confirmed that sprinklers were now in place on hydrants near "almost every fire station" in the ghetto.[205] The Superintendent of the Chicago Park District said 10 portable swimming pools had been purchased for $1,000 each.[206] And about a week later, Mayor Daley set up a 23-member citizens' committee as an alternative to a civilian review board for the Police Department.[207]

What was the underlying cause of the Negro riots in Chicago? Theories blanketed the city like confetti. It was allegedly due to grinding poverty, despair, resentment of

Dr. Willis. But there was still that nagging question of timing: *Why now?* The conditions most often cited as motives for the rioting had been grievances of long standing—grievances not of months, but of years. Why, at this particular juncture, in the presence of the Crown Prince of Nonviolence, did the Chicago riots take place?

Edward Marciniak, director of the Chicago Human Relations Commission, had a much more jarring theory. Marciniak attributed the rioting to civil rights workers who he felt had bred in teen-age gang members a disrespect for the police.[208] It was reported that one city official close to the Mayor said he and others had "begged" civil rights workers several months before to discontinue their efforts at reaching gang members. He said that the gangs had been quiescent until "agitators" began working with them.[209]

Quite obviously, the Rev. Andrew J. Young, executive director of the Southern Christian Leadership Conference, was not going to corroborate Marciniak's charge. But the Negro minister did say that most of the rioting had been done by teen-agers in the gangs, and that older gang leaders were the only ones who could control them.[210] Much of the window-smashing and store-burning on the West Side had been attributed to three youth gangs—the Cobras, the Vice Lords and the Roman Saints.[211] When the rioting had finally spent itself—and National Guardsmen were patrolling the area—Martin Luther King called leaders of these gangs to a meeting in his apartment in the ghetto.[212] For the first four hours, they poured out their grievances against the city. Young said the gang leaders "talked mainly about a desperate need for jobs." Presumably they felt an equally desperate need for political power. Rev. Young quoted them as seeing "the Negro politicians in the ghetto as pawns of the Daley machine, and want to see political power shifted to the people of the area themselves."[213]

The meeting concluded with a munificent agreement by

the gang leaders to "try nonviolence."[214] City officials cautioned that this civil rights-gang alliance was giving the gangs the prominence and importance they sought for basically criminal ends.[215] Marciniak warned that some civil rights leaders were being "naive" in thinking they had earned a measure of control over the gangs' activities.[216]

In a highly publicized meeting with Police Superintendent Wilson, leaders of the gangs pledged a truce.[217] A few hours later, five youths were shot and wounded in gang territory.[218] A week after the truce, casualties in the gang feud had climbed to two killed and 13 wounded.[219] Two weeks after the gang leaders had met with Martin Luther King and pledged to "try nonviolence," the police had to enforce a state curfew law against the warring Negro youth gangs in Chicago.[220]

The police enforced that curfew law none too soon; Stokely Carmichael had come to town to make several speeches. Carmichael told a cheering rally that Negroes should stop fighting each other. He asserted that "the only nonviolence we need is nonviolence among ourselves," and said that "we've been shooting and cutting the wrong people."[221] Carmichael was guarded by two members of the Deacons for Defense and Justice, an armed Negro group.[222] And yet the violent Mr. Carmichael had a meeting—however brief—with the nonviolent Dr. King.[223]

It may well be that the Chicago riots were among the first overt manifestations of Black Power, and that Martin Luther King had a front-row seat for the preview. This theory was based upon an incident seen and then forgotten by much of the press. It happened at King's less-than-spectacular rally in Soldier Field. During the rally, four Negro boys from a West Side gang managed to slip into the press box. In loud, insistent voices, they demanded to be heard, saying, "We came up to tell these reporters about what Black Power is, what it really means. We want to tell it like it is." The boys got on the radio, then found themselves struck dumb with stage fright. Finally they

said that *showing* would be better. The incident was recalled by a journalist for the liberal Catholic magazine
Commonweal.[224] He felt it demonstrated the way in which
Martin Luther King "had lost great face in the Negro
community." This liberal writer was convinced that "Tuesday, July 12, another group chose another way to demonstrate it—and Chicago's West Side riots began."[225] His
conclusion was not incompatible with Marciniak's accusation that civil rights workers had stirred up quiescent
gangs. In either case, it was obvious that once stirred up,
these gangs became uncontrollable; the young hoodlums
repudiated King's nonviolence, while embracing his doctrine that laws subjectively considered unjust could be disobeyed. Equally obvious, there was scant comfort in the
fact that for all his efforts, it was not Martin Luther King
who ended the Chicago riots, but the National Guard.

If King had "lost great face," it was because victories
in his Chicago campaign were frustratingly few. One of
the rare confrontation coups scored by his Southern Christian Leadership Conference occurred as a result of a rent
strike in the East Garfield section of Chicago. Following
the rent strike, an agreement was signed between a 3,000-
member Tenants Union and the Condor-Costalis Real
Estate Company, owners of 25 multiple dwelling units and
managing agent for 20 others in the ghetto. The contract
obligated the landlord to accept the union as sole collective
bargaining agent for the tenants; the company was required to take action within six months to bring its property up to the standards required by Illinois laws.[226] What
act, if any, the union agreed to have its *tenants* perform
was not at all clear—unless it was the breath-taking concession of no longer living rent-free in the apartments they
had leased.

But this was one of King's very few breakthroughs. As
the New York *Times* expressed it, "the dramatic encounter
with the power structure, a confrontation that so often
worked for Dr. King in the South, never happened in Chi-

cago."[227] For much of this period, he was a part-time campaigner—a week-end commuter who delegated much of the campaign to the very Left Rev. Bevel.[228] The *Times* duly noted the undiminished power of King's evangelistic fervor, but added that the movement's "most ardent advocate would hardly claim that he has in fact ended Chicago's slums . . ."[229]

King told an audience that there was a "wall in this city" behind which a million Negroes were kept in a ghetto "of race, poverty and human misery." Behind this wall, he said, the Negro walked the street, unemployed or underemployed, and paid more for comparable housing than whites.[230] Within the statement seemed to be at least two tacit assumptions: that these Negroes were qualified for better jobs, and that such jobs were presently available. But these were not quite the facts of working life as unfolded by John D. Gray, chairman of the Chicago Merit Employment Committee of the Chicago Association of Commerce and Industry. He offered one statistic that served to backstop Martin Luther King's contention, with the finding that several hundred thousands were working at jobs well below their potential skill capacity. But at the same time, Gray revealed that there were still about 100,000 unfilled jobs in Illinois *because of a lack of qualified people to fill them.*[231] An enlightened civil rights crusade would have dropped everything else and concentrated on training unemployed or underemployed Negroes to fill as many of those job vacancies as possible. It would have been the better part of racial statesmanship to show more interest in job headway than news headlines. But characteristically, King put confrontations first and vocational guidance second.

Chicago was something new to him. But Martin Luther King was unable to come up with any new tactics. He could only reach into his well-worn bag of tricks and conjure up the same old demonstrations. King realized from the start that he would not be able to stage demonstrations with quite the same free-wheeling abandon he had displayed in Birmingham and Selma. A "judicial backlash"[232] had begun to set in. For some time, the *Times* noted, a ritual had evolved in civil rights cases: "The state courts would uphold the Negroes' convictions for disturbing the peace, and the Supreme Court would throw the convictions out . . . by holding that the demonstrators had a right to be where they were and that their protests did not amount to an offense."[233] The first sign that the Supreme Court was beginning to lose its patience with protest excesses—their size and activities—came in 1964. At that time, there was a case involving 2,000 demonstrators in a march to the courthouse in Baton Rouge, La. An astounding reversal was made by Justice Hugo Black, who had devoted nearly a lifetime to championing civil liberties. The Supreme Court Justice broke with the majority and sounded this warning: "It is not a far step from what to many seems the earnest, honest, patriotic, kind-spirited multitude of today to the fanatical, threatening lawless mob of tomorrow."[234]

From that point, Justice Black voted in each case to uphold protestors' convictions.[235] He said that demonstrators "have no right to go wherever they want, whenever they please, without regard to the rights of private or public property or state law."[236] For over a year, Black was unable to secure a majority to uphold demonstrators' convictions. But in November, 1966, Justice Byron White switched sides, and for the first time since the civil rights movement began, a lower court conviction of Southern Negro demonstrations was upheld by the High Court. The Supreme Court ruled that policemen in Tallahassee, Florida, had acted legally when they arrested 32 demonstrators for trespassing, after the Negroes had disobeyed the sheriff's order to leave the jailhouse grounds.[237]

While this monumental decision was announced some months after King's Chicago campaign had begun, he was an astute enough judge of the political climate to recognize that the High Court would no longer automatically rubber-stamp his every action. For King, this growing coolness in judicial attitude could not have come at a more inopportune time; indeed, it must have bordered on the traumatic to discover that his old allies in Washington were no longer willing to support him in the manner to which he had become accustomed.

For probably the first time since Albany, Martin Luther King had found a foeman more than worthy of his steel. It was one master strategist facing another—Mr. Civil Rights pitted against the last of the big-city bosses (or, as Daley preferred to be known, "the first of the new leaders"). Robert A. Goldwin, a former University of Chicago political scientist, felt that "Daley's greatest political achievement is the unlikely alliance he holds together. His major support has been from Negroes and people who hate Negroes. He always supports civil rights laws, for example, which gets him the Negro vote. But he never enforces them, which gets him the votes of whites antagonistic to Negroes. Chicago has an open occupancy ordinance but it is not enforced in white neighborhoods where Negroes are unwelcome. Anyone who can succeed in doing this has to be a masterful politician."[238]

Daley had good reason to be apprehensive of the consequences if the open housing ordinance had been rigidly enforced in hostile neighborhoods. In Bridgeport, the neighborhood in which he lived, a Negro couple had recently moved into an apartment. They arrived home one night to find that all their furniture and belongings had been removed to the police station.[239] This experience was a mild one compared with the reception awaiting a few Negro families who moved into the Trumbull Park housing project in South Deering back in 1953. At that time, angry white mobs often numbered in the thousands. Some 1,200 policemen were needed to control them during disturbances that continued as long as the Negroes remained in the project. A special detail of the Police Department was quartered in an apartment in the project for five years to handle repeated bombings and other incidents. Before the turmoil subsided, property had been damaged extensively and 280 white persons had been arrested.[240] The cessation of neighborhood hostilities did not signal any change in attitude. In 1963, South Deering's two representatives in the State Legislature were the only Democrats to vote against open occupancy; the bill failed of passage by just two votes.[241]

King's open-housing targets were most of about 20 virtually all-white residential areas.[242] The majority of the homes were in the $15,000 to $30,000 bracket.[243] Many of the residents were first- and second-generation Americans whose fathers or grandfathers had come from Poland, Germany, Lithuania, and Italy.[244] Their incomes were estimated at from $7,500 to $8,500,[245] which hardly placed them in the category of the affluent power structure. Many of these residents had moved into the areas from the "inner city" as Negroes became their neighbors. At the very outset, it was agreed on all sides that feeling against housing desegregation in these areas was high.[246]

Interestingly enough, out of some 950,000 Negroes in Chicago, fewer than 2,000 were to participate with any regularity in the meetings and marches led by King.[247] Probably one reason for this lack of militancy was the feeling that many of them might never be able to take advantage of open occupancy. The average Chicago Negro family income was then $4,700 annually[248]—not nearly enough to warrant a move to an expensive apartment or a home costing $15,000 to $30,000.

By now, King-watchers were aware of the almost invariable pattern of demonstrations—a small beginning led by King's assistants with a modest number of marchers, then the gradual build-up in tempo to hundreds and then thousands of marching feet. The beginning came in late July. About 250 civil rights demonstrators marched into an all-white neighborhood to demand equality in renting and buying property. The demonstrators encountered a barrage of jeers, rocks and bottles. At one point, club-swinging police charged into a band of white hecklers.[249]

The following day, some 550 Negro and white civil

rights marchers took part in another demonstration. About 700 whites waited at Marquette Park for the demonstrators to arrive and begin the march. As the demonstrators drove up, they were jeered. Firecrackers exploded. Between 15 and 25 cars, some owned by Negro marchers, were overturned and set on fire by white youths. More than 54 persons were injured, including two policemen, and at least 14 persons were arrested. The casualty figures might have gone even higher had it not been for members of Chicago's youth gangs, who walked with the demonstrators and batted down hundreds of bricks and bottles thrown at the marchers.[250]

Still commuting to Chicago, King arrived and immediately berated the Chicago Police Department, accusing them of laxity in their efforts to protect civil rights demonstrators from their white assailants. He said the whites had caused more property damage than had Negroes in the recent racial disturbances.[251]

A joint statement by King and Raby said:

It is clear that the police were either unwilling or unable to disperse the riotous mob that so brutally attacked Negroes and whites who had come to the community to seek open housing in compliance with the law.

The failure to exercise full responsibility for full protection is especially appalling [since] huge masses of police and National Guardsmen were mobilized to put down the violence of a few hundred Negroes on the West Side.

At the height of the violence on the West Side, not more than a few cars were burned. It is clear that this bigoted mob destroyed more property on the Southwest side than did the West Side rioters.

We shall continue to demonstrate in every all-white community in Chicago in our non-violent effort to open housing for all men. In the process, we demand the full and active protection of the local police.[252]

It was not devoid of amusement that the same civil rights

leaders who had condemned "police brutality" in July now condemned "police laxity" in August. But it was totally deceptive to say that "this bigoted [white] mob destroyed more property on the Southwest side than did the West Side [Negro] rioters." Reference has already been made to a fire in the Negro riot zone which caused $100,000 damage to a bottling plant and adjacent packing company. It was equally misleading to say that the National Guard was mobilized "to put down the violence of a few hundred Negroes on the West Side." On the night of heaviest fighting between the police and Negro rioters, there was a confirmed estimate of 1,000 shots exchanged *at one corner alone* in the Lawndale section;[253] at one time, there were 5,000 Negroes in the streets.[254] The white mobs' attacks on the civil rights demonstrators were to increase in size and ferocity, but their worst excesses were in no way comparable to the trigger-happy gunmen and Molotov cocktail hurlers of the Negro riots.

Among those complaining about the police were members of the youth gangs. Thirty-eight members of South Side Negro gangs went by school bus to City Hall and complained about police methods. The group met with Hugh Osborne, deputy director of the Commission on Youth Welfare. Osborne, himself a Negro, told the young gang members, "There are people in your community who are afraid of you, God-fearing people who are afraid." Osborne replied to charges of police brutality by commenting, "If I were a police officer and I saw four or five of you coming down the street, believe me, I would get ready. There is something to say on both sides."[255]

Now King himself participated in the demonstrations. The next march took them to the Gage Park-Chicago Lawn-Marquette Park area. The area had approximately 100,000 residents, all but seven of them white (according to the not-quite color blind 1960 census). King was struck by a stone as a crowd of whites raged out of control. A special force of 960 policemen succeeded in preventing

King and about 600 civil rights demonstrators from being critically injured. At one point the white crowd numbered more than 4,000, and in more than five hours of disorder, the police clubbed and arrested scores of whites. But they could not prevent whites from attacking cars and buses with stones, firecrackers and bottles. "I've never seen anything like it in my life," said King. "I think the people from Mississippi ought to come to Chicago to learn how to hate."[256]

The civil rights marchers fared no better in the all-white Belmont-Cragin neighborhood. The police had to fight back thousands of jeering hecklers and use nightsticks to disperse angry whites who were throwing bottles, rocks, and firecrackers at both policemen and marchers. The mob screamed "White Power, White Power!" At one point, the police estimated that 3,000 to 5,000 persons were gathered near the march column. As quickly as the force of 500 policemen dispersed the crowds, the mob regrouped, and began following and taunting the marchers once again, even through a summer downpour.[257] This was the fifth time within a week that the demonstrations had met stiff resistance from whites.[258]

By now there were almost as many policemen as marchers at the demonstrations. Patrolmen surrounded the marching column to protect it from shrieking whites. But for all the precautions, a white mob of thousands was now following the marchers, jeering and cursing and hurling firecrackers, bottles, rocks, and tomatoes.[259]

The demonstrations began to attract some of the sickest groups in the country. Members of the fanatical National States Rights Party and the American Nazi Party moved through the white crowds distributing membership application forms and recruitment handbills.[260] Some white youths took to embellishing their placards with swastikas.[261] Others began yelling "We want Martin Luther Coon."[262] In Marquette Park, "Captain" John Patler of the American Nazi Party issued an inflammatory call to arms against

"Jew Commies" and "nigger scum." He exulted that "I've never seen a more responsive group of white people."[263] Nor was the Catholic Church immune from this abuse. Incensed by the sight of priests and nuns marching in the demonstrations, some white spectators shouted that they were Catholics and would stop contributing to the church unless the clergy stopped helping "niggers."[264] And some whites carried placards denouncing "Archbishop Cody and his Commie coons."[265]

But for all the handbills and recruiting forms passed out, the American Nazi Party was able to produce only one recruit in Chicago by mid-August—a part-time construction worker who said he had left the Catholic Church and Democratic Party because it was "sickening" to see both "helping the niggers."[266] The swastika-brandishing was done mostly by white teen-agers but their numerical strength was elusive, because often the same youths showed up at one demonstration after another.[267] As for their parents, reporter Donald Janson felt that "Except for agreement on anti-communism and racial segregation, there is no adult support for the American Nazi Party."[268]

The backlash was felt even by Rep. Roman C. Pucinski (D-Ill.), who in the past had voted for strong civil rights bills. Pucinski had voted the liberal position in Congress 74 per cent of the time, according to Americans for Democratic Action.[269] Nevertheless, at the height of the demonstrations in Chicago, Rep. Pucinski introduced legislation to authorize Federal courts to limit demonstrations by number of participants, times, and places.[270] "The demonstrations may be intended to [be] nonviolent," he said. "But can the organizers truly be nonviolent, knowing in their minds and hearts that their conduct will assuredly precipitate violence in others?"[271] Pucinski's Chicago district contained row after row of small houses occupied by Poles or other ethnic groups from Eastern Europe who spent Sundays caring for their homes and lawns.[272] He said that the Eastern Europeans "came to this country with the love for the land, and that 30-by-125 foot lot means everything to them." Pucinski knew "people in Chicago who have moved three or four times [to escape deteriorating neighborhoods] and now they are saying, 'I'm not going to move again. I'm going to make my stand here.' "[273] The liberal congressman blamed the reaction on "fear and lack of communication."[274] He noted that King's demonstrations had attracted unkempt people, and that when whites see them "they think these are the people who want to move in next door."[275]

Police Superintendent Wilson stated that Chicago's crime rate had risen 25 per cent since the demonstrations began. He linked the rise in crime to the need to assign hundreds of policemen to the protest marches.[276] Earlier, Wilson disclosed that patrolmen had been resigning in increasing numbers since the demonstrations began because of the "distasteful" work of protecting marchers.[277]

As the white reaction against the marches increased in fury and violence, demands grew for a halt to demonstrations. Archbishop Cody, spiritual leader of the area's three million Roman Catholics, appealed for an end to the marches.[278] The Archbishop blamed the "shameful reactions of some" for the violence that marchers had recently faced. He stated, "It is truly sad, indeed deplorable, that the citizens should ever have to be asked to suspend the exercise of their rights because of the evil doing of others. However, in my opinion and in the opinion of many men of goodwill, such is the situation in which we now find ourselves."[279] And following a two-and-a-half hour meeting between Daley and 17 union leaders, these labor officials joined the Mayor in an appeal to halt protest marches.[280] Among those issuing this appeal was Robert Johnston, regional director of the United Automobile Workers, which had given strong support to the civil rights movement. "We must try to resolve the problem without more violence," Johnston said.[281] Daley wanted the civil rights leaders to sit down with city officials, mortgage bankers, labor leaders, real estate interests and religious figures in an effort to end the impasse.[282]

At about this time, the latest march into an all-white neighborhood had evoked little more than jeers and rock throwing.[283] Bevel commented that while the demonstration appeared comparatively peaceful, "there wasn't less animosity in Bogan, just 1,000 more police."[284] Another lieutenant of King's, Rev. Jesse Jackson, termed it "acquiescence, not peace." He said "religious and political leaders have told their people to act tame and suppress their hate and not to let it show on their faces."[285]

Arrangements were now being made for King to meet with real estate, civic and political leaders.[286] But far from abating, the civil rights pressure escalated to an all-time high in community tensions.

Civil rights leaders now announced that they would demonstrate simultaneously in three all-white neighborhoods.[287] The Chicago Police Department was already reeling under the Herculean burden of protecting demonstrators in a single neighborhood; whether they could now protect marchers in three neighborhoods at the same time, and simultaneously preserve law and order in the rest of the city, was a question that assumed virtually crisis proportions.

King rejected Daley's plea for a moratorium on the marches. After a ten-hour meeting with the mayor and the Chicago Board of Real Estate, he said that city and realty spokesmen had not guaranteed open occupancy, so he would not call a moratorium.[288] The mayor made a television address in which he charged that "extremists of the Right and Left" had provoked much of the violence in the city. Daley said the extremists "live out of the community, out of the county, and in many instances out of the state." He said he had told King that a continuation of the demonstrations "would only serve as a magnet to the hate groups, whose only desire is to stir up racial violence and disorder." The mayor stated, "I have repeatedly appealed for voluntary recognition of the rights of others and to end the kind of street demonstrations which have made it impossible for the police department to adequately protect the lives and property of all citizens."[289] Unable to persuade King to modify his position, Daley no longer could afford the luxury of options; there was one course, and only one course, that he could reasonably pursue.

On August 19, 1966, the city of Chicago went to court for an injunction limiting the number and size of civil rights demonstrations.[290] The suit named Martin Luther King, his Southern Christian Leadership Conference and Al Raby's Coordinating Council of Community Organizations as defendants.[291] The city's suit asserted that if simultaneous marches continued, "it will be impossible for the police department to protect the defendants, the marchers, the public and the private property of the more than 3,500,000 citizens of the city." The suit contended that the city faced "a clear and present danger of riot" if multiple marches were not stopped.[292]

Two hours after the city filed suit, the Cook County Circuit Court granted a temporary injunction.[293] The injunction restrained King and his associates from holding marches in more than one area of the city on any one day, having more than 500 persons in a march, holding a march at night or during traffic rush hours, and holding a march without giving 24 hours notice to the police.[294] King labeled the action "a tragic expression of bad faith on the part of the city" and asserted, "We have violated injunctions in the South and may have to here."[295] He denounced it as "unconstitutional and unfair" and said that no injunction imposed on his Southern Christian Leadership Conference in the South in the past had been as restrictive.[296]

What would King's next step be? A none-too-veiled hint came from one of his top aides, the Rev. Andrew J. Young. Openly skeptical that King would win concessions at a meeting with key officials, Young had commented, "We're not too hopeful. We haven't been able to put on enough pressure yet. In Birmingham and Selma we almost needed martial law before we got anywhere."[297]

Now King was ready to unleash his ultimate confrontation weapon. The day after the injunction, he announced that in a week's time the civil rights demonstrators would march in Cicero.[298] This all-white suburban town was considered a racial tinderbox. The last time a Negro family tried to move into a flat in Cicero, in 1951, the event touched off a race riot. A mob of 5,000 whites burned the family's belongings and heavily damaged the apartment building. The rioting was halted only by calling up the National Guard. The Negro family was finally forced to move out of Cicero.[299]

Cook County Sheriff Richard B. Ogilvie said the National Guard would be needed again if King carried out his intentions. He told a news conference that Cicero's reaction would make some of the previous marches "look like a tea party."[300] The sheriff said he had sent a telegram to King, urging him to abandon his plan "in the interest of public safety." He said race hatred remained as strong as ever in this all-white middle class suburb, creating an "extremely sensitive" and "volatile" situation.[301] King refused to cancel the march. He conceded that Cicero might be the most racially sensitive of any Chicago area in which marches had been held. "But we feel," he said, "that if Chicago is to be an open city then metropolitan Chicago will have to resolve this problem. And Cicero is part of metropolitan Chicago."[302]

Cicero had less than 100 men on its police force, with a 30-man reserve.[303] Chicago had been using half its more than 10,000 policemen to maintain order during the recent Negro demonstrations.[304] Cicero's town attorney, Christy Berkos, said that he and Sheriff Ogilvie would apply for an injunction unless King called off the march or Governor Kerner sent in the Illinois National Guard.[305] Berkos wired Governor Kerner that "the probability of danger and destruction to human life and property now has become a certainty, and all efforts of the Cicero Police Department to maintain law and order would be futile."[306] At the same time, town officials denied an application from the American Nazi Party to hold a rally in front of Cicero Town Hall.[307]

Governor Kerner agreed to call up the National Guard to assist the Cicero Police in preventing clashes.[308] King's reply must have evoked gales of mirth South of the Mason-Dixon line. To the acute embarrassment of many a Northern liberal, King stated:

We appreciate Governor Kerner's concern for the protection of our march into Cicero on Sunday and his feeling that it was necessary to call out the National Guard. It is tragic, however, that we can march into Southern bastions of segregation, such as Mississippi, without armed military protection, but cannot march peacefully into a Northern suburb such as Cicero without armed escort of Guardsmen.[309]

The threat of a march into Cicero provided the remorseless pressure Rev. Young had advocated. Two days later, King and his assistants reached a unanimous agreement with Mayor Daley and Ross Beatty, head of the Chicago Real Estate Board, on a ten-point program designed to end alleged discrimination in residential renting and sales.[310] King hailed the accord as "the most significant program ever conceived to make open housing a reality in the metropolitan area."[311]

These were the terms of the agreement:

An announcement by the Chicago Real Estate Board that "in a significant departure from its traditional position" it would "withdraw all opposition to the philosophy of open occupancy legislation at the state level, provided it is applicable to owners as well as brokers."

Action by the Chicago Commission on Human Relations

against brokers who failed to comply with the city's fair housing laws, and brokers found guilty of violations would have their licenses suspended or revoked.

A pledge by the Chicago Housing Authority to begin a leasing program which placed families in their best available housing without regard to the racial character of the neighborhood.

A statement by the Cook County Board of Commissioners that the County Department of Public Aid would seek the best housing for aid recipients regardless of location, and that "the department will not be satisfied if recipients live in less satisfactory accommodations than would be available to them if they were of a different race, color or national origin."

A promise that in relocating families, the Department of Urban Renewal would place each family, regardless of color, in the best available housing, irrespective of its location.

An affirmation by the Cook County Council of Insured Savings Associations and the Chicago Mortgage Bankers Association that their policy was "to lend mortgage money to all qualified families without regard to race, for the purchase of housing anywhere in the metropolitan area."

A statement from the Department of Justice that Assistant Attorney General Roger W. Wilkins of the Community Relations Service would look into the question of continued service by the Federal Deposit Insurance Corporation and the Federal Savings and Loan Insurance Corporation to financial institutions found guilty of racial discrimination in providing public financial services.

Pledges from the Roman Catholic Archdiocese of Chicago, the Church Federation of Greater Chicago, the Chicago Board of Rabbis and the Union of American Hebrew Congregations, which co-sponsored the Chicago Conference on Religion and Race, to use their full strength "in effecting equal access to housing in the metropolitan area for all people."

Pledges from participating secular groups, including representatives of commerce, industry, banking and labor, to secure the support of their organizations for the fair housing program.

The formation by the Chicago Conference on Religion and

Race of a continuing body of representatives of religious and secular groups to "accept responsibility for the education and action programs necessary to achieve fair housing."[312]

King said that as a sign of the Chicago Freedom Movement's good faith that the agreement would be carried out, it would "defer" its plans to send 3,000 marchers into Cicero.[313] He planned to remain in Chicago, and work toward ending discrimination in employment and education. He maintained, "we are still a long way from our goal."[314]

At least one of these goals was made known the following day. Civil rights leaders had established a goal of at least one per cent Negro occupancy *in all 75 Chicago communities* by the end of eight months—April 30, 1967. That one per cent figure was to be the standard by which Negro leaders would measure the results of the ten-point agreement. There had been attempts to write the April 30 target date into the agreement, but civic leaders said they could not commit themselves to a rigid numerical goal. In addition, many rights leaders opposed the inclusion of the one per cent figure as a "quota." Nevertheless, the civil rights leaders were said to have regarded that percentage figure as "an internal checkout."[315]

Two months later, a confidential report was being circulated among members of the Chicago Freedom Movement. The report accused city leaders of broken promises on open housing in Chicago. Specifically, the report charged that four civic agencies had failed to live up to the commitments they made when the ten-point open housing agreement had been reached. A spokesman for the Chicago Freedom Movement said there was "an intentional slowdown or do-nothingism in fear of the political backlash" as well as legitimate organizational problems, the difficulty of breaking new ground, and "administrative incompetence." The "confidential" report (much of which was confidentially reprinted in the New York *Times*) included the following comments:

In the past five weeks, the follow-up committee has tested brokers in areas such as Hyde Park, South Shore, Bogan, Gage Park, Belmont Cragin, Austin and Rogers Park. In every case the white family was served and the Negro family discriminated against.

The Department of Urban Renewal committed itself to search out the best housing available, regardless of location, relocating families. In September, the department relocated 158 families, the great majority of whom were Negro, and it is not known that any were relocated into white areas. In August, the Chicago Housing Authority admitted that most of its housing for the elderly was in white areas and those buildings were all white occupancy. The authority committed itself to integrating these buildings. As of today, it seems that authority policy is still to have different waiting lists for elderly to enter authority buildings on the basis of neighborhood area.[316]

This "confidential" report was leaked to the public about a week before the general election in 1966.[317] Ed Marciniak, director of the Chicago Commission on Human Relations, said his agency had "done every one of the specific things" in the ten-point agreement except establish a year-round inspection program of real estate offices. He said that was "only a matter of days away."[318]

Mayor Daley vigorously denied that there had been any delay in implementing the agreement. He contended that "The story of foot-dragging was leaked to the press for purely political purposes."[319] Daley's consternation was perfectly understandable. The elections of 1966 were only a week away, and the Mayor's political antennae was picking up disquieting signals of a Republican upsurge. A survey by the Chicago *Sun-Times* found that "racially tense areas of Chicago and its suburbs are taking a Republican turn, especially to the benefit of Sheriff Richard B. Ogilvie [GOP candidate for president of the Cook County Board, which embraced Metropolitan Chicago]." Sheriff Ogilvie had achieved fame by arresting George Lincoln Rockwell and charging him with disorderly conduct; he had previously vowed to arrest the Nazi on sight. The Chicago paper found that in normally Democratic areas, Ogilvie and Republican Senatorial candidate Charles Percy were actually outpolling their Democratic opponents. In traditional Republican strongholds, the GOP candidates were running stronger than Republicans ever had before in major elections.[320] Daley's political machine was losing votes from white householders infuriated by the very existence of the ten-point agreement, and their opposite numbers, the rights militants, infuriated by the alleged failure to enforce its provisions. Clearly, it looked like a long, hard winter ahead for the Democratic faithful. And, in fact, when all the votes were counted, Chicago Sheriff Ogilvie proved himself the top Republican vote-getter in Cook County; he led the ticket, even outpolling Charles Percy.[321] Daley or no Daley, both Republicans carried Cook County.

Compounding the Democrats' woes was the rent strike in the 628-apartment Old Town Garden complex on the Near North Side. In the name of integration, the strikers, organized as the Tenants Action Council, began refusing to make rent payments; they charged that the owners were withholding service so whites in the integrated project would move. The end result, they contended, would be a higher-rent, all-Negro slum.[322]

The Old Town Garden complex was then 65 per cent Negro.[323] Three rent strikers had already been evicted and 127 more had been ordered out.[324] Strikers pitched tents nearby for storing furniture and housing tenants removed by court order.[325] Martin Luther King pledged the "full and absolute support" of the Chicago Freedom Movement to the rent strikers. King told a rally, "What you see here is the anatomy of the development of a slum. We mean to stop it in its tracks right now."[326]

The rent strike was supported by more than half the tenants, and did not end until the landlord agreed to sell the building to a church group when the necessary financing arrangements could be made.[327]

By November, 1966, more than 10,000 tenants in Chicago were members of various tenant unions.[328] Although none of these Chicago tenant unions was formally affiliated with the AFL-CIO, the federation's Industrial Union Department did serve as adviser to these groups.[329] The tenant unions used labor's traditional weapons—picketing and the strike, or the withholding of rents until the landlord agreed to bargain. Each building usually had a steward who organized and collected dues (usually from 10 cent to 25 cents a year), checked out tenants' complaints, and made sure the landlord carried through with promised improvements.[330] At one union meeting, a highly vocal participant was elected steward, only to move a week later because he was behind on his rent.[331]

Julian Levi, professor of urban studies at the University of Chicago, supported tenant unions, although he questioned the rent-strike tactic.[332] He believed that leases and other landlord-tenant pacts should contain specifically stated obligations and responsibilities for both parties, just as labor contracts did.[333] For centuries, of course, the tersest of leases has included this sine qua non—the solemn obligation of the landlord to give to the tenant physical possession of the property, and the equally solemn obligation of the tenant to pay the stipulated rental as long as he occupies the premises. What the rent-strikers sought was to hold the landlord to his end of the compact, while asserting the right to repudiate their own obligation. Indeed, what the tenants "union" leaders asserted was nothing less than the right to stage simultaneous sit-down strikes in hundreds or even thousands of apartments for any reason they wished, as long as they wished. It was a new variation on an old theme—a contractual disobedience that was proving surprisingly successful. By March, 1967, Martin Luther King was able to say that "Through more than a dozen collective-bargaining contracts gained by rent strike and negotiation, major property owners and management firms now are obligated to bring approximately 2,000 dwelling units up to code standards."[334]

At the same time, King disclosed that his Chicago Freedom Movement had been granted $4 million in low-cost, FHA-insured loan funds. This Federal money was to be used to acquire and rehabilitate some 500 family-sized apartments in three Chicago slum areas. Once rehabilitated, the buildings were to be turned over to housing cooperatives organized in each of the neighborhoods.[335]

For some time, one of the recurrent rallying cries of civil rights groups had been, "Take the Profit out of Slums." But did the slums really comprise profitable investments? We have already seen that the late John Bender had offered to *give* King the slum dwelling he had commandeered, if the Negro leader would also take over the mortgage payments. Was this simply an isolated occurrence involving one luckless slumlord? Not according to the Citizens Housing and Planning Council, a leading civic group in New York City. With a former contractor, Roger Starr, as its chairman, the Council had set out to prove that private capital could make an annual profit of at least 8 per cent by renovating and running slum housing. But after four years as the owner of two Manhattan tenements, the Citizens Housing and Planning Council glumly concluded that it was virtually impossible for a landlord to maintain decent living conditions in a slum area *and* make a fair profit.[336]

The Council's experiment began in late 1961, when Laurance Rockefeller donated a quarter of a million dollars to a non-profit foundation established to rehabilitate an old tenement at 92 Ridge Street, on New York's Lower East Side.[337] The Council assumed ownership of the building in December, 1962, and bought a second tenement building at 186 East Second Street.[338] Since Rockefeller's $250,000 donation was not enough to renovate both buildings, the Council took out a $45,000 mortgage.[339] The Ridge Street building was a six-story walk-up built around 1880, before indoor plumbing was required by statute.[340] The Council acquired the property for $15,500 and proceeded to spend $115,000 putting in new kitchens and bathrooms (there had been one hall toilet for every two families before renovation), replacing all electrical wiring and plumbing, replastering the public areas and patching and painting the apartment walls.[341]

Rents were almost tripled from about $23 a month for each apartment to about $65 a month.[342] As a result, tenants —unhappy over the bloated price tag of all this civic goodness—began moving out in droves. Starr disclosed that the building's largely Puerto Rican population had an annual turnover rate of 80 per cent.[343]

In spite of the rent increases, the building showed a net loss of $565.07 without depreciation, and $4,461.86 counting depreciation.[344] In the building, Starr pointed to broken windows, garbage a foot deep in the air shafts, defaced hallways and new mailboxes that already showed signs of being broken into, probably by narcotics addicts. Starr said, "The most discouraging thing is that we can't keep the building in very good condition—and we still lose money."[345]

He attributed the deficit mainly to vandalism, the high costs of maintenance and materials, and the inability to charge rents that would meet these costs. He stressed that the deficit existed even though the building had had tax abatement for 12 years, was not thoroughly rehabilitated, and paid a low rate of interest—5¼ per cent—on its mortgage.[346]

The other tenement on Second Street had been bought for $27,000, and $123,000 was spent on it for repairs that included the refurbishing of apartment walls. The building showed a cash profit of $1,647.09 the preceding year, Starr revealed, largely because it was in a better neighborhood and rents ran about $84 a month. He found vandalism less of a problem in that house because "The tenants there have a completely different attitude."[347]

In 1966, the Citizens Housing and Planning Council had made a cash profit of slightly more than $1,000 on an investment of almost $300,000. Counting depreciation, it lost $7,335 on the two buildings.[348] Starr declared, "It soon became clear that you couldn't make anything at all. It simply costs more money to keep up your property than you collect from rents at this level of the economic system."[349]

Starr was convinced that low-cost mortgages were not sufficient to attract private investment in the slums, and that some kind of outright grant was also needed.[350] He asserted, "Without subsidies, rehabilitation is a snare and a delusion. No reasonable person would invest money to rehabilitate buildings like the ones we own."[351] His solution was the all too familiar one—millions, if not billions, from Government's Horn of Plenty. Starr said that city, state, and Federal governments must provide huge subsidies to both landlords and tenants if the city's slums were ever going to be made habitable.[352] He believed that large rent supplements would be necessary to allow poor families to pay the rents the renovated buildings would require to remain a workable proposition.[353] He admitted that many decrepit slum buildings were not worth saving, but added, "the city cannot afford to tear them down, and these people have to have some place to live."[354]

Like practiced retrievers, liberals fairly leaped at this scent of greater government handouts. Not too surprisingly, many housing experts agreed with Starr that only massive government subsidies for tenants' rents and landlords' mortgages would make slum rehabilitation feasible in many areas.[355] And at about that point, the meeting of minds came to an abrupt halt. The new Housing and Development Administrator, Jason R. Nathan, termed the $300,000 outlay "piddling." He argued that the "building by building approach is not workable. Rehabilitation has to be on a vast scale encompassing entire neighborhoods."[356] His contention was upheld by Frederick W. Richmond, a philanthropist who had helped sponsor the rehabilitation of 37 tenements on 114th Street in Harlem.[357]

As for the vandalism in Starr's tenements, the fault was predictably shifted to that perennial punching bag, society. "Aren't these vandals really striking out at a lack of opportunity?" asked Nathan. And in a less than subtle hint that rent supplements were only the first step, he stated that "job training, recreational facilities and other services are also essential."[358] One of those who had worked with Starr on his experiment, Mrs. Hortense Gabel, blamed many of the problems on "bad management, of which I was a part" —a rather startling revelation, considering that Mrs. Gabel had once been New York City's Administrator of Rent and Rehabilitation.[359]

Starr's critics raved about the project on Harlem's 114th Street, where "vandalism is a minimal problem and there are no vacancies in the rehabilitated apartments."[360] But there was one crucially important difference: Starr was trying to operate at some kind of a profit; the 114th Street project was "not making a profit, but it was never intended to."[361]

The rehabilitation of minority slum areas might have seemed almost anti-social in the brave new world of integration. But it was generally agreed that even if every all-white neighborhood in every city had put out a welcome mat for Negroes, a sizable number would still have preferred to remain in the familiar surroundings of the ghetto. And rights chieftains were by no means excluded from this group. One Negro civil rights leader told Sydney Harris, of the Chicago *Daily News:* "Another reason we wouldn't care to live among you whites is that frankly you're pretty dull. Fact is, most of you are constipated. You talk tight, you walk tight, you think tight, you feel tight. It's just a drag spending a lot of time with you."[362]

This unidentified civil rights leader notwithstanding, the major thrust of the civil rights campaign was still in the area of open housing. It therefore became necessary to pose such rude questions as: Just how open would open housing be?

Certainly Morris Milgram, a pioneer in the field of integrated homes, was anything but an advocate of open housing. As far back as 1960, the New York *Post* recounted an anecdote in which this lifelong Socialist woke up in a cold sweat one night and told himself, "Milgram, you s.o.b., you're gonna wind up building houses that are just as segregated as anything that Senator Bilbo [a deceased Mississippi white supremacist] could hope for."[363] Milgram commented, "I knew right then that the only way to build integrated private housing successfully *was to set up quotas for Negro and white buyers*."[364] In other words, fight discrimination by discriminating. At that time, the key to Milgram's "controlled occupancy" was to set a quota in advance that ranged from 55 per cent to 75 per cent white, and 45 per cent to 25 per cent Negro.[365] In 1961, Milgram drew national attention when he tried to build an integrated development in Deerfield, Illinois. Local residents stopped him with a referendum that turned his site into a park.[366]

In 1966, Milgram had expanded his base of operations considerably; he was now manager of the Mutual Real Estate Investment Trust, a company which had been organized to purchase apartment buildings in all-white neighborhoods with the specific purpose of integrating them.[367] Some 1,800 investors had subscribed $1.6 million.[368] That year, his company bought three apartment buildings.[369]

All three apartment buildings were located in New York City,[370] and a captious critic might have reminded Milgram that his "benign quota" was against the law. In New York State, Milgram's quota system quite obviously violated state law against discrimination. It therefore became necessary for government officials and private developers seeking integration to approach the problem with—as the New York *Times* delicately phrased it—"subtlety."[371] Milgram's subtle approach was to achieve similar results to an outright quota through a "selective requirement" that avoided the problem of having to turn anyone down.[372] When a Negro tenant was wanted, local fair-housing groups were approached. The opening was not advertised generally. But when both white and Negro tenants were wanted, then the apartments were generally advertised.[373] In his own defense, Milgram cited the old truism that integrated buildings and developments have "tipping points"—ratios of Negro to white tenants beyond which the whites move out, and the project becomes another Negro ghetto.[374] But the fact still remained that one form of discrimination was simply being substituted for another. Negroes were still being actively recruited for certain apartments because they were Negroes, and whites for other dwellings because they were white.

Milgram told a stockholders meeting that the three buildings were in Astoria and Forest Hills, Queens, and on Ocean Parkway in Brooklyn.[375] But he refused to make public the actual addresses of the buildings. "We feel that people in integrated buildings are entitled to the same privacy as those in segregated buildings," Milgram told the meeting. "We don't want reporters knocking on the doors and photographers harassing the tenants."[376] And just possibly, Milgram did not want embarrassed state investigators knocking on his door and asking him such harassing questions as whether or not he was complying with the anti-discrimination laws.

From all accounts, the Mutual Real Estate Investment Trust was a going concern. The three apartment houses were purchased for a total of $2.2 million.[377] Now the investment trust was seeking properties in Chicago, Washington, D.C., Los Angeles and St. Louis.[378]

White opposition to housing integration was not confined to jaundiced members of the backlash. Assistant Professor Frances Fox Piven and Professor Richard A. Cloward of the Columbia University School of Social Work collaborated on a ringing dissent, in an article titled "The Case Against Urban Desegregation."[379] Piven and Cloward were convinced that "after several decades of civil rights struggle, the lot of the Negro urban poor has actually worsened in some respects . . ."[380] The professors stressed the growing hopelessness of urban integration in numerical terms. They noted that "Over the next decade or two many central cities could well become predominantly Negro, if the movement of Negroes into the city and the exodus of whites to the suburbs continue, and if the higher Negro birthrate persists."[381] Then they took cognizance of a paper George Schermer had presented to the National Committee Against Discrimination in Housing—a paper in which Schermer had estimated the number of people who would have to be moved each year to insure that a 50-50 population balance would exist in Washington, D.C., in the year 2000. (At the time the paper was presented, Washington was 63 per cent Negro.) Assuming that migration trends and birthrates remained constant, Schermer estimated that twelve thousand nonwhite families would have to be dispersed to suburban areas and four thousand white families induced to return to the District of Columbia *every year until 2000*.[382] So the integration goal would remain as illusory as ever. The educators were not convinced of the effectiveness of legal reforms; they pointed out that "many such reforms were won years before the civil rights movement but have failed completely to retard segregation. Racial zoning ordinances, for example, were struck down by the courts in 1917."[383]

Piven and Cloward were not overly enthusiastic about housing subsidies as a means of promoting integration. They wrote, "It is found that when large numbers of tenants are Negro, low-income whites desert the projects or are reluctant to apply. Projects thus tend to become high-rise brick ghettos rather than outposts of integrated living. Programs to further integration by locating projects in outlying white communities have provoked even more serious opposition. Only when white tenants predominate has any degree of community tolerance resulted."[384] The professors' most stinging salvos were reserved for urban redevelopment, which, they charged, had "resulted in the destruction of low-rental housing and low-income communities, so that many poor people are pushed farther into the ghetto."[385] They revealed that the Federal urban renewal program and the Federal highway program had together demolished close to 700,000 units, most of which were low rental, in less than 15 years.[386] They too believed that "massive subsidies must be granted for new and rehabilitated housing in the ghettos and slums."[387]

The sociological shock treatment inherent in their cold hard statistics was in no way mitigated by Piven and Cloward's conclusion: "If the Negro is to develop the power to enter the mainstream of American life, it is separatism—not integration—that will be essential to achieve results in certain institutional arenas."[388] As delineated in the article, this "separatism" had some striking points of resemblance to Stokely Carmichael's "Black Power."

The article appeared in *Social Work* magazine in January, 1967—about the time the New York *Times* admitted that not quite everything was coming up roses in Chicago's open housing circles. The grim headline told part of it: *Dr. King Plagued by Resistance and Apathy in Chicago Slums.* And an equally somber subheading told the rest: *Rights Leader's Aides Cite Some Gains But Find Problems of Northern Ghetto Tougher Than Those in the South.*[389] King had summoned Hosea Williams from the Atlanta headquarters of the Southern Christian Leadership Conference to mobilize "political power in the Negro community." In his first month there, Williams said, "I don't like Chicago. We're used to working with people who want to be freed. The Chicago Negro isn't concerned about what the power structure is doing to him. It's cold here and I'm having a lot of problems."[390] Leon Hall reported after canvassing a typical South Side block of rundown tenements, "One lady came at me with an icepick." He asserted, "This is worse than Alabama. At least you have some fresh air there."[391] Williams candidly admitted "Our time schedule is way off base, largely because of division in the Negro leadership."[392] Pouring salt on the wounds was the fact that the ten-point agreement had yet to be implemented.[393] Some civil rights skeptics charged that the mayor—seeking a fourth term on April 4—had to cope with a potential backlash from white ethnic groups, and so would go no further than politically necessary toward achievement of civil rights goals.[394] In addition, Albert Raby of the Coordinating Council of Community Organizations admitted that the long campaign to desegregate Chicago's schools and upgrade ghetto education had been a "total failure" so far.[395] It was beginning to look as if all Martin Luther King had to show for his marching feet was calluses.

One of Williams' most memorable contributions to the campaign was to make evident his enmity toward Mayor Daley. Three months before the election he told a questioner, "There is no difference between the Daley machine in Chicago and the Wallace machine in Alabama, sugar. Both are out to keep you in slavery."[396] Williams may have convinced "sugar," but very few others bought the comparison. In his campaign for re-election, Mayor Daley was supported by all four major newspapers—the Chicago News, the Chicago Tribune, the Chicago Sun-Times, and Chicago's American. The Mayor was endorsed by both the Negro newspaper, the Chicago Defender, and the Polish Daily News.[397] Several radio and television stations also endorsed Daley, as did the Negro magazines published in Chicago, Jet and Ebony.[398] On Election Day, Daley defeated his Republican opponent by 516,208 votes, a record plurality, representing 72.8 per cent of the votes cast.[399] He carried all 50 wards.[400] A second opponent, Dick Gregory, the Negro nightclub comedian, running on a frankly anti-Daley slate, got less than two per cent of the total as an independent write-in candidate.[401]

In a victory statement, Daley pledged to eliminate "every slum in the city" by the end of 1967, and to provide equality of opportunity in jobs, schools, housing and recreation. But he warned any who might have thoughts of repeating the riots that "there will be law and order in Chicago as long as I'm mayor."[402] As for the civil rights forces, a reporter noted that "Workers for the Rev. Dr. Martin Luther King's Southern Christian Leadership Conference conducted a voter registration drive in the ghettos to mobilize anti-Daley sentiment, but pulled out with little to show for their efforts."[403]

About two weeks after Daley's triumph, the leader of a group of local Negro ministers called on King to stop his civil rights marches and leave Chicago.[404] The blunt critique was expressed by the Rev. Henry Mitchell, pastor of the North Star Missionary Baptist Church, at a news conference with about a dozen other ministers who said they spoke for 50,000 Chicago Negroes. Rev. Mitchell said the civil rights marches that King had led had "created hate." He labeled King an "outsider" and said he had been a failure in Chicago. Finally, he urged that King "stay in Alabama."[405]

Two months later, the National Association for the Advancement of Colored People formally broke with King's Chicago Freedom Movement.[406] Sidney Finley, regional director of the NAACP, said that the Chicago branch had withdrawn from the CCCO earlier in the year.[407] The split had actually begun the preceding summer, when King led the open-housing marches. The Rev. Carl Fuqua, then executive secretary of the Chicago branch of the NAACP, denounced the marches as useless. When rioting occurred on the West Side, Rev. Fuqua said the time had come for King to leave town.[408] The New York *Times* noted that the NAACP had been the largest organization in the Coordinating Council of Community Organizations and revealed that "Some other groups remain members in name only, though not in all cases because of disagreement over the Chicago role and effectiveness of Dr. King."[409]

Meanwhile, the House Committee on Un-American Activities had been quietly uncovering startling evidence that a number of riots in recent years had been planned in detail by professional black nationalists and pro-Communists.[410] The committee staff closely examined riots in 1965 and 1966 in Chicago. An undercover agent gave HCUA sworn testimony that the 1965 riot was "deliberately planned in advance by certain leaders of ACT, a militant civil rights group who are also members of the Revolutionary Action Movement and are using ACT as a RAM front."[411] The HCUA study said that ACT leaders instructed their followers in the techniques of guerrilla warfare, "used teen-age gangs to carry out violence, and attended classes in Marxism conducted by Ishmael Flory, a member of the National Negro Commission of the Communist Party."[412] The House committee also blamed ACT for the Chicago riots that broke out July 12, 1966—just a few days after King's speech in Soldier Field. It said Douglas Andrews, identified as an ACT leader who had been involved in the 1965 riot, "is known to have stated on July 13 that he met with teen-age gangs the day before and arrangements had been made for them to riot in certain areas; that he was going to contact the top leader of the youth gangs to get them to start using Molotov cocktails; and that he was going to mix Molotov cocktails in a garage in the rear of his home."[413]

In all fairness, it must be reiterated that ACT was not a part of the Coordinating Council of Community Organizations. But it must also be reiterated that however lofty the motives, King's group was showing pictures of the Los Angeles riots to these youth gangs, knowing their reputation for violence, *before* the Chicago riots took place.

Chicago was not precisely Martin Luther King's Waterloo. But it was as close to a rout as anything he had seen since the painful days in Albany, Georgia. On the whole, he was probably not overcome with grief at the thought of bringing his formal campaign to a close and looking elsewhere for greener racial pastures. He found his next target area, and was to revert to the first and most effective weapon he had ever used—the one weapon in his loving arsenal that did not require an omnipresent Federal government for its success. In a sense, Martin Luther King was to come full circle in 1967, with the threat of a massive boycott that would be the steel-plated backbone of Operation Breadbasket.

CHAPTER 8

1967: Operation Breadbasket

In the year and a half that the author has spent poring over much of the literature of the civil rights movement, one theme keeps recurring—the problem of jobs. Delight is expressed over the passage of the civil rights acts, the silencing of the Southern senatorial filibusters, the growing political muscle of (for all practical purposes) a Negro voting bloc; but again and again, the talk, the fears, the apprehensions revolve about employment. Somewhere along the way, the author came across a most succinct quote by a ghetto dweller, who said, "What Ralph Bunche eats doesn't fill my stomach." This is the crux of the problem, and it is one that affects Negro militants and moderates alike in every age bracket, in every town and city. Forgetting the glittering successes of the few Negro notables who "made it," and made it big, what about the Negroes with an indifferent educational background and a less than impressive work history? Are they getting jobs? Can they hold on to the jobs they get? Can they earn a decent living for their families? What is being done for them? And much more to the point, what are they doing for themselves?

One of the most intriguing historical speculations is to ponder what the life of Negroes in America might have been if their leaders had followed the precepts of Booker T.

Washington down through the years. Once idolized by his people, his name is not often mentioned today; he has been consigned to the rubbish heap of Uncle Tomism by the militants of our time, and his teachings have been largely forgotten. But occasionally a Negro moderate takes his courage in both hands, and actually dares to discuss and defend this great teacher and great American. Thus, in May, 1964, *Negro Digest* published an article titled: "Booker T. Washington, His Defense and Vindication," written by Gordon B. Hancock, who organized the departments of sociology and economics at Virginia Union and had been a professor there for 31 years.[1] Professor Hancock felt that in one of the most trying times in American Negro history, Washington, and only Washington, arrived on the scene as "A Man With A Plan." Washington's plan was as simple as this: Having done the South's hard labor for hundreds of years, the Negro's "foot was in the door," and all he had to do was to keep pushing. Washington argued that the Negro's labor was his only commodity, and if this could be sold to advantage the Negro could gradually rise by his own efforts. This was his "gospel" of industrial education and the dignity of labor. He wanted to take the foothold Negroes had in the economic life of the nation, through his primacy in the manual arts, and exploit it to the utmost; to sell the use of proficient hands until Negroes qualified themselves to sell the product of their brains; to make the very most of their opportunities in the manual arts until they gathered strength and prepared themselves for positions of their liking.[2]

Professor Hancock wondered aloud:

According to the teachings and doctrine of Booker T. Washington, just suppose he could have sold his idea to the Negro race through its leaders! The Negro cooks would be the owners of our great eating places and establishments. Our bricklayers and carpenters would be our great contractors now. Our launderers would have charge of the great laundry industry. Instead of quarreling and fighting for the jobs that are becoming fewer and fewer by reason of competition and automation, we would now be commanding those jobs.[3]

Dr. Hancock noted that "Negro leadership has utterly rejected Washington's plan of using the manual arts and occupations as means of gaining positions, but nobody seems to be coming up with a plan to feed the Negro while he fights."[4] He recognized that the animosity toward Washington was based on the Exposition speech he made in Atlanta, when he said, "In things economic, the races in the South could be as one as the fist, but in things social they could be as separate as the fingers." Hancock asked, "What else could he have said at the time? For him to have taken the position that Martin Luther King, Jr. is taking now and saying what Negroes on every corner are saying would have meant annihilation for the Negro race."[5] The professor added that despite gains and court decisions, there was still little evidence that Negroes and whites of the South would not continue to live as one as the fist "in things economic" and as separate as fingers on the hand "in things social."[6]

Curiously, much the same admiring tribute to the vision of Booker T. Washington could be found in the pages of the ultra-militant Negro magazine, *Liberator*. A writer in that magazine lauded Washington as the man who established Tuskegee and later instituted a business program to promote cooperative business activities among his people. He wrote that Washington "stimulated the people to save for investment. He offered industrial education to the young people of his day and prepared them to become producers as well as consumers."[7] The *Liberator* writer paid homage to Washington for teaching Negroes "self-reliance and self-sufficiency. He taught them to learn the mechanics of better farming and construction work. He influenced them to improve their art in cooking, sewing, tailoring, weaving and other arts. He inspired them to purchase land, build homes and own productive enterprises."[8]

If the reader has ever perused a copy of *Liberator*, he may find this next statement little short of incredible; he is therefore invited to convince himself that in the July, 1967, issue, this magazine *attacked* Dr. W. E. B. DuBois for his destruction of the Washington doctrine. The *Liberator* writer attacked DuBois' weakening of "Dr. Washington's framework for Black Advancement. He destroyed the people's initiative and desire to pull themselves up by their own bootstraps."[9]

In recent days, a few still remember the Booker T. Washington program, although it has become less and less fashionable to mention its founding father. Thus, in 1965, Dr. Rudolph Jones, President of Fayetteville State College in North Carolina, told a meeting, "Somehow we must get it across to our young people that all work is honorable—that you do not have to be a doctor or lawyer or preacher or teacher to earn a respectable living. We must point out to them and make them aware of the many jobs in business and industries—the many jobs above the level of maid and janitor—in the downtown stores. We must convince them that they can qualify for these jobs by taking one- and two-year business courses, by going to various community colleges and technical institutes so wisely provided by our great state. In Fayetteville, graduates at the Technical Institute are placed as fast as they complete the courses. *I regret to say, however, that very few of my race are enrolled in these courses.*"[10]

Dr. Jones considered it self-evident that "it means little to be permitted to stay in a hotel if one does not have the money to pay for the night's lodging, or to be permitted to eat in a restaurant if one does not have the price of a steak dinner."[11] Amid all the demonstrations, all the sit-ins, lie-ins and jail-ins, one crucially important question should have been asked over and over again, so loudly and so insistently that an answer would finally be forced out into the public scrutiny. That question was: exactly what was Martin Luther King doing to train and educate his people to qualify for employment in the new, ever more complex and bewildering job market?

In 1962, while King was locking horns with Laurie Pritchett in Albany, Georgia, the New York *Times* was reporting that in employment, "the Negroes are in a race with time, and they know it."[12] The *Times* underscored the fact that Negroes "are still concentrated heavily in industries and occupations that are dwindling or not expanding. This is a big reason why the unemployment rate for Negroes is 11.4 per cent—more than twice that of whites."[13]

The *Times* grimly predicted, "Unless Negroes are able to make rapid and major inroads into expanding areas of employment, it would appear that many of them will become permanent candidates for relief."[14]

In 1964, Edwin C. Berry, executive director of the Chicago Urban League, was hammering away at this same theme. He admitted that in his own Chicago there had been a dramatic breakthrough in some hitherto inaccessible white-collar occupations. He wrote: "Today, we find Chicago Loop businesses affirmatively seeking Negro professional, clerical and technical help. . . . In short, we are dealing with thousands of employers who are new to the hiring of Negro workers and the same is going on all over the North. . . . In general we have noted that almost every major firm in Chicago is asking for some talented and skilled Negroes."[15] But he feared that "unemployment will increase; for the displacement of labor by machines will continue while the labor force grows at an accelerated rate as the post-war baby boom hits the labor market. A business recession would further complicate the picture and diminish the number of jobs."[16] The Urban League official came up with this statistical shocker: "Depending upon the general level of employment, one-third to one-half of the urban Negroes under current conditions are in a position to take advantage of new employment opportunities. This means also that under current conditions one-half to two-thirds are walled off from a secure position in the labor market."[17] Berry's solution would have been fiscally catastrophic; he proposed the establishment of "a massive crash-crisis program of the magnitude of the Marshall Plan. . ."[18] In Chicago alone, Berry coolly estimated that "we would have to spend a minimum of a half a billion dollars a year for the next 20 years."[19] But Berry's demands were almost Uriah Heep-like in humility, compared with that quite seriously proposed by a coalition of civil rights, religious and labor leaders in 1966. This group proposed no less than a "freedom budget for all Americans" in the amount of $185 billion to end poverty in the United States in the next ten years.[20] Martin Luther King indicated that his Southern Christian Leadership Conference might sponsor nationwide demonstrations to gain support for the plan.[21]

As early as 1963, private industry was practically moving mountains to find qualified Negro applicants, and meeting a most discouraging response. James J. McFadden, acting commissioner of labor in New York City, conceded, "There's no question about it—there is a shortage of qualified Negroes for professional and semi-professional jobs."[22] In Detroit, an employment agency reported that one company had a standing request to interview any college-trained Negro.[23] In the insurance field, the director of manpower development for the Equitable Life Assurance Society said, "I talked recently to the head of the personnel department of a large chemical company. He told me he had searched the 70 highest-ranking Negro colleges without finding a single qualified engineering applicant."[24] A California utility company asked the NAACP to help find Negro workers for jobs above the lower level. The NAACP sent 30 applicants. Fourteen failed the first test; all the others failed subsequent tests.[25] In San Francisco, the manager of an employment agency commented, "We have found that the majority of Negro applicants—even those with high school diplomas—couldn't pass the simplest clerical tests. They are not equipping themselves."[26]

The situation was no different in Philadelphia. What was different was the far-seeing vision of one man who transformed hopeless unemployment into gainful employment in an incredibly short period of time. The number involved was small, but the potential—and implications for the future —were virtually limitless.

In 1964, Philadelphia had a hard core of about 123,000 unemployed.[27] A Chamber of Commerce survey the preceding year found 15,000 skilled jobs open, and a potential demand, from expansion, of some 50,000 more.[28] The head of the local Manpower Utilization Commission had found some 4,000 certified job vacancies within the city limits.[29] But in the preceding year and a half, fewer than 1,400 workers were trained under the city's $7 million manpower grant, and only half of them got jobs.[30] This worked out to about $5,000 for each trainee.[31]

The dismal results of this government training program were not lost on Philadelphia's Negro leaders, among them the Reverend Leon Sullivan, pastor of the Zion Baptist Church. By any criteria, Sullivan was one of the most militant of all the city's civil rights leaders, and more than lived up to his nickname "The Lion of Zion." Sullivan was the leader of some 400 Philadelphia Negro ministers—the spiritual leaders of some 250,000 parishioners—who, in years past, had conducted 24 boycotts against some of the country's biggest distributors of soft drinks, foods, gasoline, and other consumer goods, and won them all.[32] In four years time, through the threat of selective buying, the ministers opened up more than 3,000 new and better jobs to Philadelphia Negroes without a single picket line or sit-in or a penny spent on litigation.[33]

Skilled Negroes were hired, but the ministers soon had to face the fact that there simply weren't enough skilled Negroes.[34] Sullivan wasted little time lambasting society or bewailing the lot of the unskilled Negro in urban America. This was a problem that no amount of rhetoric or invective would begin to solve. It was time to train Negroes to meet the demands of the job market, and there was literally no time to lose.

Accordingly, in July, 1963, Rev. Sullivan announced his plans for a training center; at the time of his announcement, he had no funds, no building, no equipment, and no teachers[35]—nothing but a stubborn man's faith in a better future for his people.

Six months later, the center formally opened. A friendly councilman got the city council to lease Sullivan an abandoned police station in a shabby part of Philadelphia for a dollar a year.[36] Thacher Longstreth, executive director of the Philadelphia Chamber of Commerce, recalled, "It was like a barn raising. Different groups of colored people each did some of the work to get the building ready. Negroes did it all themselves. This was important."[37]

The first class started on March 2, 1964, with classes in power sewing, restaurant practices, drafting and electronics.[38] Soon classes in laboratory chemistry, machine tooling, and sheet-metal work were added.[39] By holding classes day and night, close to 300 could be trained at a time, and classes were packed.[40] Even in that first year of operation, there was a waiting list of 4,500.[41] The training center was named the Opportunities Industrialization Center, or OIC, and the center was so successful that the then-head of the Area Redevelopment Administration and the chairman of the Industry Advisory Council to the President's Committee on Equal Employment Opportunity arranged for Sullivan to tell other people how to set up similar centers in their cities.[42]

From the outset, industrial advisers helped Sullivan decide which jobs were most in demand, and helped him plan courses that would give trainees the necessary special training and up-to-date skills.[43] For example, the Philadelphia branch of the Automatic Retailers of America—who distributed food to hospitals, schools, and factories—helped the center make new up-dated plans for training waitresses and counter girls, and paid for a large part of the streamlined kitchen and cafeteria equipment they recommended. Philco gave electronic equipment and manuals. Pennsalt and General Electric donated tools and heavy machinery for the machine-shop course.[44] That first year of operation, Philadelphia industry contributed a quarter of a million dollars in equipment and thousands more in cash.[45] Negro professional and business men contributed more than $50,000 and a door-to-door canvass in Negro neighborhoods raised another $50,000 in small pledges.[46] With this money and the backing of industry, the OIC applied to the Ford Foundation for a grant of $200,000 and received it soon after classes started.[47]

The Center now had a yearly budget of $300,000.[48] In sharp contrast to Federal training programs, which paid subsistence allowances, the OIC charged $25 per course, mostly for the sake of the applicant's self-respect.[49] But no one unable to pay was turned away.[50]

About a third of the trainees were drawn in by a crew of recruiters who toured pool halls, bars and cafes where out-of-work men were likely to gather.[51] As recently as January, 1968, OIC trainees were still forbidden to take any pay for training, as was done in other programs. Rev. Sullivan explained, "I want to be sure the people are not going to train just so they can get $40 or $70 a week. OIC is no WPA program. A man realizes that if he stays with the program there will be a job at the end."[52] This was no idle boast. As of early 1968, OIC had trained and found jobs for more than 4,000 men and women—80 per cent of its graduates. This ranked far ahead of most other job-training programs.[53]

Unlike Federal job training programs which invariably cost thousands of dollars per trainee, the OIC trained students for an average cost of about $550.[54] The average student was in his twenties, although there were some teen-agers and some in their fifties and sixties.[55] Every bit as important as job-training, students were taught such simple things as how to stand and sit and shake hands, how to dress and talk and present themselves acceptably. Boys in drafting class were expected to wear jackets and ties.[56] Teachers worked with all students in the three R's as well.[57]

A retired executive vice president of the Chamber of

Commerce hailed the project as "by far the greatest of its kind anywhere in the country." He stressed, "The ideas were their [the Negroes'] own. That is what is so beautiful about it. They recognized the need."[58]

By the end of the first year of operation, the OIC had:

Established a program in which 750 persons were trained annually.

Set up a "feeder" or pre-job training program designed to maintain academic incentive and to provide additional educational assistance for about 5,500 applicants on the waiting list.

Received backing as a pilot project in the Federal anti-poverty program.[59]

The OIC could point with well-deserved pride to the climb upward of a number of their students. One father of four was an unemployed laborer on public assistance when he took the course. After training at the center to be a cook, he became the cook and night manager at a small restaurant.[60] Another student, a former truck driver, was trying to support a wife and child on $50 a week; after taking the course, he qualified for a spot-welding job and earned, with overtime, between $115 and $140 weekly.[61] Civil rights leader Bayard Rustin called OIC the most revolutionary approach to Negro equality in the economic field to come along in a century.[62] By early 1967, OIC was operating on a $2 million budget and the Federal government was now providing some 85 per cent of the funds.[63] And Sullivan proudly disclosed, "Our own people, our staff, pledged $25,000 a year. That's how deeply they believe in this work."[64] Sullivan's right-hand man, the Rev. Thomas J. Ritter, said, "We don't know what drop-out means here. And we don't pay allowances; we don't have to. Many of our people walk 20 blocks to come here to learn."[65]

Assistance from private industry continued unabated. The girls in the electronics assembly class were using components and chassis units donated by a local hi-fi assembler.

Univac gave a $350,000 solid-state computer to be used for technical training. A Philadelphia philanthropist turned over a six-story building, without even asking the usual dollar a year for it.[66]

Sullivan pointed out that since 97 per cent of his students were classified as poor, OIC had added $9,000,000 to Philadelphia's consumer purchasing, and saved the state of Pennsylvania $2,000,000 in welfare costs.[67] OIC now had six centers around the city,[68] and in the imitation that was the sincerest form of flattery, the Federal government had given $5,100,000 for OIC centers in eight other cities, from Little Rock to Oklahoma City and Washington, D.C.[69] Besides this, 65 additional cities were running their own OIC operations without Federal help in such places as New Haven, Boston, Watts, Cleveland and Camden.[70]

Compared with this record of solid achievement by the OIC, Martin Luther King's "Operation Breadbasket" becomes a form of economic retrogression—a mental attitude about Big Business as hopelessly outdated as Matthew Josephson's *The Robber Barons*. The idea of an economic boycott was nothing new. In *Black Metropolis*, co-authors St. Clair Drake and Horace Cayton told how "A group of ragged pickets walking in front of a Black Belt chain store in the fall of 1929 signalized the beginning of a movement which stirred Black Metropolis as nothing had done since the [1919] Race Riot.[71] The attention of Negroes all over the country fastened on Chicago's 'Spend Your Money Where You Can Work' Campaign." This economic attack against the Woolworth stores resulted in a major victory, and "convinced the Negro community that the boycott was a useful weapon."[72]

In a more contemporary setting, *Ebony* reported, "The Operation Breadbasket method of attacking employment discrimination was first observed by Dr. King in the city of Philadelphia six years ago, and subsequently introduced to the Atlanta-based staff by a Philadelphia minister."[73] If the minister was not Rev. Leon Sullivan, it was almost

surely one of the members of the boycott group of which he
was leader before he formed the Opportunities Industrialization Center. *Ebony* wrote that shortly thereafter, Operation
Breadbasket "was under way in Atlanta and a number of
smaller Southern cities."[74] But the Negro magazine felt
that the 1929 Chicago Boycott—which had engaged the
support of churches and community organizations—could
really be considered the progenitor of Operation Breadbasket.[75]

What was—and is—Operation Breadbasket? Exactly no
more and no less than Martin Luther King wanted it to be.
In 1964—possibly seeking to allay fears of some of his
more moderate supporters—King wrote, "Negroes certainly
do not want nor could they find the path to freedom by
taking jobs from the white man. Instead, they want the
white man to collaborate with them in making new jobs.
This is the key point. Our economy, our resources are well
able to provide full employment."[76] But as we shall see,
the key point of Operation Breadbasket *in actual practice*
is that Negroes be hired for certain jobs for the principal,
if not sole reason that they are Negroes—and that to this
extent, certain specified numbers of jobs are withdrawn from
the general labor market and denied to whites.

In practice, Operation Breadbasket called for using boycotts, picketing, marches, and other tactics against selected
companies to force them to hire and upgrade Negroes.

First the Southern Christian Leadership Conference accumulated relevant data on the target company, such as its
Negro employment policies and Negro market penetration
—from the company itself, if it was willing to cooperate.
Then a delegation called on the company with specific demands. Usually these were for hiring unemployed Negroes
and upgrading Negroes already on the payroll. If the demands were resisted, the next step was negotiating with the
company. This might include some attempt at broadening
company executives' understanding of Negro problems, even
getting company officials to visit Negro slums. If negotiation failed, then the ministers organized boycotts—or as

SCLC preferred to call them, "selective buying" campaigns —in the Negro community.[77] As it developed, the boycotters' batting average ran very close to 1.000.

To head the northern division of Operation Breadbasket, King chose the Rev. Jesse Jackson of Chicago—a 25-year-old Baptist minister.[78] While working on the streets as a salesman, Jackson professed to have discovered that Negroes "live in the jaws of the beast who is a racist—demoralized by his racist spirit, contained by his militarism, and starved by his misuse of capitalism. That's the way he whips the game."[79] An admirer of Stokely Carmichael, Rev. Jackson said, "The white press accuses Stokely of preaching racism, but he is preaching nationalism, and his nationalism is good because it tells the black man he is somebody and tells the white man that he must respect everybody. Stokely is not a Christian preacher, but he is a rock crying out with truth."[80]

In the South, the SCLC claimed it had produced more than 5,000 new jobs for Negroes in Atlanta during the preceding five years.[81] In Chicago, Jackson's most effective bargaining lever was the "green power" of Chicago's one million Negroes, who spent some $2 billion a year on goods and services.[82] And he would use that lever to the hilt with private industry, in negotiations which alternated the use of the carrot and the stick, with the none too subtle wielding of an economic bludgeon.

A pioneer agreement was reached between the Chicago Freedom Movement—of which the SCLC was a major part —and High-Low Foods, Inc., a food chain with 50 outlets in Chicago, including fourteen in Negro districts.[83] The three-point agreement announced by the chain store and "Operation Breadbasket" pole-vaulted from employment to banking practices, to shelf displays and pricing policies. The company "agreed to engage in the following programs in redefining a dynamic relationship to the Negro community":

First, 183 jobs are open for new and/or upgraded employees in the several job categories within the company's operation.

These jobs will fully integrate the company's total work force and will integrate each job category within the company.

Second, goods produced and distributed by Negro manufacturers will be given equal display space and will sell at non-prohibitive mark-ups with competitive products in High-Low Food stores.

Third, commercial accounts from several High-Low stores will be transferred to two Chicago banks which have direct relationship with the Negro community.[84]

Martin Luther King exulted that the agreement with High-Low was "most significant because it shows that a large white-dominated company now understands that money spent by its Negro consumers should remain in the Negro community."[85] Like other companies which had undergone the experience, High-Low was fairly taciturn about Operation Breadbasket. Almost a year later, about all James E. Manning of High-Low Foods would say, was: "I wouldn't choose to go through it again. It takes a lot out of you. It goes on for quite a while and they are quite emotional."[86]

How emotional can be gleaned from some of the statements of Rev. Jesse Jackson, in an article devoted to this "Apostle of Economics" in *Ebony*. Jackson stated, "We live under colonialism because white people who don't live in our community own everything in it. Black people must have control of eleven per cent of Chicago." Jackson believed that "Black producers and consumers must be organized. We need striking power. Any twelve black women, organized properly, can close down one of 'the man's' chain stores."[87] Jackson claimed to be inspired by Jesus, Malcolm X, James Bevel, and Martin Luther King.[88] *Ebony* found Jackson "imposing, but never frightening; arrogant, but not offensive; impulsive, and yet disciplined."[89]

Under Jackson's leadership, Operation Breadbasket in fifteen months negotiated agreements with Chicago food chains, soft drink firms and dairies that opened some 2,000 jobs worth more than $15 million in annual income to Chicago Negroes.[90] But beyond any question, the most far-reaching agreement was that reached in May, 1967, with the Great Atlantic and Pacific Tea Company (A & P). A & P agreed to: 1) open 770 new and upgraded jobs to Negroes, including the appointment of 20 store managers and an equal number of assistant managers; 2) market the products of sixteen Negro producers and suppliers in metropolitan Chicago stores; 3) grant scavenger and extermination service accounts from a minimum of 40 stores to Operation Breadbasket for distribution to Negro-owned companies; 4) transfer the banking transactions of a minimum of 40 stores to Independence Bank of Chicago and Seaway National Bank (both predominantly-Negro banks); and 5) provide contracts for the construction and refurbishing of A & P stores throughout Chicago, and especially in the black community, to emerging Negro building organizations and related trades in the construction industry.[91]

Jackson told a press conference, "A & P has merely contracted to do today what it should have done yesterday. If this policy is carried out with honesty and determination, A & P will cease to be the *Man's* store and will become *our* store . . . No longer will we allow the colonial powers—the white owners—to take profits and leave poverty, to take joy and leave sorrow, to take our sense of dignity and leave only despair. Ultimately, the black ghetto must be controlled by black people."[92] In all, Jackson signed agreements with fourteen Chicago companies.[93]

In 1967, Illinois State Treasurer Adlai Stevenson III carried out his own boycott. Stevenson announced that state funds would be withheld from financial institutions with discriminatory lending or employment policies, and that he was placing state funds in two banks and three savings and loan institutions in the black community. "I was encouraged by the Rev. Mr. Jackson and the members of Operation Breadbasket and wanted to do everything I could," said Stevenson. The receiving institutions had all been recommended by Jackson.[94]

Seeking new companies to conquer, King and his Southern

Christian Leadership Conference began a boycott of Seal-test Dairy Products in Cleveland.[95] The company's economic felony had been its refusal to cooperate fully in providing data on colored employment. Sealtest asserted that 10 per cent of its 458 Cleveland employees were non-white, and said it had given the SCLC all the information it requested except financial data which would aid competitors.[96] During the boycott, people were urged not to buy Sealtest products and stores were urged not to stock them, with the threat that they themselves would be boycotted unless they complied.[97] After a month-long boycott, Sealtest yielded.[98] The company announced that, in Cleveland, it would provide 50 new and upgraded jobs for Negroes; make greater use of Negro-owned businesses, including banks, suppliers and sales and service companies; list all jobs with employment agencies serving the Negro community; and establish firmer recruiting contacts with Negro schools.[99] Another notable Midwest conquest took place when, with Martin Luther King gazing on benevolently, Jackson signed an agreement with Jewel Tea Company, on behalf of its hundreds of self-service food stores.[100] Under the agreement, Jewel Tea Company would either find jobs or make jobs—462 of them— and also would carry goods manufactured by Negro-owned companies on shelves of the stores in Negro districts, deposit funds in Negro banks, and hire Negro contractors to build future stores in the slums.[101]

Job gains in Eastern cities, generally speaking, have been more moderate in scope, possibly because Negroes already represented a sizable percentage of various company work forces. In October, 1967, for example, Brooklyn's "Operation Breadbasket" called off a threatened boycott when the local plant of Taystee Bread came to terms to employ 26 local youths and adults. Negroes already comprised 17 per cent of the work force in the Brooklyn plant; now the figure would be 25 per cent.[102] And again, in December, with great fanfare, Brooklyn's "Operation Breadbasket" announced another victory, in which they were hardly breaking new ground. At the time of their first meeting with officials of Continental Baking Company (producers of Wonder Bread and Hostess Cake) approximately 120 Negroes were employed by their New York bakeries. Now, under threat of boycott, Wonder Bread pledged to hire 55 additional Negro workers, and to upgrade present Negro employees in all departments. In the cases of both new employees and upgradings, the company would provide all necessary training.[103]

Insofar as the companies concerned are in interstate commerce and have a work staff in numerical excess of that specified in the statute, it is impossible to escape the conclusion that Operation Breadbasket is an open, flagrant, if not arrogant violation of the Fair Employment provision of the Civil Rights Act of 1964. But if any high-ranking Federal official is at all concerned about a campaign which coerces employers into hiring on the basis of color, the author has yet to read about it. It is equally clear that the state fair employment laws are also being violated, but again, state officials consider silence the better part of valor. These officials would, of course, be much more vocal —and start strewing subpoenas about like confetti—if the racial shoe were on the other foot, and whites formed their own Operation Breadbasket to compel lily-white hiring in the same companies. As it is, rights leaders can now inhabit the best of two possible worlds—using the fair employment laws to keep businesses from discriminating in favor of whites, while using Operation Breadbasket to force these same employers to discriminate in favor of Negroes.

What eventual end does Rev. Jesse Jackson seek for Operation Breadbasket? As close to *de facto* control of white businesses in black ghettos as the boycott threat can achieve. There is no reason why a demand for the hiring of 45 Negroes today cannot be followed by still more job demands six months or even a year from now. Similarly, the virtual dictation to the supermarkets to stock certain Negro-produced goods can be followed by new and more sweeping orders within a very short time. In effect, each of these businesses now has a new partner—a partner they did not want, and who invested not a penny in the enterprise, but who nonetheless may eventually have more power over the company than all the stockholders combined. With the constant threat of a boycott hanging over these corporate heads, one can expect more and more power being ceded to Operation Breadbasket unless someone finds the courage to tell Rev. Jackson, "This far, and no further."

Whether the corporations involved will reach this point depends upon many things—how large a percentage of their sales are made in Negro neighborhoods; how perishable their products are (one of Operation Breadbasket's first Chicago campaigns was against a dairy company which quickly came to terms, because milk must be sold quickly, or not at all);[104] whether they are in a community where there is reason to fear a white counter-boycott; whether the Negro demands are so excessive that there is no alternative but to resist them; and—perhaps most important—whether unions will object to a campaign whose employment policy is anti-white.

This last question could yet prove to be the controlling factor. Just as there is a "tipping point" beyond which white residents move out of integrated neighborhoods, it is the author's belief that there will be a "tipping point" for Operation Breadbasket, beyond which either the unions or groups of wildcat strikers will demand of their employers that the Negro-only hiring campaign be either curtailed or halted.

Not nearly enough has been said about the roles of the labor unions, in the reams of articles that have been written about job discrimination. Lyndon Johnson had barely moved into the White House when *Look* published an article titled: "Black Men, White Unions." In this article, *Look* declared, "The Negro in the North is fighting—but losing—a desperate battle for a chance at gainful employment and job training, and among the most vigorous forces opposing him are the wearers of the union label."[105] The magazine granted that there were a few notable exceptions to the rule, such

as the United Automobile Workers and the United Pack-
inghouse Workers, but grimly commented that—exceptions
excepted—"The hard fact is that organized labor, once seen
as an agent of advancement for Negro workers, has now
emerged as the unyielding bastion of white supremacy in
employment."[106] Among the prime offenders were the building trades unions. In that industry, unions did the hiring
and they hired only their members. Since few Negroes were
admitted to membership, they were thereby blocked from
getting skilled jobs in construction.[107] Even George Meany's
old local, Local 2 of the United Association of Journeymen
Plumbers and Steamfitters, at that time had not a single
Negro among its 3,300 members.[108]

Oddly enough, although the Negro was usually confined
to a segregated local in the South, he had a better chance
of getting work on a construction project there than in the
North. While Lyndon Johnson was still vice president, he
told labor leaders that the lowest number of skilled Negroes
to be found on the job anywhere in the nation—three per
cent—was in Brooklyn, in a state that was bristling with
fair employment laws. By contrast, in some Southern cities,
Negro employment in the building trades ran as high as 40
per cent.[109]

Meany and other union leaders said part of labor's problem was connected with the structure of the AFL-CIO itself. Most often it was the local that discriminated, and the
AFL-CIO had no control over the local. All it could do
was to vote to expel the parent union, which was considered
far too drastic a solution to a basically local problem.[110]

There were a few breakthroughs before the Civil Rights
Act of 1964—and its fair employment provisions—were the
law of the land. Detroit's 8,000-member Trade Labor Council (an affiliate of the Negro American Labor Council)
helped hammer out agreements with eighteen out of nineteen construction unions calling for admission of Negroes,
and ran its own program to train Negro youths for skilled
employment.[111] But Philadelphia was quite another story.

In 1965, after more than two years of intensive battling, including bloody picketing at a school construction site by civil rights workers, only three Negroes had been admitted to the 1,100-man Local 19 of the Sheet Metal Workers.[112] And in 1967, in Cleveland, membership in the building trades unions was still all but barred to Negroes. A Department of Labor survey discovered that a 1,500-man plumbers and pipefitters' local had not accepted a single Negro. Of 450 journeymen members of an electrical workers' local, only one was non-white. And a sheet metal workers union had no Negroes among its 1,250 journeymen members.[113] Writing in the Howard University *Law Journal*, New York City lawyer William B. Gould attacked the failure of the Equal Employment Opportunity Commission to solve not only the Negro issue but the seniority problem as well. He noted that most Negroes employed at automotive plants were confined to foundry work, while few were in better-paying assembly line jobs and almost none in the skilled jobs. He saw the Negro plight as one of "de facto segregated jobs," and contended that until the unions relaxed the seniority provisions, Negroes would continue to be barred from upgrading in many areas of industry.[114]

In April, 1967, Secretary of Labor W. Willard Wirtz attempted a crackdown on union apprenticeship programs when his department threatened to decertify programs that did not meet the government's non-bias regulations. Decertification would have barred apprentices from working on Federal projects at apprentice rates. At the time, Plumbers' Union President Peter Schoemann termed the threat "ridiculous gobbledygook," and the ultimatum was later withdrawn.[115] But more recently, Schoemann accomplished a virtual about-face. In December, 1967, he pledged that his union would "participate more actively in what is generally called affirmative action, meaning among other things direct efforts to notify minority group members of openings and even direct recruiting."[116] Affirmative action was the keystone of new Administration policy to place Negroes in the higher-paying construction trades.[117] A similar note was struck by labor chief C. J. Haggerty at a biennial convention of the AFL-CIO Building & Construction Trades Department. Haggerty told the convention delegates that their unions not only should take in "qualified" minority workers as journeymen, but "should institute learner or trainee programs" in the ghetto areas for youths who want to learn construction work.[118]

The change of heart had a great deal to do with a change of law—specifically with construction work in the newly-passed Model Cities program. The regulations under this law specifically required payment of "prevailing" wage rates (usually, the going union rates in the area) for construction work. At the same time, these regulations stipulated that "maximum work opportunities" must be provided for ghetto residents.[119] Adding to the potency of the pocket-book argument is the further fact that starting this year, before the government will award construction contracts in excess of $1 million, the contractor must demonstrate that minority workers will have equal job opportunities "in all trades . . . to be used on the job in all phases of the work, whether or not the work is to be subcontracted."[120] And so, if for no other reason than enlightened self-interest, the building trades unions are almost certain to modify their virtual ban on Negro members. How far the modification will go remains to be seen—depending upon how equal is "equal" as vaguely defined in government guidelines—but surely there will be some integration of these unions, if only of the token variety.

In August, 1967, the Equal Employment Opportunity Commission released the results of an industry-by-industry survey of minority hiring. It showed that in New York, the financial capital of the world, Negroes working for security and commodity brokers and exchanges did not number even one in 25. In New Orleans, the crude oil and gas industry employed only one Negro in 100 workers. In nine cities covered by this preliminary report, wholesaling, insurance, printing and publishing, communications, air travel and banking lagged behind the average in Negro employment.[121] The new chairman of the EEOC, Clifford L. Alexander, said, "With these figures, we'll be armed to the teeth. We can go to Mister X and say: 'Here's an employer in your industry who's doing twice as well as you are. Why aren't you doing better?'" Alexander said he would try to achieve conciliation with the offending employers. But if investigators didn't get an "immediate and receptive audience," Alexander vowed to increase the number of lawsuits filed under the 1964 Civil Rights Act, charging a "pattern or practice" of discrimination.[122]

One of the cities covered by this preliminary report was Chicago. And yet in January of 1968, *U. S. News & World Report* wrote that in the "booming Chicago area. . . . Jobs are going begging. Employers are trying all sorts of recruiting methods. Some are lowering qualifications for applicants. Still, not enough workers can be found to fill vacancies." In some cases, orders had to be cancelled by firms unable to find as many workers as they wanted. The metropolitan area of Chicago had an unemployment rate of 2.5 per cent, one of the lowest among the nation's large cities. The director of research for the Chicago Association of Commerce said: "Most of the unemployed now seem to be people who really don't want to work. We're trying to place people in on-the-job training programs, and finding it pretty hard to get those who'll stick." The Illinois employment service set up offices in ghetto areas. Recruiters stopped people on the street, went into pool halls, knocked on doors, visited bars. The Chicago transit authority searched for 430 bus drivers at $160 a week. Only seventeen had been hired.[123]

Within the past few years, many firms have made special efforts to hire Negro workers. All sorts of programs have been instituted, but of them all, probably the most ambitious is the Ford Motor Company experiment. It began in October, 1967, in the wake of the most devastating race riot in our country's history. Ford sent its own labor recruiters into the ghetto, waiving traditional written tests of ability, and hiring men on the spot where they lived. In effect, the company was saying that it was not waiting for men to come looking for jobs, but was taking jobs to the men.[124] Ford had just come through a two-month strike, and estimated that for its catch-up period it would need 6,500 employees.[125] The openings were publicized by press and radio.[126] Ford sent two of its interviewers into two of the city's job centers in the ghetto. These centers already had some 7,000 hard-core unemployed registered.[127] Cooperating with Ford was the Mayor's Specialized Training Employment Placement Service (STEPS) which sent typed notices to the hard-core unemployed on its lists. The notices read: "We have factory job openings paying over $3 per hour. No test will be given. Persons with police records will be considered. . . ."[128] The men filled out the simple "hourly employment application" cards that asked for basic information only. The interviews lasted about half an hour. Those who passed received a medical examination by city doctors just down the corridor.[129]

Not all who made it to Ford stayed on the job. In the engine plant a 26-year-old high school dropout who had run through a string of spot jobs—and been in jail—was at work on "minor assembly." After nine days he asked to be transferred out of the engine plant "because I don't like the job or the people." He was transferred to another section, but after thirteen days there, he never came back.[130] Another man had to be discharged for chronic absenteeism.[131]

As of January, 1968, Ford had interviewed 3,000 hardcore unemployed at the two ghetto centers. Of that total, some 1,600 were on the job, most of them in the Rouge plant; 600 were hired but "banked"—not yet on the payroll, awaiting assignment to jobs; 375 who were hired had not shown up or were taking their time about showing up for work; and 425 were rejected, mostly for medical disabilities or because their police violations had been too habitual.[132] Ford officials said they were hiring "indefinitely."[133] But an expert on the Mayor's Committee said, "One of the really terrible things that could happen would be a cutback in Ford production. Being the newest employees, these men would be the first to go."[134]

Over and over, in one article after another, in one city after another, one reads about, hears about large corporations making extraordinary efforts to find jobs or make jobs for the hard-core unemployed from the ghettos. The momentum builds constantly, spreading from one company to another, as some firms almost vie with each other to see who can place more hitherto unemployable Negroes in gainful employment. If anything in the world can halt this momentum, and dry up this vast reservoir of good will, it is the business-baiting Operation Breadbasket. Left to themselves, a number of American industries have gone above and beyond the line of corporate duty in their efforts to aid the ghetto dwellers—but with the trigger-happy Rev. Jackson's economic gun pointed at their heads, being human, they may do only what they are compelled to do, and not a whit more. It will indeed be one of history's crowning ironies if Operation Breadbasket, in the end, provides only a few paltry crumbs—or if it becomes so powerful that it ignites an irresistible backlash that will destroy the entire movement to train, educate and prepare poorer Negroes for better jobs. It would be equally ironic if history records that it was that Crown Prince of Good Will, Martin Luther King, who self-righteously killed or even wounded the goose that was just beginning to lay the golden egg.

CHAPTER 9

The Rise of Black Power

How will posterity judge Martin Luther King? Quite possibly in terms of his own professed ultimate objective—an objective it is easy to lose sight of in the feverish, almost compulsive whirlwind of activity that has marked the King Decade. King did, after all, envision a land of Canaan at the end of the civil rights rainbow. The zenith of all his marches, all his demonstrations, all his "creative" pressures, all his dramatic confrontations was to be "the Beloved Community." He instilled "the Beloved Community" into the national consciousness in *Stride Toward Freedom*, and made periodic reference to it down through the years.

As the father of the most sweeping civil rights legislation of all time; as the mahatma of civil disobedience and protracted conflict with civil authority; as the perennial planned martyr-in-residence to "police brutality," let us look at the America that Martin Luther King created.

Let us examine the America we live in, today—an America which bears the indelible imprint of King's marching feet. Let us "tell it like it is"—sweeping aside the theory and dogma and wishful thinking—and look at the reality of our lives, our country, and our future.

Under the dispassionate microscope of history, let us scrutinize Martin Luther King's Beloved Community, ten years later. When we have finished this social biopsy, let us ask ourselves:

Is Martin Luther King's "Beloved Community" now nearer or more remote than it was at the start of his career?
Are the races today closer or farther apart?
Is there now more racial trust or less?
Is there now—to quote King himself—chaos or community?

In the pages that follow, the facts will speak for themselves. And these answers will tell us whether Martin Luther King succeeded gloriously or should be ranked among the most colossal failures of all time.

THE LOS ANGELES RIOTS

If all else about it is forgotten, this much should be remembered—that one of the worst race riots in this country's history took place during a period of monumental political gain for the Negro.

On August 6, 1965, President Johnson signed into law the Voting Rights Act. It was a stunning victory for Martin Luther King and a shattering defeat for the forces of racial segregation. Glowing predictions were made that the Negro was now on the threshhold of a new era—that a miraculous new day in race relations was dawning, and that the strategically located Negro vote in the vast urban centers of the North would cast off the remaining shackles of second-class citizenship, one by one.

Less than a week later—while the first tentative steps were being taken towards a racial rapprochement—a nightmare ripped across the front pages of the nation's press. It was a Molotov cocktail with a fleabite for a wick—an orgy of violence, destructiveness and lawlessness whose immediate cause was a perfectly routine traffic arrest on a charge of drunken driving.

At first, it sounded like some macabre joke, but it was all too grimly factual that in a four-day period some died and hundreds were injured, thousands were arrested and hundreds of millions of dollars worth of property destroyed, following an attempt by a policeman to arrest a young Negro in the Watts section of Los Angeles.

On a hot smoggy Wednesday evening in August, a white California Highway Patrol officer stopped a 21-year-old Negro motorist, Marquette Frye, on suspicion of drunken driving. Some 25 persons gathered to watch.[1] The patrolman said later, "Everything was peaceful until the boy's mother arrived. She started to berate him for his condition, and this made him angry."[2] Frye refused to submit to arrest and swung at the officer.[3] The patrolman called for assistance, then drew his pistol. Frye shouted, "Go ahead, kill me!" Frye's mother jumped on the patrolman's back and tore his shirt.[4] And the crowd, now grown to about 200, moved forward, shouting and cursing.[5]

When help arrived, the patrolman was able to take the Fryes to the police station.[6] But the crowd did not disperse. Rumors of "police brutality" sped through Watts.[7] One rumor had it that the police had arrested a pregnant woman; actually she was a lady barber whose smock was mistaken for a maternity dress.[8]

By 10:00 p.m., the crowd was growing larger, pelting city buses with stones and other missiles. Then with terrible suddenness, the crowd became a mob, and rioters started fanning out into the surrounding area, breaking windows and looting stores.[9]

The following night in Watts, crowds of up to 5,000 Negroes gathered in a 20-block area that had been sealed off by some 100 policemen and more than 300 deputy sheriffs.[10] The renewed rioting came *after* civil rights leaders and clergymen had toured the neighborhood, pleading with people to stay off the streets.[11] Most of the combatants were youths, some of whom had promised another violent night.[12] In one instance, a police car was halted by Negroes who attempted to pull the occupants from the car. The officers were rescued when other police cars arrived.[13]

Robert Richardson, a Negro advertising salesman for the

Los Angeles *Times*, witnessed the rioting for eight hours. He called it "the most terrifying thing I've seen in my life," and added, "It's a wonder anyone with white skin got out of there alive." Richardson wrote that whenever a car with whites in it was seen in the area, the word spread: "Here comes whitey—get him!" The older people were egging on the teen-agers and the people in their twenties. Then, Richardson continued, "the young men and women would rush in to pull white people from their cars and beat them and try to set fire to the cars." He told of one white couple, in their sixties, who happened to be driving along. In Richardson's words, "They were beaten up and kicked until their faces, hands and clothing were bloody." He reported that "Those not hitting and kicking the couple were standing there shouting, 'Kill! Kill!' "[14] A phrase popularized by a local Negro disc jockey, "Burn, Baby, Burn," became the rallying cry of the howling, fighting, screaming mob.

During the riots, a Negro worker for CORE—Cornell Henderson—tried to help a white man, with disastrous results. Henderson said he saw the white man "knocked out and then put back in his car, and the car was overturned and set fire. I went to the car and tried to get him out but they [the Negro assailants] began to call me 'Tom' and told me to get away or they would put me in the car with him. I had to leave. I don't know whether he ever got out." Henderson saw "little kids acting like animals, carrying shotguns and saying to the police, 'Come on in and we'll kill you. Let us alone. We rule here now.' "[15]

The third night, two thousand heavily armed National Guardsmen moved into Los Angeles to battle rioters.[16] The Guardsmen—brought in to support a battered contingent of 900 policemen and deputy sheriffs—were under order to use rifles, machine guns, tear gas and bayonets if necessary.[17] One Guard spokesman said of the rioters, "They've got weapons and ammo. It's going to be like Vietnam."[18] They were greeted by crowds numbering in the thousands, and chanting, "White devils, what are you doing here?"[19]

At one point, Negro rioters charged Oak Park Hospital, where many of those injured and wounded in the riots were being treated.[20] Elsewhere, officials revealed that they had abandoned efforts to halt a fire sweeping a three-block section after Negroes hurled fire bombs and rocks at the fire fighters.[21] Negro youths later took complete control of another two-block area and set 15 fires to homes and stores. Great sections were destroyed by fires that ran unchecked.[22] Finally, 200 "Flak Suits" of bulletproof mesh armor had to be borrowed from the Camp Pendleton Marine Base.[23]

"The 150-block section of Los Angeles last night took on the appearance of a war zone with men crouching in the shadows, streets littered with debris or completely torn up, store windows broken and scorched and a pall of smoke hanging over the area," reported the New York *Times*.[24] Los Angeles Police Chief William H. Parker called it "guerrilla warfare."[25]

Scores of homeowners and apartment dwellers in the area were phoning police, asking to be evacuated from the neighborhood. A center for hundreds of refugees was set up in a church near the riot zone.[26]

Hundreds of men and children made repeated trips to stores and shops carrying off armfuls of merchandise. Children, many of them as young as three or four years old, stayed close to their parents with armloads of goods. Some adults stopped momentarily to clean blood from their feet, arms and legs, which had been cut by broken glass in showcase windows.[27] The following night, a helicopter pilot for the Los Angeles Police Department said he saw a rental auto trailer backed up to a large supermarket. Virtually the whole neighborhood was participating in the looting, with men, women and children rushing from store to trailer with armloads of booty.[28] One furniture store in the heart of the riot area was stripped so systematically and completely that it looked like an abandoned location.[29]

On the fifth day of rioting, authorities were at last able

to assert that they had gained "the upper hand."[30] By this time, the total number of arrests reached 2,255. Of these, 1,680 were adults charged with felonies; 232 adults charged with misdemeanors; 287 juveniles charged with felonies; and 56 juveniles charged with misdemeanors. The number of injured totaled 762, as the troops used rifle fire, tear gas, machine guns and bayonets to quell the onslaughts of Negro hoodlums. Losses from fires approached $200 million. And the losses from looting were as yet literally incalculable.[31] Police Chief Parker now said that the situation *in respect to the rioters* was that "we're on the top and they're on the bottom."[32] The Chief's many opponents glossed over his qualifying reference to the rioters, and made it look as if he had equated "we" with the white community, and "they" with the Negro community.

During this time, stores had reported an extraordinary weekend sale of guns in white neighborhoods, particularly on the periphery of the area. Governor Brown called the gun sales "a very dangerous thing" on the ground that most people were untrained in using firearms. But Chief Parker said he would not take it upon himself to discourage people from exercising their legal right to buy guns if they felt they needed the protection.[33]

August, 1965, may well be recorded as the month of Martin Luther King's greatest triumph and greatest humiliation. The triumph had been spread all over the front pages when President Johnson made the Voting Rights Act the law of the land. Now came the humiliation from which King would never quite recover—the positive biracial clamor for him to stay away from Watts during the riots.

Ironically, this was one of the rare occasions where King managed to utter the word "police" without immediately adding "brutality." King said that he favored the "use of the full force of the police power to quell the situation in Los Angeles."[34] He told reporters that he considered the Los Angeles riots "absolutely wrong, socially detestable and self-defeating." But he stated that "police power can only bring a temporary halt." He called for a massive program to help Negroes.[35]

King said that he would fly to Los Angeles to meet with Negro and white leaders and help create "a community of love."[36] But the love seemed to be distinctly one-sided. Governor Brown said that he hoped King would not come to Los Angeles at that time. He stated that King was associated in the public mind with civil rights turbulence elsewhere.[37] Brown's statement proved to be a political faux pas. As other public officials could have told him from gloomy personal experience, the surest way to get Martin Luther King into a given community was to urge him to stay out.

King did go to Los Angeles, and his reception by local officialdom proved to be somewhat frosty. After a meeting with Chief Parker, King commented that the chief had disagreed with "our ideas" and should be dismissed.[38] In reply, Mayor Yorty stated that "the white community would not stand for firing Chief Parker" and added he would refuse to accept the chief's resignation if it were offered.[39]

King's reception was hardly more ecstatic in the Negro community. Escorted by six police officers, he talked to a crowd of 300 in a Community Center. As he counseled nonviolence, a man identified by other Negroes as a Black Muslim yelled: "Get out of here, Dr. King! We don't want you!"[40]

The Negro magazine *Jet* wrote, "The Black Muslims are powerful enough to challenge the established Negro 'leaders' in the Watts ghetto."[41] Just how powerful was soon made painfully clear to King. *Jet* reported that "Perhaps the greatest single blow to the leadership came when Nobel Peace Prize winner Martin Luther King, Jr. was forced to invoke the name of Elijah Muhammed to gain a hearing in the riot-scarred community of Watts."[42] Watts Muslim minister John Shabazz said of the incident—perhaps only slightly tongue in cheek: "Dr. King's high intelligence, high sensitivity and innate leadership enabled him to quickly assess the mood of the black people in Los Angeles. Once he saw they were with the honorable Elijah Muhammad, he realized why the other leaders had not been able to get these peoples' ears and that the only way he could, would be by using the name of Mr. Muhammad."[43]

Had King attended one particular Black Muslim rally, he would have heard Marquette Frye, whose arrest ignited the riot, telling his audience, "These troops don't mean a thing. They haven't seen anything yet."[44] And in an interview by *Newsweek*, the 21-year-old Mr. Frye stated, "Why go over to Vietnam and get shot and fight for your country? What country? I don't have a country . . ."[45]

At the time of the rioting, a convention of 1,000 Negro Masons deplored the uprising because it "hurt the American Negro in his civil rights fight." The Negro Masons' resolution added: "We also feel that some radicals that moved into Dr. Martin Luther King's movement under false pretenses were unobserved because certainly Dr. King does not use or endorse radical tactics."[46]

What did the academic community consider the causes of the Los Angeles riots? The New York *Times* drily noted that "There were as many theories as there are sociologists today on why a depressed residential area was ripped . . . by rioting Negroes."[47] Dr. Oscar Handlin of Harvard University contended that the outbreak should not be called a race riot because it did not "involve group wars between whites and Negroes."[48] But Philip M. Hauser—head of the University of Chicago's sociology department and a civil rights activist of some standing—believed that the Los Angeles riots were definitely of racial origin even if they did not involve frontal clashes between gangs of Negroes and whites.[49] Lewis M. Killian, professor of sociology at the Florida State University, felt that "The token integration the Negro middle class are achieving has no impact on the daily life of the Negro mass, the people living in the slums. The main effect it has is to create unrest by creating new aspirations that the mass cannot realize.

The Negro in the slum is being told daily that he doesn't have to wait for change. Civil rights leaders are talking in terms of freedom now with the emphasis on the 'now'."[50] The author's own opinion is that Professor Killian came closest to delineating the underlying reasons for the riot. And curiously enough, Killian was, in effect, restating the racial forecast made by Malcolm X some time before. Malcolm had predicted that passage of the Civil Rights Act of 1964 would be followed by more, not less, violence because the gap between promise and fulfillment would lead to greater fury and frustration. As Malcolm X tersely expressed it, "A hungry man will *dislike* you if you refuse to give him help, but will *hate* you if you promise help and give him a check that bounces."[51]

Article after article in the nation's press catalogued the grim, sordid statistics. Watts contained some 80,000 people within a square of 25 blocks.[52] Twenty per cent of their homes were classified as run-down.[53] Two-thirds of its adults had less than a high-school education; 30 per cent of its children were from broken homes.[54] It had more than 500 parolees from California prisons, widespread narcotics addiction, alcoholism and prostitution.[55] The crime statistics in Watts far exceeded the city average—in the last three months, there had been 1,000 crimes, including 98 murders, rapes and felonious assaults.[56]

And yet, as the New York *Times* commented, "Exhaustive post-mortems of the riot, while spotlighting many lamentable factors in terms of poverty, unemployment, undereducation and general underprivilege *have not disclosed conditions that do not exist elsewhere.*"[57] The *Times* writer felt that the key element was the Watts Negroes' sense of isolation from those "on the other side of the freeway."[58] And there was apparently a growing body of support for this view. But later, sociologists at the University of California at Los Angeles interviewed 585 Negroes living in the riot area. In a report on the survey, the sociologists stated: "We find no relationship between social contact with whites and participation in and favorability toward the riot . . . If riot support implies hostility toward whites, our data indicate that its magnitude is unaffected by contact with white persons."[59]

What did government officials consider the causes of the Los Angeles riots? Federal officials and Whitney Young blamed Mayor Yorty, who blamed Sargent Shriver, who turned right around and blamed Mayor Yorty. Specifically, Whitney Young of the Urban League said his group had warned Los Angeles in the preceding four months that the city was not immune to violence.[60] Federal officials said they had warned Mayor Yorty as long ago as the spring that there was potential danger of racial violence in his city.[61] Whether or not this was an accurate portrayal of the situation in the spring, the racial atmosphere seemed to have improved substantially just a month before the streets of Watts were seething with "Burn, baby, burn!" A month before the riots, a correspondent wrote that in Los Angeles "The past year has been marked by an array of unspectacular but extensive efforts toward racial harmony that have been substantial enough to ease militant frictions."[62]

Mayor Yorty charged Sargent Shriver with "cutting off poverty funds" to Los Angeles.[63] In a counter-blast, Shriver replied that Los Angeles had not been short-changed in "war on poverty" dollars, and in fact had not spent some of the money it received long ago.[64] Shriver heavily emphasized the contention that Los Angeles was the only major city in the United States that had failed to organize effective local anti-poverty programs.[65] The conflict with Mayor Yorty involved the selection of representatives of the poor by open processes. In the absence of an acceptable "umbrella" agency, the Office of Economic Opportunity had channeled more than $17 million to other public and private agencies in Los Angeles. Shriver said that this sum compared favorably with the $18 million Chicago had received in Federal largesse.[66]

Shriver's boundless faith that great gobs of Federal dollars would have created enough good will to stave off a riot was touching, but perhaps not overly realistic. After all, 37 per cent of the juveniles arrested in the Los Angeles riots were being supported by welfare.[67] Furthermore, reports filed by state investigators immediately after the riots said that in Watts the hostility toward county welfare workers was second only to the hostility toward police.[68]

Leroy Collins, race relations troubleshooter for the White House, finally worked out an acceptable compromise, giving seven seats out of a 23-member policy board to community representatives.[69] With tremendous fanfare, an election was announced in which the poor would ballot for their representatives. A corps of 600 volunteers was organized to familiarize people with the election. The balloting, originally set for February 8, 1966, was postponed three weeks for additional promotional time. On election day, 25 chartered buses helped get people to 154 polling places. When it was all over, a final check of ballots indicated that less than one per cent of the eligible poor had turned out to vote. Mayor Yorty used the *mot juste*, and called the election a "costly farce."[70]

Over and over, the anguished cry of "police brutality" was raised and offered as a cause—*the* cause—of the bloodletting in Watts. And yet no one seemed able to pinpoint any flagrant physical brutality, not even the 1962 Civil Rights Commission delegation.[71] After the riots, field investigators who were interviewing Negroes to gather evidence reported that most of the complaints against the police involved "verbal abuse" or harassment, rather than physical brutality.[72] Negroes charged that most of the police of Los Angeles were Southerners. But the fact was, the great majority were native to the West Coast. They had to have an IQ of at least 110. At that time, Chief Parker's force had one Ph.D., 15 officers with masters' degrees, 15 with law degrees, 208 B.A.'s, 288 with two-year college certificates, 375 with police academy diplomas;

more than 2,000 policemen were taking outside courses.[73] The roots of the antagonism in Watts ran much deeper. Negro psychiatrist Dr. Price M. Cobbs, himself a Californian, believed that the policeman, "whether benevolent or repressive, symbolizes raw, untrammeled power. For the powerless, the powerful are a natural antagonist." As regarded the police presence in Watts, Dr. Cobbs did not consider the question of color overly relevant. He wrote: "In a Negro ghetto there could be all Negro policemen, but if the men in that ghetto were blocked in their development and aspirations, the same abrasions would occur."[74]

A veteran Los Angeles police captain said, "We're the most undermanned police force in the country."[75] The force policed 463 square miles of territory with 5,120 officers. (Compare this with New York's 30,000 police for 365 square miles.)[76] A month after the riots, the American Broadcasting Company had a poll taken in the Watts section. When residents were asked directly about police brutality, 46.8 per cent of those interviewed believed that some police brutality existed, 15.1 per cent said "none at all," and 38.1 per cent were not sure. However, the report said "a number of people did not feel that the blame for the brutality was altogether the policemen's part." When asked what might be done to prevent violence, nearly one-third of all respondents said there should be "better" police protection and "more" police protection.[77]

What was the final toll of the Watts riots? Thirty-four deaths, 1,032 injuries, the arrest of 3,952 persons, $40 million in property damage; more than 600 buildings were damaged, 200 totally destroyed.[78] The state Bureau of Criminal Identification and Investigation compiled a statistical profile of the rioters. It found that "The average convicted rioter who was placed on probation was a Negro male who had lived in Los Angeles for more than five years. He lived with his wife or relatives in a rented apartment or house . . . was a high school dropout . . . was employed as either a domestic or unskilled laborer earning from $200 to $400 a month . . . and had an arrest record."[79]

Less than three per cent of the rioters who were arrested received sentences of six months or more. All of the others convicted were given short jail sentences, fined or placed on probation.[80] To paraphrase the Churchill saying of another time, in another war: never had so many been wrist-slapped so lightly for so much.

A week after the riots, Governor Brown appointed a commission headed by John McCone, former boss of the CIA, to find the reasons for the uprising.

The eagerly awaited McCone Commission report was handed down some three and a half months later. The study was compiled by a professional staff of 29, aided by 26 consultants. The commission heard testimony from 78 sworn witnesses and its staff interviewed several hundred persons who witnessed or were arrested during the riot, and distributed questionnaires to some 10,000 teachers, social workers and others involved in the Watts area.[81]

The eight-member commission, appointed by Governor Brown, called for the following programs in its 101-page report:

A massive "emergency literacy program" for schools in "disadvantaged areas" embracing, among other things, pre-school training and "drastic reduction" of class size.

A large-scale job training and placement center to be opened in the Watts area, combined with the expansion of existing public and privately financed job training projects.

A new mechanism for processing complaints against the police, involving a strengthened civilian board of Police Commissioners and the appointment of an independent Police Inspector General.

Greatly increased mass transit facilities to enable Negroes to commute to jobs in other parts of the city.[82]

The Commission acknowledged that its proposals might seem "extensive and burdensome," but added, "We make them because we are convinced the Negro can no longer exist as he has with the disadvantages which separate him from the rest of society, deprive him of employment and cause him to drift aimlessly through life. This we feel represents a crisis in our country."[83]

The report criticized what it considered the police department's cumbersome procedure for processing complaints and for not encouraging more Negroes to join the force. At that time, only four per cent of the police department's sworn personnel were Negroes.[84] However, the report rejected charges that Chief Parker had shown any prejudice against Negroes, either by word or action, and also spurned demands for the establishment of a civilian review board.[85]

The McCone Commission report cited three "aggravating events" that recurred in the 12 months prior to the riot. These were what it called the rising encouragement of civil disobedience in connection with the national civil rights movement; the passage of Proposition 14 in California, which repealed the state's Fair Housing Act; and the widespread publicity about Federal antipoverty funds that for various reasons "did not live up to their press notices" in Los Angeles.[86]

A paragraph in the report which should have been much more widely publicized was this:

The accusations of the leaders of the national [civil rights] movement have been picked up by many local voices and have been echoed throughout the Negro community here. As we have said in the opening chapter of this report, the angry exhortations and the resulting disobedience of the law in many parts of our nation appear to have contributed importantly to the feeling of rage which made the Los Angeles riots possible.[87]

One scarcely had to read between the lines to discern the name: Martin Luther King.

After reviewing the welfare programs, the commission stated it was "profoundly disturbed by the accelerating trend of expenditure," which exceeded $400 million in Los

Angeles County. Between 1960 and 1964, when the county population increased 13 per cent, expenditures in the Aid to Families with Dependent Children Program alone rose 73 per cent.[88]

On the transportation issue, the McCone Commission found that totally inadequate mass transit handicapped Negroes in seeking jobs as well as in shopping. Only 14 per cent of Watts families owned cars, the report said, compared with more than 50 per cent in other areas.[89]

The McCone Commission made a thoroughgoing investigation of the riot and concluded that there was "no reliable evidence of outside leadership or preestablished plans for the rioting."[90] However, the report added, the sudden appearance of Molotov cocktails in great quantity and handbills aimed at inciting the Negroes indicated that, once the riot was under way, several well-organized gangs moved into action to spread the disorder.[91]

The McCone Commission grimly concluded: "So serious and so explosive is the situation that, unless it is checked, the August riots may seem by comparison to be only a curtain-raiser for what could blow up one day in the future."[92] Three months after the riots, the OEO had approved expenditures of $18 million for Los Angeles.[93] The Federal government made at least four grants to the Watts section by May of the following year.[94] Funds were approved for the Los Angeles Housing Authority to lease and rehabilitate 1,000 units of private housing for low-income families. A grant of $333,000 was made to demolish vacant and unsafe structures. Ninety-seven thousand dollars was advanced for preparation by the city of two general neighborhood renewal plans.[95] But still the seething hostility was never far below the surface. In March, 1966, the New York *Times* still found "distrust and growing hate of white society, with its visible affluence and seeming unconcern . . ."[96] The article appeared after a second, much smaller, riot took place in Watts. A Negro was arrested for throwing bricks at the car of a white teacher outside a Watts high school. The arrest was made just as students were leaving for the day. There were cries of police brutality and suddenly bricks and bottles began to fly. Within minutes, the crowd was on a rampage, with cries of "get Whitey!" The rioting went on for four hours, as from 600 to 1,000 Negroes set fires, hurled bricks and looted over a 12-block area. The riot subsided only when 200 policemen, armed with shotguns and moving shoulder to shoulder, imposed a tense truce. The toll was two dead, 20 injured, 49 Negroes arrested, and 19 buildings damaged.[97] McCone commented, "I'm afraid this is one more evidence of an unwillingness by Negroes to accept responsibilities as law-abiding citizens of our community. Until this changes, it's going to be very difficult for anyone in the community to change things."[98]

Almost a year after the Los Angeles riots, there was a "Renaissance of the Arts" held at Markham Junior High, in the heart of Watts. The festival, among other exhibits, featured a roomful of sculpture fashioned entirely from objects found among the wreckage the rioting had left. In one corner was an old hollow TV set. Inside, where its picture tube should have been, was a human skull. The name of the piece was "The Late, Late, Late Show."[99]

Eight hundred and fifty-one guns were confiscated during the Los Angeles riots in August, but one policeman said, "There are a lot more guns out there. They looted every pawn shop and sports shop in the area last summer —there are a lot more guns out there."[100]

For all anyone knows, those guns are still out there.

THE RISE OF STOKELY CARMICHAEL

Stokely Carmichael made a speech in Watts sometime after the riots; he was accompanied by *Life* writer-photographer Gordon Parks, who had followed the SNCC leader around for four months. As Parks described Carmichael's appearance in Watts: "First Stokely made a modest pitch for money. When the donations came in faster than the small buckets could hold them, Cliff Vaughs, a SNCC worker, grabbed an old leather satchel off the platform. When he opened it, his jaw dropped and he quickly snapped the bag shut. 'That damn thing is full of equalizers,' he whispered to me."[101]

A year after the Los Angeles riots, America was still groping for a reason—still sifting every clue, every lead, every racial rumbling for the one answer which would unlock all the smoldering secrets of the Black Ghetto. Everyone had his own pet explanation, not the least of which was this theory from Stokely Carmichael:

The people I blame for Watts are Martin Luther King and the Student Nonviolent Coordinating Committee, and the mass media of this country. Because you see I think that every time they saw Martin get slapped, they got mad. And every time they saw four little black kids get bombed, they got madder. And when nothing happened, boy, they were steaming. Because they knew that the reason and the only reason that those people got hit was because they were black. The only reason we are depressed in this country is because we are black.[102]

Carmichael raged: "I've had so much law and order, I swear before God I want some chaos! I want some chaos so bad I can taste it on the tip of my lips, because all I see is law and order, everywhere I go, law and order: from Canton, Mississippi, to Watts, Los Angeles, to Harlem to Chicago—nothing but law and order."[103]

The Stokely Carmichael who clamors for chaos has become a familiar figure on the national and international scene. All but forgotten is the Stokely Carmichael of the early 1960's, who joined SNCC when the Student Nonviolent Coordinating Committee was exactly what its name implied.

According to all the liberal orthodoxies of race relations, Stokely Carmichael should have been a paragon of brotherhood. He lived in an integrated neighborhood in the Bronx; he went to an exceptionally good integrated school; his father had been admitted into a union; and a white lady offered to provide financial assistance to send Stokely through college. Liberal dogma insists that nearness would make the heart grow fonder. And yet it is the very integrated Mr. Carmichael who is the chief architect of Black Power.

Carmichael was brought by his family from Trinidad to Harlem in 1952, when he was eleven years old.[104] Within a couple of years, they moved to the East Bronx, in a neighborhood where they were the only Negroes.[105] His white friends taught him "the tricks, how to break into stores, and how to steal cars." He was the only Negro member of the Morris Park Avenue Dukes and, by his own admission, became a specialist in stealing hubcaps and car radios.[106]

The Carmichael family lived in a three-room apartment.[107] Stokely Carmichael said of his father, "My old man would Tom [would act like an Uncle Tom]. He was such a good old Joe, but he would *Tom*."[108] His father, Adolphus Carmichael, was head deacon of the church, a man who "never realized people lied or cheated or were bad."[109] Adolphus was said to have been admitted into the Carpenter's Union after his wife had given the business representative $50 and a bottle of perfume (her husband was never told of the bribe).[110] Adolphus worked as a cab-driver at night and went to school to study electricity, and during the day he worked as a carpenter.[111] Stokely Carmichael's sardonic narrative concluded, "My old man was like the Man with the Hoe. He just felt that there were millions to be made in this country and he died at forty-two—just a poor black man."[112] If his father was worn out, it may well have been that he was overwhelmed by the heavy responsibility of supporting a family of eight on a meager income.[113] Ironically, the father's employment problems vis-à-vis the union might have been lessened somewhat in a state with right-to-work laws—but Stokely Carmichael's vehement left-wing orientation would never have admitted of such a possibility.

In 1956, Carmichael was admitted to the Bronx High School of Science, a school for some of the brightest children in New York.[114] He started reading Marx, Camus, Darwin, "anything that anybody mentioned," and began associating with young Socialists.[115] He was one of about 50 Negroes in the school,[116] and by all the copious rhetoric of the liberal rule-book, should have become the very model of a modern integrationist. Instead, Carmichael "learned at Science that white people, liberal white people, could be intellectually committed, but emotionally racist. They couldn't see *through*."[117] Carmichael had white friends; he was dating white girls, and going to Greenwich Village.[118] He was invited to parties on Park Avenue, at least one of which he vividly remembers. As Carmichael recalled it: "Well, his mother had a group of ladies there, and it was like I hit it off right away. She said, 'Oh, I've heard so much about you, you've got such a sense of humor, Jimmy is always talking about you, you're such a good-looking boy . . . what features you have . . .' and on and on. Finally, when I was leaving, the door was just about closed, his mother turned to the other ladies and said, 'Oh, yes, we let Jimmy hang around with Negroes.' I didn't like that."[119]

Evidently Carmichael had no greater liking for his mother's employer. In his own words: "My mother used to get up at five o'clock in the morning and fix me breakfast and then go across town and fix breakfast for 'Miss Ann.' And 'Miss Ann' was a liberal . . . She was going to give me money to go through college. She didn't understand that she was taking my mother from me when I needed her most . . ."[120] Why 'Miss Ann' was to blame for Stokely Carmichael's mother having to help support a family of eight was something the Black Power leader never quite explained. Carmichael continued: "My mother wasn't there [late in the afternoon] because she was taking care of 'Miss Ann's' children. She was giving her attention to 'Miss Ann's' children, not to me, so I developed a hatred for 'Miss Ann's' children . . . I don't know what made her think I was going to use any of *her* money to send me to college."[121] Later, he summed up this, and presumably other such experiences in one contemptuous sentence: "Liberalism is an extension of paternalism."[122]

When the sit-ins first began in 1960, Carmichael's first reaction was that they didn't know what they were doing.[123] A few months later, he became interested. And in May, he met a number of people who had been involved in the sit-ins.[124] Even at that time, Carmichael stressed, "I never took the approach we've got to teach them to love us. I thought that was nonsense from the start."[125]

Paradoxically, it was not Stokely Carmichael, but Martin Luther King, who was one of the founders of SNCC. It was in April, 1960, that representatives of student groups in the South and North met at Shaw University in Raleigh on Easter weekend and formed the Student Nonviolent Coordinating Committee. The meeting had been called by King, whose Southern Christian Leadership Conference at first underwrote it financially.[126] King was named as an adviser to SNCC, which the New York *Times* then described as "a temporary regional group established to guide the protest movement."[127]

At the outset, the Southern Christian Leadership Conference was one of SNCC's main sources of financial support.[128] Nevertheless, King and SNCC soon came to a parting of the ways because the students felt he was getting credit that should have gone to them.[129] However, King retained close ties with SNCC through one of his key assistants, Rev. James Bevel. Originally, Bevel had intended to work full-time for SNCC,[130] but for reasons lost in the folklore of the civil rights movement, he elected to join the Southern Christian Leadership Conference instead. Bevel married Diane Nash, one of the inner circle of SNCC, and in his activity with the SCLC, worked closely with the student group in Alabama and Mississippi.[131]

About a year after SNCC was formed, Stokely Carmichael was participating in the Freedom Rides.[132] He became something of a legend even among this group of hyper-activists. In 1967, he still could recall the fifty-three brutal days he spent in a Mississippi jail. In his words:

Fifty-three days. Oh, lord, fifty-three days in a six-by-nine cell. Twice a week to shower. No books, nothing to do. They would isolate us, maximum security. And those guards were out of sight. They did not play *they did not play*. The sheriff acted like he was scared of black folks and he came up with some beautiful things. One night he opened up all the windows, put on ten big fans and an air conditioner and dropped the temperature to 38 degrees. All we had on was T-shirts and shorts. And it was so cold, so *cold*, all you could do was walk around for two nights and three days your teeth chattering, going out of your mind, and it getting so cold that when you touch the bedspring, you feel your skin is gonna come right off.[133]

Carmichael became one of SNCC's most widely known field secretaries. Later, Martin Luther King recalled how he and Carmichael "had worked together in communities all across the South,"[134] and Professor Howard Zinn (who became something of a Boswell to the student group) mentioned a first meeting with Carmichael in Albany, Georgia, in December, 1961.[135]

Almost from the outset, there was considerable clerical support for the Student Nonviolent Coordinating Committee. (Its first chairman, John Lewis, was a Baptist minister.)[136] On one occasion Northern clergymen were on their way to Hattiesburg, Mississippi, to assist the student group. But it was not exactly a mutual admiration society. Some months before, a SNCC field secretary had written from Hattiesburg to the Atlanta office: "We plan to let Guyot speak . . . We are going to announce an interdenominational Bible study course that will be dedicated to the proposition that religion doesn't have to be bullshit. We hope to tie in an active image of the Christ, and what would he have done had he been here now . . . you see?"[137]

Professor Zinn thought "The ministers probably would have approved."[138]

SNCC was widely touted as the poorest of the civil rights groups, but in an emergency it almost invariably could turn to its wealthy and notable friends for sizable donations. In August, 1965, one party to aid SNCC was given in a lush Beverly Hills discotheque called "The Daisy." By the end of the evening, Marlon Brando, Richard Burton and Sidney Poitier each had parted with $5,000. Harry Belafonte and James Garner had each donated $3,500, and Paul Newman, Burt Lancaster and Mike Nichols had doled out $1,000 apiece.[139] In February, 1966, SNCC announced its annual fund-raising dinner at the New York Hilton. Tickets were $100 each, and Mrs. Harry Belafonte and Diahann Carroll were co-chairmen of the benefit. They and Lena Horne and Sidney Poitier performed in a program directed by Himan Brown.[140] (Ironically, in view of SNCC's subsequent diatribes against Zionism, Mr. Brown, for some years, has participated in the Chanukah Festival for Israel.)

A year before the Carmichael coup, northern affiliates called Friends of SNCC had 150 chapters, mostly on campuses. Friends of SNCC also helped secure the funds needed to meet the group's one million dollar annual budget.[141]

All this was at a time when the Student Nonviolent Coordinating Committee was still paying more than lip service to nonviolence. When SNCC was formed in 1960, it adopted a credo, which included these sentences: "Love is the central motif of nonviolence . . . by appealing to conscience and standing on the moral nature of human existence, nonviolence nurtures the atmosphere in which reconciliation and justice become actual possibilities."[142]

Seven years later, Carmichael, now the Keeper of the

Flame of Black Power, raged: "I don't go along with this garbage that you can't hate, you gotta love. I don't go along with that at all. Man you *can*, you *do* hate. You don't get arrested twenty-seven times. You don't smile at that and say love thy white brother."[143]

This was the same Stokely Carmichael who played a featured role in an adoring article by *Look* in 1965. *Look* wrote that "Stokely, *who believes fervently in nonviolence*, can't convince Strickland [a tough Alabama Negro], whose home arsenal includes a Browning automatic rifle, of its virtues." Carmichael was quoted as urging Strickland to put down his guns. Strickland refused. Carmichael reminded Strickland, "The Bible says to turn the other cheek." To which Strickland replied, "You turn the other cheek, and you'll get handed half of what you're sitting on."[144]

Small wonder that when Stokely Carmichael finally and formally renounced nonviolence loud and clear, his former white friends were stunned, and at first deluded themselves with the false hope that he had somehow been misquoted, or been victimized by a sensation-seeking press. They eagerly grasped at any explanation at all—all except the bare possibility that Carmichael had meant exactly what he said, and said exactly what was reported in the newspapers.

The schism in SNCC's ranks did not sprout up overnight. The organizer of the 1963 march on Washington, Bayard Rustin, saw the conflict coming during the biracial crusades in the South. He cited this example: "A Negro girl down South is working in a SNCC headquarters where she has been told about 'participatory democracy.' Get this scene—and I saw this myself. The girl is struggling to prepare a mimeographed press release which has to be out by 2 o'clock. She can't type or spell. A white girl comes in, looks at it in horror, says: 'Move over,' and knocks it off in three minutes."[145]

Rustin stressed: "That happens over and over. And then there were all those Negro boys who had been taught all their lives to leave white girls alone. And then the white girls start to arrive in droves, some of them pretty sick whites too. Again, you could see it over and over, a bunch of black and white kids sitting in a room and the Negro girls getting no attention whatsoever."[146]

Seven months before Stokely Carmichael became chairman, there were ominous signs that SNCC was conditioning children to regard all policemen as their mortal enemies. SNCC published a 50-page paperback of Negro history written by staff members and intended for use in "freedom schools." The book equated a "Tom" with anyone who informed on the movement. Modernistic drawings in the book showed policemen beating hapless Negroes and a suspender-wearing white sheriff leaning over a ballot box with a pistol.[147] While this may have been a reasonably accurate portrayal of *some* officials in *some* counties in the past, it was all too obvious that children might apply the "lesson" to *all* counties, *all* states, and *all* the country in the present. And this at a time when an official was quoted as saying, "There are not many Jim Clarks left who will try to put down a movement with simple force."[148] A case in point was Rankin County, Mississippi, which might have held a record for burned churches. Officials there turned on the air conditioning in the courthouse and *welcomed* a group of steaming Negro marchers protesting discrimination in voter registration.[149]

At this point in racial history, the civil rights movement was swiftly turning from protest to politics. And it was now that for perhaps the first time, the outside world became aware of the existence of Stokely Carmichael. In a twist of wry irony, his name appeared in the news in August, 1965, in the aftermath of the shotgun slaying of a white civil rights worker in Lowndes County, Alabama.[150] Carmichael, then SNCC's field secretary in charge of the Lowndes County movement, commented: "We want to show the people that we are not afraid of Lowndes County and that they can't run us out. We want them to know that if that is the price that has to be paid, there are some people willing to pay it."[151] At the same time, in almost the manner of a casual aside, Carmichael disclosed that there was talk of forming a new political party in the county modeled after Mississippi's predominantly Negro Freedom Democratic Party.[152]

In January, 1966, in an article in the *New Republic*, Carmichael spelled out the committee's plans in greater detail. (Parenthetically, it should be noted that Carmichael was still a field secretary, and his article appeared under the titular banner: "Thoughts of the Young Radicals.") Writing from Lowndes County, Carmichael revealed that SNCC's research department had found a curious quirk in Alabama law—the possibility of a group of citizens in any county becoming a political party in that county by running candidates for county offices and getting 20 per cent of the vote. Having done that, the county party could go on to become a state party by running candidates for state office and polling 20 per cent of that vote.[153] To this end, Carmichael announced that local "freedom parties" were being organized in ten counties stretching across Alabama's Black Belt, with plans for more of the same in twelve more counties. One hundred and fifty black Alabamans had already learned about the duties of a county sheriff and a tax assessor, with more to come.[154] At the same time, SNCC workers were advising Negroes to boycott the Democratic primary, because of a law which could be used to invalidate the independent nominating convention on the grounds that voters at the convention had also participated in the Democratic primary.[155]

Thus the all-black Black Panther Party was born, and beyond any doubt it was an all-Carmichael production. On paper at least, the chances of Negro electoral victories in Lowndes County seemed all but assured with the passage of the Voting Rights Act of 1965. Of the approximately 15,000 persons living in Lowndes County, 81 per cent were Negroes.[156] But they did not reckon with the economic

power of the white minority. In January, civil rights workers started erecting tents for Negroes who said they had
been ordered from their farm homes by white landlords
during a voter registration campaign. One local Negro
leader charged that "Several families, maybe as many as
50, have been ordered from their homes in Lowndes
County," adding, "And we'll get tents for any of them that
wants one."[157] Carmichael took the stump to urge election
of the all-Negro slate.[158] By Election Day, after a strenuous
voting campaign, 2,681 Negroes were registered to vote,
compared with 2,519 whites.[159] The New York *Times* felt
that if the white list were purged of absentees, the true
figure would be "somewhat less."[160] In any event, white
politicians in Lowndes County had little difficulty in getting
the message, and began reluctantly facing the realities of
political life. One unidentified white politician said he knew
times were changing in Lowndes County, and that he believed whites would now accept a "little integration."[161]

On Election Day, Stokely Carmichael received the not
merely bad, but practically traumatic, news. The seven
Negro candidates running as independents under the Black
Panther emblem in Lowndes County, Alabama, were defeated by white candidates by margins ranging from 273
votes to 677 votes.[162] It was a dismal defeat not only for
Carmichael, but his vaunted credo of "Black Power" as
well.

When the Black Panther Party first clawed its way
through Lowndes County, Stokely Carmichael was still a
Senior Field Secretary. By the time Election Day, 1966,
had arrived, he was the new chairman of the Student Nonviolent Coordinating Committee. Somewhere in the interim,
SNCC's pallbearers, clad in their best dungarees, bore "We
Shall Overcome" to a nitty-gritty grave, and unveiled the
warning to Whitey: "Move on over, or we'll move on over
you!"

At what exact point did the metamorphosis take place?
One could only refer to the old saw: "Those who say,

don't know; those who know, won't say." Looking back six months and even a year before Carmichael took office, there were signs of the new orientation. In June, 1965, just before his tenth arrest, SNCC Executive Secretary James Foreman warned that he did not know "how much longer we can stay nonviolent."[163]

In November of that same year, white liberal Charles Silberman wrote in *Fortune* that "SNCC members and sympathizers have been moving toward a rhetorical stance in which *any* cooperation with established organs of government or the existing political parties is decried as selling out to the Establishment . . ."[164] Pat Watters of the Southern Regional Council felt that SNCC was moving away from any devotion to nonviolence; as Watters put it: "The possibilities for success of terrorism against whites" was becoming "a topic for informal discussion."[165]

And in January, 1966, Carmichael—still marking time as head of SNCC's Alabama program—was telling the New York *Times* that SNCC felt it had spawned the New Left and did not object to the term. Equating SNCC with the New Left, he declared, "Our way is to help the poor get political power and then they can draw up their own plans."[166]

In Winter, 1966, the scattered monologues and dialogues coalesced into the position paper written by members of SNCC. It was still considered confidential in August, at which time excerpts were "leaked" to the New York *Times*.[167] It proved conclusively that SNCC's "Black Power" philosophy was no sudden impulse, but the product of months of planning.

In the SNCC position paper, white liberals were not merely criticized but torn to shreds; the tone was not simply one of disapproval but withering contempt for liberal paternalism. In the first instance, the position paper expressed the conviction that "white people coming into the movement cannot relate to the black experience, cannot relate to the word 'black,' cannot relate to the 'nitty gritty,' cannot relate to the experience that brought such a word into being, cannot relate to chitterlings, hog's head cheese, pig feet, hamhocks, and cannot relate to slavery because these things are not a part of their experience."[168] The SNCC paper contended that "One white person can come into a meeting of black people and change the complexion of that meeting . . ." because "blacks feel intimidated by whites." This was the reason that whites had to be excluded—because "whites have an intimidating effect."[169] One could concede that blacks might well feel ill at ease in the presence of whites—almost as ill at ease as whites had often been in the presence of blacks—and still decry the ludicrousness of the position paper's claim that "Negroes in this country have never been allowed to organize themselves because of white interference."[170] Whatever the situation in some, not necessarily all, Southern states, few obstacles had been placed in the path of would-be Negro organizers in the North—except, of course, the almost legendary political inertia of Northern Negroes themselves, as exemplified by the fact that less than half of the Negroes in New York City were registered to vote.[171]

One can only conjecture as to the amount of soul-searching that produced the SNCC position paper's grudging admission that whites had played "an important role in the movement. In the case of Mississippi, their role was very key in that they helped give blacks the right to organize."[172] But before the liberals could start trooping back to the fold, the position paper bluntly declared, "Since these goals have now been accomplished, their [whites'] role in the movement has now ended."[173] For any lingering whites still peering furtively through the blinds, the SNCC Black Power cabal had this word: "Further [white participation] means in the eyes of the black community that whites are the 'brains' behind the movement and blacks cannot function without whites."[174]

Almost exultantly, the SNCC black militants were burning all their white bridges behind them; they were lobbing verbal Molotov cocktails at those swollen liberal checkbooks that had kept them financially afloat for so many years. For them, the racial millennium would be reached only when "whites no longer designate roles that black people play but rather black people define white people's roles."[175] How approximately eleven per cent of the population would go about laying down the law to the other 89 per cent—in a country that still had some quaint notions about majority rule—never quite entered into the deliberations of SNCC's master planners.

SNCC was no longer pulling its punches where Whitey was concerned; it unleashed haymaker after haymaker, jab after jab, hook after hook, in a display of polemic prowess worthy of a Cassius Clay. Each sentence drew fresh blood, as when it stated: "When we view the masses of white people to view the over-all reality of America, we view the racism, the bigotry, and the distortion of personality, we view man's inhumanity to man; *we view in reality 180 million racists*."[176] (Italics supplied.) Curiously their most scathing ridicule was reserved for those whites who had worked most closely with them, as witness the statement: "There have been examples of whites who stated that they can deal with black fellows on an individual basis but become threatened or menaced by the presence of groups of blacks. It can be maintained that this attitude is held by the majority of progressive whites in this country."[177] SNCC's caustic counsel to "progressive whites" was to clean up their own Augean stables. They expressed the most scathing resentment "that most white radicals have sought to escape the horrible reality of America by going into the black community and attempting to organize black people while neglecting the organization of their own people's racist communities."[178] This was more than just rhetorical breast-beating; in the same paragraph appeared this astonishing denunciation, which could have been penned by Kwame Nkrumah and Jomo Kenyatta:

We feel that SNCC and the civil rights movement in general is in many aspects similar to the anticolonial situations in the

African and Asian countries. We have the whites in the movement corresponding to the white civil servants and missionaries in the colonial countries who have worked with the colonial people for a long period of time and have developed a paternalistic attitude toward them. The reality of the colonial people taking over their own lives and controlling their own destiny must be faced.[179]

Never had an umbilical cord been so totally, and irreparably, severed. "Whites," they declared, "are the ones who must try to raise themselves to our humanistic level."[180] This was followed by a dreary diatribe against the white man's "genocidal war in Vietnam," "neocolonialism in Africa and Latin America" and holding Negroes "in animalistic bondage over 400 years."[181] In sum, the position paper put it all down in black and white (or perhaps just black) in language so clear even the most sycophantic white supporter could have understood: "We reject the American dream as defined by white people and must work to construct an American reality defined by Afro-Americans."[182]

The bristling Whitey-phobia of the SNCC position paper (whose publication was followed by the transparently feeble objections of the SNCC hierarchy) angered, but hardly surprised, conservatives. American conservatives had always held a rather low opinion of the student group, and so were scarcely disillusioned by this latest scurrillity. But the liberal establishment went into a state of shock, mixed with the soulful lament of unrequited love. Over and over, one heard the redundant litany of deeds of almost otherworldly goodness that Big White Brother had performed for Little Black Brother. And amidst the intermittent liberal wails of self-pity one could discern the question: how could they do this to us?

At this point, it will come as no great surprise to the reader that the views contained in the position paper were championed by Stokely Carmichael.[183] At a meeting near Nashville, Tennessee, in May, 1966, the SNCC membership voted to adopt a formal policy of excluding whites from policy-making and organizational roles with the committee.[184] At this same meeting, John Lewis, SNCC's long-time chairman, made known his opposition to the new policy, and was ousted in favor of Carmichael.[185] One source said that the student committee re-elected Lewis during the early part of the meeting, but later rescinded its action and voted him out.[186]

At the time he became SNCC's new chairman, Stokely Carmichael was little more than a name to the overwhelming majority of Americans. He quickly proceeded to remedy that with large doses of demagogy in press conferences and on the roads of Mississippi.

One of Carmichael's first official acts was to refuse to participate in the White House Civil Rights Conference.[187] He blasted integration as "an insidious subterfuge for white supremacy in this country." He was in full accord with a SNCC manifesto that called for "all black Americans to begin building independent political, economic and cultural institutions [to] use as instruments of social change."[188]

With a tenderness he had never shown toward white racists, King softly disassociated himself from the black racism inherent in the new political stance of the student group. Throwing a bone to his white supporters, King stated: "While I can't agree with the move toward a kind of Black Nationalism which seems to be developing in SNCC, it is an indication of deep discontent, frustration, disappointment and even despair in many segments of the Negro community."[189]

As King had probably intended, there was nothing in the statement that would have caused Stokely Carmichael more than a momentary flicker of annoyance. In any event, it was the SNCC chieftain who had the last word, in a forum that could hardly have been more ideal for his purposes if he had designed it himself. The eyes of the country were on the setting he had picked—and after Americans half-dozed through the dog-eared clichés of Martin Luther

King, they suddenly woke with a start and realized that the master of racial drama was being upstaged by a 25-year-old with an almost too-perfect Southern drawl (which could change to New Left dialectic or New Yorkese at a moment's notice, as the locale required). And when the rerun had ended and the performers stalked off the stage, it was not King but Carmichael who was taking most of the curtain calls and garnering most of the critical reviews.

It began, as did many of the milestones in civil rights history, with an act of violence. The loner of the civil rights movement, James Meredith, was walking along U.S. Highway 51, two miles south of Hernando, Mississippi. His walk was a personal pilgrimage aimed at promoting Negro voter registration; it was also a test to learn whether he and other Negroes still had reason to fear Mississippi whites.[190] Meredith got his answer. He was shot in the back from ambush—hit in the head, neck, shoulder, back and legs by more than 60 birdshot pellets.[191] The assailant, who was not a Mississippian, could not say why he had fired the shots.[192] For some time, Meredith had been "out of sight, out of mind," but now he was front-page news again, and as such, the object of a virtual foot-race between King and Carmichael to see who could get to the hospital first. King crossed the finish line slightly ahead of the new leader of SNCC.

The reasons for the stampede to Meredith's bedside were all too transparently obvious. As the New York *Times* pointedly reminded its readers, "In recent years, every major civil rights bill has been spurred to Congressional passage by acts of violence in the South. Last week, the Meredith shooting in Mississippi created new pressure for enactment of President Johnson's 1966 civil rights measure."[193] As Rep. Emanuel Celler, a sponsor of the bill commented: "There are times when the civil rights movement has no greater friend than its enemy."[194]

If events had progressed in the usual way, one could

almost have written the ending before Martin Luther King
had put on his marching shoes. A massive march would
have taken place. The marchers would have met stiff resistance along the way from white segregationists, culminating in bloodied heads, and, with luck, the use of fire
hoses and/or police dogs. Overjoyed, the civil rights leaders would have implored Washington to send Federal
troops, Congress would have been deluged with mail, delegations, resolutions and stinging editorials demanding the
immediate passage of the Civil Rights Act of 1966. The
few Southern Congressional diehards opposing it would
have been beaten down, and the bill would have passed
with the kind of top-heavy majority that party whips dream
about. This had been the unfailing pattern for years, and
King was straining every nerve to follow the script faith-
fully. But it all came to pieces on the roads of Mississippi,
when Stokely Carmichael added two incendiary words to
the dialogue.

The morning after the shooting, King was on his way
to the Memphis hospital where Meredith was recuperat-
ing from his wounds. Floyd McKissick of CORE accompanied King to the hospital, and Carmichael arrived a little
later that same day.[195] According to King, the discussion
with Meredith centered around plans for a larger Mississippi march, its character and logistics.[196] But Pete Hamill,
a reporter for the New York *Post*, told a more disillusion-
ing story. Writing from Mississippi, Hamill said that King,
Carmichael and McKissick viewed the attack on Meredith
as "something of value" which could put new life in a
"civil rights movement which has seemed to be petering
away."[197] The *Post* reporter continued:

But when it turned out that Meredith had received only super-
ficial wounds and was—according to officials of William F.
Bowld Hospital—able to go home, they protested vigorously.
Instead of starting the march at Coldwater on schedule at
10 a.m., King, Carmichael and McKissick went to the hospital
and talked with great vigor about the need for Meredith to

help keep the march going. Obviously, if Meredith were well enough to fly back to New York, the deep national outrage which made Selma possible would probably fizzle. So would the march on Jackson, to which they were strongly committed.[198]

Hamill cited reliable sources within the movement who said that "the leaders wanted Meredith to stay in the hospital as long as possible; as long as he stayed, his value as a symbol would continue. The hospital, however, said that Meredith was able and well enough to leave and that his bed could be used by other patients."[199]

For three hours, Hamill wrote, King, McKissick and Carmichael tried to convince Meredith to remain in the hospital.[200] Meredith rejected their demands, left the hospital and flew to New York. In the middle of a press conference in New York, as he was reading a statement, Meredith suddenly fainted.[201] A physician examined him and found that he had suffered nothing more serious than a fainting spell; a hospital authority attributed it to the emotional stress of the past few days.[202] The New York *Post* reporter thought Meredith's fainting spell had been at least partially caused by the pressure exerted on Meredith by King, McKissick and Carmichael. Three people who had been in and out of Meredith's hospital room in Memphis said this pressure had been "tremendous."[203]

A few days later, both houses of the Mississippi legislature adopted a resolution deploring the "unfortunate and criminal shooting" of Meredith.[204]

King expressed confidence that the civil rights movement would stage a march that would rival the one from Selma to Montgomery.[205] At first, it seemed very much like old times, with hordes of reporters beating a path to Mississippi and then hanging on King's every word. The three civil rights chiefs got off to a rousing start as they took up James Meredith's march to Jackson. Three Mississippi troopers told them to hike along the side of the road instead of the pavement. When they refused, the troopers

began pushing and shoving the marchers.[206] Now civil
rights partisans were rushing to Mississippi in droves, and
began talking of a march of hundreds if not thousands,
and a variety of goals.[207] King hoped the march would
help pass the pending civil rights bill—a bill which provided stiffer penalties for those who injured civil rights
workers.[208] SNCC was primarily interested in using the
march as a "good organizing tool."[209] And Stokely Carmichael left no doubt that the organizing was to be along
racial lines. From the first lap of the march, the SNCC
chief was urging Negroes to seize power in areas where
they outnumbered whites. "I'm not going to beg the white
man for anything I deserve," he said. "I'm going to take
it."[210] And McKissick, denouncing the failures of the nation's policymakers, said they ought to break the Statue
of Liberty's legs "and throw her in the Mississippi."[211]

With the march just barely begun, four civil rights
groups signed a "manifesto" demanding that President
Johnson send Federal voting registrars into 600 Southern
counties; that Congress provide a "freedom budget" involving "billions" in aid for low-income Negroes; that the pending civil rights bill be amended to require states and
counties to hire Negro law enforcement officers and put
Negroes on jury lists in direct proportion to their population ratio.[212] The "manifesto" was signed by Martin Luther
King, Floyd McKissick, Stokely Carmichael, and Arthur
Thomas, head of the Delta Ministry (an affiliate of the National Council of Churches).[213] Roy Wilkins and Whitney
Young had flown in to see Meredith, but did not sign the
document.[214]

At the beginning, the marchers—varying, day by day,
from a few dozen to a few hundred—were protected by
Mississippi state highway patrolmen. On one of these days,
twenty of these patrolmen moved ahead of the column,
urging whites to "keep calm" and occasionally inspecting
cars for firearms.[215]

The march was a rag-tag, on-again, off-again affair. King

left the march for a few days, and then was back at the head of the column.[216] Carmichael went to Arkansas, but said he would be back later.[217] McKissick had planned to return to New York at one point, but then decided to stay on for another day.[218] This may have been one of the reasons why an exasperated Charles Evers of the Mississippi NAACP snapped, "I don't want this to turn into another Selma where everyone goes home with the cameramen and leaves us holding the bag."[219]

Evers charged that someone had signed his name to the march "manifesto" without his permission after he had declined to sign the document "because it was too critical of President Johnson." He added, "And I feel that the money that's going to be spent on the march would be more beneficial to Negroes if it were spent on voter registration and voter education." Evers couldn't quite see "how walking up and down a hot highway helps" and was convinced that "Mississippi has been exploited enough by Negroes and whites who want to raise money and get publicity."[220] But he indicated that he might join the column himself if he became convinced that the out-of-state marchers would remain in Mississippi and help with Negro voter registration drives.[221]

The New York *Times* felt that "The marchers are providing the first major convention of civil rights activists since the drive against segregation in Selma, Ala., more than a year ago . . ."[222] If it was a convention, one of the major subjects on the agenda was the role, if any, whites would play in the movement. While staff workers from the Southern Christian Leadership Conference thanked Northern whites who came South to march, SNCC wondered aloud if whites ought to be on the march at all.[223] The division even permeated King's own ranks. One of King's top aides complained that "Instead of drawing the Negro community together, they [white organizers] divide it by trying to make too many decisions." But another of King's top aides, the Rev. Ralph Abernathy, told a Negro meeting, "If you got any notions that Negroes can solve our problems by ourselves, you got another thought coming. We welcome white people."[224]

Now King was back on the march, after two days in Chicago. Presumably he was replying to Evers when he told reporters: "We aren't here to engage in a publicity stunt. We are here because things are not right in this state."[225] He announced that plans were being made to assign civil rights organizers to several parts of the state after the march was over.[226]

What looked like the movement's first solid success took place in Grenada, Mississippi. City and county officials appointed four Negro voting registrars and promised nighttime and neighborhood voting registration for Negroes. The six Negro registrars worked through the day and into the night and registered more than 500 Negroes.[227]

State Highway Patrolmen were still protecting the marchers, in accordance with the policies of Governor Paul Johnson, who felt that racial incidents hurt business in Mississippi and resulted in increased civil rights activity.[228] To King, the cooperation of the state police was all part of a sinister plot. He called it "a more sophisticated form of resistance to racial desegregation."[229] And it must have been positively maddening for him to see the marchers hiking along highway shoulders that had been freshly mown by state highway maintenance crews to make marching easier and faster.[230]

And then, very suddenly, Governor Johnson reversed his policy. Proclaiming that "We aren't going to wetnurse a bunch of showmen all over the country," the Governor reduced the march's escort from about twenty highway patrol cars to four.[231] His announcement came as the marchers were in the vicinity of Greenwood, "one of the worst communities in the United States for Negroes," according to a member of SCLC.[232]

It was in Greenwood that Charles Evers, now satisfied that the march was a "good thing," joined the column.[233]

And it was in Greenwood that Stokely Carmichael started a racial—if rhetorical—conflagration that may not be extinguished in our lifetime. Five times Carmichael shouted, "We want black power!" And as the audience applauded enthusiastically, Carmichael ranted: "Every courthouse in Mississippi ought to be burned down to get rid of the dirt."[234] Martin Luther King was not there to hear it; he had flown back to Chicago for another brief visit.[235]

When Governor Johnson cut back on the highway patrol escort, he also called upon the local police to take over the responsibility for the marchers.[236] Almost at once, white resistance to the march stiffened. In Greenwood, the police jailed three march leaders, a white man used a gun to order supply trucks for the column off the roadside, and Stokely Carmichael was jailed on charges of trespassing when he attempted to erect tents on public school property.[237] But shortly after, the City Commission allowed the marchers a campsite at a park for Negroes.[238]

King came back to the march, but almost all that he could do or say was drowned out by the chants of "Black Power! Black Power!" He appealed for an end to talk of "black power" among some Negro leaders, to little avail.[239]

There developed a fierce competition between the Black Power advocates and the Freedom Now partisans. Speakers on each side did their utmost to persuade the crowds to chant their slogan the loudest.[240] King considered the term "unfortunate because it tends to give the impression of black nationalism." It was King's belief that "Black supremacy would be equally as evil as white supremacy."[241]

Certainly, on the marching line, "Black Power" was not conceived of as nonviolent; among some marchers, it evoked a yell for "white man's blood."[242]

The next town in the line of the march was Philadelphia, Mississippi, the town in which Deputy Sheriff Cecil Price was among eighteen white men charged with depriving three murdered civil rights workers of their civil rights under a Federal statute of 1870.[243] (In 1967, he would be found guilty by an all-white Federal court jury.)[244] The march was part of a memorial service for the three—Michael H. Schwerner, Andrew Goodman, and James E. Chaney—whose bodies had been found in an earthen dam two years before. Here, a white crowd assaulted the marchers and there was an exchange of gunfire when marauding whites invaded the Negro community.[245]

The next stop on the march itinerary, Indianola, was the birthplace of the White Citizens Council. There were no incidents. More than 100 whites stood quietly on the sidewalk as the Negroes, while waiting for King, began shouting "black power—black power."[246] A SNCC field secretary told the crowd, "When people say, 'What do you want?' don't say 'freedom,' say 'black power.'" Like a racist community sing, he shouted, "What do you want?" The crowd replied: "Black Power." But when SCLC's Rev. Abernathy arrived at the rally, he also asked Negroes what they wanted. When some yelled "black power," he ordered, "say 'freedom.'" The Negro crowd then obligingly shouted, "Freedom."[247]

At a rally in Yazoo City, King was reported to have "lashed out at the student committee's policy of advocating 'black power' and at the Deacons for Defense and Justice, which urges Negroes to arm themselves in self-defense."[248] King "lashed out" all right, but a considerable part of this attack sounded more appropriate for a Black Muslim treatise than an integrationist's speech. King told his audience, "Some people are telling us to be like our oppressor, who has a history of using Molotov cocktails, who has a history of dropping the atomic bomb, who has a history of lynching Negroes. Now people are telling me to stoop down to that level. I'm sick and tired of violence. I'm tired of the war in Vietnam. I'm tired of Molotov cocktails."[249]

In announcing a second march in Philadelphia, King emphasized that it would be nonviolent, and said anyone not committed to that philosophy would not be allowed to participate. Carmichael and McKissick professed to agree

"100 per cent."[250] Nevertheless, twice in two nights, Mississippi Negroes met violence with violence, wounding a few would-be white bully boys in the process. "They got to realize," Charles Evers stated, "that we're not going to take it any more."[251]

From a political standpoint, the results of the march thus far had been spotty, uneven, and generally disappointing. Then the marchers reached Canton, Mississippi—in Madison County—and the movement was right back on Page One. The headlines fairly screamed: "Mississippi Police Use Gas To Rout Rights Marchers!"[252] If one had read far enough down the columns, persevering until he had reached the last few paragraphs, he would have discovered that the tear and irritant gas was used only as a last resort, and only then after warning had been given. To understand what *really* happened that day, it is necessary to keep in mind that the gassing was almost the *last* in the chain of events that took place in Madison County. Let us lay the headline aside for the moment, back up, and start from the beginning.

Let us start with the civil rights marchers demanding the right to use the grounds of a Negro elementary school in Canton as a campsite.[253] Let us listen to the Superintendent of Schools, explaining that school property "could be used only for school-sponsored events."[254] Let us quote Attorney General Katzenbach's statement that the demonstrators had been offered alternative sites by the city of Canton[255]—a statement quickly confirmed by Andrew Young, executive director of the Southern Christian Leadership Conference.[256] Then let us listen to Stokely Carmichael telling a crowd: "They said we couldn't pitch tents on our own black school ground. We're going to do it now."[257] Let us follow this Pied Piper of Chaos leading more and still more Negroes, until at one point as many as 3,500 persons were on the school property.[258] Let us view the state troopers warning the marchers over microphones, "You will not be allowed to erect the tents—if you do you will be removed."[259] And then let us re-read that headline, and put in proper perspective the troopers' grim decision to use gas to clear the school grounds.

Madison County Attorney Goza readily acknowledged, "This was a rough decision but these people had been told twenty times not to do it. This is not a campsite, this is public property dedicated to education. The Boy Scouts couldn't use it. The church couldn't use it."[260]

Just before the tear gas was fired, the Rev. Richard McSorley, S.J., professor of social justice at Georgetown University, asked Assistant Attorney General John Doar: "Isn't there something you can do?" Doar replied, "What can I do? Neither side will give an inch."[261]

There had been drenching showers that day, and the ground was soaked. With the tents already removed by the police, the marchers would have had no shelter at all but for a Roman Catholic mission that turned over its gymnasium to the Negroes.[262]

The following day, Martin Luther King reached a compromise with Canton officials. No further attempt was made to pitch tents on the Negro schoolgrounds, but the marchers were permitted to hold a meeting there. Boos greeted the announcement that the tents were already on their way to the next stop, and the Negroes would have to rough it one more night on the concrete floor of the Catholic mission gymnasium.[263]

Now King and a racial entourage of 300 returned to Philadelphia, Mississippi, to show "that we can stand before you without fear after we were beaten and brutalized the other day." This time, more than 100 heavily armed state highway patrolmen and local law enforcement officers were on hand to provide protection from some 1,500 to 2,000 whites. The Mayor told the marchers that he did not want "any trouble," and then lent his electric megaphone to the march leaders for their speeches.[264]

At this point, the forgotten man, James Meredith, joined the march, the first time he had participated since he was

shot[265] (it was somewhat analogous to a banquet attended
by everyone except the guest of honor). Meredith rode in
a car during the last two miles on the advice of doctors.
"I'm not armed," Meredith said, "because the Mississippi
Highway Patrol Chief has accepted all responsibility for
security. He has given me his word."[266]

It was hoped that the march could be ended with a
bang, but it was really more like a pallid pop. A crowd of
eight to ten thousand turned out for a rally featuring
Anthony Franciosa, Marlon Brando, Burt Lancaster,
Sammy Davis, Jr., and Dick Gregory.[267] SNCC workers,
recruiting right to the end, distributed bumper stickers
bearing a picture of a lunging panther, and the legend
humbly proclaiming "We're the greatest."[268]

The long march was officially brought to a close in Jackson, as 12,000 to 15,000 singing, shouting marchers
crowded around the State Capitol and demanded immediate and sweeping reforms in the treatment of Negroes.[269]
Hundreds of National Guard troops, state highway patrolmen and other officers looked on, with tear gas and riot
guns at the ready.[270]

A much more meaningful show was being played back-
stage. March leaders barred Charles Evers and other
NAACP leaders from speaking at the rally. The reason
given for the exclusion was that Evers had repudiated the
"march manifesto."[271] Among those voting for the exclusion
were CORE and SNCC. King's Southern Christian Leadership Conference had voted against the limitation.[272] Whitney Young of the Urban League was allowed on the
platform, but only after he had agreed to sign the manifesto.[273]

The battle of the slogans went on, unabated. SNCC
passed out placards that said "Move on Over or We'll
Move on Over YOU." SNCC supporters repeatedly roared:
"Black power, black power." Southern Christian Leadership Conference supporters tried to drown them out with
shouts of "Freedom Now," and distributed hundreds of

plastic American flags. The sight of the flags enraged SNCC field secretary Willie Ricks, who rushed into the march column and demanded "Give me those flags. That flag does not represent you."[274]

Did the march do any good? "Oh, I think so," King replied. "It's just unfortunate we weren't able to get across the incredible conditions, the degradation Negroes live under in Mississippi, because of all the focus on dissension within."[275]

One of King's top aides, the Rev. Bernard Lee, commented, "We've learned a lesson from this march." The lesson was that "We can't work with SNCC, or for that matter with CORE either. This time it was unavoidable. We had to pick up the march once Meredith was shot. And SNCC was here when we arrived. But we've learned. From now on we'll keep Stokely [Carmichael] off Dr. King's coattails. Did you notice that every time the cameras were running, there was Stokely right next to Dr. King?"[276]

In the dizzying span of three short weeks, the Mississippi march had made a national figure of Stokely Carmichael and provided a national forum for "Black Power!" It was Carmichael who dominated the march, Carmichael who electrified the crowds with his chants of "Black Power," Carmichael who was being hailed as a new Malcolm X. As King stood by, mildly mouthing the old sagging platitudes, press power was building up black power as the tidal wave of the racial future.

If King balked at the heretical idea of dissociating himself from the student committee, it was because, as the New York *Times* noted, such an action "would strip him of much of the youthful support he needs to mount successful demonstrations."[277] Other Negro leaders would denounce the Student Committee implicitly, if not explicitly, but King would perch precariously on the fence, blandly ignoring Stokely Carmichael sawing away at the posts.

In *Where Do We Go From Here: Chaos or Community*,

King quoted Carmichael as saying, "Martin, I deliberately decided to raise this issue on the march in order to give it a national forum and force you to take a stand for Black Power." To which King laughingly replied, "I have been used before. One more time won't hurt."[278]

Certainly the American public had been used before—and before that—by Martin Luther King, and now "one more time" in Mississippi. New York *Post* reporter Hamill wrote of King, McKissick and Carmichael that "None of them became involved in his [Meredith's] march through Mississippi until he was shot."[279] The point was well taken, and amply confirmed a year later when Meredith resumed his march on U.S. Highway 51, from the same spot where he had been ambushed.[280] This time, Meredith was not shot, and this time, to no one's great surprise, he marched without the company of Martin Luther King, Floyd McKissick, or Stokely Carmichael.

By now, the entire country was asking (with the degree of personal urgency depending upon one's proximity to a Negro neighborhood) "What is Black Power?" Carmichael's own answers seemed to vary with the audience he was addressing or the publication which was interviewing him. In the mass-circulation Negro magazine *Ebony*, Lerone Bennett, Jr., wrote that Carmichael regarded Black Power as "a black declaration of independence. . . . In its simplest form, it is the demand for majority control in areas where black people are in the majority and a proportional share (20 per cent where the black population is 20 per cent of the total) of key decision-making posts in areas where they are in the minority. If conceded or taken, this would mean black control in several Black Belt counties and Southern cities and eventual black control in Baltimore, Washington, Newark and other major American cities that will soon have black majorities."[281] According to Bennett, Carmichael insisted that power exercised by black people would "be power exercised not for racial ends but for the most advanced social interests of the day—decent housing, decent jobs, democratic decision-making."[282]

But it was quite another Stokely Carmichael, chanting a considerably more racist tune, who had this to say in the militant-oriented *Negro Digest:* "We have to build a strong base to let them know if they touch one black man driving his wife to the hospital in Los Angeles, or one black man walking down a highway in Mississippi, or if they take one black man who has a rebellion and put him in jail and start talking treason, we are going to disrupt this whole country."[283] Carmichael wrote that the Muslim leader, Elijah Muhammad, "represents a great section of the black community. Honor him."[284] As for whites who considered themselves friends of the Negroes, "We haven't had the chance to say whether or not that man is stabbing us in the back or not. All those people who are calling us friends are nothing but treacherous enemies . . ."[285]

What program did Black Power offer? "None," Carmichael promptly admitted. Writing in the *New York Review of Books*, he conceded:

We have no infallible master plan and we make no claim to exclusive knowledge of how to end racism; different groups will work in their own different ways. SNCC cannot spell out the full logistics of self-determination but can only address itself to the problem of helping black communities define their needs, realize their strength and go into action along a variety of lines which they must choose for themselves.[286]

But a writer for the socialist magazine *Dissent* shrewdly noted that in some instances, "SNCC and CORE were substituting themselves for the Negro masses they claim to be responding to. They declare in favor of 'letting the people decide,' but their impatience and ideology drive them to try to decide for the people."[287]

This socialist writer was unimpressed by Carmichael's proposal that "Black Money" go into "the communal pocket," and that through the threat of rent strikes and boycotts, black ghetto residents force "an exploitative storekeeper to sell them, at minimal cost, a building or a shop that they will own or improve cooperatively . . ." The socialist called Carmichael's moral vision "admirable, but his social understanding fuzzy," in that a viable separatist black economy would mean "Negroes would have to take control of General Motors and U. S. Steel: hardly an immediate prospect and utter fantasy as long as Carmichael proposes to 'go it alone.' "[288]

As for Martin Luther King, he engaged in a running debate with himself on the whole subject. If one read his book *Where Do We Go From Here*, and turned to page 36, one found him labeling Black Power "a call to black people to amass the political and economic strength to achieve their legitimate goals." On page 38, he considered Black Power as "a call for the pooling of black financial resources to achieve economic security . . . a psychological call to manhood." But then on page 44, King effectively rebutted himself, and wrote: "Beneath all the satisfaction of a gratifying slogan, Black Power is a nihilistic philosophy born out of the conviction that the Negro can't win. It is, at bottom, the view that American society is so hopelessly corrupt and enmeshed in evil that there is no possibility of salvation from within."[289]

King considered the most destructive feature of Black Power "its unconscious and often conscious call for retaliatory violence." Then, shuddering at the blasphemous thought of "guilt by association," he hastened to add that he was not referring to Stokely Carmichael, who, he said, opposed "aggressive violence."[290]

In one of his rhetorical attacks on violent rebellion, King summoned up hellish visions of genocide, in supposed retaliation by fiendish whites. King wrote:

Anyone leading a violent rebellion must be willing to make an honest assessment regarding the possible casualties to a minority population confronting a well-armed, wealthy majority with a fanatical right-wing that would delight in exterminating thousands of black men, women and children.[291]

Re-read the above passage from his book, and then try to reconcile it with the public image of Martin Luther King as one of the most moderate of all civil rights leaders.

Probably one of the most disarming defenses of Black Power was made by Donald R. Hopkins, Assistant Dean of Students at UCLA, at Berkeley. Hopkins asked the reader to picture a poor Negro family "standing in the squalorous shamble of a living room in a tenement dwelling . . . then ask yourself which philosophy, the civil rights philosophy or the Black Power philosophy is more likely to get the floor swept first. I submit the clear answer is the Black Power philosophy." Dean Hopkins maintained, "Should for any reason whatsoever, due to pride, anger, love, whatever, 70 percent of the black slum dwellers decide to sweep their own floors and patch their own walls, a social revolution would be heralded that would resound around the world."[292]

But one got a much bloodier concept of Black Power from Dr. Nathan Hare, professor in the Department of Sociology and Anthropology at Howard University, and a sometime mentor of Stokely Carmichael. Dr. Hare wrote: "We foresee a black *blitzkrieg*—already shown bubbling last summer in Omaha, Chicago, Cleveland and elsewhere —making America a giant, mushrooming Watts, in which this country will either solve its problems or get the destruction it deserves."[293]

Another tireless champion of Black Power has been Sterling Stuckey, chairman of the Amistad Society, called by *Negro Digest* "perhaps the most vital of the independent associations concerned with extending knowledge and appreciation of Negro history."[294] To Stuckey, "Black power presupposes the essential identity of interests of people of African descent in America and abroad. An affirmation of

Pan-Africanism in its original sense, the mystique of black power is symbolic of the blazing vision which carried Malcolm X across the continent of Africa, forging links."[295]

Seven months before the formation of the Black Power Conference in Newark, the clergyman who was to be its chairman, Dr. Nathan Wright, Jr., discussed "The Creative Possibilities of Black Power." Dr. Wright, who was Executive Director of the Department of Urban Work in the Newark Diocese, wrote, "Our religious and national heritage, as well as the persistent experience of family life, speaks to the equitable principle of taking from each as he is able and providing for each as is his need."[296] This was, of course, only a slight paraphrase of the old Communist dogma, "from each according to his ability, to each according to his need."

Perhaps the most astute comment about Black Power was made by one of America's most renowned historians, C. Vann Woodward, speaking before a group of socialist scholars. (The speech was quoted by William Styron, author of The Confessions of Nat Turner, in a letter to the New York Times in 1966). Woodward stated, "I am more and more impressed with the association of extremist doctrines of separation with Caribbean and West Indian leaders and origins. . . . I am thinking also of a contemporary constellation of fledgling prophets who hail from Trinidad, St. Thomas, Jamaica and other glamorous West Indian vacation spots."[297]

Woodward went on:

The slogans of black nationalism, and go-it-alone, and bring-Whitey-to-his-knees have some color of historical logic behind them in islands where the population is 90 per cent or more black. They have no historical logic and no place in the historical experience of the country where the population is 90 per cent white. Three and a half centuries of American experience have bred in the American Negro a realism that is a product of his own history, not that of the West Indies, and he knows it in his very bones and marrow—whatever slogans he shouts in the hysteria of street riots, and whatever preachments of apocalyptic blood baths and racial Armageddons he may occasionally cheer.[298]

What is Black Power? Still, the question was asked. And still, there was no definitive answer, least of all from the man who had shouted the phrase into history in Greenwood, Mississippi.

In December, 1966, Carmichael sardonically declared, "Black people by their actions will define Black Power, and the people of this country will just have to wait and find out."[299]

The people of this country found out when the New Left assembled in Chicago on Labor Day weekend, 1967, to hold a convention of the National Conference for New Politics. It was a vengeance-riddled recreation of the saying, "All men are created equal, but some are more equal than others."

Possibly King had some premonition of impending racial disaster at this New Left gathering, for which he had agreed to deliver the keynote address.[300] In any case, almost two months before the National Conference for New Politics opened its convention, King had already begun dissociating himself from the group. He said that his presence as keynote speaker did not imply endorsement of any decisions the five-day conference might make because he would not be participating in its deliberations. Languidly holding the New Left at arm's length, he stated, "I am related to the convention merely as a guest speaker at its mass rally."[301]

It was really not quite that simple for a man of Martin Luther King's prominence to address an ultra-left-wing gathering—allow the sponsors to use his name as a drawing card for financial and political support—and then softly croon "Don't Blame Me" if the convention adopted resolutions that he found personally embarrassing. It was even less ingenuous of King to pretend that the speech was his one and only link with the National Conference for New Politics. Two days before he issued his verbal disclaimer, the New York *Times* had listed King and Stokely Carmichael as members of the national council of the New Politics conference.[302] Furthermore, while King himself might not have been on the convention floor, members of his SCLC did attend the conference (undoubtedly with his blessing) and did take part in the convention actions. The same article quoted Michael Wood, chairman of the convention steering committee, to the effect that while the Communist Party had not been invited to the convention, their members would not be excluded if they came as observers.[303] The Communists did not have to be asked twice. They sent in observers,[304] without a word of protest from Mr. Wood. There were also two representatives from TASS, and one each from the Bulgarian News Service and *The Worker*.[305]

Meeting at the Palmer House in Chicago, the National Conference for New Politics was comprised of some 3,000 people representing 200-odd groups[306] (with the emphasis on *odd*). Included were Women Strike for Peace, the Mississippi Freedom Democratic Party, the Summit County [Ohio] Adequate Welfare Committee, the Bergen County Democratic Council, and the Camden Citizens for Peace in Vietnam, to name only a few. Most delegates were under thirty. There was even a high school caucus. On the 25-man steering committee were David Frost, who ran for the U. S. Senate on a peace ticket in New Jersey, Dr. Benjamin Spock, representatives of SNCC and the Southern Christian Leadership Conference.[307]

Votes were distributed according to the number of activists the participating organizations had back home. On that basis, of the 33,500 votes distributed in the convention, about 5,000 represented black organizations.[308]

The ostensible purpose of the convention called by the National Conference for New Politics was to defeat President Johnson in 1968 and ultimately forge a new political "third force" in the nation.[309]

In his keynote address, Martin Luther King urged that the 1968 election be made "a referendum on the war" in Vietnam. He declared, "The American people must have an opportunity to vote into oblivion those who cannot detach themselves from militarism, those who lead us not to a new world but drag us to the brink of a dead world."[310] It was the same old serving of warmed-over similes, delivered to a not overly enthralled audience. A writer for the *New Republic* said King's speech "was such a bore to the delegates that they started to walk out of the hall ten minutes before it was finished."[311] A contributor to the *New Leader* found "support for Dr. King [as a third-party candidate] dissipated after his opening-night speech. He not only failed to fire emotions but the black militants and white radicals wrote him off as passé . . ."[312] Even the *New Yorker* found cause for ennui in his keynote speech, "a long and, for him, rather flat peroration, in a tired voice," and added that "As he spoke, some local Negro teen-agers shouted threats and insults at him from the back of the room."[313] King left the convention the following morning;[314] however, his Southern Christian Leadership Conference still had members present at the convention.

While the New Politicians inside the Chicago Coliseum were listening to the dulcet tones of Martin Luther King, outside a bongo group was chanting "Kill Whitey . . . Kill Whitey . . . Kill Whitey . . . Kill Whitey. . . ."[315]

At the National Conference for New Politics convention, there was the White Radical Caucus, the White Revolutionary Caucus, the Black Caucus, the Radical Alternatives Caucus, the Poor People's Caucus, the Women Strike for Peace Caucus, the Mobilization Caucus, the Labor Caucus, the California Caucus, the anti-King-Spock Caucus.[316]

There was one other added attraction. In the words of the *New Yorker*, "there were some local criminals who, despite the determination of the 'radicalized' to view them as revolutionaries, pursued their isolated acts of mugging in the elevators and vandalism in the halls . . ." These worthies further expressed their dissent by stealing three hundred dollars from the delegation of the Mississippi Freedom Democratic Party.[317]

Of all the groups and all the caucuses, it was the Black Caucus that reigned supreme—Black Supremacy taunting the Uriah Heeps in white radical ranks who performed nothing less than a groveling surrender. It was patently obvious even for so ultra-Left a magazine as the *Nation* that "What the whites offered the blacks was contempt for the white middle class—springing from self-contempt— that affirmed something about the power of being black."[318]

Even before the conference started, black militants complained that they were being excluded from pre-conference decision-making and barred from participating in drafting resolutions.[319] This in spite of the fact that no actual "decision-making" had yet taken place,[320] and that in any case nine of the twenty-five members of the convention steering committee were Negroes, as well as six of the twenty-four members of its executive board.[321]

The Convention's Committee on Resolutions deplored the alleged lack of black representation on the Steering Committee. Martin Peretz, an instructor in government at Harvard and a member of the convention's executive board, objected, "You are trying to railroad chaos through this convention," and scored the committee's "militant ignorance."[322] Eventually, more than half the Committee on Resolutions walked out to form a Whites in Support of the Black Caucus.[323]

It was to avoid further protests that the steering committee allowed Negroes to form a Black Caucus, financed by the National Conference for New Politics but operating as an autonomous unit within the conference.[324] Moderate blacks and black nationalists joined forces to form the Black Caucus, and if New Left integrationists sometime wake up screaming in the middle of the night, it may be that they are recalling their ignominious humiliation at the hands of the black minority in that weird convention.

At the outset, two-thirds of the Black Caucus opposed

the militants and voted *not* to walk out of the conference.[325] Then the militant minority persuaded most Black Caucus members to accept their position,[326] and from then on were in control. At the first full day of conference sessions, they set up a counter meeting, called the Black Peoples Convention. They met at a white Methodist church after the militants failed to secure a Negro church.[327]

Floyd McKissick of CORE set the tone as succinctly as anyone when he proclaimed, "Black people can't be a plank in someone else's platform. They must be the platform itself."[328]

"From the beginning of the convention," the *New Yorker* correspondent wrote, "the 'radicalized' whites had resolutely refused to deal with any competent or intelligent Negroes—any rational Negroes, as it turned out—as authentic blacks. Non-failed non-whites were simply regarded as sell-outs to the system, and ignored."[329] The "chairman" of the Black Caucus (for whom none of the Negroes could remember having voted) was Carlos Russell, a former Brooklyn poverty worker.[330] Russell conceded that the group did not pretend to represent black people all over the country.[331] His group included African nationalists, attired in African shirts and faletas; Northern ghetto militants; representatives of Martin Luther King's Southern Christian Leadership Conference in high-priced suits and ties; women from the Mississippi Freedom Democratic Party; and young men from SNCC in "black power" T-shirts.[332]

On the second day of the convention, the blacks sent word out of their secret caucus that they would be willing to participate in the convention if the white delegates accepted in toto a list of demands, which started out with this declaration:

We, as black people, believe that the United States system is committed to the practice of genocide, social degradation, to the denial of political and social self-determination of black people, and cannot reform itself. There must be revolutionary change. Revolutionary change does not mean systematic exclusion of blacks from the decision-making process as was done here in this convention.[333]

The Black Caucus considered it proper to make certain demands of the rest of the convention because "this exclusion raises serious doubts that white people are serious about revolutionary change."[334] The Negroes then made thirteen demands of the convention:

50 per cent Negro representation on all conference committees.

A conference slogan not of "Peace and Freedom," but "Freedom and Peaceful."

Support of the concept of self-determination for black people.

"Total and unquestionable support" to all so-called wars of national liberation in Africa, Latin America and particularly in Vietnam.

Condemnation of the "imperialistic Zionist war. This is not to imply anti-Semitism."

Restoration of Representative Adam Clayton Powell, Democrat of Manhattan, to the chairmanship of the House Education and Welfare Committee.

Assistance to indigenous local freedom and political organizations in voter registration, political education and the election of black candidates whom black people select.

Support of black control of the political, economic and social institutions in black communities.

A call to "all so-called freedom loving white people who wish to strike a blow for humanity to unshackle their minds from old conceptual structures and deal anew with the 20th century facts of black liberation efforts."

"Immediate reparation for the historic, physical, sexual, mental and economic exploitation of black people."

Organization of "white civilizing committees in all white communities to humanize the savage and beast-like character that runs rampant through America, exemplified by George Lincoln Rockwell and Lyndon Baines Johnson."

Support of all resolutions of the Newark Black Power convention.

Support of a bill by Representative John Conyers, Jr., Democrat of Michigan, to rebuild Detroit's black communities, "destroyed by Gestapo police tactics and Army occupation."[335]

The Black Power Caucus demanded that its program be accepted unamended by 1:00 p.m. If the white delegates refused, the Negroes said they would walk out.[336]

Several Negroes who wished to speak against the adoption of the thirteen proposals were hustled from the room by enforcers from the Black Caucus, and threatened and silenced outside.[337]

In the genteel vocabulary of the New Left, a New Jersey organizer told the Conference that if a bunch of whites had presented him with thirteen points on a take-them-or-leave-them basis, he would have replied, "Shove it!" He saw no reason to give a different answer to blacks.[338] Other whites strongly criticized the reference to "Zionist imperialism."[339] Nevertheless, there was tremendous sentiment to vote for the entire thirteen-point package as a gesture of trust and sympathy for the suffering Negroes. A sympathetic observer wrote in the New York *Times* magazine: "It was passion, not strategy, that carried the day. As one NCNP planner described it, 'An extraordinary development took place. The walls of the Palmer House began to drip with guilt.' "[340]

The *Times* observer wrote: "So far as a generous sampling of opinion could determine, nobody in the Palmer House that Saturday had read" the resolutions passed by the black power conference in Newark.[341]

Perhaps this explained why in the "debate," such as it was, the 2,100 delegates never once discussed the merits of the Newark pronouncements.[342] Nobody could remember what the Newark Black Power resolutions said, *and some of them were, in fact, secret.*[343] Later, the *New Republic* revealed that one of the Newark Resolutions threatened that blacks would disrupt the economy unless there was a Federal guaranteed wage.[344]

The anti-Zionist resolution should not have surprised anyone who heard Dick Gregory (the Negro militant and sometime comedian) at the opening session. Gregory said that he had received complaints from B'nai B'rith for some of his statements about Jews.

"Every Jew in America over 30 years old knows another Jew that hates Negroes," Gregory declared, "and if we hate Jews, that's just even, baby."[345]

Through an aide, Martin Luther King sent a last-minute appeal to drop the anti-Israel plank from the thirteen proposals.[346] The Black Caucus recommended only that the principle be changed to condemn the Israeli government, instead of "imperialistic Zionist war."[347] Some of the New Politics' largest contributors, including Harvard instructor Martin Peretz, indicated they were through with the group and walked out.[348] The *New Yorker* found these well-publicized departures "a kind of daily ritual; the few responsible whites at the convention often found themselves walking out, only to walk right back in, and out again."[349]

Much of the opposition to the Israel resolution seemed to center around a fear that liberal money would now be scared off.[350] A Newark organizer said he thought they would have to reckon with the possibility that most of the money except the Communist Party money would now withdraw from the Conference, but that there was no point in being fussy about where money for local organizing was coming from.[351]

The *New Leader* found irony in the fact that "the black militants kept deriding white liberals and Jewish money, yet the conference organizers had raised some $6,000 to feed, house and transport scores of black people to the convention."[352]

All thirteen proposals passed the convention by a 3-to-1 margin.[353] The subservient white majority viewpoint was neatly summarized by Dr. Bertram Garskoff, a psychology professor from Michigan State University, who said "to create revolution . . . anything goes."[354] The convention voted to approve the proposals and to give the blacks "sole" power to amend them.[355]

A writer for the *National Observer* found "Many black militants were surprised by the surface unity; they had assumed that their demands were so exorbitant they couldn't possibly be met."[356]

The *Nation* found the blacks "not only contemptuous of the whites for the ease with which they capitulated but offended by what they regarded as a more subtle and pernicious form of paternalism."[357] Other reactions were scarcely more flattering. One national leader privately referred to the white surrender as "self-flagellation."[358] And King's long-time aide, the Rev. James Bevel, later dismissed the white delegates as "Masochistic Fascists."[359]

By now, the black militants were ridiculing the National Conference for New Politics as a "paper tiger." And now they demanded no less than 50 per cent of the convention votes.[360] Instead of the 5,000 or so votes they had been given on the basis of the numbers of activists they allegedly represented, the Black Caucus now demanded no less than 28,498 votes—as many as all the white delegations represented.[361] Since the Black Caucus was acting as a bloc, this would mean effective control of the convention.[362]

The Communists and their dialectic comrades-in-arms had been on the fringes of this entire Fringe Convention. Then one after another of them got the microphone to urge 50 per cent of the vote for the Black Caucus.[363] Very quickly, other Communist Party stalwarts followed suit, along with their young serfs from the W. E. B. DuBois Clubs.[364] "My God," a convention staff member exclaimed, "they've surfaced!"[365] Among the Communists attending the convention was Claude Lightfoot, chief of the Communist Party in Illinois.[366]

It was the Communists and the DuBois Club representatives who emerged as the chief spokesmen for the Black Caucus demands.[367] "I hope they have the guts to turn it down," said a NCNP planner.[368] But given the Far Left orientation of most of the delegates, the outcome was inevitable. By a top-heavy margin of 2-to-1, the Black Caucus carried the day and won 50 per cent of the votes at the convention.[369] If the symbol of the Black Caucus was a panther, that of the white delegates could well have been a chicken, and a rather puny chicken at that. A woman from Wisconsin stood up and sadly burned her delegation card. "This is the old politics, not the new politics," she said, and went home.[370]

Carlos Russell, chairman of the Black Caucus, exulted, "We have just shown the nation that black people can fight." Then he formally took over the meeting, in the words of a New York *Times* observer, "on behalf of a group which represented, at best, a sixth of the convention's constituency and had no noticeable program beyond the humiliation of their white comrades."[371]

Now James Foreman of SNCC delivered a speech to the 2,000 delegates, which the New York *Times* called "the strongest demand for separate Negro political action under full Negro control that the convention had yet heard."[372]

Speaking for the Black Caucus, Foreman declared:

"We and we alone have the responsibility to wage our own war of liberation as we see fit. No one, absolutely no one in the world or the United States, has the right to dictate to us the forms of our struggle.

"We insist on our right to define the manner in which we will fight our aggressors. It is our right, our responsibility, and anyone who does not like it can go to hell.

"The dispossessed must assume direction and give leadership to the new politics. If you're not going to support us, you go your merry way, and we're going to liberate you whether you want to be liberated or not."[373]

When a white girl delegate rose, and called "point of order," Foreman replied: "There are no points of order." Someone shouted, "Is this a dictatorship?" and the SNCC leader said, "Yes, and I'm the dictator." At that point, about two dozen white delegates walked out of the Palmer

House ballroom in protest. Foreman then insisted none too convincingly that he had only been joking.[374]

A most perceptive commentary on the convention was offered by Henry Etzkowitz and Gerald Schatlander, instructors in sociology at Northeastern and Boston University, respectively: one of them had been a delegate, and the other a "close observer" at the New Politics Convention. Etzkowitz and Schatlander wrote: "We saw the SNCC-CORE black caucus 'whitemail' radicals and liberals into total submission. The super black-power advocates threw the guilt of the KKK and the White Citizens Council at whites. Many white radicals and liberals accepted this guilt as their own." The sociology teachers considered the outcome of the convention "the first real transformation of 'black power' from rhetoric to reality," and foresaw a backlash from many white radicals and a withdrawal of support from the New Politics organization. They revealed that "in an ironic double-reverse turnabout," the white revolutionary caucus at the convention refused to admit Negroes to its meeting. Etzkowitz and Schatlander glumly predicted, "Since CORE-SNCC black radicals could not possibly accept a militant integrationist black candidate such as Martin Luther King, and since the white radicals cannot work within the realities of the historic two-party system, they are all condemned to the self-fulfilling prophecy of their own powerlessness."[375]

In a "News Bulletin: To our friends, From: The SCLC Staff" dated November, 1967, King's group protested that:

Serious distortions by the press have created an impression that SCLC was part of a group at the Chicago conference of New Politics which introduced a resolution condemning Israel and unqualifiedly endorsing all the policies of the Arab powers. The facts are as follows:

1. The staff members of SCLC who attended the conference (not as official delegates) were the most vigorous and articulate opponents of the simplistic resolution on the Middle East question. As a result of this opposition the Black Caucus modi-

fied its stand and the convention voted to eliminate references to Zionism and referred to the executive board the matter of final wording. This change was the direct result of the spirited opposition on the floor by Hosea Williams, Southern Director of SCLC.[376]

The author has no reason to disbelieve the above statement. But the ugly fact still remains that members of the Southern Christian Leadership Conference—with the full knowledge of Martin Luther King—were part of a Black Power Caucus that made a racist conquest of a convention in which they were clearly a small numerical minority; they were part of a Black Caucus which compared the President of the United States to the then leader of the American Nazi Party, and supported all so-called wars of national liberation and everything that had come out of the Newark Black Power convention. These members of SCLC could have cast the most decisive vote of all, with their feet, and walked right out of the convention. But lacking courage or conviction, they stayed and became willing catspaws for the Black Militants. In that November, 1967, News Bulletin, King's group trumpeted: "SCLC will continue tirelessly to denounce racism, whether its form is white supremacy or anti-Semitism." Surely it was no oversight that the SCLC Bulletin failed to denounce the black racism which had turned this groveling Far Left convention into a virtual satellite of SNCC.

Many tears were shed for the abysmal failure of the convention of the National Conference for New Politics, but the author remains dry-eyed. With its Left-of-Left constituency—with its paeans of praise for Ho Chi Minh—no group has ever more richly deserved the fiasco that marked its meetings. If there is any tragedy connected with the whole shoddy affair, it is in the aura of pseudo-respectability that surrounded the convention because of the presence of members of the Southern Christian Leadership Conference, and the fact that Martin Luther King delivered the keynote address. Undoubtedly at the outset, a great many Americans—unaware of King's addiction for the Far, Far Left—believed the convention was simply a gathering of liberal "doves"; it was not until SNCC forced the passage of the thirteen resolutions that the cold and ugly truth seared its way into the national consciousness.

Above all people, Martin Luther King should have been able to foresee the pro-Communist, anti-white, anti-Semitic outcome of the convention in view of the sordid headlines being made by the Student Nonviolent Coordinating Committee. If he had not gotten the message from any other source, he could have learned from Gene Roberts, Southern correspondent for the New York *Times*, that "Rarely is a SNCC office without a handful of copies of such publications as *The Worker* or *People's World*, both organs of the Communist Party; *Freedomways*, a Marxist magazine; *The Militant*, a Trotskyite newspaper; *The National Guardian*, which is oriented toward both the Soviet Union and Communist China."[377] This same article revealed that "in the summer of 1964, children of well-known Communists and radicals became SNCC volunteers."[378] In 1965, Pat Watters of the racially moderate Southern Regional Council, wrote: "Everyone always says there are no Communists in positions of influence in the civil rights movement. But now they know this is hard to say. Clearly there is no reason why some skilled undercover man couldn't become a leader; *indeed, in SNCC such a fellow would seem to have found a perfect set-up.*"[379] (emphasis added)

A few months after becoming national chairman of SNCC, Stokely Carmichael announced that his organization would "join hands" with the Revolutionary Action Movement.[380] J. Edgar Hoover has described the Revolutionary Action Movement (or RAM) as "a highly secret all-Negro, Marxist-Leninist, Chinese-Communist-oriented organization which advocates guerrilla warfare to obtain its goals . . ."[381] RAM's official publication, *Black America*, stated: "When war breaks out in the country, if the action is directed toward taking over institutions of power and 'complete annihilation of the racist capitalist oligarchy,' then the black revolution will be successful. . . . The revolution will 'strike by night and spare none.' Mass riots will occur in the day with the Afro-Americans blocking traffic, burning buildings, etc. Thousands of Afro-Americans will be in the street fighting: for they will know that this is it."[382]

On February 16, 1967, in testimony before the House Appropriations subcommittee, J. Edgar Hoover stated, "In espousing his philosophy of black power, Carmichael has been in frequent contact with Max Stanford, field chairman of the Revolutionary Action Movement. . . ." The FBI chief added that Carmichael had "afforded Stanford assistance and guidance in forming a Black Panther party in New York City."[383] It was at just such a meeting—in which Carmichael and Stanford shared the same platform —that the RAM field chairman said the U. S. could be brought down with "a rag and some gasoline and a bottle"[384]—the ingredients of a Molotov cocktail.

In a background story on RAM, the New York *Times* included among its variously described aims "selective assassination of whites and Negroes . . ."[385] A month later, a stunned America learned that this aim was no empty rhetoric. In June, 1967, twelve men and four women in New York City were arrested on charges of conspiring to murder moderate civil rights leaders Roy Wilkins and Whitney Young.[386] It was charged that all the defendants were members of the Revolutionary Action Movement. Among those arrested was Max Stanford.[387] The Queens District Attorney's Office said that ten rifles, a machine gun, three carbines, a shotgun, four knives and three metal arrows had been found in the home of one of the defendants.[388]

To this day, Stokely Carmichael has not uttered a word of criticism against Max Stanford and the Revolutionary

Action Movement; it must therefore be assumed that SNCC and the RAM are still "joining hands."

The arrests took place two months before the convention of the National Conference for New Politics—but King manifested not the slightest uneasiness about the murderous company Stokely Carmichael keeps. Indeed, over the years, in the tons of pronouncements oozing out of the King verbiage mills, it would be difficult to find more than the mildest criticism of SNCC at all.

In the face of the voluminous evidence, King stolidly maintained his determination to see no evil, hear no evil, speak no evil of Stokely Carmichael and SNCC—even when the evil was virtually at his own doorstep, in his own home city of Atlanta. It happened just a few months after Carmichael became the head of SNCC. The Atlanta police shot and seriously wounded a Negro suspected of a car theft, after he had ignored their warning to stop.[389] Within three hours of the shooting, more than 400 Negroes, including about ten members of SNCC, were milling through the streets in a Negro neighborhood, chanting "Black power" and "police brutality."[390] When Atlanta Mayor Ivan Allen, Jr. climbed upon a police car to talk to the Negroes, they surged toward him and rocked the car repeatedly. Soon the mayor, shaken but uninjured, tumbled to the street, as some rioters screamed "White devil! White devil!" The mayor urged Negroes to "go home, please go home. . . . This is a good city. Help keep it that way, and go home." But members of the student committee urged Negroes, "Don't go—stay here and protest police brutality."[391]

The first SNCC member to arrive in the area was Stokely Carmichael; he rushed in only minutes after the 1:30 p.m. shooting of the suspect.[392] Carmichael found Negroes preparing to demonstrate, and told them: "We're going to be back at 4 o'clock and tear this place up."[393] That day in Atlanta, rioting Negroes fought the police with bricks and bottles. Sporadic violence continued into the

night, and by midnight the injury toll stood at fifteen.[394]
Atlanta Police Chief Jenkins said, "It is now the Nonstu-
dent Violent Committee. We must and will deal with it
accordingly."[395] And Mayor Allen declared, "If Stokely
Carmichael is looking for a battleground, he created one
last night, and he'll be met in whatever situation he cares
to create."[396]

Martin Luther King had been in Chicago while the Negroes were rioting in Atlanta.[397] His reaction followed the
well-worn pattern of bowing stiffly in the direction of law
and order, while reserving a bear hug for the student committee. Those white liberals still mesmerized by the King
name could point to the first sentence of his statement: "It
is still my firm conviction that a riot is socially destructive
and self-defeating. On the other hand," and here SNCC's
adroit King-watchers had learned to perk up their ears,
"while condemning riots it is just as important to condemn the conditions which bring riots into being." In a
speech which, by now, had all the spontaneity of a com-
puter, King continued, "A riot is the desperate language of
the unheard. What has America failed to hear? It has
failed to hear that the economic plight of the Negro has
worsened and that the promises of equality have not been
met."[398]

Meanwhile Stokely Carmichael was arrested and charged
with two misdemeanors—inciting to riot and disorderly conduct.[399] His bond was set at $11,000 (later reduced to
$10,000) and he was held in City Jail.[400] At first he re-
fused to post bond, and announced that he would remain
in jail "indefinitely."[401] Then, having milked the imprisonment for all the publicity value possible, he abruptly
changed his mind about being a "political prisoner" and
posted bond.[402]

Asked about Carmichael's role in the riots, King timidly
replied, "I would not want to pass on that. The matter is
in the courts, and under our system of justice, a man is
innocent until proven guilty."[403] And yet King had never

hesitated to declare the guilt of white segregationist defendants long before a final verdict had been reached.

By now, resentment against SNCC had spread to many parts of Atlanta's Negro community. In the Vine City community, about two miles from the scene of the riot, Negroes burned an outdoor stand filled with SNCC literature.[404] Several Negroes in Vine City reportedly threatened to "run SNCC out."[405] And a new community organization was formed in Summerhill, the riot area. Its first action was to pass out 700 door stickers saying "I am a good neighbor." Putting this sticker on a door meant that the student committee was not welcome at that house.[406]

As ever, King's modus operandi was to denounce the authorities (always a safe target) and to absolve SNCC of wrongdoing, even if it meant adding fuel to the still simmering racial fires. King conceded that, having been away from Atlanta, he was unable to weigh the reported resentment by Atlanta's Negro community against SNCC.[407] But this in no way inhibited him from saying that while Negro residents "are as disgusted with slums as much as anyone else, they do not want violence, tear gas or a camp occupied by police in their community. They feel this [SNCC's involvement] might lead to these conditions."[408]

In Federal Court, Stokely Carmichael admitted having made a radio broadcast in which he urged Negroes to "turn out and tear up the city."[409] But in a neat semantic somersault, he told the court he had meant that Negroes should come out and protest in an effort to "tear up their old way of life."[410] The Federal Court threw out Carmichael's contention, along with one of the laws under which he had been arrested. The Court held unconstitutional an Atlanta disorderly conduct ordinance under which he and dozens of other Negroes had been convicted after the rioting. But the judges delayed the effect of their decision for 60 days to permit enactment of a legal ordinance, if the city wanted to take such action. The court ruled that Carmichael had failed to prove his charge that the prosecution was aimed only at discouraging civil rights activities. As for the state law under which Carmichael had also been arrested, the three judges simply declined to pass on its legality.[411]

Shortly after the rioting began, one of Martin Luther King's top aides, the Rev. Hosea Williams, told a news conference that he was urging a massive campaign of non-violence.[412] He was promptly contradicted by the Rev. Samuel W. Williams, chairman of the Atlanta chapter of the NAACP, a leader of the Atlanta Summit Leadership Conference, and a member of the board of the Southern Christian Leadership Conference. Rev. Williams pointedly commented that "Dr. King does not go anywhere unless the local leaders ask him in. We have not made any such request and we do not intend to."[413]

Step by inexorable step, Martin Luther King was building bridges between the Southern Christian Leadership Conference and the Student Nonviolent Coordinating Committee. To be sure, King evinced some distress at the growing anti-white, anti-Semitic sentiments of the student committee; but he still allowed his aides to "join hands" with SNCC and others, to create the demagogic Black Caucus at the National Conference for New Politics. And this only a few months after SNCC published a newsletter so flagrantly anti-Semitic that it evoked that very rarest of protests from liberal never-never land—a denunciation by the Anti-Defamation League of *left-wing* extremism.

In 1967, that sizable group of Americans receiving their copy of *Facts*, Volume 17, No. 5, published by the Anti-Defamation League of B'nai B'rith, must have received the shock of their liberal lives. Reading between the lines, one could almost hear the cry: How Art Thou Fallen From Heaven, O Lucifer. In any case, there was the indictment in living black and white. For the first time within the memory of many a man, the Anti-Defamation League was devoting reams of space to an unbridled attack on a Negro organization.[414] After overcoming the first faint feeling that the sky was falling down, the Anti-Defamation League's avid fans read: "It is ironic that the Student Non-Violent Coordinating Committee (SNCC), which has become a black racist and left-wing revolutionary organization, and the National States Rights Party (NSRP), a white racist, anti-Negro, anti-Jewish, neo-Nazi organization, have both permitted themselves to become mouthpieces for Arab propaganda groups which are registered as foreign agents with the United States government."[415] The Anti-Defamation League report maintained that "SNCC, via its June-July 1967 *Newsletter*, and NSRP via its August 1967 issue of *The Thunderbolt*, both turned to Arab propaganda sources for material on which to base their attacks on Jews, Zionists, and the State of Israel and their charges of anti-Arab atrocities committed during the Arab-Israeli wars."[416] The Anti-Defamation League listed fifteen paragraphs from the SNCC newsletter, side by side with an equal number of paragraphs from *Do You Know? Twenty Basic Facts About the Palestine People*, issued by the rabidly anti-Semitic Palestine Liberation Organization almost a year before; the two sets of paragraphs were substantially similar, and in some instances, virtually identical.[417]

A cartoon in the SNCC newsletter depicted Major General Moshe Dayan, the Israeli Defense Minister, with dollar signs—rather than stars—on his shoulders.[418] Another cartoon showed a hand, marked with the Star of David and a dollar sign, tightening a rope that was fastened around the necks of Egyptian President Gamal Abdul Nasser and Muhammad Ali (the Muslim name of Cassius Clay).[419] In a phrase that vividly recalled the anti-Semitic hate sheets of the Thirties, SNCC's newsletter charged that "the famous European Jews, the Rothschilds, who have long controlled the wealth of many European nations, were involved in the original conspiracy with the British to create the 'state of Israel' and are still among Israel's chief supporters."[420]

SNCC program director Ralph Featherstone poured oil (Arabian, no doubt) on the troubled waters when he said that the Student Committee was not interested in indicting all Jews but "only Jewish oppressors" such as "those Jews in the little Jew shops in the [Negro] ghettos."[421] Later, he stated that "Israel is, and always has been, the tool and foothold for American and British exploitation in the Middle East, and Africa."[422]

The Anti-Defamation League pointed out that "The SNCC *Newsletter* was not the first time that SNCC or its spokesmen had been accused of anti-Semitism in their writings and in their public statements."[423] The League quoted this statement by Stokely Carmichael in the September 22, 1966 issue of the *New York Review of Books:* "Black people do not want to 'take over' this country. They don't want to 'get whitey'; they just want to get him off their backs as the saying goes. It was for example the exploitation by Jewish landlords and merchants which first created black resentment towards Jews—not Judaism."[424] And again in November, 1966, at a public rally in Los Angeles, Carmichael said: "Negroes cut up and shoot each other every weekend and the police don't get too excited about that; but you let just one Negro get a Molotov cocktail and throw it at some Jew's liquor store and they call out the whole damn National Guard."[425] Anyone who follows the Anti-Defamation League reports has a right to ask why it took the B'nai B'rith organization almost a year to denounce the black bigots in SNCC. The question becomes all the more pointed when one recalls that virtually any and all anti-Semitic kooks who label themselves—or are labeled—as right wingers are quickly condemned by the Anti-Defamation League, almost while the print is still drying on their revolting little papers.

For some years, the Anti-Defamation League has issued doom-laden warnings of *Danger on the Right.* May the overwhelming majority of responsible right-wingers now look forward to an Anti-Defamation League tome entitled *Danger on the Left?*

Not unexpectedly, some long-time Jewish apologists for SNCC—who had formerly looked with an indulgent eye upon Black Power—took strong exception when its leaders started facing toward Mecca. Harry Golden, one of the South's leading champions of civil rights, resigned from SNCC "because of the increasing use of anti-Semitism and their echoing the ideas found in the Ku Klux Klan and the American Nazi Party."[426] Golden protested that the cartoons in the SNCC newspaper "are obscene and this comes in ill grace from an organization from which two Jewish boys, Schwerner and Goodman, along with Mississippi Negro Cheney were murdered while doing field work for SNCC in Philadelphia, Miss."[427]

One of the strongest objections to Golden's remarks came not from the student committee (which seemed not overly disconsolate at Golden's departure) but Nathan Schwerner, father of one of the murdered civil rights workers. Schwerner appeared in a rally in New York's East Village before an estimated crowd of 2,800, mostly white. In the seating arrangements for SNCC-dominated meetings that had now become de rigueur, the first rows belonged to the angry young Negroes—and they wanted to hear only Rap Brown. One of them called out "We want Brother Rap," as Schwerner told the audience, "I wish to record the fact that my immediate family and I personally resent the use of my son's name in any public castigation of SNCC." Schwerner said of the SNCC newsletter, "I did not consider it anti-Semitic, but solely anti-Zionist." He hurried away after his speech.[428]

Another notable resignation from SNCC was tendered by Theodore Bikel, the actor, folksinger, and one of the national vice presidents of the American Jewish Congress. Bikel declared that he could no longer be part of "any organization which condones injustice, let alone commits it," and pledged that henceforth he would "fight on the side of those who, like Dr. Martin Luther King, speak with the voice of sane and deliberative determination . . . to unite men as brothers, not divide them by the litmus test of color."[429]

But the problem was that Martin Luther King was assiduously carrying water on both shoulders, in two discernibly leaky containers. King condemned black anti-Semitism but refused to end his ties with the student group's black anti-Semites. King praised Jews as the "strongest allies for social justice," but did not directly criticize the blatantly anti-Semitic SNCC newsletter. King still needed SNCC as much as (if not more than) that black power group needed him. So Bikel may have salved his conscience by resigning from SNCC, but in his association with Martin Luther King, he would never really be that far away from the Student Nonviolent Coordinating Committee.

Certainly King's faint-hearted remonstrances stood in sharp contrast to Whitney Young's forthright statement that "SNCC's view of Israel-Arab relations would just be an unfortunate distortion of history and logic, if it did not contain vicious anti-Semitic overtones."[430] And Roy Wilkins considered it "a sad development that young Negroes, seeking to overcome the injustices suffered by their race, should employ against the Jews the same hateful distortions and lies that have been used for 350 years against their own kind."[431]

Some Jewish organizations reacted with the benign paternalism that was almost as degrading as it was divorced from reality. A case in point was the rose-colored glasses clung to by the National Community Relations Advisory Council, which coordinates nine national Jewish agencies and 80 local Jewish Community councils concerned with interracial problems. This national Jewish organization urged American Jews to patch up their differences with Negroes for the good of both peoples; in its words, "For the Jewish community to be deflected from its support and advocacy of equality for Negroes on the ground that Negroes are anti-Semitic would not only be self-defeating but to repudiate a fundamental tenet of Jewish tradition—equal justice for all."[432]

But Rabbi Richard L. Rubinstein, director of the Hillel Foundation at the University of Pittsburgh, remained very much unconvinced. In an article appearing in the *Recon-structionist* magazine, and quoted in the *Jewish Post and Opinion*, Rabbi Rubinstein called upon Jews to "withdraw from the Negro revolution in America, and become more conservative in their traditional fight for social change."

Rabbi Rubinstein said the black "revolution will have to play out its own drama with its own cast, its own inner compulsions, and, I believe, its own tragic end." Rabbi Rubinstein stated, "Three years ago the Negro revolution was an internal struggle for Negro rights within America. Today it has become part of a worldwide movement in which SNCC members have aligned themselves with the largely non-white agrarian masses which are committed to overwhelm the white capitalistic world dominated by America." The rabbi concluded that "Their long range aim is the revolutionary defeat of America by China and the 'oppressed' peoples who follow her lead."[433]

The activities of the Student Nonviolent Coordinating Committee split the civil rights movement, and shattered whatever lines of communication had existed between the older moderates and the young radicals. Roy Wilkins felt that further cooperation between the NAACP and civil rights groups advocating black power had become virtually impossible.[434] Wilkins denounced black power as black racism that could lead to a "black death." Wilkins disclosed that it was the NAACP and its branches that had supplied the food, the housing and transportation along the route of the Mississippi march. At the rally in Jackson, the local NAACP branch had taken on the responsibility of preparing food and drinks for more than 10,000 persons.[435] It was Charles Evers of the Mississippi branch of the NAACP who had paid out $300 in bail money for Stokely Carmichael. And it was Charles Evers who hired a truck which was converted into a speaker's platform, *and then was barred from speaking on that platform.*[436] Wilkins said of the Mississippi march, "The whole business showed the NAACP again how difficult it is to have genuine cooperation on an equal responsibility basis with groups that do not have the same commitments and which may very well be pursuing certain goals that have nothing to do with civil rights at all."[437]

In the furor over Black Power, debate on the new civil rights bill came almost as an afterthought. Somewhere, sandwiched in-between Stokely Carmichael's most recent diatribes, came the reminder that the Congress was considering a civil rights bill which would prohibit discrimination by race, color or creed in the sale or rental of housing. But 1966 was not exactly a vintage year for civil rights bills. In August, 1966, *Newsweek* reported that the Louis Harris polling organization found that about 46 per cent of whites objected to having a Negro family next door. Seventy per cent thought the Negro was trying to move too fast, while more than half of the big-city whites admitted feeling uneasy on the streets.[438] In September, 1966, Harris said, "Back in 1963, two out of every three white college-educated liberal people—mainly in the North—were in sympathy to the civil rights movement. On the eve of this summer, in May of this year, you found just about 50 per cent of these white liberals who were sympathetic—a slippage. But at the end of this summer, it's scarcely more than one in four who feel sympathetic any longer. There's been disenchantment among your white liberals with the civil rights movement."[439]

In a mood of stony realism, Martin Luther King admitted that he did not expect Congress to pass the civil rights bill. "I am pessimistic," he said. "I don't feel we'll get it through this year. They feel we are split up. We can't say to Congress anymore: 'You've got to pass this bill.' "[440]

On September 14, 1966, the Senate failed by a margin of ten votes to cut off a filibuster against the civil rights bill.[441] The key figure in the defeat was Senator Everett Dirksen, who had expressed his opposition to the measure in unequivocal terms and attacked it on the Senate floor as "a package of mischief." The President tried to change

Dirksen's mind during a 90-minute conversation, but without success.[442] Never had there had been so much obvious uneasiness about any civil rights act. On three of the first five days of Senate debate, the chamber was unable to muster a quorum, possibly because mail from constituents at home had run heavily against the bill—with some ratios going as high as 40 to 1.[443]

A month after the Civil Rights Bill of 1966 was quietly laid to rest, seven national Negro leaders affixed their names to a three-quarter page advertisement called "Crisis and Commitment." It was heralded by much of the press as a repudiation of Black Power; as for the author, he remains much more impressed by their intentions than the statement upon which they eventually agreed.

The document made four basic points:

1. We are committed to the attainment of racial justice by democratic process . . .
2. We repudiate any strategies of violence, reprisal or vigilantism and we condemn both rioting and the demagoguery that feeds it . . .
3. We are committed to integration, by which we mean an end to every barrier which segregation and other forms of discrimination have raised against the enjoyment by Negro Americans of their human and constitutional rights . . .
4. As we are committed to the goal of integration into every aspect of the national life, we are equally committed to the common responsibility of all Americans, both white and black, for bringing integration to pass . . ."

The statement was signed by Roy Wilkins of the NAACP; Whitney Young of the Urban League; A. Philip Randolph, President of the Brotherhood of Sleeping Car Porters; Mrs. Dorothy Height, president of the National Council of Negro Women; Bayard Rustin, director of the A. Philip Randolph Institute; Amos T. Hall, executive secretary of the Conference of Grand Masters, Prince Hall Masons of America; and Hobson Reynolds, Grand Exalted

Ruler, Improved Benevolent and Protective Order of Elks of the World.[444]

A name that was conspicuously missing was that of Martin Luther King.[445]

The following day, King endorsed the statement of principles.[446] This action was not nearly as courageous as it sounded. After all, "Crisis and Commitment" never once mentioned Stokely Carmichael, Black Power, or the Student Nonviolent Coordinating Committee. So King came out four square against violence, and, at minimal risk to himself, *seemed* to be attacking the Student Committee without ever saying it in so many words. During his news conference, King did mention black power, but only to refer to it as a confusing phrase.*[447] Again, he took care not to condemn any groups which had adopted the term. And again he seemed to have learned nothing from the defeat of the civil rights act on Capitol Hill.

There is reason to believe that Martin Luther King alienated still more white supporters by his opposition to the war in Vietnam. For the most part, in 1966 he was still soft-pedaling his opposition, relying more on speeches and resolutions than more overt demonstrations. Nevertheless, he hardly helped the cause of civil rights when the Southern Christian Leadership Conference called on the President to abandon the ruling military government of South Vietnam, and consider withdrawing from the country altogether.[448] At that time, a poll by Louis Harris showed that four out of ten Americans were unfavorably disposed toward civil rights groups opposing the Vietnam war.[449]

Civil rights or Vietnam? Martin Luther King would spend the next few agonizing months trying to reach a decision. And soon a once adoring America would discern

---

* It should be noted that the phrase "black power" was not coined by Stokely Carmichael. Years before, Richard Wright had used it as the title of a novel, and starting in November, 1965, Lerone Bennett, Jr., used it as the title for a series of articles about Negro political power in the South right after the Civil War. Bennett's "black power" articles in *Ebony* denounced the integrated political leadership of that era.

a few chips in the composition of its first plaster saint. Soon America would be witnessing a grotesque inversion of nonviolence, with human blockades telling Pentagon guards, "We Shall Not Be Moved"; demonstrators chanting, to the vast delight of the Viet Cong, "Ain't Gonna Study War No More"; and above it all, Martin Luther King vowing "We Shall Overcome" the Commander in Chief of the Armed Forces, and the President of the United States.

CHAPTER 10

The Vietnam Protests and Black Anarchy

In years to come, future generations may well ask themselves if in 1967, like some latter-day Nero, Martin Luther King fiddled with the Vietniks while Newark and Detroit burned.

The record is clear that for almost two years, King toyed with the idea of joining the peace movement. As early as July, 1965, at a civil rights rally in Petersburg, Virginia, he warned that unless the Johnson Administration found a way to negotiate peace in Vietnam, he might mass his civil rights followers in "teach-ins" and "peace rallies."[1] In August of that year, he said he was planning to appeal directly to Ho Chi Minh, President Johnson, the Viet Cong and the Saigon government to halt the war.[2] Even at this early stage of the anti-Vietnam protests, King acknowledged that he was under "great pressure" from peace groups to join their campaign as they had joined in his.[3] It was not generally known that pacifist leaders had contributed both money and personnel to King's Selma campaign. For example, the Fellowship of Reconciliation had representatives in the Selma demonstrations[4]—and it was from this pacifist group that the late A. J. Muste surfaced to become Founding

Chairman of the Spring Mobilization Committee to End the War in Vietnam. For that matter, King's wife had been active in the peace movement—particularly Women Strike For Peace—for many years.[5] On June 8, 1965, in a rally in New York City sponsored by SANE, Mrs. King had been one of the speakers.[6]

Characteristically, King's response at that time was an ambivalent one. He was not yet prepared to commit any overt acts in support of the peace movement, but he could and did place his considerable powers of oratory at the Vietniks' disposal. Thus, in 1965 King expressed regret that Hanoi and Peking had not "responded with a positive attitude" toward negotiations on Vietnam, but this did not deter him from advocating a UN seat for Red China.[7]

In August, 1966, King described as "very definitely" more important than the war in Vietnam, his proposal for a $100 *billion* "Marshall Plan" in America to get rid of conditions allegedly causing Negro riots and unrest.[8] Negro leaders , he said, could not stop riots—only "progress" could do that.[9] A week and a half later, the board of directors of King's Southern Christian Leadership Conference attacked, for the second time that year, America's involvement in Vietnam. SCLC called upon the President to de-escalate the war unilaterally, to see if there was a positive response from the Viet Cong. It also contended that "Negroes suffer double the unemployment rate of whites, double the poverty, and double the combat responsibility to fight for the society that inflicts this discrimination on them."[10] King stepped up the attack in November, 1966, at the University of Pittsburgh, where he charged that about 40 per cent of the combat troops in Vietnam were Negro, although only about 10 per cent of this country's population was Negro. King said Negroes were drafted because they did not have sufficient education to gain an exemption or could not afford to attend college.[11] In December of that year, King declared, "The security we profess to seek in foreign adventures, we will lose in our decaying cities. The bombs in Vietnam explode at home; they destroy the hopes and possibilities for a decent America."[12]

In January, 1967, the wife of one of Martin Luther King's top aides told Negro reporters of her recent trip to North Vietnam. She was Mrs. Diane Nash Bevel, wife of the SCLC's Rev. James Bevel. A former SNCC stalwart, Mrs. Bevel had white reporters barred from her press conference because "I do not intend to have the white press interpret to black people what I have to say." She called the war in Vietnam an "economic war with racial overtones,"[13] an accusation her husband was to echo just a week later.

On January 27, 1967, the Rev. James Bevel went on leave of absence from the Southern Christian Leadership Conference to become national director of the Spring Mobilization Committee to End the War in Vietnam.[14] Bevel said he would work full-time in the anti-war movement and that his participation had the "full support" of King.[15] Bevel stated, "Each passing day makes more and more plain to millions of Americans the hollowness and wickedness of this war of oppression against a foreign colored people, which parallels in military terms what has been done to the American Indians and the colored people of America for centuries."[16]

Some months later, in *Harper's*, reporter David Halberstam wrote:

The far-left groups who organized the peace march went for Bevel because they wanted King. King had seemed interested himself, but very slightly so. They contacted Bevel and they found he was interested and ended up coming to their meetings. "Then the question was," one of them said, "could he deliver King? He said he could and promised, but weeks went by and no King. We began to wonder. Then finally he came through."[17]

Why was it so important to get King? Because, as one peace organizer said, "There were a lot of people we felt wanted to come in on this, you know, good-hearted Americans for whom someone like King would make it easier, be a good umbrella. We could then call some of these unions and church groups and just middle-aged people who were nervous about coming in, who wanted to come in a little bit, but didn't like the whole looks of it, and we could say, Look here, we've got King, and it makes them all breathe easier. They think, 'Why it's King, it's all right, it's safe.' "[18]

Why in 1967 did Martin Luther King help forge an alliance of civil rights activists and their friends in the "peace-now" movement? A carefully considered answer was suggested by the prestigious liberal organization, Freedom House of New York City. Freedom House began by saying that King's "reasons for attempting to divert the civil rights movement to a new alliance can only be speculated on,"[19] but it seems to the author a most sound speculation. Freedom House theorized that "The racial revolution had slowed, the sounder and more thorough forces like the NAACP and the Urban League were once again in the forefront of genuine progress, the 'Black Power' militants were facing bankruptcy in both influence and finances. King's own position in the headlines had been considerably eroded. NBC's Frank McGee commented, 'His disappointment is verging on bitterness.' "[20] Freedom House went on, "What is not in any doubt is that King chose to team up with militants like Stokely Carmichael . . . And, most clearly, King emerged as the public's spear-carrier of a civil disobedience program that is demagogic and irresponsible in its attacks on our government."[21]

King lost little time aiming that spear at the more moderate leaders of the civil rights movement. He hurled his shaft at Whitney Young of the Urban League in early March, 1967, at a fund-raising dinner in Great Neck, Long Island. It was an evening of speeches, questions and answers, featuring Martin Luther King, Whitney Young, and John Morsell of the NAACP. The subject of Vietnam came up, and King replied with a criticism of the war, the morality of it, and what it was doing to America. Young was

asked the same question, and he disagreed. Young stressed
that he couldn't speak for the Urban League, but his own
personal position was that communism had to be stopped
just as Hitler should have been stopped in World War II.
As the evening was breaking up, Young and King got into
a brief but very heated argument. Young told King his position was unwise since it would alienate the President. King
angrily replied, "Whitney, what you're saying may get you
a foundation grant, but it won't get you into the kingdom of
truth." Young quite angrily told King that he was interested in the ghettos and King was not. "You're eating
well," Young told King. King's response was that he opposed the war precisely because of what it was doing to the
ghettos. The argument became so heated that King's lawyer
quickly broke it up.[22]

Afterwards, King regretted the argument and phoned
Young to apologize.[23] Young continued his attempts to dis-
suade King from joining the peace movement, in a mara-
thon phone conversation that went on until 3:30 one March
morning.[24] And even Bayard Rustin—whose list of left-wing
affiliations has adorned many a page of the *Congressional
Record*—argued in vain that King at least ought to get out
of the Spring Mobilization March.[25] But they were both
wasting their breath. On March 25, 1967, Martin Luther
King led his first anti-war demonstration in Chicago, where
he called on "all those who love peace" to "combine the
fervor of the civil rights movement with the peace movement." King declared, "We must demonstrate, teach and
preach, until the very foundations of our nation are
shaken."[26]

Now the non-Communist peace groups could breathe
easier and get ready to march in the Spring Mobilization,
just three weeks away. It was King, it was all right, it was
safe.

At this point, there was still time, however little, for
King to turn back from the path he had chosen. There was
one more way-station before the Spring Mobilization—a

speech at New York City's Riverside Church—at which he could still shift rhetorical gears, reverse his position, and join the moderates of the civil rights movement. But Martin Luther King was no longer listening to Roy Wilkins and Whitney Young—if, indeed, he ever had.

The Viet Cong could never have hoped to win on the battlefield any victory to equal its triumph that April day in Riverside Church. On that day, Martin Luther King walked out of Birmingham, Selma and Chicago, into the arms of Hanoi, in nothing less than an unconditional surrender. It was a total capitulation, from first to last. It was not at all necessary for the Communist propaganda apparatus to force-feed him; King gladly and willingly swallowed the Viet Cong party line whole, and come back for more.

That day in New York's Riverside Church, Martin Luther King spoke to an overflow crowd of more than 3,000, who gave him a standing ovation at the beginning and end of his talk.[27] Acknowledging that "many persons have questioned me about the wisdom of my path . . . ," King declared, "I knew that America would never invest the necessary funds or energies in rehabilitation of its poor so long as adventures like Vietnam continued. . . . So I was increasingly compelled to see the war as an enemy of the poor and to attack it as such."[28] King told his audience, "we have been faced with the irony of watching Negro and white boys on TV screens as they kill and die together for a nation that has been unable to seat them together in the same schools. So we watch them in brutal solidarity burning the huts of a poor village, but we realize that they would never live on the same block in Detroit. I could not be silent in the face of such cruel manipulation of the poor."[29]

Then came King's verbal Molotov cocktail, which has been quoted and requoted around the world by the Communist press. King spoke of his counsel to "rejected and angry young men" that "social change comes most meaningfully through nonviolent action. But they asked," King went on, "and rightly so—what about Vietnam? Their questions hit home, and I knew that I could never again raise my voice against the violence of the oppressed in the ghettos without having first spoken clearly to *the greatest purveyor of violence in the world today—my own government*"[30] (italics added).

King deplored American determination that Ho Chi Minh "should not unify the temporarily divided nation."[31] His most scathing abuse was reserved not for Ho, but "one of the most vicious modern dictators—our chosen man, Premier Diem."[32] King charged that the South Vietnamese people "consider us—not their fellow Vietnamese—the real enemy. They move sadly and apathetically as we herd them off the land of their fathers into concentration camps where minimal social needs are rarely met. They know they must move or be destroyed by our bombs. So they go—primarily women and children and the aged."[33]

His rolling cadences now enlisted for the duration in behalf of the Viet Cong, Martin Luther King said of the South Vietnamese: "They watch as we poison their water, as we kill a million acres of their crops. They must weep as the bulldozers roar through their areas preparing to destroy the precious trees. They wander into the hospitals with at least 20 casualties from American fire-power for one Viet Cong-inflicted injury. So far we may have killed a million of them—mostly children. They wander into the towns and see thousands of the children, homeless, without clothes, running in packs on the streets like animals. They see the children degraded by our soldiers as they beg for food. They see the children selling their sisters to our soldiers, soliciting for their mothers."[34]

King escalated still further his verbal atrocities, as he asked, "What do they [the peasants] think as we test out our latest weapons on them, just as the Germans tested out new medicine and new tortures in the concentration camps of Europe?"[35]

King glorified the Communist rulers of Hanoi as "the men who led the nation to independence against the Japanese and the French, the men who sought membership in the French Commonwealth and were betrayed. . . . It was they who led a second struggle against French domination at tremendous costs and then were persuaded to give up the land they controlled . . . as a temporary measure at Geneva."[36]

King set forth a five-point program "to atone for our sins and errors in Vietnam . . .":

1) end all bombing in North and South Vietnam;
2) declare a unilateral cease-fire in the *hope* that such action will create the atmosphere for negotiation;
3) take immediate steps to prevent other battlegrounds in Southeast Asia by curtailing our military build-up in Thailand and our interference in Laos;
4) realistically accept the fact that the National Liberation Front has substantial support in South Vietnam and must thereby play a role in any meaningful negotiations and in any future Vietnam government;
5) set a date that we will remove all foreign troops from Vietnam in accordance with the 1954 Geneva agreement.[37]

For one brief, fleeting moment, King's simple, childlike faith in the Viet Cong seemed to waver, as he suggested, "Part of our ongoing commitment might well express itself in an offer to grant asylum to any Vietnamese who fears for his life under a new regime which included the Liberation Front."[38]

Martin Luther King recommended "to all who find the American course in Vietnam a dishonorable and unjust one" that they become conscientious objectors. He expressed great pleasure "that this is the path now being chosen by more than seventy students at my alma mater, Morehouse College. . . ."[39]

King declared that "our greatest defense against communism is to take effective offensive action in behalf of justice. . . ."[40] While reading this excerpt, the author was irresistibly reminded of an anecdote he heard many years

ago—that Stalin, told that the Pope opposed him, coolly
replied, "And how many divisions does the Pope have?"

Somewhere along the way, one began wondering whether
King was still speaking as an American, or professed instead some other, paramount allegiance. This uneasy feeling
was in no way mollified by King's claim to speak "as a citizen of the world," and his call "for a worldwide fellowship
that lifts neighborly concern beyond one's tribe, race, class
and nation. . . ."[41]

King departed from his prepared text to say that his
speech was not an "attempt to make North Vietnam or the
National Liberation Front paragons of virtue."[42] And he
added that while both may have reason to be suspicious of
the United States, "conflicts are never solved without trust-
ful give and take."[43] At the same time, in his delivery, King
also dropped several paragraphs from the prepared text,
one of which charged that U.S. policy would lead to an
American colony in Vietnam and could goad Red China
into a war which would permit the U.S. to bomb Peking's
nuclear installations.[44] The Washington *Post* saw both the
addition and the deletion as "last-minute attempts by Dr.
King to tone down his sharp criticism of U.S. actions in
Vietnam," but noted that King "all but exonerated the Hanoi
government and the Viet Cong for their roles in the war."[45]

Negro journalist Carl Rowan, former director of the U.S.
Information Agency, wrote that President Johnson, reading
the wire-service reports of King's address, flushed with
anger.[46] A Presidential aide shouted, "My God, King has
given a speech on Vietnam that goes right down the Commie
line!"[47]

Sharing Rowan's dismay was the Washington *Post*, for
years one of Martin Luther King's most eloquent and influential supporters. The *Post* editorialized that King's
Vietnam speech "was filled with bitter and damaging
allegations and inferences that he did not and could not
document." It observed that King had "flatly charged the
government with sending Negroes to fight and die in ex-

traordinarily high proportions relative to the rest of the population. But Negro troops constitute 11 per cent of the enlisted personnel in Vietnam (10.5 per cent of the population was Negro in 1960). Negro casualties are higher than this (22.5 per cent of those killed in action) because of higher Negro enlistment for elite corps and higher rate of Negro reenlistment." The editorials cited King's assertion that "the United States may have caused a million civilian casualties in Vietnam—mostly children—but he did not give any supporting authority for this statement." That newspaper referred to a flat statement by King "that 'our officials know' that less than 25 per cent of the members of the National Liberation Front are Communists—but he neglected to say what officials or where they said it." The Washington *Post* referred to statements that King had inserted in his prepared text, but could not quite bring himself to say aloud in Riverside Church—that America's "minimal expectation was to occupy it [Vietnam] as an American colony," and that men would "not refrain from thinking" that our "maximum hope was to goad China into a war so that we may bomb her nuclear installations." The editorial stressed that "It is one thing to reproach a government for what it has done and said; it is quite another to attribute to it policies it has never avowed and purposes it has never entertained and then to rebuke it for these sheer inventions of unsupported fantasy." Reluctantly, but unavoidably, the *Post* concluded: "Dr. King has done a grave injury to those who are his natural allies in a great struggle to remove ancient abuses from our public life; and he has done an even graver injury to himself. Many who have listened to him with respect will never again accord him the same confidence. He has diminished his usefulness to his cause, to his country and to his people. And that is a great tragedy."[48]

Still another of King's "natural allies" sharply attacked him for having compared U.S. practices in Vietnam with those of the Nazis during World War II. The head of the

Jewish War Veterans of America, Malcolm Tarlov, called it "utterly incredible that Dr. King's denunciation of our government should manifest itself in such an ugly parallel." Tarlov emphasized that his group did not question King's right to dissent, "But we consider his extremist tirade to reveal an ignorance of the facts, pandering to Ho Chi Minh, and an insult to the intelligence of all Americans." The Jewish War Veterans' Commander found it "indeed sad that so respected a national leader should have voiced his dissent so irresponsibly. His speech could have been written in North Vietnam."[49]

A few days later, Dr. Ralph J. Bunche, himself a Nobel Peace Prize winner, stated that King should not try to lead both a civil rights campaign and a crusade against American involvement in Vietnam. Bunche declared, "In my view, Dr. King should positively and publicly give up one role or the other."[50] Bunche was a director of the NAACP, and that group's 60-member board of directors voted unanimously to oppose King's effort to merge the civil rights and peace movements. Bunche himself had moved to toughen the language of the NAACP resolution by denouncing the merger attempt as a "serious tactical mistake."[51] Walter Reuther, another NAACP director, supported the Bunche proposal.[52] As Carl Rowan expressed it, "King delivered a one-sided broadside about a matter on which he obviously has an abundance of indignation and a shortage of information." Perhaps even more disturbing was Rowan's revelation that "Key members of the House and Senate have been told by the FBI that King is listening most to one man who is clearly more interested in embarrassing the U.S. than in the plight of either the Negro or the war-weary people of Vietnam."[53]

Now King gave all-out support to the Spring Mobilization Committee to end the war in Vietnam—totally ignoring the documented public knowledge that if ever a parade kept Open House for the Communists, their sympathizers, and political satellites—emblazoning that fact with all but neon signs—it was the Spring Mobilization Committee.

Consider its origins, and some of its most vocal organizers and organizations, as disclosed by the House Committee on Un-American Activities. According to the organizers' claims, 257 persons attended the meeting held at the University of Chicago, December 28–30, 1966, to discuss the idea of a nationwide student strike and other forms of demonstrations against the war in Vietnam.[54] The delegates came from 16 states, Puerto Rico and Canada, and from 49 different colleges and universities.[55] The House Committee on Un-American Activities stated:

"The organizers of the conference have openly admitted that representatives of the following Communist organizations took part in the conference:

"Communist Party, U.S.A.
"W. E. B. DuBois Clubs of America
"Progressive Labor Party (the Peking-oriented faction of the U.S. Communist movement)
"Socialist Workers Party (the Trotskyist Communists)
"Young Socialist Alliance (youth branch of the Socialist Workers Party)
"Youth Against War and Fascism (youth arm of the Workers World Party, a Trotskyist splinter group)
"*National Guardian* (published by Weekly Guardian Associates)."[56]

Among the speakers were Bettina Aptheker—described by HCUA as "probably the most widely known Communist in the United States"—and Charles Cobb of the Student Nonviolent Coordinating Committee.[57] The Rev. James Bevel, for years one of Martin Luther King's top aides, was one of the sponsors of the meeting.[58]

Bevel's credentials for participation in this gathering of the Far Far Left were impeccable. He was the signer of a public appeal for funds to furnish the DuBois Clubs' "Freedom Center" clubhouse in Chicago,[59] and joined as co-plaintiff with the DuBois Clubs in their suit to restrain the Subversive Activities Control Board from holding hearings on that group (the hearings had been requested by the

Attorney General).[60] His wife, Diane Nash Bevel, had made an unauthorized trip to Hanoi.[61]

The Chicago Conference shrilled that in Vietnam, the United States was waging a "war of aggression." It said the war in Vietnam waged by the United States "is a racist war, a murderous war against a colored people . . . an illegal war [and] but one symptom of a diseased society."[62] A decision was made to adopt a "Call to Vietnam Week" in 1967.[63] During Vietnam Week, demonstrations were to concentrate on these issues:

(1) Bringing the GI's home now;

(2) Opposing the draft, and supporting the right of individuals to refuse to cooperate with the military system; and

(3) Ending campus complicity with the war effort.[64]

Vietnam Week was to be held April 8–15, 1967.[65] To make certain all the Communist faithful would be fully informed about the operation, the Student Mobilization Committee placed an ad in the March 12, 1967, issue of *The Worker*.

The Committee pleaded with the paper's Communist readers to contribute money and time. The ad was headed: "The CIA Doesn't Support Us! We Need You!"[66]

To the House Committee on Un-American Activities there could be no question about the fact that the week of April 8–15 "was chosen as Vietnam Week primarily, if not exclusively, because the Spring Mobilization Committee had designated April 15 as the day of its massive demonstrations against the U.S. Government."[67]

That ad by the Student Mobilization Committee in *The Worker* made it clear there was complete cooperation between the Student Committee and the Spring Mobilization Committee. It stated that the Student Mobilization Committee had been working for two months "to bring thousands of students to New York and San Francisco for the April 15th demonstrations."[68] It boasted of "amazing progress" on the Student Committee's part—contact with over 300 campuses; the mailing of 50,000 calls; 30,000 Student Mobilizers, 50,000 pledge cards; and thousands of buttons, posters and stickers.[69] In addition, a flyer printed by the national office of the Student Mobilization Committee in March stated in just so many words that it was organizing student participation in anti-war activities "as part of the national Spring Mobilization against the war. . . ."[70]

The Spring Mobilization Committee to End the War in Vietnam was formed at a meeting held in Cleveland on November 26, 1966.[71] About 150 persons attended the meeting.[72] The HCUA report disclosed that sponsors of the group included the ubiquitous Bettina Aptheker; Arnold Johnson, public relations director of the Communist Party; James R. ("Bob") Lindsay, Communist Party candidate for city councilman of San Jose, Calif.; Ben Dobbs, a leader of the Southern California District of the Communist Party; Robert Treuhaft and Benjamin Dreyfus, attorneys who have been identified as members of the Communist Party; identified Communist Party members Malvina Reynolds, Don Rothenberg and Al Richmond, executive editor of the Communist Party's West Coast newspaper, *People's World*.[73]

The House Committee on Un-American Activities made the important point: "There are, of course, many non-Communists who are sponsors of the Spring Mobilization Committee. It is probable that thousands of such persons will support its April 15 demonstrations. Not one of the top officers of the committee is known to be a Communist. With this excellent cover, there is little doubt but that the many Communists who are giving their all-out support to the group's activities will succeed in hoodwinking many persons who are sincere pacifists, liberals and critics of U.S. policy in Vietnam into supporting the April 15 demonstrations."[74]

The House Committee on Un-American Activities acknowledged that "Pacifist elements are involved in Vietnam Week, in the Student Mobilization Committee, the Spring Mobilization Committee. . . . Generally speaking, however, genuine pacifist elements and organizations in this country are relatively small and weak. Alone, they have never succeeded in staging a major demonstration. While the sincerity of these groups in agitating for peace in Vietnam and elsewhere is not to be questioned, it is clear that they have played, and are playing, a minor role in Vietnam Week and in other anti-Vietnam-war demonstrations that have taken place in this country in recent years."[75]

The President of the Spring Mobilization Committee was the late A. J. Muste, once described by J. Edgar Hoover as a man "who has long fronted for Communists."[76] Muste was one of a small group of alleged "independent observers" selected by the Communist Party to attend their 16th Antional Convention in 1957. At the conclusion of the convention, Muste joined other members of the group in attesting to the "democratic manner" in which the convention had been conducted.[77] It therefore should scarcely have shocked the moderates in the peace movement that Muste urged the Spring Mobilization Committee to adhere firmly to its policy of welcoming Communists into its ranks. He wrote: "We adhere to the policy of 'non-exclusion' [of Communists] first and most of all, because it is right in principle. . . . People of the Left (Communists with or without quotation marks) should be permitted and expected to function normally in the political life of the country." Besides, Muste was horrified by the possibility that "In practice, a non-Communist coalition is in danger of becoming an anti-Communist one. . . ." But Muste's most compelling reasons for refusing to exclude Communists was that without them, the Spring Mobilization Committee would collapse. He wrote: "What no doubt clinches the matter is that if we were to abandon the 'non-exclusion' principle we would quickly disintegrate. . . ."[78]

The House Committee on Un-American Activities considered it self-evident that Dr. Martin Luther King's agreement to play a leading role in the April 15 demonstrations in New York City, and his freeing Rev. James Bevel from his key position in the Southern Christian Leadership Conference to head up the Spring Mobilization Committee, are evidence that the Communists have succeeded, at least partially, in implementing their strategy of fusing the Vietnam and civil rights issues in order to strengthen their chances of bringing about a reversal of U.S. policy in Vietnam."[79] *

HCUA concluded: "The Communist propaganda apparatus throughout the world will capitalize in every way possible on the Vietnam Week and April 15 demonstrations. The global publicity given to them by the Communist propaganda machine will have the following effects:

(a) It will give aid and comfort to Communists everywhere, particularly in Vietnam.

(b) Among non-Communists, it will tend to create the false impression that a truly large segment of the U.S. population is vehemently opposed to this country's policy in Vietnam.

(c) U.S. leaders will be faced with greater difficulties in

---

* Two days before the parade, Michael Laski, head of a Peking-oriented group called the Communist Party, U.S.A., told reporters that "HCUA is a committee of the U.S. government but it happens to have the correct facts in this instance." According to Laski, "A coalition of the Socialist Workers Party and the revisionist [i.e., Moscow-oriented] Communist Party has effective control of the Fifth Avenue Peace Parade Committee." Laski said that at a meeting on March 19, at which he was present, Bevel ceded control of the parade to these two groups. Laski told the press, "Mr. King receives financial support from organizations and individuals that are tied with the revisionist party. He knows what is happening and so does Bevel. . . . Martin Luther King is not a Communist but he is working in alliance with them." The incident was recounted in the May 2, 1967, issue of *National Review*, which felt that Laski was to be believed. For himself, the author remains dubious about Communist press conferences in spite of *NR*'s logical argument that "among certain new types on the hard Left who follow the Peking line of open conflict, there is no policy of subterfuge." The author prefers to focus upon the devastating information unearthed by the House Committee on Un-American Activities, without reference to the Laski press conference. Given the history of the past 20 years, he considers it a safer policy to go on considering Communists of all stripes "Masters of Deceit," fully capable of lying about anyone or anything, at any time, for any reason. However, in the interests of a complete account of the Vietnam protests, he has felt it desirable to bring the Laski statements to the attention of the reader.

convincing our allies of the correctness of this country's policy in Vietnam.[80]

On April 15, 1967, the Spring Mobilization Committee massed thousands of anti-war demonstrators, who marched through the streets of Manhattan and then assembled in front of the United Nations building to hear scathing denunciations of United States policy in Vietnam.[81] It was the largest peace demonstration staged in New York since the Vietnam War began—so large that it took four hours for all the marchers to leave Central Park for the United Nations Plaza.[82] The parade was led by Martin Luther King, Dr. Benjamin Spock and Harry Belafonte, plus other civil rights and religious figures, all of whom linked arms as they moved out of the park at the head of the line.[83]

An hour before the parade started, about 70 young men gathered in an area of Central Park to burn their draft cards.[84] A number of girls burned half of their husbands' or boy friends' draft cards while the men burned the other half.[85] In another part of the park, a group calling itself the United States Committee to Aid the National Liberation Front of South Vietnam built a 40-foot-high tower of black cardboard tubing. They then attached Viet Cong flags to it, with a gold star in the center.[86] Elsewhere in the park, demonstrators methodically set fire to an American flag while onlookers cheered.[87]

This was too revolting, even for a jaded American public. As outrage over the burning of an American flag grew, King attempted to wash his hands of the entire incident. He declared that the Spring Mobilization Committee could not "condone" such actions.[88] King's fastidious disclaimer may have satisfied some of the more starry-eyed liberals on the national scene, but conservatives were hardly deceived. The extent of Communist infiltration of the parade had become a matter of national and even international knowledge well before the paraders began their dreary procession. It was just too ludicrous for King to participate in a parade that fully accepted Communist support, and then voice a genteel surprise when the Redniks followed the party line with slavish fidelity.

If the remaining moderates in the peace movement could not quite bring themselves to read the definitive report, "Communist Origin and Manipulation of Vietnam Week," printed on March 31, 1967, by the House Committee on Un-American Activities, they could at least have read page 3 of the New York *Times* on the morning of the parade. If they had read this page, they would have found the *Times* quoting a spokesman for the Communist Party, who said that for the first time since the 1940's, "there'll be a number of us marching under the banner of our party." They would have found the same article reiterating the fact that along with moderate groups, "Trotskyites, anarchists, Communists and Maoists" had joined the Spring Mobilization.[89]

Among the messages of congratulation received by the Spring Mobilization Committee was a cable from Premier Pham Van Dong of North Vietnam. The message—dated April 12, three days before the parade—read in part: "Glad learn broad section of American people are organizing a 'spring mobilization' to demand United States government stop war of aggression in Vietnam and bring American troops home."[90] Appearing on NBC's "Meet The Press," the day after the parade, Secretary of State Dean Rusk bluntly stated that the "Communist apparatus" was working hard in support of anti-war demonstrations in the United States and elsewhere. Rusk said, "I have no doubt at all that the Communist apparatus is very busy indeed in these operations all over the world and in our own country. But I do not mean to say by that that all those who have objections to the war in Vietnam are Communists. But the world-wide Communist movement is working very hard on this." Asked if he had evidence, the Secretary of State replied, "I am giving you my responsible personal view that the Communist apparatus is working very hard on it."[91]

How many marchers participated in the Spring Mobilization parade? The police estimated that between 100,000 and 125,000 people took part in the rally.[92] King commented, "I have no quarrel with the police estimate, just an absolute denial of the accuracy of it."[93] King contended that his years of participation in demonstrations had given him wide experience in estimating the size of crowds—"perhaps" he modestly added, "more experience than the New York police." King declared: "There were fully 300,000 and perhaps 400,000 people in the demonstration," and claimed he spoke to as many as "125,000 persons in the United Nations Plaza. . . ."[94] Deputy Police Commissioner Jacques Nevard termed King's 125,000 figure in U.N. Plaza "a physical impossibility." Deputy Commissioner Nevard pointed out, "First of all, the space between police barriers on First Avenue (or United Nations Plaza) from 47th Street to 44th Street was 64 feet wide and extended south 650 feet. Assuming that the crowd here was in maximum density—at one person for every three square feet—there would have been approximately 13,860 persons. On 47th Street, where the crowd was held between barriers 62 feet apart and extended back 500 feet, it works out to about 10,330 persons. And on the side streets 44th, 45th and 46th Streets, we figure a maximum density of 5,700 persons. We come up with about 29,000 at the peak in U.N. Plaza."[95]

Freedom House gave this incisive analysis of the march and the marchers:

The parade itself had all the earmarks of the old-style "Popular Front" rallies of the 1930's. The majority of the marchers may have been motivated by their devotion to the cause of peace, but the Communists were clearly in evidence among the parade managers. They told people where to go, kept the paraders in some semblance of order, led the chanting and sloganeering. It would be absurd to describe the demonstration as "Communist" or even "Communist-controlled," though the premier of North Vietnam cabled his congratulations to the parade's organizers. It would also be foolish, and dangerous, to ignore the Communists' participation or their rising hopes for exploiting King and other non-Communists for their own ends in the future.[96]

Reading and watching and hearing about the Fifth Avenue parade and the burning of an American flag, the mood of many Americans was one of impotent rage—a feeling of helplessness to communicate to the nation and the world that the motley mob participating in the Vietnam protests did not represent the true face of this country. There was a deeply felt desire to *do* something—to *say* something—but what and how? It remained for two men to translate this grass-roots indignation into one of the prouder chapters of contemporary American history. The first of these men was Ray Gimmler, an ex-Marine and now a New York City Fire Captain. Gimmler wanted a parade which would be non-partisan in character, formed solely to support the soldiers in Vietnam.[97] One of the first men he turned to was Charles Wiley, author, lecturer and, as it developed, a maker of Instant Miracles. Certainly, it was nothing short of miraculous to accomplish all that they did in so little time. In less than a month, Gimmler and Wiley had to plan, organize, and assemble thousands of marchers, secure pledges of marching contingents, map out a parade route and staging areas for dozens of organizations, secure all the necessary permits, have thousands of handbills printed and distributed, and let the New York metropolitan area know of the existence of the committee and its headquarters. The Committee to Support Our Boys in Vietnam shot up almost overnight, and it was an all-volunteer affair. The fragile finances of the committee were such that Gimmler had to pledge his own home to have two telephones installed in the group's headquarters.[98] On May 12, 1967, Captain Gimmler and others raised the American flag in the Sheep Meadow in Central Park at the same spot where one had been burned by Vietniks the month before.[99] The Committee received endorsements from former President Eisenhower, Richard Nixon and General William Westmoreland.[100] And then came the day of the parade—a day on which Charles Wiley had absolutely refused to predict how many would march to support the men in Vietnam. The newspapers told the story, and by any criteria it was a resounding success. Without a single big name to put on the committee letterhead; with a negligible budget; with a crisis schedule from start to finish—the Parade Committee to Support Our Boys in Vietnam put over 70,000 marchers on the street, some waiting as long as seven hours to get in the line of march (including the author, who was marching with the New York State Conservative Party). Some newspapers put the figure as high as 250,000 marchers.[101]

For a brief moment in time, a parade *supporting* the war effort in Vietnam was front-page news, seen and heard around the world, but for only a brief moment. And then with stunning rapidity, the national spotlight was focused again on the Vietniks and Martin Luther King.

The New York *Times* noted that King's opposition to the war in Vietnam had so consumed him "that he has drawn closer to such 'black power' organizations as the Student Nonviolent Coordinating Committee and the Congress of Racial Equality. . . ."[102] King had once sworn off any alliance with these groups as long as they espoused the doctrine of racial separation, "but now he seems to feel that the peace effort outweighs other considerations."[103]

King left the platform of the Spring Mobilization before Stokely Carmichael began his inflammatory speech;[104] nevertheless, he accepted Carmichael's embrace of welcome into the fold.[105] The day after the march, King attended a secret strategy caucus of civil rights leaders, government men and foundation angels, convened by the Field Foundation in New York. The issues discussed would have appealed to the Martin Luther King of the Birmingham and Selma campaigns: jobs, vote registration, and implementing programs already on the books.[106]

At this meeting, King vowed that he would be spending no more than three to five per cent of his time on peace and asked the caucus leaders for a second date nine days later to talk about their civil rights problems some more.[107] But two days before that second session was to take place, King and Dr. Spock announced a "Vietnam Summer" project to put 10,000 volunteers in the field, drumming up opposition to the war.[108] That second meeting of civil rights leaders suddenly seemed pointless; it never came off. A member of the Urban League commented, "The Movement is back where it began. It's us and the NAACP."[109]

Vietnam Summer was the brainchild of a group of Harvard faculty members, students and local residents in Cambridge, Mass. The acting director of the project was Chester Hartman, an assistant professor in the department of city planning at Harvard.[110] Hartman said that, in May, an army of field organizers would be moving across the country seeking 10,000 volunteers for peace organizing efforts in their home communities.[111] King declared, "I give my absolute support to those who initiated this move." He was seconded by Dr. Benjamin Spock and Robert Scheer, managing editor of *Ramparts*.[112] King called for an "escalation of our opposition to the war in Vietnam," and went on, "There comes a time when silence is betrayal, and today we are involved in one of the most bloody and cruel wars in history. It is poisoning the soul of our nation and has isolated our nation morally and politically."[113] King insisted that he had never advocated a merger of the civil rights and peace movements—something of an exercise in semantics, since only three weeks before, he had spoken to a reporter about "a realization of the interrelatedness of racism and militarism and the need to attack both problems rather than leaving one."[114]

The Spring Mobilization had barely ended its tawdry march before King was making startling front-page headlines—warning the country that at least ten cities across the country could explode in racial violence that summer.[115] Among the cities he named was Newark.[116] But a week later, as if there were really no cause for alarm, Martin

Luther King joined Vietnam Summer and turned his back on the Long Hot Summer he himself had predicted. He said he believed "it is more important that I should be concerned with the survival of the world" than with integration.[117] And with this bit of rhetorical swagger, King grandly threw ten American cities to the racist wolves in the smoldering Negro ghettos.

King's old marching partner, Rev. James Bevel, threw his weight behind Vietnam Summer in an address delivered at an all-Negro conference being held in the Watts district of Los Angeles. Bevel urged his audience to join "thousands" refusing to be drafted, and called on Negroes to "fill up the jails." Now billed as national director of the Spring Mobilization, Bevel said that Negroes should be prepared to "face charges of treason."[118]

In August, Martin Luther King disclosed that the nationwide campaign for a referendum on the war in Vietnam was now under way in a dozen areas. He stated that "Vietnam Summer volunteers and other antiwar groups are already working to place similar initiatives on the ballot in Seattle, Portland, San Francisco, Berkeley, Cleveland, New York, Cambridge, Marin County, Calif., and the state of Wisconsin."[119] On Labor Day weekend, to no one's great surprise, the *New Republic* noted that along with people from SNCC, CORE, the Southern Christian Leadership Conference, the W. E. B. DuBois Clubs and the Communist Party, there was "a large contingent who had come from the Vietnam Summer Project" at the National Conference for New Politics in Chicago.[120]

A few days before that Labor Day weekend meeting, opponents of the war in Vietnam announced plans for a huge October demonstration in Washington to "shut down the Pentagon."[121] The organizers of the demonstration said they believed it would be "the most serious antiwar protest in American history."[122] Spearheading the demonstration was the National Mobilization Committee to End the War in Vietnam (the new name for the old Spring Mobilization

Committee).[123] At this news conference, the Rev. Thomas Lee Hayes, executive director of the Episcopal Peace Fellowship, read a statement which warned, "We will gather in a massive anti-war presence, and some will take on the most serious responsibility of direct dislocation of the war machine." The committee statement said that one goal would be to "shut down the Pentagon. We will fill the hallways and block the entrances. Thousands of people will disrupt the center of the American war machine. In the name of humanity we will call the war makers to task."[124] A national coordinator of the committee, Professor Robert Greenblatt, on leave from Cornell, declared that the committee was also preparing petitions in effect charging the United States with genocide in Vietnam.[125]

Among supporters of the march to the Pentagon were H. Rap Brown, successor to Stokely Carmichael as national chairman of SNCC; David Dellinger, one of the top leaders of the Spring Mobilization, who had defied U.S. travel bans for trips to Cuba, Red China, and North Vietnam; Dagmar Wilson, of Women Strike for Peace, who considered these demonstrations a "second front"; and Jerry Rubin, who had close ties with the pro-Peking Progressive Labor Party, and had once suggested that "treason, deliberate sabotage of the war machine" might be used as an anti-war tactic.[126] Rubin told organizers, "The peace movement is no longer one of mere protest and demonstrations. We are now in the business of wholesale and widespread dislocation of the American society. Our immediate objective is to close down the Pentagon. We will provoke an incident that has worldwide repercussions, whatever its outcome."[127]

Among the prominent Communists who were on the administrative committee were:

Stewart Edward Albert, of the pro-Peking Progressive Labor Party;
Vincent Benjamin Copeland, editor of *Workers World*, a Communist-oriented paper;

Harry Ring, assistant editor of *The Militant*, a paper of the
Socialist Workers Party;

Morris Chertov, Socialist Workers Party candidate for Connecticut State Treasurer in 1960;

Frederick Wolf Halstead, Socialist Workers Party Candidate
for President in 1968;

Arnold S. Johnson, public relations director, Communist Party,
U.S.A.; and

Phyllis A. Kalb, a self-declared Communist in student campaigns at Brooklyn College in 1966.[128]

This probably helped to explain the sharp drop in support from clergymen who had serious reservations about
the outcome of the October demonstration. To be sure, there
was some clerical representation among the functionaries
of the October march—among them Msgr. Charles Owen
Rice, pastor of the Holy Rosary Parish in Pittsburgh[129]—but
for the most part, the consensus seemed to be expressed by
Rabbi Richard G. Hirsch, director of the Social Action
Center of Reform Judaism, who said that many religious
groups were "not having anything to do with it." While
these groups opposed war on moral grounds, Rabbi Hirsch
said, "they are not prepared to go along with these people
who think everything the United States does is wrong and
everything Hanoi does is right."[130]

One of the most notable absentees from the October
demonstrations was Martin Luther King. Neither he nor
his Southern Christian Leadership Conference endorsed it.[131]
But King's long-time aide, Rev. James Bevel—organizer
of the Spring Mobilization, and still on leave from the
SCLC—willingly remained to work as national director of
the committee.[132] And there can be little doubt that the
parade organizers exploited Bevel's ties to the SCLC to
the hilt, to build support and prestige for the demonstrations against the Pentagon. Nor can there be any doubt that
Martin Luther King never uttered a word of public protest
against his assistant's participation in the October march.

A week and a half before the October parade, syndicated

columnists Evans and Novak wrote that Secretary of State Dean Rusk had told a group of New York executives that the government had detailed intelligence on Communist control of the peace movement, but "we haven't made public the extent of our knowledge. We didn't want to set off a new McCarthyism."[133]

On October 21, 1967, some 54,000 demonstrators gathered at the Lincoln Memorial.[134] Then, at 2:15, the march leaders stepped off for the Pentagon across the Potomac River. For three hours, the trek continued across Memorial Bridge. There was a rope at the top of the steps at the Mall side, separating the demonstrators from United States marshals, who were backed up by military policemen.[135] Some of the demonstrators carried American flags, and some carried flags of the Viet Cong.[136] One SNCC official asked for a moment of silence in memory of Che Guevara.[137]

The police set up three defense lines to keep out the thousands of demonstrators who were trying to storm the Pentagon, shouting obscenities and taunting the forces on guard there. Some threw eggs and bottles as darkness fell.[139] James Reston wrote that "The personal vilification of President Johnson alone was almost enough to retrieve his declining fortunes at the polls." There were signs that read "LBJ the Butcher," "Johnson's War in Vietnam Makes America Puke," and "Beat Army." Reston wrote, "It is difficult to report publicly the ugly and vulgar provocation of many of the militants. They spat on some of the soldiers in the front line at the Pentagon and goaded them with the most vicious personal slander." Reston noted that "Many of the signs carried by a small number of the militants and many of the lines in the theatrical performances put on by the hippies are too obscene to print." Reston saw some of the protestors as sincere pacifists opposing the Vietnam conflict "because it seems to them a senseless war. . . ." Others, he wrote, disliked the war "at the moment because there is no chance of American defeat. They probably would like it if the United States were being beaten. . . ."[140]

The nominal leadership of the march included, by their own admission, Communists and Communist sympathizers,[141] but an authorized government official said there was no evidence that the Communists were in charge or that there were more than " a very, very few" of them in influential roles.[142] But it is one of the more melancholy historical truisms that Communists have never needed more than "a very, very few" in influential roles. The government would only have had to refer to them as "agrarian reformers" to make the sophistry complete.

The news dispatch did not make clear whether the "authorized government official" made his statement before or after 4:30 p.m., at which time the line in front of the Pentagon was breached by a group consisting, in part, of the U.S. Committee to Aid the National Liberation Front, carrying the NLF flag.[143]

Walter Teague, of the Revolutionary Contingent, quickly assembled a group of 200 to make the first assault on the Pentagon. Wearing a white crash helmet and flanked by two comrades carrying 15-foot-high flagstaffs with Viet Cong flags, he told his followers to "link arms, link arms." This they did as they slammed into the troops.[144]

The great majority of those arrested chose to plead nolo contendere (no contest). Three United States Commissioners—Federal committing magistrates—levied typical fines of $10 (most of which were paid by representatives of the National Mobilization Committee) and imposed suspended jail terms of five to ten days. The Mobilization Committee said it had received hundreds of contributions to its bail and fine fund for arrested demonstrators.[145]

Later, the Johnson Administration revealed that it had developed detailed contingency plans to rush 25,000 or more Army troops to Washington's slums, had the anti-war demonstration spilled over into the city. A Defense Department official said there had been reports that representatives of black power groups would split off from the bulk of demonstrators after the rally at Lincoln Memorial, and, instead of marching to the Pentagon, would go to various Negro neighborhoods in Washington and seek to stir up the inhabitants. A number of large bulldozers were lined up at nearby Fort Meyer and kept ready for possible movement into the city. The bulldozers would have been used in clearing crowds off streets. As it developed, they weren't needed, but as the Defense Department official commented, "We just couldn't sit back and allow another Detroit to happen in Washington."[146]

The Administration was lavish in its disclosures about contingency plans, but disturbingly tight-lipped about the extent of Communist influence in the march on the Pentagon. About a week after the Pentagon demonstration, House Republican leader Gerald Ford was at the White House for a private briefing of Congressional GOP leaders. At this briefing, Johnson read from what appeared to be a report on the demonstrators, and the House Republican leader was convinced that the President clearly had implied that Communists were instrumental in directing the stormy anti-war protest.[147] Ford urged that the President make public this report on the demonstrators. He said the President had told an aide that there appeared to be no reason why the disclosure should not take place.[148] But the next day, Ford related, White House officials resisted release of the report.[149] When Ford asked why, Attorney General Ramsey Clark visited him and argued against making it public.[150]

In a speech on the floor of the House, Rep. Ford called upon the President to "order a full report made to the American people on the extent of Communist participation in organizing, planning and directing" the march on the Pentagon.[151] His request was supported by two more GOP leaders, Leslie Arends of Illinois and Frank Bow of Ohio, both of whom had been present at the briefing and heard the President read the report.[152] All three leaders were convinced by the document that Hanoi had organized the march on the Pentagon.[153] But the Johnson Administration still refused to release the report or otherwise document the charges, saying that to do so would fuse a "McCarthyist" witch hunt.[154]

On the other hand, Hanoi was far less coy about the inestimable propaganda value of the protest. North Vietnamese spokesmen termed the demonstrations "valuable support" for and "a great encouragement" to North Vietnam.[155] The official newspaper of the North Vietnamese Communist Party, *Nhan Dan*, went even further; in the words of the New York *Times*, the *Nhan Dan* editorial "also seemed to suggest that Hanoi would like to play some direct role in the anti-war movement in the United States."[156] The *Nhan Dan* editorial stated, "*By coordinating actions on both fronts in Vietnam and the United States* and stepping up the struggle against their common enemy, the Vietnamese and American peoples will unquestionably defeat the U.S. imperialist aggressors." *Nhan Dan* exulted that the "campaign in the U.S. for an end to Johnson's aggressive war in Vietnam has entered 'a stage of active resistance.' "[157]

It bears repeating that the man who organized the march on the Pentagon in October, 1967, was the same man who had organized the Fifth Avenue parade in April—the Rev. James Bevel, still on leave from the Southern Christian Leadership Conference and whose chief, and perhaps sole, claim to fame was his long and trusted association with Martin Luther King. King did dissociate himself from the march on the Pentagon, but not from the Rev. James Bevel.*

In New York, Ray Gimmler and Charles Wiley, as officials of the newly formed National Committee for Responsible Patriotism, let the world know that those who marched

---

* Before his death, Martin Luther King had agreed to be the keynote speaker at an anti-Vietnam rally in New York on April 27, 1968. On that date, his wife, Coretta King, spoke in his place at Sheep Meadow in Central Park. She told the wildly applauding audience: "I come to you in my grief only because you keep alive the work and dreams for which my husband gave his life. I come now, hoping you might strengthen me for the lonely road ahead." In her address, Mrs. King read "10 Commandments on Vietnam," written by her husband, which were found on a scrap of paper in his pocket on the day he was killed. She believed

on the Pentagon did not speak for this country. The marching feet in Washington were answered by marching feet in the New York metropolitan area—marching to declare support for American fighting men in Vietnam.

Many thousands marched in the Bronx, Brooklyn, and suburban areas; in Newark alone, the police estimated that 50,000 persons marched and 40,000 watched. "We are claiming the biggest grassroots movement in the history of this country," said Wiley. At his suggestion, many motorists drove with their headlights on in daytime to show their support for American servicemen. City officials ordered police drivers to keep their car lights turned *off* in daytime, an order some policemen cheerfully flouted. John J. Cassese, president of the Patrolmen's Benevolent Association, expressed deep satisfaction that some of "the fellows have their lights on, and rightfully so—we are Americans first." He warned, "if action is taken against one patrolman, you'll hear from the PBA like you've never heard before." In the Bronx, a group of youths burned a flag—a Viet Cong flag.[158]

The law-abiding never get nearly as much press coverage as the lawless. The patriotic never quite make the journalistic grade, compared with the nihilists. In column inches, number of articles and follow-up stories, those trying to breach the Pentagon received three to four times the news

---

that Martin Luther King might have prepared his Vietnam decalogue for the rally.

King's "Ten Commandments on Vietnam" read:

Thou shalt not believe in a military victory.
Thou shalt not believe in a political victory.
Thou shalt not believe that they—the Vietnamese—love us.
Thou shalt not believe that the Saigon Government has the support of the people.
Thou shalt not believe that the majority of the South Vietnamese look upon the Viet Cong as terrorists.
Thou shalt not believe the figures of killed enemies or killed Americans.
Thou shalt not believe that the generals know best.
Thou shalt not believe that the enemy's victory means communism.
Thou shalt not believe that the world supports the United States.
Thou shalt not kill.

Even in death, Martin Luther King was providing the Viet Cong with one of its most stunning propaganda victories of the war.

space almost grudgingly allotted to those defending the American presence in Vietnam. To conservatives this is an old and morosely familiar story—but the renewed realization of it becomes all the more disheartening when our servicemen become the targets of verbal sniping by our home-grown Viet Cong.

It was one of the more curious anomalies that the Vietnam protests, while a source of passionate concern to Martin Luther King, seemed to leave the overwhelming majority of Negroes cold (and, in all frankness, the same statement would have to be made for the parades to support our men in Vietnam). Negro moderates, as exemplified by Roy Wilkins and Whitney Young, had already indicated their desire to give the Vietnam protests the widest of possible berths— but while some Negro militants like Stokely Carmichael and Rap Brown were conspicuous in the line of parade, their participation made little apparent impact on many of their supporters and allies. And nowhere was this more evident than in the march on the Pentagon. The Washington Committee for Black Power had voted unanimously to dissociate itself from the October 21st Mobilization. Their reasons were bluntly racist. As the committee told the *Amsterdam News:* "Future mobilization against the war in Vietnam in which black people participate will be black-led and black-organized. The Washington Committee for Black Power will urge all black people in America to boycott the October 21st Mobilization and instead attend the 'Black Power Week End' as an honest and meaningful black activity."[159] And some months earlier, in Washington, the Rev. Channing E. Phillips, a Negro opponent of the war, said he wished the majority of Negroes objected to the country's Vietnam policy, but had concluded that they did not. He thought Negroes were probably "less exercised" about the war, at least in Washington, than were whites.[160]

As always, Negroes were more concerned with the nitty-gritty issues—jobs, housing, schools, vote registration— while King took a separate fork in the road, and almost literally, from a racial viewpoint, went his own way. King's speeches in Selma and Birmingham could, and did, turn out large numbers of Negroes to march, to contribute, to go to jail. But for all his most fiery oratorical efforts, the percentage of Negroes participating in the two mammoth Vietnam protests in 1967 was surprisingly small. King had painted himself into a corner—and now seemed unable to make any meaningful move.

King knew that the summer of 1967 promised to be the longest and hottest yet. In mid-April of 1967, he himself had warned that at least ten cities across the country could explode in racial violence. Among the cities he named were Cleveland, Chicago, Los Angeles, Oakland, Washington, Newark and New York.[161] He exclaimed, "I'll still preach nonviolence with all my might but I'm afraid it will fall on deaf ears."[162] But purely racial matters, in general, and the Long Hot Summer in particular, did not loom very large on his list of priorities. King showed considerably greater interest in haggling with New York Deputy Commissioner Jacques Nevard about the number of marchers in the Spring Mobilization Parade on Fifth Avenue. And when he did address himself to race problems, he seemed to have an infinite capacity for making a tense situation even worse.

In June, 1967, King's contribution to better race relations in Cleveland was to assert that "brutality and oppressive methods" by the Cleveland police appeared to invite riots. King said that the city's Negro areas "are almost moving toward a police state now," and told a news conference that "Wagon loads of armed police who patrol the Negro areas at night give the impression the police department is the agency that keeps the Negro oppressed."[163] King stonily maintained that 99 per cent of all riots were started by willful or ignorant police action. "Certain segments of the police seem almost to be inviting a riot," he stated.[164] And earlier King stated, either give the Negroes "their freedom or exterminate them."[165]

With a Negro, Carl Stokes, running for mayor of Cleveland, the situation in that city remained under control, racially. But Negroes in Newark, Detroit, and elsewhere were quick to get the message—and the advance exoneration from guilt—from the Crown Prince of Nonviolence, a contingency Roy Wilkins had foreseen some months before. Wilkins had described King's warning of impending race violence in ten cities as dangerous, asserting that the danger lay in the possibility that "less disciplined persons" might interpret such warnings as *encouragement* to riot.[166]

J. Edgar Hoover saw the same tragic result of King's headline-hunting. In May, he cautioned that civil rights leaders who named cities where riots might occur that summer were issuing an "open invitation" to violence. Hoover wrote that civil rights leaders who preached nonviolence and at the same time spoke of the possibility of violence were, in effect, inviting "hotheads and rabble rousers . . . to move into action on cue. It puts them on notice that they are *expected* to riot."[167]

With Newark sitting on a racial tinderbox, the very last thing that unhappy city needed was Martin Luther King busily adding more fuel to the fire next time. That Newark was a sociological disaster area was beyond dispute. A city of nearly 400,000, it had an unemployment rate of 8.2 per cent—more than double the national average.[168] In the city of Newark's application to Congress for Federal Model Cities funds, it wrote, "among major American cities, Newark and its citizens face the highest percentage of substandard housing, the most crime per 100,000 of population, the heaviest per-capita tax burden, the sharpest shifts in population and the highest rate of venereal disease, new cases of tuberculosis and maternal mortality."[169]

These problems alone were enough to comprise an urban crisis, but in addition, the application went on, "Newark is second among major cities in population density, second in infant mortality, second in birth rate, seventh in absolute number of drug addicts and has a rate of unemployment persistent enough and high enough to make it one of only five cities in the nation qualified for special assistance under the Economic Development Act." Compounding the population density, the application noted, was the fact that Newark had only 23 square miles, the smallest land area among major American cities, and almost 25 per cent of the city was covered by Newark Airport, Port Newark or almost uninhabited meadowlands.[170]

Months later, liberals would run down this list of grievances, and then point the finger of responsibility at the city administration for the Newark race riots. And yet even with the best will in the world, it was difficult to see how the mayor and/or Newark City Council could be blamed for the high Negro birth rate, the increase in crime, the high rate of venereal disease, the smallest land area among major American cities and the burgeoning number of drug addicts (some of whom had shredded practically all the mailboxes from the lobby walls of a Negro housing project in search of welfare and social security checks).[171]

And while the rate of unemployment was undoubtedly a serious problem, its existence had very little to do with racial discrimination in hiring. The crux of the job problem was that, as Donald Malafronte, administrative assistant to the Mayor put it, "Newark is essentially a white-collar town. Most of the Negroes are unskilled." He added that "The white unemployment rate and Negro unemployment rate are just about the same."[172]

Admittedly, there were legitimate causes for hostility among the city's Negroes—hostility that still should have stopped far short of a wick, a bottle, a match and gasoline. There were at least two prime bones of contention sticking in the throats of ghetto residents. In the almost holy name of Urban Renewal, the city had revealed plans to turn a 14-block slum area over for initial construction of the New Jersey College of Medicine and Dentistry. To the city, it was an unparalleled opportunity to upgrade the area. To the ghetto, it was a thinly disguised pretext for Negro removal. It was certainly an arguable proposition that in this case, at least, the bulldozers of progress would be creating at least three new problems for each one they purported to solve.

A second dispute involved the mayor's attempt to have a white City Councilman, James Callaghan, who was a high school graduate, appointed as secretary to the Board of Education. Negro groups favored the appointment of Willard Parker, a Negro accountant who was the City Budget Director and a graduate of Cornell University.[173] Again, Negroes certainly had a valid position, but they hardly aroused white sympathy for their candidate by their bull-in-a-China-shop tactics. At one hearing, Negroes tore up a stenographic record, destroyed a wall map, hurled a tape recorder to the floor and threw eggs at the board.[174] The Board of Education had to adjourn its meeting without deciding on the appointment.[175]

Most of this wanton destruction of public property was done by a Colonel Hassan of the Black Man's Volunteer Army of Liberation, from Washington, D.C. The police escorted Hassan outside, immediately, but did not arrest him.[176] The story was told by William Millard, a Negro detective in the intelligence unit of the Newark Police Department. This is what Millard told the Senate Judiciary Committee:

We took him [Colonel Hassan] downstairs in the lobby of the city hall and it was agreed by the superior officers and the corporation counsel not to make an arrest because if we locked him up, there was a possibility that terrible violence could have broken out in the city hall. It was packed with people who were at least demonstrating this kind of an attitude by shouting, and it was decided not to make the arrest.[177]

This failure to arrest Colonel Hassan was corroborated by Leonard Kowalewski, president of the State of New Jersey Fraternal Order of Policemen, also testifying before the Senate Committee:

Senator McClellan. Under circumstances like that, what keeps the man from being arrested?

Mr. Kowalewski. Unofficial orders, not written, but verbal, no arrest regardless of what happens, no arrest. Don't antagonize them. This is about what it means. Don't antagonize them.

Senator McClellan. I am talking about somebody that you don't recognize associated with the race movement, the civil rights movement or one of these organized groups that are out agitating . . . somebody that you won't associate with that element coming in there and start wrecking the furniture, would he be arrested?

Mr. Kowalewski. Immediately . . . He would be locked up immediately, because you just don't have the right to do that.[178]

This same Colonel Hassan had addressed "the black brothers and sisters of Newark, N.J.," on April 28, 1967. At this meeting, Colonel Hassan told his audience that the U.S. government would eventually put all Negroes in concentration camps. He said the concentration camps were already built at former Army bases.[179] Later, Colonel Hassan was at a youth rally held at Mount Zion Church in Newark. Present, among others, were Hassan, a former head of Essex County CORE, and the president of the Newark NAACP. At this meeting, Hassan said he had an army that would do whatever it has to do. "The people here can't do it," Hassan stated, "so my army will have to do it."[180] Hassan had also been observed with members of the poverty program.[181]

Notwithstanding these ominous rumblings in the ghetto on May 28, 1967, Mayor Hugh Addonizio said through an aide, "I do not believe there will be any mass violence in Newark this summer."[182] But three days before, Newark Police Director Dominick Spina had sent a telegram to anti-poverty Director Sargent Shriver, vehemently protesting the "use of resources and manpower of an agency of OEO for the purpose of fomenting and agitating against the organized and democratic government and agencies of the city of Newark." Spina bluntly warned that the "acceleration of this practice by this anti-poverty agency will lead to riots and anarchy in our city."[183]

Spina asked for an immediate response, but it took Shriver more than two weeks to reply by letter. In his letter, Shriver denied Spina's charges and absolved the accused OEO agency of any wrong-doing.[184]

By no stretch of the imagination could Dominick Spina be considered a northern Bull Connor. Spina graduated with both arts and law degrees from the University of Newark Law School.[185] One of his proudest accomplishments was that he had spread racial integration throughout his force. His outer office walls were adorned with plaques and testimonials, including one from the Urban Better Relations Society for his efforts for racial harmony. For four years, Spina had carried on a citizens observer corps that let citizens ride in patrolling police cars.[186]

By July, 1967, virtually all 1,400 Newark policemen had attended the community relations school in the Newark Police Academy, listening to talks by various civic leaders, clergymen, and representatives of the attorney general.[187]

The rank and file were as apprehensive of an impending conflict in Newark as their police director. Almost a month before the Newark riot, the executive board of the Newark Chapter of the New Jersey Fraternal Order of Police wrote to Mayor Addonizio, "our city is virtually an 'Armed Camp.'" The letter went on, "Should a riotous condition be brought about by circumstances beyond your control, or anyone else's for that matter, it is our opinion that our police department is not properly equipped to handle any riot of tremendous magnitude such as those we see appearing in other major cities throughout the country. . . . By not being properly equipped we mean that there are no shotguns or riot guns within the Newark Police Department. There is doubt as to the ample supply of tear gas to sustain a riot lasting several days. Also and most important, the riot helmets that are to be provided and distributed to the men are completely and totally inadequate. They are not suitable against the weapons that have been used by mobs recently in other cities. We strongly feel that the present helmet is not adequate against flying glass, Molotov cocktails, and rocks that come from all directions. . . . Therefore, Your Honor, we respectfully request that you change the present riot helmet in the city's possession to one used and provided in other cities that have had previous experience in riot control. . . . We further request that this city provide riot guns, shotguns and an ample supply of tear gas; and that the members of the department be taught the proper use of this equipment."[188]

The letter was hand-delivered to the Mayor on June 18, 1967.[189] Addonizio ordered that a survey be conducted, and that if the need were there, the city council would be asked for an emergency appropriation to provide the necessary equipment for the patrolmen.[190] Three days before the riot, the finished survey was put on the mayor's desk, but the mayor did not have the time to read the recommendations of the police director and the chief of police.[191]

But the Newark City Council found the time to hear an anti-poverty worker make a speech which could almost have been ghost-written by Stokely Carmichael and Rap Brown. The anti-poverty worker told the Newark City Council:

There is going to be blood running in the streets of Newark like there has never been anywhere else in America. . . . You will pay the supreme price, and the city, the state and the nation will know that in Newark, N.J., six supposedly upright citizens became the instrumentality for the worst kind of blood bath that America has ever seen.

You know that your actions are wrong, you know that you are perpetrating the worst kind of fraud, and yet you are hell-bent on doing it. So I am simply saying to you that when the blood runs thick, don't come to me and ask why, because the reason for it will be the action that you take.[192]

This incendiary diatribe was delivered only a few days before the outbreak of the Newark riots.

As had now become Standard Operating Procedure in the nation's ghettos, the Newark riot began following a routine traffic arrest, which, by itself, would have made boring traffic reading on any police blotter. It started Wednesday night, July 12, 1967, with the arrest of a stocky, goateed Negro cab driver with even the routine name of John Smith. His name was on an official list for revocation of his driver's license.[193] The arrest took place in Newark's predominantly Negro Fourth Precinct, and occurred while a score of taxicabs were cruising by.[194]

Suddenly the cab radios began carrying a false rumor that Smith had been fatally beaten.[195] As the rumor spread, angry Negroes gathered outside the precinct police station and hurled stones and bottles. Negro and white community leaders and James I. Threatt, Negro executive director of the Newark Human Rights Commission, sought to quiet the 200 or so persons. Someone threw a gasoline-filled bottle against the building; others threw rocks and bottles. The police ran outside and used flying wedges to disperse the crowd.[196]

By 2 a.m. Thursday morning, more than 50 carloads of Negroes had fanned out of the tenement district to the heart of the city.[197] Other bands of Negroes went through a heavily Negro neighborhood in Newark, smashing windows and looting stores. The swiftly moving gangs of looters smashed dozens of store windows, strewed merchandise on the sidewalks, and moved on. Burglar alarms could be heard all over the area.[198]

Thursday night, crowds again gathered at the precinct station, drawn by leaflets calling for a rally. Threatt told the demonstrators that a long-sought Negro goal was about to be achieved. The city of Newark was going to promote Lieutenant Edward Williams, who would become the city's first Negro police captain. "Who needs that?" somebody scoffed. More bottles and rocks were hurled at the station house while TV cameras filmed the action. A Negro woman picked up a stick and carefully jammed it between the bars to break all the basement windows of the station house.[199]

Newark Police Director Spina was in command. After some 45 minutes, he sent the precinct police out into the crowd armed with nightsticks. The scattered crowd spilled back into the streets.[200] The police began widening the "no man's land" around the station house, as some of the mob shouted at white policemen, "Kill them devils," while another yelled at Negro policemen, "You Uncle Toms got to come home tonight."[201]

"Isn't it true," Senator McClellan asked Kowaleski, "that these agitators and riot inciters have become a privileged class in this country, where the law is not enforced against them, where they are above law?" Kowalewski replied, "Senator McClellan, you can walk around the city streets of Newark and carry a machete and not get locked up by the Newark police because you are told that the machete is a part of the Mau Mau uniform."[202]

Kowalewski testified that the Newark police had been instructed not to use guns during the whole first night and seven or eight hours of the second night of the Newark riots. He told the Senate committee, "The police were told to stand by and let these people release their pent-up emotions and then if we can we will gather and contain them."[203]

Thousands of Negroes collected along a 20-block stretch of debris-covered Springfield Avenue, a street lined with cheap furniture stores, bars, pawnshops, and a few Moslem mosques. As quickly as the police could quell one flare-up of looting, bands of looters would strike at stores in another section. The police said Negroes were looting every store in the area that contained anything of value in its window.[204]

Appliance stores were stripped bare. Baby carriages were stolen and some of them piled high with loot. Liquor stores were broken into and looted. A toy store was set afire by a Molotov cocktail and the blaze quickly spread to two adjoining stores.[205] The looters said they saw very little, if anything, wrong in their "self-service shopping." One Negro woman, guarding a family business with a "Soul Brother" sign, defended the looting on the grounds that "these white stores have been robbing these people for years and Negro businessmen can hardly beg, borrow or steal their way to renting a place on the street."[206]

During the early stages of the Newark riot, when the police had not yet been authorized to take aggressive action, a police car radioed, "We're sitting ducks out here. They're hitting us with everything. Give us the word. Let us shoot." Another radio car broke in: "We're getting bombed here. What should we do?" The dispatcher's terse reply was "Leave."[207]

Mayor Addonizio finally instructed policemen to return gunfire when fired upon, or otherwise placed in jeopardy, and to take more drastic action to quell the Negro mobs.[208] And at 2:20 a.m., Friday morning, the mayor telephoned New Jersey Governor Richard Hughes, and told the Governor that the rampaging Negroes had produced an "ominous situation." He asked the Governor to send in National Guardsmen and state troopers, and the Governor agreed.[209] As he spoke to the Governor, shotgun-wielding policemen guarded firemen who were fighting a raging blaze at Broad and Market Streets, the center of downtown Newark.[210]

Shortly after 6 p.m. Friday night, National Guardsmen and policemen—wearing bullet-proof vests and advancing behind armored cars, including an eleven-ton personnel carrier—opened fire on the top floors of the Stella Wright housing project, from where a sniper had killed a policeman. Fires raged in adjacent buildings, and sniper fire delayed fire trucks approaching the scene. As his men battled the flames, a battalion chief said, "Plenty of bullets were firing around their heads."[211]

Fire Chief Edward Wall appeared before the Senate Judiciary Committee in a dual capacity—as a representative of the Newark Fire Department, and also as a spokesman for the International Association of Fire Chiefs. Chief Wall told the committee, "We found 33 instances of sniper fire being directed at either companies operating at fires [in Newark] or fire stations themselves."[212] Chief Wall testified that at times, as many as three Newark fire companies had been pinned in their quarters by sniper fire.[213] Wall added, "This to my way of thinking seems to indicate a planned pattern, to negate the fire protection in the area. They hold down the fire companies, keep them in quarters, and then set fires."[214]

Fire Chief Wall stated that in spite of police protection which formed a protection ring around the firehouses, "the gunfire in the area was unbelievable. It was very much like being on a battlefield."[215] Wall told the Senators: "In the city of Newark, we had 35 fire-fighters injured during the riots from injuries sustained through non-fire instances—in other words, rock- and bottle-throwing."[216] He stressed that Coke bottles or beer bottles were filled with sand, and became a "deadly instrument when heaved by a young thug."[217] And he made it perfectly clear that the firemen "were injured regardless of race or color. In the city of Newark, we have, I believe, 33 Negro firemen and one officer, who all served very valiantly during the fire. They were subjected to as much harassment and punishment as any other fireman or fire officer."[218]

In the racial inferno that was Newark, a National Guard captain who commanded a company of helicopter-borne infantry stood in the street with a cocked .45-caliber pistol in his belt. He stated, "They put us here because we're the toughest and the best. We haven't put anybody on the rooftops. If anybody throws things down on us, then it's shoot to kill—it's either them or us and it ain't going to be us."[219]

Now Governor Hughes took personal charge of the riot-control operation, saying that New Jersey's largest city was in a state of "open rebellion." The Governor declared, "The line between the jungle and the law might as well be drawn here as well as any place in America."[220] The line was drawn not a second too soon. Fire headquarters reported more than 70 fires Friday night, and 100 fires the night before. The snipers had not even spared the Newark City Hospital from their attacks.[221] And the New York *Times* wrote of Newark that "the usually bustling city of some 400,000 looked like a war zone."[222]

After an inspection tour, the Governor said that he had found most repellent the "holiday atmosphere" among the looters. Roving bands of defiant young Negroes, some wearing shiny new clothes that they had stolen, light-heartedly went through the debris-cluttered streets.[223] A newsman watched one band of looters cart off 75 to 100 TV sets in less than ten minutes. One of them said, "Man, this is better than Watts."[224]

One of the most bizarre journalistic accounts of the Newark snipers was found in the pages of *Life*. *Life* reporters had a clandestine meeting with members of an organization of snipers near the outskirts of the riot zone. The Newark snipers belonged to a group formed by young civil rights workers in Mississippi in 1965. One of their members, a former law student at an Eastern university, said there were more than 50 members of this sniper group now active in and around the city. More than half of them were from Newark. Others had been moved in for the action, from California, Ohio and Pennsylvania. The snipers freely discussed their contacts with the pro-Peking RAM (Revolutionary Action Movement) and saw themselves as a kind of composite Robin Hood. As the former law student phrased it, "While the police are busy tearing buildings apart looking to kill snipers, our people are getting color television sets, refrigerators, clothes—whatever they couldn't afford, they got it."[225] Their people also got burned-out buildings, the destruction of millions of dollars in property, two dozen deaths, countless injured and arrested, serious food shortages, and a legacy of terror, horror, and hatred that would haunt the ghetto for years to come.

At one point, three white men driving in a car along Springfield Avenue approached a crowded intersection. A Negro holding a chunk of wood tried to pull open the driver's locked door. Another Negro jumped in front of the slowly-moving car and when it halted, leaped to the side, snapped off the radio aerial and tossed it at the passenger side of the road. A volley of rocks thudded against the car as it sped away.[226]

At a news conference Friday evening, Mayor Addonizio was asked if he thought the rioting was being "led or controlled." The Mayor replied, "Up to early this afternoon, I thought it was unorganized and the work of just the criminal element. But I have just met with about 35 clergymen and they indicated to me that it might be controlled, possibly by people from outside."[227]

Kowalewski testified that well over 50 per cent of those arrested during the riots were found to have previous criminal records.[228] *Life* gloatingly reported a city official's admission that in almost half of these cases, the records consisted simply of arrests but no convictions[229]—but then the same statement could have been made about various members of the Cosa Nostra.

The food shortage in the Central Ward had now become acute. Food suppliers were afraid to drive their trucks into the neighborhood.[230] Thousands of Negro residents lined up to receive emergency food supplies, brought in under the watchful eyes of the National Guard and distributed by volunteers from the City Housing Authority, civil rights groups and anti-poverty organizations. Many Negroes were still too frightened to leave their homes. But thousands of others stood in line for up to four hours to be given a quart of milk, half a cabbage, some other vegetables, and a small portion of salami or bologna.[231]

Throughout the Newark riots, the verbal sniping at the police had been almost as hateful as the sniping from rooftops. Now the National Guardsmen and police were accused of harassing peacemakers and smashing the windows of Negro-owned stores.[232] Governor Hughes called the charges "hearsay" but said he would investigate.[233]

Nearly half of Newark was still an occupied zone.[234] National Guard troops and the police hunted house to house for snipers after gunfire took three more lives.[235] Newark City Hospital came under sniper fire for the third straight night. Doctors and nurses dropped to the floor during ten minutes of sniping.[236] Governor Hughes said the police estimated that as many as 25 snipers were operating in the ghetto.[237] Neither the Governor nor the Mayor said he had any evidence of a conspiracy by an outside group, but the Governor said that "the rather expert sniping, the jumping from place to place—the cruel and despicable efficiency with which this sniping occurred—indicates some organization and some coordination between those criminals participating in it."[238] Governor Hughes charged that many of the rioters were "committing violence because they hate America."[239]

On Tuesday, July 18, Governor Hughes stated: "The restoration of order is accomplished. While sniping incidents continue, it is grinding to a halt." With the Governor's announcement that "the rioting and looting are over," National Guard units and state troopers began moving out of Newark. Hughes ordered the withdrawal of the 3,000 guardsmen and 375 state policemen at the fervent plea of Negro leaders.[240] Almost simultaneously, police headquarters and City Hall received more than 100 telephone calls protesting the withdrawal as "premature."[241] Their fears were well-founded. Less than three hours after the Governor's order went into effect, a city fire truck answering an alarm came under such heavy sniper fire it had to turn back.[242] After the main body of state police and guardsmen had left the city, thieves backed up trucks at an appliance shop, a furniture store, and an iron works, and began moving out considerable quantities of loot.[243]

The Newark riots took a grisly toll of 26 lives, the last of these the same day the Governor had proclaimed that "the restoration of order is accomplished." Of these 26 dead, only two were white—a fire captain shot in the back by a sniper while fighting a blaze in the riot area,[244] and a policeman—cited for saving a drowning child in 1964—who died two hours after being shot through the chest by a sniper.[245] The rest of the death toll included Negro children and women, looters and gunmen.[246]

Mayor Addonizio was irritated by news from Washington that Newark police officials had protested to the Office of Economic Opportunity months before that some Newark anti-poverty workers were "acting in a manner which might create a riot." Of this police action, he said, "We'll certainly remind them that there's only one Mayor in Newark."[247] And yet, in almost the same breath, the Mayor himself charged that the tensions that erupted in racial rioting had been "fueled by the rash of wild and extremist statements and behavior of the past 10 to 12 weeks in our city." And in what could virtually serve as a carbon copy of Police Director Spina's telegram to Sargent Shriver in May, Addonizio said that some statements by workers in the city's anti-poverty agency were "contributing actions."[248]

Newark's anti-poverty agency, the United Community Corporation (UCC), was an autonomous body.[249] In its three years of operation, the UCC had received $10 million to $12 million for such anti-poverty programs as Head Start, Legal Aid, youth and senior citizen recreational programs, and educational and job training programs for large numbers of Negroes.[250] At least 90 per cent of this money came from the Federal government,[251] but apparently these mountains of millions generated only the most minimal good will in Newark's Negro ghetto. Newark police believed that a leaflet giving instructions on how to make a Molotov cocktail was run off on mimeograph machines in a Newark anti-poverty office.[252] And beyond dispute, some of the most radical elements in the Negro community had found their way into Newark's anti-poverty agency, among them Willie Wright, a member of the UCC board.

The riot fever in Newark spread to neighboring communities, including the city of Plainfield. After martial law had been imposed and on order of Governor Hughes, police and the National Guard conducted a house-to-house search in Plainfield for 46 stolen rifles.[253] Three of these rifles were found.[254] Upon hearing of this search, anti-poverty board member Willie Wright declared that he was telling Newark's Negroes "to get yourselves a piece of gun and put it in the bottom drawer or something and have it fully loaded, and then if some joker breaks into your home like they did in Plainfield, let him have it."[255] Wright stated that it was his "firm conviction that complete chaos will have to prevail in the streets of American cities, and blood will have to flow like water before the black man will become an accepted citizen of this society."[256]

The Federal Office of Economic Opportunity asked Newark's UCC to suspend Wright pending an investigation of his statements, and immediately disavow any sympathy with statements that would precipitate violence.[257] In reply all 17 members of the executive committee of Newark's anti-poverty agency voted against suspending Wright.[258] UCC President Timothy Still piously proclaimed, "This agency cannot police the private views of its members." Furthermore, he continued, "Mr. Wright was elected to the board at the annual UCC Meeting in 1965. If the board of trustees so desires, they may consider Mr. Wright's fitness to serve, but they are the only ones authorized to do so."[259] At this point, following a meeting with Miss Josephine Nieves, Regional Director of OEO, the Office of Economic Opportunity withdrew its demand for the suspension of Willie Wright.[260]

A week and a half later, at a UCC meeting, Wright took the floor and made anything he had said before seem tepid by comparison. Wright now said that he not only advocated Negroes arming themselves, but asserted, "Just a six shooter won't be enough. Get yourself a machine gun, cause you're gonna need it. Every black man should buy a tank and put it in his back yard."[261]

In Washington, Sargent Shriver had told every local anti-poverty agency that he would insist upon the withholding of funds from any group that encouraged or tolerated employees taking part in rioting.[262] But he was said to be "resigned to the fact that he was 'legally powerless' to force Mr. Wright's suspension, because he was an elected official."[263] Shriver asked UCC President Timothy Still to state publicly that Wright's statement did not reflect official anti-poverty policy. Delighted to get off the hook at this bargain price, Still glibly declared that Wright had been speaking for himself.[264] But in view of Still's own previous statements, his tardy disclaimer was of dubious validity. Shortly after Wright made his statement, Timothy Still stated, "When anybody—the police, the National Guard, or a criminal—breaks into a man's home without a warrant, they should be prepared to get shot. If they broke into my home and started breaking it up and pushing my wife and kids around, I'd start shooting. I might get killed on the spot, but a man has to be a man."[265]

The Long Hot Summer had become even longer and hotter for Newark's sterling anti-poverty warriors in the UCC. The mercury now soared a little higher when the Police Athletic League withdrew as a co-sponsor with the UCC of a summer play program in Newark funded by the Federal government to the tune of $268,000.[266]

In his letter of resignation as head of the project, Detective Charles Meeks asserted that extremists, alcoholics, narcotics addicts, and a prostitute had been hired to work with children in the summer play program. Meeks wrote that members of the Black Man's Volunteer Liberation Army had been hired for the program, that children had been sent to camp where there was left-wing indoctrination, and that Meeks himself had been reduced to a "figurehead" status.[267] Almost a month later, the Office of Economic Opportunity notified the Newark anti-poverty agency that it would be cut off from Federal funds unless it thoroughly reorganized itself according to a list of stipulated standards within 30 days.[268]

It had been common knowledge for quite some time that there was little, if any, love lost between the UCC and the

Newark city government. But this was not any stereotyped struggle between liberal or ultra-liberal forces on the one hand, and conservative, or ultra-conservative forces on the other. The *National Observer* wrote that Newark city officials "can state that the city is one of the most liberal in the country. ('There are no right-wing Republicans here,' one says. 'I'm a liberal Democrat and I'm on the right wing.')"[269]

The city could hardly have been more zealous in its financial outlays for the Negro poor. Welfare expenditures in Newark increased in the years 1941–1963 by 400 per cent.[270] Public assistance to the poor rose nearly six-fold in 20 years.[271] Newark had the highest per capita expense for urban renewal projects of any of the nation's top 50 cities. For each person, $277 was being spent.[272] And yet, the New York *Times* reported, "Many anti-poverty workers in the field feel, however, that the hard truth of the matter is that no amount of money can do the job." The *Times* quoted an anti-poverty worker who despairingly commented, "We can only hold the line," and then pointing towards the rubble of the riots, concluded, "White America will just have to get used to this."[273]

Raymond Moley saw unemployment and inadequate housing as the paramount problems in Newark's Negro ghetto, but in a terse, no-nonsense analysis, he put to rest the prevailing sociological shibboleths that had thrown more heat than light on the entire problem.

Of the unemployment problem, Moley commented, "The economy of the Newark area simply could not meet the need of jobs for the people who came to live there."[274] This was confirmed, however unconsciously, by a Newark official who told the *Daily News*, "A big problem is matching the jobless with jobs they can handle." This official disclosed that unemployment in Newark had dropped from 14 per cent in 1962 (when there were no riots) to seven per cent in 1967 (when there were).[275]

As for the housing problem, it was scarcely a startling new development on the Newark scene. Moley pointed out that "in Newark, the problem of slums has been known for many years. The files of the Newark Public Library are crammed with material on the subject which runs back to the turn of the century . . . In 1946 the housing authority of Newark reported on conditions that are even now the target of comment."[276]

Three or four years before the Newark riots, members of the Urban Studies Center of Rutgers University began an intensive study of the slums, with special emphasis upon Newark. The director of the project, Professor George Sternlieb, showed that over the past 20 years, the Newark property tax rate per $100 of valuation had more than doubled. Sternlieb found that in Newark, "In the face of rent level plateaus, the increasing level of the tax rate . . . has reduced the profitability of slum investment." The inevitable result was that "the typical landlord response has been to reduce maintenance and avoid additional investment."[277]

Not only were the chances of higher rents—to cover increased maintenance costs—virtually nil; some Negro tenants were complaining bitterly that the rents they were presently paying were much too high. The *Afro-American* quoted one lady who protested that the rents at Hayes Project were unreasonable: "This is supposed to be low-income, public housing," she said, "but I pay $85 a month, and I don't even have a job." Asked what she would consider a reasonable rent, she replied, "about $30 a month."[278]

But vocally, at least, the main thrust of Negro unrest still followed the well-worn trail of almost every racial disturbance since the Los Angeles riots. In Newark, as elsewhere, it was the same old cry of "police brutality," and the same refusal or inability to substantiate these charges in meetings with police authorities. At the height of the rioting, Newark's Human Relations Commission said it had received dozens of telephone calls complaining of unnecessary clubbings and beatings. But none of the complainants went to the office to file formal charges.[279]

A month later, 18 Negroes filed suit in U.S. District

Court asking that a Federal receiver take over and operate the Newark Police Department on the grounds that the police had consistently discriminated against Negroes. Associated with the suit were the American Civil Liberties Union, the Newark Legal Services Project, the Law Center for Constitutional Rights, and the Scholarship, Education and Defense Fund for Racial Equality (formerly a part of CORE). The suit charged that the Newark police, the New Jersey State Police, and the National Guard had deliberately destroyed Negro-owned property and used "massive and unlawful deadly force against members of plaintiffs' class when said force was unnecessary" during the riots. The Executive Director of the ACLU in New Jersey, Henry M. diSuvero, said his office had more than 200 statements from Negro residents charging police abuses. He said they had not been turned over to the police because Negroes in Newark "have no trust in the police."

Newark Public Safety Director Spina termed the court action "ridiculous" and said, "I don't believe I have had more than seven or eight complaints of abuse of authority and these are being investigated." Spina added, "These are the kind of negative complaints which frustrate law enforcement and make it more and more difficult for a police department to carry on its work."[280]

Less than a week later, in an address that deserved far more attention than it received, diSuvero revealed the real reason for this absurd lawsuit. Speaking to students at the New York University School of Law, diSuvero disclosed that a "significant factor" in bringing the suit had been the belief that awareness of it would curb any further alleged police excesses. The ACLU official commented that with the case pending in Federal court, lawyers had the right to demand immediate depositions from the police in connection with any new charges of brutality. He emphasized, "In effect, we created our own review board." DiSuvero said that the very complications that the police encountered in defending an anti-brutality lawsuit could deter any more of the same police actions. He told the law students that either the accused policeman would have to spend his own money hiring a lawyer to defend what could be a complicated case, or else municipal lawyers who would have to fight the case would tell the police chief to "tell your guys to knock it off" because of all the trouble it involved.[281] The implications of diSuvero's lawsuit were all too chillingly clear; with or without a scintilla of evidence, the mere *charge* of wrongdoing would be enough to tie a policeman's hands, and this in a city ripped to shreds by riotous racists.

The battle now shifted somewhat from police brutality to fear of impending canine brutality. A bill came up in the Newark City Council to allocate $21,000 for a K-9 Corps for the Police Department[282] Police Director Spina and most of his policemen wholeheartedly supported the use of dogs, and the two Negro City Councilmen just as wholeheartedly opposed it.[283] On September 6, 1967, the City Council cast a 7 to 2 vote against the K-9 Corps—before a predominantly non-white audience.[284] Two weeks later, the Council Chamber was crowded with whites supporting the use of dogs—and this time the Council voted *for* the bill by 7 to 2.[285] In October the Newark City Council again reversed itself and voted down the K-9 Corps.[286] The Negro newspaper, the *Amsterdam News*, carried the story side by side with a voice from the past—Bull Connor, now President of the Alabama Public Service Commission and a state Democratic committeeman. Connor asked Federal funding for the training of police dogs in the belief that dogs are "more humane than a gun," and that many deaths in Northern riots would not have occurred if the police had used dogs as he did during Birmingham's racial demonstrations four years before. Connor recalled, "Most of the newspapers gave me a fit for using dogs. Now nearly every city in the United States is getting them. I should have got a patent on them."[287]

More than a few journalistic pot-shots were being taken at Governor Hughes during this time, because he had the temerity to reiterate his conviction that his "hard line" against the Negro rioters in Newark was "absolutely" correct and that "no amount of deprivation" in the Negro slums justified mob burning, looting, and murder.[288] The Governor frankly declared, "We want a new signal, a new understanding to go out in New Jersey. There is to be an unconditional dedication to law enforcement. We will not have physical attacks on the police, and there will be no ifs, ands, or buts about it."[289] But in the eyes of apologists for Negro excesses, Hughes may have redeemed himself somewhat when he asked his administration to investigate the feasibility of dropping employment qualifications where possible in an attempt to recruit jobless Negroes for state positions[290] (the feasibility of dropping employment qualifications for jobless whites never quite entered into the conversation).

The Most Reverend Thomas A. Boland, Archbishop of Newark, visited the riot area, and shortly after, the Roman Catholic Archdiocese announced its sponsorship of a new housing and rehabilitation program for the slum-dwellers. The program envisaged the expenditure of as much as $50 million in state and Federal funds for low- and middle-income housing over a two-year period.[291] And in November, ground was broken in Newark for the first housing project undertaken as part of a billion dollar urban rehabilitation program announced by insurance companies. Cosponsored by Prudential Insurance Company, the state of New Jersey and the city of Newark, the project was to be a 270-unit, $4.5 million, middle-income co-op.[292]

There was still the venerable complaint that there were too few Negroes in the National Guard. The state of New Jersey proposed to solve that problem with a sizable dosage of reverse discrimination. Governor Hughes revealed that the Army had approved a request by New Jersey to increase the strength of its National Guard by five per cent, *with the increase consisting wholly of Negroes*.[293] There were currently 7,000 young men, most of them white, who were on the Guard's waiting list. Major General James F.

Cantwell, the chief of staff of the New Jersey National Guard, asserted that the Negro recruitment drive would not interfere with the present waiting list, because Negroes would be recruited specifically for the newly authorized overstrength. However, the general acknowledged that Negroes on the waiting list would jump ahead of whites into the Guard's new overstrength component.[294] A senior Guard officer, who asked not to be identified, told the New York *Times* that this "may very well violate Federal anti-discrimination statutes."[295] As for Governor Hughes, he simply refused to comment on the legality of the Negro recruitment drive.[296]

General Cantwell expressed the hope that white youths on the waiting list would be "understanding," but he conceded that "there might be a legal challenge" from any one of the whites on the list who faced a daily risk of being drafted by the Army while awaiting induction in the Guard.[297] David M. Satz, Jr., the United States Attorney for New Jersey, at first declined comment, but finally opined that provisions of the Equal Employment Opportunities Act could outweigh the anti-discrimination provisions of the United States Civil Rights Code.[298] All of which seemed to corroborate the suspicion that under the Equal Employment Opportunities Act, Negroes were more equal than whites.

Both Federal and state governments pulled out all the stops to push, pull, coax, or drag more Negroes into the New Jersey National Guard. The campaign was hailed as a success by the Pentagon,[299] but the results fell far short of the goal. The test program permitted New Jersey to acquire a five per cent overstrength—amounting to 865 openings reserved exclusively for Negroes. But some four months after Hughes' announcement, only 381 Negroes had been enlisted for the New Jersey Guard[300]—about 45 per cent of the total number the government had sought.

In an ironic twist of circumstance, Governor Hughes' growing unpopularity in the Newark ghetto may have guaranteed the success of the largest and most diverse group of Negro civil rights activists ever to assemble in the United States. Shortly after the end of the riots—almost while the rubble was still being cleared away—the National Conference on Black Power was scheduled to hold a four-day meeting in Newark. The Governor stated that he could not think of a worse time or place for such a meeting.[301] Result: more than three times the number expected were present,[302] as about 400 persons representing 45 civil rights groups in 36 cities attended.[303] Roy Wilkins, Whitney Young, and Martin Luther King were not present, but their organizations were represented;[304] King's chief aide in Chicago, the Reverend Jesse Jackson, was present in his capacity as the guiding hand behind Operation Bread-basket.[305] Floyd McKissick and H. Rap Brown were there. Ron Karenga was there, as head of US, a Watts-based organization said to recruit and train Negroes for revolution. William H. Booth, head of New York City's Commission on Human Rights, was there.[306] And there to lend a bizarre, if not surrealistic note to the delegate list were two high-ranking officers of the New York City Police Department. They attended Black Power sessions as "official representatives" of the police department, but only *after* they had already revealed plans to attend the conference on their own.[307] One of these Negro police officers said he was at the conference "to learn, observe, and take part and to contribute whatever I can."[308]

Organizer of the meeting was Dr. Nathan Wright, Jr., executive director of the Department of Urban Work of the Episcopal Diocese of Newark.[309] A four-hour mass meeting of militant speechmaking at the Mount Zion Baptist Church ended the first conference day. Newark's Commissioner of Human Rights, Alfred Black, set its tone by stating, "A black man today is either a radical or an Uncle Tom."[310]

The ultra-militant *Liberator* wrote that there was increasing suspicion of "black people who will even allow the label of 'middle-class' to be placed upon them."[311]

Leaders of the Black Power Conference asserted that

white people were basically responsible for the racial violence in Negro ghettos. "Bad conditions make for violence," said Floyd McKissick. "White people control the government, the money, and the ghettos. They should be made to answer that question."[312]

Living dangerously, the white press made valiant efforts to cover the Black Power Conference. About thirty newsmen were gathered for a press conference in the Cathedral House at the Episcopal Diocese, the headquarters for the meeting. Suddenly a dozen screaming participants of the Black Power meeting invaded the news conference, overturned television cameras, and sent the newsmen scurrying to safety, some by the windows of the first-floor room. A few minutes after the disorder, four carloads of policemen, some armed with shotguns, pulled up outside. But when a crowd of delegates gathered near them, a police inspector yelled, "Get all the police out of here," and the police withdrew. Afterward Dr. Wright coyly informed the newsmen, "Obviously we regret this incident very much."[313]

Dr. Wright stated that fifty major American corporations helped finance the National Conference on Black Power.[314] He refused to name the corporations, but said that "they were not pressured" into making contributions. Wright would only describe the corporations as being "major industries" and say that they were "white-owned."[315]

If the executive officers of the fifty major American corporations had read the August, 1967, issue of *Liberator*, they would have had spelled out in chapter and verse exactly what they were financing. They would have learned that the following resolutions were endorsed by the body of delegates as a whole:

Black-controlled financial institutions (banks, insurance companies, savings and loan associations) to provide funds for credit unions, housing loans, etc.

Selective buying to force job upgrading and a nationwide "buy-Black" move.

Election of 12 Black Congressmen.

Paramilitary training for Black youths.

A Black National Holiday to honor such heroes as Malcolm X.

A Black University with subsidiary colleges in every city.

A school for Black political organizers.

Boycott of magazines that carry ads for hair straighteners and skin lighteners.

Boycott of all Olympic games and other sports until Muhammad Ali's lawful heavyweight title is restored.

A refusal to accept birth control programs on the ground that any such attempt seeks to exterminate Black people.[316]

Well after the Newark riots had ended—and the National Conference on Black Power had folded its racist tent, and stolen away—an almost suffocating smog of suspicion, hostility, and hatred still continued to blanket the city. The Long Hot Summer had come to a close, but emotions still smoldered. In October, nine students were injured and a dozen others arrested after two consecutive days of fighting at Barringer High School, the largest in Newark.[317] More than 75 detectives and uniformed policemen raced to the school, along with Mayor Addonizio, Police Director Spina, and Superintendent of Schools Franklyn Titus.[318] Barringer, a three-year-old, $6.5 million school, had a student population of 2,540 with at least 40 per cent of it Negro enrollment.[319] The *Amsterdam News* wrote of Barringer: "Today the school is figuratively surrounded with low-cost housing projects, rooming houses, and overcrowded apartment houses crawling with hundreds of potential Afro-American and Spanish-speaking students."[320] The free-for-all at Barringer began when two girls started fighting over a seat in the cafeteria.[321] Later a melée erupted in the cafeteria, requiring more than 75 policemen to keep order.[322] Although both white and Negro students were involved, the Mayor stoutly denied that racial conflict was a cause of the violence.[323]

The New York *Times* had a differing view, though: "Although the fighting was not along racial lines at first," it wrote, "it later developed into a black versus white conflict in the school . . ."[324] At one point, policemen on horseback kept roaming groups of white and Negro students from clashing at Barringer.[325]

Racially, Barringer High had a short but stormy history. In the process of building this million-dollar school, Barringer was plagued by a work stoppage, fist fights, and sit-ins and lay-ins when complaints were made that the builder was discriminating against skilled and professional Negro workmen.[326] And as recently as a month before the fracas, many of the whites at City Hall in support of the K-9 Corps were Barringer High School students.[327]

In an effort to ease the tension following the two days of violence, Barringer High School students were dismissed early.[328] Some of the school's teachers were scheduled to have a meeting with the Mayor to seek authority to remove unruly students from class and from the school if necessary. There was a report that half of the teaching staff would not come to class if these demands were not met.[329] Subsequently, at the recommendation of the Mayor, the Board of Education did give teachers greater authority to dismiss disruptive students.[330] But Barringer's problems were far from solved. In November, about 1,800 of the students stayed away from school to protest a resurgence of violence. This boycott by more than two-thirds of the student body had been suggested by the president of the Barringer Parent-Teachers Association because the school was "unsafe."[331] Just how unsafe was conceded by the Vice Principal, who disclosed that fist fights had occurred in the school, that a former student was seen carrying a gun in the building, that one teacher had been struck by a student, and that a student with a knife had reportedly been disarmed at the school.[332]

A few days later, there was virtually normal attendance by pupils and teachers as Barringer High School enjoyed what the acting Principal called "an edgy peace." A few more policemen were stationed at the school entrances, and school bus drivers served as supervisors in the cafeteria. And over the public address system, the student body heard the Assistant Superintendent of Schools make a plea for peace and understanding coupled with a warning that violators would be dealt with severely.[333]

In a sense, Barringer High was Newark in miniature. In the city, as in its largest high school, "edgy" was the word that described it all. Three months after the riots, the New York *Times* wrote, "the prevailing mood of Newark is an edgy puzzlement, what appears to be a directionless ferment in the Negro community and a sometimes belligerent and sometimes apologetic uneasiness among the whites." A white clergyman who worked in the Negro community said gloomily, "We're nowhere out of the woods. Could we have another riot? Sure." And a Negro anti-poverty worker showed a companion how groups of whites and Negroes passed on the sidewalk now; self-consciously and silently, they walked around each other.[334] In this traditionally liberal city, a white politician observed, "The John Birch Society scheduled one of its movies, and the crowd was so big they had to have two shows."[335] As for Mayor Addonizio, he expected the suburbs to help solve Newark's problems. "Look," said the Mayor, "we had a riot in Newark. That's not going to go away. If those people out there [in the suburbs] don't do something to help out, it might soon be in their backyard."[336]

This could prove to be more than mere political verbiage. Newark law enforcement officials revealed that less than 100 of the 1,000 guns stolen during the rioting there had been recovered despite intensive searching.[337] The twin combustibles of Black Power and Gun Power could yet inflame the surrounding suburban areas, whether they "help out" Mayor Addonizio or not.

Five days of rioting in Newark left 26 persons dead, more than 1,200 injured, and more than 1,300 arrested; property damage was estimated in excess of $10 million.[338]

Martin Luther King's prediction of racial turmoil in Newark had borne ghastly fruit.

What city would next be victimized by race riots? It became a macabre guessing game. City after city was listed as possible targets of The Fire This Time. But not many seriously believed that less than a week after the Newark riots had ended, a new, more terrible, and even more anarchic riot would break out in a city long considered a model in race relations. A race riot in Detroit in 1967 with Jerome Cavanagh as Mayor? It seemed all but inconceivable.

Mayor Cavanagh was helped into office initially by Detroit's half-million Negroes.[339] His first step as Mayor was to appoint as Police Commissioner a former State Supreme Court Justice known for his liberal views, and much respected by the Negro community.[340] With Cavanagh in City Hall, Detroit began hiring and promoting more Negro police, integrated two-man patrol cars, and the police commisioner supervised meetings with Negro groups to discuss police problems.[341] Cavanagh appointed a number of Negroes to important posts: as controller, secretary of the Department of Public Works Commission, head of the Mayor's Commission on Children and Youth, and later Deputy Police Commissioner.[342] In 1963, Mayor Cavanagh led a Freedom March of 150,000 Negroes and whites down Woodward Avenue.[343] Cavanagh's projects for the ghettos and intensive lobbying in Washington had brought Detroit more than $185 million in Federal grants.[344] Long before the advent of the Federal legislation, the city of Detroit's rat eradication program reduced rat bites from 123 in 1951 to 17 in 1965.[345] And in 1966, the Detroit City Council *unanimously* adopted an ordinance requiring the city to write non-bias employment directives in all contracts.[346]

Detroit had the country's largest chapter of the NAACP —with 18,000 members.[347] Also the most successful fund-raising chapter, it had collected $130,000 in 1966 at the annual "Fight for Freedom Dinner."[348] As far back as 1960, more than 57 per cent of Detroit's Negroes owned automobiles, and about 41 per cent owned their own homes.[349] The New York *Times* wrote: "These homes are spread through such a large area of the city that it is difficult to talk of a Negro ghetto in Detroit."[350] This was so obviously the case that a white banker commented, "If there's a ghetto, I live in it."[351]

Well before Los Angeles teetered on the brink of race riots, *Negro Digest* featured an article titled, "A City's Pride: Detroit's 'Bright Young Men' in Washington." The article showed that in Washington, D.C., "Detroit is represented by more able and experienced young Negro men in responsible government positions than any other major city in the country." And when John Conyers, Jr., was elected to Congress the preceding fall, two "firsts" were recorded. It was the first time since Reconstruction that two Negroes from one state sat in the House of Representatives, and the first time in history that two Negroes from a single Northern city served in Congress. As for the education and employment picture—and this was two years before the riots—*Negro Digest* wrote: "Partly because of the unions—and Negro strength in them—racial segregation and favoritism have been far less frequent in the factories of Detroit than those of any other city. Negroes and whites worked side by side and, in many cases, shared the same schools and neighborhoods, and it was difficult under these circumstances for whites to assume superiority."[352]

If any city, North or South, came even reasonably close to de facto integration, it was Detroit, especially with the Golden Boy of Urban Race Relations, Jerome Cavanagh, at the helm. It seemed so safe to assume that Detroit was less likely to have a riot than other cities. "We've got a lot going for us," was a common statement by Negro and white leaders.[353] Mayor Cavanagh was this certain that Detroit would remain racially peaceful in 1967: two months before the riots began, a biography prepared by his staff glowingly stated that the Mayor's "enlightened policies have spared Detroit the civil upheavals that have struck other cities."[354]

But there were discernible signs of slippage in Cavanagh's political popularity. After losing to G. Mennen Williams in the Democratic Senatorial primary, suspicions had grown in Detroit that the Mayor was no longer very interested in his job, and was seeking a Federal appointment. There was also a vigorous movement to recall Cavanagh from office on the ground that he was lax in dealing with the city's growing crime rate.[355] His apparent boredom with the city was such that, returning to City Hall after a trip around the world the preceding winter, one cynical reporter asked him: "Mr. Mayor, what brings you to Detroit?"[356]

There was one serious conflict between Cavanagh and much of Detroit's Negro community. Ironically, the issue was one of Negro representation, not on the state or Federal level, but in the Detroit Common Council. Since the abolition of the old ward system half a century ago, the nine-man Detroit council had been elected at large, and only two Negroes had been able to win. There was now only one Negro in the council, the Rev. Nicholas Hood. Many Detroit Negroes argued that with less than 40 per cent of the population, they could not expect to win more than one at-large race. They wanted a return to the ward system in the belief that, by concentrating Negro votes in several wards, they could probably elect three Negro councilmen.[357]

Mayor Cavanagh opposed a return to the ward system because "I can get much more done—for the inner city and for the Negro community—with the at-large system. The ward system would balkanize the city. If we wanted to scatter small public housing projects around the city as we're doing now, some councilman from a primarily white area would say, "Oh no, not in my area."[358]

His somewhat paternalistic arguments failed to impress Rep. John Conyers, one of Detroit's two Negro congressmen. Conyers denounced the Mayor's attitude as "typical of the white liberal. To elect even one Negro at large, we need support from white liberals and particularly the United Auto Workers, the real power here. The candidate needs union votes, but also union money, because it costs more to run for the council at large here than it does for Congress. This means he has to be anointed by our white 'friends.' That won't do any more."[359]

But Conyers was positively moderate, compared with the Rev. Albert C. Cleage, Jr., pastor of the Central United Church of Christ in Detroit. This was the only known black nationalist Christian church in the nation, worshipping a black Messiah.[360] (Cleage wore an African amulet, instead of the cross.)[361] Writing in *Liberator* a month before the riots, Rev. Cleage stated, "No one can deny that Malcolm [X] certainly told the truth when he said that the white man is a beast."[362] Cleage believed that "Dr. King led black people to understand that integration could never come to pass. He helped black men to understand that 'the man' is an enemy. When Dr. King said, 'My dream has turned into a nightmare,' he was speaking for all of us."[363] Cleage told his ultra-militant flock, in *Liberator*, "We demand the right to live any place we wish and unless we are given that right, we will take it. And when we take it, we will still live together because we don't want to live with white people. . . . Until we get power, Malcolm X is just a memory. When we do get power, we can put his statue up in every city *because the cities will belong to us*."[364] (Emphasis added.)

In his state of blissful euphoria, it is not known whether Mayor Cavanagh ever read Rev. Cleage's racist exhortation to his black militant faithful. Other black militants preferred to work secretly behind the scenes, biding their time until the opportune moment. In a series published in the *Detroit News*, a leading Negro liberal, Louis Lomax, charged that the Detroit riots were masterminded by a "Black Power revolutionary organization." Lomax said that "Operation Detroit" got under way several weeks before the riots. Posing as magazine salesmen, revolutionaries fanned out across the Negro areas to recruit bomb-throwers. As Lomax told it, the battle plan was as simple as this: "Remain as obscure as possible until police-ghetto dynamics provide the proper setting for 'the revolution.'" Lomax said that a Negro reporter who had infiltrated the group "was so frightened by what he saw and heard that he refused to write the series." Lomax wrote that certain white liberals had given the riots undercover support because they felt "that the only way to solve the problems of the ghetto was to burn it down."[365]

There had been trouble in the ghetto in recent years, but it had all been kept under control. In 1963, a patrolman shot and killed a six-foot, 193-pound prostitute known ironically as "Saint Cynthia." The patrolman said "Saint Cynthia" had pulled a knife, but Negro groups demonstrated nonetheless.[366] And three years later there was "the riot that didn't happen." It "didn't happen" on August 9, 1966, in the Kercheval section of East Detroit.[367] On that date, the Afro-American Youth Movement tried to exploit the arrest of three of their members in a street corner fracas in order to start a full-scale riot. But in two nights of unrest, there was little serious violence, and under official orders *not a shot was fired by the police*.[368] There was little property damage, and the Detroit *News* hailed the police for their "iron self-discipline."[369] So an ugly racial situation was averted in Detroit in 1966, but potential troublemakers would now have reason to believe that in future disturbances, the police would again be forbidden to use their weapons.

If there was trouble, where would it start? Newsmen who knew Detroit knew the answer; they predicted it would begin at 12th and Clairmount.[370]

The 12th Street area is honeycombed with "blind pigs"—

Detroitese for after-hours speakeasies. In recent months, one of the most active blind pigs in town had been on the second floor of a shabby brick building at 9125 12th Street, above a printing company. At the top of a flight of stairs was a door marked "The United Civic League for Community Action,"[371] but their denizens were united only in their thirst for alcoholic refreshment. A year before, the police had raided the spot; but recently the operators had become more cautious, and the plainclothesmen had had difficulty getting a man inside to make the "buy" necessary for prosecution.[372]

At 3:45 a.m. on July 23, 1967, a Negro plainclothesman managed to get in by joining two regular women customers as they came up the stairs. He purchased a beer for 50 cents. By prearrangement, other policemen then burst through the door and found, not the expected 30 customers, but 83 persons.[373] Even at that hour, 12th Street was alive. About 50 persons—among them prostitutes, pimps, con men and numbers runners—had gathered on the sidewalk in front of the printing company. A report quickly spread on the streets that the police had clubbed one man and kicked a woman. The crowd outside began stoning the police. The officers did not retaliate, but took the patrons to jail; as their car pulled away, a thrown bottle crashed through their back window.[374]

A young onlooker recalled, "Those first hours when the cops pulled out were just like a holiday. All the kids wandered around sayin' real amazed like, 'The fuzz [police force] is scared; they ain't goin' to do nothin.' "[375]

A Negro hurled a brick through a plate glass window at the Esquire Clothing Store. When the police did not return, a handful of Negroes entered the store through the shattered window and emerged with armfuls of hats, shoes and shirts. Others rushed into the store, as well.[376]

Detroit had 4,500 policemen to deal with a population of 1,640,000, and also more than 700,000 civilians moving in and out of the city every day.[377] Detroit Police

Commissioner Ray Girardin somewhat belatedly admitted, "We had been prepared for any large masses of demonstrators, but not for arsonists, looters and snipers spread over so much of the city. We have not even provided adequate communications facilities so that policemen can work together. Only a few officers have walkie-talkies. For antisniper work we had to *borrow* six armored cars."[378] The first day, the police were ordered to hold their fire, and fifteen of them were injured even as they gave ground to the Negroes and ignored most looting.[379]

Many of Detroit's Negroes turned angrily on the police—this time not alleging police brutality, but police leniency. The Negroes complained that the police should have cracked down harder and faster on the rioters when the trouble first began. The Negroes said that firm action early Sunday morning when the looting began could have stopped the orgy of breaking and burning later Sunday and Monday.[380] Longworth Quinn, editor of Detroit's Negro newspaper, the *Michigan Chronicle*, ran an eight-column banner headline reading, "It Could Have Been Stopped." Quinn was convinced that "if the police had stopped looting when it centered on one 12th Street block early Sunday, when the mood was allowed to become a Roman holiday, the riot could have been prevented."[381]

One of the ghetto dwellers said that when one police car rolled up at 4 o'clock Sunday morning with its siren going, at the time the looting of Jack's Esquire Clothing Store began, "50 kids piled out of that store." But later, when Negroes realized that the police were not going to stop them, the gathering of mobs, looting and burning intensified.[382] Other Negroes made this same point—that crowds joined in the riot only after they realized that the police were not cracking down. Children told newsmen they knew that Mayor Jerome P. Cavanagh had ordered the police not to shoot.[383]

Later Monday, Mayor Cavanagh graciously authorized policemen to defend themselves. "Their safety is at stake,"

he said, "and if they must return fire, it must be."[384] But
by now the outbreak had spread to other sections of the
city, and there were not enough policemen or firemen to
prevent looting and burning.[385] Governor Romney ordered
1,500 National Guardsmen, backed by tanks, to quell the
riot,[386] but even that was not enough to bring peace to
the besieged city. Romney declared a state of public emergency in Detroit and its two self-contained suburbs, High-
land Park and Hamtramck.[387] By now, a four-mile section
of Woodward Avenue had been plundered by looters, and
a three-mile section of Grand River Avenue was hit by
looting and fire-bombing which raged along 18 blocks of
12th Street.[388] The destructive fury reached almost to the
city limits. In at least one area, the fire ranged in a solid
sheet for more than 10 blocks.[389]

The front-page story in Tuesday's New York *Times* was
that "President Johnson rushed 4,700 Army paratroopers
into Detroit at midnight last night as Negro snipers besieged two police stations in rioting that brought near
paralysis to the nation's fifth largest city."[390] But by that
newspaper's own showing, the President seemed to be in no
rush at all; it took the White House a leisurely 22 hours to
make up its mind that Federal troops were needed, and
needed to be *used*.[391]

It began shortly after 2 a.m. on Monday in the office
of Police Commissioner Ray Girardin. Governor Romney
burst into the office to find Mayor Cavanagh talking on
the phone to Vice President Humphrey.[392] The Mayor
thought the situation was beyond control of state and local
police and also of the National Guard, and wanted to know
how to go about getting Federal troops. Humphrey suggested that Cavanagh call Attorney General Ramsey
Clark.[393] The Mayor briefed Governor Romney on his
phone conversation, and then quickly called the Attorney
General. Clark said he thought Federal troops could be
made available, but felt that the law required that the request come from the Governor. Romney then got on the

phone. He said he asked the U.S. Attorney General what steps he could take to get Federal troops; he recalled that "Clark assured me that an oral request would be sufficient."[394] Governor Romney then made the oral request, and, in cooperation with the Mayor, arranged for a 4 a.m. press conference to announce that Federal troops would be coming to Detroit.[395]

In Romney's words, "While the press conference was under way, Clark called me and I left the press conference to talk to him. The Attorney General indicated then that he had to have a written request." Romney then rushed back into the conference room, reassembled the reporters and told them that the situation had changed, and that he was not sure, then, whether the Federal troops would be coming.[396]

It was highly probable that the Johnson Administration was worried about setting a precedent that could have Federal troops being sent all over the country, all summer, and so insisted on Governor Romney complying with the wording of the Federal statute "to the letter."[397]

The Federal Statute, Section 331, Chapter 15, Title 10, of the United States Code, says:

Whenever there is an insurrection in any State against its government, the President may, upon the request of its Legislature or of its Governor if the Legislature cannot be convened, call into Federal service such of the militia of the other states in the number requested by that State, and use such of the armed forces as he considers necessary to suppress the insurrection.

At about 8 a.m., the Governor showed the Mayor and his staff a copy of the telegram he had drafted. In the telegram, Romney stated that he "recommended" (rather than requested) the use of Federal troops. The Governor also avoided the use of the word "insurrection."[398] Romney was most reluctant to use the word "insurrection" in applying and writing for Federal troops because he felt this might invoke escape clauses in insurance policies and prevent hundreds of property owners from being reimbursed for their losses.[399]

At 8:30 a.m., the Governor called Attorney General Clark and read him the telegram. The Attorney General told Romney that the telegram wasn't adequate.[400]

Romney came back with a shorter telegram which contained the word "request," but wrote around the word "insurrection." The Johnson Administration accepted the telegram even though the word "insurrection" was not used.[401]

By mid-afternoon, the first of 4,700 paratroopers were on their way to Selfridge Air Force Base near Detroit. But the Johnson Administration stipulated that they were not to go into action until Cyrus R. Vance, the President's representative, arrived on the scene for a first-hand inspection.[402] Vance felt that Federal troops should not be committed until all the National Guard forces had been deployed. But Mayor Cavanagh flatly disagreed, insisting that Federal troops be sent into the city immediately.[403] Vance stuck by his decision, however, and agreed at about 10 p.m. only to shift about 1,800 troops into a temporary "staging area" at the state fair grounds just inside the city limits.[404] At 10:20, Vance recommended the signing of the Presidential Proclamation calling upon the rioters to disperse, which Johnson did at 10:31.[405] At that time, the orders to the Federal troops were that none was to receive ammunition until assembly at the fair ground, that none was to load his weapon until ordered by an officer and that no one was to shoot until shot at.[406] The President instructed Vance to make one final appeal for order on Detroit television at about 11 p.m.[407]

At 11:22 p.m., with both state and Federal officials having now recommended that Federal troops move in, the President signed the Executive Order authorizing the Army to move into the riot area and to take command of National Guard forces.[408] At 11:56, Johnson went on a national television hookup to describe his action and his great regret, and to denounce the lawlessness. The President said that the Federal government had "no alternative but to respond since it was called by the Governor of the state and presented with proof of his inability to restore order."[409] In all, it took 22 hours for the President to send Federal troops to the city after Romney's first request was made. Mayor Cavanagh wryly commented, "We were all very civilized while the city burned."[410]

The first Federal troops appeared on the streets around 2 a.m., Tuesday.[411] Romney charged that the failure of Army troops to appear on Detroit streets before that time hurt efforts to control the riots, since Sunday and Monday were the days and nights of greatest destruction and violence. He stated that Attorney General Clark kept changing his mind about what was needed to get Federal troops.[412] Clark agreed with the Michigan Governor on one point—that an oral request for Federal troops would have been sufficient. But he defended his demand that the Governor had actually to *request* the troops and not merely recommend that they be sent, and that the word "insurrection" be used to describe the riots.[413] The Attorney General did not indicate why the troops were finally sent without use of that word.[414] Vance got into the argument with the contention that the legal provisions under which the President might Federalize the National Guard and dispatch Federal troops to the scene "were not understood by the officials of the state of Michigan." He said that Romney could have asked for Federal help on the grounds that "a state of insurrection" existed in Michigan or that "there was domestic violence he was unable to suppress."[415] The argument was apparently getting a bit too hot for the White House. Vance emphasized that the decision finally to send the troops in that night had been his and that the President had signed the necessary Executive Order after being requested to do so by Mr. Vance.[416] It was one of the more unconvincing statements of the time, implying as it did that Lyndon Johnson, a jealous guardian of Presidential prerogatives, danced like a puppet on a string while Vance operated the controls.

In the manner of a divine dispensation, Martin Luther King said that he supported the President's use of Federal troops to deal with rioting in Detroit. "I am very sorry that Federal troops had to be called in," King stated. "But there's no question that when a riot erupts it has to be halted."[417]

As had now become Standard Operating Procedure in these cases, the burned-out city was found guilty of inciting to riot. "Revolts come out of revolting conditions," said King. "A riot is the language of the unheard. It is a suicidal act—that last desperate act—when the Negro says, 'I'm tired of living like a dog.' Every single breakout [of racial violence] without exception has substantially been ascribed to gross unemployment, particularly among young people."[418] King's pre-packaged comments were run off the same tired old rhetorical assembly line, and showed the usual cavalier disregard for the facts. A survey of arrestees found that those rioters who were employed (the majority) were earning an average of $117 a week, and included building and car workers, waiters and college students.[419]

It was quite apparent that King had no desire to go beyond lip service to his dream of nonviolence. Asked if he planned to go to Detroit or other cities hit by racial violence, King said he would not.[420]

In no other city in the country were the policemen as shackled by their superiors as in Detroit, most especially at the outset of the riots. The president of the Detroit Police Officers Association, Carl Parsell, maintained that the arrival of troops was delayed by jockeying between Mayor Jerome Cavanagh and Governor George Romney. He said: "We have a Democratic mayor who wants to run for Governor against a Republican. They both wanted all the credit they could get, but did not want to make mistakes, so the decision to get the troops was made and changed from one hour to the next."[421] Parsell said hundreds of guns stolen from pawnshops got into the hands of rioters because of senseless delays by top officials in removing firearms from the shops.[422] Charging that the Detroit police department was completely unprepared for such civil disorder, Parsell said: "Our men were given shotguns, then told: 'Don't load them. Put them in the trunks of your cars because if these people see them, they might get excited and nasty.' "[423] The Detroit policemen's spokesmen continued: "After the first night, we were told to take containing action to hold the riot within a 100-block area. We were told: 'Don't go in. Don't do anything. Don't shoot.' Looting seemed no longer to be a crime. One white Cadillac made five trips to Saks Fifth Avenue department store carrying away loads of stuff. People just walked in and out of the broken windows with their arms full."[424]

U.S. News & World Report wrote, "The Detroit uprising was the nearest thing to civil war that the U.S. has witnessed in more than 100 years."[425] This was no overstatement. Tanks rumbled into Detroit's East Side to rescue more than 100 policemen and National Guardsmen who were trapped inside the precinct houses. Negro snipers fired into windows and doors, and policemen and Guardsmen fought back with machine guns, shotguns and high-velocity rifles.[426] "It looks like Berlin in 1945," said Mayor Cavanagh.[427] Variety stores and shops of every description were in flames over a 14-square-mile area of the city.[428] Scores of Negroes fled their homes, among them the Rev. Nicholas Hood, Detroit's only Negro Councilman. He said that his family had been threatened. Along with other Negro leaders, Hood had tried but failed to bring the rioting under control.[429] At one time seven refugee centers were in operation.[430]

Along one section of Grand River Avenue, where Negroes and Southern whites live in adjoining neighborhoods, stores were raided by biracial bands.[431] Governor Romney remarked that Detroit had scored a first in having "integrated looting."[432]

By Wednesday, no fewer than 950 buildings had been destroyed or heavily damaged by fire, the police said, and at least 1,500 more had been looted for a total property loss of more than $150 million, making it the costliest riot in the nation's history.[433] By then, injuries stood at nearly 900 and arrests at 2,700.[434] In the now familiar pattern, the looters first stripped the stores of all they could carry and then set fire as they fled the buildings.[435] In some places, the looting appeared to be organized, with a leader directing the operation. One eyewitness gave this description:

When the looters finished stealing and generally tearing up a shop, a man who seemed to be the leader would give a whistle, a special "match-man" would set all the debris on fire and the looters would move out. They seemed to know just where to head for next.[436]

On Thursday, Negro snipers waged a daylight guerrilla operation, but National Guard tanks and armored personnel carriers brought it under control.[437] The night before, hundreds of National Guardsmen had taken up positions in store-fronts along 12th Street, where it all began. Armed helicopters swooped low over buildings in attempts to frighten away would-be snipers.[438]

Some policemen and National Guardsmen could count the hours of sleep that they had had in the last four days on their fingers. During the early hours of the morning, some National Guardsmen took advantage of a lull and sprawled on sidewalks for a few minutes of rest. One wrapped himself from head to foot in a tarpaulin, which might have been dropped by fleeing looters. Another Guardsman commented, "People keep coming up and asking if that's a corpse. I tell them he's dead all right—dead for sleep."[439]

The looting and smashing did not always follow strict racial lines. Some stores with "Soul Brother" painted on the window were spared, while others were looted.[440] Among the offices ransacked was that of U. S. Rep. Conyers, a Negro Democrat who had been an outspoken advocate of civil rights.[441] Later, Conyers said of the alienated youths in the Negro ghetto, "They don't relate to our society. They are so alienated they almost need psychiatric care."[442]

The destruction was almost unbelievable. Grand River Avenue, a major artery on the West Side of the city, had a three-mile stretch of broken windows or blackened stores.[443] And a county official said of the arrests, "We arraigned more people in the past four days than in the first six months last year."[444]

In the jail cells, there were few, if any, signs of regret. Many of the prisoners seemed to take a kind of psychotic pride in the extent of the destruction. A teen-ager, told about the havoc that had been wrought on 12th Street, could not hide the grin on his face. "They burn it down, huh? They burn it down, oh man!" Another prisoner said, "You should have been here on Monday night. We had a party. The police just let you go in and get anything you wanted." He said he had carried a transistor radio with him so he could hear when the police were ordered to shoot. Another prisoner wanted to know if they had started to rebuild 12th Street. "It won't do them no good," he said. "They'll just burn it down again. But they ain't going to build it up anymore, I'll bet on that."[445]

In Detroit, "Burn, baby, burn" was more than a slogan: it was a cold, calculated plan of wholesale destruction that regarded firemen as mortal enemies on the battlefield. The wanton savagery visited upon the firemen of Detroit, if written as fiction six months before the riots, would have been rejected out of hand by any editor as utterly unbelievable.

To be sure, Detroit firemen had been subjected to vicious treatment in Negro neighborhoods since at least 1963. In that four-year period, it had become common for Detroit firemen to answer an alarm, find a crowd standing around the hydrant, and face curses and thrown objects and be prevented from hooking up their hoses. In 1966, Engine Co. 13 was stoned away from a blaze while trying to fight it. Ladder Co. 15 arrived at a fire, was encircled by jeering Negroes, and prevented from moving forward or backward.[446]

But all this was mere frolic compared with the ordeal of the firemen of Detroit during the riots. Detroit firemen, who normally answer 125 alarms a day, responded to 209 one day, 617 the next, 177 the next, and 105 on the following day when order was finally restored.[447] Detroit committed all 131 pieces of its equipment, plus 56 engines from 41 surrounding cities.[448]

Firemen worked from Sunday to Wednesday without relief, flopping exhaustedly on the ground or collapsing on their rigs' seats to sleep a few minutes when they could. Many fell over from exhaustion. At least one had a heart attack. Some actually went to sleep on their feet, leaning against a building while still holding a hose on a fire.[449] Among the casualty list notations were: "Cardial arrythmia; developed chest pains after fire." "Passed out, striking rig, coronary heart disease." "Exhaustion, chest pain." "Exertional exhaustion."[450]

Early Tuesday, firefighter Carl E. Smith took a fatal bullet between the eyes some six miles from the place where firemen were first stoned Sunday morning. Smith died during a gunfire exchange between snipers and National Guardsmen while running to reach his rig.[451] Only a short while before, he had been stricken with acute appendicitis while on duty and rushed into a hospital for surgery. He was still on recuperation leave when the alarm came, and need not have responded at all, but he insisted that he was well enough to join his company.[452] A thousand firemen were at his funeral.[453]

In a very few instances, firemen had the protection of residents of the burning areas. In one case, about 20 Negro members of one block club armed themselves with rifles and deployed around firefighters to protect them from harassment. Vowed Lennon Moore, one of the block club members, "They say they need protection, and we're damn well going to give it to them."[454] But these instances were tragically rare.

Now the order was out: no one to go up an aerial. It was a too easy, tempting target.[455] Before the week was out, 537 structures had been demolished or damaged—far the greater part demolished.[456]

Executive Chief Charles Quinlan ordered that no company was to continue toward a fire if it met hostility on the way—nor was it to pause at any fire location if threatened upon arrival there. A second order was that all fire companies were to get out of a rectangular area a mile and a half wide. Within that area, there were fires burning which normally would have called for three, four, and even five alarms. But in no part of that area could firefighters and their apparatus be counted safe.[457] Even civilians just trying to help were as likely to stop a bullet or a knife. One young white civilian was helping firemen hold a two-and-a-half-inch line on a fire when a Negro youth walked up, stabbed him, and ran off. Luckily, the civilian recovered. One of the firemen thought, "The reason he [the Negro] didn't stab me was that maybe he thought my coat was too thick; the white kid was just wearing a T-shirt. . . . You can't fight a fire and guard your rear too; you turn your head and a wall's liable to fall on you."[458]

The National Guardsmen started riding with the firemen, and developed their own drill: "Arrive at a fire; hit the pavement; swiftly scan the scene for sniper possibilities; deploy to the spots where they could do the most good."[459]

The scene was graphically described by Earl Berry, President of the Detroit Firefighters' Union, in testimony before the Senate Judiciary Committee. Asked why so many of the snipers and rock-throwers had not been caught, Berry replied:

I was on 12th Street in the city of Detroit early Sunday. In fact, I spent four days, the first two days on 12th Street. And when you see these people running down the street, and you are responding with apparatus, and I was on the back of an aerial truck, and you see these bottles come—many of our people were hit by bottles. They throw the bottles and keep going. There is no way of stopping them or getting after them. The police were busy. The looting was going on. I think this is one of the main reasons they threw the bottles at us at this time. There was much laughter at the firefighters trying to perform their duties.[460]

Concluding his testimony, Berry stressed that "The aerial company I was riding with most of the time, we had seven or eight firefighters on the truck, and we also had four National Guardsmen on the apparatus, and we still came under sniper fire, and they never did run down the person that was firing at us."[461]

And if they had been caught? Detroit's courts, implementing Michigan and local law, generally meted out token punishment for interfering with firemen. As one fire fighter put it: "The courts fine them $25 when they threaten and stone us. Now who the hell minds a $25 fine?"[462]

The ghastly scorecard of deaths, injuries, and destruction of property proved the Detroit riots far and away the worst in American history. At least 43 persons were killed—31 of them Negroes. About 2,000 persons were injured. About 1,400 fires were reported, and about 1,700 stores looted. Property damage ran upwards of 250 million dollars. *U.S. News & World Report* estimated that the total cost could eventually approach one billion dollars.[463]

The deadliest crossfire the National Guardsmen had to face came from some newspapers and even some senior Federal officers who turned their most caustic verbal artillery on the defenders of a ravaged city. While some of the comments may have had merit, other statements resembled a critique of Elliot Ness for persecuting Al Capone.

Early in August, a memorandum listing a number of

lessons in riot control learned in Newark and Detroit was sent by the Department of the Army to the Continental Army Command for distribution to National Guard units. Among the lessons listed in the memorandum were the following:

The necessity to insure that troops and police treat all civilians fairly and that they strictly follow orders on whether they are to use their weapons and to what extent and in what circumstances they are allowed to employ them.

The need for troops and policemen at all echelons to report what they see in their sectors to their superiors to insure that the responsible commanders have the information they require to make decisions.

The use of nonlethal tear gas shells or small teams of marksmen to suppress snipers rather than mass firing by large groups of policemen and troops.

The need to saturate areas where looting and rioting are going on with large numbers of troops and policemen as quickly as possible to gain control of the situation.[464]

Officials noted that some of the troops or police in Detroit had shot out the street lights when they were being fired on, in order to make it more difficult for the snipers to hit them. But the officials felt that the loss of the street lights only made it more difficult in the end to find the snipers and put them out of action.[465]

More than a month after the riots, the Detroit *Free Press* charged that most of the 43 deaths could have been prevented. The newspaper said that the National Guard "was involved in a total of 11 deaths in which nine innocent people died."

The article continued: "Eighteen of the 43 riot victims were shot and killed by Detroit police, and of that number, 14 have been confirmed as looters in the *Free Press* investigation. The other four are a sniper, a possible but unconfirmed arsonist and two of the three men shot and killed in the Algiers Motel."

The Detroit *Free Press* made a finding that "At least six of the victims were killed by the National Guard, five of them innocent, the victims of what now seem to be tragic accidents. In five more cases, both police and National Guardsmen were involved and it is impossible to say definitely whose bullets were fatal. Four of these victims were innocent of any wrongdoing."

As for some of the others, "Two more persons, both looters, were shot and killed by storeowners. Three more were killed by private citizens; murder warrants have been issued in two of those cases and a warrant decision is pending in the third. And two looters died when fire swept the store from which they were stealing."

The *Free Press* said it had concluded that "both the number of snipers active in the riot area and the danger that snipers presented were vastly overstated." The newspaper felt that "Both city and Army authorities acted to try to keep the death toll at a minimum, though they did so in different ways. In both cases, their efforts were not successful, and permitted unnecessary death."

It was all part of a 24,000-word article published in that newspaper. Three reporters interviewed more than 300 persons and read hundreds of documents before coming to what the newspaper called "the inescapable" conclusion that "a majority of the riot victims need not have died."[466] Unfortunately, in the midst of a riot the police and Guardsmen did not have the leisure time to conduct interviews, read documents, and confer with the Detroit *Free Press*. With bullets flying about, and block after block being put to the torch, the police and troops had to use instant judgment and make split-second decisions about the use of force; that some of these decisions, in hindsight, may subsequently have proven erroneous should have reflected adversely upon the would-be destroyers of the city, not upon those who attempted to save it.

The attacks against the National Guard now came from the two senior Army officers who had been in charge of suppressing the riots. Assertions that Michigan National Guardsmen were nervous and trigger-happy were made by Lt. Gen. John L. Throckmorton, commander of the 18th Airborne Corps, and Maj. Gen. Charles P. Stone, who had served as General Throckmorton's deputy in Detroit, in testimony before a House Armed Services Subcommittee.[467] One of the generals' complaints was that National Guardsmen had not obeyed orders to unload their weapons—an order that Representative Porter Hardy, Jr. (D-Va.) flatly labeled "preposterous." Hardy accused General Throckmorton of needlessly risking the lives of the Guardsmen, and stated, "I don't see how you as a general officer could issue any order like that to a man working for you."[468] General Throckmorton testified, "I was confronted with a group of trigger-happy, nervous soldiers in the National Guard. I had no intention of seeing those soldiers shoot innocent civilians or children." He said that he had decided that the best way to deal with snipers was to have the troops unload their weapons until the snipers were located and then to fire only on command of an officer.[469] Subcommittee Chairman F. Edward Hebert (D-La.) commented that he did not see how a Guardsman could be expected to "take cover if fired upon and await the arrival of an officer." Hebert asked General Throckmorton whether he wanted to "take cover, too." His face flushed, the general replied, "I gave those orders, sir. I don't disagree with them."[470] Which was not precisely a direct answer to a direct question.

General Throckmorton testified that in an effort to get his order to unload weapons enforced, he had had National Guard officers mimeograph it and issue a copy to each of their troops on Wednesday night. Representative Hardy asked, "Why didn't you have the offenders court-martialed?" The reply was, "You can't court-martial ninety per cent of a force."[471]

A far different view of the National Guardsmen was expressed by Governor Romney, in a letter to chairman

Hebert. Romney wrote that the Guardsmen had performed "with honor and distinction" despite the fact that they "were handicapped by late commitment, lack of equipment, and a type of riot duty never before encountered."[472]

The Michigan Governor wrote, "Experience in Watts, Newark and Detroit convinces me that a force of 12,000 Army National Guard, with the command, control and support elements required to conduct sustained operations in two urban areas, is the minimum requirement for the State of Michigan."[473] During the Detroit riot, 8,200 guardsmen were on duty.[474] The Federal response was to propose that the Michigan National Guard be *reduced* by 717 men, along with the elimination of some command capability.[475]

One serious charge may never be fully resolved in or out of the courtroom, but become a *cause célèbre* in the ghetto—the charge that two Detroit policemen cold-bloodedly murdered unarmed Negroes. The grave accusation—that three young apparently unarmed Negroes were deliberately killed by the police—was made a few days after the riot. The three were found dead early Wednesday morning at the Algiers Motel, near the riot scene.[476] At first, police officials said the three were apparently shot to death in an "exchange of gunfire with snipers." But after an investigation, it was disclosed that the three were gunned down with shotguns at close range, probably in the rooms where their bodies were found.[477] One Negro, Robert Greene, who said he was at the scene of the shooting, was questioned by Detroit authorities. Greene believed a National Guard warrant officer had killed two of the three men. He said the officer, who was one of a group raiding the motel, took the two Negroes into nearby rooms one at a time. He said he then heard shots. But authorities who heard a tape recording of Greene's statement found it contained inconsistencies.[478]

On August 7, two Detroit policemen were charged with the murder of two of the Negroes. The arrested officers were Patrolman Ronald August and Patrolman Robert Paille.[479] None of the witnesses saw the shooting of the dead Negroes. Nor did any witness say he saw any guns at the motel except those carried by the lawmen,[480] although the police said that there had been sniper fire coming from the motel annex.[481]

A National Guardsman testified at an examination hearing that Detroit policemen had been hitting Negroes and taking them into rooms, pretending to kill them, in order to frighten others remaining in the hallway.[482] He testified that he had seen a policeman hand a shotgun to August, and say, "You want to kill one?" He said that he saw August go into a room with a Negro, heard a shot, and then what sounded like the thud of a falling body. He testified that he had then seen Patrolman August come out of the room.[483] The Guardsman testified, "At this time I got scared. I believe I told the policeman this was strictly their business," and left soon after.[484]

In his own behalf, Patrolman August submitted a statement to the court in which he admitted killing the Negro, but claimed self-defense.[485] In a formal statement to the police, two weeks before the examination hearing, August claimed that he had shot the Negro, but only after he had grabbed for the patrolman's shotgun. In the statement, August said that he was part of a raiding team that had searched the motel for weapons or snipers. The officer stated, "He grabbed my shotgun," and that he yelled "Let go" and tried to shoot, but that the safety was on. August said that he finally released the shotgun's safety, and fired as the Negro again tried to grab the weapon.[486] An assistant prosecuting attorney admitted that he would have had no case if the two accused patrolmen had not gone to their superiors.[487]

In the ghetto court of public opinion, the patrolmen will be considered guilty by many, regardless of any verdict reached by the judiciary. It is to be devoutly hoped that the officers are in fact innocent of this awful charge—but even

if judge and jury were to find them guilty, this still would
not, and should not, detract from the magnificent courage
and dedication of the overwhelming majority of the Detroit
police force, at a time when they were subjected to an
almost superhuman ordeal. The malfeasance of one judge
does not invalidate the entire judiciary system, and, now
or in the future, the possible misconduct of a handful of
patrolmen cannot invalidate the tremendous importance of
effective police work in our communities.

What became of those who were arrested during the
Detroit riots? In all, 7,231 persons were arrested—6,407
Negroes and 824 whites. Nearly half were released without
charges being filed. Of the 4,180 persons bound over for
trial, 1,014 were charged with misdemeanors and upon a
plea of guilty were sentenced to the time they had already
spent in jail. A total of 3,166 persons were charged with
felonies. Of this number 1,134 were to go on trial in spring,
1968. Charges were dismissed against 888 persons, while
379 were allowed to plead guilty to lesser charges and then
were sentenced to the time they had spent in jail, plus
court costs. Four months after the riots, only some 40 adults
were still in jail, and most of them were being held for
previous crimes.[488]

Who ever said that crime doesn't pay?

H. Rap Brown visited the West Side of Detroit five
weeks after the riot had broken out; he was greeted by enthusiastic throngs of Negroes who smashed a box office
window and pushed through blocked doors in efforts to
get into the small theater where he spoke. Spectators were
jammed in the aisles, and at least 2,000 more yelled outside as Brown shouted, "The honkie [white man] is your
enemy." Brown told the cheering crowd that Detroit rioters
"did a good job" and that this city's riot would "look like a
picnic" when Negroes united.[489]

Brown urged Detroit Negroes "to get a gun . . . arm
yourself for the troubled days ahead." Shortly after, 150
rifles were taken from a sporting goods store.[490] In all, De-

troit police informed congressional probers that nearly all of the 2,700 guns stolen during the Detroit riots are still missing.[491]

In January, 1968, the Michigan Crime Commission—a 57-member unit appointed by the Governor—cited planned efforts by organized groups as a major reason why the Detroit riots "exploded to tragic proportions."[492] The report did not specify the groups, but one commissioner said the reference was to black nationalists.[493] Specifically, the report stated, "Certain organized elements seeking to expand and exploit a civil disturbance engaged in extensive planning and preparation to enable them to seize upon what otherwise may have been a limited incident of public disorder."[494]

The Michigan Crime Commission's report said lack of adequate police intelligence about the plans of those responsible for expansion of the riots contributed to the difficulties.[495]

The Commission recommended a toughening of Michigan's laws dealing with rioting. Among the proposals:

Create and expand "adequately staffed, well-financed intelligence units" in police forces to assist in preventing groups from taking advantage of civil disorder.

Permit police wiretapping in cases involving organized crime or corrupt public officials.

Give witnesses better immunity from prosecution.

Outlaw interference with on-duty firemen.

Outlaw possession of Molotov cocktails and other incendiary devices.

Vigorously regulate sale of handguns.

Give mayors, sheriffs and the state police director power to proclaim states of emergency and temporarily control traffic, public assembly and sale of liquor and guns.[496]

Could Martin Luther King have halted the riots? It was certain that he could not. And it was almost equally certain that the riots in Newark and Detroit—the death, destruction, and almost incredible social savagery of the participants; the incalculable loss in blood and dollars; the racial hatred that may never die—all this is part of the House that King Built. The dividing line between super-militant nonviolence and super-militant violence was always an artificial and unnatural one, propped up, pasted together by the charisma of one man. It was inevitable that sooner or later the artifice and charisma would come unstuck, the dam would break, and the flood of seething hostility engendered by Birmingham and Selma would overflow the Negro ghettos, and finally the cities themselves. The civil disobedience glorified by Martin Luther King—the concept that each man had the right to put a kind of Good Housekeeping Seal of Approval on laws that met with his favor, and reserve the right to disobey "unjust" laws or even "unjust" officers of the law—was more than enough to kindle the spark of rebellion, if not revolution, among young militants who simply stopped turning the other cheek, and started battling those who had been called their oppressors. It was King who, by the very nature of nonviolent dynamics, was compelled to *force* reluctant police to arrest him. It was King who raised the cry of police brutality in the South, and thereafter made *every* police action in *every* ghetto racially suspect. As surely as the child is father to the man, nonviolent resistance in the South sired the violent resistance in the North. Stokely Carmichael's comments about the Los Angeles riots could as easily be applied to Newark and Detroit:

You see, the people I blame for Watts are Martin Luther King and the Student Nonviolent Coordinating Committee, and the mass media of this country. Because, you see, I think that every time they saw Martin get slapped, they got mad. And every time they saw four little black kids get bombed, they got madder. And when nothing happened, boy, they were steaming. Because they knew that the reason, and the only reason that those people got hit was because they were black. The only reason we are depressed in the country is because we are black.[497]

It was King's own refinement of the Chinese Water Torture —with drop after drop of daily demonstrations, confrontations, and planned crises, beating relentlessly down on the heads of potentially violent ghetto residents until they reached the racial breaking point. King's approval of the use of troops to quell riots was, at best, a superfluous gesture—a gesture that meant less than it seemed to say, since he never so much as hinted that the rioters' actions violated the law, and the law must be obeyed by *all* citizens. King never hurled a Molotov cocktail, but he never stopped faulting society for those who did. King never looted a store, but he never stopped defending those who felt that poverty gave them a license to steal. King never hid on a roof with a rifle and sniped at the police, but he never stopped picturing the police department as a sort of homegrown Gestapo. King never drove a white businessman out of a Negro neighborhood, but he never strongly condemned the black racism that put the torch to white-owned stores and spared the "Soul Brothers."

The author does not count himself as an admirer of George Romney. But the Governor did make a statement at the National Association of Counties meeting that deserves to be requoted. "We must enforce the laws firmly, fairly, and in proper time," he said. "There can be no such things permitted as a little looting, a little rioting, a little sniping, a little arson. We must be firm in this resolve."[498] By the same token, America has learned the hard way that —Martin Luther King to the contrary—there can be no such things permitted as a little law-breaking, a little civil disobedience, a little flouting of police regulations, because a little nonviolence inevitably incites more than a little violence.

The days of free and easy—and often amused—indulgence of civil rights excesses are over. In today's riot-prone society, law-breaking—of the civil or criminal variety—is a luxury this nation can no longer afford. Not if we want to go on having a nation.

CHAPTER 11

The Legacy of Martin Luther King

≱⅌⅌⅌⅌⅌⅌⅌⅌⅌⅌⅌⅌⅌⅌⅌⅌⅌⅌

(This last chapter is a mixture of documented fact and personal opinion. To underscore this, it is written in the first person.)

In the days following the tragic death of Martin Luther King, much was said about the legacy he left his country. Some called it a legacy of love. Some called it a legacy of peace. For myself, I am perfectly willing to grant his brilliance, his basic sincerity, his charismatic effect upon perhaps hundreds of thousands of Americans—and still regretfully conclude that primarily Martin Luther King left his country a legacy of lawlessness. His concept of civil disobedience was exquisitely embroidered with "love" and "good will," but stripped to its essentials it was the concept that every man could be his own judge and jury and legislator—that no law was binding upon any American unless he could "conscientiously" obey it. It was the concept that a minority had the right to flout the law—day after day, week after week, month after month, if need be—to force its will upon the majority. It was the doctrine that Martin Luther King could harness the forces of lawlessness to compel the passage of law—never realizing that his doctrine of civil disobedience might well contain the seeds of destruction of every gain the Negro has ever made, or ever hopes to make. The success of Martin Luther King's doctrine of civil disobedience in the legislative field rested upon a belief that whites would be compelled to obey laws, while Negroes would be allowed to disobey them. But civil disobedience can boomerang upon its user; it can as easily provide whites with a rationale for disobeying any or all of the civil rights legislation spawned during the King era. King realized—and made a legion of mayors and sheriffs realize—that virtually any law can be rendered null and void if enough people choose to disobey it. To underscore the point, he was quite ready to push a city to the brink of martial law to force the abandonment of laws he opposed, and the passage of laws he favored. In essence, it was a form of political blackmail—an ultimatum that unless favorable action was taken, the normal processes of law enforcement would not be permitted to function.

King's first act of civil disobedience created the first small crack in the wall of law enforcement. Each succeeding act of civil disobedience widened that crack in the wall, and weakened its foundations. Today, for the second time in our history, America is a house divided—but this time the division is not between freedom and slavery, but between law and lawlessness. In effect, these are two biracial societies, not physically separated, but often dwelling side by side in the same cities, the same neighborhoods, even the same families.

Our house is divided for all the world to see, and now we are compelled to see it as well. We see it in the fanatical excesses of the anti-Vietnam movement. We see it in colleges where student body militants virtually seize power from the school administration. We see it in the rantings and ravings of Stokely Carmichael, who was practically permitted to incite the sacking of the nation's capital without spending so much as a day in prison. We see all this and more, and we know that the forces of law and order are on the defensive—and losing more and more precious ground each day to the forces of a civil disobedience, until it borders on anarchy. This is all part of the unhappy legacy left us by Martin Luther King—the doctrine that a man can invoke beliefs of conscience to place himself above the law. It is our American nightmare, and could some day be the death of our country and our democracy.

It is only a short step from the doctrine of civil disobedience to the criminal disobedience of the Negro riots. The more articulate rioters would probably say that they are simply invoking their right to disobey "unjust" policemen, exacting retribution from "unjust" storekeepers, and in general, declining to cooperate with "an unjust society." The liberal's protest that the rioters are being violent, while Martin Luther King was nonviolent, wholly misses the point. Once you permit a man to disobey laws he dislikes, you cannot later disapprove of the *form* that disobedience takes or the *motivation* behind it.

In compelling the abject surrender of law enforcement in community after community, in demonstration after demonstration, civil disobedience became the unwitting midwife of the urban riots. In both cases, it was mob action making impossible the orderly functioning of government. In both cases, it was taking a grievance into the streets instead of the voting booth. The riots have been generally described as aimless, but I think that once they get under way, there is a very definite aim—one of de facto separation, in the sense of a black community so in control of its institutions that it is practically a government within a government. This is the heart and soul of Black Power—the Balkanization-in-fact of each city with a numerically significant Negro population. This is the real meaning of the Negro demand for "control of the community," and as always the most militant members of the Negro community will be able to call upon the guilt-ridden liberals for sympathy and support.

The liberal double-standard in race relations was probably never more evident than it is today. To liberals, whites may not segregate themselves—that is racism—but Negroes may segregate themselves—that is black nationalism. Whites may not vote on the basis of color—that is backlash—but Negroes may vote on the basis of color—that is racial solidarity. Employers may not hire whites because of their color—that is bigotry—but employers may hire Negroes because of their color—that is positive discrimination. Positions which would have been unthinkable ten years ago are now eagerly embraced by liberals today. And as always, it was Martin Luther King and/or his assistants who bridged the gap between liberal doctrine and black racism. Through such groups as the National Conference for New Politics, it was Martin Luther King providing the bridge that linked the liberals to the Far Left, and helped bestow the mantle of leadership on the most demagogic, violent elements in the Negro community.

Today, anyone who suggests, however timidly, that Negro rioters be condemned and punished can expect an apoplectic reaction from the typical white liberal. The new racial orthodoxy of liberalism absolves Negro rioters from so much as a twinge of remorse, and lays the guilt at the door of virtually every white man, woman, and child in America.

In a statement on the report of the Commission on Civil Disorders, Dr. Arthur S. Flemming, president of the National Council of Churches, said: "We must confess the guilt of racism so clearly identified by the members of the commission, ask for forgiveness, and proceed to do everything possible to rectify the conditions that confront us as a result of our sins."[1] A dissenting view was given by Wilbur J. Cohen, Secretary of Health, Education, and Welfare in President Johnson's cabinet. Cohen called the Commission's emphasis on "white racism" a vast oversimplification, and noted that "black racism, brown racism and red racism" existed at the same time. Cohen suggested that some of the energy used in rioting "could be directed toward building organizations [among and by the disadvantaged] to help themselves get jobs and education." He added, "I believe this was by-passed in the commission's report."[2] Vice President Humphrey reacted with equal coolness to this aspect of the Commission Report. Humphrey stated, "To say that 'white society condones' inequity comes dangerously close to a doctrine of group guilt. Let us not fall into the error of condemning whole societies—white or black, or German or Arab or Chinese. Let us not look for scapegoats."[3] And civil rights leader Bayard Rustin said "there can be only two responses" to the Commission's "white racism" charge. On the one hand, he said, there are certain whites with a "guilt complex," masochists anxious to let the Negro know of their guilt—"these are the kinds of whites that disgust me and offend other Negroes." On the other hand, Rustin said, "there are more healthy people who, however, admit racism is so deep and profound a problem that they can simply put out and do nothing." The civil rights leader felt that "What we know about racism is that we all have it, that we all are capable of exercising it."[4]

Many liberals who long ago decided that "God Is Dead" now worship a new Deity—the Report of the National Advisory Commission on Civil Disorders. This is their Holy Writ and they genuflect at its biracial shrine in their words, in their actions, and in the pressures they exert on local police to observe its dogma. To question the report has become an all but unforgivable blasphemy, which subjects the apostate to charges of "racism," "backlash," or worse. But as a matter of conscience, the author must live dangerously and express his view that there is little in the U.S. Riot Commission Report to command confidence. One can begin with the very composition of membership in the Commission. The Negro population was well represented by Senator Edward Brooke of Massachusetts, Rep. James Corman of California, and Roy Wilkins of the NAACP. White liberals were represented by Gov. Otto Kerner of Illinois, chairman, and Mayor John Lindsay of New York, vice chairman, to name only two. There was one law enforcement officer on the panel, Herbert Jenkins, Chief of Police of Atlanta, Georgia, and known as one of the most liberal police chiefs in the country.[5] The only group that was not represented was the conservative community—the millions and millions of conservatives who shared Barry Goldwater's belief that portions of the 1964 Civil Rights Act were (at best) unwise and unworkable, or, at worst, unconstitutional. Given the makeup of the panel, one needed no crystal ball to divine that its report would repeat every hoary liberal cliché about the race problem in America, with little danger of an opposing viewpoint being expressed on the panel. This becomes all the more significant, in view of the Commission's statement, "We are charged by the President with the responsibility to examine this condition and to speak the truth, *as we see it.*"[6]

In relation to the news media, the Commission recommends:

Improve coordination with police in reporting riot news through advance planning and cooperate with the police in the designation of police information officers, establishment of information centers *and development of mutually acceptable* guidelines for riot reporting and the conduct of media personnel.

Accelerate efforts to ensure accurate and responsible reporting of riot and racial news, *through adoption by all news gathering organizations of stringent internal staff guidelines.*[7]

In effect, the U.S. Riot Commission is asking for censorship during a riot, and quite obviously the minimizing of the extent and seriousness of rioting by the columnists and reporters and editorialists of that city. From the muzzling of the press, it could be only a short step to the kind of totalitarianism the Commission presumably wishes to avoid.

The U.S. Riot Commission sees as the major goal "the creation of a true union—a single society and a single American identity."[8] This desire to stifle diversity has an Orwellian ring to it—a 1984 in which individuality and differences

in aptitude, intellect, and background would be regarded
as virtually subversive. Conservatives cannot view with
equanimity the bleak prospect of think-alike, act-alike human marionettes dancing on the strings pulled by Big
Brother in Washington.

In its report, the U.S. Riot Commission noted:

In formulating this report, we have attempted to draw on all
relevant sources. During closed hearings held from August
through December, we heard over 130 witnesses, including
federal, state and local officials, experts from the military
establishment and law enforcement agencies, universities and
foundations, Negro leaders and representatives of the business
community. . . . [We] took sworn testimony in nine of the cities
investigated and from Negro leaders and militants across the
country. Expert consultants and advisors supplemented the
work of our staff in all the areas covered in our report.[9]

Again, the question arises: Did the Commission take testimony from conservative sources or did they fail to consider
such testimony "relevant"? It is all very well to say that
the Commission took sworn testimony from "Negro leaders
and militants" but few, if any, of the witnesses are quoted
in the report, thus making impossible a rebuttal from more
informed or reliable sources. As for the Commission hearing "over 130 witnesses," the number involved is meaningless, unless we know precisely what they said, and whether
in fact they represented various shades of the political
spectrum, including conservative thought and policy. Certainly if the overwhelming majority of the witnesses called
were as liberal as the panel, it was nothing more than a
mutual admiration society, with the "experts" simply con-
firming views that had already been held by the Commission
members before they were even appointed to their posts.
The Star Chamber aspect of the proceedings (as far as the
public is concerned) is confirmed by the Panel's admission
that:

Since some information was supplied to the Commission on a confidential basis, a fully annotated footnoted copy of the Profiles cannot be made public at this time but will be deposited in the Archives of the United States.[10]

In view of the top-secret testimony of many of their witnesses, we are being asked to take a great deal of the commission's report on blind faith—something which the author is unwilling to do in view of the gravity of the problem and the ideologically loaded liberal composition of the panel. The U.S. Riot Commission Report should be chewed very gingerly, and *not* swallowed whole.

During the days of disorder and rioting that followed the slaying of Martin Luther King, there was clearly a new policy of police and military restraint in the cities that came under siege. The new concept willingly accepts looting to avoid killing, with the hope that overwhelming law enforcement manpower will reduce loss of property.[11] This policy, which also encourages the heavy use of tear gas to disperse rioters, is largely the work of Attorney General Ramsey Clark, and one of the documents he relied on in his planning was the report of the President's National Advisory Commission on Civil Disorders.[12]

Under ancient common law, it is justifiable to defend property by force, even by killing, to forestall a serious crime such as robbery, burglary or arson.[13] A federal official commented, "The law hasn't changed, but the way it's being enforced has changed tremendously." The official went on, "That old stuff about 'looters will be shot on sight' is for the history books and maybe the movies. It's for people who don't know how it is to be in a riot where if you shoot they shoot back, and you've got a lot of dead cops and troops along with the dead citizens."[14] It would of course be welcome news to the criminals of any city that the police will not be allowed to shoot them for fear that they might shoot back.

A Justice Department lawyer said, "We are going to be greatly misunderstood. Our critics think we are just being thoughtful of Negro hoodlums. . . . We say that this is a matter of effectiveness as well as saving lives. There really is no alternative, and the people who are saying 'Why didn't you shoot' don't understand that yet." He added, "The other side has guns."[15] It is predictable that if local law-enforcement authorities are either unable or unwilling to defend law-abiding citizens, those citizens may well avail themselves of their common law right and arm themselves in their own defense, even forming protective organizations to guard a given neighborhood, with or without the blessing of the President's National Advisory Commission on Civil Disorders.

It must be stressed that this policy of official "restraint" during riots is not only the policy of the federal government. Through a series of closed training meetings by the Justice Department and the International Association of Chiefs of Police at Airlie House, in Warrenton, Virginia, it has become the policy of many local police authorities throughout the country. More than 400 police chiefs attended these meetings.[16]

On one occasion, during the riots in Washington, the police came upon looters in the act of window-smashing and burning but withdrew rather than use their guns. There were not enough policemen to control the situation without gunplay, so the Public Safety Commissioner, Patrick V. Murphy, pulled his men out to avoid shooting.[17]

Long before the Negro riots became an established part of our national life, fourteen states had enacted laws that require cities to pay for riot damage resulting from their officials' failure to quell disturbances. These laws are still on the books, but officials in these states are complaining that their cities can be bankrupted by them, and probably many of these laws will either be repealed or sharply modified in their scope and coverage.[18] Eventually, the federal government may be called upon to pay the bills resulting from its pacifist policy toward rioters and looters.[19]

The performance of policemen in Chicago after the riots which followed King's assassination was praised by some officers of the Illinois National Guard and the federal troops which were brought in to help restore order.[20] During this time, more than 200 buildings were destroyed or badly damaged in Chicago, with losses estimated by insurers at $9 million.[21] Before the rioting, Daley had said that disorder in Chicago would no longer be tolerated, and he thought that orders to policemen to shoot arsonists and looters were in effect.[22] But he found out later that the police had been under instructions to use their discretion as to whether to shoot.[23] In the Chicago rioting, at least seven persons died and several hundred were injured. More than 3,000 people were arrested.[24] After the riots, Daley met with city department heads behind closed doors and asked Police Superintendent James Conlisk why the police had not shot looters and arsonists. Conlisk was said to have replied, "Mr. Mayor, you issued no such orders."[25] Daley then issued a formal order to Conlisk that in the future arsonists and looters were to be shot. In the case of arsonists, Mayor Daley said, Chicago policemen were instructed to "shoot to kill." In the case of looters, policemen were to "shoot to maim or cripple" so that they may be detained.[26] The order noted that arson, attempted arson, burglary, and attempted burglary were forcible felonies, and stated: "Such force as is necessary, including deadly force, shall be used to prevent the commission of these offenses and to prevent the escape of the perpetrators."[27] Daley described arson as "the most hideous crime" and said he was bewildered that only sixteen people had been arrested on arson charges during the rioting. He said, "There is something wrong. If anyone doesn't think this was a conspiracy, I don't understand."[28] When a reporter asked Daley what should be done about young looters—some only children—the Mayor replied, "You wouldn't want to shoot them." He suggested that Chemical Mace be used to "detain them."[29]

Daley called the conditions in the Chicago schools the day after the assassination "indescribable. The beating of girls. The slashing of teachers. The general turmoil. And payoffs and extortions [by students]. . . . Principals tell what's happening and they are told to forget it."[30]

The Rev. Jesse Jackson, director of Operation Breadbasket and a key aide to Martin Luther King at the Southern Christian Leadership Conference, called Mayor Daley's orders to shoot looters and arsonists "a fascist's response." Jackson called riots "illegal but not illegitimate"[31]—a predictable response coming from one who championed the arrogant lawlessness of civil disobedience.

In New York, Mayor Lindsay had this comment about the orders of Mayor Daley: "We are not going to turn disorder into chaos through the unprincipled use of armed force. In short, we are not going to shoot children in New York City."[32] In the upside-down world of John Lindsay, it was not those who violated law but those who vigorously enforced the law who were inviting chaos and were even unprincipled. As for his declaration against shooting children, Mayor Daley had not advocated this course of action, preferring instead to use the temporarily disabling chemical spray, Mace. Mayor Lindsay was also opposed to using Mace on rioters, and for any remaining skeptics at the news conference, he invited them to repent by reading the report of the National Advisory Commission on Civil Disorders.[33] In Washington, Attorney General Clark said that Daley's order could lead to "a very dangerous escalation of the problems we are so intent on solving." Clark restated his position that deadly force was not permissible "except in self-defense or when it is necessary to protect the lives of others."[34]

When one reads statements such as these from the highest law enforcement official in the land, it is readily apparent why it has become so excruciatingly difficult to recruit more police and keep veteran policemen on the force. Overworked, underpaid, the subject of the most vicious harassment and vilification from self-appointed community leaders, and now expected to face the crime epidemic in our cities virtually unarmed—with all this it is miraculous that we have any policemen at all. One thing is certain—the Attorney General's cavalier disregard for the enforcement of law in our cities can benefit no one but the criminals and those who will now begin to see that crime pays, and pays handsomely, and entails only negligible risk.

Mayor Daley received over 4,000 telegrams and letters after he issued that order. A spokesman said the communications were overwhelmingly in favor of his stand, and came from all parts of the country.[35] It took rare courage to take the position that Daley did, and it is the author's belief that the mayor deserved the gratitude of everyone who prefers the rule of law to the rule of the jungle.

Presumably on the premise that nothing was so bad that a federal spokesman could not make matters worse, the President's adviser on consumer affairs, Miss Betty Furness, entered the arena. Miss Furness said the slum violence made clear "the poor are being swindled, or feel they're being swindled" by their neighborhood merchants. She said that inferior quality goods, overpricing, high interest rates, and fraudulent practices were common in the slums and asked, "Is it so startling that stores were burned in Watts [in 1965] where the mark-up on television sets ranged as high as 160 per cent above prices for the exact model in other parts of Los Angeles?"[36] We can perhaps expect nothing better from a lady whose chief claim to public fame consisted of opening refrigerator doors in television commercials. If she had taken the trouble to communicate with slum merchants, she would probably have discovered that a greater number of credit risks, increased pilfering and higher insurance rates all push up the cost of doing business in the slums, and that this cost necessarily is passed along to the consumer. Even in those cases where the ghetto residents had valid grievances against a particular store owner, their recourse could hardly have been simpler—stop buying in that store, boycott it, encourage the establishment of competitive enterprises.

After the riots, Mayor Lindsay praised himself effusively for the minimal disturbances in New York City. Then a few disenchanted voices began to be heard from Negro merchants in the Negro community. Speaking for Harlem merchants, Hope R. Stevens, president of the Uptown Chamber of Commerce, said, "Everybody is happy no one has been wounded. It is recognized that that would have exacerbated the situation. But there is considerable criticism from many merchants over the fact that in many instances groups of policemen were observed to stand and look on while vandals and looters were free to break in and take away merchandise without hindrance. In fact, vandalism and looting went on without any preventive measures in instances where, the merchants feel, the police could have intervened with normal police measures that would not have threatened the lives of anyone." Stevens pointed out that virtually all the looting and vandalism were committed by persons 14 to 21, and said that police seemed unable to cope with the disorder, even though all sections of the communities were demanding that order be maintained.[37]

A few days later, the charges became considerably more blunt. In New York City, 100 Negro and Puerto Rican operators of small businesses charged that Mayor Lindsay had minimized the damage caused by arson and looting in the six days after the assassination. They also declared that police protection was inadequate and that "an attitude of appeasement and condoning seemed to perpetuate the trouble." Many of these merchants said they had been wiped out by looters. A spokesman for the Mayor sputtered, "This is completely untrue. It's ridiculous. What damage there was can be seen and cannot be hidden." But perhaps Mayor Lindsay —as vice chairman of the U.S. Riot Commission—just didn't want to see it. This meeting was called by the Small Business Development and Opportunities Corporation in Harlem (which had been set up under the Economic Opportunity Act of 1964). Orrin Judd, chairman of the corporation's Brooklyn division, said many Negro and Puerto Rican merchants stayed in their stores throughout the night during the six-day period guarding them against looters. Judd said, "Hundreds of stores were totally destroyed." Louis Hernandez, an official of the Bedford-Stuyvesant Puerto Rican Merchants Association, said he felt Mayor Lindsay was "minimizing what has happened." He stated, "The mayor makes it seem as if nothing is going on. But places in Brownsville [in Brooklyn] look like they were bombed out and you can see the shells of small stores—groceries, beauty parlors, barbershops, restaurants—that are no longer in business." Hernandez said the stores were "bankrupted in a few minutes because the police acted too slowly."[38]

What could well be a history-making claim against the city of New York has been made by Larry Sonboleh, owner of the Atlas Men's Wear Store on Nostrand Avenue in Brooklyn. Sonboleh charged that the police had "failed, refused and neglected" to provide adequate protection on the night of April 5, when looters broke into his store and carried away suits, sports outfits, shirts, and other items from his stock of merchandise. The looters had ripped off an iron gate to enter the store. This had set off an alarm system that directly notified the police that the door was opened. Sonboleh said he telephoned the 80th Precinct immediately but had been given "vague excuses" about taking any action against the looters. His attorney said, "Since it was apparently decided that a hands-off policy was necessary to curb further outbreaks, the city has an obligation to pay those who have been hurt." Mr. Sonboleh is suing New York City for $250,000 for refusing to protect his property;[39] he apparently is unmoved by a police official's explanation that no command to stop the looting had been given because the outnumbered police would have had to start shooting.[40]

Support for the concept of restraint in riot control has

come from one of the most respected voices of American conservatism—William F. Buckley, Jr. Buckley reviewed the arguments pro and con, and seemed most impressed by the assertion that "we're better off letting a few dozen or hundred teen-agers cart away the contents of a few dozen stores, than induce the holocaust that would result from noisy physical arrests." Buckley concluded, "On balance my own sympathies tend to lie—reluctantly—with the utilitarian position." Buckley felt that the "purists" failed to reckon with the actualities which were that "even as the U.S. is apparently incapable of effecting its will in Vietnam, it is, as of the moment, at least incapable of effecting its will in the major cities of the U.S. . . . if the police are engaged in arresting and removing people by the hundreds or thousands, they are effectively removed from the scene."[41]

Mr. Buckley terms his position "the bitterest gall for an American conservative to drink."[42] One wishes that he had resisted the potion for yet a while longer. From a moral viewpoint, one may question whether one man has the right to give away another man's property. From a pragmatic viewpoint, one must expect the criminal to regard this as appeasement, and to keep raising the price for peace in the community. Today it can be "a few dozen stores," tomorrow much larger ones, and the day after, private homes. Today it can be "a few dozen or hundred teen-agers," tomorrow, triple or quadruple that number. And for those who wish to resist, some will reply that anything—*anything* —is preferable to a holocaust—until finally the depradations become as serious as the chaos it is supposed to avoid. Perhaps the greatest shortcoming in Mr. Buckley's position is that he fails to reckon with the reaction of the white community. There is a potentiality for violence among some whites, and it is not inconceivable that they may begin organizing in armed bands to provide the protection which City Hall is no longer willing to give. Mr. Buckley fears a holocaust emanating from a Negro minority. Perhaps he should be even more concerned about possible armed resistance emanating from a white majority.

Mr. Buckley's column was written in his usual calm and logical style. The problem is that he may not be dealing with calm and logical people. A most perceptive article about those who riot was written by Robert N. McMurry, a psychologist with an international reputation and head of an industrial psychology and personnel consulting firm. Dr. McMurry wrote that "From a psychological point of view, recent riots have tended to be marked by behavior which can only be described as berserk. At the height of these disorders, many of those taking part have clearly cast aside all civilized restraints. In their activities, they give free expression to the most primitive, atavistic impulses."

Dr. McMurry feels that it was predominantly from two groups—"the irresponsible and the psychopathic personalities—that the majority of the rioters, the vandals, the looters, the arsonists and the potential killers come." He wrote that "to many persons rioting has now become respectable. Society increasingly is condoning rioting as a justified expression of a way of life. This in turn rationalizes violence." He wrote that advocates of violence such as Stokely Carmichael and Rap Brown were given wide publicity, and their positions endorsed by some clergymen. "In consequence, owing to this shift in the mores of society, the consciences of many no longer contain restrictions against rioting, violence, arson and even murder. Hence, the individuals feel no guilt." Dr. McMurry was convinced that "Only forceable restraints and the creation of a sincere conviction in them that punishment for transgressions will be quick, certain and intolerably painful will have any deterrent effect." He acknowledged that "this may entail some infringements of these persons' civil rights. No more so, however, than is the case of those who must be hospitalized because they are mentally ill."[43]

To many Americans, there is virtually no problem in the world that cannot be solved through gargantuan infusions of cash, three or four study committees, and hundreds or thousands of bureaucrats expressing 9-to-5, Monday-through-Friday sympathy and concern. We have seen all

of these panaceas simultaneously applied to the problems of
Negroes, and we have seen that all of them combined are
about as effective as a band-aid on a bleeding ulcer.

Like Ponce de Leon searching for the Fountain of Youth,
we keep searching for The Master Solution that will solve
the problems of the Negro people. But I believe there is no
answer. I believe there is no solution, and we are tragically
deluding ourselves—and the objects of our concern—if we
think there is. In my opinion, what the Negroes need is
something that no government, no people, no open-end
checkbook can give them. They need self-respect, self-
esteem, a sense of *personal* worth and *personal* achievement.
It cannot be legislated. It cannot be handed down by the
courts. It must come from within the minds and hearts of
some 22 million Negroes.

Far from helping the Negroes, I believe the millions we
have poured into the ghettos serve only to increase their
sense of dependence, personal inadequacy, self-hatred, and
ultimate hatred of the giver. It only confirms their somber
social prognosis that they can't "make it" on their own. And
this is the greatest single failure of liberalism in this country—the demoralizing paternalism that clashes head-on with
the fierce Negro desire to pay his own bills, be self-support-
ing, and stand on his own two feet. The typical liberal
response shows that the liberal has learned nothing; he
simply escalates his errors and compounds his misjudgment
of Negro aspirations by offering still more money, still more
help, still more of everything. And all the while he stoutly
refuses to hear what more and more Negroes are all but
shouting in his ears—that the hand-out philosophy of liberalism has not only lost its relevance in the civil rights struggle,
but is actually making a bad situation even worse.

After all these years and all these demonstrations, we
still don't quite see the Negro as a human being. To many
of us he is a cause, a living reproach, a larger-than-life
martyr or a smaller-than-life caricature—anything but a
person, an individual. If we could look at the Negro as a

human being—with the usual quota of human virtues and human faults—we could applaud him when he's right, criticize him when he's wrong. We could reserve the right to like some Negroes and dislike others, without being criticized as crypto-racists. Most important of all, we could get up off our knees and tell Negroes that—like whites—they are responsible for their own personal welfare, and must share at least some of the responsibility for their generally lower economic status. And here we would have to say that, like fingerprints, no two cases of Negroes are exactly alike in the field of employment. Where Negroes had the ability to perform a certain job, and were denied it solely because of their color, their complaints of discrimination were valid and factual. But what of cases where Negroes were not qualified, or, if they were qualified, had a spotty work history, or ran head-on against nepotistic union hiring practices that have similarly frustrated many a white applicant? What if the Negroes had the ability, but lacked the training or education? The suppositions can be multiplied ad infinitum, so one cannot automatically ascribe to discrimination failure to hire a Negro. This is all the more obvious when you consider how widely employment practices, vis-à-vis the Negro, have varied from state to state, from city to city, from union to union, and sometimes from industry to industry within the same city.

The economic problem is compounded in Negro families where there are many mouths to feed. From the Bureau of Labor Statistics, we learn that a certain salary might be adequate to feed, house and clothe a family of four, but would be inadequate for a family of six. The now-classic case is that of Stokely Carmichael, whose father worked day and night while his mother worked as a maid in a struggle to support a family of eight. It is, I know, a sensitive area, but in view of the broadsides leveled against society, it is necessary to restate the somber economic equation—large family plus small salary equals poverty, a poverty which is at least partially self-imposed. And not even the most paternalistic liberal has maintained that society can control the size of a family.

We must bluntly label as nonsense the concept that whites are "the oppressor" class, and Negroes "the oppressed." In so doing, we must recall to mind an article by James Baldwin, titled "The Dangerous Road before Martin Luther King," which was written in 1961. In this article, King was quoted as saying of the South, "Perhaps four or five per cent are to be found on either end of the scale—either actively for or actively against desegregation; the rest are passive adherents. The sin of the South is the sin of conformity."[44] In other words, the overwhelming majority were simply standing on the sidelines and not actively oppressing anyone. This is something we must remember, even at the expense of deflating the enormous egoism that believes whites have been almost constantly preoccupied with the Negro. In the North, I believe whites have generally been more "passive" than "passive adherent." I believe many Northern whites just didn't care about Negro problems, and that while this attitude, in retrospect, may have been most unfortunate, not even Martin Luther King—with all his rhetorical sorcery—could make "apathy" synonymous with "oppression." On and on goes that venerable cliché that "society" is to blame for most, if not all, of the Negro's problems. But to me, society is a sum total of the living, and it is reasonable to ask how many Americans *now living* are responsible for the Negro's plight. Those who enslaved the Negroes have long since departed this earth, and it is a social absurdity to seek to indict their progeny through a form of retroactive guilt. It is even more absurd to expect feelings of guilt in today's sons or grandsons of immigrants who came to this country long after the Civil War, and themselves had to struggle to make their way. We come back to the four or five per cent who are activists, and it is simply standing reason on its head to use the deeds of a motley few to justify a blanket condemnation of the rest of the country. Many whites—and, I suspect, most Negroes

—have traditionally been more concerned about their own immediate personal and family problems, and often unconcerned about the larger events taking place in America and in the world.

Despite the avalanche of headlines, news stories, and follow-up articles over the last ten years, it is still accurate to say that the vast majority of Negroes in this country have never participated in a demonstration led by Martin Luther King, or for that matter, CORE or SNCC. There may have been tremendous sympathy and support for these demonstrations in the Negro community, but civil rights activists have always comprised only an infinitesimal percentage of this country's Negro population. To this day, the Southern Christian Leadership Conference is still basically what its name implies—a grouping of community leaders, rather than a grass-roots organization.

We should also bear in mind that the overwhelming majority of Negroes in each of the communities concerned did not participate in the Los Angeles, Newark, and Detroit riots. The validity of this statement is self-evident enough, but it becomes much more difficult to discern the reasons— or indeed, if there are any reasons at all. Again, I don't think there is any one answer to explain it, because I do not think Negro responses have Pavlovian predictability. *Liberator* maintains that "The insurrections could never have gained the momentum they did without the support of the entire black community."[45] But "entire" may be much too big a word. While some undoubtedly supported the riots, others may have been reluctant to turn on their "brothers" no matter how much they have disagreed with them, while others may have feared bodily harm if they did not at least pretend to sympathize with the rioters. But admittedly all this is sheer speculation; no one really knows.

In a sense, most of the Negro ghettos in this country are like little Vietnams—with moderates and ultra-militants contending for ultimate dominion of an amorphous population. The moderates cling to their age-old dream of some form of integration, or at least some form of social partnership with white America. The ultra-militants frankly want all-black ghettos, as nearly independent of the larger white community as possible, in fact, even if not in name. The militants presumably would have no objection to Whitey paying the costs of government (welfare included) as long as the actual power and rule of government stays in black hands—their black hands. On the theoretical level, these are varying interpretations of freedom and how it is to be achieved. Translated into action, we could some day see extreme militants calling for little black confederacies in the ghettos, with pan-African loyalties.*

The struggle between moderate and militant is of far more than academic importance. Its outcome will some day decide whether whites can go on living in some parts of our cities. If my statement sounds unduly alarmist, consider the case—the showcase, if you please—of the New York City educational system, I.S. (Intermediate School) 201.

This $5 million building, opened in 1966 in Harlem, was to be a showcase of integrated and high-quality education.[46] This was the pledge, and later the New York Times was to term it "a demonstration in unredeemable promises."[47] At its opening, the school was to have a 20 per cent white enrollment—but there was no rush of white students to the ghetto.[48] At the outset, its faculty was nearly half Negro. The school was constructed on elevated stilts, and was air conditioned throughout.[49] The pupil-teacher ratio was to be at 24 to 1 (the city-wide average was 33 to 1), with 55 teachers handling about 598 students.[50] But far from being delighted, certain community figures found

---

* It should be noted here that Black Power militants are not talking about segregation, which, whether de facto or de jure, at least acknowledges the authority of the city government to rule and maintain order in all neighborhoods, black and white. What most Black Power militants want is separation—in effect, their own government, their own laws, with all the local control and power the ghetto would have if it were a sovereign state. Some militants even talk of having part or all of a state ceded to them as a black province.

it unforgiveable that a white principal, Stanley Lisser, had been appointed to head the school. Demands were made for a Negro principal and decisive control over curriculum, hiring and firing.[51] Protest demonstrations were led by various community groups, and later joined by Stokely Carmichael and Floyd McKissick.[52]

There was never any reasonable question of Lisser's credentials or his dedication. His evenly integrated teacher staff had been hand-picked. The school had twice the usual help of school aides and a full-time "community relations specialist" to promote "closer parent and citizen involvement in the school program." I.S. 201 had language laboratories, a social studies curriculum that did not neglect Negro and Puerto Rican history and culture, musical instruments and typing classes.[53] The Board of Education had said I.S. 201 would be "one of the best in the nation,"[54] but four months after its opening, near-bedlam prevailed in some of its classes. Ten- to thirteen-year-old pupils were darting around the rooms at will, punching one another in horseplay and ignoring the teachers' occasional pleas for order, if not attention. So often had pupils in the hallways turned out the lights, that switches operated by keys were to be installed. So often had pupils ripped down or defaced hallway display boards than many teachers were discouraged from putting much effort into the next exhibit.[55]

Six months after East Harlem parents and others had tried to force his ouster, the white principal resigned.[56] Asked whether he would have accepted the post at I.S. 201 if he had known what was in store, he replied, "If I knew I would be powerless to personally solve certain problems that are outside the school, no, I would not have."[57] Now a group called the Parent-Community Coordinating Committee demanded to see "parents and community participating fully in the selection of his successor as well as all the other aspects of the school's operation."[58]

That these strident militants sought nothing less than control of the school became even more obvious during the

New York City teachers' strike in 1967. The leader of a group of Harlem parents, Queen Mother Moore, told nine teachers who had picketed I.S. 201, "You'd better not ever show your faces here at this school again. We know you. We recognize you and we don't want you here, ever again. If anyone of you ever dare return to this school to teach our children we'll take you apart. And we do mean apart. You're unfit and undecent [sic] to teach our children. Get out of here and stay out of here."[59]

During the teachers' strike, H. Rap Brown came to Harlem and held a news conference outside of I.S. 201. A reporter asked, "Is it true that you advocate seizing control of I.S. 201 and other public schools in Negro areas?" Brown answered, "Yes, we should control public education. Now we should take over the schools and not relinquish them." Brown went inside I.S. 201 briefly. While inside, Harlem parents spread-eagled before the entrance to prevent white reporters and white policemen from entering behind Brown. The *Amsterdam News* noted that "White policemen did not force their right or the issues; they stepped aside, and Afro-American policemen followed Brown inside, where he stayed 7 minutes." After he came out, a reporter asked him, "Are things very close to anarchy inside the school?" Brown shot back, "You white people keep on talking about anarchy and that's exactly what you're going to get. Nothing more and nothing less."[60]

After the strike ended, John Marsh, president of the United Federation of Teachers chapter at I.S. 201, was met at the door by Negro militant Ralph Bess, who blocked his path and shouted, "Over my dead body." Marsh turned away and left. Later it was announced that he had requested and would be granted a transfer.[61]

Marsh charged that "hate Whitey" programs were conducted at the school during the teachers' strike. He also declared that the community planning board was making a "power grab" for control of I.S. 201.[62]

At the school, those teachers who had gone on strike now

faced the threat of "screening" by the experimental community planning board, dominated by parents and other Harlem residents. The executive secretary of the planning board, David Spencer, said the teachers who participated in the strike would be screened "to determine their attitudes and motivation for returning to schools in the 201 complex," and added, "We will decide who will work here."[63]

Joining in support of the planned screening was Herman B. Ferguson.[64] He was the former assistant principal who had been suspended from his post in Jamaica after being arrested as a member of the RAM, charged with plotting the assassination of Roy Wilkins and other Negro moderates. To no one's great surprise, Ferguson passed the screening with flying black colors. Asked if Ferguson had been hired by the I.S. 201 Planning Board, Spencer replied, "Yes, he has been retained as our advisor. He is being paid. We hired him for his professional competence. . . . Mr. Ferguson is a fine and brilliant man."[65]

At this point, the reader may be wondering who paid the bills for the Planning Board. This parents' organization was lavishly financed by a $57,000 Ford Foundation grant, funded in order to find ways to involve community parents in local schools.[66] If the Ford Foundation is at all distressed that its grant pays the salary of a gentleman accused of membership in a murder plot, it is keeping awfully quiet about it.

The United Federation of Teachers warned that "as a last resort," it would tell teachers not to serve at I.S. 201 and four other Harlem schools, to protect them from "vigilante committees." Albert Shanker, the union president, said he had instructed teachers at the five schools not to submit to "screening" by the planning board.[67] Faced with this threat, the planning board said that the board would not screen teachers but would hold "a conference with each teacher personally." It conceded that the planning board was not "in a position to terminate anyone's services." But it also disclosed that teachers "who find it too difficult or too tense here" would be "encouraged" to seek transfers to other schools.[68]

Fred M. Hechinger of the New York *Times* found a startling change in community educational attitudes. In 1964, civil rights leaders and Negro spokesmen had said that nothing but city-wide integration with a short-term timetable was acceptable. A massive boycott followed to enforce these demands, paralyzing the schools in the process.[69] Now Negro groups were willingly accepting de facto segregated schools, and demanding that they be given a powerful part in administering these neighborhood schools.[70] Largely at the insistence of Negro groups years before, the Board of Education had instituted an open enrollment program which gave parents the option to have their children transported to distant schools, provided there was space. Yet now when the Board announced it was curtailing this program, the Negro reaction was one of indifference.[71]

Occasionally, one still heard a voice in the wilderness, like that of Dr. Kenneth B. Clark, professor of psychology and one of the pioneer proponents of school integration. Clark maintained, "The fact that the Black Power groups are shouting for the most rigid form of segregation will not make segregation any better."[72] But he seemed to have scant vocal support in the Negro community.

Hechinger felt that "slogans, such as 'Black is beautiful' " —made popular by the Rev. Dr. Martin Luther King, Jr.— have reinforced demands to place ghetto schools under Negro leadership. As the voice of the ghettos passed from the integration-minded, old-line civil rights organizations to those with a Black Power slant, the demands for such separatist power entered the educational scene as well."[73]

The separatist influence had clearly permeated the ranks of the African American Teachers Association, which called for "self-control, self-determination and self-defense for the schools in the black community."[74] But just as clearly this group did not speak for all Negro teachers, as was shown at a meeting of the United Federation of Teachers. There, a Negro teacher charged that a militant group not representative of the total community had "usurped" control of the I.S. 201 district "by intimidation."[75]

In November, 1967, East Harlem parents, teachers and supervisors voted to elect representatives to an experimental board which would run I.S. 201. The election was sponsored by the same I.S. 201 Planning Board which had hired Herman Ferguson. A total of 400 parents, 142 teachers and eleven supervisory employees voted, choosing one supervisor, five teachers, and ten parents to the governing board. Five community representatives would later be chosen by the ten parents. Of all the parents registered to vote, only one-third cast their ballots.[76] The acting principal of I.S. 201, Miss Beryl Banfield, a Negro, voted in the election, commenting afterward, "We support the board and the board has given us good support."[77] The board's support must have been invaluable. Three months later, Miss Banfield went on medical leave.[78] By February of this year, only about a dozen of the original 58 teachers were still there. Most of the teachers were substitutes who had never taught before their present assignments.[79] A New York *Times* reporter visited the I.S. 201 building, and on the second and third floor found a state of near-bedlam during the between-periods class changes, and many youngsters wandering around when classes were in session. According to district records, 22 pupils had been transferred out of I.S. 201 since September at their parents' request; the pupils said they had been attacked by other children inside the school. In December, a father struck a teacher in his classroom. The day before, the teacher had "slapped" the man's son to get him to stop "repeatedly punching a girl."[80] Superintendent of Schools Bernard Donovan said that the *Times* report was "accurate."[81]

With the acting principal on medical leave, a vacancy existed at I.S. 201 and there was a power struggle to fill it. The chief consultant to the parent-dominated governing board held a news conference to announce the "appointment"

of a new principal. He said the appointment was effective
the day before. Superintendent of Schools Donovan said,
however, that he had specifically "instructed" the governing
board that it had not yet received official recognition from
the Board of Education. The School Superintendent thereupon directed a District superintendent to take personal
charge of the school.[82]

The news conference of the governing board was dis-
rupted briefly when some angry mothers of children at I.S.
201 accused the board of not really consulting parents in the
"selection" of a new principal. One of the parents charged,
"This governing board is worse than the Board of Education."[83]

Inside the school, teacher morale was apparently at an
all-time low. One young Negro teacher watched pupils
shoving, fighting and yelling during a change of classes.
She said, "This isn't a school, this is a jungle." As she spoke,
a magazine hurtled out of a classroom and landed near her.
Another teacher shouted at a group of youngsters engaged
in horseplay to "cut that out!" The teacher waved a yardstick at the children, and they moved a short distance away,
then carried on as before. A visitor asked this teacher, "Do
you really use that stick?" The teacher replied, "What do
you think?" The visitor asked, "What kind of education
goes on here?" The teachers laughed and walked away.[84]

This paragraph was written February 7, 1968. Just four
days before, a new teacher turned down his assignment to
I.S. 201 because of an anti-white play personally presented
in the school auditorium by LeRoi Jones, the fanatically
white-hating Negro writer. As the teacher described it, a
major character in the Jones play poses questions that are
answered by a chorus. These are the questions and answers:

"Who murdered the black man?"
"Whitey, whitey."
"Who should we lynch?"
"Whitey, whitey."

A Negro pupil sitting nearby told the teacher, "We're talking about you, but we'll let you live." After just one day in I.S. 201, the teacher went to district headquarters and pleaded, "Take me out of there." The teacher was reassigned.[85]

On the college level, Negro youth is not lynching Whitey, but is lynching the ideal of the integrated society. Dean David B. Truman has warned that there exists "a very real danger that Negroes at Columbia will become a college within a college." He discussed the establishment of an all-Negro fraternity at Columbia as an example of "self-imposed segregation."[86] A member of this all-Negro fraternity acknowledged that "here at Columbia we were attacked on all sides by those who said that we were resegregating ourselves apart. Yes, that's about the size of it."[87] Columbia's Afro-American Society brought H. Rap Brown to the campus, where he addressed a standing-room-only audience. The black students raised $1,300 from ticket sales which has been given to SNCC to provide bail and legal fees for seven SNCC workers arrested in a draft protest.[88]

At New York University, the Black Allied Student Association boasted, "We have brought this black student black power into a national group on a national scale." Black unity and black power are always the twin themes of their paper, and topping their list of sponsored campus speakers have been James Foreman of SNCC and parents and administrators of I.S. 201.[89] There are black power organizations at Dartmouth, Yale, Brown, Providence, Harvard, Amherst, Tufts, University of Massachusetts, and Brandeis.[90]

Beyond any doubt, we will be hearing from these young Black Power zealots after they leave the campus. Some of them will enter the ranks of the Black Nationalists, and many of them will work with SNCC. Within the next few years, the future leaders of the city ghettos will come from their ranks. And, given the state of their adoration for Stokely Carmichael, Rap Brown, and the late Malcolm X, it may very well be that what has already transpired in our urban areas is as nothing compared with what lies ahead. In the end, black power could generate a ferocious and permanent black racism that would make Bull Connor and Jim Clark look like apostles of brotherhood. Carmichael himself said of the more rabid young Negroes in Watts:

"Those kids will be calling me Uncle Tom in a few years. People think *I'm* militant. Wait until those kids grow up! There are young cats around here who make me look like a dove of peace."[91]

Professor Arnold Toynbee recently wrote: "the idea of integration—the Martin Luther King idea of integration by nonviolent means—is being beaten by the idea of violence and setting up an anti-community within the community. This could lead to a kind of permanent civil war within the principal cities of the U.S., with the Negro anti-communities having their own civilization, their own way of life. That's what America seems to be heading for."[92]

The Vietnam parallel has been chillingly drawn by Col. Robert B. Rigg (Ret.), a former U.S. Army Intelligence officer who helped prepare a long-range strategic forecast at the U.S. Army Institute of Advanced Studies (in 1958, his book *War: 1974* made predictions that have become realities in Vietnam). Writing in *Army* magazine, in January, 1968, Col. Rigg pointed out that "Man has constructed out of steel and concrete a much better 'jungle' than nature has created in Vietnam." The Army Intelligence officer believed that in cities such as Chicago, New York, Detroit, Newark, Oakland, and Los Angeles, "such cement-and-brick 'jungles' can offer better security to snipers and city guerrillas than the Viet Cong enjoy in their jungles, elephant grass and marshes." Col. Rigg wrote that "Police, National Guard, and active Army units could hardly carry out successful clear-and-hold operations in the steel-and-concrete jungles of high-rise buildings without resorting to a campaign that would almost reach the destruction experienced by Stalingrad . . . . what tank or bulldozer is going to flatten an old 20-story apartment or office building that is sniper-ridden by night and vacant by day?" An expert who has specialized in planning for the future, Rigg believes that "If present trends persist, it is possible that in the next decade at least one major metropolitan area in the United States could be faced with guerrilla warfare of such intensity as to require sizable U.S. Army elements in action, and National Guard units on active duty for years." Col. Rigg considers it essential that the ghettos be penetrated by police intelligence, application of military intelligence, and reliance on traditional FBI methods. He is convinced that "Today's trend implies that very soon American troops will be maneuvering in metropolitan areas to an extent more than ever before imagined. Here they will be required to learn about and memorize details of many metropolitan communities, their buildings, streets, alleyways, roof-tops and sewers, just as once they learned the use of terrain features of open country." The sight of such maneuvers in several cities, the Colonel hopes (but it seems no more than a hope), could possibly "prove a deterrent to urban insurrection."[93]

The absolute necessity for no-nonsense law-enforcement in the years to come could hardly be more obvious. But the most heroic efforts of our police will be worse than useless if the lawbreakers and rioters in our midst are set free, or wrist-slapped by our judges and again turned loose on society. And here we come to what may well be the most controversial portion of the book—one which will probably call down upon me the icy wrath of most liberals and a number of conservatives. With deep regret—but equally with a sense of deep urgency—I am forced to suggest that the weakest link in society's defense against the lawless is our Federal judiciary, and most especially our Supreme Court. Time after time, we have seen criminals' convictions reversed, not because the evidence did not establish their guilt, but because the Court disapproved of the *means* by which the evidence was obtained. A policeman must now almost have a lawyer at his side to advise him as to the procedural steps to be taken to avoid running afoul of the latest judicial edict. New York District Attorney Frank Hogan has said that recent Supreme Court decisions have "significantly increased the chances that a criminal will escape judgment."[94] The scales of justice are now clearly weighted in favor of the criminal, and the first order of business must now be to redress the balance. Various laws may be proposed in the Congress to curb the High Court's power, but any such law must eventually come before the Court itself, and can hardly expect to meet with a dispassionate reception. As a practical matter, the Supreme Court can, and does, nullify any law for any reason, or (in the case of a Per Curiam opinion) no reason at all. The Court accounts to no one, is responsible to no one, has absolute power to reverse law and—in effect—write law, and its judges may, if they choose, hold office for the rest of their lives. In a country which prides itself on democratic procedure, one can hardly imagine a more autocratic establishment, constituting, as it does, a super-legislature whose judge-made law can never be vetoed, never repealed. As Professor Philip B. Kurland of the University of Chicago Law School has commented, "The Justices are stretching the Judicial process to try to translate their notion of an ideal society into reality."

The people of this country have the right to elect members of the legislative branch and the head of the executive branch of the Federal government. I propose that they now have the same right to elect the members—all members—of the Federal Judiciary, up to, and including, the members of the Supreme Court. To those who will object that the Constitution contains no such authority, I would reply that the Constitution was not conceived of as an all-perfect document or no provision would have been included for its amendment. (For example, I rather think that most liberals and most conservatives alike would shudder at the thought of the Constitution without the amendments known as The Bill of Rights.)

At present, the country is divided into ten Judicial Circuits, with each of the nine Supreme Court judges holding a dominant judicial position in each circuit (one justice sitting in both the eighth and tenth circuits). I propose the passage of an amendment to the Constitution which would require direct election of all nine Supreme Court justices every six years. The justices would run for office from the various Judicial Circuits in which they now function as Circuit Justices. As with any other election, varying political parties could run their own candidates. I believe this is the only way to have a Federal judiciary more responsive to the will of the people, and it will be a long overdue measure to instill the democratic process into the most undemocratic branch of our Federal government.

Predictably, the hue and cry will be raised that we will be injecting politics into the judiciary. But to say this is to assume that members of our judiciary are god-like figures handing down their decisions from some Olympian height—an overly romantic concept which I think the Justices themselves would be the first to deny. In any case, "politics" is nothing more or less than an unpleasant synonym for the art of government, and it hardly seems shocking to propose that *all* branches of government rule with the consent of the governed—even our hitherto sacrosanct Supreme Court.

At this point, the mechanics of my proposal are flexible, and subject to change. What is not subject to change is the basic concept—the (to me) logical extension of the voting process to what may well be the single most powerful branch of the Federal government.

What would I hope to accomplish? My expectations are very modest ones. I would expect that if Supreme Court Justices knew that they would have to answer to the voters for their decisions, they might think twice before handing down some of their more outrageous edicts. They might consider more carefully the right of society to be protected from the lawless, and stop shackling the police in the exercise of their duties. If they did not—and exhibited the regal disdain for their constituency they now reserve for their critics—the electorate could simply turn them out of office at the next election.

It is also possible that highly qualified state or lower court judges—who might never have reached the High Court under the Presidential appointment system—could now at least be considered for Supreme Court office. I am thinking of some latter-day Judge Learned Hand—often called "the 10th Justice of the Supreme Court" because of his widely recognized legal brilliance and ability, but who never received an appointment to that highest judicial office.

I hope the reactions to my proposal will not all be visceral, and I certainly hope the responses to it will not be guided by racial considerations. The ultra-militants, black and white, would like nothing better than a polarization of racial views on the subject of law and order. But we must not allow ourselves to be pushed into this trap. We must never forget that the lawless members of society come from all racial and religious groups, and that the vast majority of Americans, black and white, are urgently concerned that the lives and property of all be protected from criminals, whatever their color, race, or origin. To cite just one example, white New Yorkers must realize that Harlem residents are as incensed about the increase in crime as they are. Hardly an issue of the *Amsterdam News* goes by without graphic evidence of that fact. In October, 1967, over 700 Harlem residents jammed an anti-crime rally, proclaiming: "We're afraid to walk the street; we're terrified in our homes."[95] Many petitions have been signed in Harlem protesting not "police brutality," but the lack of police in their areas. The *Amsterdam News* has bluntly called for "restoring the legitimate, unbiased use of firearms by our police, the return of the right of a man to defend his home against robbers and demand more concerted efforts against criminals, white or black, old or young."[96] To which I, for one, am more than happy to say, "Amen."

In the long struggle to restore law and order in our cities, we must not be deterred by the servile comments of the White Toms—those white sycophants who will invariably defend in Negroes, because they are Negroes, conduct they would find indefensible in whites. The clergy seems to have more than its share of White Toms—like the general board of the National Council of Churches, which blamed big city riots on "white masters who have long dominated in the ghetto."[97] Others have displayed similar subservience to the worst excesses of the militants. The president of the National Conference of Christians and Jews said racial violence struck more than 100 cities in 1967 because "the pernicious doctrine of white superiority finally wrecked the patience and the hopes of American Negroes."[98] And *Liberator* quoted with obvious approval Robert Kennedy, who, in 1964, had this to say:

We must recognize that the young in many areas of the world today are in the midst of a revolution against the status quo. . . . They will prevail, they will achieve their idealistic goals one way or another. If they have to pull governments tumbling down over their heads, they will do it. But they are going to win a share of a better, cleaner world.[99]

In the present religious milieu, Martin Luther King has not been made a saint—yet. But a new catechism book in Chicago praises him effusively. One section of the catechism, accompanying a picture of a Selma, Alabama, civil rights march, tells Catholic children: "In this picture we see Negro and white people marching together. They are marching for better homes, jobs and schools for the Negro people. One of the leaders of the Negro people is a brave man named Martin Luther King. He is a Christian minister from Alabama. He preaches the message of Jesus, 'Love one another.' Some people do not like the Rev. King. They say he is a troublemaker, but no matter what some people may say, he continues to tell everyone to keep on seeking justice. Rev. King is a brave Christian." Angry Catholic laymen demanded an FBI investigation of the Roman Catholic Archdiocese of Chicago. Supporters of the new catechism called the critics "John Birchers."[100]

About all that can be said with certainty about America's racial future is that nothing is certain—nothing except more tenseness, more distrust and hostility, and above all, Longer and Hotter Summers. It has now become almost platitudinous to say that there will be more and still more riots in America's cities, and I think that the government must bear part of the responsibility for these riots. Oozing good intentions at every benevolent pore, the government has helped virtually to demolish the influence of Negro moderates in the ghettos. The prime Negro moderate argument against rioting was that the government would punish rioters, while white backlash would inhibit any further racial gains. But after every major riot, just the reverse happened. In effect, government rewarded the rioters, looters, and Molotov cocktail throwers by starting to rebuild the property the militants themselves had destroyed, instituting all sorts of sweeping job programs. And most of the rioters barely had their wrists slapped, if at all. The advocates of nonviolence once boasted that they could accomplish in weeks or months what it took years to achieve through court litigation. The rioters can now boast that they did even better—that they got promises of favorable government and business action in a matter of days. The lesson will hardly be lost on Negroes, and ironically it will be government that has helped build the power and following of militants in the ghettos, while simultaneously pulling the rug out from under the moderates.

Certainly while the militant rank and file is fiercely, almost devoutly, loyal to its self-appointed messiahs, the defections in the ranks of the moderates are reaching alarming proportions. Every year, more strenuous efforts are made to oust Roy Wilkins from his post with the NAACP. He and Whitney Young are the only real moderates in positions of leadership today, and I think that their days as effective moderate leaders may be numbered. Already they are being stigmatized, in some quarters, as Uncle Toms, and few will reach out to catch their mantle if and when they fall. This is not to say that there are no Negro moderates in the ghettos, but that where they exist they are largely disorganized and demoralized, and not nearly as articulate and persuasive as their ultra-militant counterparts. And in the inner, as in the outer city, a few demagogic activists can exert an influence out of all proportion to their numbers.

Just how demagogic these activists can be was savagely displayed in October, 1967, at the 31st Annual State Conference of the New York NAACP. It all started when most of the adult delegates voted to table a resolution by a teenager, Gerald Taylor, putting the state conference on record as opposing the Vietnam war and calling for a cease-fire. The older delegates said such a resolution was not consistent with national NAACP policy. At this state conference, fifty of the youth delegates seized control of the floor and drowned out the proceedings with senseless noise for eighteen minutes before order was restored. Led by Taylor, who had helped to organize a similar demonstration at the NAACP's National Convention, the youths sang, clapped their hands and shuffled around the room. The *Amsterdam News* reported, "Most of the 180 adult delegates, representing 70 branches throughout the state, seemed frozen in fear as the 19-year-old Taylor directed his youthful supporters to 'turn on the pressure until they give us what we want.'" Infuriated at the blocking of his resolution, Taylor rushed to the platform, and said, "I'm hot, baby. I dig all this talk but you've got to realize we are ready for action. How, in the name of God, can you support war?" Finally, the presiding officer announced that a decision had been reached to reconsider the youths' complaint. The adults agreed to do business with the teen-agers who won their point by a vote of 107 to 72.[101] There have been

rumblings of militant discontent from the so-called
oung Turks" on the national NAACP level. Indeed,
sources close to the NAACP estimate that the Young Turks
have about 20 members on the 60-member national board.[102]

Presumably, Whitney Young of the Urban League has
been put under similar pressure from the ultra-radicals. I
would like to think that it was only under such extreme
pressure that the usually responsible Young stated that "the
greatest freedom that exists for Negroes in this country is
freedom to die in Vietnam."[103] From a long-range viewpoint,
much more disturbing than Young's absurd outburst was
the declaration by spokesmen for the National Urban
League that they are ready to work with all groups, including
"black power" advocates in constructive programs in the
nation's ghettos.[104] If through this program, the "black
power" supporters get a foot in the door of the National
Urban League, Whitney Young may just wake up some
fine day and find himself outside looking in.

In the power struggle going on in the nation's ghettos,
moderates could expect little if any meaningful support from
Martin Luther King. The reason had been obscured by
many of his idolators, but had been pinpointed by Jackie
Robinson in the most forthright fashion. "Nonviolent
though he may be," wrote Robinson, "Martin King is one of
the most militant men in the world."[105]

The New York *Times* editorialized, "Once the spark of
massive law-defiance is applied in the present overheated
atmosphere, the potentiality for disaster becomes overwhelming."[106] The editorial was written during the Long Hot
Summer of 1967; there is no reason to believe that the racial
climate has since cooled to any appreciable degree. If anything, it has become considerably hotter.

After that summer had ended—and the Detroit riots had
run their bloody course—a clergyman spoke with Mrs. Rosa
Parks, the lady who launched Martin Luther King's career
in Montgomery by refusing to get up from her bus seat.
Mrs. Parks, who now lives in Detroit and works in Rep.

John Conyers' local office, was asked, "What can the churches do?" She replied, "Maybe nothing at all. You may be too late."[107]

We would do well to give careful consideration to the words of Daniel Patrick Moynihan, director of the Harvard-MIT Joint Center for Urban Affairs. With refreshing candor, he has called on his fellow liberals to "overcome the curious condescension which takes the form of sticking up for and explaining away anything, howsoever outrageous, which Negroes, individually or collectively, might do." Moynihan said of the Negro revolt:

All the signs declare that the violence is not ended. Worse still, a new set of signs tells us something that is painful, even hateful, to have to hear: We must prepare for the onset of terrorism. Indeed, it may already have begun. How widespread and how successful remains to be seen, but the probability is so great that ignoring it would be an act of irresponsibility or of cowardice.[108]

Moynihan believes that the violence at home and abroad threatens the social order of the country, and that liberals must make a new alliance with conservatives who share this concern. He acknowledged that "the politics of stability are not at first exciting. It is only when we come to see how very probably our national life is at stake that the game acquires a sudden interest."[109]

I believe both conservatives and liberals must actively seek out and invite into this new alliance Negroes who are equally concerned with preserving the social order—Negroes who will have the moral courage to defy the Black Power groups in order to participate in Operation Urban Survival. It may be an uneasy alliance of political rivals, but an alliance it must be—one of the most crucial in our nation's history.

We must no longer delay. We must no longer excuse or temporize. We must no longer hope that, like a bad dream, the impending crisis will either right itself or go away. We must stop fawning on black racists, and take them literally at their hateful word. We must support the right of all our cities—and all our citizens, black and white—to live in peace, to prosper, to be protected from those who would destroy from within. We must support the police as our first line of defense. We must support this country as still the last best hope of the world. And as a solemn covenant with generations yet unborn, we shall *not* be overcome.

The Highlander Folk School

✿✿ ✿✿ ✿✿ ✿✿ ✿✿ ✿✿ ✿✿ ✿✿ ✿✿ ✿✿ ✿✿ ✿✿ ✿✿ ✿✿ ✿✿ ✿✿ ✿✿ ✿✿ ✿✿

(One of the most famous pictures of Martin Luther King was never taken in any photography studio. It shows King sitting alongside three rather renowned gentlemen—one of them a member of the Communist Party—at a 1957 Labor Day seminar at the Highlander Folk School. Much has been written about it, still more speculated or surmised. What follows is a factual presentation of the events concerning the School, its personnel, its relevance to the civil rights struggle—and, of course, THE PHOTO.)

Highlander Folk School was founded in 1932 by Myles Horton and Rev. Don West in Monteagle, Tennessee; they were joined shortly after by James Dombrowski. Rev. West did not stay long at Highlander; he went on to become Socialist State Secretary for Georgia, and "graduated" to three important positions in the Communist Party in the South.

Paul Crouch, who had been one of the top Communist Party functionaries in the South, testified before a Senate subcommittee: "The Highlander Folk School is a school operated at Monteagle, Tenn., ostensibly as an independent labor school, but actually working in close cooperation with the Communist Party." Crouch testified that he, Dombrowski, and Horton had made arrangements for the Communist

Daily Worker to be "carried where all the students would be able to see it, and I was later informed by Mildred White that this was done and that there was considerable reading of the *Daily Worker*."

Before this same Senate subcommittee, Crouch testified that he had asked Myles Horton to become a member of the Communist Party, and that Horton replied, "I am doing you just as much good now as I would if I were a member of the Communist Party. I am often asked if I am a Communist Party member and I always say 'no.' I feel much safer in having no fear that evidence might be uncovered to link me with the Communist Party."

Asked by Senator James Eastland about Highlander official James Dombrowski, Crouch replied, "I have met officially with him on a number of occasions as head of the Communist district bureau of Tennessee . . . at this conference Mr. Dombrowski gave me the impression of being completely pro-Communist and anxious to collaborate with the Communist Party and follow its leadership, without taking the risk of actual Party membership." Called before this same Senate subcommittee, Dombrowski denied that he had ever been a member of the Communist Party, but he freely acknowledged signing a petition which called for amnesty for the top Communist leaders convicted under the Smith Act. He added, "I make no apologies for that."

On the board of directors of Highlander Folk School was Aubrey Williams. In a speech at Madison Square Garden in 1947, Williams had this to say of the government's loyalty program:

What they demand is that any man who admits to being a member of the Communist Party be fired immediately on the grounds that no man can be loyal to the United States and be a Communist. It is my belief that it is precisely at this point that we take our stand and defend the right of any Communist to maintain his position as an employee of the government of the United States. To take any less position than this is to throw overboard such primary rights as the freedom to think and to hold whatever beliefs one chooses.

Eight years later, Williams' name was attached to a brief *amici curiae* on behalf of the Communist Party at the October, 1955 Term of the U. S. Supreme Court.

All of these facts—including the hearings before the Senate Subcommittee on Internal Security—were matters of public information *before* Martin Luther King attended that Labor Day weekend seminar at the Highlander Folk School in 1957.

At this point, a word of caution is in order. The Highlander Folk School was never cited as subversive by any Federal authority, and undoubtedly many who attended its courses, and later took up the cudgels in a rather mindless defense of it, were non-Communists. The issue was not whether Highlander was an out-and-out Communist training school. What was at issue was whether Highlander, under the pleasant guise of a meeting place for integrationists, had allowed itself to be infiltrated, if not used, by members of the Communist Party, and all this with the knowledge and cooperation of top officials in the school.

Certainly a sizable number of those who participated in that Labor Day weekend seminar at Highlander were not members of the Communist Party. But, mixed in with these non-Communists were a number of well-known fellow travellers. And the gentleman sitting next to Martin Luther King in that now-famous photo was Abner W. Berry, a high-ranking leader of the Communist Party, and for years a feature writer for the *Daily Worker*. Writing in the *Worker*, Berry left no doubt as to the reason he, a veteran Communist, had come to Highlander. In his words:

Here for four days, Negro and white leaders of the South, representing millions of Southerners, had the precious communications established with each other that had been disconnected during the past few years.

Berry wrote in the *Daily Worker* that Aubrey Williams spoke "prophetically" when he stated that from what was then taking place in the South, it was "only a short step to general violence" and that "the stuff out of which rebellions are made" was definitely being planted.

It was in this atmosphere that Martin Luther King was one of the two featured speakers at the closing session of the Highlander Folk School seminar.

Later, King would make light of his attendance at this meeting. He said he had been at the school only once, and then for only an hour. "If I was trained there," he said, "it was mighty short training."

But King's interest in and support of Highlander Folk School did not end with his speech at the seminar. In its 27th Annual Report, Highlander quoted, with obvious relish, King's high praise for its workshops. Said King: "You have given the South some of its most responsible leaders in this great period of transition." In 1961, King's Southern Christian Leadership Conference and the Highlander Folk School joined forces to train Negro leaders for the civil rights struggle. And one of the South's most liberal newspapers, the Atlanta *Constitution*, revealed that King's own program director, the Reverend Andrew Young, had received training at Highlander. This same newspaper also disclosed that Highlander School had received support from the International Union of Mine, Mill and Smelter Workers, a union which had been found by the Subversive Activities Control Board to be Communist-infiltrated.

On February 16, 1960, Tennessee Circuit Judge Chester C. Chattin revoked the charter of the Highlander Folk School, but not on grounds of subversive activity. The three grounds cited for closing the school were: that Myles Horton had operated it for private gain; that intoxicating beverages had been sold on the premises; and that Tennessee's segregation laws "as applied to private schools" were constitutional and valid. An appeal was taken to the Tennessee

Supreme Court, which upheld the revocation of charter on the first two grounds. In October, 1961, the U.S. Supreme Court denied a hearing to Highlander, so the school was compelled to give up its charter. But almost at the same time, like phoenix rising out of the ashes, the school reported that a state charter had been granted to the Highlander Research and Education Center, with headquarters in Knoxville, where it is still very much in business today, with Myles Horton still officiating as its president.

In February, 1968, the Highlander Research and Education Center was able to boast that "six of seven Mississippi Freedom Democratic Party candidates elected to office in Mississippi and twelve of fifteen of the regular Democrats, were in Highlander Candidate Training Workshops." And Stokely Carmichael, who rarely has a good word for Whitey these days, fairly gushes with admiration for Myles Horton. Carmichael said that he had been taught the black power concept by Myles Horton. The SNCC leader has recalled, "I used to think the way to fight discrimination was with love, until Myles taught me you need power, not love."

Today, while conservative organizations struggle for a favorable Internal Revenue Service ruling, the Highlander Research and Education Center is gloriously tax-exempt, and has been since 1961. One of Highlander's admirers has breathlessly reported, "Many tapes of Highlander workshops over the years are currently being transcribed for the archives of the state of Tennessee, where they will be available to scholars of the future."

It is, of course, too much to hope that the archives of the state of Tennessee will also include for "scholars of the future" a transcript of ex-Communist official Paul Crouch's sworn testimony that the old Highlander Folk School "is a school operated at Monteagle, Tenn., ostensibly as an independent labor school, but actually working in close cooperation with the Communist Party."

Sources:

Senate Internal Security Subcommittee, *Southern Conference Educational Fund, Inc.*, March 18, 19, and 20, 1954.

Daily Worker, September 10, 1957, p. 5.

New York Times, March 23, 1965, p. 28.

"27th Annual Highlander Report," Oct. 1, 1958–September 30, 1959.

New York Times, February 23, 1961, p. 28.

Congressional Record, August 2, 1963, p. 13972.

New York Times, February 17, 1960, p. 20.

New York Times, April 6, 1961, p. 39.

New York Times, October 10, 1961, p. 85.

Letter from Highlander, addressed to "Dear Friend of Highlander," signed by C. Conrad Browne, Executive Vice President, and dated February 9, 1968.

National Review, September 20, 1966, pp. 914 and 915.

Highlander News (undated, but received in 1968).

Notes

CHAPTER ONE A BULLET IN MEMPHIS

1. New York *Times*, December 5, 1967, p. 1. Also see New York *Times*, March 31, 1968, Magazine Section, p. 30.
2. *Look*, April 16, 1968, p. 25.
3. New York *Times*, March 31, 1968, Magazine Section, p. 30.
4. *Amsterdam News*, January 27, 1968, p. 21.
5. *Look*, op. cit., p. 24.
6. Ibid.
7. Ibid., p. 25.
8. Ibid., p. 24.
9. New York *Times*, August 30, 1964, Magazine Section, p. 62.
10. *Look*, op. cit., p. 24.
11. New York *Times*, March 31, 1968, Magazine Section, p. 60.
12. Ibid.
13. *Amsterdam News*, March 9, 1968, p. 3.
14. New York *Times*, December 5, 1967, p. 1.
15. Ibid., p. 32.
16. *Amsterdam News*, March 9, 1968, p. 2.
17. Ibid.
18. *Human Events*, January 20, 1968, p. 35.
19. New York *Times*, March 31, 1968, Magazine Section, p. 67.
20. New York *Times*, March 20, 1968, p. 43.
21. Ibid.
22. New York *Times*, March 27, 1968, p. 24.
23. *Newark Evening News*, March 28, 1968, p. 18.
24. *Christianity and Crisis*, January 22, 1968, p. 324 ff.
25. *What Manner of Man*, by Lerone Bennett, Jr. (Chicago: Johnson Publishing Co., 1964), p. 210.
26. *U.S. News & World Report*, December 25, 1967, p. 32 ff.
27. New York *Times*, August 29, 1967, p. 12.
28. New York *Times*, March 4, 1968, p. 29.
29. Ibid.
30. Ibid.
31. Ibid.
32. New York *Times*, March 31, 1968, Magazine Section, p. 58.
33. Ibid., p. 64.
34. *Look*, op. cit., p. 25.
35. Ibid.
36. Ibid.
37. Ibid.
38. New York *Times*, March 31, 1968, Magazine Section, pp. 57 and 58.

39. Ibid., p. 62.
40. *Amsterdam News*, April 6, 1968, p. 14.
41. Ibid.
42. New York *Times*, April 7, 1968, p. 65.
43. Ibid.
44. New York *Times*, April 17, 1968, p. 24.
45. New York *Times*, March 7, 1968, p. 33.
46. Ibid.
47. Ibid.
48. Ibid.
49. Ibid.
50. Ibid.
51. New York *Times*, March 29, 1968, p. 1.
52. Ibid.
53. New York *Times*, March 31, 1968, News of the Week in Review, p. 2E.
54. Ibid.
55. Ibid.
56. Ibid.
57. Ibid.
58. Ibid.
59. New York *Times*, March 29, 1968, p. 29.
60. Ibid., p. 1.
61. New York *Times*, March 31, 1968, News of the Week in Review, p. 2E.
62. Ibid.
63. New York *Times*, April 4, 1968, p. 30.
64. Ibid.
65. Ibid.
66. New York *Times*, April 5, 1968, p. 24.
67. Ibid.
68. New York *Times*, September 21, 1958, p. 1.
69. *Amsterdam News*, April 13, 1958, p. 37.
70. New York *Times*, September 21, 1958, p. 40.
71. Ibid. Also see New York *Times*, October 25, 1958, p. 8.
72. New York *Times*, April 5, 1968, p. 26.
73. New York *Times*, April 5, 1968, pp. 1 and 24.
74. Ibid.
75. Ibid.
76. Ibid.
77. Ibid.
78. Ibid.
79. Ibid.
80. Ibid.
81. *U.S. News & World Report*, April 22, 1968, p. 32.
82. Ibid., p. 29.
83. New York *Times*, April 7, 1968, p. 62.
84. *U.S. News & World Report*, April 22, 1968, p. 29.
85. Ibid.
86. New York *Times*, April 6, 1968, p. 22.
87. *U.S. News & World Report*, April 22, 1968, p. 50.
88. New York *Times*, April 6, 1968, p. 22.
89. *U.S. News & World Report*, April 22, 1968, p. 29.

90. New York *Times*, April 6, 1968, p. 23.
91. *U.S. News & World Report*, April 22, 1968, p. 29.
92. New York *Times*, April 6, 1968, p. 1.
93. *U.S. News & World Report*, April 22, 1968, p. 29.
94. New York *Times*, April 6, 1968, p. 1.
95. New York *Times*, April 6, 1968, p. 23.
96. *U.S. News & World Report*, April 22, 1968, p. 32.
97. Ibid., p. 33.
98. *Human Events*, April 27, 1968, p. 2.
99. New York *Times*, April 8, 1968, p. 33.
100. *U.S. News & World Report*, April 22, 1968, p. 29.
101. Ibid., p. 28.
102. New York *Times*, March 31, 1968, News of the Week in Review, p. 2E.
103. New York *Times*, April 6, 1968, p. 28.
104. Ibid.
105. Ibid.
106. Ibid.
107. Ibid.
108. New York *Times*, April 9, 1968, p. 37.
109. New York *Times*, April 6, 1968, p. 28.
110. Ibid.
111. New York *Times*, April 6, 1968, pp. 1 and 23.
112. Ibid.
113. New York *Times*, April 6, 1968, p. 27.
114. New York *Times*, April 5, 1968, p. 26.
115. Ibid.
116. New York *Times*, April 8, 1968, p. 34.
117. New York *Times*, April 6, 1968, p. 28.
118. New York *Times*, April 9, 1968, p. 38.
119. New York *Times*, April 9, 1968, p. 37.
120. New York *Times*, April 8, 1968, p. 34.
121. New York *Times*, April 5, 1968, p. 26.
122. New York *Times*, April 9, 1968, p. 35.
123. New York *Times*, April 5, 1968, p. 1.
124. Ibid.
125. Ibid., p. 26.
126. Ibid.
127. New York *Times*, April 8, 1968, p. 33.
128. Ibid.
129. *Amsterdam News*, April 13, 1968, p. 49.
130. New York *Times*, April 9, 1968, p. 1.
131. Ibid., p. 34.
132. Ibid.
133. New York *Times*, April 8, 1968, p. 1.
134. Ibid., p. 32.
135. Ibid.
136. Ibid.
137. Ibid.
138. Ibid.
139. New York *Times*, April 6, 1968, p. 23.
140. Ibid., p. 1.
141. Ibid.

142. Ibid.
143. Ibid., p. 23.
144. Ibid.
145. Ibid.
146. Ibid.
147. New York *Times*, April 7, 1968, Main Section, p. 63.
148. New York *Times*, April 8, 1968, pp. 1 and 30.
149. Ibid., p. 30.
150. New York *Times*, April 9, 1968, p. 36.
151. New York *Times*, April 8, 1968, p. 30.
152. New York *Times*, April 9, 1968, p. 36.
153. Ibid.
154. New York *Times*, April 8, 1968, p. 1.
155. Ibid., p. 31.
156. Ibid., p. 1.
157. New York *Times*, April 9, 1968, p. 36.
158. Ibid., p. 1.
159. Ibid., p. 36.
160. Ibid.
161. New York *Times*, April 12, 1968, p. 20.
162. New York *Times*, April 8, 1968, p. 31.
163. "Maryland Affairs" column by Richard Homan, *Washington Post*,
     April 16, 1968.
164. New York *Times*, April 12, 1968, p. 20.
165. "Maryland Affairs" column by Richard Homan, *Washington Post*,
     April 16, 1968.
166. New York *Times*, April 12, 1968, p. 20.
167. "Maryland Affairs" column by Richard Homan, *Washington Post*,
     April 16, 1968.
168. Ibid
169. Ibid.
170. New York *Times*, April 10, 1968, p. 1.
171. Ibid.
172. New York *Times*, April 10, 1968, pp. 1, 33, 34.
173. Ibid., p. 33.
174. Ibid.
175. Ibid., p. 95.
176. Ibid., p. 32.
177. Ibid.
178. Ibid.
179. Ibid.
180. Ibid., p. 33.
181. New York *Times*, April 9, 1968, pp. 1 and 35.
182. A copy of this memo is in the author's possession.
183. *Amsterdam News*, April 13, 1968, p. 27.
184. Ibid.
185. New York *Times*, April 10, 1968, p. 36.
186. New York *Times*, April 9, 1968, p. 35.
187. New York *Times*, April 10, 1968, p. 38.
188. New York *Times*, April 10, 1968, p. 35.
189. *U.S. News & World Report*, April 29, 1968, p. 44.
190. *U.S. News & World Report*, April 22, 1968, p. 12.
191. New York *Times*, April 6, 1968, p. 25.

192. Ibid.
193. New York *Times*, April 11, 1968, p. 1.
194. Ibid.
195. New York *Times*, April 12, 1968, p. 18. Also *U.S. News & World Report*, April 22, 1968, p. 10.
196. New York *Times*, April 11, 1968, p. 35. Also see New York *Times*, April 12, 1968, p. 19.
197. Ibid.
198. New York *Times*, April 18, 1968, p. 1.
199. Ibid.
200. Ibid
201. Ibid.
202. New York *Times*, April 20, 1968, p. 1.
203. Ibid.
204. New York *Times*, April 20, 1968, p. 31.
205. Ibid.
206. Ibid.
207. New York *Times*, April 23, 1968, p. 33.
208. New York *Times*, April 24, 1968, p. 31.
209. New York *Times*, April 26, 1968, p. 22.
210. New York *Times*, April 28, 1968, Main Section, p. 45.
211. New York *Times*, April 11, 1968, p. 34.
212. New York *Times*, April 19, 1968, p. 8.
213. *Look*, April 16, 1968, p. 24.

CHAPTER TWO   TO PRISON, WITH LOVE

1. Lerone Bennett, Jr., *What Manner of Man* (Chicago: Johnson Publishing Co., 1964), pp. 33–34.
2. Ibid., p. 74.
3. Martin Luther King, Jr., *Stride Toward Freedom* (New York: Harper & Brothers, 1958), p. 102.
4. New York *Times*, Magazine Section, August 25, 1963, p. 9.
5. *Saturday Review*, April 3, 1965, p. 16.
6. *Stride Toward Freedom*, op. cit., p. 85.
7. New York *Times*, July 9, 1961, Magazine Section, p. 45.
8. New York *Times*, November 27, 1960, p. 95.
9. New York *Times*, January 22, 1961, Magazine Section, p. 72.
10. New York *Times*, November 27, 1960, p. 95.
11. New York *Times*, January 22, 1961, Magazine Section, p. 72.
12. New York *Times*, September 10, 1961, Magazine Section, p. 119.
13. Ibid.
14. See the New York *Times*, May 17, 1963, p. 10.
15. Ibid.
16. *New Yorker*, May 1, 1965, p. 35.
17. Ibid.
18. Ibid., p. 36.
19. *Vital Speeches*, October 1, 1964, p. 768.
20. Ibid., p. 767.
21. Ibid., p. 768.
22. Ibid., p. 767.

23. Ibid.
24. Ibid., p. 768.
25. Ibid.
26. New York *Times*, July 30, 1964, p. 1.
27. *Vital Speeches*, op. cit., p. 768.
28. New York *Times*, May 8, 1963, pp. 1, 28.
29. New York *Times*, July 9, 1961, Magazine Section, p. 8.
30. *Stride Toward Freedom*, op. cit., pp. 211–212.
31. Ibid., p. 212.
32. Ibid.
33. Ibid., p. 213
34. Ibid., pp. 102–103.
35. Ibid., p. 103.
36. Ibid., p. 217.
37. New York *Times*, September 13, 1964, p. 66.
38. *Stride Toward Freedom*, op. cit., p. 174.
39. *Saturday Evening Post*, November 7, 1964, p. 10.
40. *What Manner of Man*, op. cit., p. 206.
41. Ibid., p. 210.
42. New York *Times*, August 5, 1962, Magazine Section, p. 52.
43. *What Manner of Man*, op. cit., Appendix.
44. Ibid.
45. Ibid.
46. *Stride Toward Freedom*, op. cit., p. 216.
47. Ibid., p. 103.
48. New York *Times*, April 17, 1960, p. 32.
49. Quoted in *National Review*, July 14, 1964, p. 580.
50. *The Nation*, March 3, 1962, p. 191.
51. New York *Times*, September 10, 1961, Magazine Section, p. 25.
52. Ibid., p. 118.
53. *Vital Speeches*, November 15, 1965, p. 74.
54. *Vital Speeches*, March 15, 1967, p. 327.
55. *Stride Toward Freedom*, op. cit., pp. 219–220.

CHAPTER THREE   THE MONTGOMERY BUS BOYCOTT

1. *What Manner of Man*, op. cit., p. 77.
2. *Stride Toward Freedom*, op. cit., p. 43.
3. New York *Times*, March 4, 1956, News of the Week in Review, p. 6E.
4. Ibid., p. 41.
5. Ibid., p. 40.
6. Ibid., pp. 40–41.
7. Ibid., p. 148.
8. Ibid.
9. Ibid., p. 47.
10. Ibid., p. 48.
11. Ibid., p. 49.
12. Ibid.
13. Ibid.
14. Ibid.

15. New York *Times*, March 4, 1956, News of the Week in Review, p. 6E.
16. *Stride Toward Freedom*, op. cit., p. 52.
17. Ibid., pp. 63–64.
18. Ibid., p. 64.
19. Ibid., p. 75.
20. Ibid.
21. New York *Times*, December 16, 1956, Magazine Section, p. 48.
22. Ibid.
23. Ibid.
24. New York *Times*, March 4, 1956, News of the Week in Review, p. 6E.
25. Ibid.
26. New York *Times*, December 16, 1956, Magazine Section, p. 8.
27. Ibid.
28. Ibid.
29. *Stride Toward Freedom*, op. cit., p. 77.
30. New York *Times*, December 16, 1956, Magazine Section, p. 8.
31. New York *Times*, March 4, 1956, News of the Week in Review, p. 6E.
32. New York *Times*, April 3, 1956, p. 21.
33. New York *Times*, December 22, 1956, p. 18.
34. New York *Times*, March 21, 1956, p. 28.
35. *Stride Toward Freedom*, op. cit., p. 80.
36. Ibid.
37. Ibid.
38. Ibid.
39. Ibid.
40. Ibid.
41. New York *Times*, December 16, 1956, Magazine Section, p. 8.
42. New York *Times*, April 3, 1956, p. 21.
43. New York *Times*, December 16, 1956, Magazine Section, p. 8.
44. Ibid.
45. Ibid.
46. Ibid.
47. Ibid., p. 48.
48. *Stride Toward Freedom*, op. cit., p. 135.
49. Ibid., p. 140.
50. Ibid.
51. Ibid.
52. New York *Times*, December 16, 1956, Magazine Section, p. 50.
53. Ibid.
54. *Stride Toward Freedom*, op. cit., p. 122.
55. Ibid., p. 126.
56. Ibid.
57. Ibid., pp. 127–128.
58. Ibid., p. 130.
59. Ibid., pp. 55 and 72.
60. New York *Times*, August 7, 1956, p. 18.
61. Ibid.
62. Ibid.
63. Ibid.
64. Ibid.

65. New York *Times*, September 18, 1956, p. 13.
66. Ibid.
67. New York *Times*, September 20, 1956, p. 14.
68. *Stride Toward Freedom*, op. cit., p. 225.
69. New York *Times*, September 22, 1956, p. 38.
70. New York *Times*, October 27, 1956, p. 10.
71. New York *Times*, June 24, 1957, p. 6.
72. New York *Times*, May 5, 1966, p. 30.
73. *Stride Toward Freedom*, op. cit., p. 151.
74. Ibid., p. 152.
75. Ibid., p. 153.
76. Ibid., p. 142.
77. Ibid.
78. Ibid., p. 146.
79. Ibid.
80. Ibid., p. 147.
81. Ibid.
82. Ibid.
83. Ibid., p. 148.
84. Ibid., pp. 148–9.
85. Ibid., p. 149.
86. New York *Times*, October 14, 1956, Main Section, p. 51.
87. *Stride Toward Freedom*, op. cit., p. 160.
88. New York *Times*, December 16, 1956, Magazine Section, p. 48.
89. New York *Times*, December 22, 1956, pp. 1 and 11.
90. New York *Times*, December 24, 1956, p. 6.
91. New York *Times*, December 27, 1956, p. 1.
92. New York *Times*, December 29, 1956, p. 1.
93. Ibid.
94. New York *Times*, December 30, 1956, p. 1.
95. New York *Times*, January 1, 1957, p. 15.
96. New York *Times*, January 3 ,1957, p. 27.
97. New York *Times*, January 10, 1957, p. 24.
98. New York *Times*, January 11, 1957, p. 1.
99. Ibid.
100. *Time*, January 21, 1957, p. 15.
101. *Stride Toward Freedom*, op. cit., p. 179.
102. New York *Times*, January 12, 1957, p. 38.
103. New York *Times*, January 14, 1957, p. 14.
104. New York *Times*, January 17, 1957, p. 25.
105. New York *Times*, February 28, 1957, p. 14.
106. New York *Times*, February 2, 1958, p. 65.
107. New York *Times*, December 7, 1958, Main Section, p. 59.
108. *What Manner of Man*, op. cit., p. 77.
109. Ibid., p. 210.
110. Ibid., pp. 97 and 98.
111. New York *Times*, December 7, 1958, p. 59.

CHAPTER FOUR 1962: CHECKMATE IN ALBANY, GEORGIA

1. *U.S. News & World Report*, September 3, 1962, p. 44.
2. Ibid., pp. 44 and 45.

3. Ibid., p. 45.
4. New York *Times*, August 13, 1962, p. 13.
5. *Saturday Evening Post*, June 15, 1963, p. 18.
6. Ibid.
7. *U.S. News & World Report*, op. cit., p. 43.
8. Ibid., p. 46.
9. Ibid., p. 43.
10. *Stride Toward Freedom*, op. cit., p. 150.
11. New York *Times*, July 30, 1963, News of the Week in Review, p. 5E.
12. New York *Times*, December 24, 1961, News of the Week in Review, p. 5E.
13. *SNCC: The New Abolitionists*, by Howard Zinn (Boston: Beacon Press, 1964), p. 126.
14. Ibid., p. 127.
15. Ibid., pp. 127–8.
16. Ibid., p. 128.
17. Ibid., pp. 129 and 130.
18. Ibid., p. 130.
19. Ibid.
20. Ibid.
21. Ibid.
22. Ibid.
23. Ibid., pp. 130 and 131.
24. New York *Times*, December 17, 1961, pp. 1 and 46.
25. Ibid., p. 46.
26. New York *Times*, December 18, 1961, pp. 1 and 31.
27. Ibid., p. 1.
28. Ibid., p. 31.
29. Ibid.
30. Ibid.
31. New York *Times*, December 24, 1961, News of the Week in Review, p. 5E.
32. New York *Times*, December 19, 1961, p. 1.
33. Ibid., p. 24.
34. Ibid.
35. Ibid.
36. Ibid., pp. 1 and 24.
37. Ibid., p. 24.
38. Ibid.
39. New York *Times*, January 28, 1962, p. 65.
40. Ibid.
41. Ibid.
42. New York *Times*, January 31, 1962, p. 19.
43. New York *Times*, February 3, 1962, p. 9.
44. New York *Times*, February 4, 1962, p. 74.
45. Ibid.
46. Ibid.
47. Ibid.
48. New York *Times*, March 3, 1962, p. 22.
49. Ibid. Also see New York *Times*, March 8, 1962, p. 17.
50. New York *Times*, August 18, 1962, p. 44.
51. Ibid.
52. New York *Times*, May 29, 1965, p. 10.

53. New York *Times*, February 4, 1962, p. 74.
54. Ibid.
55. *Wall Street Journal*, September 6, 1962, p. 1.
56. Ibid., p. 16.
57. Ibid., p. 1.
58. *Saturday Evening Post*, June 15, 1963, p. 18.
59. New York *Times*, August 18, 1962, p. 44.
60. Ibid.
61. New York *Times*, July 11, 1962, p. 1.
62. Ibid.
63. New York *Times*, July 12, 1962, pp. 1 and 18.
64. Ibid., p. 18.
65. New York *Times*, July 13, 1962, p. 10.
66. Ibid.
67. *Congressional Record*, July 20, 1962, p. 14247.
68. New York *Times*, July 18, 1962, p. 30.
69. New York *Times*, July 22, 1962, p. 1.
70. New York *Times*, July 23, 1962, p. 13.
71. New York *Times*, July 25, 1962, pp. 1 and 22.
72. New York *Times*, July 26, 1962, p. 13.
73. Ibid.
74. Ibid.
75. New York *Times*, July 28, 1962, p. 1.
76. Ibid.
77. New York *Times*, August 10, 1962, p. 6.
78. New York *Times*, August 5, 1962, News of the Week in Review, p. E5.
79. New York *Times*, August 4, 1962, p. 11. Also see New York *Times*, August 16, 1962, p. 18.
80. New York *Times*, August 11, 1962, pp. 1 and 41.
81. Ibid., p. 41.
82. Ibid.
83. New York *Times*, August 12, 1962, p. 1.
84. Ibid.
85. New York *Times*, August 15, 1962, p. 34.
86. New York *Times*, September 1, 1962, p. 20.
87. New York *Times*, (Western Edition), March 14, 1963, p. 7.
88. Ibid.
89. Ibid.
90. Ibid.
91. New York *Times*, June 16, 1963, News of the Week in Review, p. E3.
92. *What Manner of Man*, op. cit., p. 130.
93. *Saturday Evening Post*, June 15, 1963, p. 18.
94. *Look*, November 17, 1964, p. 64.
95. New York *Times*, August 10, 1963, p. 1.
96. Ibid.
97. Ibid., p. 7.
98. Ibid.
99. New York *Times*, December 24, 1963, p. 38.
100. New York *Times*, July 22, 1966, p. 35.
101. Ibid.
102. Ibid.

103. Ibid.
104. Ibid.
105. New York *Times*, August 10, 1963, p. 7.
106. New York *Times*, January 24, 1965, p. 39.

CHAPTER FIVE   1963: WAR IN BIRMINGHAM,
                AND THE CIVIL RIGHTS ACT

1. *What Manner of Man*, op. cit., p. 132.
2. New York *Times*, September 22, 1963, News of the Week in Review, p. E3.
3. *Time*, September 27, 1963, p. 18.
4. *U.S. News & World Report*, September 30, 1963, p. 39.
5. New York *Times*, May 20, 1963, p. 21.
6. New York *Times*, May 26, 1961, p. 32.
7. *Why We Can't Wait*, by Martin Luther King, Jr. (New York: Harper & Row) 1963, 1964), p. 103.
8. Ibid., p. 102.
9. *Why We Can't Wait*, op. cit., p. 104.
10. Ibid., p. 102.
11. New York *Times*, May 11, 1963, p. 24.
12. New York *Times*, May 20, 1963, p. 21.
13. *What Manner of Man*, op. cit., p. 151.
14. New York *Times*, May 11, 1963, p. 8.
15. New York *Times*, April 11, 1963, p. 21.
16. *The Nation*, March 9, 1964, p. 231.
17. *Editor and Publisher*, May 18, 1963, p. 12.
18. Ibid.
19. Ibid. Also see New York *Times*, April 17, 1963, p. 22.
20. New York *Times*, April 17, 1963, p. 22.
21. *Editor and Publisher*, op. cit., p. 12.
22. New York *Times*, April 16, 1963, pp. 1 and 17.
23. Ibid.
24. New York *Times*, May 9, 1963, p. 17.
25. *Why We Can't Wait*, op. cit., p. 49.
26. Ibid.
27. Ibid., p. 50.
28. Ibid., p. 51.
29. *Saturday Evening Post*, June 15, 1963, p. 16.
30. New York *Times*, April 6, 1963, p. 20.
31. New York *Times*, April 9, 1963, p. 53.
32. New York *Times*, April 13, 1963, pp. 1 and 15.
33. *Why We Can't Wait*, op. cit., p. 45.
34. Ibid., pp. 45 and 46.
35. Ibid., p. 47.
36. Ibid.
37. Ibid., p. 51.
38. Ibid.
39. Ibid.
40. *What Manner of Man*, op. cit., p. 134.
41. New York *Times*, May 5, 1963, p. 82.

42. New York *Times*, November 7, 1963, p. 30.
43. *Public Papers of the Presidents of the United States: John F. Kennedy 1963* (Washington, D.C.: U.S. Government Printing Office, 1964), pp. 483–484.
44. Ibid., p. 484.
45. *What Manner of Man*, op. cit., p. 151.
46. Ibid., p. 132.
47. New York *Times*, April 7, 1963, p. 55.
48. New York *Times*, April 6, 1963, p. 20.
49. New York *Times*, April 7, 1963, p. 55.
50. Ibid.
51. New York *Times*, May 26, 1963, p. 58.
52. New York *Times*, April 11, 1963, p. 21.
53. New York *Times*, April 12, 1963, p. 1.
54. Ibid.
55. New York *Times*, April 13, 1963, p. 1.
56. Ibid., p. 15.
57. New York *Times*, April 14, 1963, p. 46.
58. Ibid.
59. Ibid.
60. Ibid.
61. Ibid.
62. *Why We Can't Wait*, op. cit., p. 82.
63. Ibid.
64. Ibid., p. 87.
65. Ibid., p. 91.
66. Ibid., p. 93.
67. Ibid.
68. Ibid.
69. *Saturday Evening Post*, June 15, 1963, p. 19.
70. New York *Times*, April 15, 1963, p. 1.
71. New York *Times*, April 21, 1963, p. 70.
72. Ibid.
73. New York *Times*, April 27, 1963, p. 9.
74. Ibid.
75. New York *Times*, May 1, 1963, p. 26.
76. Ibid.
77. New York *Times*, May 3, 1963, p. 1.
78. New York *Times*, May 4, 1963, p. 8.
79. Ibid.
80. Ibid.
81. New York *Post*, September 7, 1967, p. 14.
82. Ibid.
83. New York *Times*, May 4, 1963, p. 1.
84. Ibid., p. 8.
85. New York *Times*, May 5, 1963, pp. 1 and 82.
86. Ibid.
87. Ibid., p. 82.
88. Ibid.
89. Ibid.
90. New York *Times*, May 7, 1963, pp. 1 and 33.
91. New York *Times*, May 8, 1963, p. 1.
92. Ibid., p. 28.

93. Ibid.
94. New York *Herald Tribune*, May 9, 1963, p. 24.
95. New York *Times*, May 11, 1963, p. 1.
96. New York *Times*, May 16, 1963, pp. 1 and 22.
97. New York *Times*, May 11, 1963, p. 9.
98. Ibid.
99. New York *Times*, August 3, 1963, p. 18.
100. *Why We Can't Wait*, op. cit., p. 52.
101. New York *Times*, May 10, 1963, p. 14.
102. New York *Times*, August 3, 1963, p. 18.
103. Ibid.
104. Ibid.
105. New York *Times*, October 17, 1965, p. 79.
106. New York *Times*, May 13, 1963, p. 1.
107. New York *Times*, May 13, 1963, pp. 1 and 24.
108. New York *Times*, July 22, 1963, p. 16.
109. New York *Times*, May 13, 1963, p. 24.
110. Ibid., p. 1.
111. New York *Times*, May 14, 1963, p. 27.
112. Ibid., p. 26.
113. New York *Times*, May 17, 1963, p. 14.
114. New York *Times*, May 15, 1963, p. 26.
115. Ibid.
116. New York *Times*, May 16, 1963, p. 1.
117. New York *Times*, May 19, 1963, News of the Week in Review, p. 10E.
118. New York *Times*, May 21, 1963, pp. 1 and 18.
119. New York *Times*, May 21, 1963, p. 1.
120. New York *Times*, May 23, 1963, pp. 1 and 19.
121. New York *Times*, May 24, 1963, p. 1.
122. New York *Times*, May 24, 1963, p. 30.
123. New York *Times*, May 26, 1963, pp. 1 and 59. Also see New York *Times*, June 7, 1963, p. 30.
124. New York *Times*, June 15, 1963, p. 22.
125. New York *Times*, July 30, 1964, p. 12.
126. New York *Times*, November 13, 1964, p. 23.
127. New York *Times*, March 6, 1964, p. 27.
128. *What Manner of Man*, op. cit., p. 78.
129. *Negro Digest*, May 1964, p. 46.
130. New York *Times*, May 26, 1963, p. 59.
131. *Vital Speeches*, July 1, 1963, p. 547.
132. *Public Papers of the Presidents of the United States*, op. cit., p. 484.
133. Ibid., p. 486.
134. New York *Times*, June 11, 1963, p. 36.
135. New York *Times*, July 17, 1963, p. 14.
136. Ibid.
137. New York *Times*, July 22, 1963, p. 16.
138. Ibid., p. 1.
139. New York *Times*, July 24, 1963, p. 17.
140. New York *Times*, August 11, 1963, News of the Week in Review, p. 8E.
141. *Wall Street Journal*, July 16, 1963, p. 10.

142. New York *Times*, September 1, 1963, Main Section, p. 40.
143. New York *Times*, September 22, 1963, News of the Week in Review, p. 1E.
144. New York *Times*, September 8, 1963, News of the Week in Review, p. 1E.
145. Quoted in New York *Times*, ibid., p. 11E.
146. New York *Times*, September 22, 1963, News of the Week in Review, p. 1E.
147. New York *Times*, September 16, 1963, p. 1.
148. *Time*, September 27, 1963, p. 17.
149. New York *Times*, September 16, 1963, p. 1.
150. New York *Times*, September 17, 1963, p. 1.
151. *Time*, September 27, 1963, pp. 17 and 18.
152. *U.S. News & World Report*, September 30, 1963, p. 40.
153. New York *Times*, September 29, 1963, News of the Week in Review, p. 11E.
154. New York *Times*, September 22, 1963, pp. 1 and 72.
155. New York *Times*, September 26, 1963, p. 29.
156. Ibid.
157. Ibid.
158. New York *Times*, October 5, 1963, p. 10.
159. Ibid.
160. New York *Times*, September 17, 1963, p. 25.
161. Ibid.
162. Ibid.
163. New York *Times*, September 20, 1963, p. 1.
164. New York *Times*, September 18, 1963, p. 27.
165. New York *Times*, September 28, 1963, p. 22.
166. New York *Times*, September 29, 1963, p. 79.
167. Ibid.
168. New York *Times*, October 6, 1963, News of the Week in Review, p. 5E.
169. New York *Times*, October 7, 1963, p. 36.
170. *United Press International* dispatch, March 31, 1966.
171. New York *Times*, March 16, 1964, p. 25.
172. New York *Times*, August 29, 1963, p. 16.
173. Ibid.
174. New York *Times*, June 5, 1964, p. 1.
175. Ibid.
176. New York *Times*, June 20, 1964, p. 10.
177. New York *Times*, July 3, 1964, p. 1.

CHAPTER SIX   1965: WAR IN SELMA,
              AND THE VOTING RIGHTS ACT

1. *What Manner of Man*, op. cit., p. 87.
2. *The Nation*, September 23, 1961, p. 178.
3. New York *Times*, June 26, 1961, p. 9.
4. Ibid.
5. New York *Times*, February 9, 1965, p. 17.
6. New York *Times*, February 10, 1965, p. 18.

7. Ibid.
8. New York *Times*, February 14, 1965, Section 4, p. 2E.
9. New York *Times*, October 13, 1963, Main Section, p. 77.
10. *SNCC: The New Abolitionists*, op. cit., p. 149.
11. Ibid.
12. Ibid.
13. Ibid.
14. Ibid., p. 163.
15. New York *Times*, October 8, 1963, p. 37.
16. New York *Times*, July 6, 1964, p. 19, and July 7, 1964, p. 20.
17. New York *Times*, May 13, 1963, p. 24.
18. New York *Times*, October 13, 1963, Main Section, p. 77.
19. New York *Times*, September 30, 1964, p. 22.
20. New York *Times*, November 6, 1964, p. 26.
21. New York *Times*, November 5, 1964, p. 33.
22. Ibid., p. 1.
23. Ibid., p. 33.
24. New York *Times*, February 14, 1965, News of the Week in Review, p. 5E.
25. *Saturday Review*, April 3, 1965, p. 16.
26. New York *Times*, January 3, 1965, p. 20.
27. Ibid.
28. New York *Times*, January 19, 1965, pp. 1 and 20.
29. New York *Times*, January 20, 1965, p. 18.
30. New York *Times*, January 21, 1965, p. 1.
31. New York *Times*, January 4, 1965, p. 58.
32. New York *Times*, February 14, 1965, News of the Week in Review, p. 5E.
33. New York *Times*, February 6, 1965, p. 10.
34. New York *Times*, January 20, 1965, p. 1.
35. New York *Times*, January 23, 1965, p. 18.
36. Ibid.
37. New York *Times*, January 24, 1965, p. 40.
38. New York *Times*, January 28, 1965, p. 15.
39. New York *Times*, January 29, 1965, p. 9.
40. New York *Times*, January 31, 1965, p. 55.
41. Ibid.
42. New York *Times*, January 31, 1965, p. 49.
43. New York *Times*, February 2, 1965, p. 1.
44. New York *Times*, February 5, 1965, p. 15.
45. New York *Times*, February 6, 1965, p. 10.
46. New York *Times*, February 3, 1965, pp. 1 and 23.
47. New York *Times*, February 6, 1965, p. 1.
48. Ibid.
49. New York *Times*, February 4, 1965, p. 22.
50. New York *Times*, February 13, 1965, p. 1.
51. New York *Times*, February 11, 1965, p. 1.
52. New York *Times*, February 12, 1965, p. 58.
53. New York *Times*, February 16, 1965, p. 18.
54. New York *Times*, February 17, 1965, p. 35.
55. New York *Times*, February 26, 1965, p. 14.
56. Ibid.

57. New York *Times*, February 21, 1965, p. 52.
58. New York *Times*, February 23, 1965, p. 16.
59. Ibid.
60. New York *Times*, February 24, 1965, p. 28.
61. Ibid.
62. Ibid.
63. New York *Times*, March 5, 1965, p. 29.
64. New York *Times*, March 7, 1965, p. 46.
65. New York *Times*, March 8, 1965, pp. 1 and 20.
66. New York *Times*, March 9, 1965, p. 23.
67. Ibid.
68. *Newsweek*, March 22, 1965, p. 18.
69. Quoted in *Time*, March 19, 1965, p. 71.
70. Ibid.
71. Ibid.
72. New York *Times*, March 9, 1965, p. 1.
73. New York *Times*, March 8, 1965, p. 1.
74. Ibid., pp. 1 and 20.
75. *Reader's Digest*, August, 1967, p. 128.
76. New York *Times*, March 8, 1965, p. 20.
77. Ibid.
78. Ibid.
79. Ibid.
80. New York *Times*, March 10, 1965, p. 1.
81. New York *Times*, March 10, 1965, p. 22.
82. Ibid.
83. Ibid.
84. *Congressional Record*, March 18, 1965, p. 5444.
85. Ibid., p. 5443
86. New York *Times*, March 10, 1965, pp. 1 and 22.
87. New York *Times*, March 10, 1965, p. 22.
88. Ibid.
89. Ibid.
90. Ibid.
91. Ibid.
92. Ibid.
93. Ibid.
94. Ibid.
95. New York *Times*, March 12, 1965, p. 1.
96. Ibid., p. 19.
97. Ibid., pp. 1 and 19
98. *Congressional Record*, March 17, 1965, p. 5303.
99. Ibid.
100. Ibid.
101. New York *Times*, March 10, 1965, p. 1. Also New York *Times*, March 12, 1965, p. 18.
102. New York *Times*, March 11, 1965, p. 1.
103. New York *Times*, March 12, 1965, p. 1.
104. Ibid., p. 18.
105. Ibid.
106. New York *Times*, March 14, 1965, p. 63.
107. Ibid., pp. 1 and 63.
108. New York *Times*, June 26, 1965, p. 13.

109. Ibid.
110. Ibid.
111. New York *Times*, March 21, 1965, News of the Week in Review, p. 7E.
112. Ibid.
113. New York *Times* Magazine, May 2, 1965, p. 54.
114. New York *Times*, March 24, 1965, p. 33.
115. Ibid.
116. Ibid.
117. New York *Times*, March 10, 1965, p. 23.
118. New York *Times*, March 16, 1965. p. 1.
119. New York *Times*, March 21, 1965, News of the Week in Review, p. 1E.
120. New York *Times*, March 17, 1965, p. 27.
121. New York *Times*, March 11, 1965, p. 1.
122. Ibid., p. 21.
123. New York *Times*, March 15, 1965, p. 1.
124. Ibid., p. 22.
125. New York *Times*, March 16, 1965, p. 31.
126. New York *Times*, March 17, 1965, p. 26.
127. Ibid.
128. New York *Times*, March 18, 1965, p. 1.
129. Ibid., p. 20.
130. Ibid.
131. Ibid.
132. New York *Times*, March 19, 1965, p. 20.
133. New York *Times*, March 21, 1965, News of the Week in Review, p. 1E.
134. Ibid.
135. New York *Times*, March 19, 1965, p. 20.
136. Ibid.
137. New York *Times*, March 21, 1965, p. 1.
138. New York *Times*, March 21, 1965, p. 76.
139. New York *Times*, April 4, 1965, Section IV, p. E7.
140. *Negro Digest*, July, 1967, pp. 64 and 67.
141. *Congressional Record*, March 29, 1965, pp. 6261–2.
142. New York *Times*, March 22, 1965, p. 1.
143. New York *Times*, March 22, 1965, p. 26.
144. Ibid.
145. New York *Times*, March 17, 1965. p. 28.
146. Ibid.
147. New York *Times*, March 28, 1965, News of the Week in Review, p. 6E.
148. New York *Times*, March 17, 1965, p. 28.
149. Ibid.
150. Ibid.
151. New York *Times*, March 22, 1965, p. 27.
152. New York *Times*, March 26, 1965, p. 1.
153. Ibid.
154. Ibid.
155. New York *Times*, March 19, 1965, p. 34.
156. New York *Times*, March 22, 1965, p. 27.
157. New York *Times*, March 22, 1965, p. 1.

158. Ibid.
159. Ibid.
160. New York *Times*, May 4, 1965, p. 58.
161. New York *Times*, March 26, 1965, p. 1.
162. Ibid.
163. New York *Times*, March 27, 1965, p. 1.
164. New York *Times*, April 4, 1965, p. 60.
165. New York *Times*, April 18, 1965, News of the Week in Review, p. 12E.
166. Ibid.
167. New York *Times*, March 27, 1965, pp. 1 and 10.
168. New York *Times*, March 27, 1965, p. 11.
169. New York *Times*, March 27, 1965, p. 1.
170. New York *Times*, Main Section, March 28, 1965, p. 58.
171. New York *Times*, April 15, 1965, p. 27.
172. New York *Times*, April 21, 1965, p. 1.
173. New York *Times*, May 5, 1965, p. 33.
174. New York *Times*, October 22, 1965, p. 28.
175. New York *Times*, May 6, 1965, p. 1.
176. New York *Times*, May 9, 1965, p. 41.
177. Ibid.
178. Ibid.
179. New York *Times*, October 23, 1965, p. 1.
180. New York *Times*, December 4, 1965, p. 35.
181. Ibid.
182. New York *Times*, December 4, 1965, pp. 1 and 35.
183. Ibid., p. 1.
184. New York *Times*, March 11, 1966, p. 18.
185. New York *Times*, October 21, 1966, p. 25.
186. New York *Times*, April 28, 1967. p. 30.
187. New York *Times*, August 8, 1967, p. 15.
188. New York *Times*, January 17, 1966, p. 17.
189. *National Review*, April 20, 1965, p. 325.
190. Ibid.
191. Ibid., p. 326.
192. Ibid.
193. Ibid., p. 324.
194. Ibid., p. 326.
195. Ibid.
196. Ibid.
197. New York *Times*, May 6, 1965, p. 24.
198. New York *Times*, March 27, 1965, p. 10.
199. *Time*, April 2, 1965, p. 21.
200. New York *Times*, March 29, 1965, p. 1.
201. Ibid.
202. Ibid.
203. New York *Times*, March 30, 1965, p. 46.
204. Ibid., pp. 1 and 28.
205. Ibid.
206. Ibid.
207. New York *Times*, March 31, 1965, p. 17.
208. *Negro Digest*, July, 1967, pp. 64 and 65.
209. New York *Times*, March 23, 1965, p. 28.

210. New York *Times*, June 6, 1965, p. 52.
211. Ibid.
212. *U.S. News & World Report*, April 5, 1965, p. 38.
213. New York *Herald Tribune*, May 27, 1965, p. 22.
214. New York *Times*, May 12, 1965, p. 1.
215. *Congressional Record*, August 4, 1965, p. 19444.
216. Ibid.
217. Ibid.
218. Ibid., p. 19445.
219. Ibid.
220. New York *Times*, April 18, 1965, Magazine Section, p. 79.
221. Ibid.
222. Ibid., p. 80.
223. *U.S. News & World Report*, April 5, 1965, p. 39.
224. Ibid., pp. 39 and 40.
225. Ibid., pp. 40 and 41.
226. New York *Times*, March 17, 1965, p. 44.
227. *National Review*, April 20, 1965, p. 321.
228. Ibid.
229. Ibid., p. 322.
230. Ibid.
231. New York *Times*, August 10, 1965, pp. 1 and 14.
232. New York *Times*, August 19, 1965, p. 17.
233. New York *Times*, August 13, 1965, p. 19.
234. New York *Times*, March 1, 1966, p. 43.
235. Ibid.
236. Ibid.
237. Ibid.
238. Ibid.
239. Ibid.
240. *New South*, Spring 1966, p. 74.
241. Ibid., p. 75.
242. New York *Times*, April 17, 1966, p. 63.
243. Ibid.
244. Ibid.
245. Ibid.
246. Ibid.
247. New York *Times*, April 14, 1966, p. 27.
248. New York *Times*, May 5, 1966, p. 30.
249. Ibid.
250. New York *Times*, August 11, 1965, p. 20.
251. New York *Times*, March 6, 1966, p. 76.
252. Ibid.
253. New York *Times*, May 3, 1966, p. 33.
254. New York *Times*, March 6, 1966, Main Section, p. 76.
255. New York *Times*, May 6, 1966, p. 1.
256. Ibid.
257. Ibid.
258. Ibid.
259. Ibid., pp. 1 and 66.
260. New York *Times*, May 18, 1966, p. 24.
261. Ibid.
262. New York *Times*, May 26, 1966, p. 40.

263. New York *Times*, February 28, 1967, p. 40.
264. New York *Times*, April 30, 1966, p. 14.
265. Ibid.
266. New York *Times*, May 30, 1966, p. 8.
267. New York *Times*, June 1, 1966, p. 24.
268. Ibid.
269. Ibid. Also see New York *Times*, May 30, 1966, p. 8.
270. New York *Times*, June 1, 1966, pp. 1 and 24.
271. New York *Times*, May 30, 1966, p. 8.
272. New York *Times*, November 9, 1966, p. 33.
273. New York *Times*, April 20, 1966, p. 27.
274. New York *Times*, May 4, 1966, p. 28.
275. New York *Times*, April 20, 1966, p. 27.
276. New York *Times*, April 30, 1966, p. 14.
277. New York *Times*, November 10, 1966, p. 30.

CHAPTER SEVEN   1966: CHICAGO AND "OPEN HOUSING"

1. *Negro Digest*, May, 1967, p. 7.
2. Ibid.
3. *Ebony*, December, 1964, p. 76.
4. Ibid.
5. Ibid.
6. Ibid.
7. New York *Times*, June 26, 1963, p. 12.
8. New York *Times*, July 5, 1963, p. 1.
9. *Time*, September 18, 1964, p. 73.
10. *Human Events*, October 15, 1966, p. 667.
11. Ibid.
12. New York *Times*, July 7, 1966, p. 22.
13. *Time*, September 18, 1964, p. 73.
14. *Human Events*, op, cit .
15. *Negro Digest*, April, 1963, pp. 21, 24, 26.
16. Ibid., p. 29.
17. Ibid., pp. 21, 29, 30.
18. Ibid., p. 21.
19. Ibid., p. 32.
20. *U.S. News & World Report*, August 2, 1965, p. 55.
21. Ibid.
22. Ibid., p. 54.
23. Ibid.
24. Ibid., p. 55.
25. New York *Times*, October 17, 1965, News of the Week in Review, p. 5E.
26. New York *Times*, July 28, 1965, p. 40.
27. Ibid.
28. *U.S. News & World Report*, August 2, 1965, p. 54.
29. Ibid.
30. New York *Times*, July 28, 1965, p. 40.
31. New York *Times*, June 10, 1965, p. 24.
32. Ibid.

33. New York *Times*, May 28, 1965, p. 19.
34. New York *Times*, May 29, 1965, p. 10.
35. New York *Times*, May 30, 1965, Main Section, p. 34.
36. New York *Times*, June 9, 1965, p. 29.
37. New York *Times*, June 10, 1965, p. 24.
38. New York *Times*, June 12, 1965, p. 16.
39. New York *Times*, June 13, 1965, p. 65.
40. New York *Times*, June 19, 1965, p. 14.
41. New York *Times*, July 31, 1965, p. 50.
42. New York *Times*, July 1, 1965, p. 27.
43. Ibid.
44. New York *Times*, July 2, 1965, p. 32.
45. Ibid.
46. New York *Times*, July 3, 1965, p. 7.
47. Ibid.
48. New York *Times*, July 6, 1965, p. 23.
49. New York *Times*, July 7, 1965, p. 19.
50. New York *Times*, October 17, 1965, News of the Week in Review, p. 5E.
51. New York *Times*, October 11, 1965, p. 44.
52. New York *Times*, October 12, 1965, p. 33.
53. Ibid.
54. Ibid.
55. *Jet*, October 21, 1965, p. 23.
56. New York *Times*, October 12, 1965, p. 33.
57. New York *Times*, October 17, 1965, News of the Week in Review, p. 5E.
58. Ibid.
59. New York *Times*, October 12, 1965, p. 33.
60. New York *Times*, October 17, 1965, News of the Week in Review, p. 5E.
61. *Jet*, October 21, 1965, p. 20.
62. New York *Times*, October 28, 1965, p. 32.
63. Ibid.
64. New York *Times*, November 7, 1965, p. 130.
65. Ibid.
66. New York *Times*, July 15, 1965, p. 26.
67. New York *Times*, August 12, 1965, p. 15.
68. Ibid.
69. New York *Times*, September 2, 1965, p. 20.
70. New York *Times*, October 11, 1965, p. 44.
71. New York *Times*, July 8, 1965, p. 36.
72. Ibid.
73. New York *Times*, July 25, 1965, p. 39.
74. New York *Times*, July 26, 1965, p. 12.
75. New York *Times*, July 27, 1965, p. 18.
76. *Negro Digest*, March 1966, p. 55.
77. Ibid., p. 57.
78. New York *Times*, July 27, 1965, p. 18.
79. Ibid.
80. Ibid.
81. New York *Times*, August 1, 1965, p. 59.
82. New York *Times*, August 14, 1965, p. 9.

83. Ibid.
84. Ibid.
85. Ibid., p. 1.
86. Ibid.
87. Ibid.
88. New York *Times*, August 15, 1965, p. 1.
89. New York *Times*, August 14, 1965, pp. 1 and 9.
90. Ibid., p. 9.
91. Ibid.
92. Ibid.
93. Ibid.
94. New York *Times*, August 16, 1965, p. 18.
95. New York *Times*, September 9, 1965, p. 20.
96. New York *Times*, August 14, 1965, p. 9.
97. New York *Times*, July 17, 1966, Main Section, p. 60.
98. *U.S. News & World Report*, September 6, 1965, p. 40.
99. Ibid., p. 38.
100. New York *Times*, November 6, 1965, p. 12.
101. New York *Times*, February 6, 1966, Main Section, p. 77.
102. New York *Times*, October 11, 1965, p. 44.
103. Ibid.
104. New York *Times*, January 8, 1966, p. 22.
105. Ibid.
106. Ibid.
107. New York *Times*, January 21, 1966, p. 27.
108. New York *Times*, January 27, 1966, p. 37.
109. New York *Times*, January 21, 1966, p. 27.
110. New York *Times*, January 27, 1966, p. 37.
111. Ibid.
112. Ibid.
113. New York *Times*, February 1, 1966, p. 24.
114. Ibid.
115. Ibid.
116. New York *Times*, February 25, 1966, p. 18.
117. Ibid.
118. New York *Times*, February 24, 1966, p. 75.
119. Ibid.
120. Ibid.
121. Ibid.
122. New York *Times*, February 25, 1966, p. 18.
123. Ibid.
124. Ibid.
125. Ibid.
126. Ibid.
127. New York *Times*, March 5, 1966, p. 10.
128. Ibid.
129. New York *Times*, April 6, 1966, p. 28.
130. Ibid.
131. Ibid.
132. *Time*, March 25, 1966, pp. 18 and 19.
133. Ibid., p. 19.
134. New York *Times*, April 6, 1966, p. 28.
135. New York *Times*, April 28, 1966, p. 34.

136. New York *Times*, March 24, 1966, p. 33.
137. Ibid.
138. Ibid.
139. Ibid.
140. Ibid.
141. Ibid.
142. New York *Times*, March 25, 1966, p. 37.
143. New York *Times*, May 22, 1966, p. 43.
144. New York *Times*, March 24, 1966, p. 33.
145. Ibid.
146. *Human Events*, February 5, 1966, p. 94.
147. Ibid.
148. Ibid.
149. Ibid.
150. Ibid.
151. New York *Times*, March 24, 1966, p. 33.
152. Ibid.
153. Ibid.
154. Ibid.
155. Ibid.
156. Ibid.
157. Ibid.
158. New York *Times*, February 11, 1966, p. 21.
159. New York *Times*, May 3, 1966, p. 28.
160. Ibid.
161. Ibid.
162. Ibid.
163. New York *Times*, April 21, 1966, p. 24.
164. Ibid.
165. Ibid.
166. *Look*, June 14, 1966, p. 71.
167. Ibid.
168. New York *Times*, June 9, 1966, p. 58.
169. *Look*, op. cit., p. 75.
170. New York *Times*, July 11, 1966, p. 1.
171. New York *Times*, July 9, 1966, p. 8.
172. Ibid.
173. Ibid.
174. New York *Times*, June 16, 1966, p. 27.
175. New York *Times*, July 9, 1966, p. 8.
176. New York *Times*, July 10, 1966, p. 54.
177. Ibid.
178. New York *Times*, July 7, 1966, p. 22.
179. New York *Times*, July 11, 1966, p. 1.
180. New York *Times*, July 12, 1966, p. 26.
181. New York *Times*, July 11, 1966, p. 19.
182. Ibid.
183. Ibid., p. 1.
184. New York *Times*, July 12, 1966, p. 26.
185. *Newsweek*, July 25, 1966, p. 17.
186. New York *Times*, July 13, 1966, p. 1.
187. Ibid., p. 39.
188. Ibid., p. 1.

189. Ibid.
190. Ibid., p. 39.
191. Ibid.
192. New York *Times*, July 14, 1966, p. 1.
193. Ibid., p. 23.
194. New York *Times*, July 15, 1966, p. 1.
195. New York *Times*, July 16, 1966, pp. 1 and 8.
196. Ibid., p. 8.
197. Ibid.
198. *Human Events*, July 30, 1966, p. 484.
199. New York *Times*, July 16, 1966, p. 8.
200. Ibid.
201. New York *Times*, July 24, 1966, News of the Week in Review, p. 1E.
202. New York *Times*, July 16, 1966, p. 8.
203. New York *Times*, July 17, 1966, p. 60.
204. New York *Times*, July 16, 1966, p. 8.
205. New York *Times*, July 18, 1966, p. 17.
206. Ibid.
207. New York *Times*, July 26, 1966, p. 22.
208. New York *Times*, July 20, 1966, p. 23.
209. Ibid.
210. New York *Times*, July 17, 1966, p. 60.
211. Ibid., p. 1.
212. Ibid., p. 60.
213. Ibid.
214. Ibid., p. 1.
215. New York *Times*, July 20, 1966, p. 23.
216. Ibid.
217. New York *Times*, July 23, 1966, p. 9.
218. Ibid.
219. New York *Times*, July 29, 1966, p. 12.
220. New York *Times*, July 30, 1966, p. 11.
221. Ibid.
222. Ibid.
223. Ibid.
224. *Commonweal*, August 5, 1966, p. 492.
225. Ibid., p. 493.
226. New York *Times*, July 16, 1966, p. 8.
227. New York *Times*, July 10, 1966, p. 54.
228. Ibid.
229. Ibid.
230. New York *Times*, July 30, 1966, p. 11.
231. New York *Times*, July 31, 1966, Financial Section, p. 13F.
232. New York *Times*, November 20, 1966, News of the Week in Review, p. 6E.
233. Ibid.
234. Ibid.
235. Ibid.
236. Ibid.
237. Ibid.
238. New York *Times*, September 11, 1966, Magazine Section, p. 192.
239. Ibid., p. 182.

240. New York *Times*, August 22, 1966, p. 37.
241. Ibid.
242. New York *Times*, August 7, 1966, p. 47.
243. Ibid.
244. Ibid.
245. Ibid.
246. Ibid.
247. New York *Times*, August 28, 1966, News of the Week in Review, p. 5E.
248. Ibid.
249. New York *Times*, July 31, 1966, p. 56.
250. New York *Times*, August 1, 1966, pp. 1 and 15.
251. New York *Times*, August 2, 1966, p. 12.
252. Ibid.
253. *Commonweal*, August 5, 1966, p. 493.
254. New York *Times*, July 15, 1966, p. 1.
255. New York *Times*, August 6, 1966, pp. 1 and 52.
256. Ibid.
257. New York *Times*, August 8, 1966, pp. 1 and 55.
258. Ibid.
259. New York *Times*, August 15, 1966, p. 16.
260. New York *Times*, August 8, 1966, p. 1.
261. New York *Times*, August 13, 1966, p. 8.
262. New York *Times*, August 6, 1966, p. 1.
263. New York *Times*, August 21, 1966, News of the Week in Review, p. 5E.
264. New York *Times*, August 6, 1966, p. 52.
265. New York *Times*, August 22, 1966, p. 1.
266. New York *Times*, August 21, 1966, News of the Week in Review, p. 5E.
267. New York *Times*, August 22, 1966, p. 1.
268. New York *Times*, August 21, 1966, News of the Week in Review, p. 5E.
269. New York *Times*, September 21, 1966, p. 33.
270. Ibid.
271. Ibid.
272. Ibid.
273. Ibid.
274. Ibid.
275. Ibid.
276. New York *Times*, August 18, 1966, p. 31.
277. New York *Times*, August 17, 1966, p. 23.
278. New York *Times*, August 11, 1966, p. 23.
279. Ibid.
280. New York *Times*, August 12, 1966, p. 20.
281. Ibid.
282. Ibid.
283. New York *Times*, August 14, 1966, p. 48.
284. Ibid.
285. Ibid.
286. Ibid.
287. Ibid.
288. New York *Times*, August 20, 1966, p. 23.

289. Ibid., pp. 1 and 23.
290. Ibid., p. 1.
291. Ibid., p. 23.
292. Ibid.
293. Ibid., p. 1.
294. Ibid.
295. Ibid.
296. New York *Times*, August 21, 1966, p. 47.
297. New York *Times*, August 16, 1966, p. 16.
298. New York *Times*, August 21, 1966, p. 47.
299. New York *Times*, August 22, 1966, p. 37.
300. Ibid. Also see New York *Times*, August 23, 1966, p. 35.
301. Ibid.
302. Ibid.
303. New York *Times*, August 24, 1966, p. 34.
304. Ibid.
305. Ibid.
306. Ibid.
307. Ibid.
308. New York *Times*, August 25, 1966, p. 24.
309. Ibid.
310. New York *Times*, August 27, 1966, pp. 1 and 17.
311. Ibid., p. 1.
312. New York *Times*, August 27, 1966, p. 17.
313. Ibid., p. 1.
314. Ibid., p. 17.
315. New York *Times*, August 28, 1966, Main Section, p. 50.
316. New York *Times*, October 29, 1966, p. 17.
317. Ibid.
318. Ibid.
319. New York *Times*, November 2, 1966, p. 25.
320. *Human Events*, October 1, 1966, p. 626. Also New York *Times*, September 10, 1966, p. 14.
321. New York *Times*, October 8, 1967, p. 60.
322. New York *Times*, September 4, 1966, p. 54.
323. Ibid.
324. Ibid.
325. Ibid.
326. Ibid.
327. *Wall Street Journal*, November 16, 1966, p. 1.
328. Ibid.
329. Ibid.
330. Ibid.
331. Ibid.
332. Ibid., p. 23.
333. Ibid.
334. *Christian Science Monitor*, March 14, 1967, p. 9.
335. Ibid.
336. New York *Times*, March 9, 1967, p. 1.
337. Ibid., p. 34.
338. Ibid.
339. Ibid.
340. New York *Times*, March 9, 1967, p. 34.

341. Ibid.
342. Ibid.
343. Ibid.
344. Ibid.
345. Ibid.
346. Ibid.
347. Ibid.
348. Ibid., p. 1.
349. Ibid.
350. Ibid., p. 34.
351. Ibid., p. 1.
352. Ibid.
353. Ibid., p. 34.
354. Ibid.
355. New York *Times*, April 16, 1967, p. 79.
356. Ibid.
357. Ibid.
358. Ibid.
359. Ibid.
360. New York *Times*, March 17, 1967, p. 40.
361. Ibid.
362. *Jet*, April 20, 1967, p. 30.
363. New York *Post*, March 8, 1960, p. 41.
364. Ibid.
365. Ibid.
366. New York *Times*, October 30, 1966, Section 8, p. 1.
367. Ibid.
368. Ibid.
369. Ibid.
370. Ibid.
371. Ibid., p. 8.
372. Ibid.
373. Ibid.
374. Ibid., pp. 1 and 8.
375. Ibid., p. 1.
376. Ibid.
377. Ibid.
378. Ibid.
379. *Social Work*, January 1967, pp. 12–21.
380. Ibid., p. 12.
381. Ibid., p. 13.
382. Ibid.
383. Ibid.
384. Ibid., p. 14.
385. Ibid., p. 15.
386. Ibid., p. 16.
387. Ibid.
388. Ibid., p. 12.
389. New York *Times*, January 16, 1967, p. 22.
390. Ibid.
391. Ibid.
392. Ibid.
393. Ibid.

394. Ibid.
395. Ibid.
396. Ibid.
397. New York *Times*, April 5, 1967, p. 30.
398. Ibid.
399. Ibid., p. 1.
400. Ibid., p. 30.
401. Ibid., p. 1.
402. Ibid., p. 30.
403. Ibid.
404. New York *Times*, April 20, 1967, p. 38.
405. Ibid.
406. New York *Times*, June 30, 1967, p. 15.
407. Ibid.
408. Ibid.
409. Ibid.
410. *Human Events*, August 12, 1967, p. 500.
411. Ibid.
412. Ibid.
413. Ibid.

CHAPTER EIGHT   1967: OPERATION BREADBASKET

1. *Negro Digest*, May, 1964, p. 10.
2. Ibid., pp. 7 and 8.
3. Ibid., pp. 8 and 9.
4. Ibid., p. 9.
5. Ibid., p. 8.
6. Ibid.
7. *Liberator*, June, 1967, p. 11.
8. Ibid.
9. Ibid.
10. *Vital Speeches*, February 15, 1966, p. 271.
11. Ibid.
12. New York *Times*, August 12, 1962, News of the Week in Review, p. 8E.
13. Ibid.
14. Ibid.
15. *Negro Digest*, September, 1964, p. 7.
16. Ibid., p. 8.
17. Ibid., p. 9.
18. Ibid., p. 10.
19. Ibid., p. 11.
20. New York *Times*, October 27, 1966, p. 1.
21. Ibid., p. 20.
22. *U.S. News & World Report*, August 12, 1963, p. 28.
23. Ibid.
24. Ibid., p. 29.
25. Ibid.
26. Ibid.

27. *The Reporter*, December 17, 1964, p. 15.
28. Ibid.
29. Ibid.
30. Ibid.
31. Ibid.
32. Ibid.
33. Ibid.
34. Ibid.
35. Ibid.
36. Ibid., pp. 15 and 16.
37. *U.S. News & World Report*, January 1, 1968, p. 58.
38. *The Reporter*, December 17, 1964, p. 16.
39. Ibid.
40. Ibid.
41. Ibid.
42. Ibid., p. 15.
43. Ibid., p. 16.
44. Ibid.
45. Ibid.
46. Ibid.
47. Ibid.
48. Ibid.
49. Ibid.
50. Ibid.
51. *U.S. News & World Report*, January 1, 1968, p. 59.
52. Ibid.
53. Ibid., p. 58.
54. New York *Times*, February 15, 1965, p. 21.
55. *U.S. News & World Report*, January 1, 1968, p. 58.
56. *The Reporter*, December 17, 1964, p. 17.
57. Ibid.
58. New York *Times*, February 15, 1965, p. 21.
59. Ibid.
60. Ibid.
61. Ibid.
62. *Christian Herald*, January, 1967, p. 28.
63. Ibid., pp. 32 and 56.
64. Ibid., p. 56.
65. Ibid.
66. New York *Post*, March 11, 1967, p. 28.
67. *Time*, March 3, 1967, p. 25.
68. Ibid.
69. Ibid., p. 26.
70. New York *Post*, March 11, 1967, p. 28.
71. *Ebony*, August, 1967, p. 79.
72. Ibid.
73. Ibid.
74. Ibid.
75. Ibid.
76. *Saturday Evening Post*, November 7, 1964, p. 10.
77. *Business Week*, August 19, 1967, p. 37.
78. *Ebony*, August, 1967, p. 78.
79. Ibid., p. 86.

80. Ibid.
81. *Business Week*, op. cit., p. 37.
82. Ibid., p. 38.
83. New York *Times*, November 26, 1966, p. 32.
84. Ibid.
85. Ibid.
86. *Business Week*, op. cit., p. 38.
87. *Ebony*, op. cit., p. 78.
88. Ibid., p. 86.
89. Ibid.
90. Ibid., p. 78.
91. Ibid., pp. 78 and 79.
92. Ibid., p. 79.
93. *Business Week*, op. cit., p. 37.
94. Ibid., pp. 84 and 86.
95. *Afro-American*, July 22, 1967, p. 15.
96. Ibid.
97. Ibid.
98. *Business Week*, op. cit., p. 37.
99. Ibid.
100. *Ebony*, op. cit., p. 79.
101. Ibid. Also see *Business Week*, op. cit., p. 38.
102. *Amsterdam News*, October 21, 1967, p. 27.
103. *Amsterdam News*, December 23, 1967, p. 25.
104. *Ebony*, op. cit., p. 79.
105. *Look*, December 17, 1963, p. 43.
106. Ibid.
107. Ibid.
108. Ibid., pp. 43 and 44.
109. Ibid., p. 44.
110. Ibid., p. 46.
111. Ibid.
112. *Jet*, October 21, 1965, p. 53.
113. *Human Events*, July 22, 1967, p. 459.
114. *Jet*, April 20, 1967, p. 15.
115. *Business Week*, December 9, 1967, p. 134.
116. Ibid., p. 133.
117. Ibid.
118. Ibid.
119. Ibid., p. 134.
120. Ibid.
121. *Business Week*, August 12, 1967, pp. 128 and 130.
122. Ibid., p. 130.
123. *U.S. News & World Report*, January 22, 1968, p. 93.
124. New York *Times*, January 28, 1968, Magazine Section, p. 27.
125. Ibid., pp. 27 and 42.
126. Ibid., p. 42.
127. Ibid.
128. Ibid.
129. Ibid.
130. Ibid., p. 47.
131. Ibid.
132. Ibid., p. 50.

133. Ibid., p. 48.
134. Ibid.

CHAPTER NINE   THE RISE OF BLACK POWER

1. New York *Times*, August 13, 1965, p. 26.
2. New York *Times*, August 15, 1965, News of the Week in Review, p. 1E.
3. New York *Times*, September 4, 1965, p. 22.
4. Ibid. Also New York *Times*, August 15, 1965, News of the Week in Review, p. 1E.
5. Ibid.
6. Ibid.
7. New York *Times*, August 15, 1965, News of the Week in Review, p. 1E.
8. New York *Times*, October 28, 1965, p. 27.
9. New York *Times*, August 15, 1965, News of the Week in Review, p. 1E.
10. New York *Times*, August 13, 1965, p. 1.
11. Ibid., p. 26.
12. Ibid.
13. Ibid., p. 1.
14. New York *Times*, August 14, 1965, p. 8.
15. New York *Times*, August 15, 1965, p. 80.
16. New York *Times*, August 14, 1965, p. 1.
17. Ibid.
18. Ibid.
19. Ibid.
20. Ibid.
21. Ibid., p. 8.
22. Ibid. Also New York *Times*, August 15, 1965, p. 1.
23. New York *Times*, August 16, 1965, p. 16.
24. New York *Times*, August 14, 1965, p. 8.
25. Ibid.
26. Ibid.
27. New York *Times*, August 15, 1965, Main Section, p. 79.
28. New York *Times*, August 16, 1965, p. 17.
29. Ibid., p. 1.
30. Ibid.
31. Ibid., pp. 1 and 16.
32. Ibid., p. 16.
33. Ibid.
34. New York *Times*, August 15, 1965, p. 66.
35. Ibid.
36. New York *Times*, August 17, 1965, p. 16.
37. Ibid.
38. New York *Times*, August 20, 1965, p. 16.
39. Ibid.
40. New York *Times*, August 19, 1965, p. 16.
41. *Jet*, September 16, 1965, p. 50.
42. Ibid.

43. Ibid.
44. *The New Leader*, August 30, 1965, p. 4.
45. *Newsweek*, December 13, 1965, p. 31.
46. New York *Times*, August 19, 1965, p. 16.
47. New York *Times*, August 14, 1965, p. 8.
48. New York *Times*, August 17, 1965, p. 17.
49. Ibid.
50. Ibid.
51. *National Review*, March 23, 1965, p. 239.
52. New York *Times*, August 29, 1965, Main Section, p. 55.
53. New York *Times*, August 15, 1965, News of the Week in Review, pp. 1E and 2E.
54. New York *Times*, August 22, 1965, News of the Week in Review, pp. 1E and 2E.
55. Ibid., p. 2E.
56. New York *Times*, August 15, 1965, News of the Week in Review, p. 1E.
57. New York *Times*, August 29, 1965, p. 54.
58. Ibid.
59. *U.S. News & World Report*, September 11, 1967, p. 41.
60. New York *Times*, August 16, 1965, p. 17.
61. New York *Times*, August 17, 1965, p. 17.
62. New York *Times*, August 15, 1965, News of the Week in Review, p. 1E.
63. New York *Times*, August 19, 1965, p. 16.
64. Ibid.
65. Ibid.
66. Ibid.
67. *Reader's Digest*, May 1966, p. 68.
68. Ibid.
69. New York *Times*, August 24, 1965, p. 15.
70. New York *Times*, March 4, 1966, p. 16.
71. *Time*, August 27, 1965, p. 11.
72. New York *Times*, August 20, 1965, p. 17.
73. *Time*, op. cit., p. 11.
74. *Negro Digest*, July 1967, p. 70.
75. *U.S. News & World Report*, August 30, 1965, p. 61.
76. Ibid.
77. New York *Times*, September 4, 1966, p. 54.
78. New York *Times*, March 16, 1966, p. 39.
79. New York *Times*, September 4, 1966, p. 52.
80. Ibid.
81. New York *Times*, December 7, 1965, p. 26.
82. Ibid., p. 1.
83. Ibid., p. 26.
84. Ibid.
85. Ibid.
86. Ibid.
87. Ibid.
88. Ibid.
89. Ibid.
90. Ibid.
91. Ibid.

92. *Reader's Digest*, May 1966, p. 71.
93. New York *Times*, November 28, 1965, p. 67.
94. New York *Times*, May 18, 1966, p. 50.
95. Ibid.
96. New York *Times*, March 20, 1966, News of the Week in Review, p. 2E.
97. Ibid.
98. New York *Times*, March 17, 1966, p. 26.
99. New York *Times*, June 12, 1966, Magazine Section, p. 84.
100. New York *Times*, May 29, 1966, News of the Week in Review, p. 2E.
101. *Life*, May 19, 1967, pp. 76B and 77.
102. *New South*, Summer 1966, p. 76.
103. Ibid.
104. New York *Times*, August 5, 1966, p. 10.
105. *Who Speaks for the Negro*, by Robert Penn Warren, (New York: Random House, 1965) p. 391.
106. Ibid. Also see *Esquire*, January, 1967, p. 133.
107. Ibid.
108. Ibid.
109. Ibid.
110. Ibid.
111. Ibid.
112. Ibid.
113. Ibid.
114. Ibid.
115. Ibid. Also see New York *Times*, August 5, 1966, p. 10.
116. *Who Speaks for the Negro?* op. cit., p. 392.
117. *Esquire*, January 1967, p. 133.
118. Ibid.
119. *Who Speaks for the Negro?* op. cit., p. 393.
120. *New South*, Summer, 1966, p. 78.
121. Ibid., p. 79.
122. New York *Times*, August 5, 1966, p. 10.
123. *Who Speaks for the Negro?* op. cit., p. 397.
124. Ibid.
125. Ibid., p. 398.
126. New York *Times*, August 29, 1963, p. 20. Also see *SNCC: The New Abolitionists*, op. cit., p. 33.
127. New York *Times*, April 18, 1960, p. 21.
128. New York *Times*, June 30, 1963, News of the Week in Review, p. 5E.
129. Ibid.
130. *SNCC: The New Abolitionists*, op. cit., p. 60.
131. Ibid., p. 14.
132. New York *Times*, June 25, 1967, Magazine Section, p. 45.
133. *Esquire*, January 1967, p. 134.
134. *Where Do We Go From Here: Chaos or Community*, by Dr. Martin Luther King, Jr. (New York: Harper & Row, 1967), p. 27.
135. *The Nation*, October 5, 1963, p. 193.
136. New York *Times*, June 25, 1967, Magazine Section, p. 44.
137. *SNCC: The New Abolitionists*, op. cit., p. 102.

138. Ibid.
139. New York *Times*, August 29, 1965, Drama Section, p. 9X.
140. New York *Times*, February 24, 1966, p. 31.
141. *Saturday Evening Post*, August 28, 1965, pp. 80 and 82.
142. *SNCC: The New Abolitionists*, op. cit., p. 221.
143. *Esquire*, op. cit., p. 134.
144. *Look*, November 16, 1965, p. M22.
145. New York *Post*, June 23, 1967, p. 45.
146. Ibid.
147. New York *Times*, August 15, 1965, Main Section, p. 69.
148. New York *Times*, June 20, 1965, News of the Week in Review, p. 4E.
149. Ibid.
150. New York *Times*, August 23, 1965, p. 19.
151. Ibid.
152. Ibid.
153. *New Republic*, January 8, 1966, p. 22.
154. Ibid.
155. New York *Times*, May 3, 1966, p. 46.
156. New York *Times*, January 1, 1966, p. 15. Also see New York *Times*, October 31, 1966, p. 22.
157. Ibid.
158. New York *Times*, May 3, 1966, p. 32.
159. New York *Times*, October 31, 1966, p. 22.
160. Ibid.
161. Ibid.
162. New York *Times*, November 9, 1966, p. 25.
163. *Saturday Evening Post*, August 28, 1965, p. 81.
164. *Fortune*, November, 1965, p. 255.
165. Ibid.
166. New York *Times*, January 10, 1966, p. 11.
167. New York *Times*, August 5, 1966, p. 10.
168. Ibid.
169. Ibid.
170. Ibid.
171. New York *Post*, June 22, 1967, p. 37.
172. New York *Times*, August 5, 1966, p. 10.
173. Ibid.
174. Ibid.
175. Ibid.
176. Ibid.
177. Ibid.
178. Ibid.
179. Ibid.
180. Ibid.
181. Ibid.
182. Ibid.
183. Ibid.
184. Ibid.
185. Ibid.
186. New York *Times*, May 17, 1966, p. 22.
187. New York *Times*, May 24, 1966, p. 28.
188. New York *Times*, May 28, 1966, p. 1.

189. Ibid.
190. New York *Times*, June 7, 1966, p. 1.
191. New York *Times*, June 12, 1966, News of the Week in Review,
     p. 1E.
192. Ibid.
193. Ibid.
194. Ibid.
195. *Where Do We Go From Here: Chaos or Community*, op. cit., p. 24.
196. Ibid.
197. quoted in *Human Events*, June 18, 1966, p. 387.
198. Ibid.
199. Ibid.
200. Ibid.
201. Ibid. Also see New York *Times*, June 9, 1966, p. 32.
202. Ibid.
203. *Human Events*, op. cit. p. 387.
204. New York *Times*, June 11, 1966, p. 19.
205. New York *Times*, June 8, 1966, p. 1.
206. Ibid.
207. Ibid., p. 26.
208. Ibid.
209. New York *Times*, June 9, 1966, p. 33.
210. New York *Times*, June 8, 1966, p. 26.
211. Ibid.
212. New York *Times*, June 9, 1966, p. 1.
213. Ibid.
214. Ibid., p. 33.
215. Ibid.
216. New York *Times*, June 11, 1966, p. 19.
217. New York *Times*, June 10, 1966, p. 35.
218. New York *Times*, June 11, 1966, p. 19.
219. Ibid., p. 1.
220. Ibid., pp. 1 and 19.
221. Ibid., p. 19.
222. New York *Times*, June 12, 1966, pp. 1 and 82.
223. Ibid., p. 82.
224. Ibid.
225. New York *Times*, June 13, 1966, p. 32.
226. Ibid.
227. New York *Times*, June 15, 1966, p. 1. Also see New York *Times*,
     June 16, 1966, p. 35.
228. Ibid.
229. Ibid.
230. Ibid.
231. New York *Times*, June 17, 1966, pp. 1 and 33.
232. Ibid., p. 33.
233. Ibid.
234. Ibid.
235. Ibid.
236. Ibid.
237. Ibid., p. 1.
238. Ibid., pp. 1 and 33.
239. New York *Times*, June 21, 1966, p. 30.

240. *Where Do We Go From Here: Chaos or Community*, op. cit., pp. 29–30.
241. New York *Times*, June 21, 1966, p. 30.
242. Ibid.
243. New York *Times*, June 22, 1966, p. 25.
244. New York *Times*, December 30, 1967, p. 1.
245. New York *Times*, June 22, 1966, p. 1.
246. New York *Times*, June 22, 1966, p. 25.
247. Ibid.
248. New York *Times*, June 22, 1966, p. 25.
249. Ibid.
250. New York *Times*, June 23, 1966, p. 23.
251. Ibid.
252. New York *Times*, June 24, 1966, p. 1.
253. Ibid., p. 1.
254. Ibid., p. 20.
255. New York *Times*, June 25, 1966, p. 15.
256. Ibid.
257. New York *Times*, June 24, 1966, p. 20.
258. Ibid.
259. Ibid., p. 1.
260. Ibid., p. 20.
261. Ibid.
262. Ibid.
263. New York *Times*, June 25, 1966, p. 1.
264. New York *Times*, June 25, 1966, p. 15.
265. New York *Times*, June 26, 1966, p. 1.
266. Ibid., p. 40.
267. Ibid.
268. Ibid.
269. New York *Times*, June 27, 1966, p. 1.
270. Ibid.
271. Ibid., p. 29.
272. Ibid.
273. Ibid.
274. Ibid.
275. *The Reporter*, July 14, 1966, p. 12.
276. Ibid., pp. 12 and 16.
277. New York *Times*, June 28, 1966, p. 23.
278. *Where Do We Go From Here: Chaos or Community*, op. cit., p. 31.
279. *Human Events*, June 18, 1966, p. 387.
280. New York *Times*, June 25, 1967, pp. 1 and 54.
281. *Ebony*, September, 1966, p. 28.
282. Ibid., p. 30.
283. *Negro Digest*, October, 1966, p. 58.
284. Ibid. p. 59.
285. Ibid., p. 58.
286. *New York Review of Books*, September 22, 1966, p. 5.
287. *Dissent*, January–February, 1967, p. 75.
288. Ibid., p. 72.
289. *Where Do We Go From Here: Chaos or Community*, op. cit., pp. 36, 38, 44.

290. Ibid., p. 54.
291. Ibid., pp. 56 and 57.
292. *Negro Digest*, December, 1966, p. 6.
293. *Negro Digest*, November, 1966, p. 91.
294. *Negro Digest*, November, 1966, p. 24.
295. Ibid., p. 84.
296. *Negro Digest*, December, 1966, p. 15.
297. New York *Times*, October 9, 1966, Magazine, pp. 42 and 156.
298. Ibid.
299. New York *Post*, June 19, 1967, p. 33.
300. New York *Times*, July 9, 1967, Main Section, p. 38.
301. New York *Times*, July 11, 1967, p. 17.
302. New York *Times*, July 9, 1967, Main Section, p. 38.
303. Ibid.
304. New York *Times*, August 31, 1967, p. 23.
305. *The New Republic*, September 16, 1967, p. 11.
306. New York *Times*, September 24, 1967, Magazine Section, p. 28.
307. Ibid.
308. Ibid.
309. New York *Times*, September 1, 1967, p. 15.
310. Ibid.
311. *The New Republic*, September 16, 1967, p. 10.
312. *The New Leader*, September 11, 1967, p. 8.
313. *New Yorker*, September 23, 1967, p. 71.
314. Ibid.
315. New York *Times*, September 24, 1967, Magazine Section
316. *New Yorker*, op. cit., p. 68.
317. Ibid., p. 56.
318. *The Nation*, September 25, 1967, p. 276.
319. *The New Leader*, September 11, 1967, p. 6.
320. *New Yorker*, op. cit., p. 57.
321. Ibid.
322. Ibid., p. 65.
323. Ibid.
324. *The New Leader*, op. cit., p.6.
325. Ibid.
326. Ibid.
327. Ibid.
328. New York *Times*, September 24, 1967, Magaz
329. *New Yorker*, op. cit., p. 57.
330. *The Nation*, September 25, 1967, p. 274.
331. *The New Republic*, op. cit., p. 10.
332. *The Nation*, op. cit., p. 274.
333. *The New Republic*, op. cit., p. 10.
334. New York *Times*, September 3, 1967, p.
335. Ibid.
336. *The New Leader*, September 11, 1967
337. *New Yorker*, op. cit., p. 80.
338. New York *Times*, September 24, 196
339. Ibid.
340. Ibid., p. 125.
341. Ibid., p. 124.
342. *The Nation*, op. cit., p. 274.

343. *The New Republic*, September 16, 1967, p. 10.
344. Ibid.
345. New York *Times*, September 3, 1967, p. 18.
346. *The Nation*, September 25, 1967, p. 275.
347. Ibid.
348. *New Yorker*, op. cit. p. 79.
349. Ibid.
350. Ibid., p. 80.
351. Ibid., p. 87.
352. *The New Leader*, op. cit., p. 7.
353. New York *Times*, September 24, 1967, Magazine Section, p. 125.
354. *The New Leader*, op. cit., p. 7.
355. *The Nation*, op. cit., p. 274.
356. *The National Observer*, September 11, 1967, p. 14.
357. *The Nation*, op. cit., p. 275.
358. Ibid.
359. *New Yorker*, op. cit., p. 86.
360. *The New Leader*, op. cit., p. 7.
361. New York *Times*, September 24, 1967, Magazine, p. 125.
362. Ibid.
363. Ibid.
364. Ibid.
365. Ibid.
366. *New Yorker*, op. cit., p. 81.
367. New York *Times*, September 24, 1967, Magazine, p. 125.
368. Ibid.
369. Ibid.
370. Ibid.
371. Ibid.
372. New York *Times*, September 4, 1967, p. 15.
373. Ibid.
374. Ibid.
375. New York *Times*, September 23, 1967, p. 30.
376. *SCLC News Bulletin*, November, 1967.
377. New York *Times*, September 25, 1966, Magazine Section, p. 119.
378. Ibid., p. 122.
379. Ibid., p. 119.
380. New York *Times*, July 29, 1966, p. 13.
381. Hearings Before a Subcommittee of the Committee on Appropriations, House of Representatives, Part 1, February 16, 1967, p. 618.
382. *Human Events*, July 1, 1967, p. 3.
383. Hearings Before a Subcommittee of the Committee on Appropriations, op. cit.
384. *Human Events*, September 10, 1966, p. 579.
385. New York *Times*, May 17, 1967, p. 30.
386. New York *Times*, June 22, 1967, p. 1.
387. Ibid.
388. Ibid., p. 25.
389. New York *Times*, September 7, 1966, pp. 1 and 38.
390. Ibid., p. 1.
391. Ibid.
392. Ibid., p. 38.

394. Ibid., p. 1.
395. New York *Times*, September 8, 1966, p. 1.
396. Ibid., p. 36.
397. Ibid.
398. Ibid.
399. New York *Times*, September 9, 1966, p. 1.
400. Ibid. Also see New York *Times*, September 10, 1966, p. 1.
401. New York *Times*, September 10, 1966, p. 1.
402. New York *Times*, September 16, 1966, p. 34.
403. New York *Times*, September 12, 1966, p. 49.
404. New York *Times*, September 10, 1966, p. 14.
405. Ibid.
406. Ibid.
407. New York *Times*, September 12, 1966, p. 49.
408. Ibid.
409. New York *Times*, October 2, 1966, Main Section, p. 82.
410. Ibid.
411. New York *Times*, December 14, 1966, p. 37.
412. New York *Times*, September 13, 1966, p. 26.
413. Ibid.
414. *Facts*, October 1967, Vol. 17, No. 5 (Anti-Defamation League of B'nai B'rith).
415. Ibid., p. 421.
416. Ibid.
417. Ibid., pp. 428–430.
418. Ibid., p. 423.
419. Ibid.
420. Ibid.
421. Ibid., pp. 422 and 423.
422. New York *Times*, August 16, 1967, p. 28.
423. *Facts*, op. cit., p. 423.
424. Ibid.
425. Ibid.
426. New York *Times*, August 22, 1967, p. 24.
427. Ibid.
428. New York *Post*, August 30, 1967, p. 3.
429. New York *Times*, August 17, 1967, p. 27.
430. *Amsterdam News*, August 19, 1967, p. 1.
431. New York *Times*, August 18, 1967, p. 18.
432. *Amsterdam News*, November 4, 1967, p. 24.
433. *Amsterdam News*, December 9, 1967, p. 45.
434. New York *Times*, July 8, 1966, p. 1.
435. Ibid., p. 16.
436. Ibid.
437. Ibid., p. 1.
438. quoted in New York *Times*, August 16, 1966, p. 24.
439. New York *Times*, September 28, 1966, p. 26.
440. New York *Times*, September 12, 1966, p. 49.
441. New York *Times*, September 15, 1966, p. 1.
442. Ibid., pp. 1 and 27.
443. Ibid., p. 27.
444. New York *Times*, October 14, 1966, pp. 27 and 35.
445. Ibid.

446. New York *Times*, October 15, 1966, p. 14.
447. Ibid.
448. New York *Times*, April 14, 1966, p. 1.
449. Ibid., p. 6.

CHAPTER TEN   THE VIETNAM PROTESTS AND
              BLACK ANARCHY

1. New York *Times*, July 19, 1965, p. 12.
2. New York *Times*, August 13, 1965, p. 1.
3. Ibid., p. 2. Also see New York *Times*, August 15, 1965, p. 73.
4. New York *Times*, August 15, 1965, p. 73.
5. Ibid.
6. Ibid.
7. New York *Times*, September 11, 1965, p. 9.
8. New York *Times*, August 2, 1966, p. 12.
9. Ibid.
10. New York *Times*, August 12, 1966, p. 16.
11. New York *Times*, November 3, 1966, p. 29.
12. New York *Times*, December 16, 1966, p. 33.
13. New York *Times*, January 21, 1967, p. 3.
14. New York *Times*, January 28, 1967, p. 3.
15. Ibid.
16. Ibid.
17. *Harper's*, August, 1967, p. 49.
18. Ibid.
19. Freedom House News Letter, May, 1967.
20. Ibid.
21. Ibid.
22. *Harper's*, op. cit., p. 49.
23. Ibid.
24. *Newsweek*, May 15, 1967, p. 33.
25. Ibid.
26. New York *Times*, April 2, 1967, News of the Week in Review,
    p. 11E. Also see New York *Times*, March 26, 1967, p. 44.
27. New York *Times*, April 5, 1967, p. 1.
28. *Current*, May, 1967, pp. 32 and 33.
29. Ibid., p. 33.
30. Ibid., pp. 33 and 34.
31. Ibid., p. 35.
32. Ibid.
33. Ibid.
34. Ibid.
35. Ibid.
36. Ibid., p. 36.
37. Ibid., p. 37.
38. Ibid.
39. Ibid.
40. Ibid. p. 38.
41. Ibid., pp. 36, 38, 39.
42. *Congressional Record* (unbound), April 5, 1967, p. H3581.

43. Ibid.
44. Ibid.
45. Ibid.
46. *Reader's Digest*, September, 1967, p. 38.
47. Ibid.
48. The Washington *Post*, April 6, 1967, Editorial page. Quoted in *Current*, op. cit., pp. 39 and 40.
49. New York *Times*, April 6, 1967, p. 10.
50. New York *Times*, April 13, 1967, p. 1.
51. Ibid., pp. 1 and 32.
52. Ibid., p. 32.
53. *Congressional Record* (unbound), April 17, 1967, p. A1835.
54. House Committee on Un-American Activities, *Communist Origin and Manipulation of Vietnam Week*, March 31, 1967, p. 22.
55. Ibid.
56. Ibid.
57. Ibid., pp. 15 and 24.
58. Ibid., p. 26.
59. Ibid.
60. Ibid.
61. Ibid.
62. Ibid., p. 29.
63. Ibid., p. 28.
64. Ibid., p. 29.
65. Ibid., p. 30.
66. Ibid., p. 49.
67. Ibid., p. 36.
68. Ibid., p. 49.
69. Ibid.
70. Ibid., p. 50.
71. Ibid., p. 33.
72. Ibid.
73. Ibid., pp. 34 and 35.
74. Ibid., p. 35.
75. Ibid., pp. 53 and 54.
76. Ibid., p. 34.
77. Ibid.
78. Ibid., p. 36.
79. Ibid., p. 53.
80. Ibid., p. 54.
81. New York *Times*, April 16, 1967, p. 1.
82. Ibid.
83. Ibid.
84. Ibid., p. 2.
85. Ibid.
86. Ibid.
87. Ibid.
88. New York *Times*, April 17, 1967, p. 26.
89. New York *Times*, April 15, 1967, p. 3.
90. New York *Times*, April 19, 1967, p. 5.
91. New York *Times*, April 17, 1967, p. 9.
92. New York *Times*, April 17, 1967, p. 26.
93. Ibid.

94. Ibid.
95. New York *Times*, April 19, 1967, p. 3.
96. Freedom House News Letter, op. cit.
97. New York *Times*, May 3, 1967, p. 2.
98. Ibid.
99. New York *Times*, May 13, 1967, p. 10.
100. Ibid.
101. New York *Times*, May 14, 1967, pp. 1 and 3. Also see *Newark News*, May 14, 1967, p. 1.
102. New York *Times*, May 7, 1967, News of the Week in Review, p. 6E.
103. Ibid.
104. *Newsweek*, May 15, 1967, p. 33.
105. Ibid.
106. Ibid.
107. Ibid.
108. Ibid.
109. Ibid.
110. New York *Times*, April 24, 1967, p. 14.
111. Ibid.
112. Ibid.
113. Ibid.
114. Ibid. Also see New York *Times*, April 2, 1967, p. 76.
115. New York *Times*, April 17, 1967, p. 1.
116. Ibid.
117. New York *Times*, April 24, 1967, p. 14.
118. New York *Times*, May 28, 1967, Main Section, p. 44.
119. New York *Times*, August 12, 1967, p. 28.
120. *New Republic*, September 16, 1967, p. 9.
121. New York *Times*, August 29, 1967, p. 12.
122. Ibid.
123. Ibid.
124. Ibid.
125. Ibid.
126. *Human Events*, November 4, 1967, p. 694.
127. *Human Events*, September 23, 1967, p. 593.
128. New York *Times*, October 20, 1967, p. 2.
129. New York *Times*, August 29, 1967, p. 12.
130. New York *Times*, October 20, 1967, p. 2.
131. Ibid.
132. New York *Times*, August 29, 1967, p. 12.
133. Quoted in New York *Times*, October 20, 1967, p. 2.
134. New York *Times*, October 22, 1967, p. 58.
135. Ibid.
136. Ibid.
137. Ibid.
138. Ibid.
139. Ibid., p. 1.
140. New York *Times*, October 23, 1967, pp. 1 and 32.
141. New York *Times*, October 22, 1967, p. 58.
142. Ibid.
143. New York *Times*, October 23, 1967, p. 32.
144. *Human Events*, November 4, 1967, p. 699.

145. New York *Times*, October 24, 1967, p. 9.
146. New York *Times*, November 22, 1967, p. 9.
147. New York *Times*, November 23, 1967, p. 2.
148. Ibid.
149. Ibid.
150. Ibid.
151. Ibid.
152. New York *Times*, November 29, 1967, p. 12.
153. Ibid.
154. Ibid.
155. New York *Times*, October 26, 1967, p. 6.
156. Ibid.
157. Ibid.
158. New York *Times*, October 23, 1967, pp. 1 and 32.
159. *Amsterdam News*, October 7, 1967, p. 31.
160. New York *Times*, April 16, 1967, News of the Week in Review, p. 3E.
161. New York *Times*, April 17, 1967, p. 1.
162. Ibid.
163. New York *Times*, June 10, 1967, p. 19.
164. Ibid.
165. New York *Times*, May 17, 1967, p. 32.
166. New York *Times*, April 21, 1967, p. 26.
167. New York *Times*, June 1, 1967, p. 24.
168. New York *Times*, May 29, 1967, p. 15.
169. Ibid.
170. Ibid.
171. New York *Times*, July 27, 1967, p. 21.
172. New York *Times*, July 22, 1967, p. 10.
173. New York *Times*, May 29, 1967, p. 15.
174. Ibid.
175. Ibid.
176. Senate Committee on the Judiciary, *Antririot Bill—1967*, Part 1, August 4, 1967, pp. 265 and 266
177. Ibid., p. 266.
178. Ibid., August 7, 1967, pp. 368 and 369.
179. Ibid., August 4, 1967, p. 265.
180. Ibid., p. 266.
181. Ibid., p. 267.
182. New York *Times*, May 29, 1967, p. 15.
183. *Human Events*, August 5, 1967, p. 495.
184. Ibid.
185. New York *Times*, July 20, 1967, p. 29.
186. Ibid.
187. Senate Committee on the Judiciary, op. cit., August 7, 1967, p. 406.
188. Ibid., pp. 361 and 362.
189. Ibid., p. 361.
190. Ibid., p. 364.
191. Ibid., p. 365.
192. *Human Events*, August 5, 1967, p. 495.
193. New York *Times*, July 20, 1967, p. 29.
194. Ibid.
195. Ibid.

196. Ibid.
197. New York *Times*, July 13, 1967, pp. 1 and 26
198. Ibid.
199. New York *Times*, July 20, 1967, p. 29.
200. Ibid.
201. New York *Times*, July 14, 1967, p. 34.
202. Senate Committee on the Judiciary, August 7, 1967, op. cit., pp. 371 and 372.
203. Ibid., pp. 378 and 379.
204. New York *Times*, July 14, 1967, p. 34.
205. Ibid.
206. New York *Times*, July 15, 1967, p. 10.
207. New York *Times*, July 14, 1967, p. 34.
208. Ibid., pp. 1 and 34.
209. Ibid., p. 1.
210. Ibid.
211. New York *Times*, July 15, 1967, p. 1.
212. Senate Judiciary Committee, op. cit., Part 2, August 30, 1967, p. 828.
213. Ibid.
214. Ibid.
215. Ibid., pp. 828 and 829.
216. Ibid., p. 831.
217. Ibid., p. 830.
218. Ibid., p. 831.
219. New York *Times*, July 15, 1967, p. 11.
220. New York *Times*, July 15, 1967, p. 1.
221. Ibid.
222. Ibid., p. 10.
223. Ibid.
224. *Newsweek*, July 24, 1967, p. 22.
225. *Life*, July 28, 1967, pp. 27 and 28.
226. New York *Times*, July 15, 1967, p. 10.
227. Ibid.
228. Senate Judiciary Committee, op. cit., Part 1, August 7, 1967, p. 381.
229. *Life*, July 28, 1967, p. 27.
230. New York *Times*, July 17, 1967, p. 22.
231. Ibid.
232. New York *Times*, July 17, 1967, p. 23.
233. Ibid.
234. Ibid., p. 1.
235. Ibid.
236. Ibid., p. 23.
237. Ibid.
238. Ibid.
239. Ibid.
240. New York *Times*, July 18, 1967, p. 1.
241. Ibid.
242. Ibid. p. 22.
243. Ibid.
244. Ibid.
245. *Time*, July 21, 1967, p. 17.

246. Ibid.
247. New York *Times*, July 19, 1967, p. 42.
248. Ibid., p. 1.
249. New York *Times*, July 25, 1967, p. 22.
250. Ibid.
251. Ibid.
252. *Human Events*, August 5, 1967, p. 484.
253. New York *Post*, August 4, 1967, p. 6.
254. Ibid.
255. Ibid.
256. New York *Times*, August 4, 1967, p. 12.
257. Ibid.
258. New York *Post*, op. cit.
259. New York *Times*, August 4, 1967, p. 12.
260. New York *Times*, August 5, 1967, p. 10.
261. New York *Times*, August 18, 1967, p. 19.
262. Ibid.
263. Ibid.
264. Ibid.
265. New York *Post*, op. cit.
266. New York *Times*, August 22, 1967, p. 23.
267. Ibid.
268. New York *Times*, September 23, 1967, p. 14.
269. *National Observer*, July 24, 1967, p. 12.
270. *Human Events*, August 19, 1967, p. 518.
271. Ibid.
272. New York *Daily News*, July 15,1967, p. 4.
273. New York *Times*, July 23, 1967, News of the Week in Review,
    p. 1E.
274. *Human Events*, August 19, 1967, p. 518.
275. *Daily News*, op. cit.
276. *Human Events*, August 19, 1967, p. 518.
277. Ibid.
278. *Afro-American*, July 22, 1967, p. 4.
279. New York *Times*, July 15, 1967, p. 10.
280. New York *Times*, August 25, 1967, pp. 1 and 22.
281. New York *Times*, August 31, 1967, p. 18.
282. *Amsterdam News*, October 14, 1967, p. 28.
283. Ibid.
284. *Amsterdam News*, October 14, 1967, p. 2.
285. Ibid.
286. Ibid.
287. Ibid.
288. New York *Times*, August 3, 1967, p. 1.
289. Ibid.
290. Ibid.
291. New York *Times*, September 21, 1967, p. 43.
292. *Amsterdam News*, November 18, 1967, p. 48.
293. New York *Times*, August 17, 1967, p. 1.
294. Ibid., p. 27.
295. Ibid.
296. Ibid.
297. Ibid.

298. Ibid.
299. *Amsterdam News*, December 23, 1967, p. 37.
300. Ibid.
301. New York *Times*, July 21, 1967, pp. 1 and 34.
302. Ibid., p. 1.
303. Ibid.
304. Ibid.
305. Ibid., p. 34.
306. Ibid.
307. New York *Times*, July 22, 1967, p. 11.
308. Ibid.
309. New York *Times*, July 21, 1967, p. 1.
310. New York Times, July 22, 1967, p. 11.
311. *Liberator*, August, 1967, p. 9.
312. New York *Times*, July 22, 1967, p. 1.
313. New York *Times*, July 23, 1967, p. 18.
314. New York *Times*, July 25, 1967, p. 21.
315. Ibid.
316. *Liberator*, August, 1967, p. 9.
317. New York *Times*, October 12, 1967, p. 39.
318. Ibid.
319. New York *Times*, October 15, 1967, Main Section, p. 69.
320. *Amsterdam News*, December 2, 1967, p. 31.
321. New York *Times*, October 13, 1967, p. 21.
322. Ibid.
323. Ibid.
324. New York *Times*, October 15, 1967, Main Section, p. 69.
325. Ibid.
326. *Amsterdam News*, December 2, 1967, p. 31.
327. Ibid.
328. New York *Times*, October 13, 1967, p. 21.
329. Ibid.
330. New York *Times*, October 15, 1967, Main Section, p. 69.
331. New York *Times*, November 17, 1967, p. 38.
332. Ibid.
333. New York *Times*, November 21, 1967, p. 36.
334. New York *Times*, October 14, 1967, p. 1.
335. Ibid., p. 54.
336. Ibid.
337. *Human Events*, October 7, 1967, p. 637.
338. New York *Times*, July 18, 1967, p. 1.
339. *Time*, September 24, 1965, p. 24.
340. Ibid. Also see New York *Times*, July 25, 1967, p. 19.
341. Ibid.
342. New York *Times*, July 25, 1967, p. 19.
343. *Time*, September 24, 1965, p. 24.
344. New York *Times*, July 25, 1967, p. 19.
345. *U.S. News & World Report*, August 14, 1967, p. 35.
346. *Jet*, October 13, 1966, p. 50.
347. New York *Times*, August 27, 1967, Magazine, p. 41.
348. Ibid.
349. Ibid.
350. Ibid.

351. Ibid., pp. 41 and 43.
352. *Negro Digest*, May, 1965, pp. 21, 23, 31.
353. New York *Times*, July 25, 1967, p. 19.
354. New York *Times*, August 27, 1967, Magazine, p. 48.
355. New York *Times*, July 25, 1967, p. 19.
356. Ibid.
357. New York *Times*, August 27, 1967, Magazine, p. 51.
358. Ibid.
359. Ibid.
360. New York *Post*, September 26, 1967, p. 45.
361. New York *Times*, January 28, 1968, Magazine Section, p. 48.
362. *Liberator*, June, 1967, p. 6.
363. New York *Post*, September 26, 1967, p. 45.
364. *Liberator*, June, 1967, p. 7.
365. *Human Events*, September 2, 1967, p. 548.
366. New York *Times*, August 27, 1967, Magazine, p. 46.
367. Ibid.
368. Ibid., pp. 46 and 48.
369. Ibid., p. 48.
370. New York *Times*, July 25, 1967, p. 19.
371. New York *Times*, August 27, 1967, Magazine, pp. 43 and 44.
372. Ibid., p. 44.
373. Ibid.
374. Ibid. Also see New York *Times*, July 30, 1967, News of the Week in Review, p. 1E.
375. New York *Times*, August 27, 1967, Magazine, p. 44.
376. New York *Times*, July 30, 1967, News of the Week in Review, p. 1E.
377. *Saturday Evening Post*, September 23, 1967, p. 10.
378. Ibid.
379. New York *Times*, July 24, 1967, p. 15.
380. New York *Times*, July 26, 1967, p. 1.
381. Ibid., pp. 1 and 18.
382. Ibid., p. 18.
383. Ibid.
384. New York *Times*, July 24, 1967, p. 15.
385. New York *Times*, July 26, 1967, p. 18.
386. New York *Times*, July 24, 1967, p. 1.
387. Ibid., p. 15.
388. Ibid.
389. Ibid., p. 1.
390. New York *Times*, July 25, 1967, p. 1.
391. New York *Times*, July 30, 1967, p. 50.
392. Ibid.
393. Ibid.
394. Ibid.
395. Ibid.
396. Ibid.
397. Ibid.
398. Ibid.
399. Ibid., p. 1.
400. Ibid., p. 50.
401. Ibid.

402. Ibid.
403. Ibid.
404. Ibid.
405. Ibid.
406. Ibid.
407. Ibid.
408. Ibid.
409. Ibid.
410. Ibid.
411. New York *Times*, August 1, 1967, p. 17.
412. Ibid., pp. 1 and 17.
413. New York *Times*, August 2, 1967,, p. 16.
414. Ibid.
415. New York *Times*, September 13, 1967, p. 32.
416. New York *Times*, July 30, 1967, p. 50.
417. New York *Times*, July 26, 1967, p. 19.
418. Ibid.
419. *National Review*, August 22, 1967, p. 907.
420. New York *Times*, July 26, 1967, p. 19.
421. *U.S. News & World Report*, August 7, 1967, p. 25.
422. Ibid.
423. Ibid.
424. Ibid.
425. Ibid., p. 23.
426. New York *Times*, July 25, 1967, p. 1.
427. Ibid.
428. Ibid., p. 19.
429. Ibid.
430. New York *Times*, July 26, 1967, p. 18.
431. New York *Times*, July 25, 1967, p. 19.
432. *The National Observer*, July 31, 1967, p. 1.
433. New York *Times*, July 26, 1967, p. 18.
434. Ibid.
435. Ibid.
436. *U.S. News & World Report*, August 7, 1967, p. 24.
437. New York *Times*, July 27, 1967, p. 1.
438. Ibid.
439. Ibid., p. 18.
440. New York *Times*, July 28, 1967, p. 10.
441. New York *Times*, July 27, 1967, p. 18.
442. New York *Post*, August 4, 1967, p. 5.
443. New York *Times*, July 28, 1967, p. 10.
444. Ibid.
445. New York *Times*, July 29, 1967, p. 8.
446. *The National Observer*, September 4, 1967, p. 1.
447. Ibid., p. 11.
448. Ibid.
449. Ibid.
450. Senate Judiciary Committee, op. cit., Part 2, August 30, 1967.
     p. 835.
451. Ibid., p. 834.
452. Ibid., pp. 834 and 835.
453. *The National Observer*, September 4, 1967, p. 11.
454. New York *Times*, July 24, 1967, p. 15.

455. Senate Judiciary Committee, op. cit., Part 2, August 30, 1967, p. 833.
456. Ibid.
457. Ibid., p. 834.
458. *The National Observer*, September 4, 1967, p. 1.
459. Senate Judiciary Committee, op. cit., Part 2, August 30, 1967, p. 836.
460. Ibid., p. 837.
461. Ibid., p. 839.
462. *The National Observer*, September 4, 1967, p. 1.
463. *U.S. News & World Report*, August 7, 1967, p. 24.
464. New York *Times*, August 6, 1967, Main Section, p. 51.
465. Ibid.
466. Quoted in the New York *Times*, September 5, 1967, p. 32.
467. New York *Times*, August 23, 1967, p. 1.
468. Ibid., pp. 1 and 31.
469. Ibid., p. 31.
470. Ibid.
471. Ibid.
472. New York *Times*, August 23, 1967, p. 30.
473. Ibid.
474. Ibid.
475. Ibid.
476. New York *Times*, August 1, 1967, p. 17.
477. Ibid.
478. Ibid.
479. New York *Times*, August 8, 1967, pp. 1 and 24.
480. New York *Times*, August 15, 1967, p. 42.
481. New York *Times*, August 1, 1967, p. 17.
482. New York *Times*, August 16, 1967, p. 27.
483. Ibid.
484. Ibid.
485. New York *Times*, August 17, 1967, p. 25.
486. Ibid.
487. Ibid.
488. New York *Times*, November 27, 1967, p. 52.
489. New York *Times*, August 28, 1967, p. 60.
490. *Human Events*, October 7, 1967, p. 637.
491. Ibid.
492. *U.S. News & World Report*, January 15, 1968, p. 16.
493. Ibid.
494. Ibid.
495. Ibid.
496. Ibid.
497. *New South*, Summer, 1966, p. 76.
498. New York *Times*, August 1, 1967, p. 17.

CHAPTER ELEVEN   THE LEGACY OF MARTIN LUTHER KING

1. *Human Events*, April 13, 1968, p. 7.
2. Ibid.
3. Ibid.
4. New York *Times*, April 28, 1968, p. 36.

5. *Report of the National Advisory Commission on Civil Disorders* (New York: Bantam Books, 1968), p. xvii.
6. Ibid., p. 31.
7. Ibid., p. 21.
8. Ibid., p. 23.
9. Ibid., p. 33.
10. Ibid., p. 108.
11. New York *Times*, April 14, 1968, Main Section, pp. 1 and 61.
12. Ibid.
13. Ibid.
14. Ibid.
15. Ibid.
16. Ibid.
17. New York *Times*, April 13, 1968, p. 13.
18. Ibid.
19. Ibid.
20. New York *Times*, April 16, 1968, p. 30.
21. Ibid.
22. Ibid.
23. Ibid.
24. Ibid.
25. Ibid.
26. Ibid.
27. Ibid.
28. Ibid.
29. Ibid.
30. Ibid.
31. Ibid.
32. New York *Times*, April 17, 1968, p. 1.
33. Ibid., p. 29.
34. New York *Times*, April 18, 1968, p. 40.
35. New York *Times*, April 19, 1968, p. 22.
36. New York *Times*, April 19, 1968, p. 16.
37. New York *Times*, April 12, 1968, p. 19.
38. New York *Times*, April 16, 1968, pp. 1 and 27.
39. New York *Times*, April 25, 1968, p. 33.
40. Ibid.
41. New York *Post*, April 18, 1968, p. 38.
42. Ibid.
43. *Nation's Business*, October, 1967, p. 72 ff.
44. *Harper's*, February, 1961, p. 40.
45. *Liberator*, August, 1967, p. 37.
46. *Jet*, October 13, 1966, p. 16. Also see New York *Times*, October 4, 1967, p. 37.
47. New York *Times*, October 4, 1967, p. 37.
48. Ibid. Also see *Jet*, op. cit.
49. *Jet*, op. cit.
50. Ibid.
51. New York *Times*, January 23 ,1967, p. 23.
52. New York *Times*, September 22, 1966, pp. 1 and 50.
53. New York *Times*, January 23, 1967, p. 23.
54. Ibid.
55. Ibid.
56. New York *Times*, March 11, 1967, p. 33.

57. Ibid.
58. Ibid.
59. *Amsterdam News*, September 16, 1967, pp. 1 and 38.
60. Ibid., pp. 1 and 38.
61. New York *Post*, September 29, 1967, pp. 1 and 3.
62. Ibid.
63. Ibid.
64. Ibid.
65. *Amsterdam News*, October 7, 1967, p. 43.
66. New York *Times*, November 11, 1967, p. 37.
67. New York *Times*, October 3, 1967, p. 36.
68. Ibid.
69. New York *Times*, October 4, 1967, p. 37.
70. Ibid.
71. Ibid.
72. Ibid.
73. Ibid.
74. Ibid.
75. New York *Times*, November 16, 1967, p. 56.
76. New York *Times*, November 11, 1967, p. 37.
77. Ibid.
78. New York *Times*, February 1, 1968, p. 1.
79. Ibid., pp. 1 and 26.
80. Ibid., p. 26.
81. New York *Times*, February 2, 1968, p. 32.
82. Ibid.
83. Ibid.
84. New York *Times*, February 1, 1968, p. 1.
85. New York *Times*, February 3, 1968, pp. 1 and 30.
86. *Columbia Daily Spectator*, April 26, 1967, p. 1.
87. *Amsterdam News*, November 25, 1967, p. 38.
88. Ibid.
89. *Amsterdam News*, December 2, 1967, p. 43.
90. *Amsterdam News*, December 16, 1967, p. 47.
91. *Life*, May 19, 1967, p. 77.
92. *Life*, December 8, 1967, p. 108B
93. *U.S. News & World Report*, January 15, 1968, pp. 68–71.
94. *Nation's Business*, October 1967, p. 86.
95. *Amsterdam News*, October 28, 1967, pp. 1 and 46.
96. *Amsterdam News*, September 30, 1967, p. 16.
97. *Human Events*, September 30, 1967, p. 610.
98. *Amsterdam News*, November 18, 1967, p. 8.
99. *Liberator*, August, 1967, p. 16.
100. New York *Times*, August 6, 1967, Main Section, p. 47.
101. *Amsterdam News*, October 28, 1967, pp. 1 and 46.
102. New York *Times*, October 23, 1966, Main Section, p. 70.
103. New York *Times*, August 26, 1967, p. 23.
104. New York *Times*, August 27, 1967, Main Section, p. 72.
105. *Amsterdam News*, October 7, 1967, Feature Page.
106. New York *Times*, August 17, 1967, p. 36.
107. *The National Observer*, September 25, 1967, p. 17.
108. *U.S. News & World Report*, October 9, 1967, p. 22. Also see New York *Times*, November 1, 1967, p. 46.
109. Ibid.

Index

240. *Where Do We Go From Here: Chaos or Community*, op. cit., pp. 29–30.
241. New York *Times*, June 21, 1966, p. 30.
242. Ibid.
243. New York *Times*, June 22, 1966, p. 25.
244. New York *Times*, December 30, 1967, p. 1.
245. New York *Times*, June 22, 1966, p. 1.
246. New York *Times*, June 22, 1966, p. 25.
247. Ibid.
248. New York *Times*, June 22, 1966, p. 25.
249. Ibid.
250. New York *Times*, June 23, 1966, p. 23.
251. Ibid.
252. New York *Times*, June 24, 1966, p. 1.
253. Ibid., p. 1.
254. Ibid., p. 20.
255. New York *Times*, June 25, 1966, p. 15.
256. Ibid.
257. New York *Times*, June 24, 1966, p. 20.
258. Ibid.
259. Ibid., p. 1.
260. Ibid., p. 20.
261. Ibid.
262. Ibid.
263. New York *Times*, June 25, 1966, p. 1.
264. New York *Times*, June 25, 1966, p. 15.
265. New York *Times*, June 26, 1966, p. 1.
266. Ibid., p. 40.
267. Ibid.
268. Ibid.
269. New York *Times*, June 27, 1966, p. 1.
270. Ibid.
271. Ibid., p. 29.
272. Ibid.
273. Ibid.
274. Ibid.
275. *The Reporter*, July 14, 1966, p. 12.
276. Ibid., pp. 12 and 16.
277. New York *Times*, June 28, 1966, p. 23.
278. *Where Do We Go From Here: Chaos or Community*, op. cit., p. 31.
279. *Human Events*, June 18, 1966, p. 387.
280. New York *Times*, June 25, 1967, pp. 1 and 54.
281. *Ebony*, September, 1966, p. 28.
282. Ibid., p. 30.
283. *Negro Digest*, October, 1966, p. 58.
284. Ibid. p. 59.
285. Ibid., p. 58.
286. *New York Review of Books*, September 22, 1966, p. 5.
287. *Dissent*, January–February, 1967, p. 75.
288. Ibid., p. 72.
289. *Where Do We Go From Here: Chaos or Community*, op. cit., pp. 36, 38, 44.

189. Ibid.
190. New York *Times*, June 7, 1966, p. 1.
191. New York *Times*, June 12, 1966, News of the Week in Review, p. 1E.
192. Ibid.
193. Ibid.
194. Ibid.
195. *Where Do We Go From Here: Chaos or Community*, op. cit., p. 24.
196. Ibid.
197. quoted in *Human Events*, June 18, 1966, p. 387.
198. Ibid.
199. Ibid.
200. Ibid.
201. Ibid. Also see New York *Times*, June 9, 1966, p. 32.
202. Ibid.
203. *Human Events*, op. cit. p. 387.
204. New York *Times*, June 11, 1966, p. 19.
205. New York *Times*, June 8, 1966, p. 1.
206. Ibid.
207. Ibid., p. 26.
208. Ibid.
209. New York *Times*, June 9, 1966, p. 33.
210. New York *Times*, June 8, 1966, p. 26.
211. Ibid.
212. New York *Times*, June 9, 1966, p. 1.
213. Ibid.
214. Ibid., p. 33.
215. Ibid.
216. New York *Times*, June 11, 1966, p. 19.
217. New York *Times*, June 10, 1966, p. 35.
218. New York *Times*, June 11, 1966, p. 19.
219. Ibid., p. 1.
220. Ibid., pp. 1 and 19.
221. Ibid., p. 19.
222. New York *Times*, June 12, 1966, pp. 1 and 82.
223. Ibid., p. 82.
224. Ibid.
225. New York *Times*, June 13, 1966, p. 32.
226. Ibid.
227. New York *Times*, June 15, 1966, p. 1. Also see New York *Times*, June 16, 1966, p. 35.
228. Ibid.
229. Ibid.
230. Ibid.
231. New York *Times*, June 17, 1966, pp. 1 and 33.
232. Ibid., p. 33.
233. Ibid.
234. Ibid.
235. Ibid.
236. Ibid.
237. Ibid., p. 1.
238. Ibid., pp. 1 and 33.
239. New York *Times*, June 21, 1966, p. 30.

290. Ibid., p. 54.
291. Ibid., pp. 56 and 57.
292. *Negro Digest*, December, 1966, p. 6.
293. *Negro Digest*, November, 1966, p. 91.
294. *Negro Digest*, November, 1966, p. 24.
295. Ibid., p. 84.
296. *Negro Digest*, December, 1966, p. 15.
297. New York *Times*, October 9, 1966, Magazine, pp. 42 and 156.
298. Ibid.
299. New York *Post*, June 19, 1967, p. 33.
300. New York *Times*, July 9, 1967, Main Section, p. 38.
301. New York *Times*, July 11, 1967, p. 17.
302. New York *Times*, July 9, 1967, Main Section, p. 38.
303. Ibid.
304. New York *Times*, August 31, 1967, p. 23.
305. *The New Republic*, September 16, 1967, p. 11.
306. New York *Times*, September 24, 1967, Magazine Section, p. 28.
307. Ibid.
308. Ibid.
309. New York *Times*, September 1, 1967, p. 15.
310. Ibid.
311. *The New Republic*, September 16, 1967, p. 10.
312. *The New Leader*, September 11, 1967, p. 8.
313. *New Yorker*, September 23, 1967, p. 71.
314. Ibid.
315. New York *Times*, September 24, 1967, Magazine Section, p. 28.
316. *New Yorker*, op. cit., p. 68.
317. Ibid., p. 56.
318. *The Nation*, September 25, 1967, p. 276.
319. *The New Leader*, September 11, 1967, p. 6.
320. *New Yorker*, op. cit., p. 57.
321. Ibid.
322. Ibid., p. 65.
323. Ibid.
324. *The New Leader*, op. cit., p.6.
325. Ibid.
326. Ibid.
327. Ibid.
328. New York *Times*, September 24, 1967, Magazine Section, p. 124.
329. *New Yorker*, op. cit., p. 57.
330. *The Nation*, September 25, 1967, p. 274.
331. *The New Republic*, op. cit., p. 10.
332. *The Nation*, op. cit., p. 274.
333. *The New Republic*, op. cit., p. 10.
334. New York *Times*, September 3, 1967, p. 18.
335. Ibid.
336. *The New Leader*, September 11, 1967, p. 7.
337. *New Yorker*, op. cit., p. 80.
338. New York *Times*, September 24, 1967, Magazine Section, p. 124.
339. Ibid.
340. Ibid., p. 125.
341. Ibid., p. 124.
342. *The Nation*, op. cit., p. 274.

343. *The New Republic*, September 16, 1967, p. 10.
344. Ibid.
345. New York *Times*, September 3, 1967, p. 18.
346. *The Nation*, September 25, 1967, p. 275.
347. Ibid.
348. *New Yorker*, op. cit. p. 79.
349. Ibid.
350. Ibid., p. 80.
351. Ibid., p. 87.
352. *The New Leader*, op. cit., p. 7.
353. New York *Times*, September 24, 1967, Magazine Section, p. 125.
354. *The New Leader*, op. cit., p. 7.
355. *The Nation*, op. cit., p. 274.
356. *The National Observer*, September 11, 1967, p. 14.
357. *The Nation*, op. cit., p. 275.
358. Ibid.
359. *New Yorker*, op. cit., p. 86.
360. *The New Leader*, op. cit., p. 7.
361. New York *Times*, September 24, 1967, Magazine, p. 125.
362. Ibid.
363. Ibid.
364. Ibid.
365. Ibid.
366. *New Yorker*, op. cit., p. 81.
367. New York *Times*, September 24, 1967, Magazine, p. 125.
368. Ibid.
369. Ibid.
370. Ibid.
371. Ibid.
372. New York *Times*, September 4, 1967, p. 15.
373. Ibid.
374. Ibid.
375. New York *Times*, September 23, 1967, p. 30.
376. *SCLC News Bulletin*, November, 1967.
377. New York *Times*, September 25, 1966, Magazine Section, p. 119.
378. Ibid., p. 122.
379. Ibid., p. 119.
380. New York *Times*, July 29, 1966, p. 13.
381. Hearings Before a Subcommittee of the Committee on Appropriations, House of Representatives, Part 1, February 16, 1967, p. 618.
382. *Human Events*, July 1, 1967, p. 3.
383. Hearings Before a Subcommittee of the Committee on Appropriations, op. cit.
384. *Human Events*, September 10, 1966, p. 579.
385. New York *Times*, May 17, 1967, p. 30.
386. New York *Times*, June 22, 1967, p. 1.
387. Ibid.
388. Ibid., p. 25.
389. New York *Times*, September 7, 1966, pp. 1 and 38.
390. Ibid., p. 1.
391. Ibid.
392. Ibid., p. 38.
393. Ibid.